From your friends at

South Texas Money Management

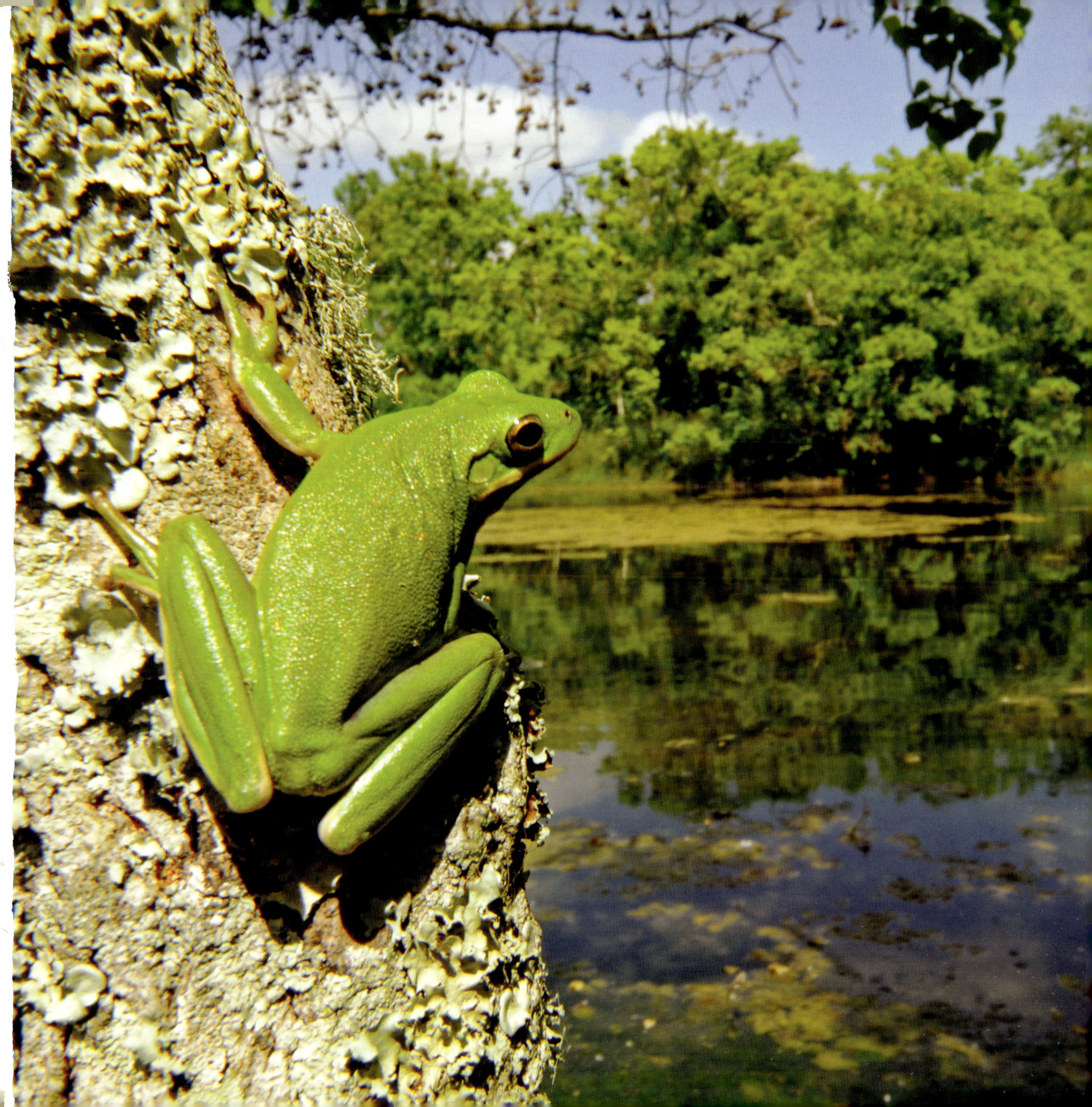

Dear Fellow Wildlife Enthusiast...

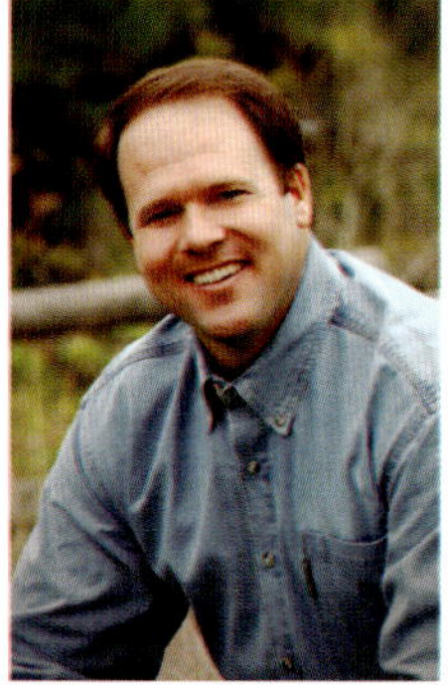

Texas is blessed with an extraordinary amount of treasures, particularly of the natural kind. Within our state may be found some of the most biologically varied and irreplaceable habitats in all of the western hemisphere. As Texans, we take great pride in the diversity of our lands and waters and recognize that their safe stewardship is a responsibility we owe to the generations that follow.

Nowhere is that ecological uniqueness and commitment to its conservation more self evident than in Texas' fabled Coastal Bend. From its fields, farms, prairies, pastures, woodlands, marshes, and refuges abound populations of birds, fish and game that are the quarry of many a sportsman and the pursuit of many a nature enthusiast.

Supporting it all, are the region's private landowners. It is a group that includes seventh and eighth generation descendents of pioneering farming and ranching families who have outlived and outlasted an imposing and impressive litany of droughts, hurricanes, floods, and erratic agricultural markets that prompted less hardy souls to seek refuge further inland. While some are long to the land, others are reborn or recently acquainted to it.

Irrespective of tenure, they are bound by a love of the land, the region, and all that is found within it. Individually and collectively, they do much to ensure the area's fish, wildlife, lands, and waters are well managed for the benefit of all who care about the future of its' wild things and wild places. And, while they didn't ask for it, let me respectfully suggest that their quiet and determined stewardship merits our most profound gratitude.

Thanks to a most innovative contest sponsored by the Images for Conservation Fund, the nearly singular beauty and richness of the Coastal Bend can be enjoyed by all in the pages of this book. Through the Pro-Tour of Nature Photography, teams of professional nature photographers and Coastal Bend landowners have collaborated to capture the signature beauty, color, and majesty of the flora and fauna found beyond the region's ranch gates. I trust you will find the imagery as memorable and awe inspiring as I do.

The Images for Conservation Fund is celebrating its second official "Pro-Tour" contest. In doing so, it has built upon other similar ventures in Texas sponsored by the Valley Land Fund and the Coastal Bend Land Trust. Their genesis comes from a shared premise that we must find creative ways to recognize and reward those landowners who safeguard our precious natural heritage, as well as educate the rapidly growing number of citizens who lack even the most basic of connections and exposure to the natural world. It is without doubt a laudable, yet ambitious, charge. After you peruse this book, I hope you will concur that through the lens of these highly skilled photographers, and the exemplary stewards on whose lands the photos were collected, that charge is made possible.

On behalf of all of us at the Texas Parks and Wildlife Department, I offer my utmost thanks to all who look after the land and to those who have brought it to us in such an inspirational array of photographic images. Thanks for caring about Texas' wildlife and wild places. They need you more than ever.

Carter Smith
Texas Parks and Wildlife Department

Published by
Images for Conservation Fund (ICF)
2112 W. University Drive, #801
Edinburg, Texas 78539
Phone: 956-381-1264
Fax: 956-380-2472
Email: icfprotour@aol.com
www.imagesforconservation.org

Editor: Gail M. Hoffman
Story Editor: David Sikes
Writers: Gail M. Hoffman, Jenna B. Hoffman, Alicia M. Hoover, Mary O. Parker
Book Designer: Judy Robertson Designs

ISBN 78-1-61584-334-3
First Printing, 2009
Printed in the U.S.A.

IMAGES FOR CONSERVATION | BOOK TWO

Coastal Bend of Texas Edition

Species identification: Wildlife Diversity Program, Texas Parks and Wildlife Department: Andy Gluesenkamp – herpetologist, Jackie Poole – botanist, Cliff Shackelford – ornithologist, John Young – mammalogist; John Findeisen – Inland Fisheries; Bastiaan "Bart" Drees – Texas AgriLife Extension Service; Allen Dean – Texas AgriLife Research; Forrest Mitchell, Texas Agrilife Research
Photo credit for first page: Ulrich | Green Treefrog | Pierce Ranch
Photo credit for inside dust jacket: Larry Jones Photography

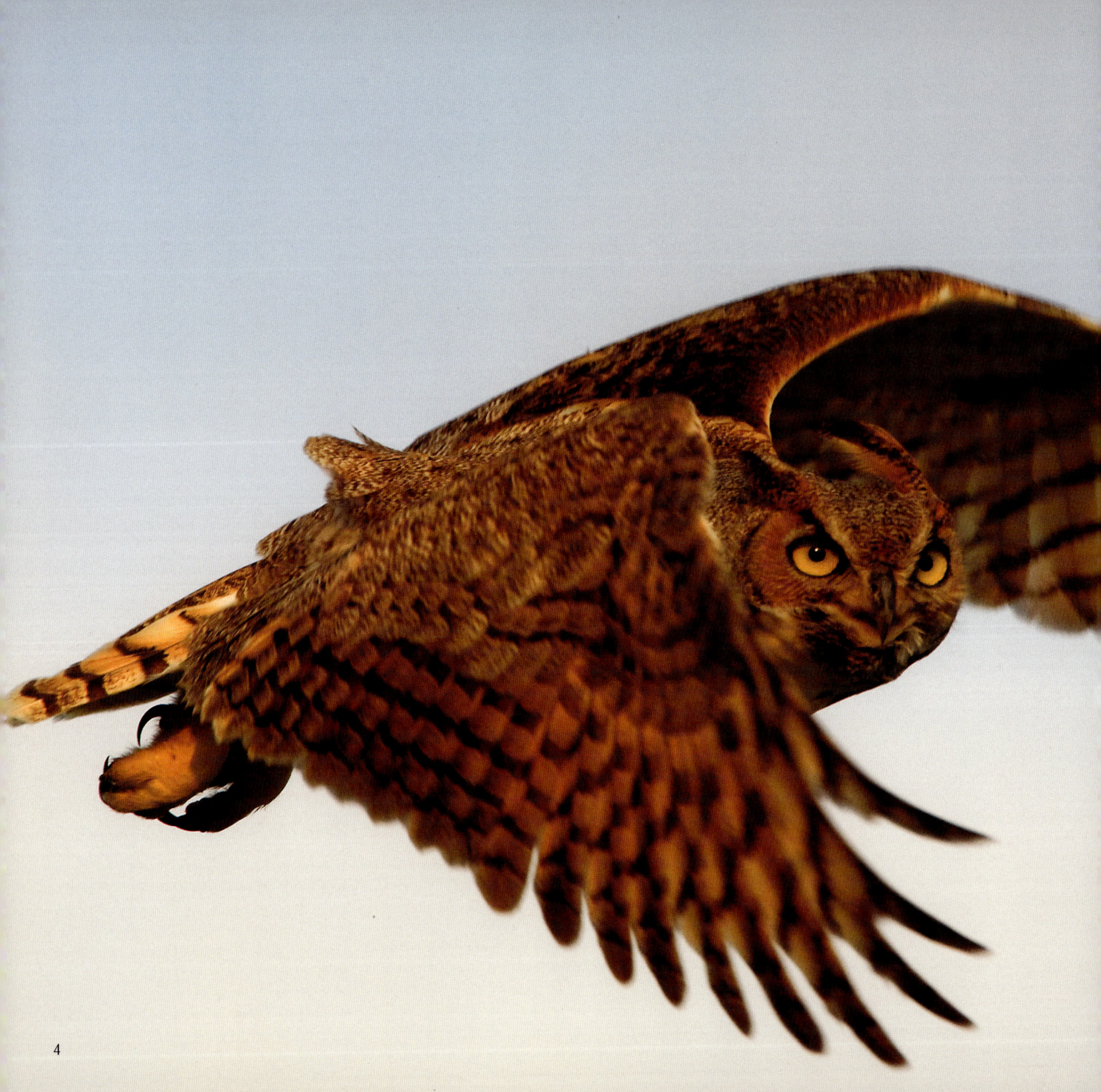

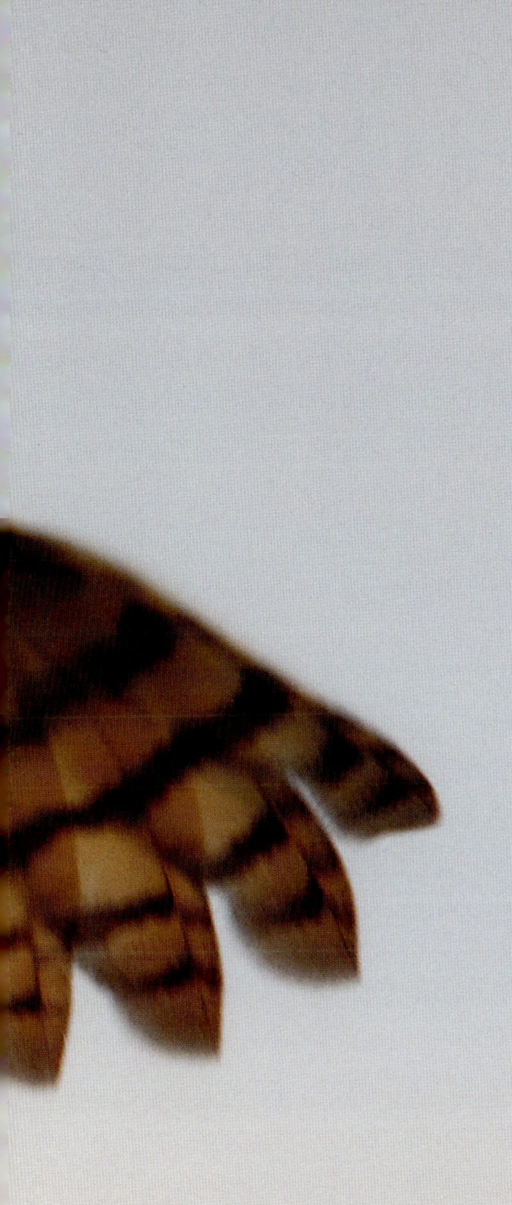

AEP Texas, an electricity delivery company serving south and west Texas, is proud to be an original sponsor of the Images for Conservation Fund Pro-Tour of Nature Photography.

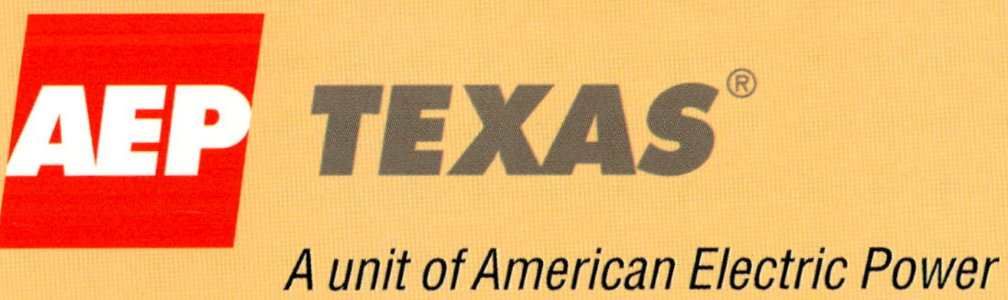

Hahn | Great Horned Owl | Pedrotti-Sorgente Ranch

About Images for Conservation Fund...

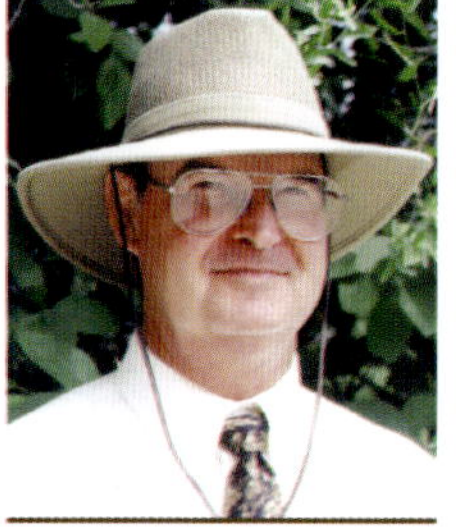

Images for Conservation Fund (ICF) 2008 Coastal Bend of Texas Pro-Tour proved that we have developed a sustainable model. If there were one word to describe the reason for the success of the 2008 Pro-Tour, it would be leadership. Thanks to the ICF Board, our sponsors, volunteers, landowners, photographers and staff we continued the conservation event of the 21st Century. The tournament took on an international flavor as photographers from Spain, Holland and Canada joined the already talented group of U. S. photographers.

In the 2008 Coastal Bend of Texas Pro-Tour, 20 teams created some of the most beautiful images ever produced, showcasing one of the richest eco-systems in North America. Our landowners immersed themselves in the competition and enriched their knowledge of the wildlife sharing the land with them. The photographers and their images changed forever the thinking and attitudes of many of the participating landowner families about individual species. Animals that previously were immediately killed on sight now have been granted full protection on the ranch and are viewed as providing future economic benefits.

In the past great photography was limited by the complexity of the camera equipment and the expense of the film. The ability to control the use of light and the film, camera and lenses prevented the general public from producing quality photography. Then there was the time lag between when the image was captured and then viewed by the photographer and finally shared with friends, family and the world. Only patient, dedicated and artistic individuals took great nature photographs.

With the introduction of digital cameras and micro processors, nature photography is open to millions of people and the Internet allows the immediate sharing of images. The direct result is the creation of a new recreational industry of nature photo tourism.

The future of conservation lies in the development and expansion of recreational nature photography. Every recreational industry of any economic importance has developed from a professional competition, and the industry model that best represents our goal is golf. The game itself requires large expanses of green area, a great deal of patience and is never fully conquered. That is nature photography. Potentially millions of acres of privately owned wildlife habitat will be preserved by opening the gates to recreational nature photographers willing to pay a true "green fee."

We reached a milestone in 2008 with the successful organization of the Texas Hill Country Nature Photography Alliance. The 2006 Texas Hill Country Pro-Tour introduced the industry, and Bob Petersen, ICF Vice Chairman, led several of the ranches in developing the Alliance to market nature photography to the region.

ICF is committed to the growth of this new industry as the most viable way to bring economics to the conservation of private lands and in helping landowners who want to move forward. We currently have member ranches in the Texas Hill Country, the Coastal Bend and the Lower Rio Grande Valley of Texas. It's happening.

John F. Martin

John F. Martin, 2009
Founder, Images for Conservation Fund

Introduction...

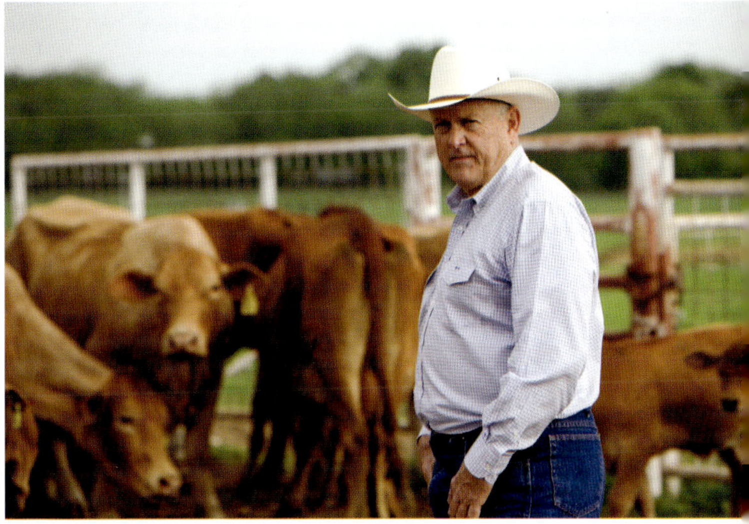

Rugged mountains, sweeping vistas, salt spray misting across sandy shores are just a few of the sights you can expect to encounter as you cross the varied terrain we are all proud to call our home, Texas. Texas is a land of diversity in every aspect. The description of animal species found in Texas range from the scaly armadillo, the sleek Jaguarundi, the bristled feral hog to the playful raccoon.

Our region is home to some of the most beautiful wildflowers in the country; the State Flower the Bluebonnet is surrounded by Indian Paint Brush, Texas Thistle, Coreopsis and Purple Flame Flower which combine to create a blanket of native Texas wildflowers that annually draw tourists to enjoy the panoply of color.

Texas is known for its vast array of avian splendor. Springtime in the Coastal Bend welcomes a host of migratory Tropical birds that provide a feast to the eyes of birders of all ages. These birds are on their annual migration back to Mexico, but stop along their way to indulge on the remnants of past grain harvests and the abundance of insects rampant in the fields.

All these elements combine to create a landscape of color, texture and activity all depicted in the 2008 Pro-Tour of Nature Photography: Coastal Bend Edition. The 20 Landowner and Professional Photographer teams partnered to create a depiction of wildlife unique to the Coastal Bend.

The imagery created reminds me why I am proud to be a Texas rancher. The task inherent with being a landowner is to ensure the native qualities we all enjoy remain intact. The maintenance of the wildlife that makes Texas unique is what we strive to pursue through the Images for Conservation Fund. I encourage each of you to read the stories, study the photos and share this beautiful book with your friends and family. Remind them how important good stewardship of our land is for now and for future Texans.

Nolan Ryan
Hall of Fame Pitcher and Texas Rancher

Dedication to David Langford...

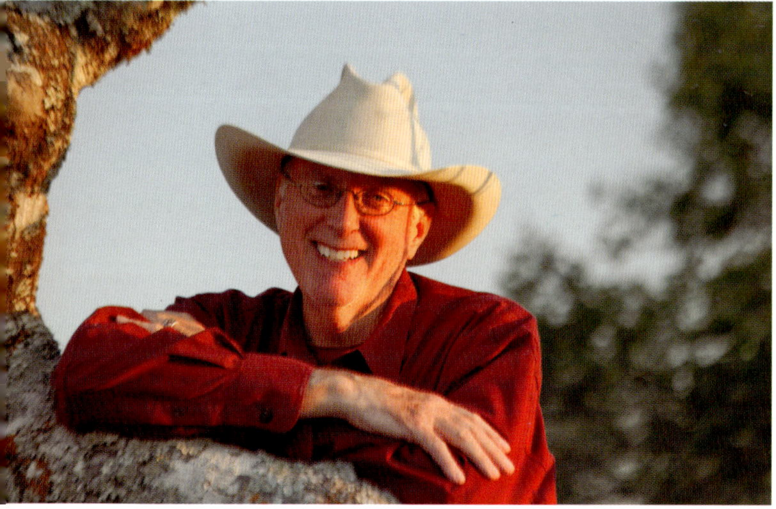

Photo credit Laurence Parent

In a world of many whiners and few doers, David K. Langford stands out as a doer – with little patience for hand-wringers. Langford understands the problems an increasingly urban society pose for wild, open spaces – and he confronts them head on.

As Executive Vice President of the Texas Wildlife Association for twelve years, and then fading only slightly into the background in an emeritus role in 2002, Langford showed up in Austin, Washington and anywhere a voice was needed on behalf of wild places in Texas, especially those managed by private land stewards.

Before his career at TWA, Langford made his living as a photographer. That, coupled with the heritage of being a member of a six-generation ranching family in Kendall County, gives Langford a perspective of how important it is for private landowners to, as he says, "open the front gates," to photographers and other public. Opening those gates is a vital step in combating the natural resource illiteracy of modern urbanites. Stepping onto well-cared-for land gives city folk a better understanding of the relationship between what happens on the range and how it affects the greater public good. The images in this book are proof of how that private/public partnership works.

Our private lands are priceless, but not free. There are no government-paid park rangers out fixing fences or clearing brush. The fees from photographers and others in the rapidly growing "Nature Tourism" segment are re-invested to maintain and keep the resources intact.

David K. Langford understands what's at stake in conserving the land behind the gates and keeping them open to the flow of commerce and understanding. All good Marines understand that, as he often reminds us, "failure is not an option."

Langford and his wife Myrna live on their family's ranch between Comfort and Fredericksburg. They are blessed with two children, and their families, which include four grandchildren.

David Baxter
Consulting Features Editor, Texas Wildlife Association

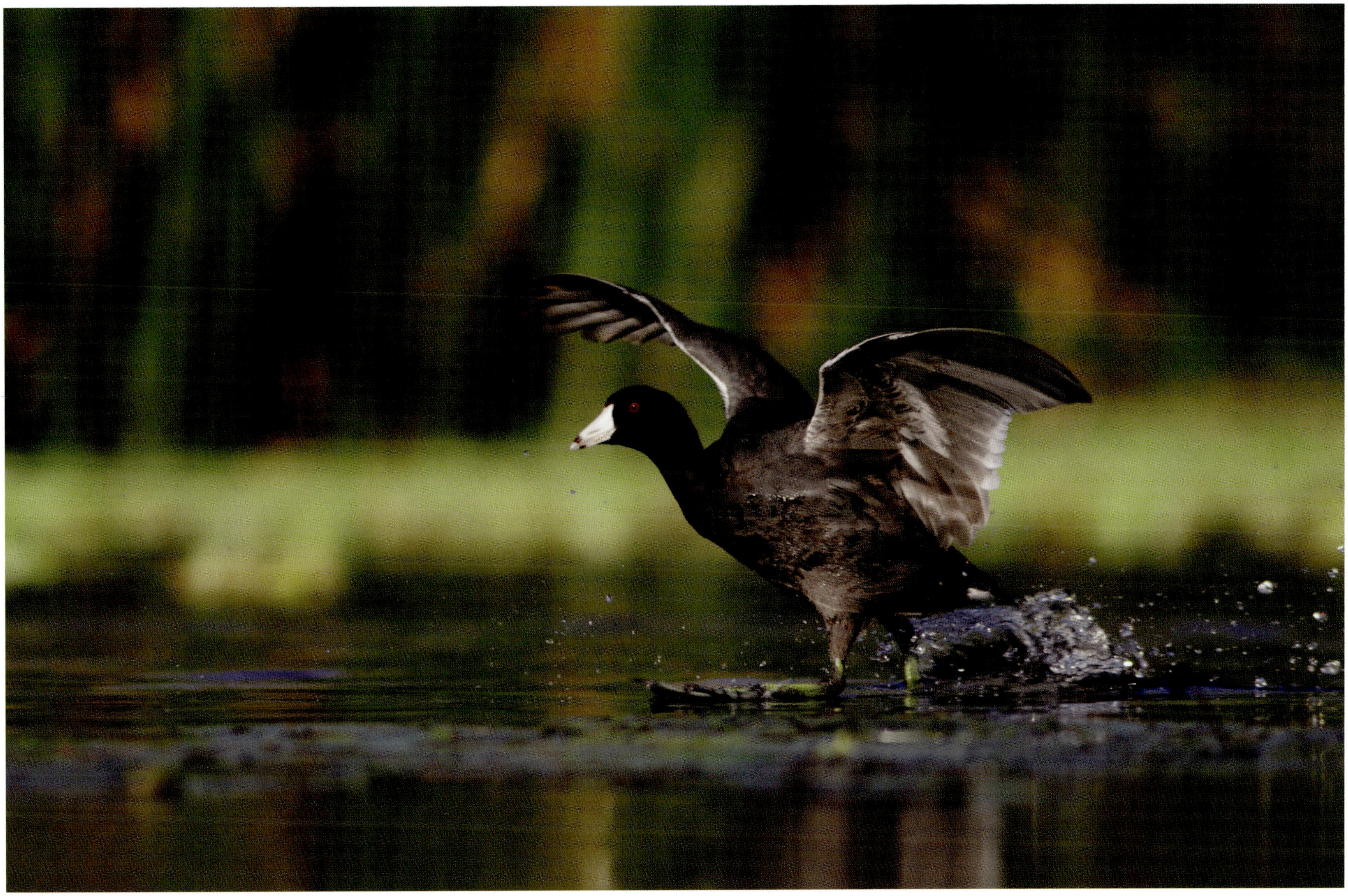

Nussbaumer | American Coot | Fennessey Ranch

As your local bank, we understand your needs

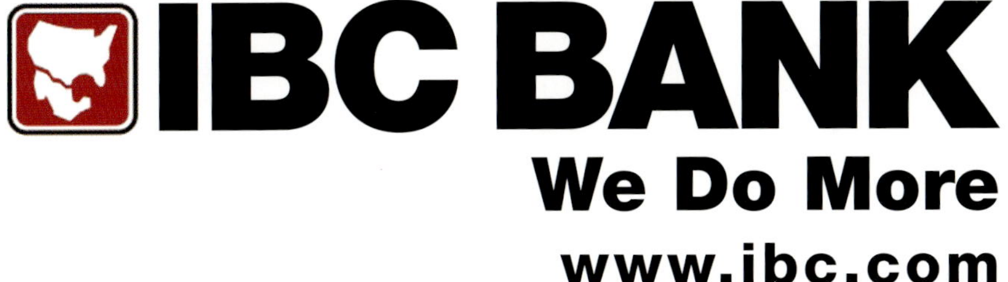

About Fennessey Ranch...

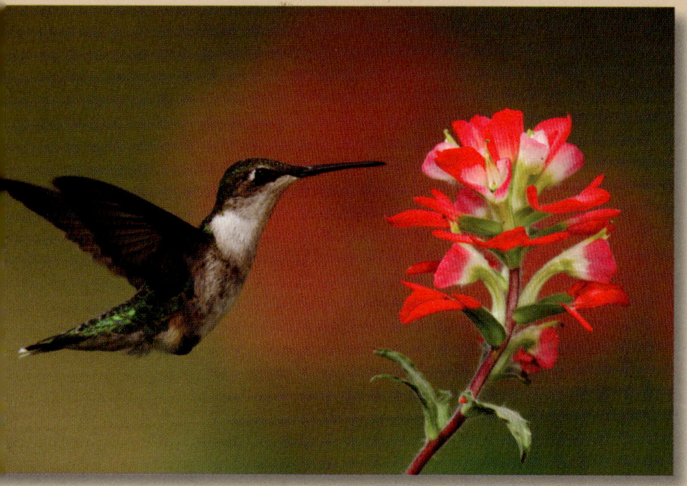

Nussbaumer | Ruby-throated Hummingbird (female) with Indian Paintbrush

The Fennessey Ranch offers the kind of diversity that nature photographers long to shoot. The habitat here spans the gamut from coastal prairies to river woodlands, which includes 400 bird species, 16 plant communities, 50 reptiles and amphibians, 70 kinds of moths and butterflies and nearly every native mammal that calls South Texas home.

Such biodiversity is possible because of the Fennessey's wetlands, meadows, lakes, riparian woods and brush lands. The ranch is bordered on three sides by a U-shaped portion of the Mission River. For nine miles, the river meanders through the property, providing its inhabitants with just about every flavor that seasons South Texas.

The Fennessey Ranch's owner, Brien O'Connor Dunn, certainly began with some great raw ingredients. The ranch has been in the family since 1834. But it's the enhancements that make this property so special. Creating so much eye candy for a photographer's lens wasn't easy.

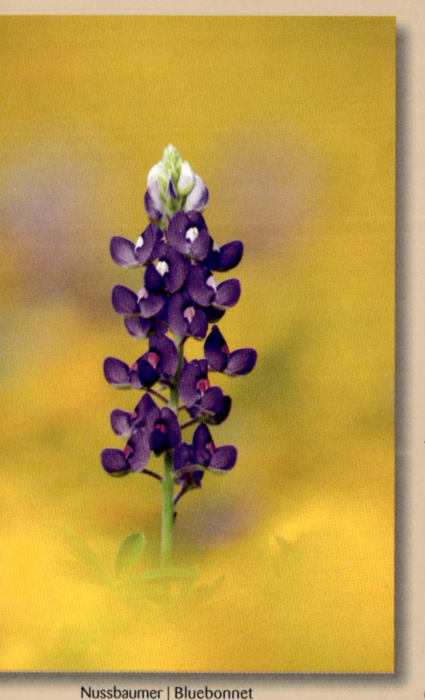

Nussbaumer | Bluebonnet

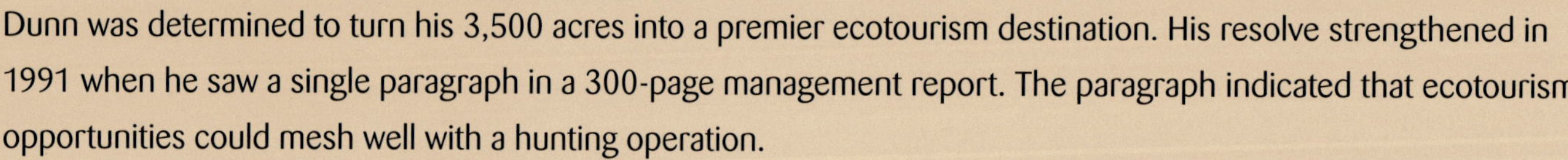

Dunn was determined to turn his 3,500 acres into a premier ecotourism destination. His resolve strengthened in 1991 when he saw a single paragraph in a 300-page management report. The paragraph indicated that ecotourism opportunities could mesh well with a hunting operation.

"I took that one paragraph and made it my life's work," he said.

Since then, this passionate land steward has worked to nurture what nature provided.

"It's back-breaking work," Dunn said. "And one of the toughest things about doing this is keeping yourself from falling out of love with why you started this in the first place."

Ranch manager Sally Crofutt said she's never seen Dunn falter during nearly two decades of pursuing his quest to pioneer this industry.

"When it comes to traditional ways of making a living at ranching, the vacation is over," Crofutt said. "The glory days of cattle and oil and gas leases are gone even though the days of paying property taxes never will be."

Dunn and Crofutt insist that the only way to preserve native habitats is to figure out a way to make them profitable.

A huge part of Dunn's life's work has been in creating what he calls an environmental Disneyland. Part of the plan of building such a theme park has included sharing the Fennessey's bounty through the eyes of some of nature's most passionate advocates: photographers.

Dunn sees the Pro-Tour as an effective tool for bringing awareness to conservation issues and for providing much-needed funds to ranch owners.

"This contest is near and dear to Brien's heart," Crofutt said. "He's always felt that photo contests like it are so important because they introduce ranchers to their own ecosystems. At the very least it's fun for a rancher to document what's on his place. At the very most it's one more avenue for bringing in some revenue, a way for private landowners to keep the land in the family."

And that's the way it's worked at the Fennessey. By capturing the Pro-Tour's Grand Prize in 2008, it truly was a win-win situation for the Fennessey whose glory was showcased by the exquisite images of photographer Rolf Nussbaumer, who vibrantly brought the ranch's abundance into focus.

For Dunn, sharing his ranch this way reaches far beyond the cash payoff. It's really not nearly as much fun unless you get to share it with others, he said.

Sally Crofutt
Bayside, TX
[e] fenranch@sbcglobal.net

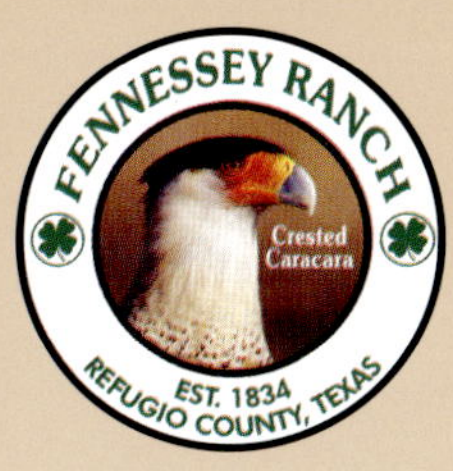

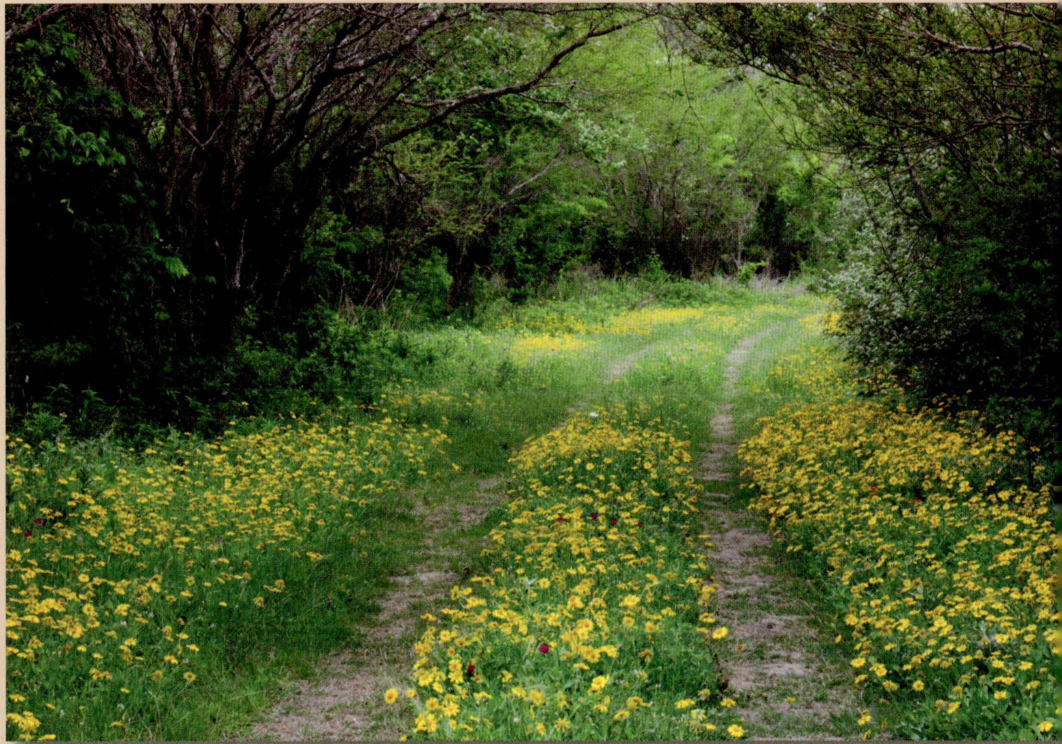

Nussbaumer | Huisache Daisy

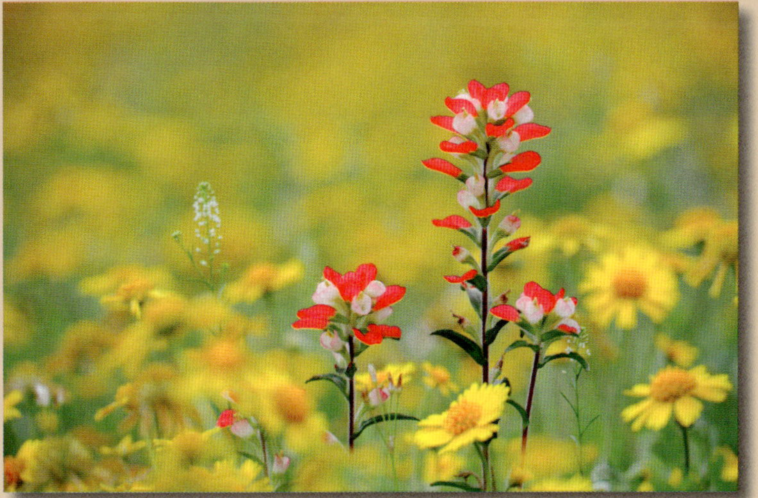

Nussbaumer | Indian Paintbush and Huisache Daisy

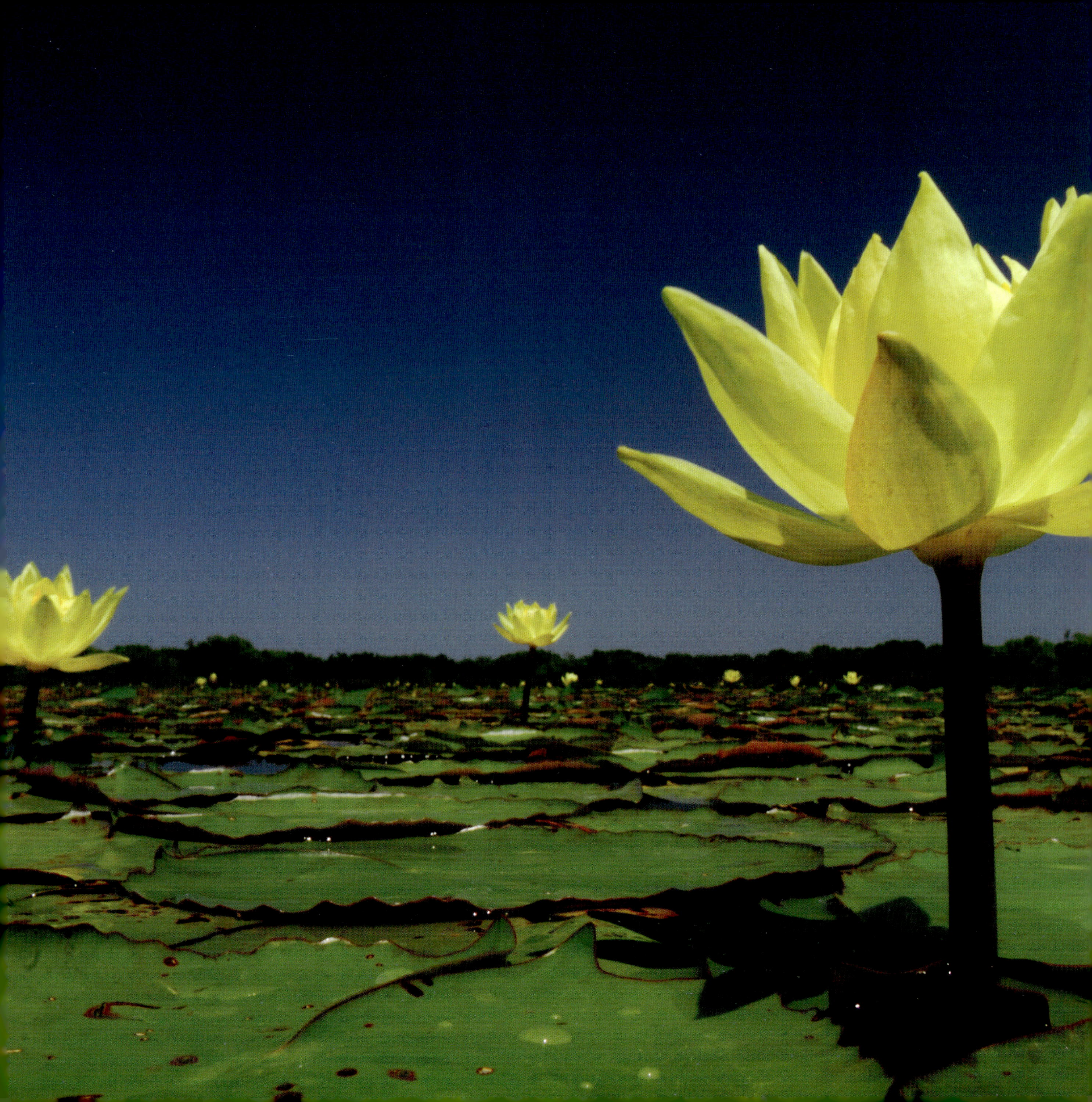

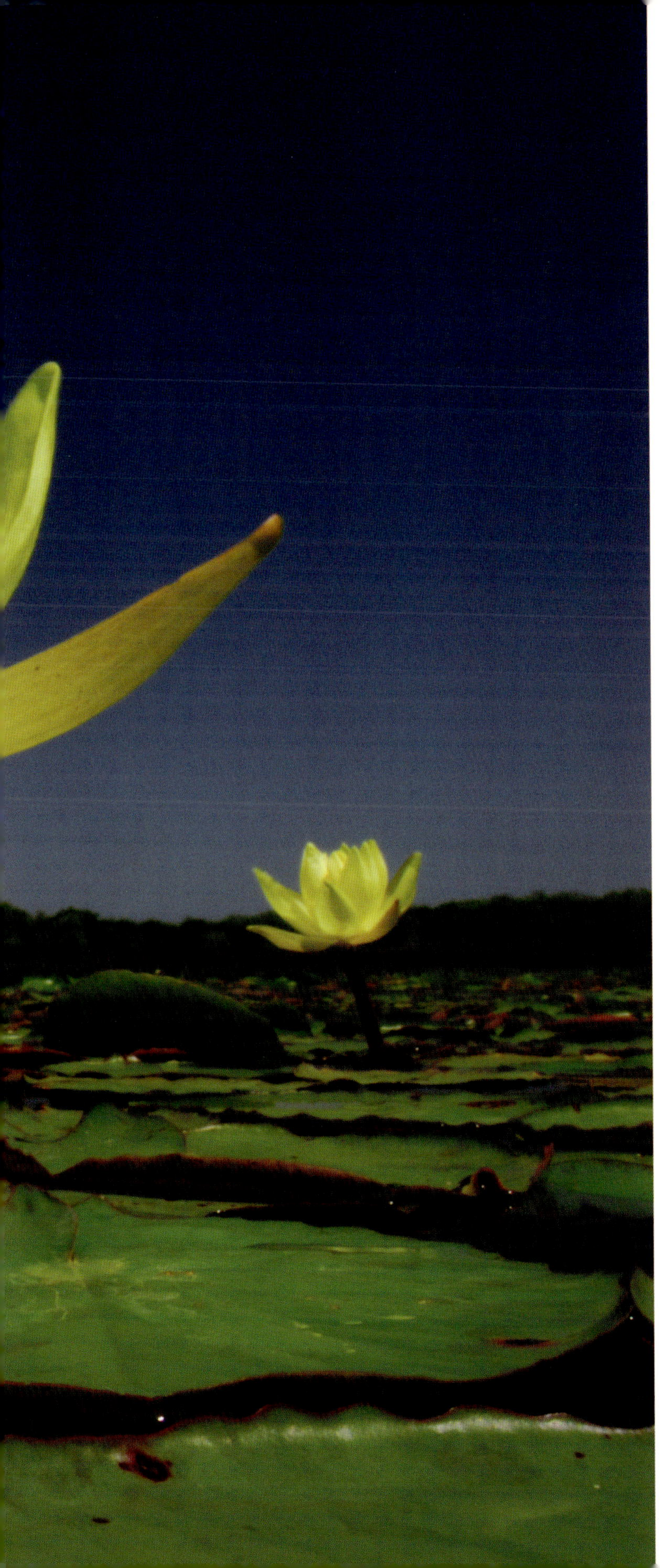

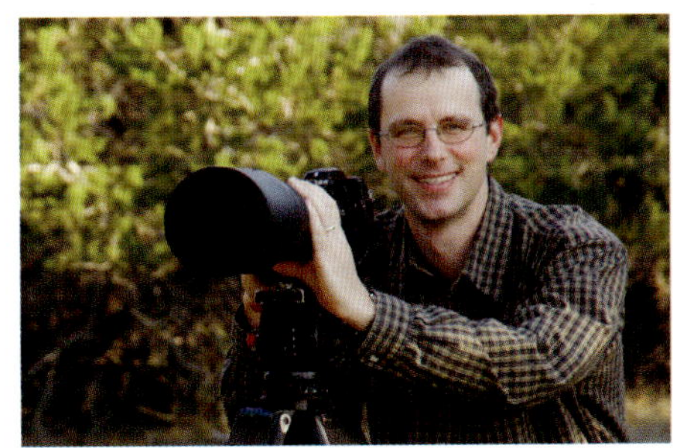

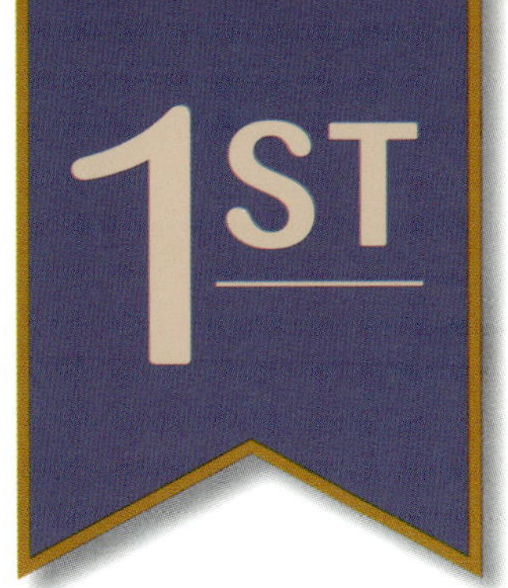

Rolf Nussbaumer

"Most of the time," says Rolf Nussbaumer, who spent his Pro-Tour month learning the intimate nuances of the Fennessey Ranch, "an image starts without my camera."

He elaborates, "When a subject catches my eye for some reason, I need to spend some time finding out what that reason is. For example, with a flowering plant, is it the stem? The shape? The color? Is there a thin colored line going through it that enhances it somehow?" It's all about what he calls the "enhancement factor."

"I'll look at it from different angles trying to determine exactly what it is that makes it special. I'm always trying to find the uniqueness of my subject and then to enhance that with my picture." He adds with a soft chuckle, "Of course, that works better with stationary things."

But, to Rolf, the bottom line is making sure that "uniqueness" is magnified rather than lost in the photographic translation – a translation, he stresses, that must also convey his unique way of seeing. "I have always wanted my approach to be my very own. I've never tried to imitate other photographers' approaches. I'm basically a nature-lover first and a photographer second."

Rolf's been a nature-lover since childhood and a nature-lover with a camera since 14 when he roamed the Swiss countryside "taking pictures to share with other people." There, he took what he considers some of his first "real" photos of a bird called a European Dipper.

Throughout his life, Rolf says, "Photography was a hobby that let me be out in nature where I could watch stuff." But, in 2002 when he moved to Texas it became much more than that, he says, "I figured I would try it since it was always something I'd wanted to do for a living. I'd won the Valley Land Fund and the contest gave me enough courage to say, 'Let's give it a shot.'" And, thus, quite literally he did.

Today, when he's taking his shots, he explains, "I always try to keep it to a minimum on the equipment side. I do like to do set-ups with flashes and with the infrared beam, but I'm not the guy who needs to have 20 different lenses."

New Braunfels, TX
www.rolfnussbaumer.com
[e] rolfnussbaumer@sbcglobal.net

Nussbaumer | Water Lilies

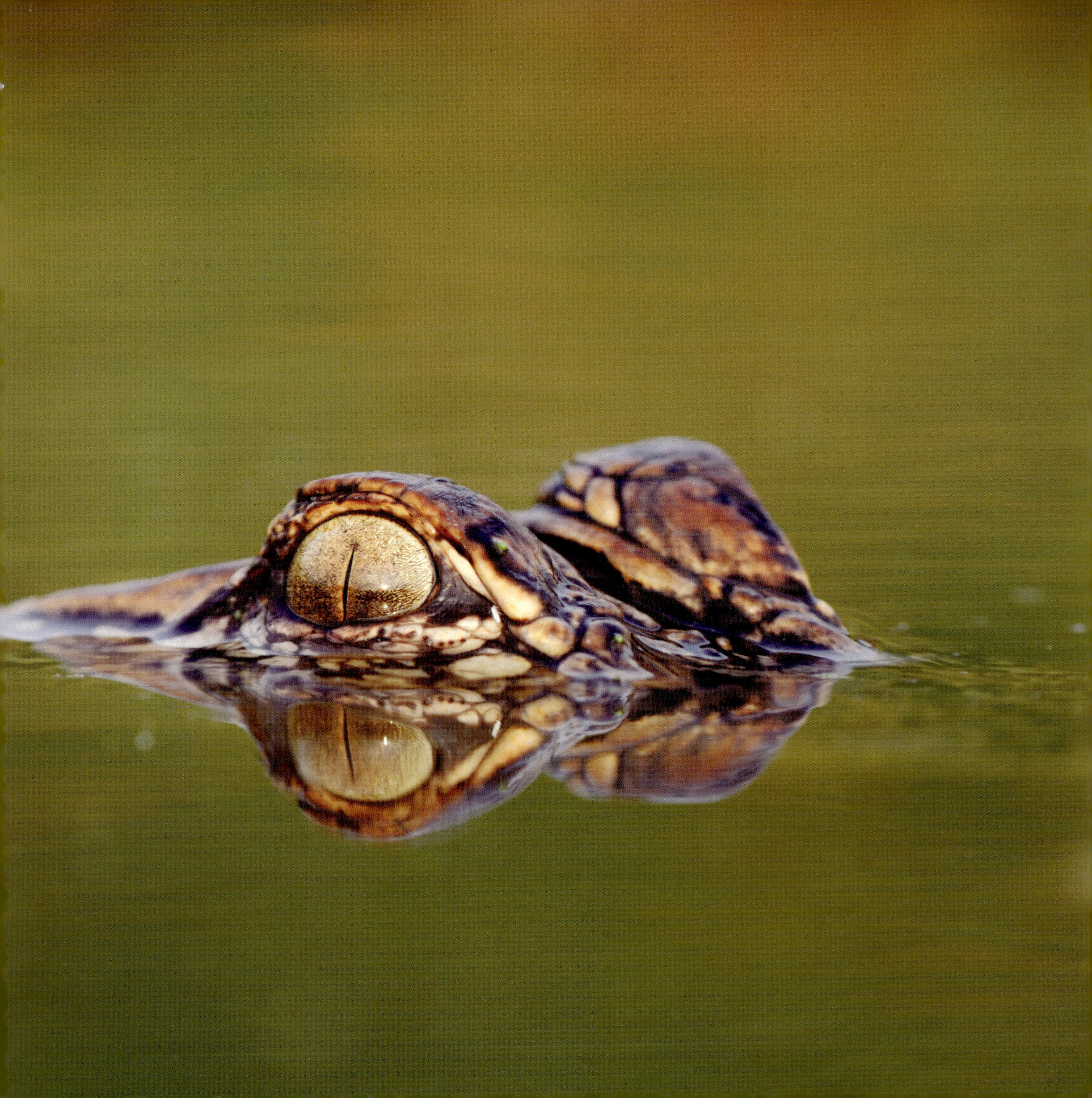

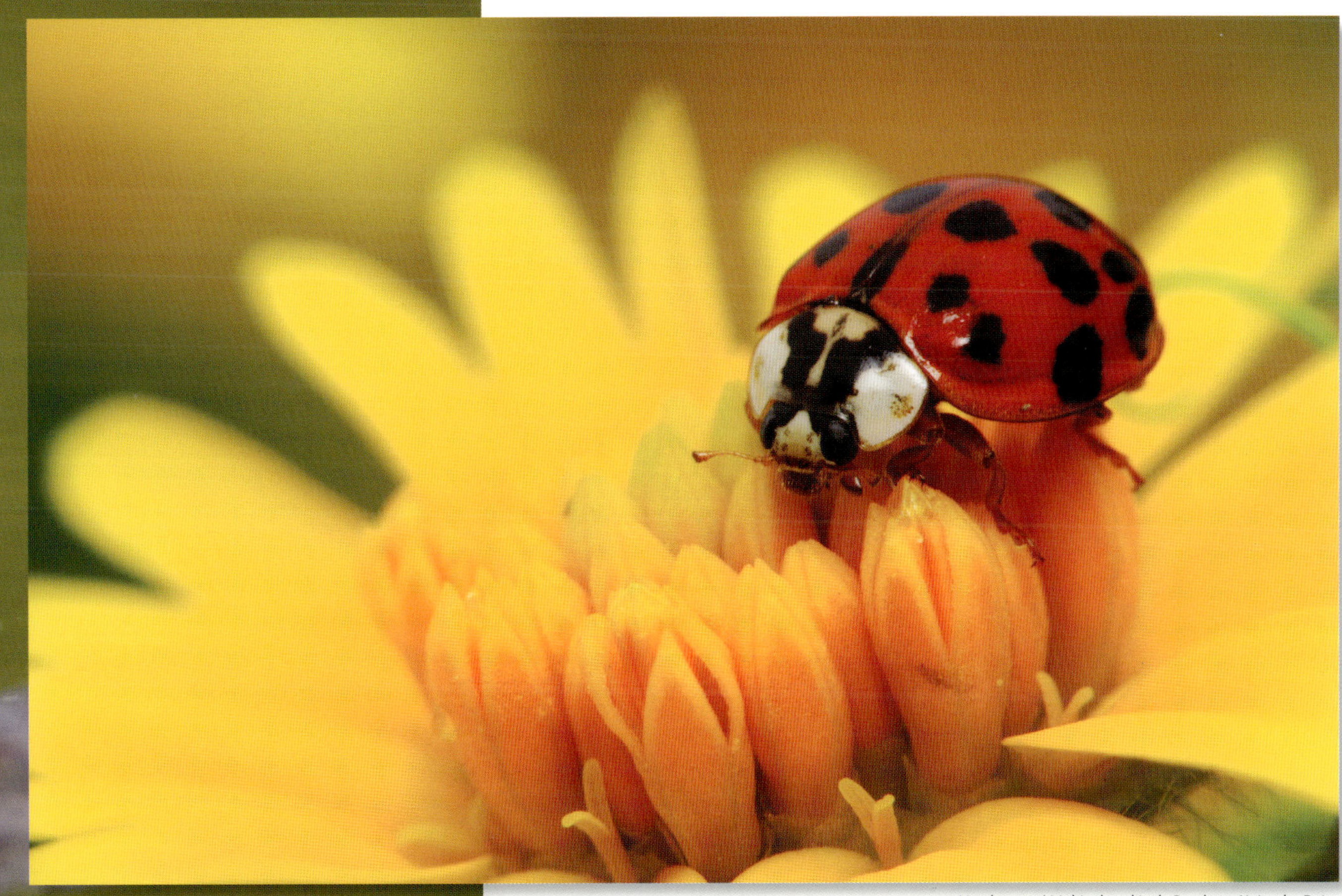

Nussbaumer | Multicolored Lady Beetle on Huisache Daisy

Nussbaumer | American Alligator

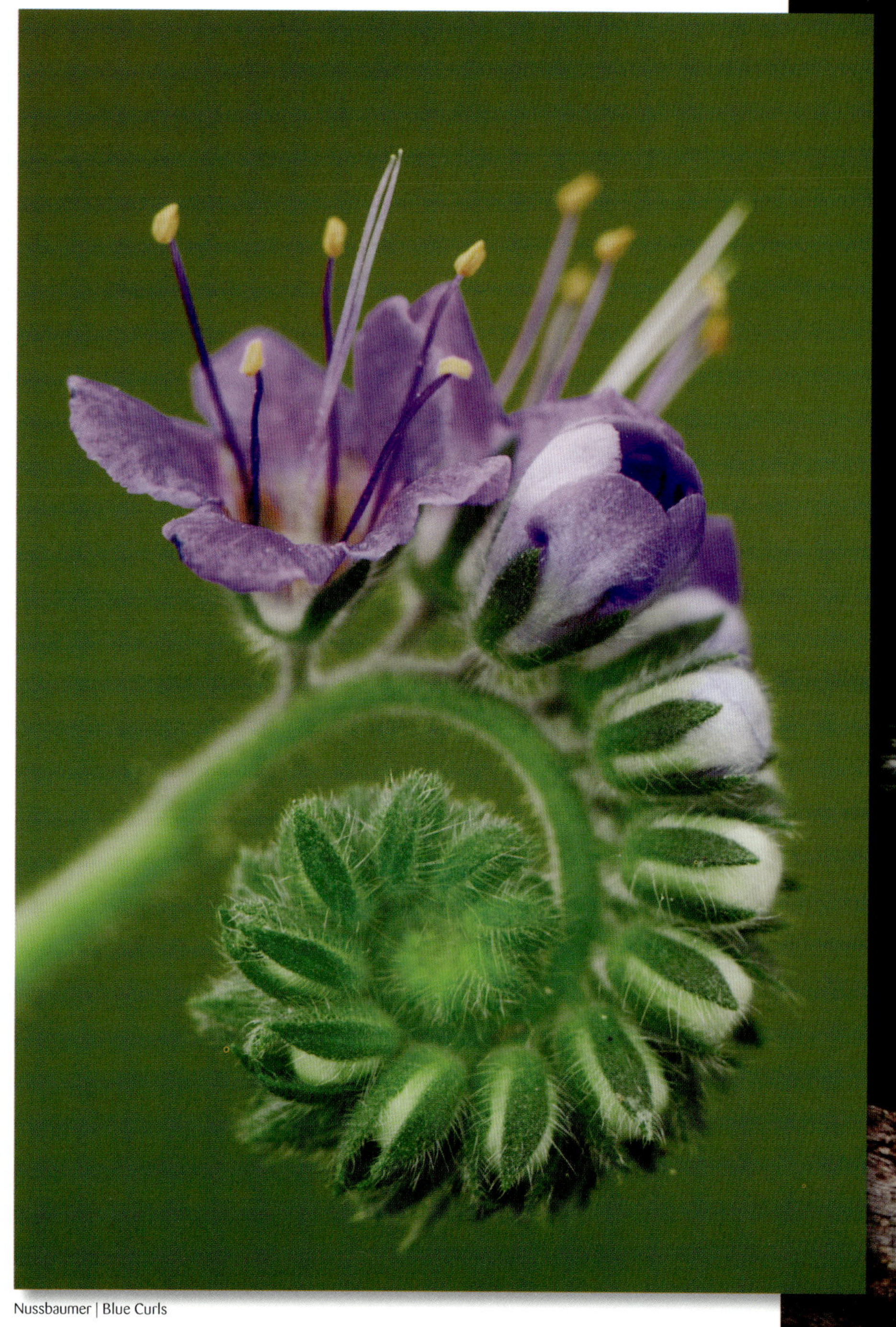

Nussbaumer | Blue Curls

Nussbaumer | Eastern Fox Squirrel

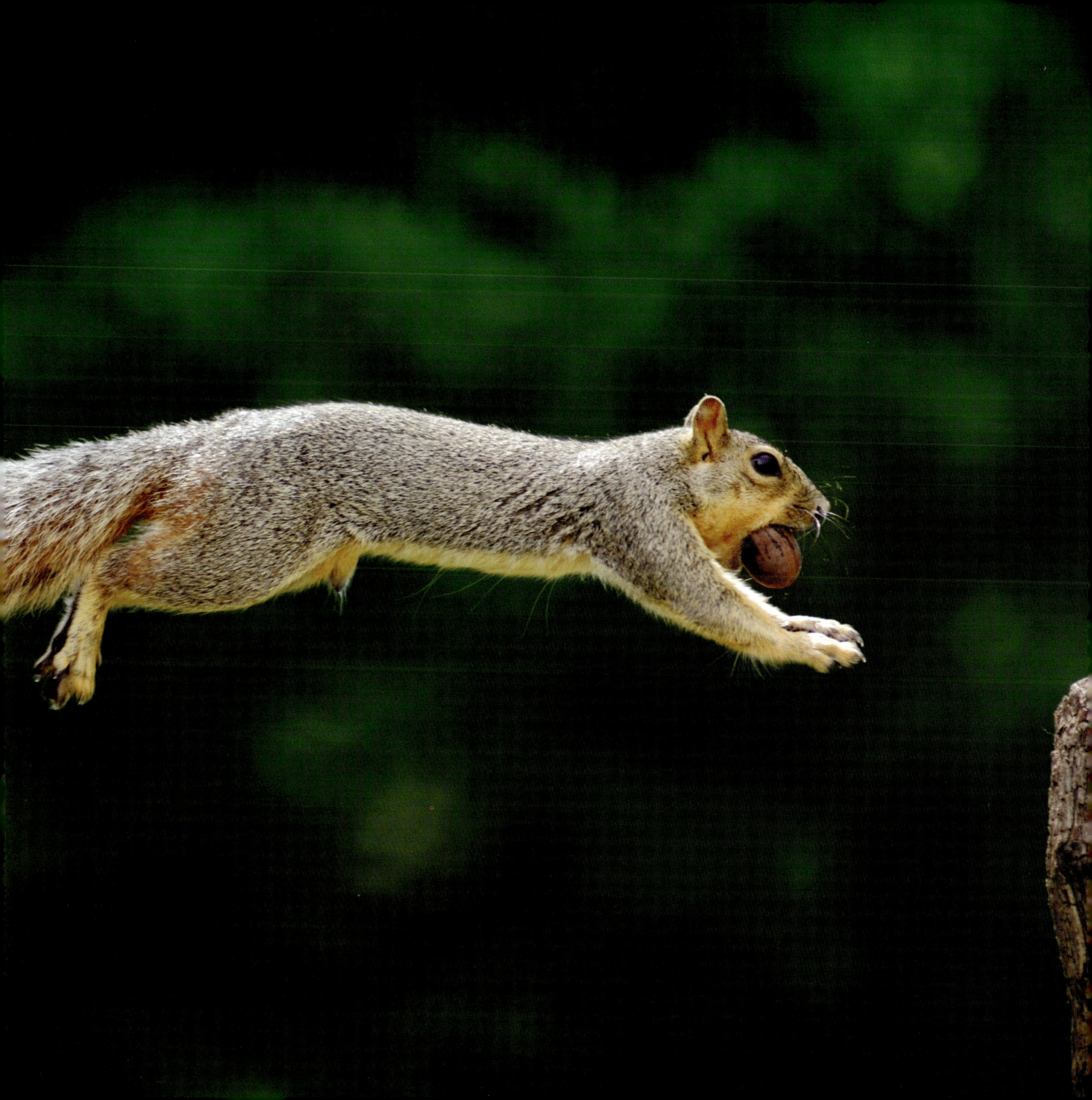

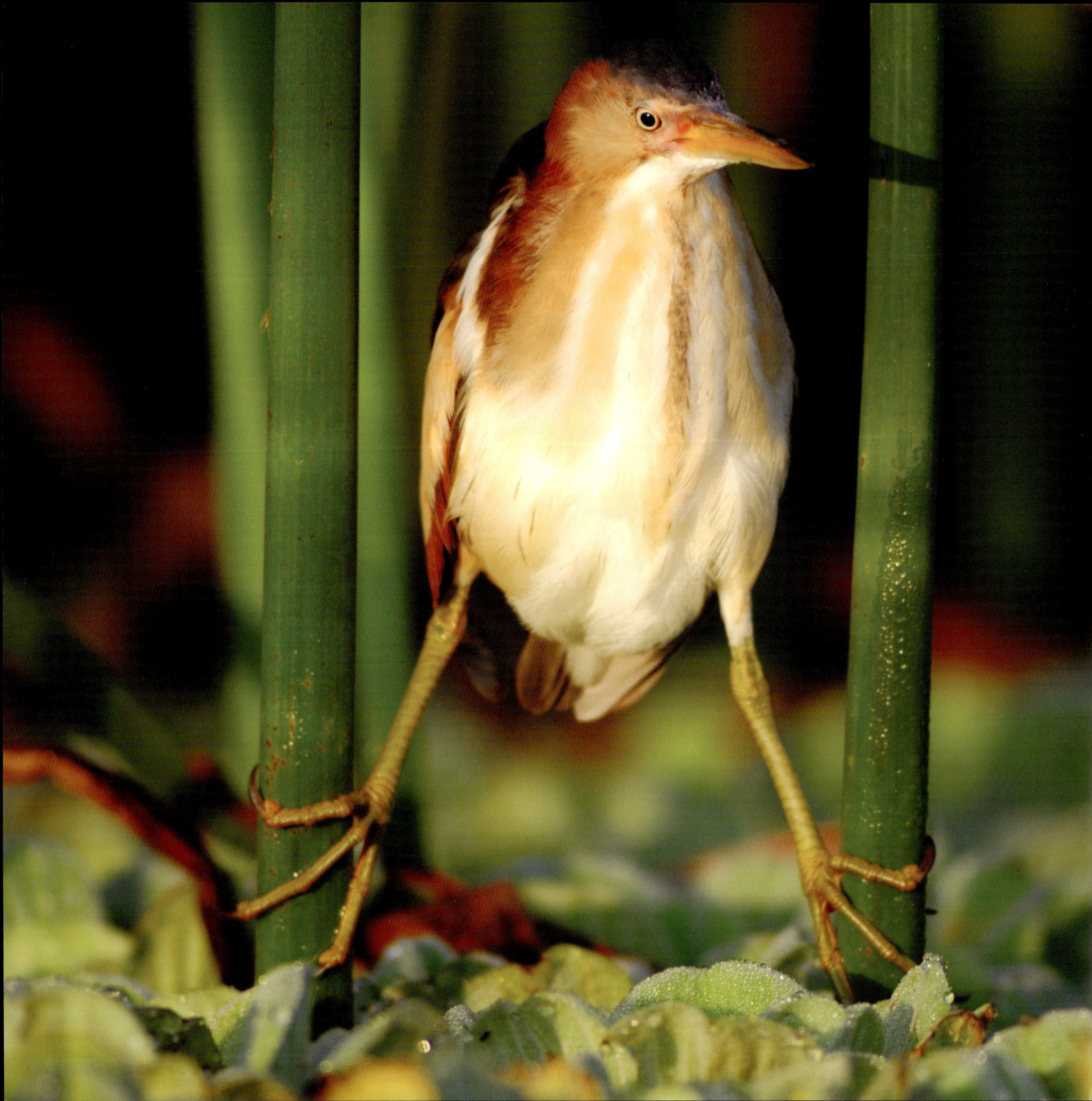

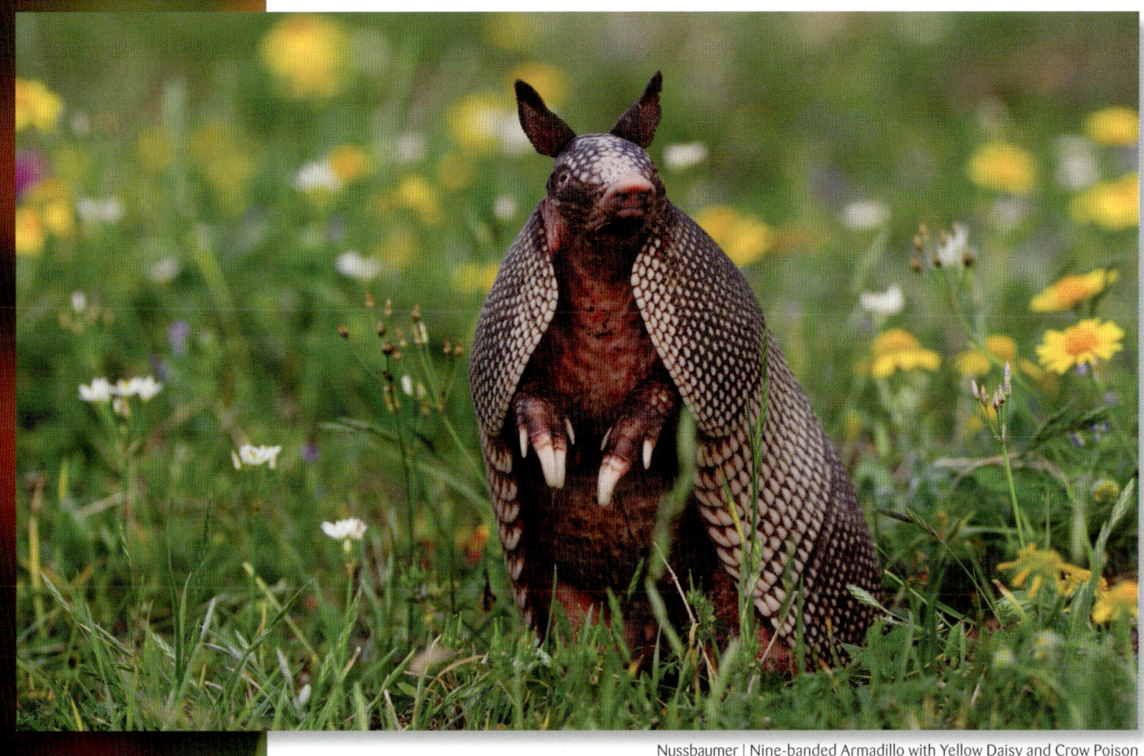

Nussbaumer | Nine-banded Armadillo with Yellow Daisy and Crow Poison

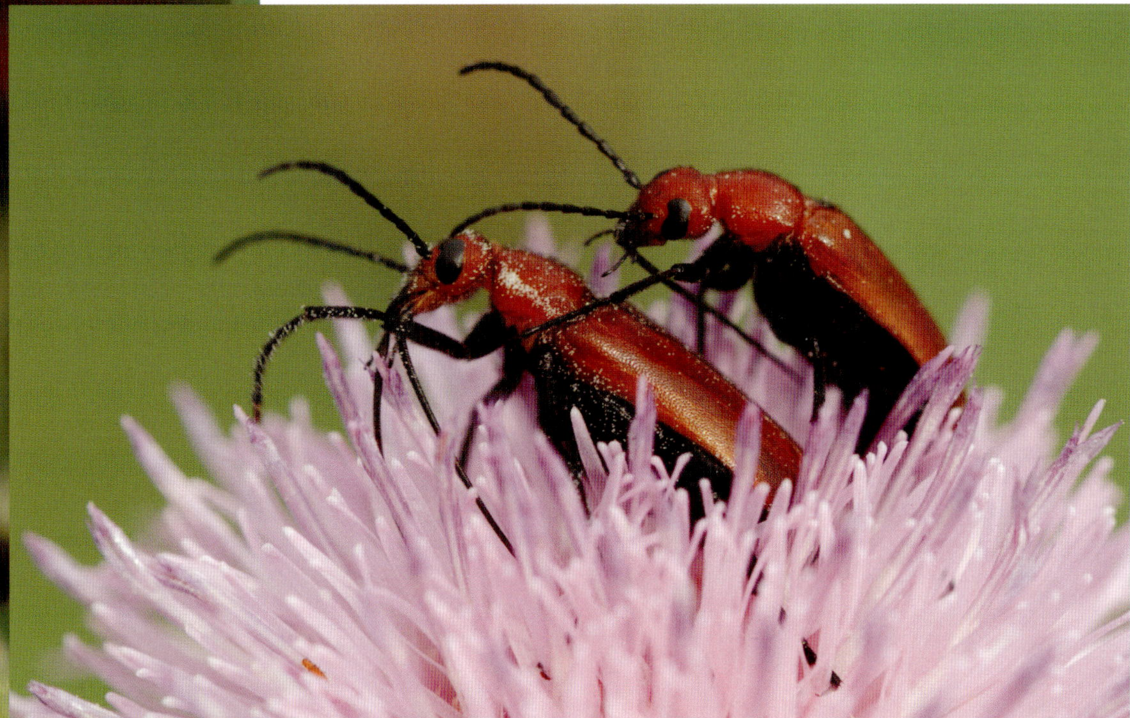

Nussbaumer | Soldier Beetles on Texas Thistle

Nussbaumer | Least Bittern standing above Water Lettuce

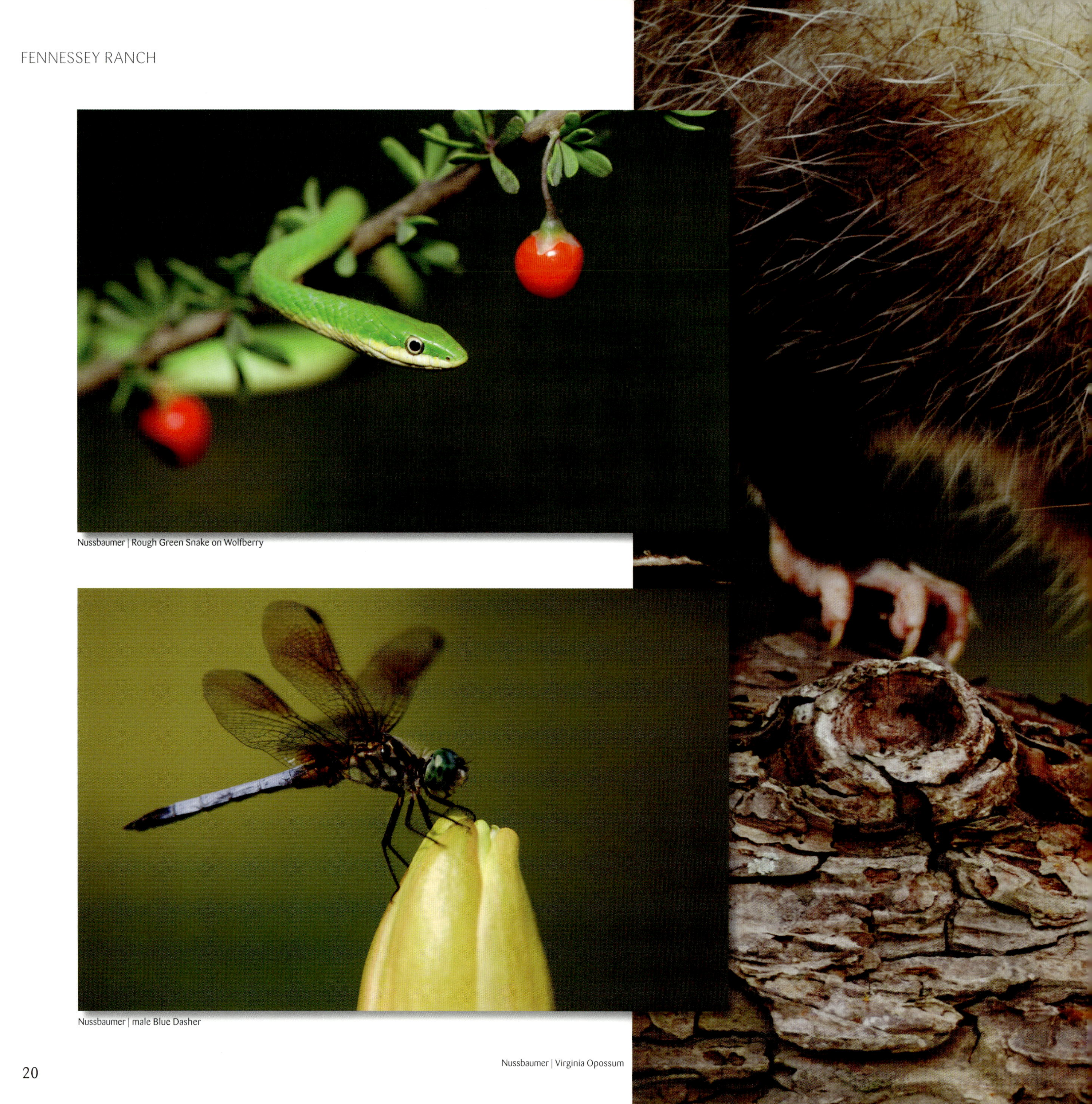

Nussbaumer | Rough Green Snake on Wolfberry

Nussbaumer | male Blue Dasher

Nussbaumer | Virginia Opossum

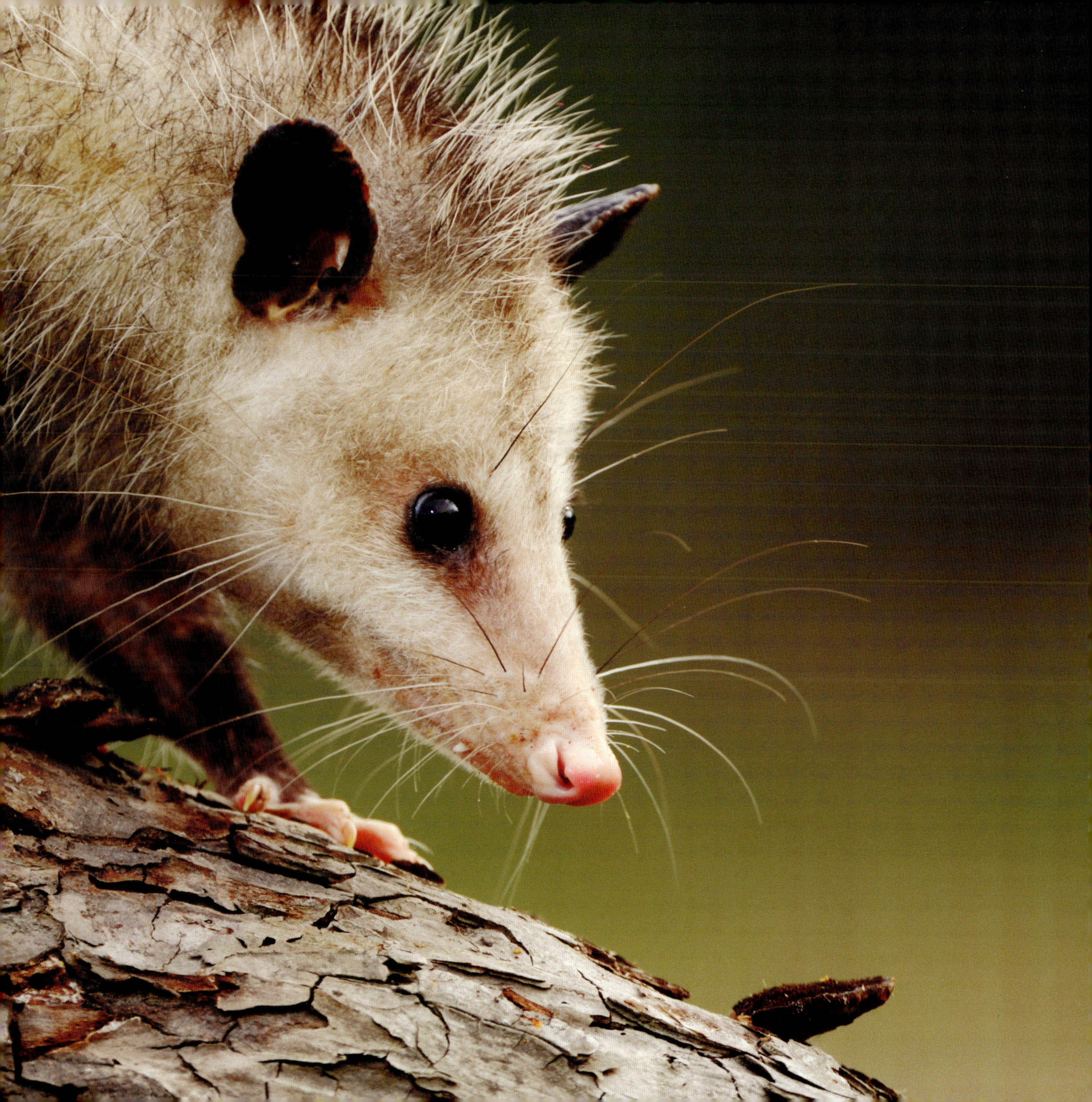

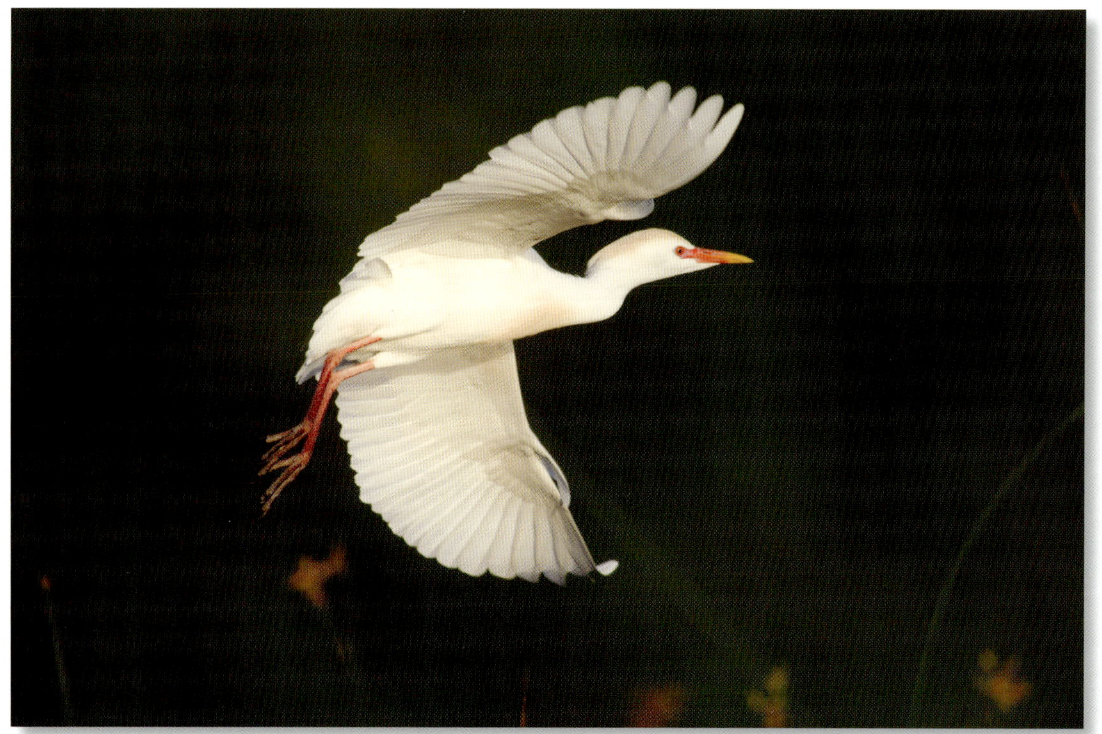

Nussbaumer | Cattle Egret

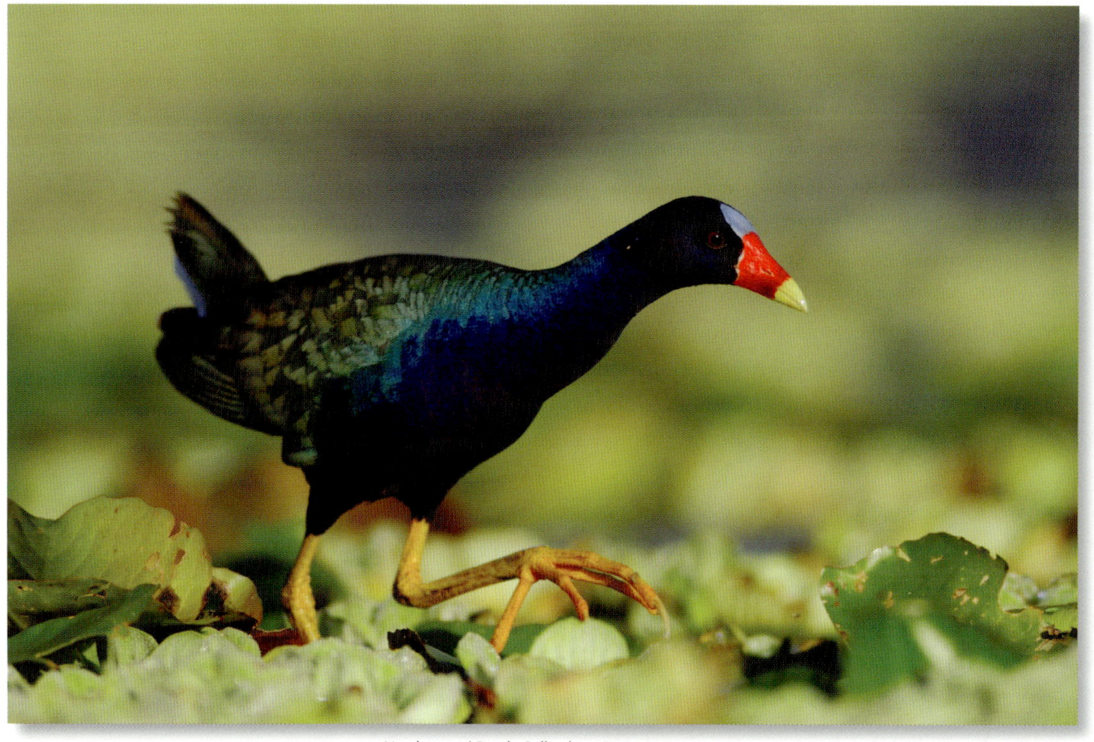

Nussbaumer | Purple Gallinule on Water Lettuce

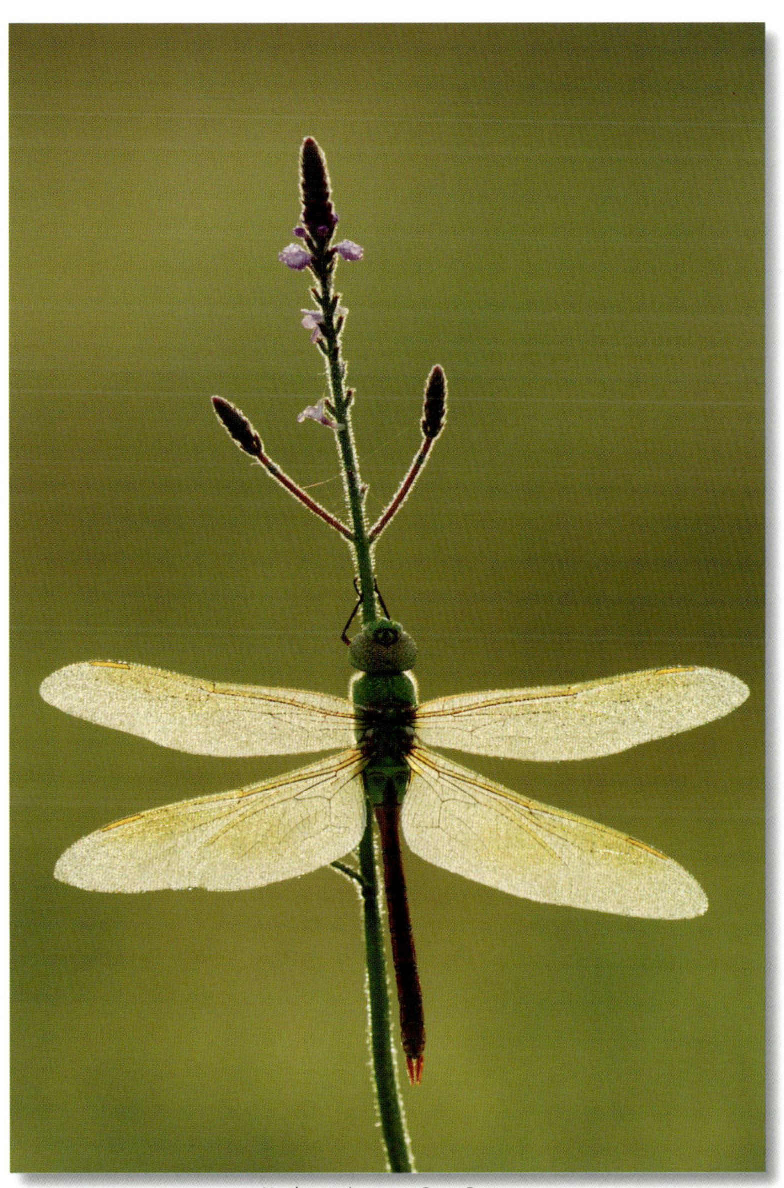

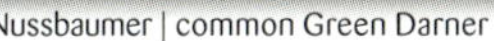
Nussbaumer | common Green Darner

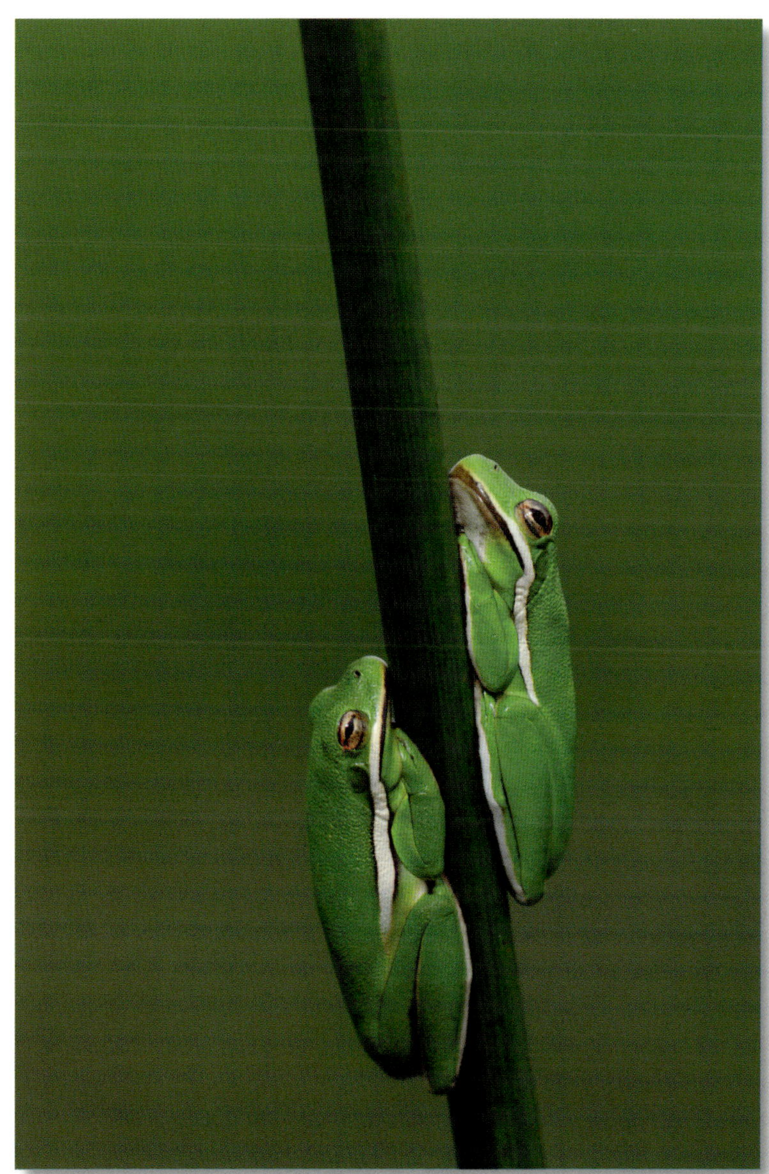
Nussbaumer | Green Treefrogs

About Mustang Ranch...

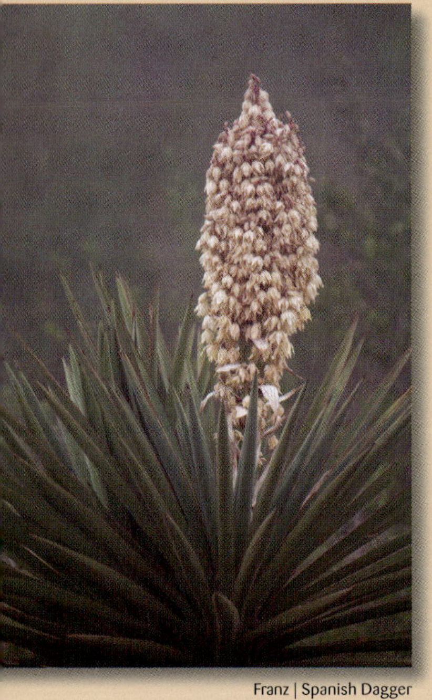
Franz | Spanish Dagger

Hugo, Laura and Omar Berlanga's ranching journey began 16 years ago with the acquisition of land that would become known as the Mustang Ranch. The family said the name was a logical fit because this region of Duval County originally was called the Wild Horse Desert. That and the fact that Omar Berlanga is a graduate of Southern Methodist University, which most Texans know is home to the SMU Mustangs.

In the 1940s, caliche destined for Corpus Christi Naval Air Station was mined from the Wild Horse Desert, giving the land much of its uncharacteristic contours. Scars left by the excavation of caliche required more than 60 years of healing before the natural vegetation returned. What remains on parts of the ranch is a landscape with brushy canyons and hills that today provides an outstanding wildlife habitat for a broad variety of plants and animals. Under the direction of Texas Parks and Wildlife biologists, the Berlangas are developing a commercial hunting business and a scientific white-tail breeding operation to enhance their herd. Through the years they also have enhanced the ranch's wildlife habitat, provided service water and added several food plots.

The Mustang Ranch began as a cattle operation, but recurring severe droughts forced the family to focus on native wild game management as an alternative. Located in southern Duval County outside of San Diego, The Mustang Ranch is an ideal location for a concerted conservation effort.

The family's primary focus today is the conservation of wildlife, scientific deer breeding and game management. These activities have not stopped the Berlangas from deriving a great deal of recreational pleasure from their rural getaway. Many weekends at the ranch are spent with friends and family. They have found that each day offers something new to be gleaned from exploring the countryside.

Hugo, Laura and Omar strive to keep the ranch as natural as possible. Since the day they purchased the ranch their mission has been to maintain its natural state and enhance the native plant species with a goal to add more acreage if possible. Their desire is that such lands never develop in a way that destroys the natural habitat.

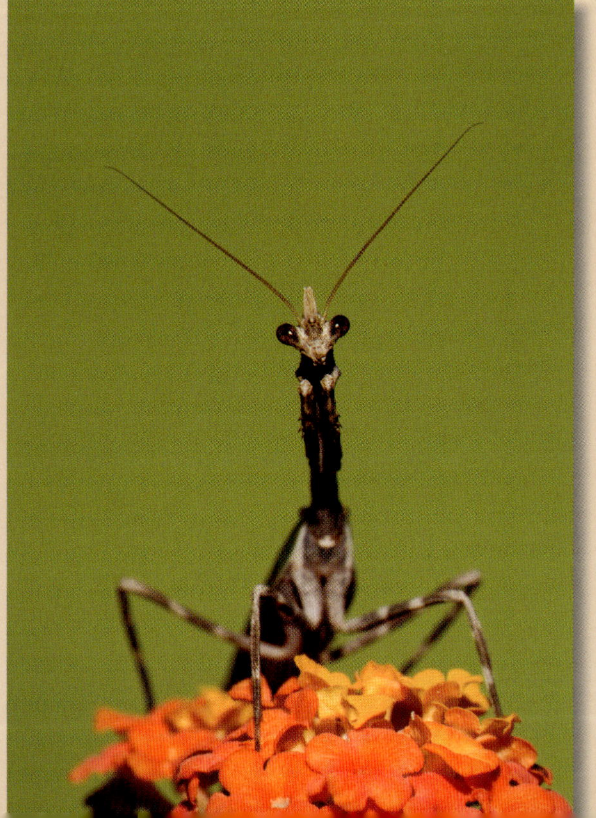
Franz | Preying Mantid on Texas Lantana

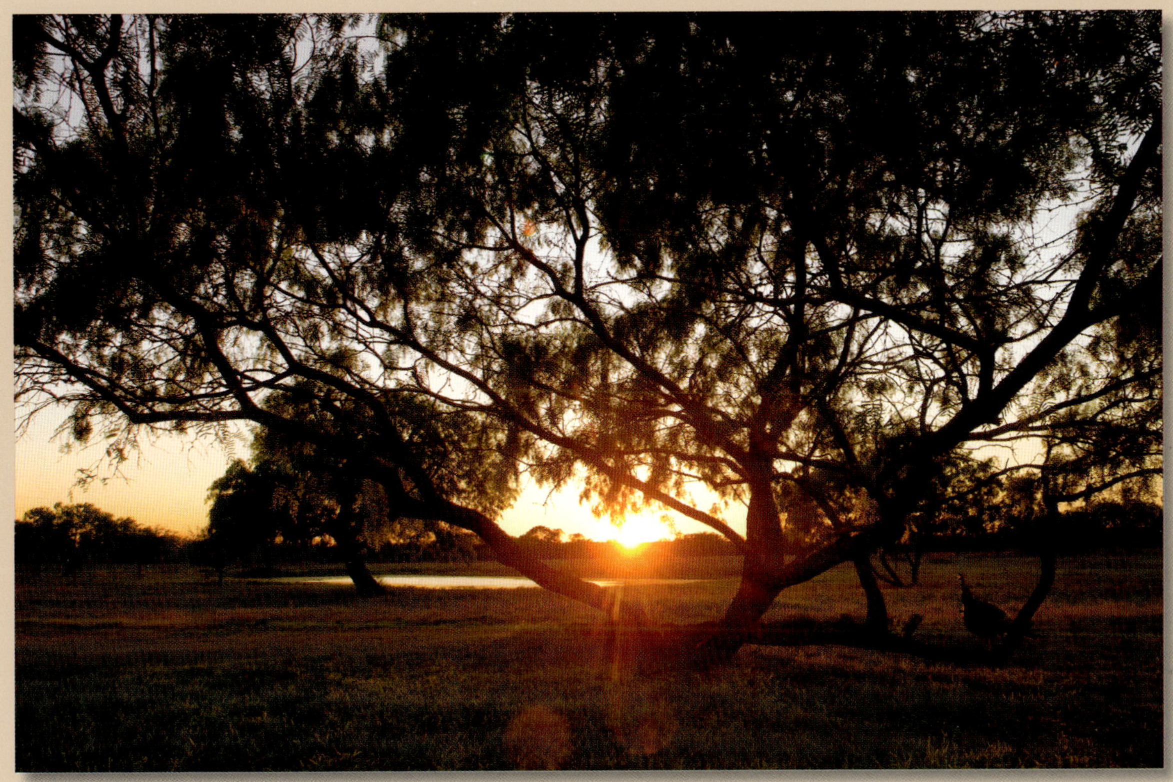

Franz | Mesquite tree

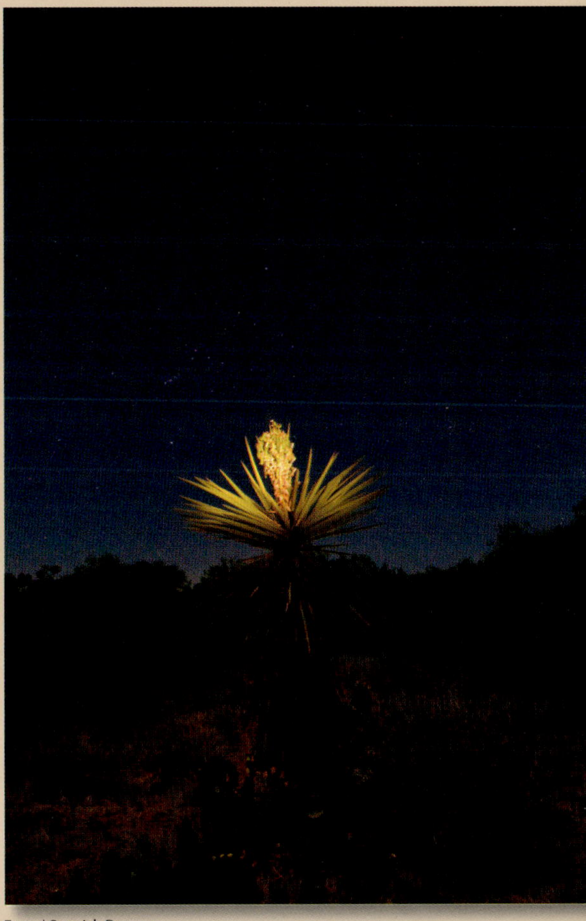

Franz | Spanish Dagger

This weekend retreat and ultimately the Berlangas' future retirement home is a conservation model for other ranchers to emulate. The Berlangas chose to participate in the Pro-Tour after their success in the 2003 Coastal Bend Wildlife Photo Contest. The family's efforts can be seen not only in the legacy of conservation on their ranch, but in the lasting and striking images created by photographers who visit there.

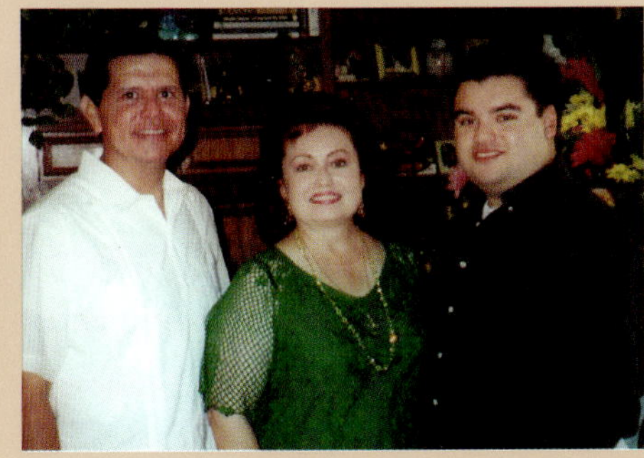

Hugo and Laura Berlanga, Omar Berlanga
Corpus Christi, Texas
[e] bbcberlanga@yahoo.com

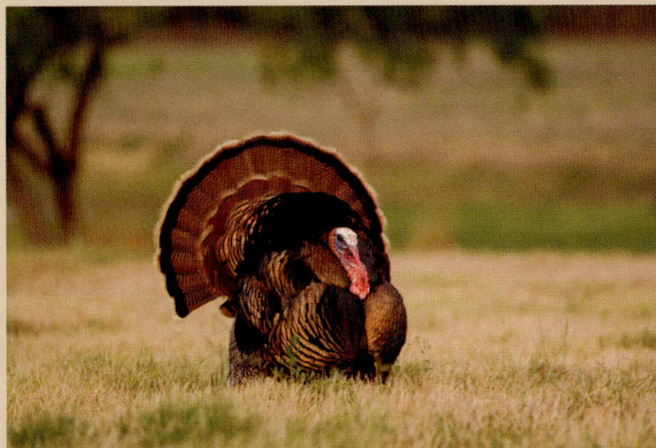

Franz | Wild Turkey

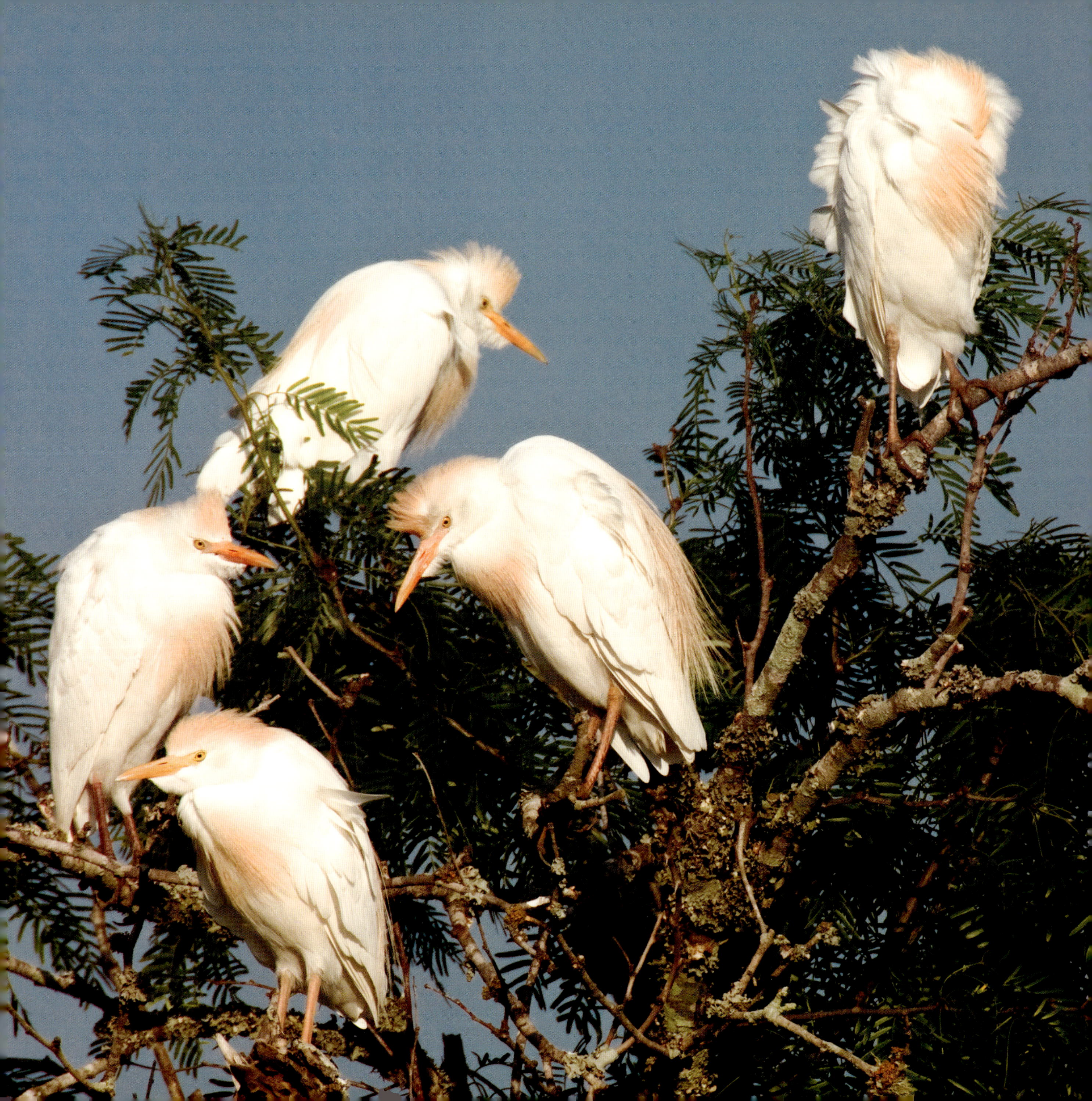

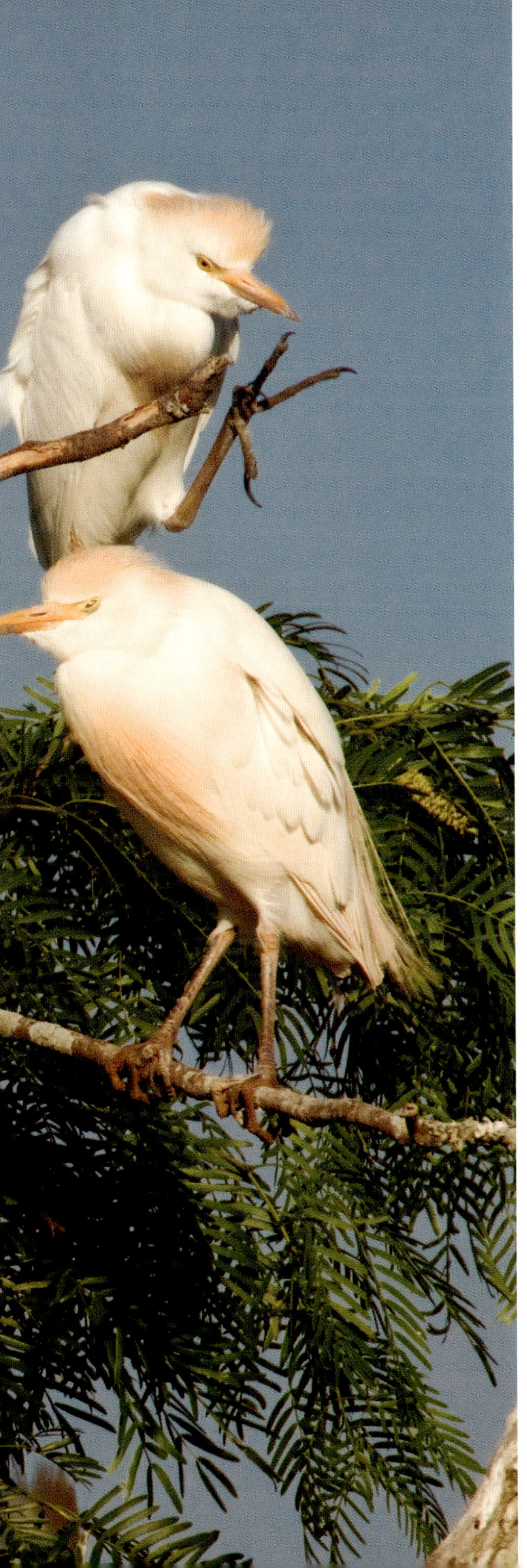

Franz | Cattle Egret in Mesquite

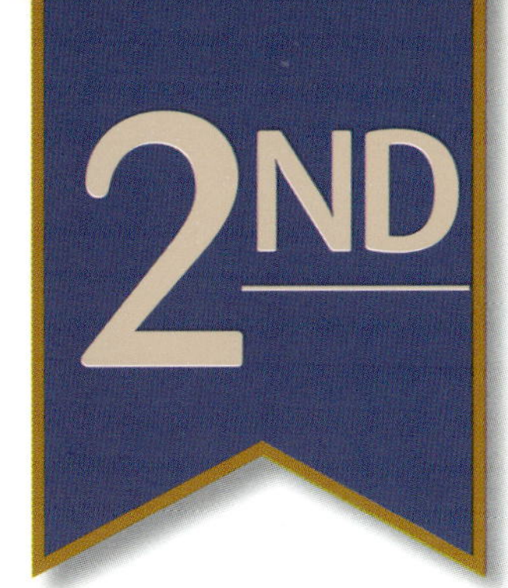

D. Robert Franz

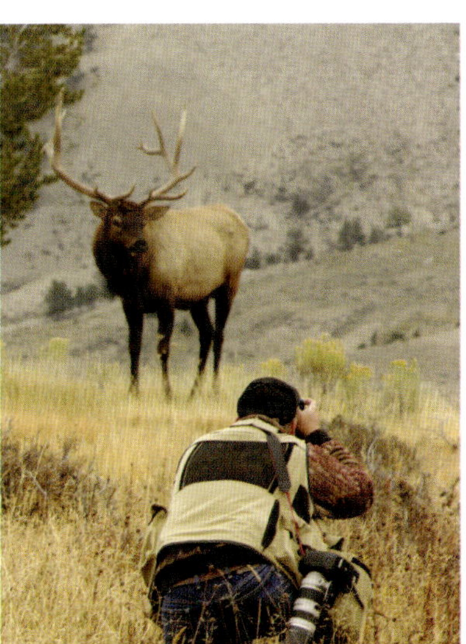

To D. (Dale) Robert Franz it's icing on the cake when he can tell a tale with his photographic eye. "When I'm out there photographing," he explains, "I'm not exclusively after a story, but I really like it when the image tells one."

Dale's own story is one of obsession. He admits that being obsessive can "get in your way at times" but, "it's what you need if you want to make really good pictures. Especially during this contest I needed it. Because of heavy predator control at the ranch Coyotes and Bobcats and such only came out at night. As tired as I could be, I had to be obsessive about staying up at night if I was going to get any of those kinds of shots."

Those weren't the only shots that kept him up at night on the Mustang Ranch. "There was a particularly frustrating situation where I had these nesting Barn Owls and I knew exactly what photo I wanted. I'd been working at it for a while and had tried several times to get a shot. The owls just would not cooperate," he says with chagrin. "At this point I was up every night, checking on the infrared equipment, hanging from a ladder in the middle of the night. There were weather issues and technical problems with my triggering device."

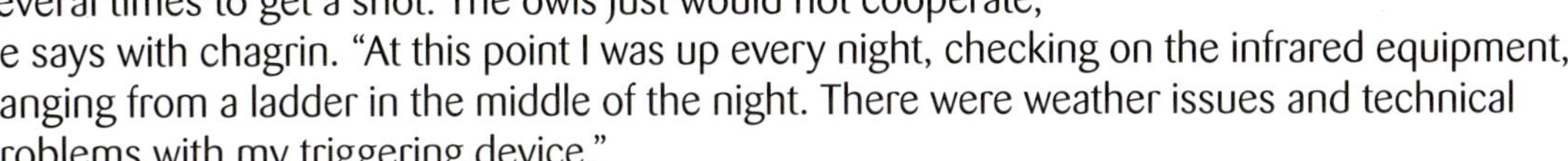

"But," he says with a sigh, "I finally got the image."

"Although," he adds, "it wasn't the one I wanted but it was pretty good. It was of the owl flying at you straight on with a rabbit in its mouth."

"Even as a child I was always running around with a camera taking photographs of nature." However, it wasn't until college that he picked up a camera with true intention. "I was a wildlife biology major and they suggested we get a 35mm camera. When I finished my degree it was tough to get a job in my field and photography seemed to be my only way to have a job working with wildlife."

Since 1989 he's been using the camera professionally. He "cut his teeth" as a film photographer and because of this, he says, "I think in terms of getting the exposure and composition right in the camera instead of going back and fixing it."

These days, he admits, it's difficult for him to simply enjoy wildlife without thinking about what shots he could be taking. "But, the truth is, I also sometimes really need some time away from my camera. Sometimes I just need to put it down."

Cody, Wyoming
www.franzfoto.com
[e] drobertfranz@msn.com

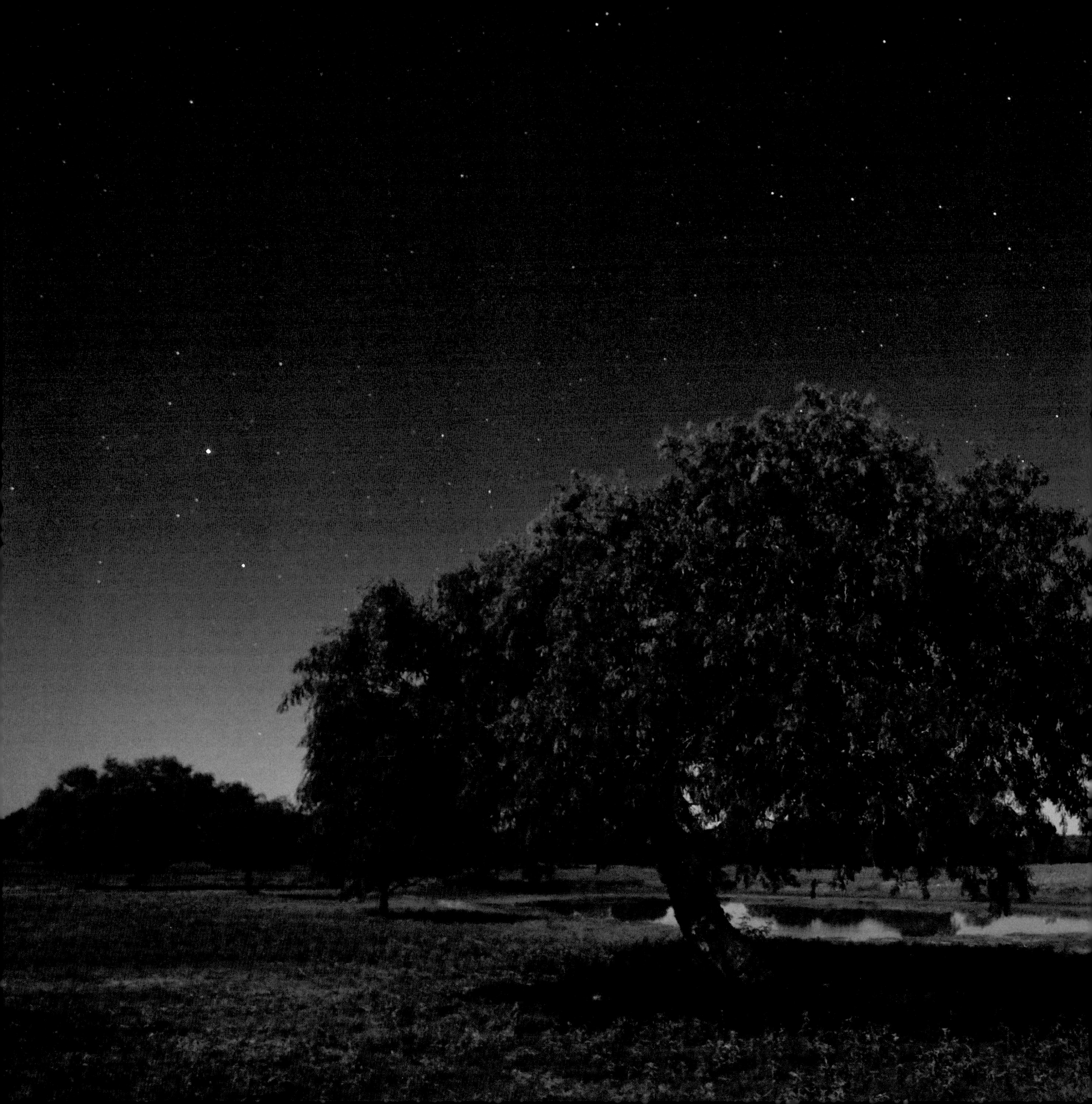

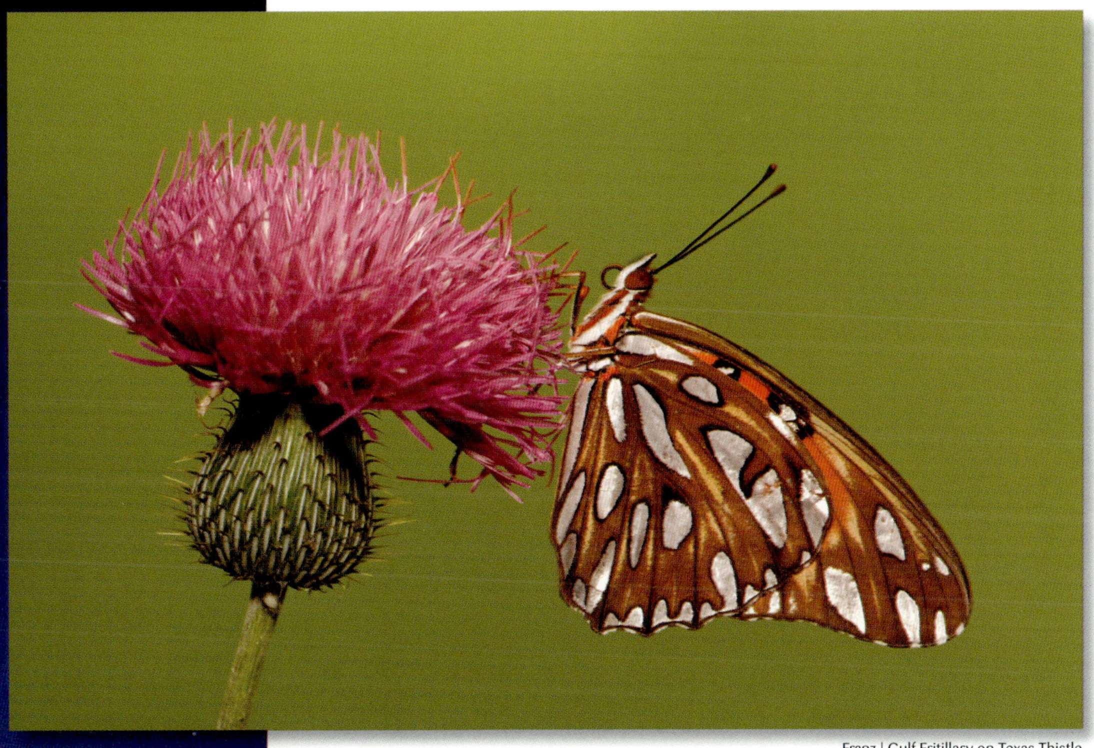

Franz | Gulf Fritillary on Texas Thistle

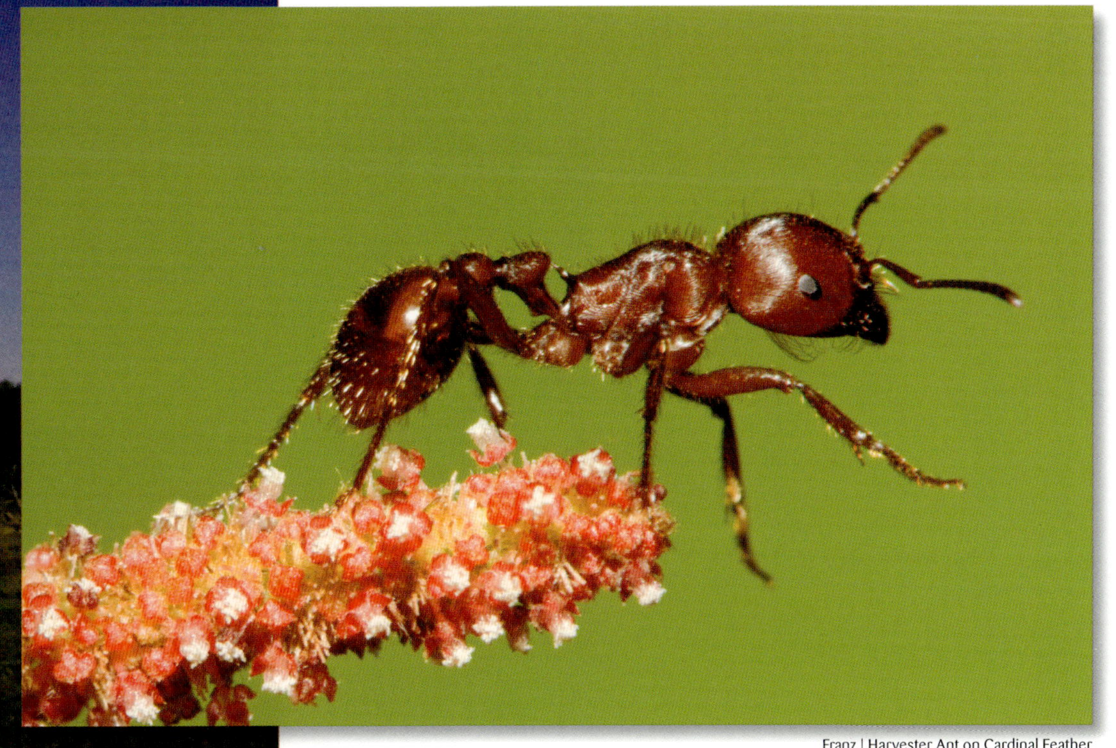

Franz | Harvester Ant on Cardinal Feather

Franz | Live Oak tree

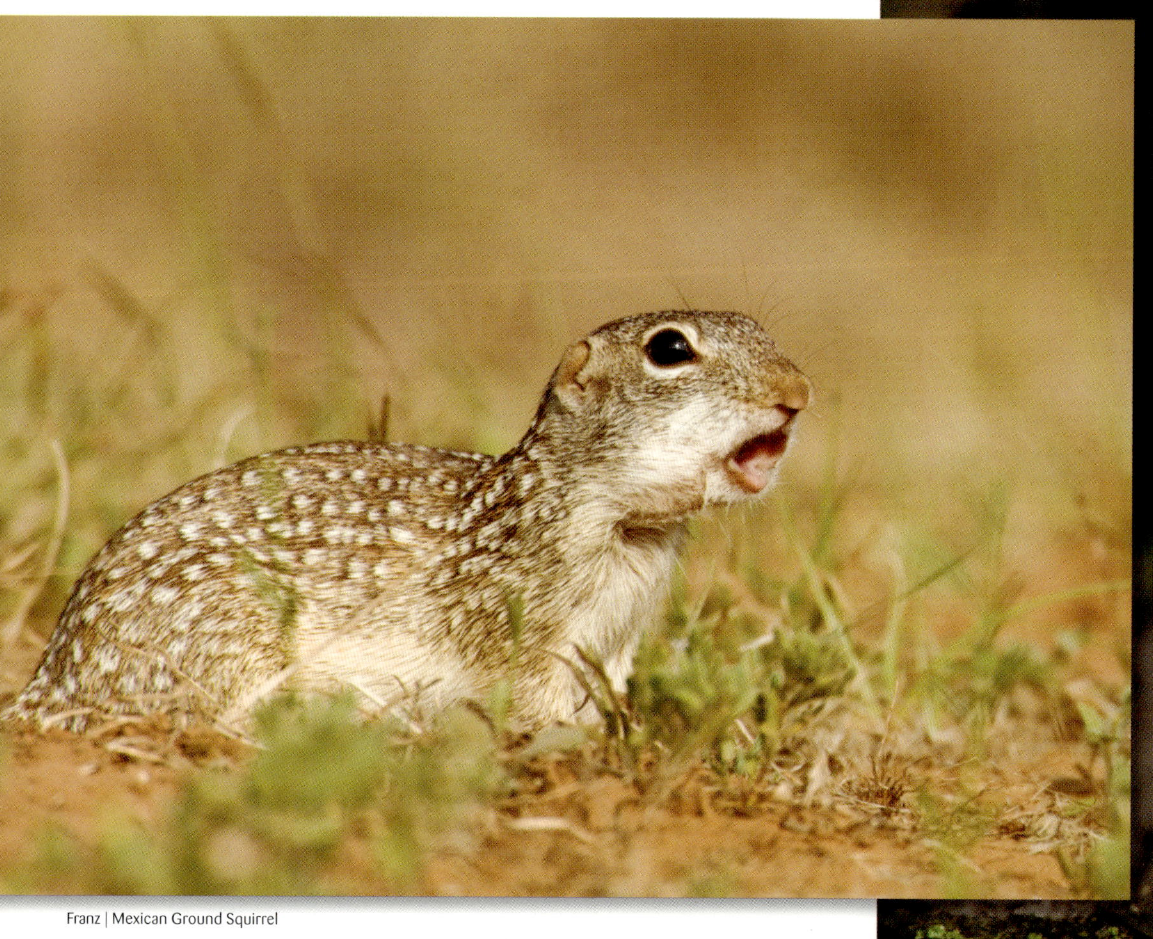

Franz | Mexican Ground Squirrel

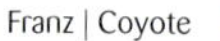

Franz | Coyote

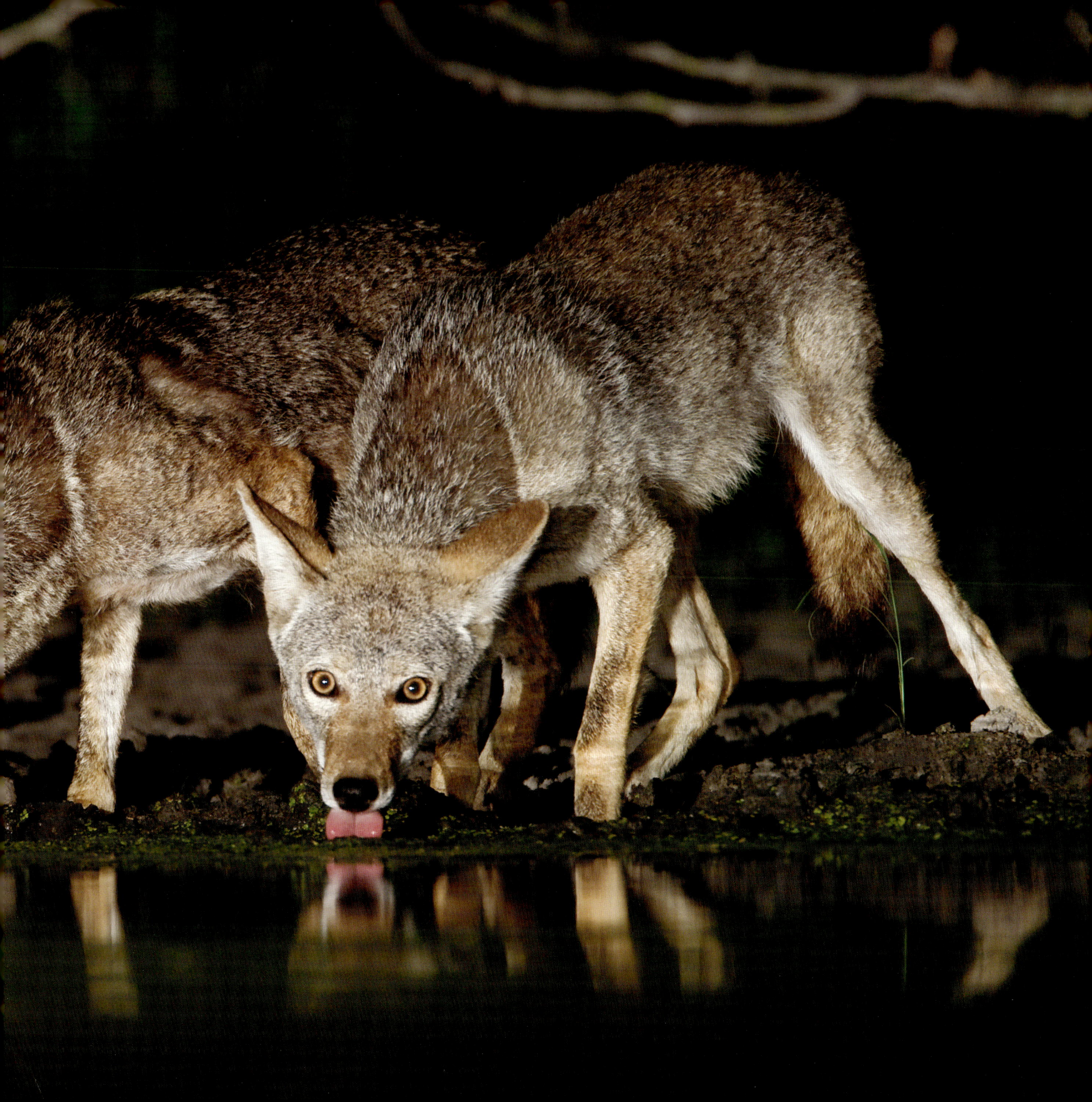

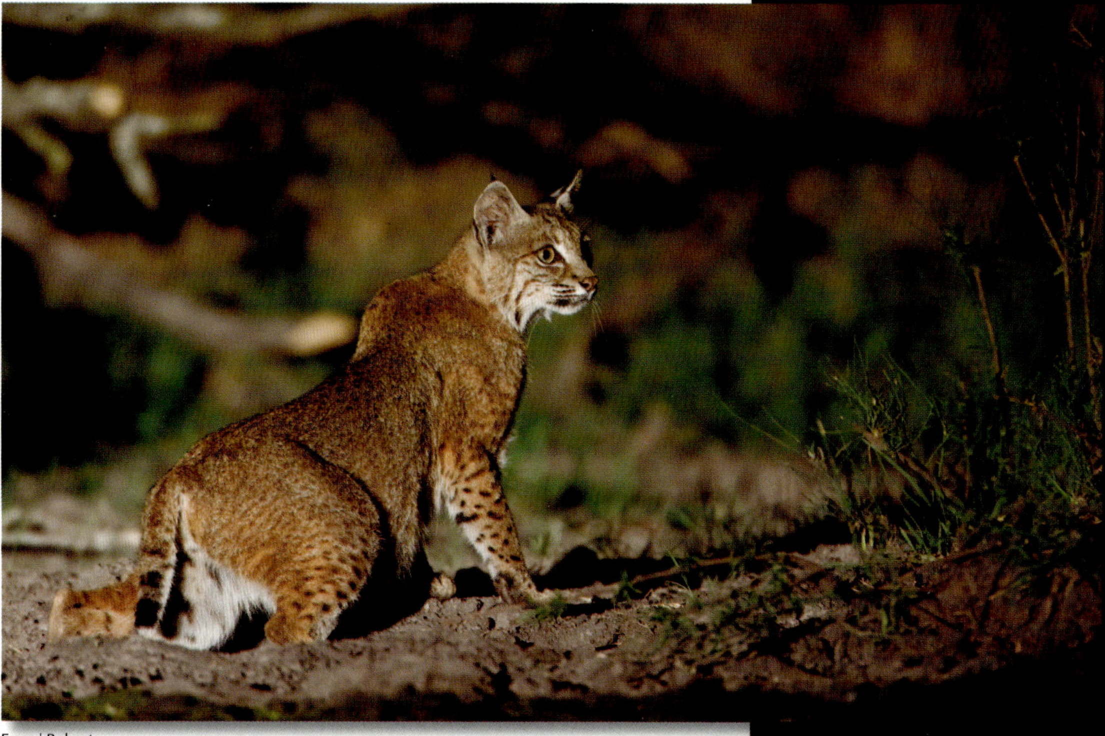

Franz | Bobcat

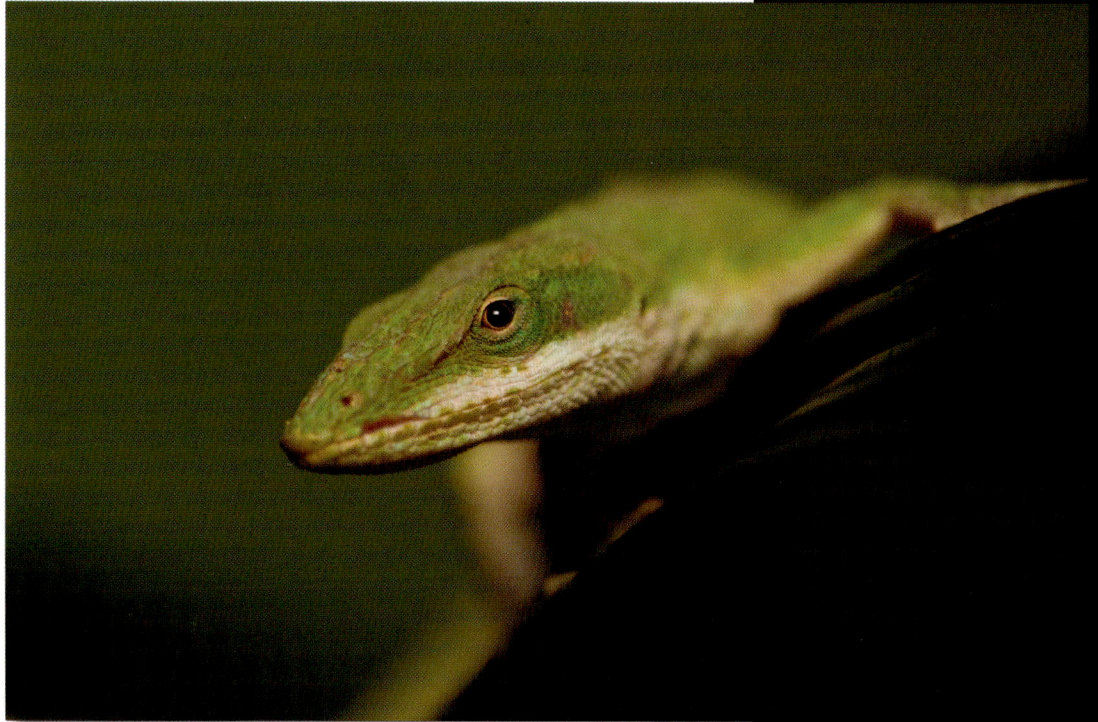

Franz | Green Anole

Franz | Barn Owl

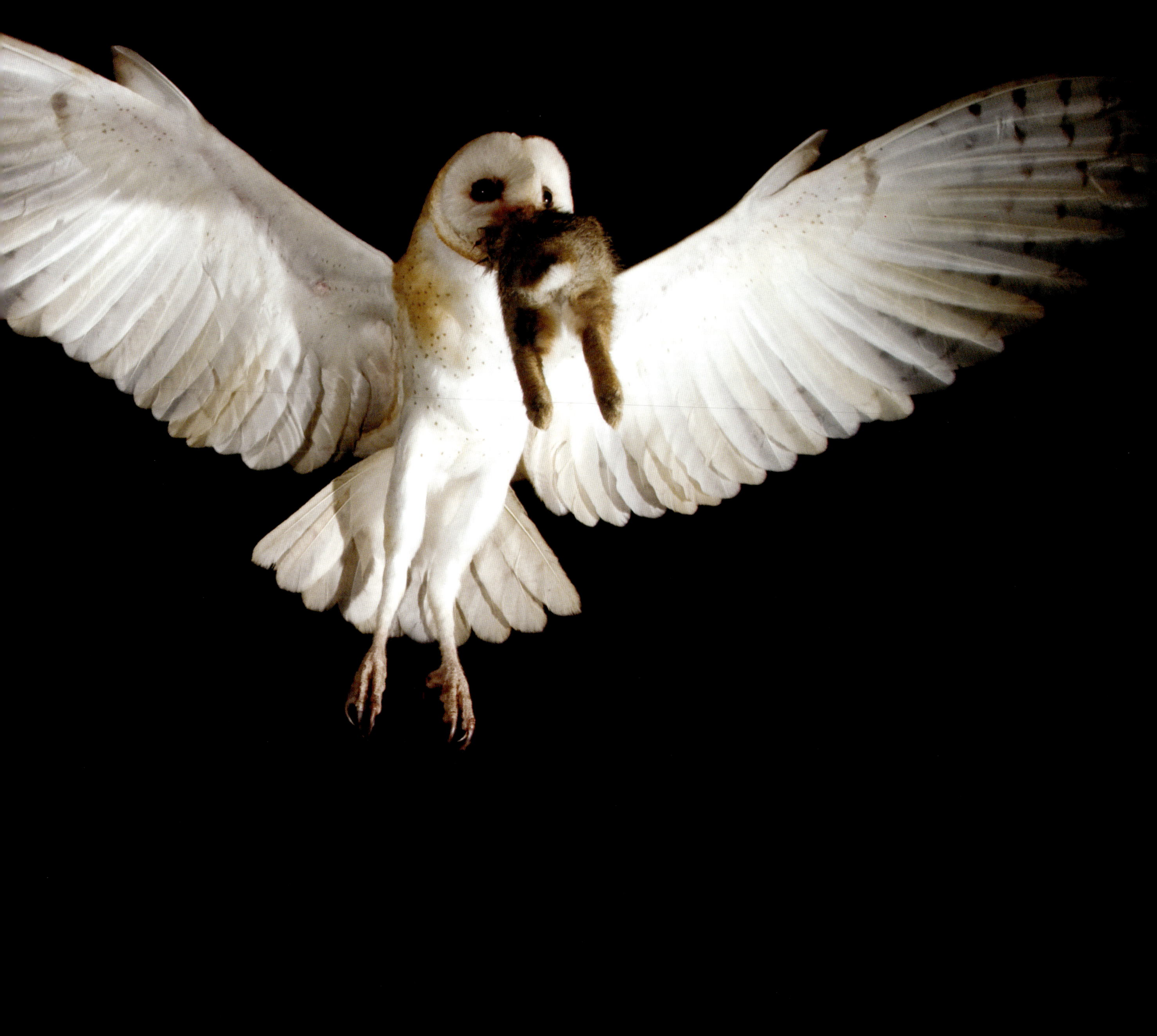

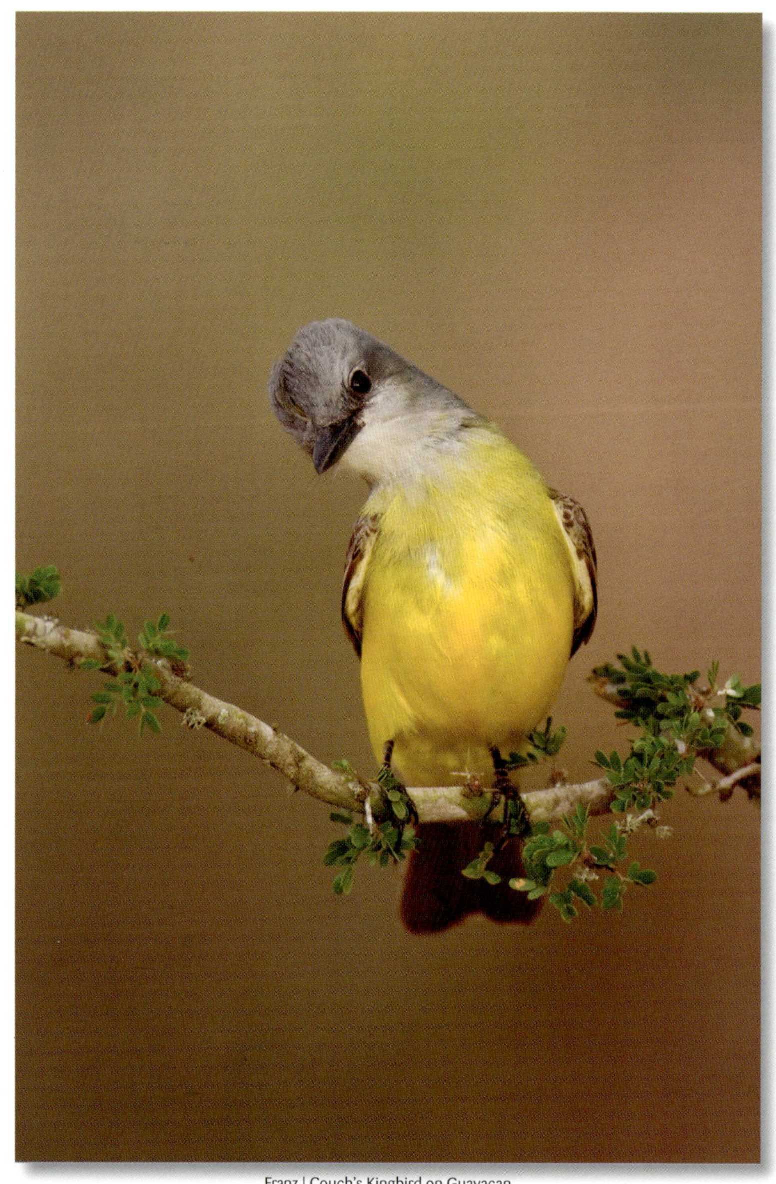

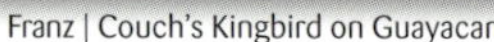
Franz | Couch's Kingbird on Guayacan

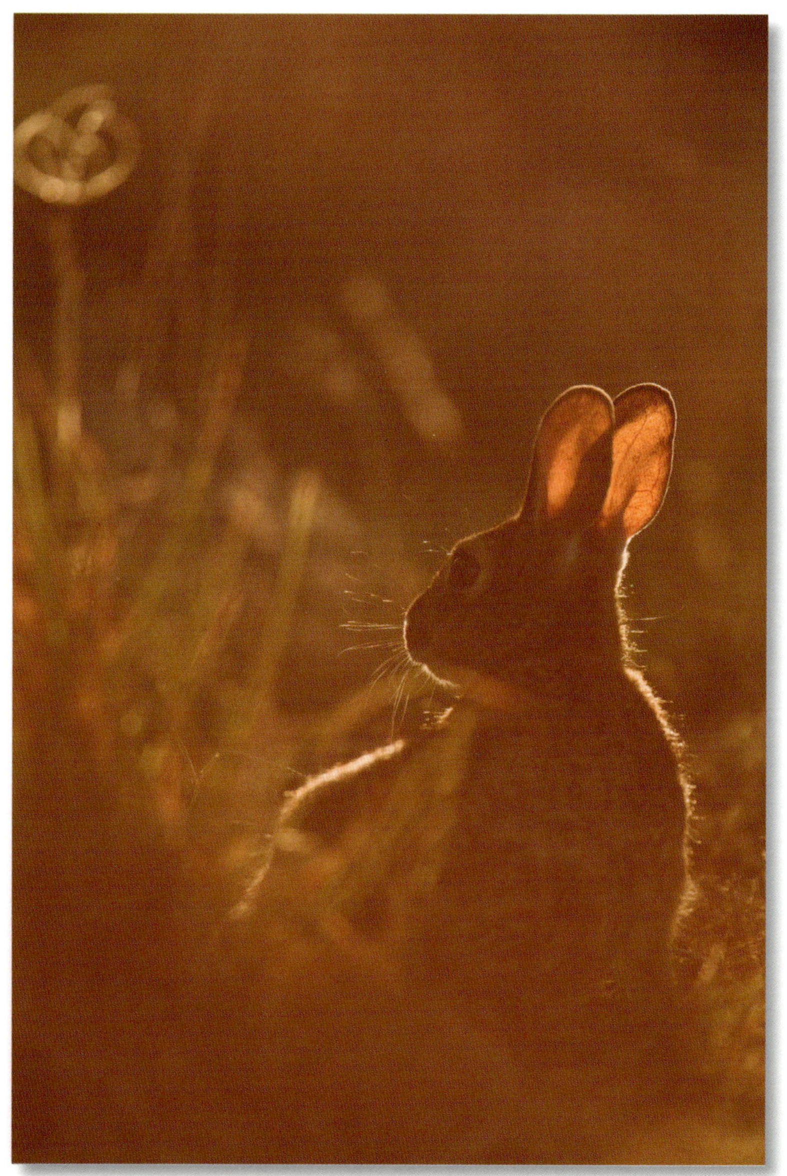
Franz | Eastern Cottontail Rabbit

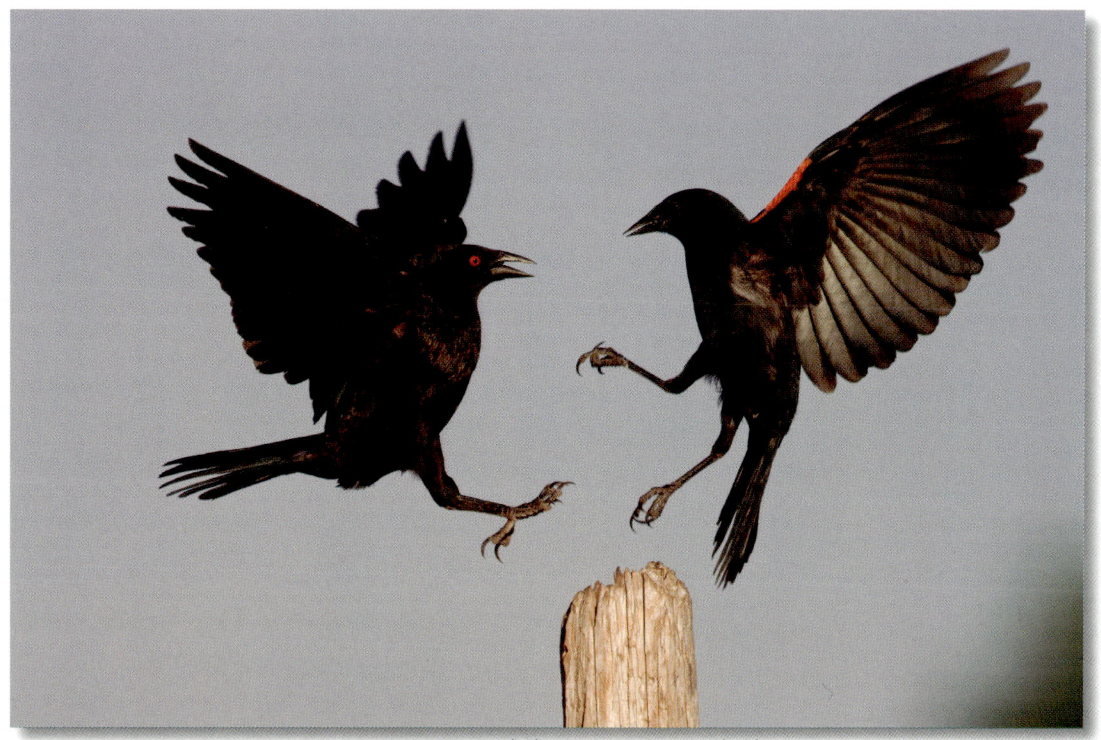

Franz | Bronzed Cowbird (left) and Red-winged Blackbird (right)

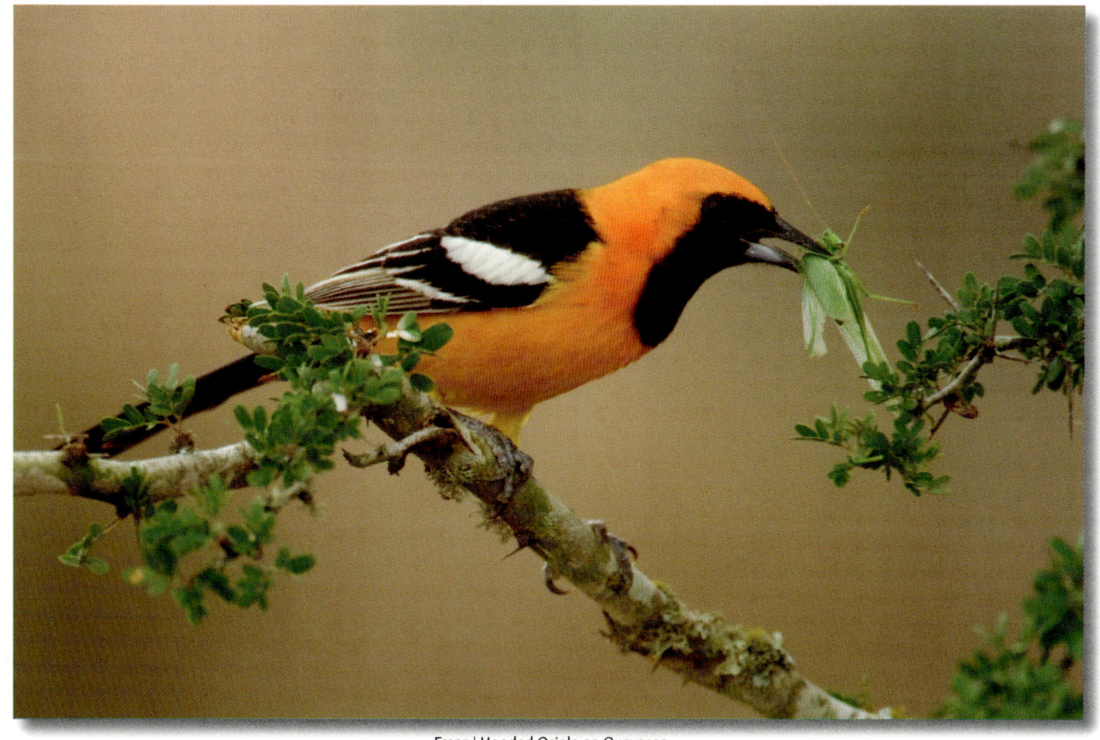

Franz | Hooded Oriole on Guayacan

About Welder Wildlife Foundation...

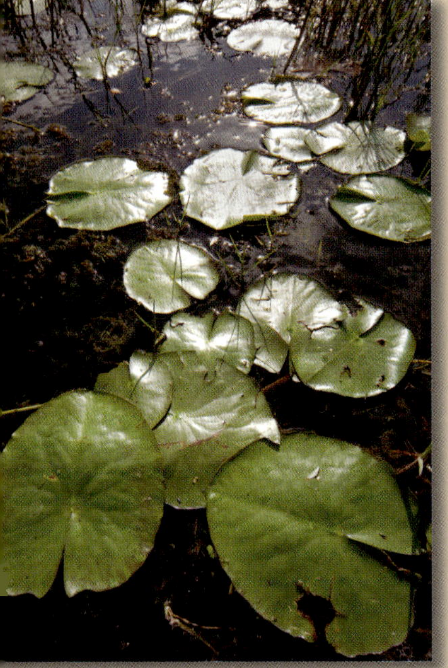

Hendrickson | Water Lilies

A simple white stucco structure with a red tile roof marks the Welder Wildlife Foundation Refuge and headquarters just outside Sinton. It's difficult to imagine from this unassuming landmark in rural San Patricio County that the research conducted here has an international reach.

Beyond the gate house on U.S. Highway 77 is a compound that includes several residences, an outdoor rotunda, a dormitory and an administration building with specimen collections, laboratory, library, museum, and lecture hall. The refuge itself encompasses 7,800 acres of prime wildlife habitat, spanning the Tamaulipan Biotic Province, a transitional zone between coastal prairies and marshes and the Rio Grande Plain vegetation areas. The Aransas River serves as the Refuge's northern boundary for 15 miles as it serpentines toward Copano Bay along the coast. Through geologic history the river has gradually moved northward leaving remnants of the prehistoric channel that form several oxbow lakes on the refuge. The largest of these, Big Lake, covers 130 acres when full.

Varied soil types and topography provide diverse habitats for the abundant wildlife found on this unique geographical location. Lakes, prairie, riparian forest, marshes, chaparral, and Mesquite savannah make up the natural habitats.

White-tailed Deer, Rio Grande Turkeys, bobwhite quail, rabbits, Javelinas, Coyotes, and Bobcats are common residents on the Welder Wildlife Refuge. Many species of non-game birds, reptiles, and amphibians also thrive here. Legions of avian species abound especially during winter and long migration periods. Approximately 400 birds have been recorded on the Refuge and it's not unusual for a trained student to identify 75 species in a day's time.

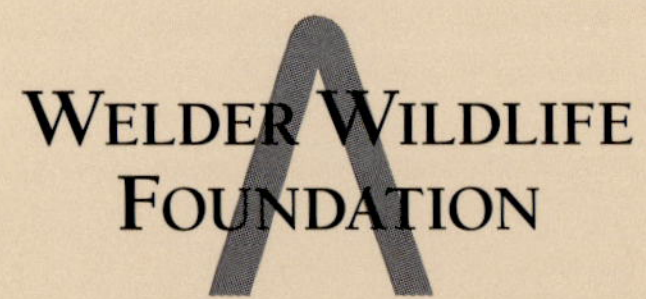

Created through the will of Robert Hughes Welder, the Rob and Bessie Welder Wildlife Foundation was established in 1954 as a uniquely Texan, private wildlife research and conservation institution, gaining national and international recognition through its graduate student research program. WWF is a private, non-profit foundation funded by an endowment, contributions, cattle income, and interest from investments. The Refuge is a portion of a Spanish grant received by Don Felipe Roque De La Portilla in 1834. This would serve as a springboard for the Welder family in this area. Today the Foundation continues its mission through its dedicated trustees, directors, staff and students.

Hendrickson | Gulf Coast Toad with Huisache Daisy

Annually, an average of 10 carefully selected graduate students from universities across the U.S. and Canada are granted fellowships to conduct research and pursue advanced degrees in wildlife conservation and management. Research topics, theses, and dissertations are as varied as the range of living organisms they study. Conducted on the Welder Wildlife Refuge, or elsewhere, all research shares a focus on conservation of native wildlife and their natural habitats. The research strives to provide examples of good land stewardship to promote the wise use of our natural resources throughout the South Texas ranching community. The Foundation uses grazing to manage vegetation and prescribed fire to manage brush on rangelands. The goal is to provide a diversity of plant species in native grassland and brushland for abundant wildlife species present on the Refuge.

The Welder Wildlife Foundation has developed plans for a new education facility to enhance educational programs on the Refuge. This facility will also improve storage and display areas for biological specimens. A new museum is also planned to showcase the conservation of natural resources.

The Refuge sponsors guided tours for the public, school field trips, conservation workshops for school teachers and lectures by wildlife specialists.

Terry Blankenship
Sinton, Texas
[e] tblankenship@welderwildlife.org

Hendrickson | Bullfrog and male Rambur's Forktail

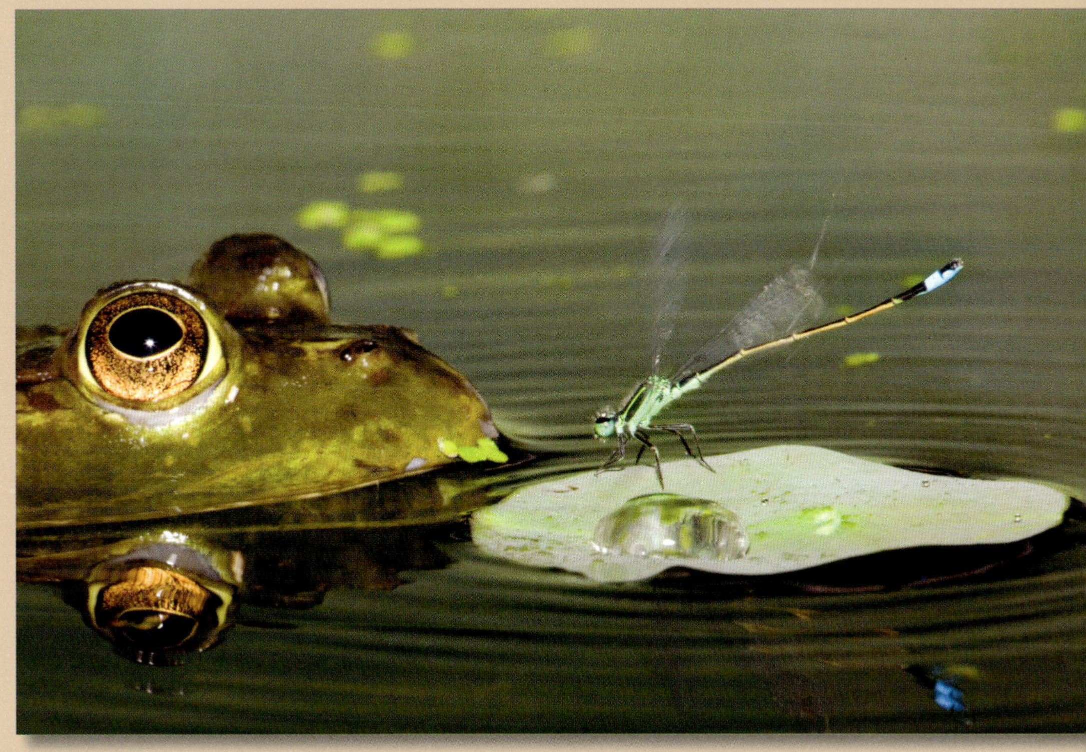

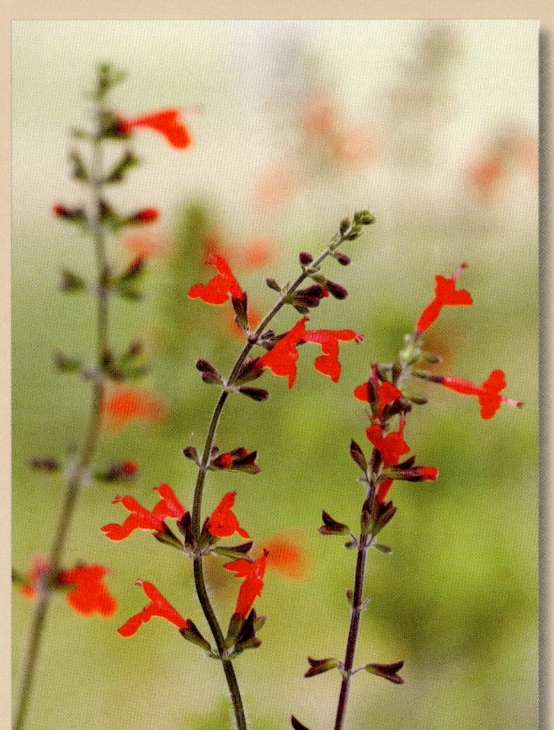

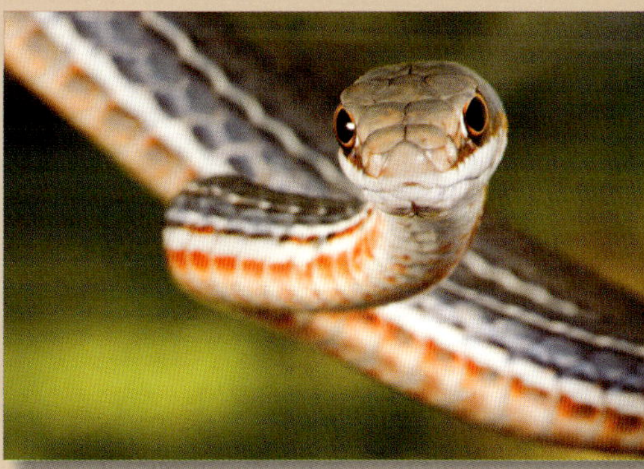

Hendrickson | Schott's Whipsnake

Hendrickson | Tropical Sage

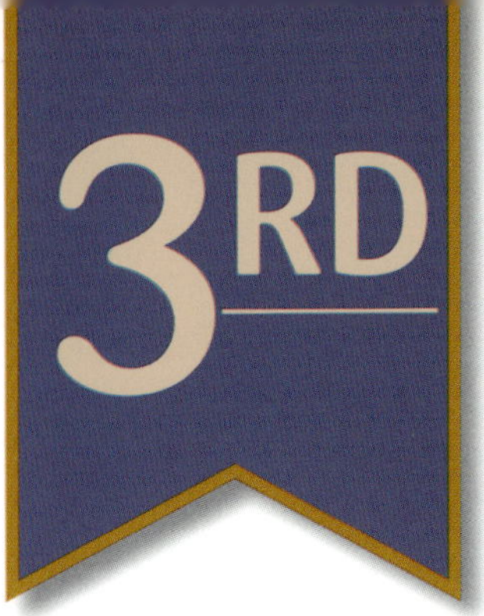

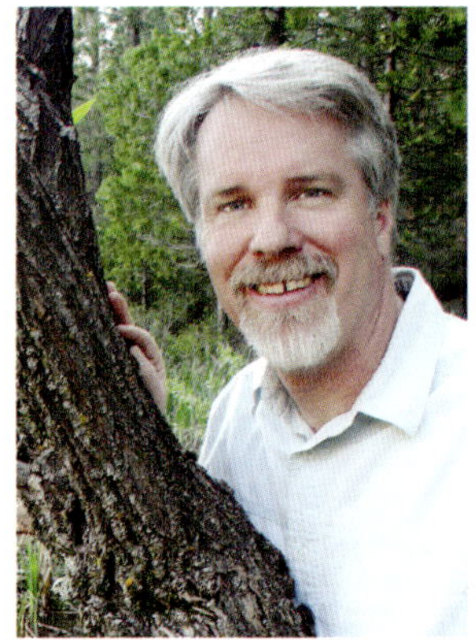

John Hendrickson

"I really see myself as more of a naturalist than a nature photographer. Photography is one of the tools I use to bring people to nature," John explains.

He was brought to nature, in part by "my grandfather, who was a naturalist. He gave me a Blue Morpho butterfly from Brazil and it opened up the world to me; knowing where the different butterflies came from helped me learn my geography."

Another adult was also instrumental in determining the course of John's life. "When I was in second grade my teacher introduced me to Lincoln Van de Griendt, who was a photographer and professor of Ornithology at UC Berkeley. After he talked to our class, my teacher, knowing I was interested in nature, encouraged me to write him a letter."

The college professor received the second-grader's note on the same day he also received the news that he had only about three months to live. "Van de Griendt's wife told me he connected the two events. He asked my parents if he could come out and show me some things."

When he came, he brought his books about falconry, hawks, and other birds. When the professor died, he left his ornithology books to John.

John tells of two especially memorable moments during his days at the Welder Wildlife Foundation. The first was during a storm when, he confides, "I was really the most scared that I was going to die. There I was in this blind in the middle of nowhere. My blind was tied to barbed wire to secure it and this lightning storm came. The first bolt was so close there were sparks on the barbed wire and it disrupted the electronics of my camera. That camera died that day."

When he talks about the other special contest memory, his voice calms, "I was in a marsh when I heard a sound like someone trying to start a flooded outboard. I saw a couple of alligators, a big one and a small one, and they were mating, doing a kind of rumble with their throats while the water around them kinda vibrated. One of them lifted its head and tail out of the water, amidst the sunrise and the mist. I started taking photos."

Clipper Mills, CA
[e] tpjuan@excite.com

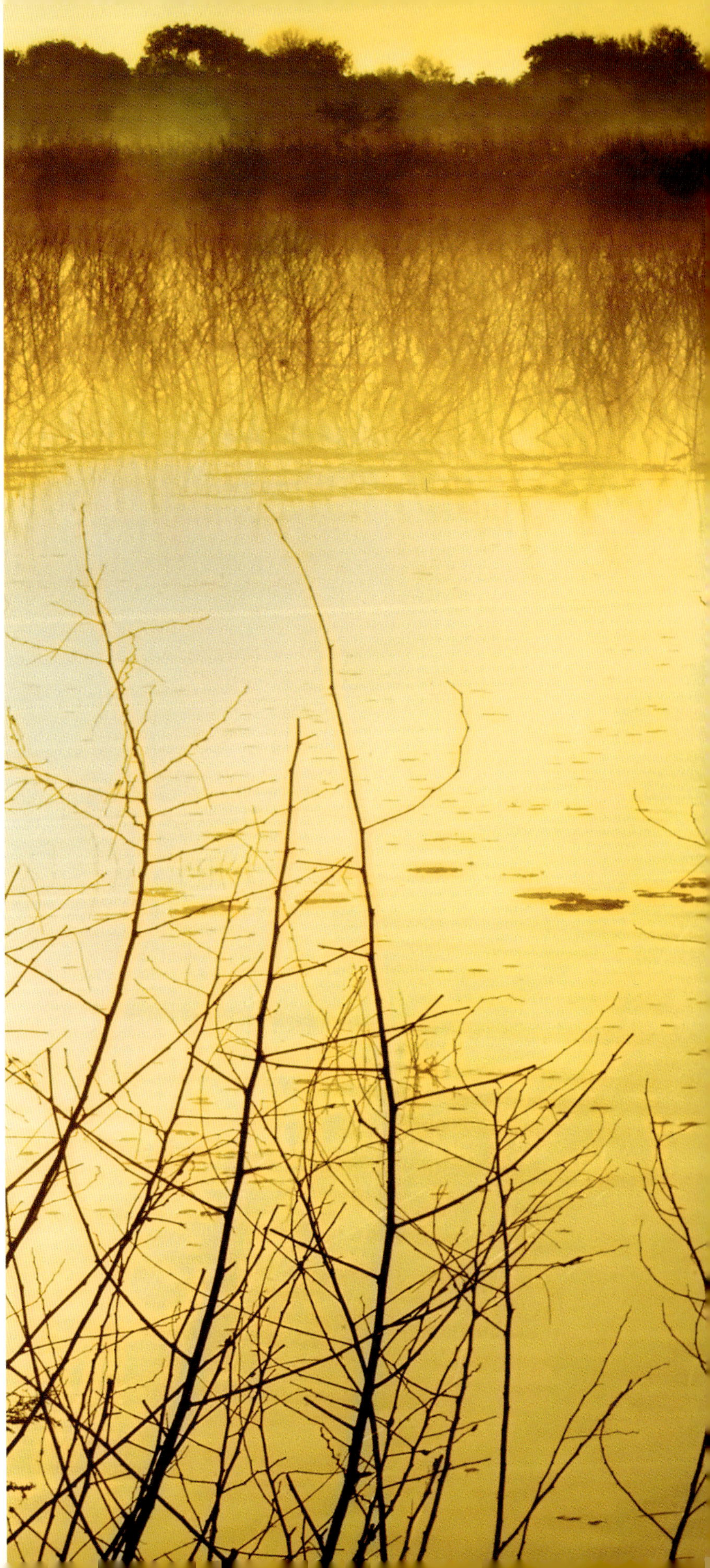

Hendrickson | American Alligator

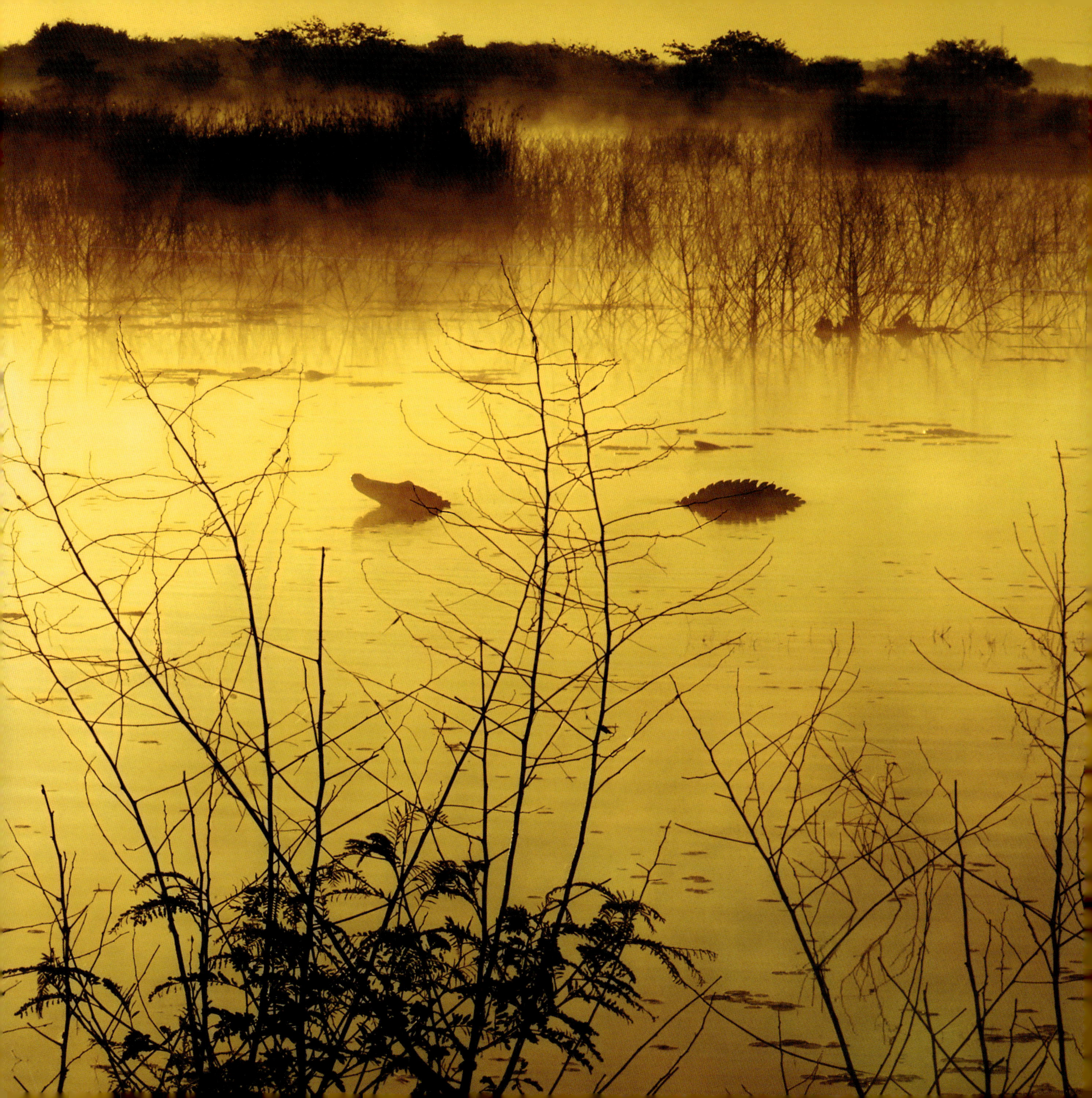

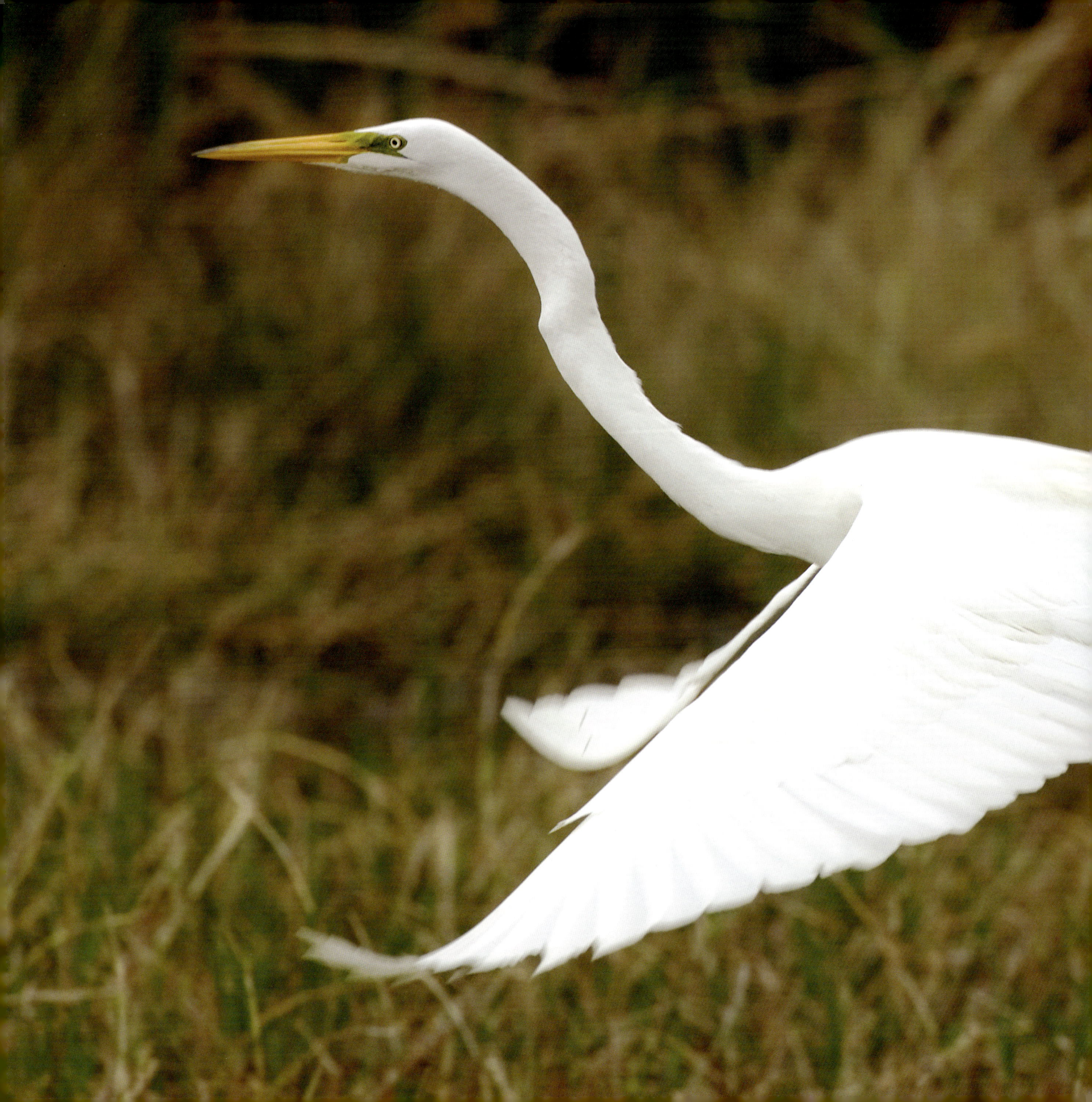

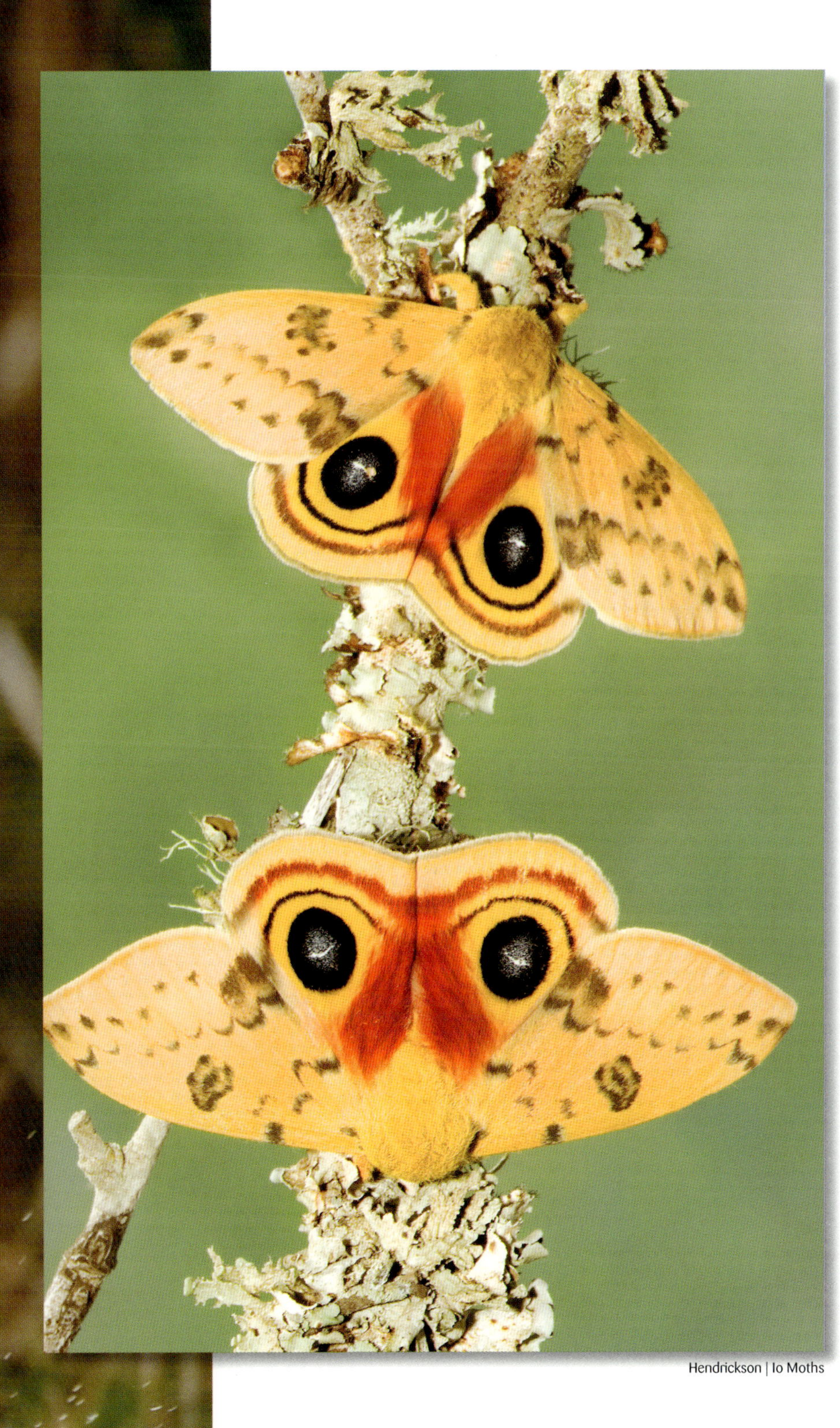

Hendrickson | Io Moths

Hendrickson | Great Egret

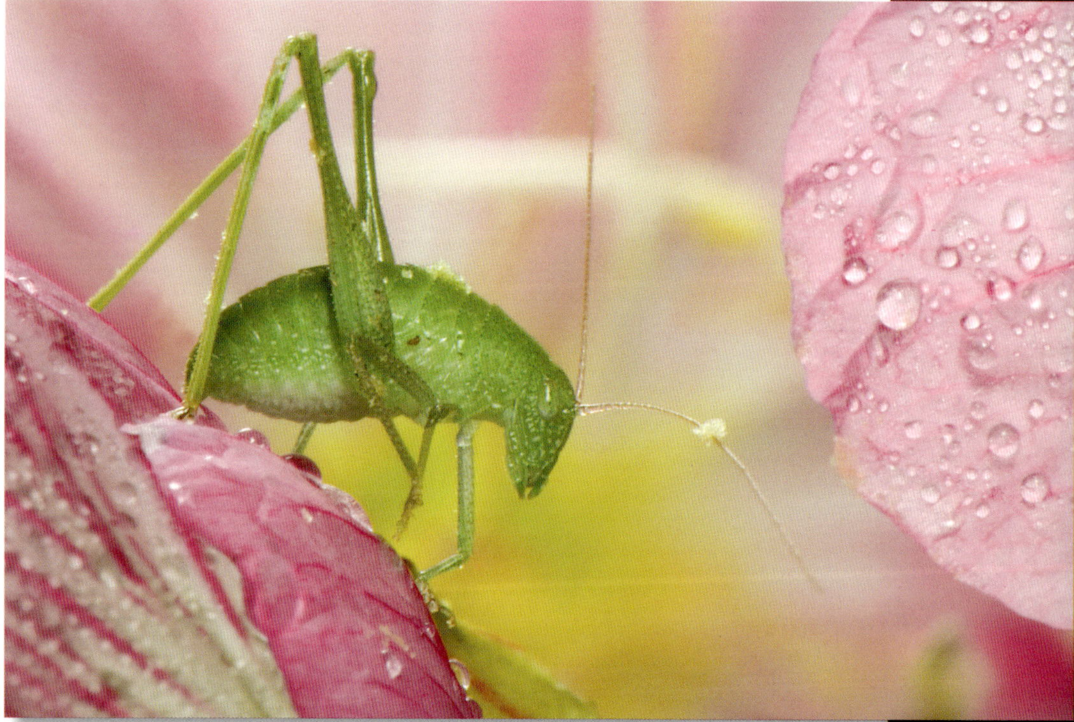

Hendrickson | Cricket Nymph on Pink Evening Primrose

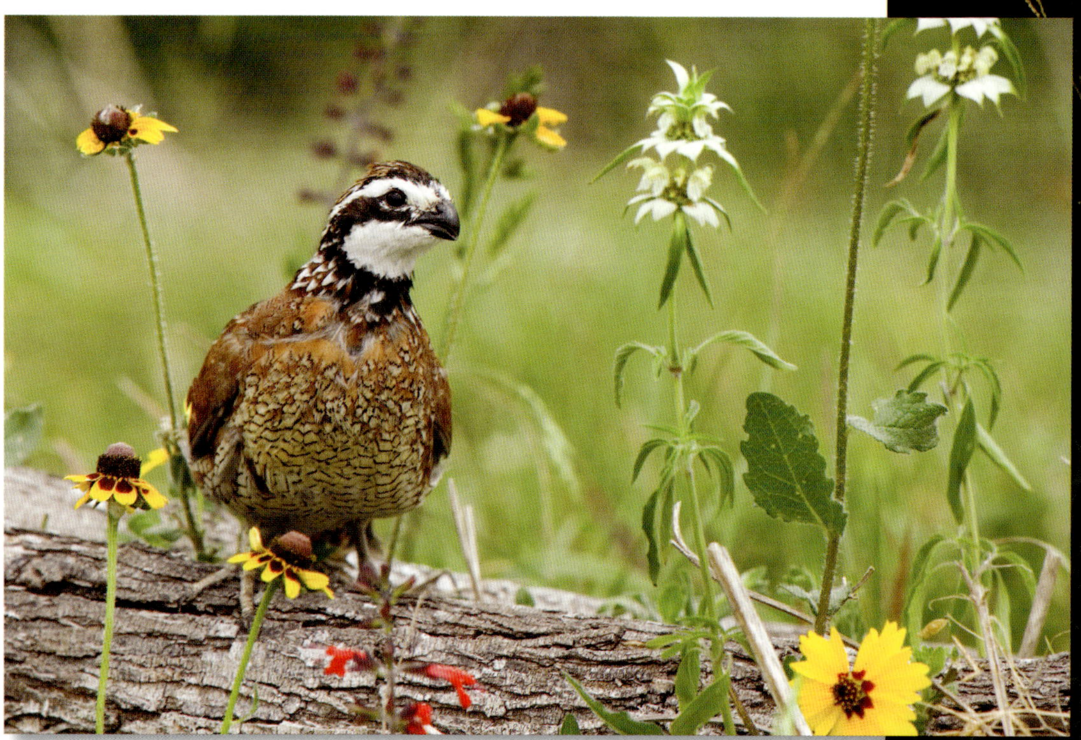

Hendrickson | Northern Bobwhite surrounded by Horsemint, Tropical Sage, Tickseed, and Brown-eyed Susan

Hendrickson | Common Raccoon

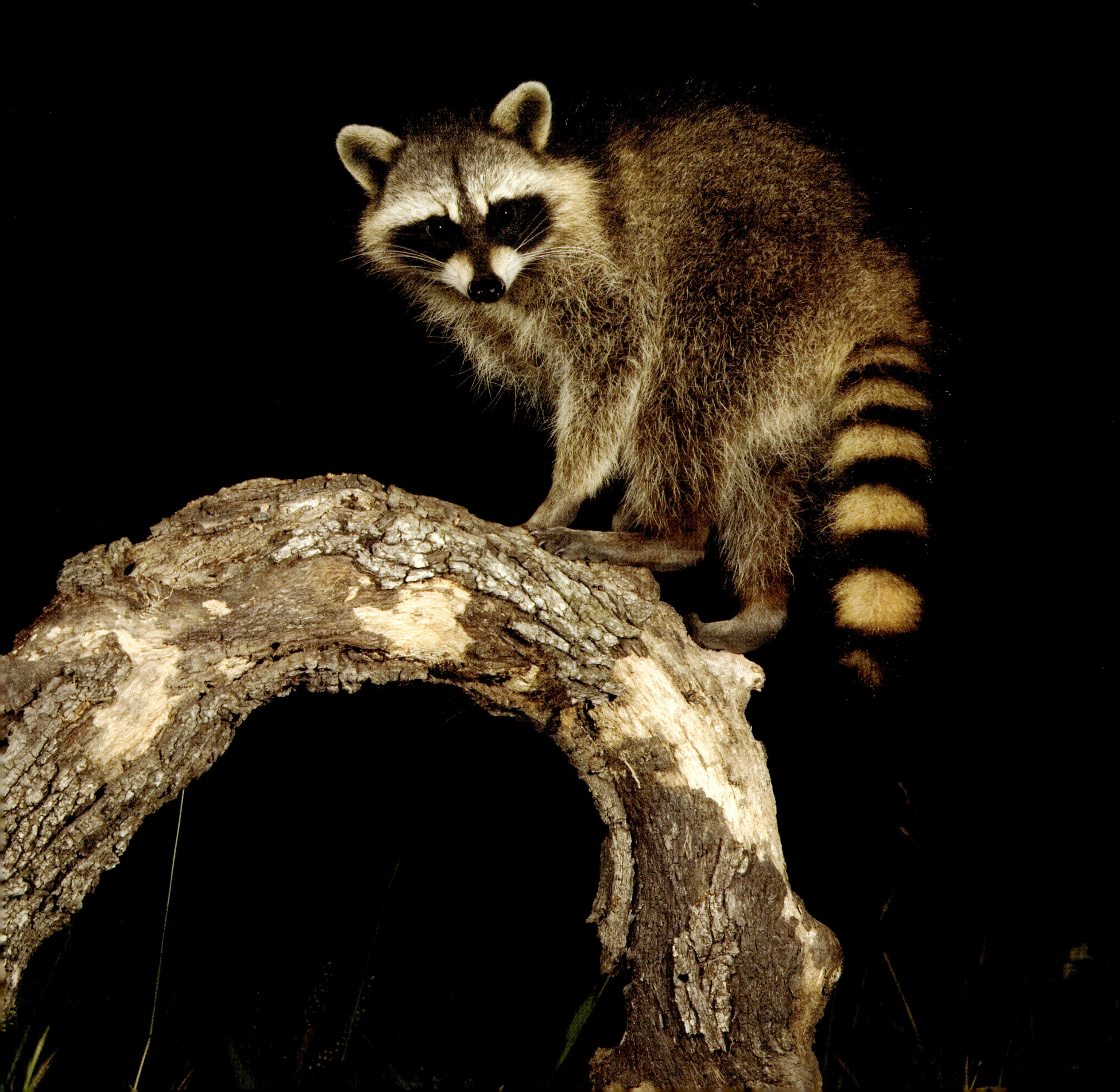

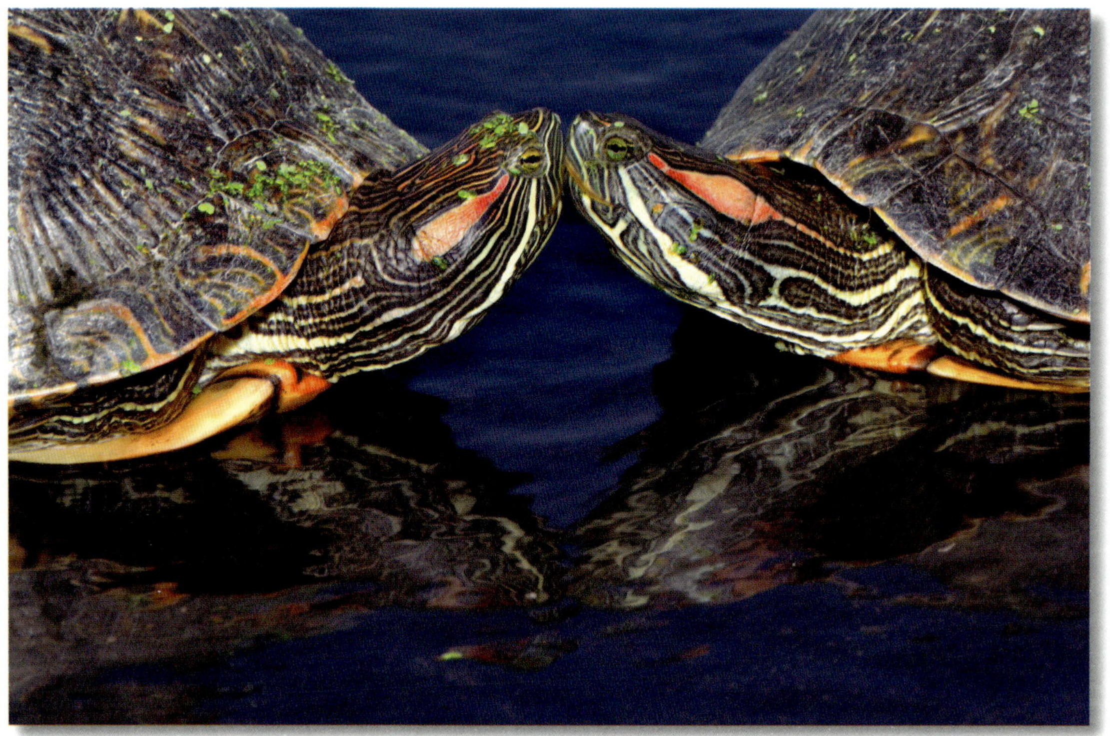

Hendrickson | Red-eared Sliders

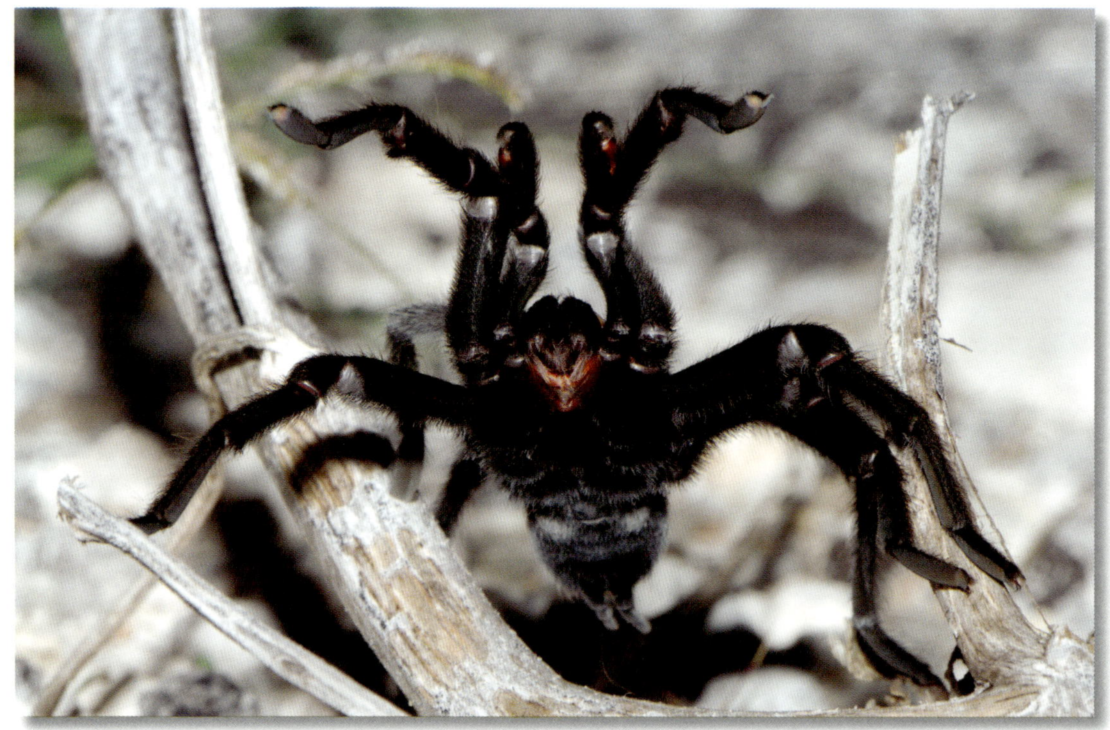

Hendrickson | Tarantula

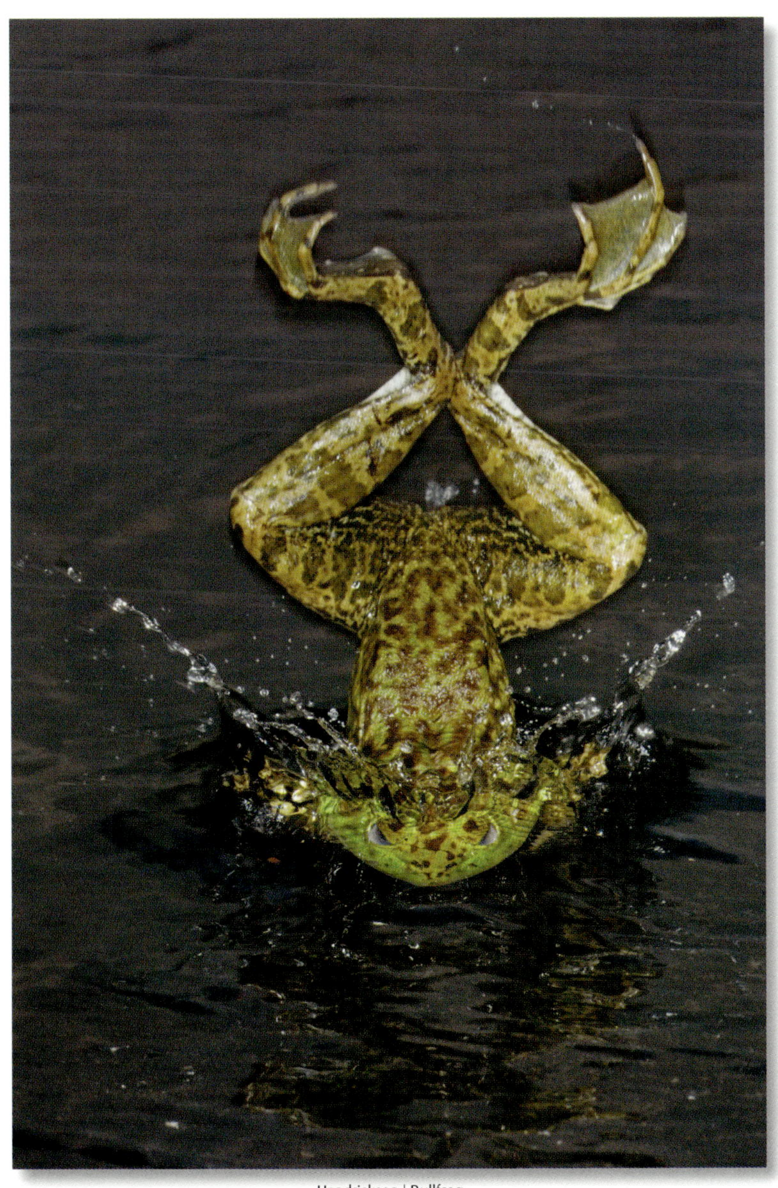

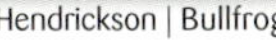
Hendrickson | Bullfrog

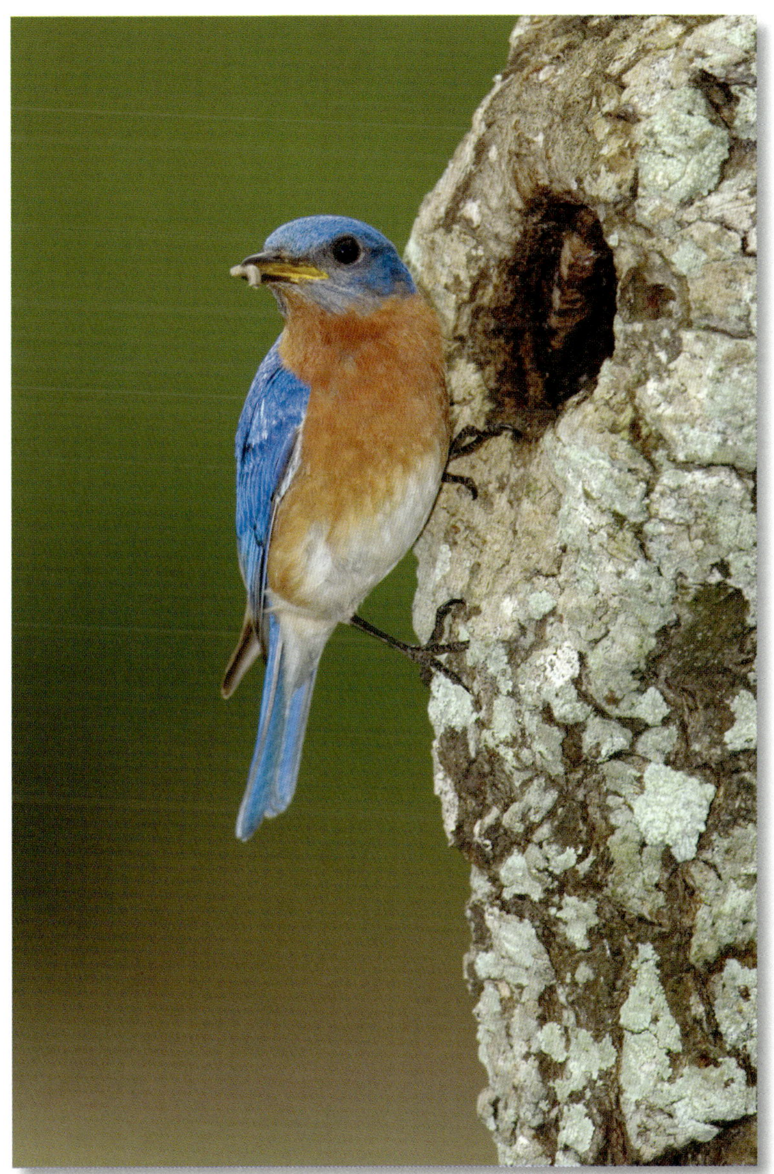
Hendrickson | Eastern Bluebird

About Borchers Ranches...

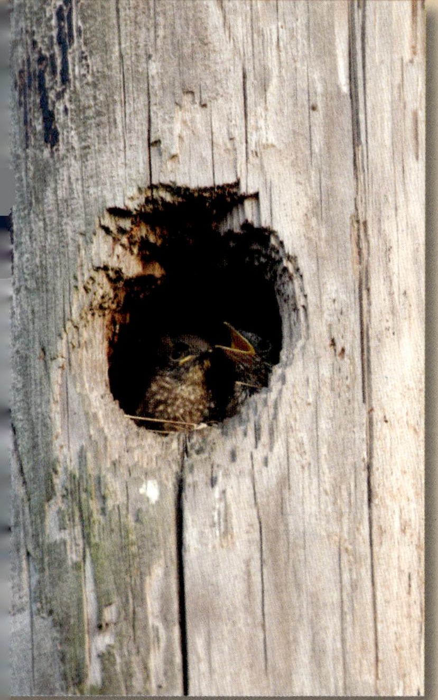

Sloat | Eastern Bluebird nestlings

Lavaca County's coastal landscape seemed the ideal location for a ranch, according to William H. and Otto R. Borchers' grandparents, Otto and Emma Buergner Borchers. Having grown up during the 1800s farming the Yorktown area, they realized the farming life was not for them. They preferred cattle. So in 1907 they purchased land near Cuero along the Lavaca River from the Bushell family. In 1915 they added additional tracts and expanded the cattle operation. Eventually their sons, William, Otto and Henry, joined them and together they accumulated almost 40,000 acres. History has it that William lost 1,200 head of cattle in the freeze of 1924. On the heels of that loss came the Great Depression. The cattle market became so depressed during those hard times that once after transporting a herd of cattle to market in Fort Worth, the family received a bill for shipping their livestock rather than a check for the beef they had sold. But the family learned to economize and eventually the industry rebounded, allowing them to continue their ranching heritage. Today, William and Otto R. Borchers are joined by Otto's wife Betty Ann in the family cattle business.

Live Oak, Black Jack Oak and Post Oak trees thrive in the sandy soil of this brush country ranch. The family has cleared some areas, but natural vegetation provides ample habitat for native game to live in complete obscurity. Today F-1 cattle share the ranch with White-tailed Deer, thanks to the Borchers' deer feeding program. The family also has prohibited hunting on 3,000 acres of the property. Some of the land has been cleared. But when asked if he would consider farming these pastures, Otto's response is an unequivocal "no," citing that handling cattle is much easier than handling crops. "At least they can walk off the truck on their own."

The Borchers family hopes to preserve as much of the ranch's natural vegetation as possible. Otto is concerned that past clearing may have caused irreparable harm to the habitat. But he feels the ends justified the means.

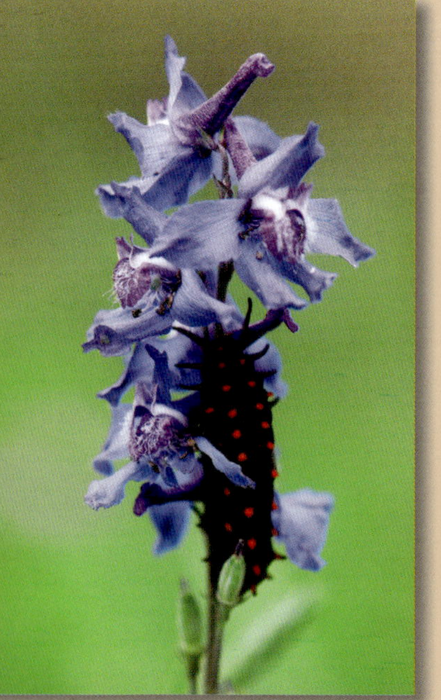

Sloat | Pipevine Swallowtail Caterpillar on Larkspur

Sloat | Phlox

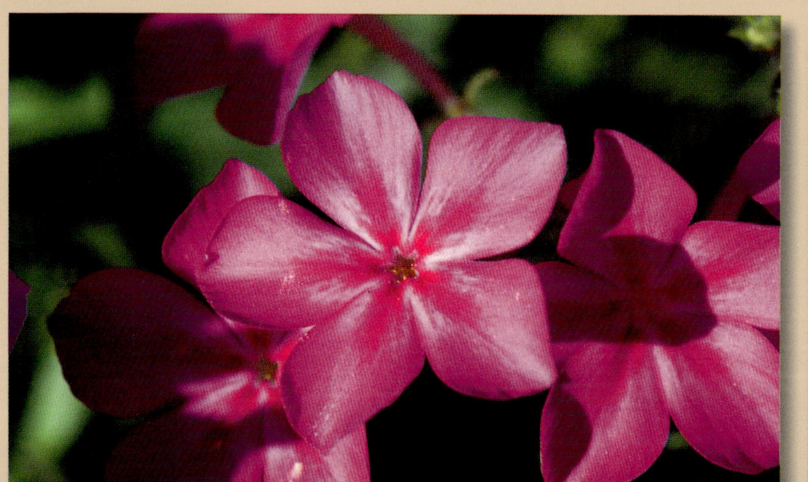

Sloat | Cattle Egret

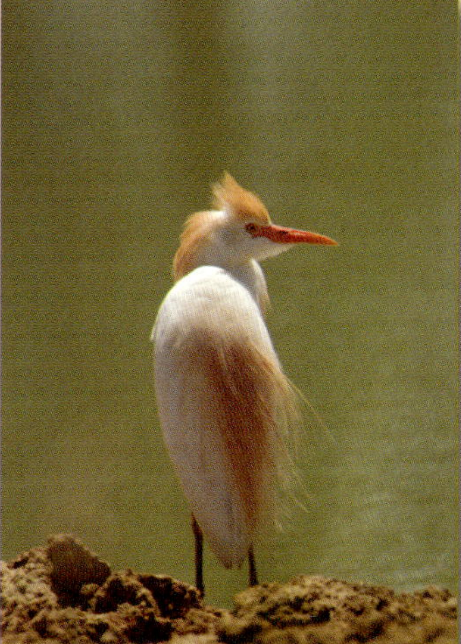

The clearing was done to provide greater visibility to certain sections of the property. If there is a pretty spot hidden in a bramble who would ever know about if you didn't clear a little bit? Ultimately the family is happy some of the more beautiful spots on the ranch are accessible for everyone to enjoy.

The family's hopes are that generations to come will continue this ranching tradition and resist the urge to divide the property into smaller parcels. Once it's cut up you can never put it back together again, Otto said. You see too many large tracts of land subdivided when estates are settled. Once that happens, those wide expanses of Texas are gone forever.

The Borchers have enjoyed their new venture into nature photography. And from this they've learned there is more to do on their land than punch cattle.

Otto R., Betty Ann & William Borchers
Yoakum, TX

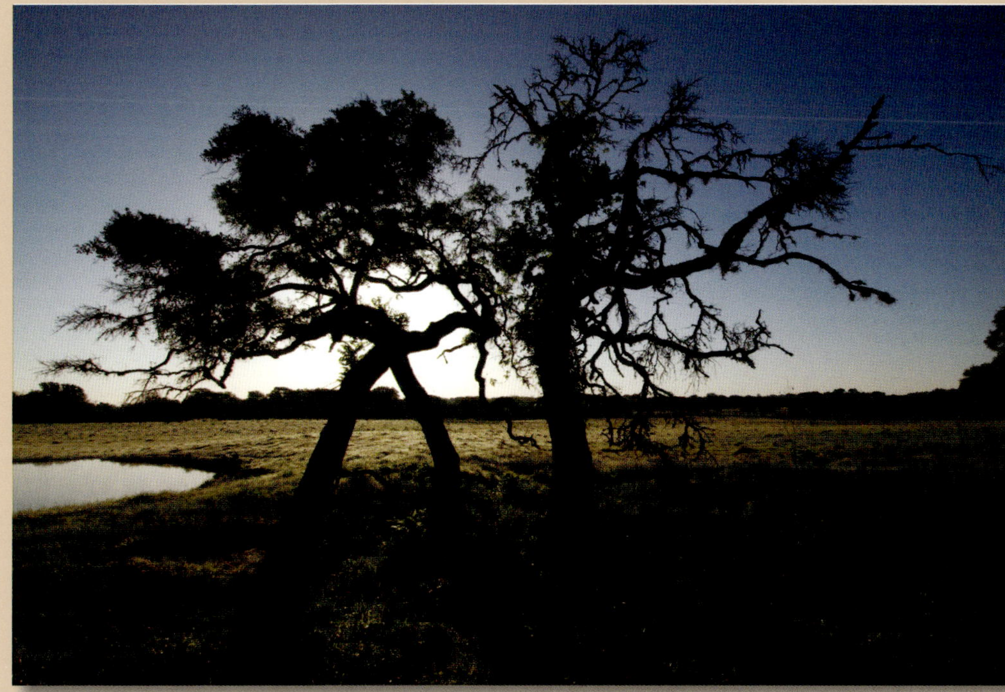

Sloat | Live Oak tree

Sloat | Resurrection Fern and Lindheimer Prickly Pear

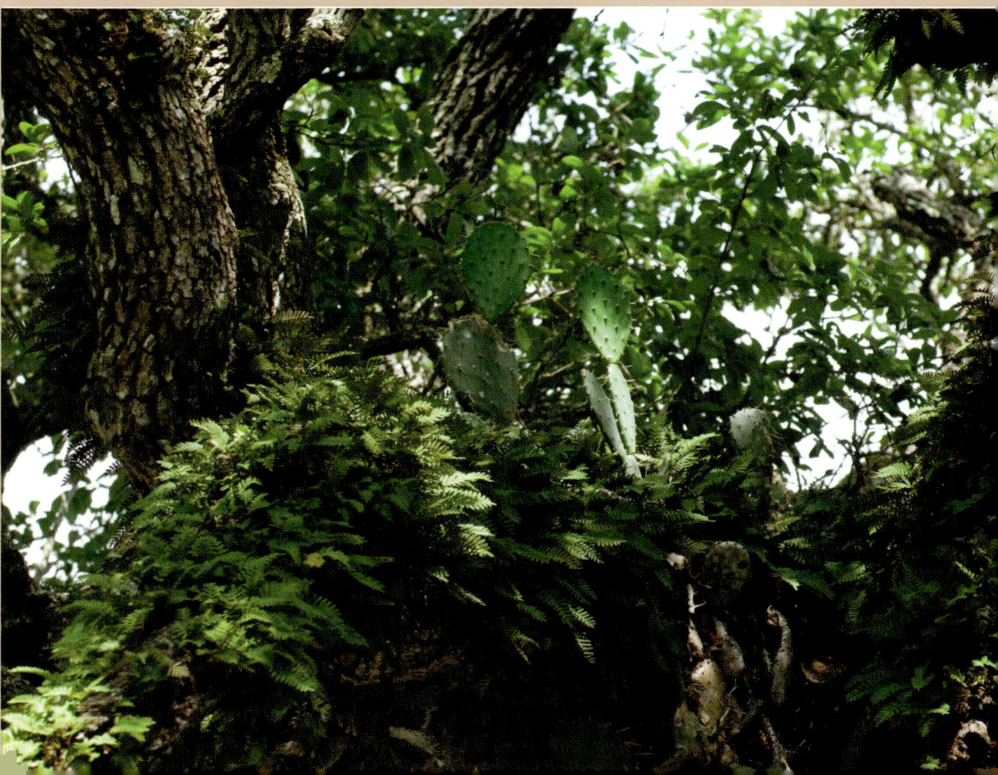

Sloat | Eastern Fox Squirrel

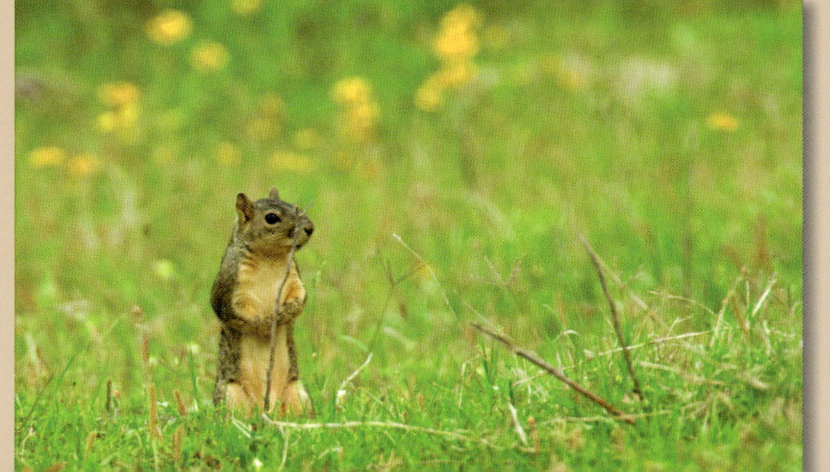

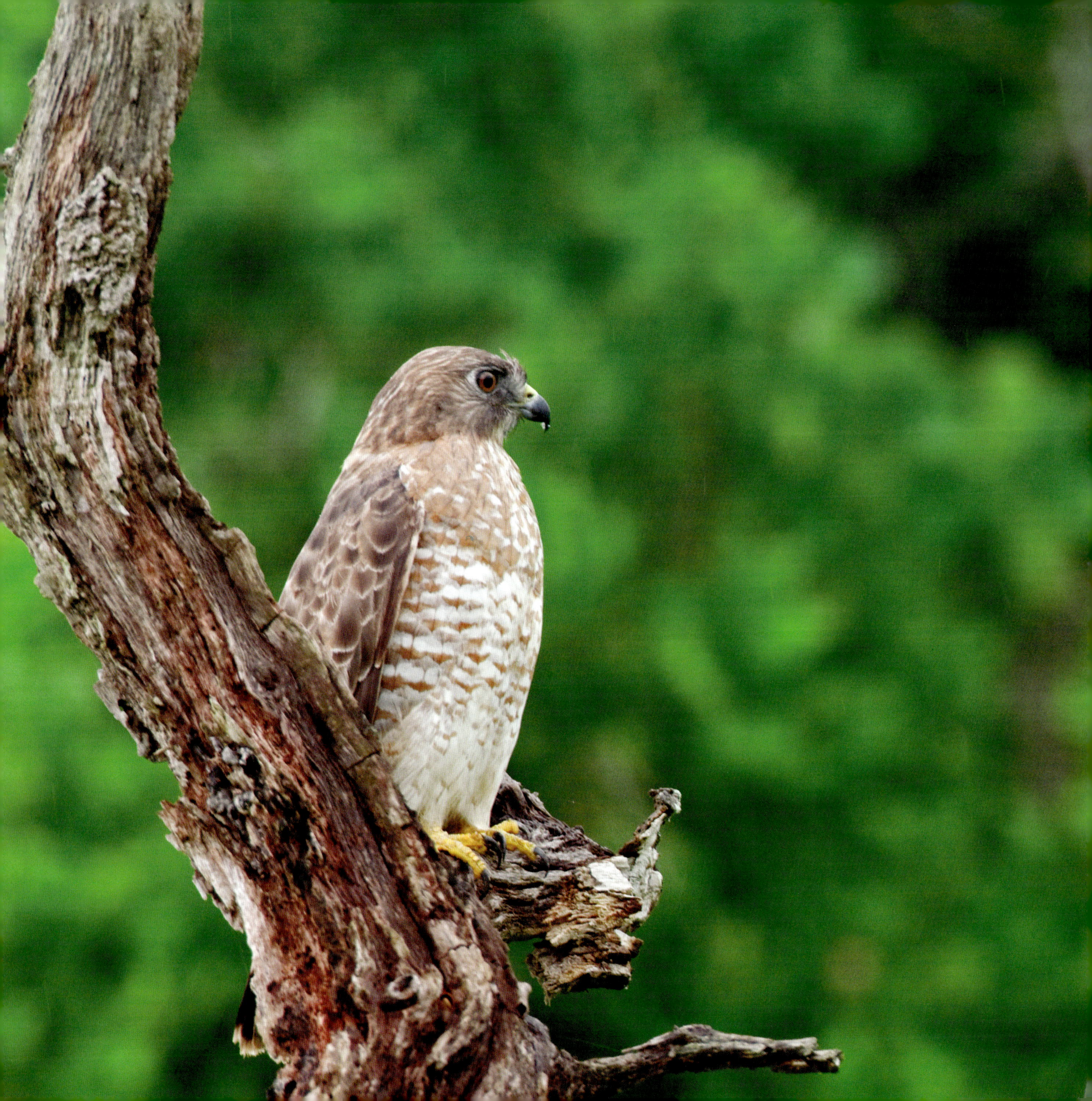

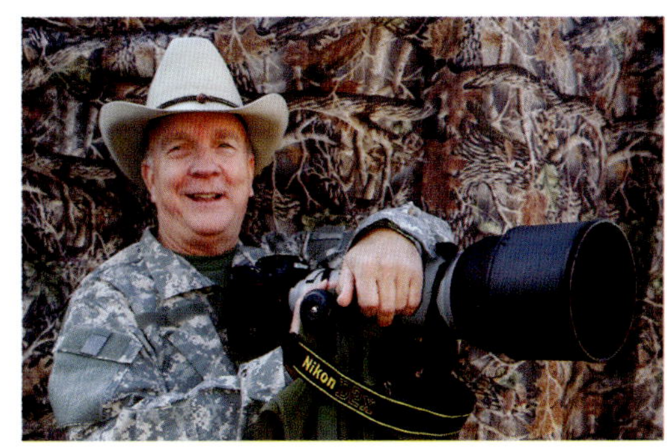

Mike Sloat

When Mike Sloat was a teenager in the 1960's he helped clear brush off the Borchers' Ranch, the same place where, in 2008, he would spend 30 days as a photographer.

"From 14 to 17 years old, I lived on a ranch about five miles from Borchers. It's sad to see how much has changed about the region. I saw a lot more wildlife out there when I was a kid. I remember having Gray Wolves, Ocelots and Black Bear."

Mike says that's why it's so very important to bring awareness to what's left. "By the time I left, I think the folks on Borchers' came to have a more appreciative view of the wildlife they're blessed with."

One of his favorite contest memories involves a Timber Rattlesnake. Like most ranchers they were not too fond of them. But, he talked them into "petting" a rattler he'd caught. "They were amazed at how you could feel it breathe, with its beauty, its patterns. If they'd killed him, they would have never had that experience."

Another special bit of Pro-Tour wonder was when Mike came across a baby fawn near a timber line. "The mother was at a narrow opening and was acting strange. Suddenly this little spot popped up. She nudged it and I knew she was telling it to get back in but it didn't. Instead it went into the timber. So, I followed to get a better shot when I almost stepped on another fawn. It was about a foot away and just about a day old."

"I like to use images to capture wildlife so I can show people what they're missing and how it behaves." He's been capturing images and sharing them professionally for 42 years.

The Pro-Tour "makes you open your own eyes. It provides a unique opportunity being in one spot for so long. I'm regularly reminded of how small one is in the environment, but when you're out there for 30 days straight you really feel that even more."

"And," he adds, "it's good to be reminded of this."

Fort Worth, TX
www.txswoutdoorphotography.com
[e] blackhawk048@msn.com

Sloat | Broad-winged Hawk

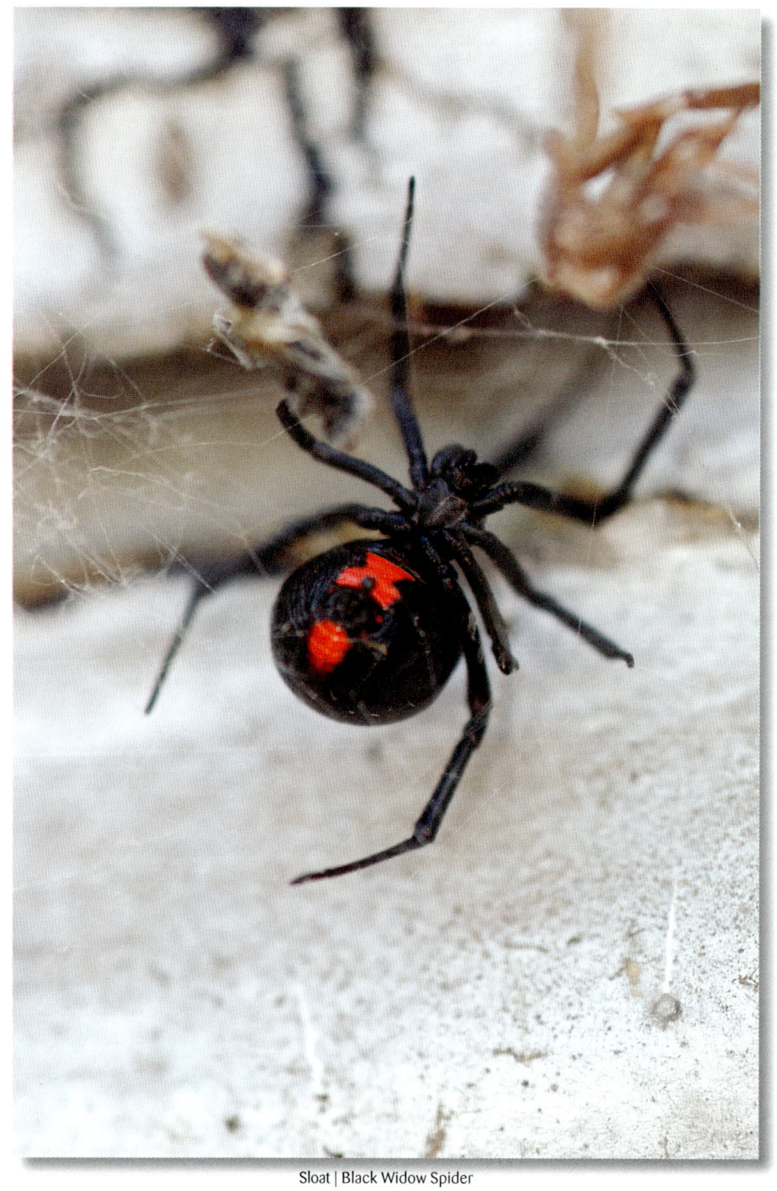
Sloat | Black Widow Spider

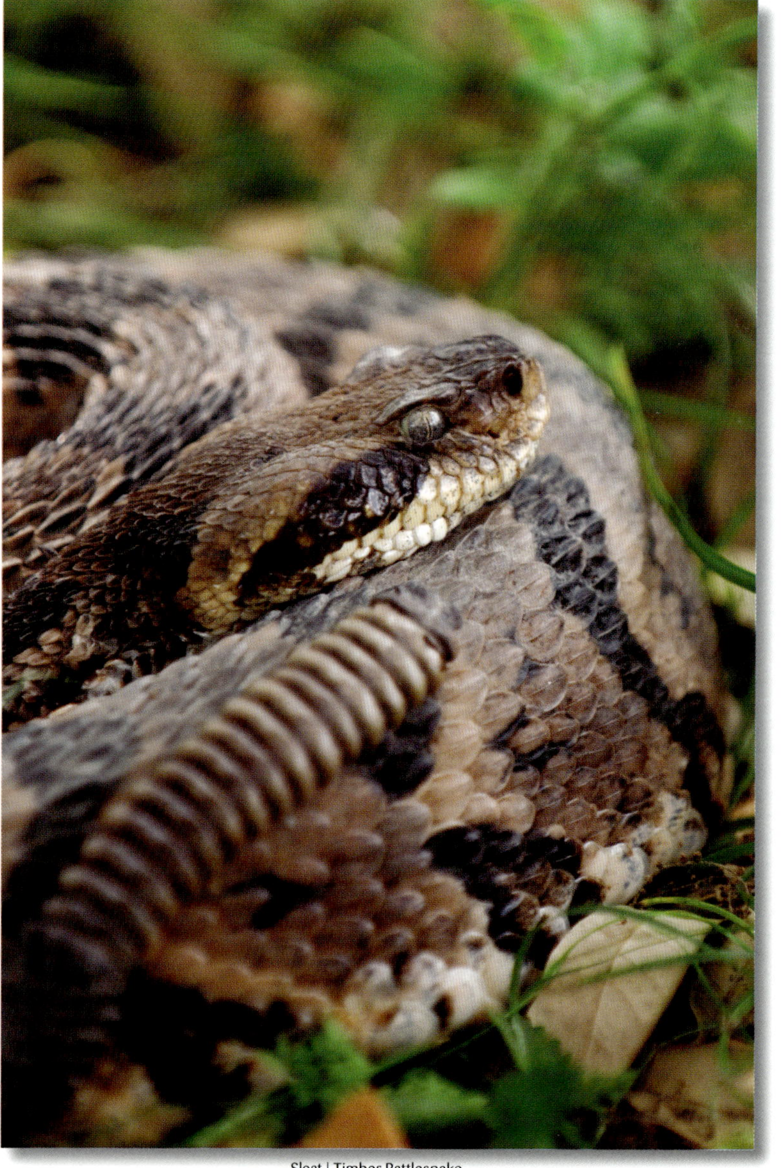
Sloat | Timber Rattlesnake

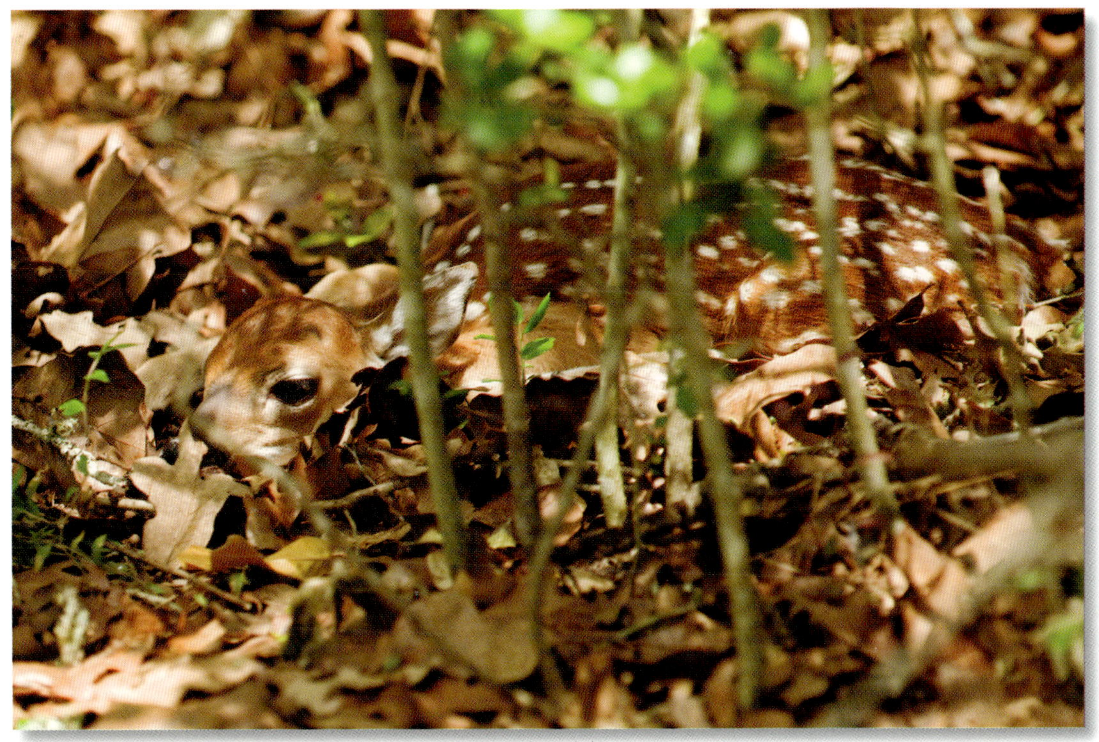

Sloat | White-tailed Deer

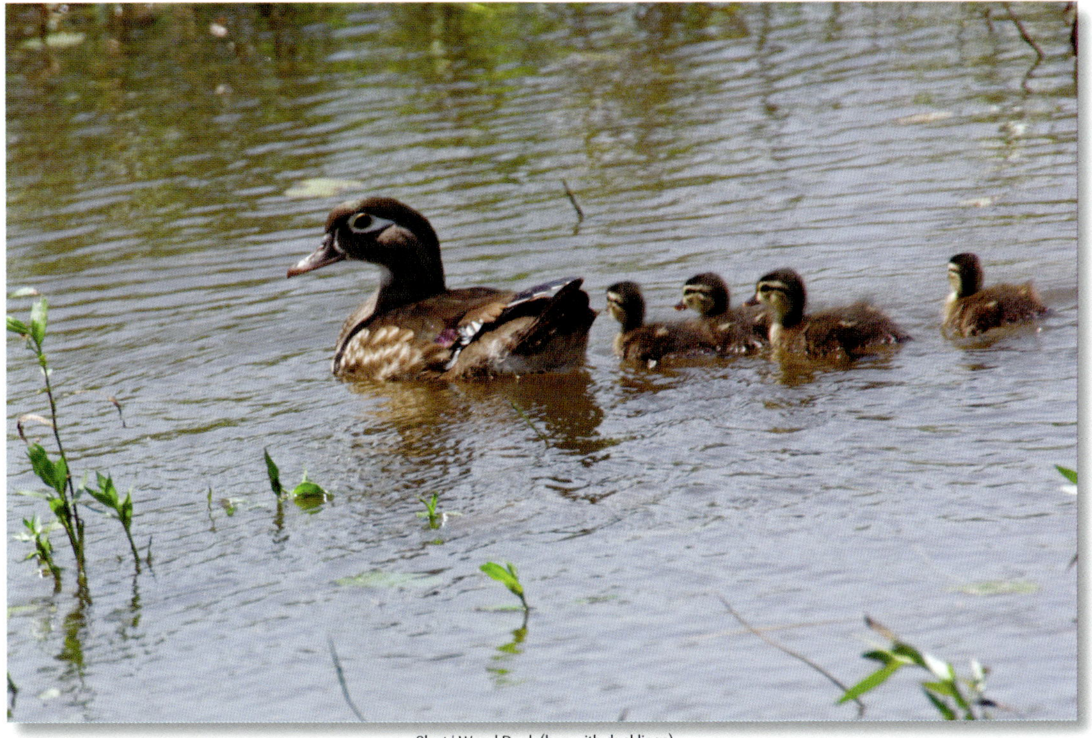

Sloat | Wood Duck (hen with ducklings)

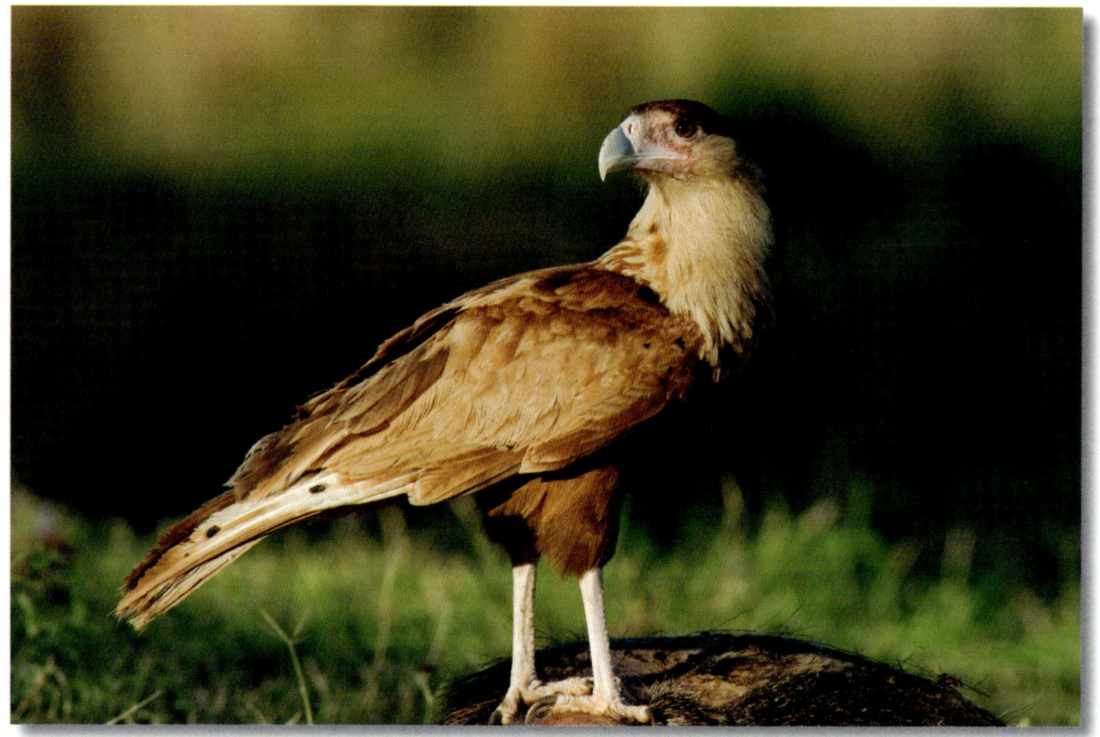

Sloat | juvenile Crested Caracara

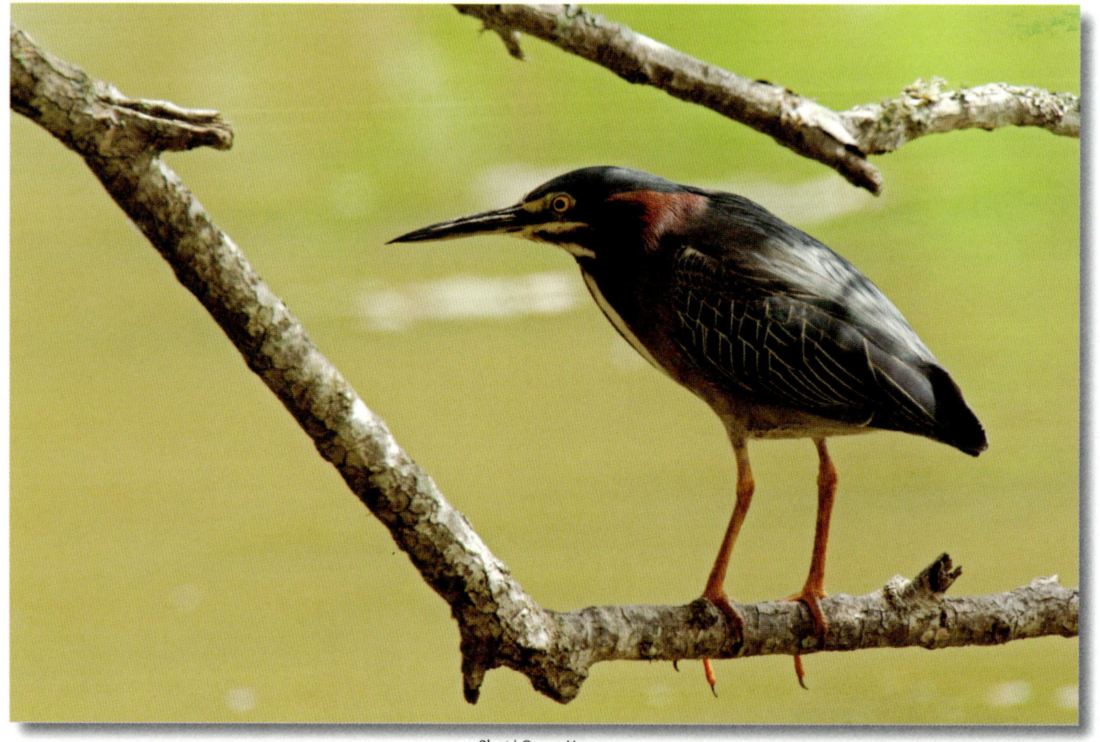

Sloat | Green Heron

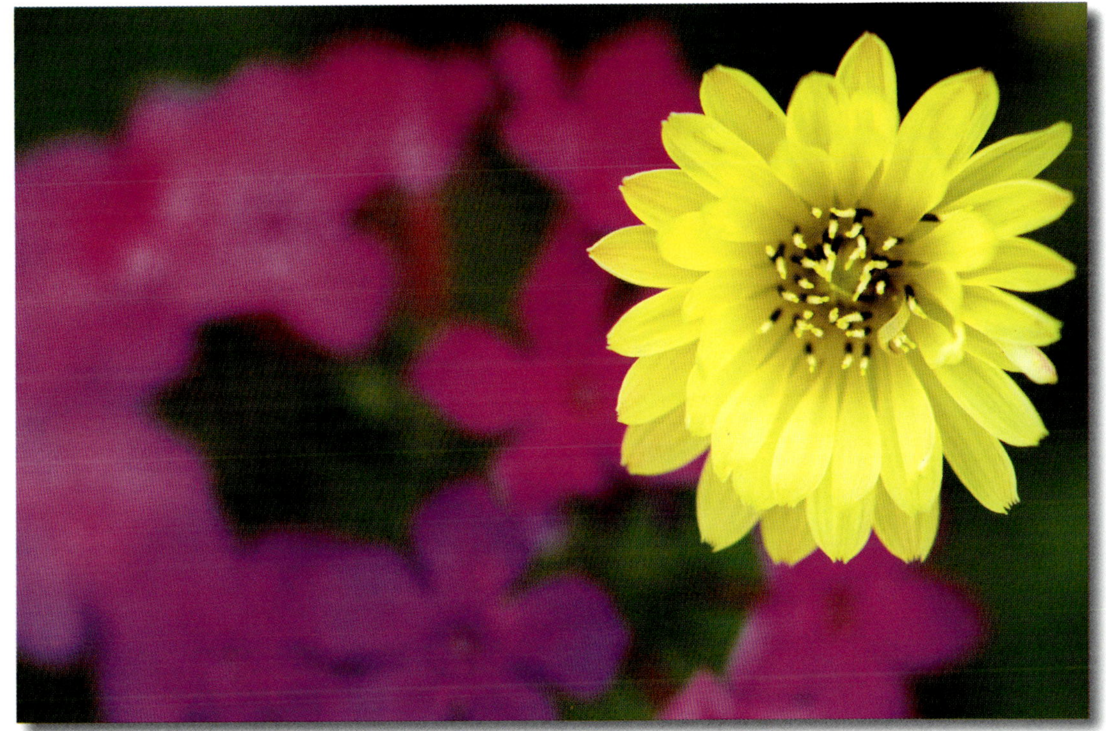

Sloat | False Dandelion

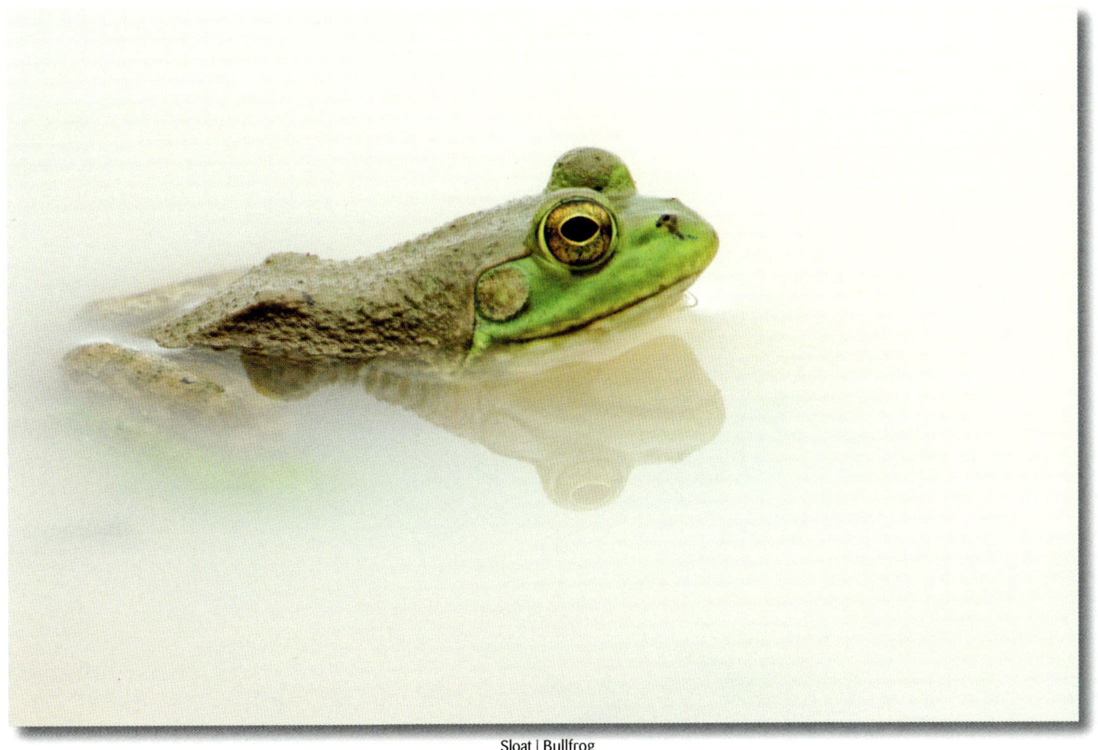

Sloat | Bullfrog

About Butler Family Ranches...

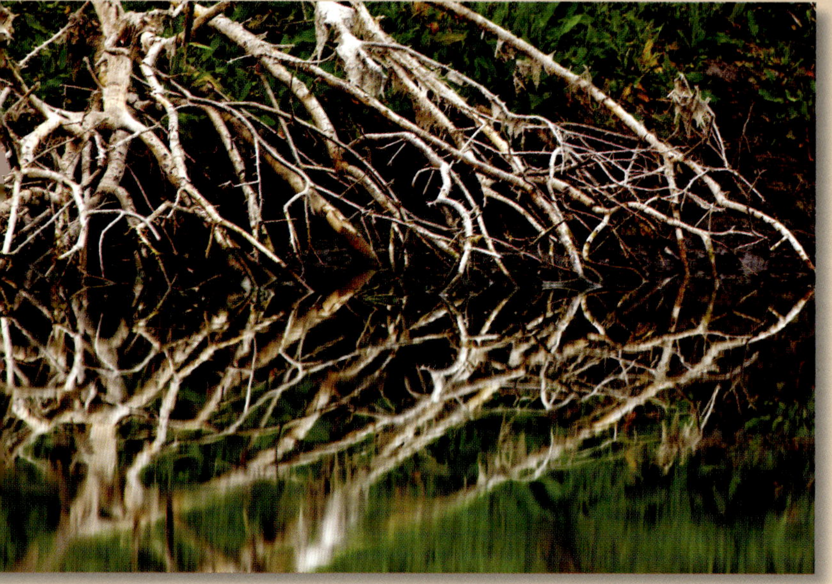

Steele | unknown tree roots

The Butler family sustains a legacy of ranching in Karnes and Live Oak counties since the arrival of their ancestors in 1852. Fifth generation owners Sue Butler Carter and her sister Pat Butler Literati, partnered with their cousin Julie Butler Beck and her husband Gus for the ICF Coastal Bend Pro-Tour. Their ranches comprise 1,800 acres of native brush, cacti and rolling grassland shaded by Mesquite trees and majestic Live Oaks. During years with normal rainfall, the spring landscape becomes a lush kaleidoscope of wild flowers, providing essential pollen and nectar for bees and migrating butterflies.

Sue, Pat and Julie's great-great grandfather, William Green Butler, was a leading pioneer in the trail driving industry. This Civil War veteran organized cattlemen and thousands of cattle to make many long, treacherous journeys through Texas and on to Kansas cattle towns.

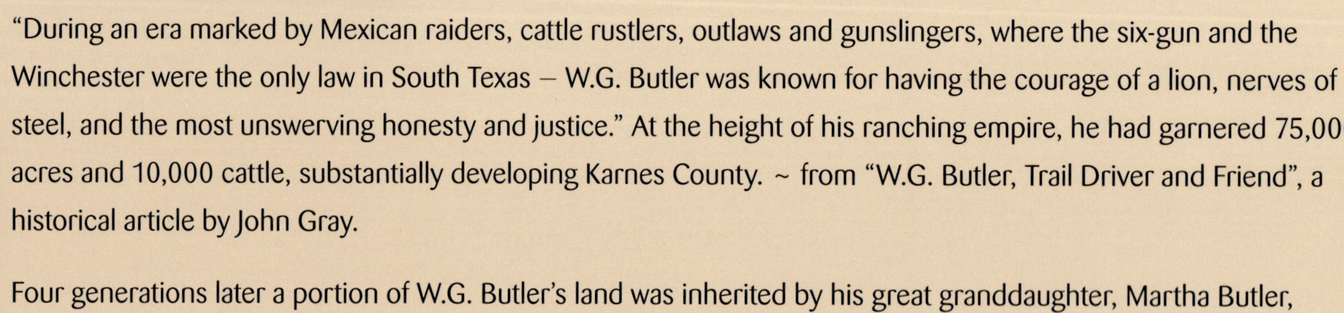

"During an era marked by Mexican raiders, cattle rustlers, outlaws and gunslingers, where the six-gun and the Winchester were the only law in South Texas – W.G. Butler was known for having the courage of a lion, nerves of steel, and the most unswerving honesty and justice." At the height of his ranching empire, he had garnered 75,000 acres and 10,000 cattle, substantially developing Karnes County. ~ from "W.G. Butler, Trail Driver and Friend", a historical article by John Gray.

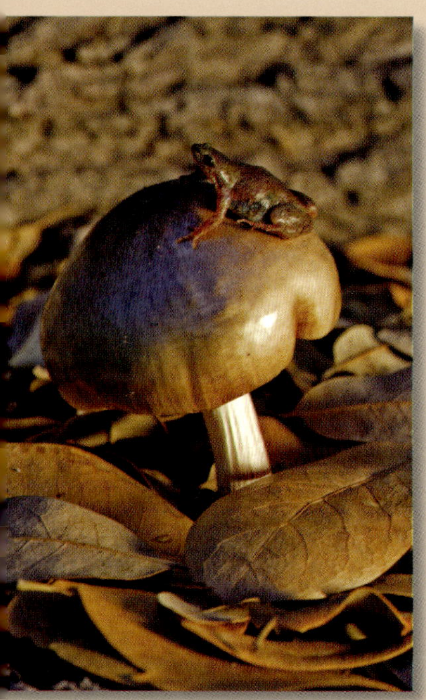

Steele | Great Plains Narrowmouth Toad on mushroom in Live Oak leaves

Four generations later a portion of W.G. Butler's land was inherited by his great granddaughter, Martha Butler, from her father, Marvin Butler. Martha, as did her father, endeavored to protect and improve the habitat for cattle and wildlife. In 1977 Martha was named Outstanding Wildlife Conservationist by the Karnes-Goliad Soil and Water Conservation District. Practices such as brush management, planting native grasses and adding watering tanks were established with cost-share assistance through the Agricultural Stabilization and Conservation Service. When Sue, Pat and Julie inherited part of the ranch from their Aunt Martha, they also acquired a sense of honor and enduring gratitude ingrained in their family's love of the land.

The Butler Ranches have been a gathering place for the families. Sue and Pat's father, Bill Butler, and Julie's father, Ted Butler, have enjoyed the good fortune of celebrating their 80th birthdays at the ranch. "Going to the ranch" has been the family mantra for generations. In the gracious comfort of Aunt Martha's quaint ranch house, guests relax on a wide sleeping porch that faces southeast, as cool breezes prevail from the Gulf 100 miles away. Just off the porch, Green Jays, thrashers, cardinals and woodpeckers can be easily photographed from what Sue calls the best little bird blind in Texas. Two seasonal creeks run through the ranch, converging behind the house.

This rustic dwelling surrounded by nearly 600 acres has beckoned Sue to visit regularly for peace and renewal, especially since the death in 2007 of her beloved husband, Tom Carter, whose favorite pastime was fishing at the ranch.

Observing wildlife is a recreation shared by all of the Butler family. Spotting wildlife is an untiring pleasure to the nature seeker. But Sue says she'll never forget the thrill of seeing a Mountain Lion beside a creek near the house.

While outdoors, Sue likes to both photograph and watch birds, noting that 115 species of birds have been spotted on the property. Preserving the wildlife habitat continues to be a primary focus on the Butler Family Ranches. Minimal land was previously cleared for Coastal and Klein grasses, leaving acres of undisturbed brush. An effort is under way to replace the Coastal with native grasses, including Little Bluestem, Side-oats Grama, and Alamo Switchgrass. In 2003 the ranch was recognized by the Family Land Heritage program, honoring families dedicated to agriculture and their land for more than 100 years.

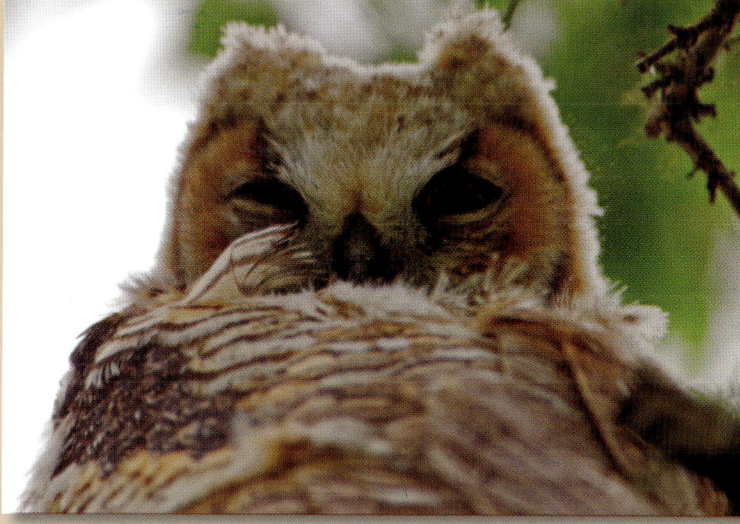
Steele | immature Great Horned Owl

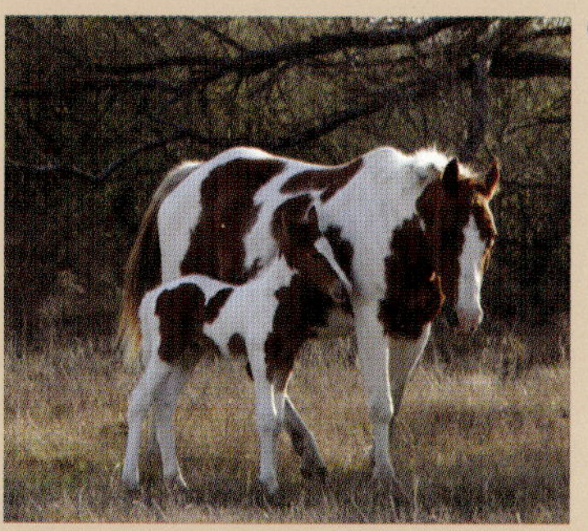
Curly & Sugar

Sue Butler Carter, Pat Butler Literati, Julie and Gus Beck
La Vernia, TX
[e] suecarter@satx.rr.com

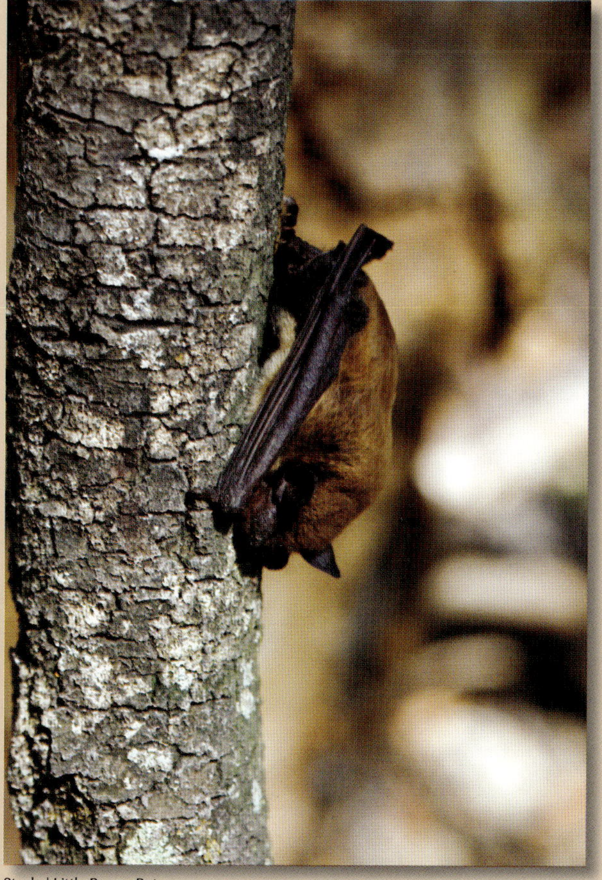
Steele | Little Brown Bat

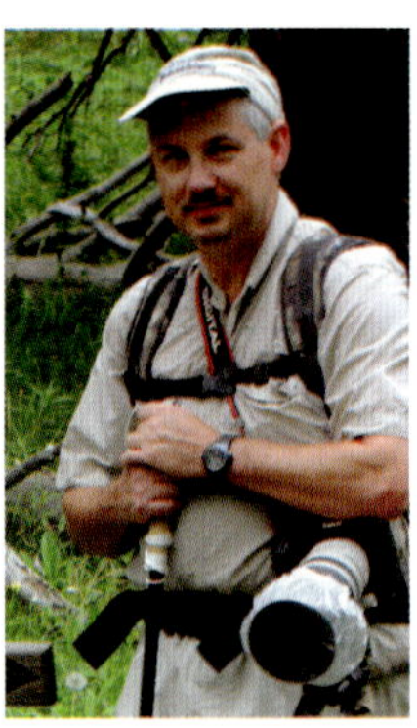

Todd Steele

How many professions allow you to sit and sip a glass of wine with a family of Common Raccoons? Very few. One of photographer Todd Steele's favorite contest memories at the Butler Family Ranches took place after the sun went down. "I still miss sitting up at nights drinking wine with the coons," he laments.

"Over the course of a week I spent time with a group of raccoons that came out around nine o'clock to feed. They got used to me so I could sit on the ground and photograph them feeding from a few feet away. In a few instances they would approach the camera gear for a closer look and I would have to shoo them away."

After long nights up with the nocturnal critters, Todd says marathon-style catnaps were necessary to keep up his endurance, "I'd doze off 15 – 20 minutes and wake up refreshed. That's how I made it for days at a time on so little sleep at night."

As a photographer, he finds it even easier to press himself to the limit because "I get a lot of enjoyment out of it. I don't view it as work. I just have this desire to get out there. There's so much out there that you never really get tired of it. Each picture is different."

He sees more contests like the Pro-Tour in his and others' futures. "A few years back," he says, "no one would have believed that guys flicking plastic worms at bass would be competing in tournaments where prize money for a single contest can exceed a million dollars."

"I believe we will see a metamorphic evolution of nature photography contests much like other competitive tournaments." And, he for one, intends to stick around to enjoy it.

Katy, TX
www.toddsteelephotoart.com
[e] nancy@toddsteelephotoart.com

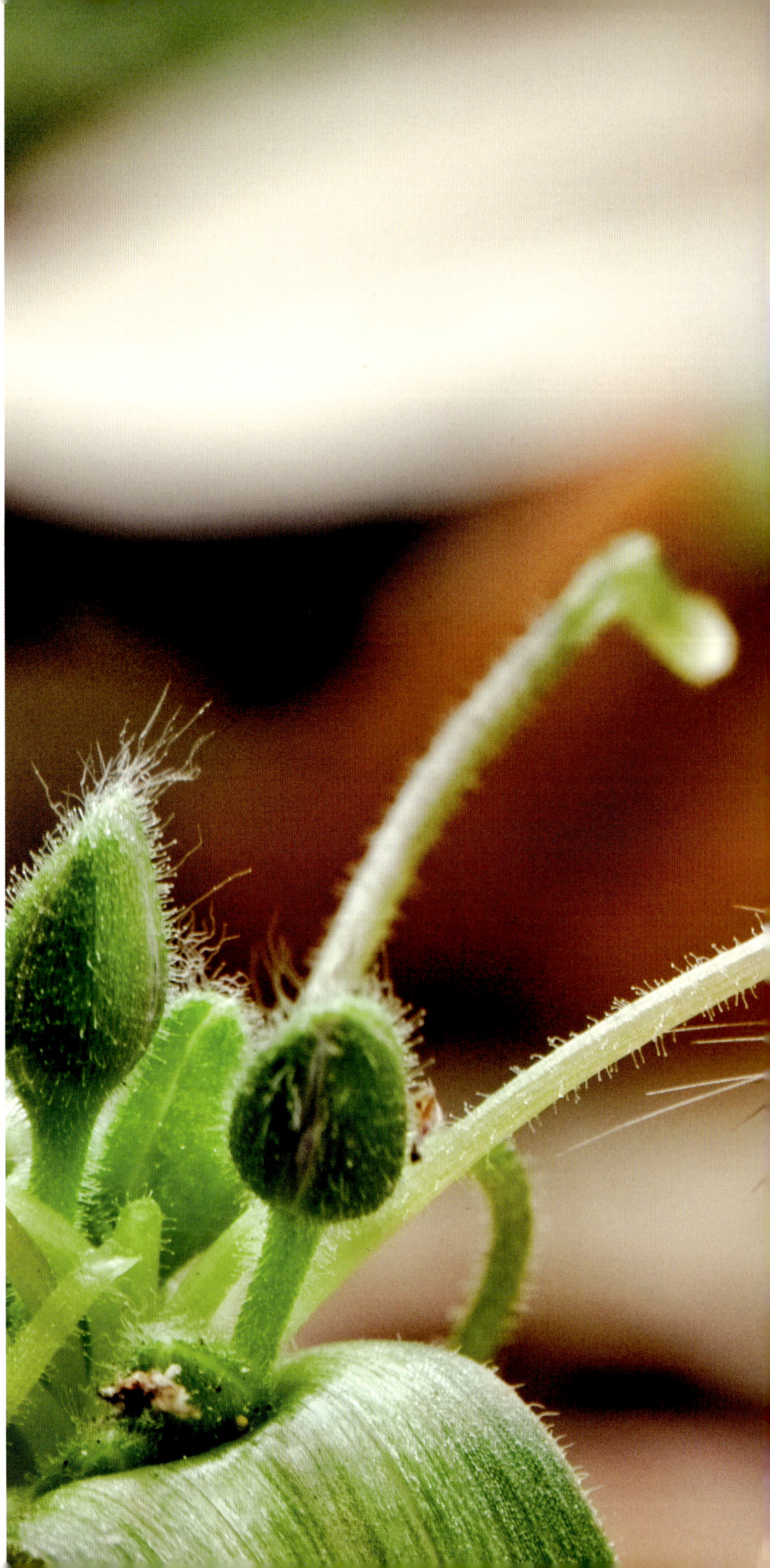

Steele | Saltmarsh Caterpillar on Spiderwort

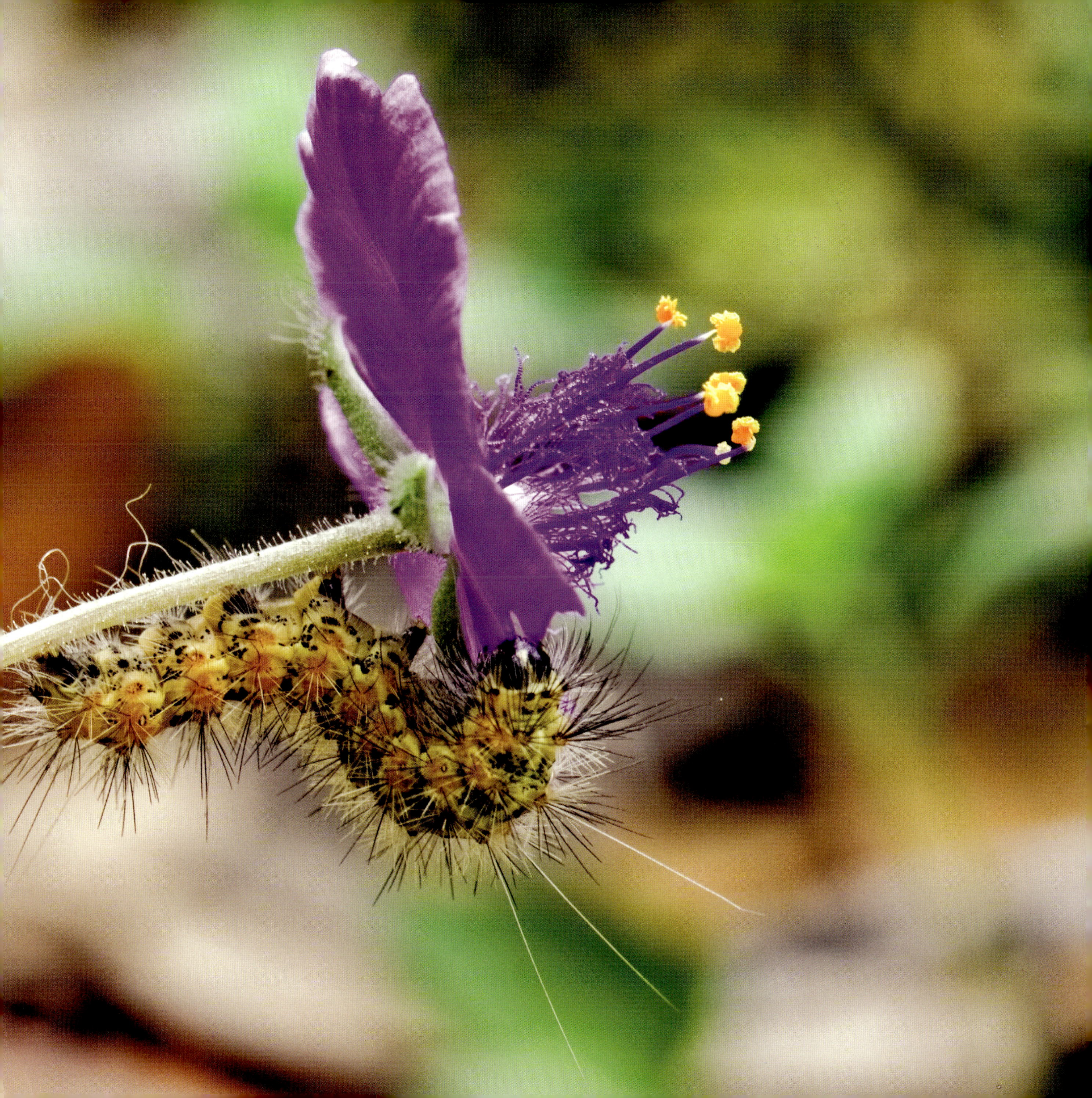

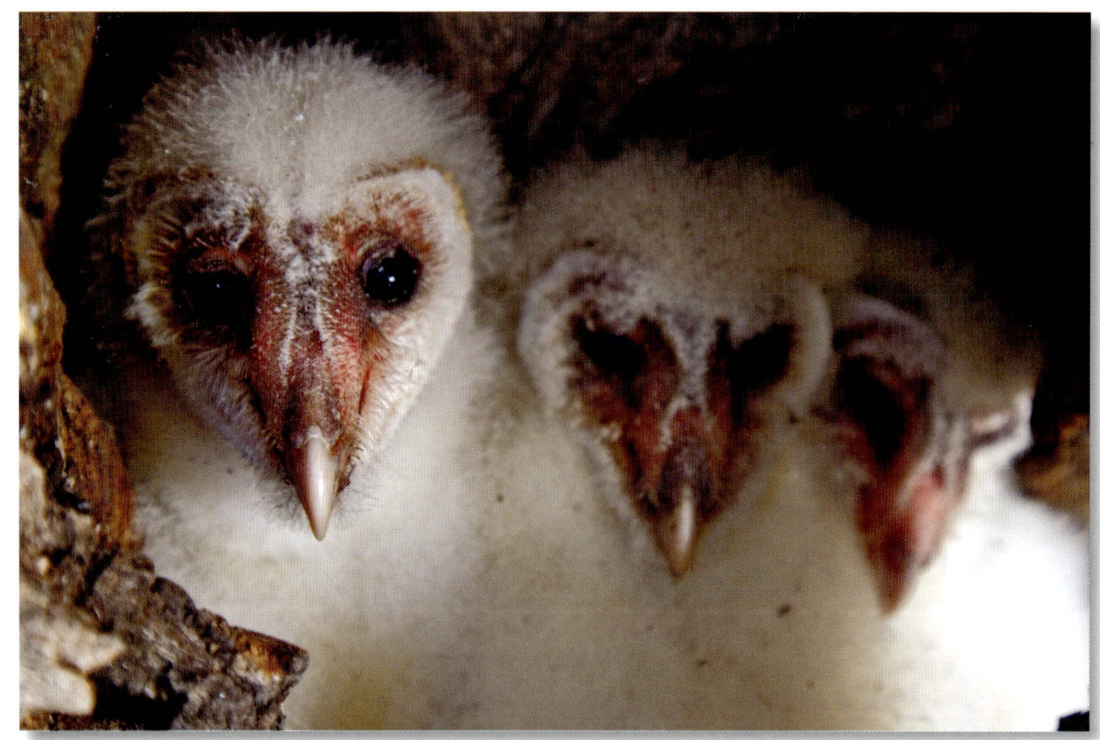

Steele | Barn Owl nestlings

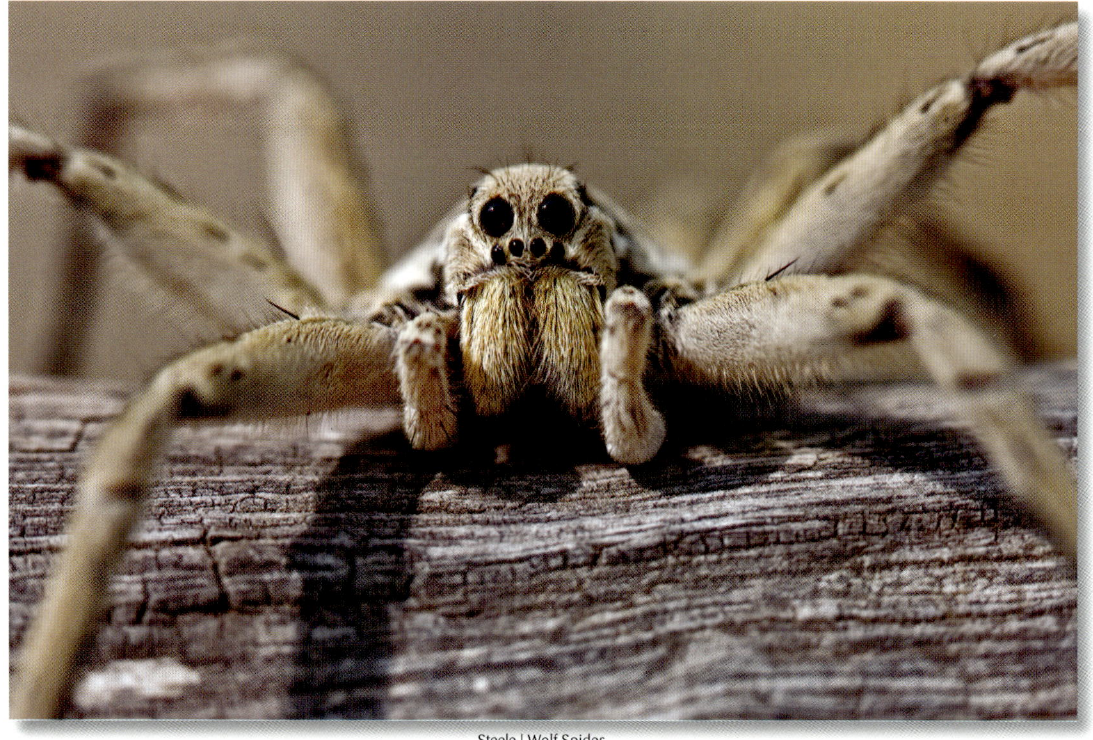

Steele | Wolf Spider

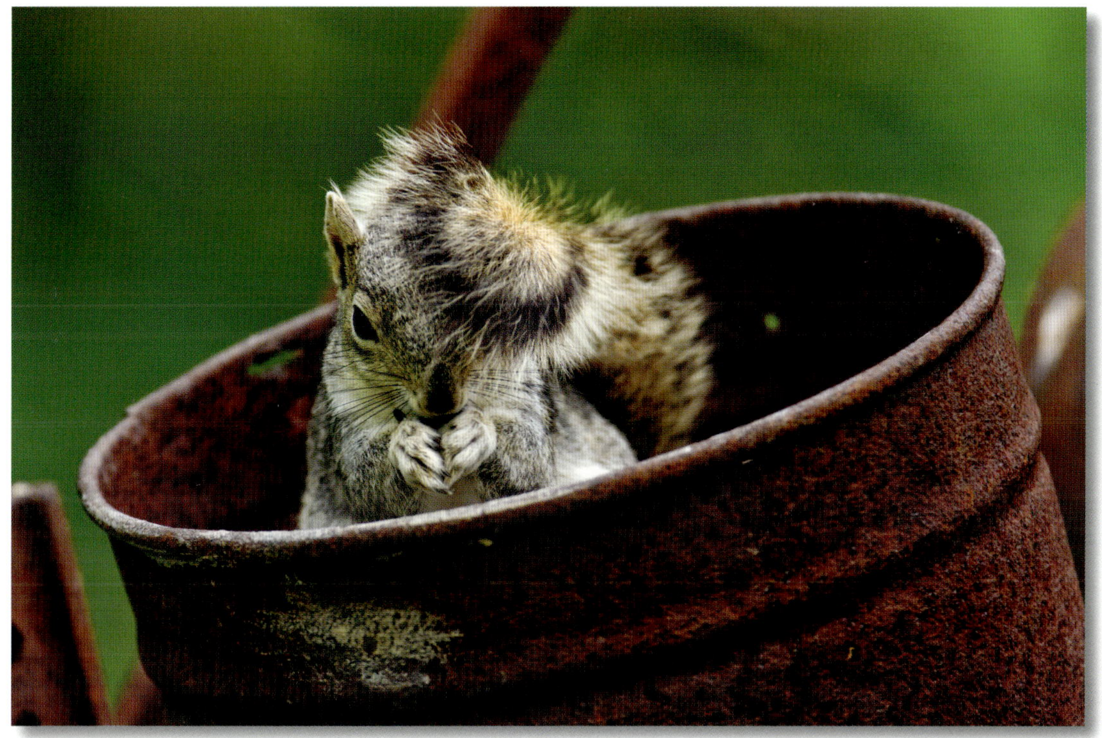

Steele | Gray Squirrel

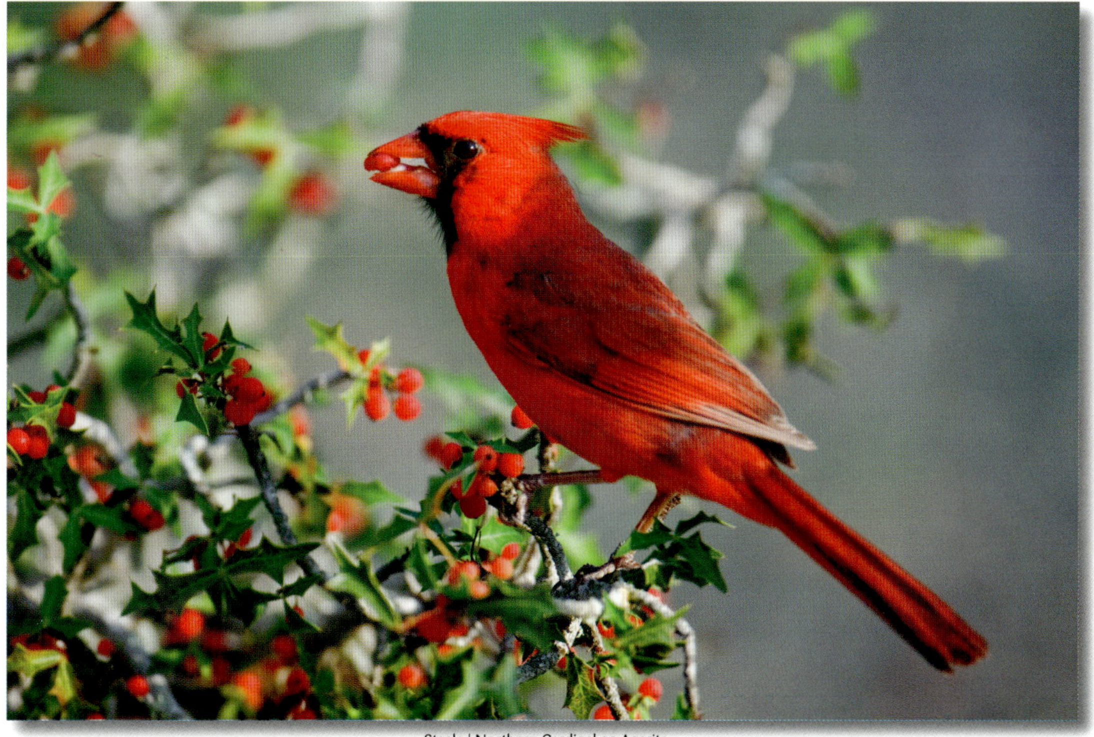

Steele | Northern Cardinal on Agarita

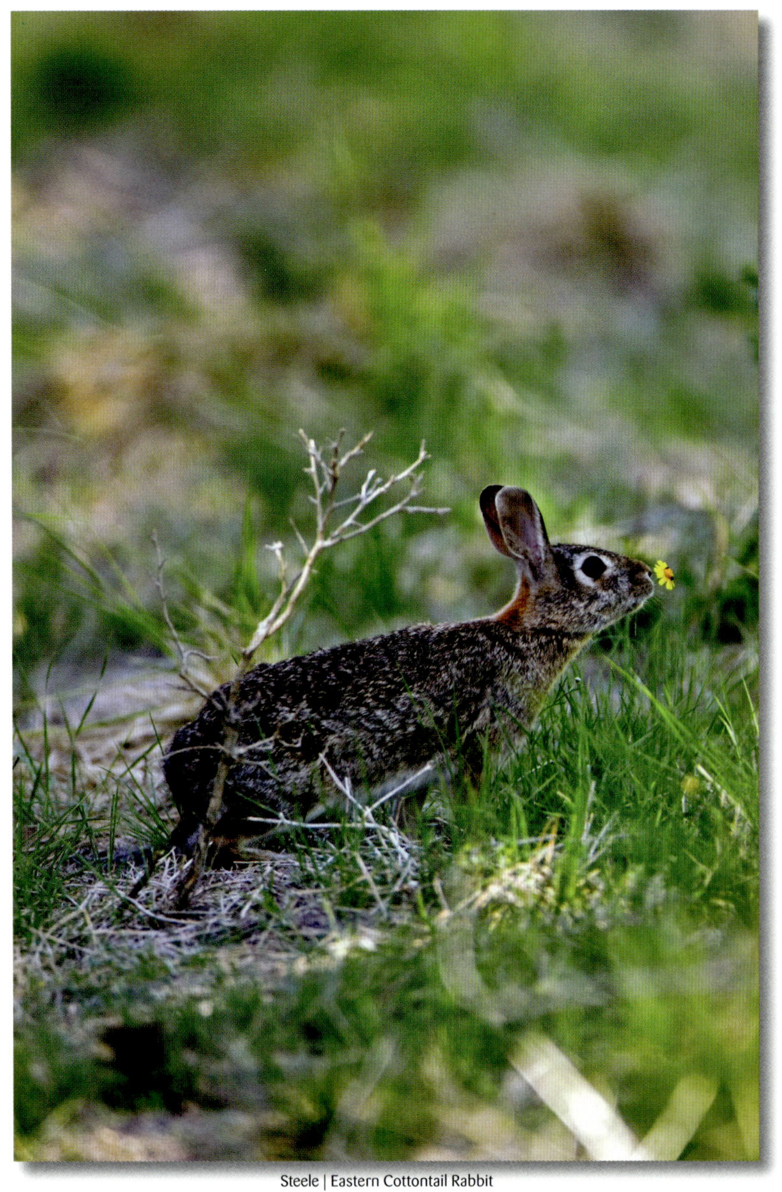

Steele | Eastern Cottontail Rabbit

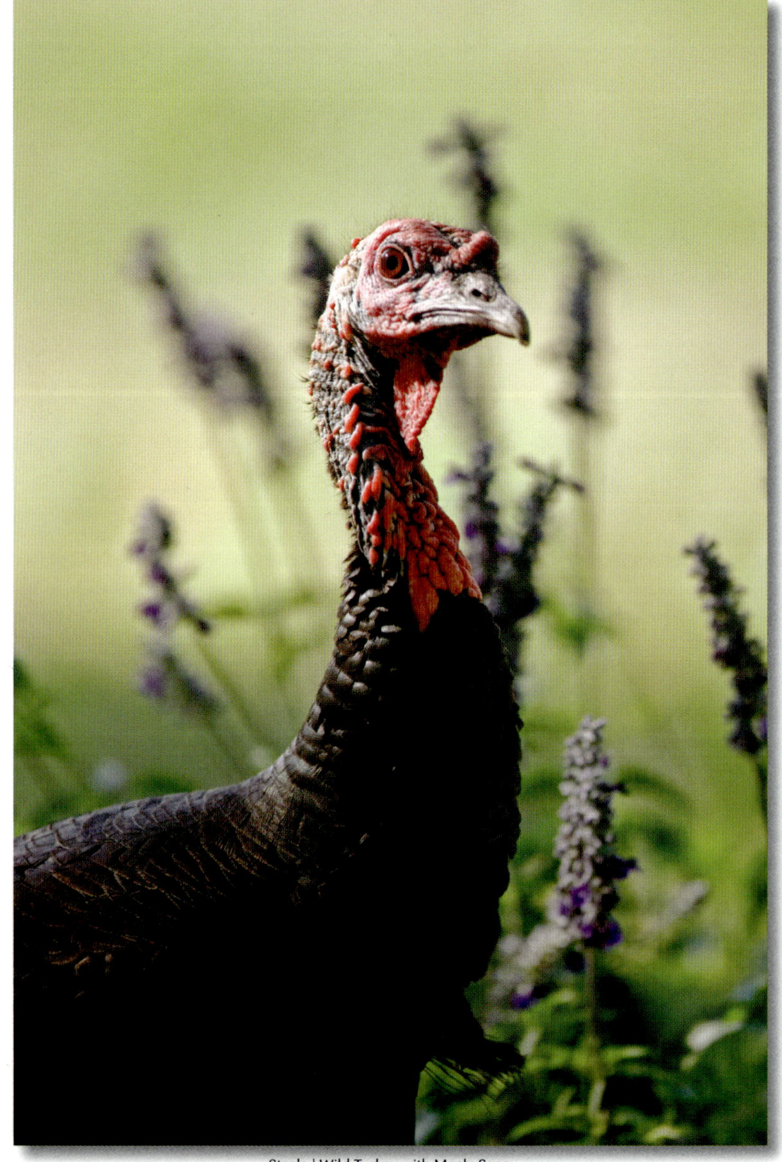

Steele | Wild Turkey with Mealy Sage

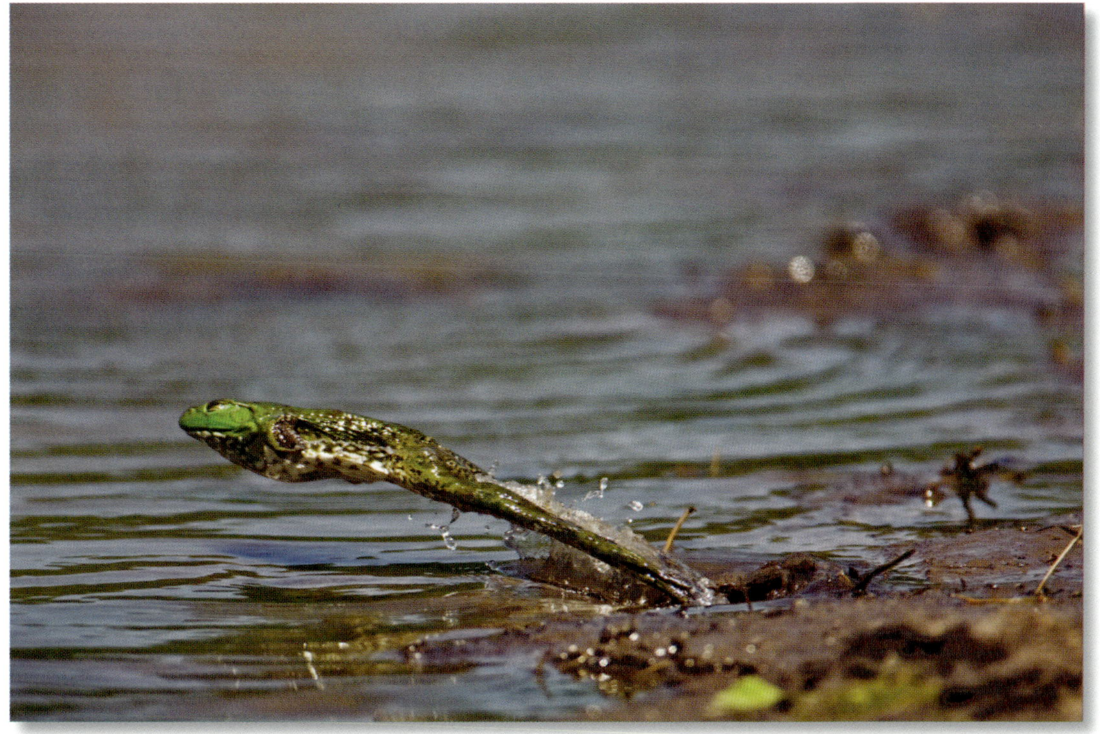

Steele | Bullfrog

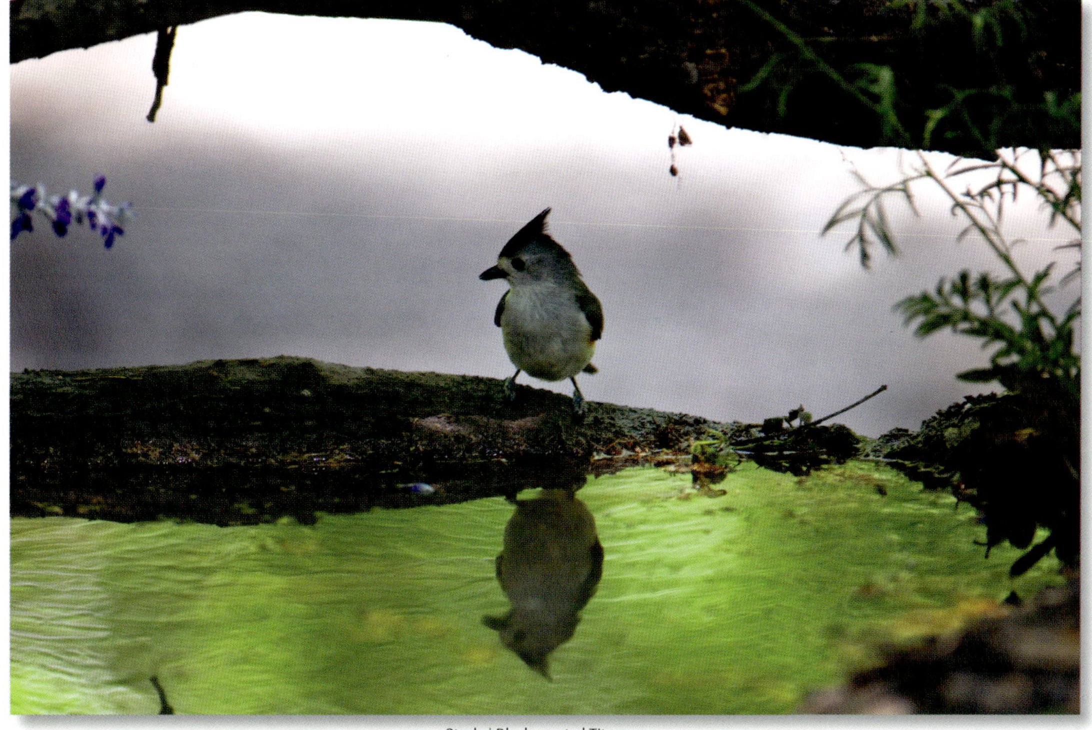

Steele | Black-crested Titmouse

About Coleto Creek Project...

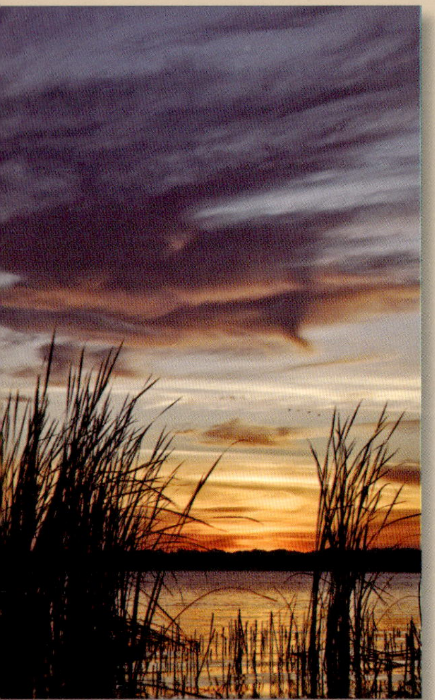
Szafranski | reeds

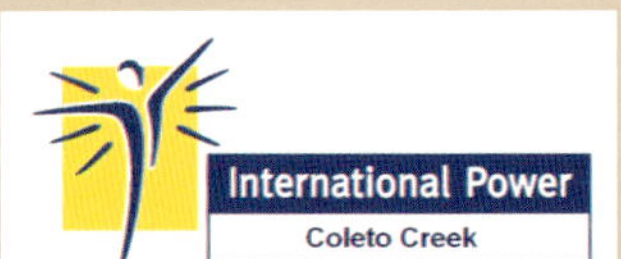

IPA – Coleto Creek Natural Area consists of 1,500 of 5,000 acres of coastal prairie and Post Oak and Live Oak savannahs along the Coleto Creek Reservoir near Fannin.

A service road carries visitors over the dam and across the reservoir from Coleto Creek Park. Located between Goliad and Victoria on the Texas Independence Trail, this natural landscape still bears a resemblance to earlier days when the Battle of Coleto Creek took the lives of many brave Texians during the Texas Revolution against Mexico. Today, tall native grasses and wooded stands of oak and Mesquite adorn the property, managed by the Guadalupe-Blanco River Authority.

The reservoir was created in 1980 to serve a power plant located on the western shores of the 3,100-acre impoundment. The following year, Coleto Creek Reservoir and Park opened to the public, providing year round family recreation with multi-use campsites, cabins, hiking and biking nature trails, world class bass fishing, a 200-foot lighted pier and a boat ramp to access the lake. Fishing tournaments, mountain biking, reunions, school trips and an annual photo contest number among the events offered at this inviting destination.

Chief Ranger Wilfred Korth has overseen land stewardship at the park and private natural area since its inception nearly 30 years ago. Attentive to every facet of park life, he has observed natural wonders manifest from fields of enchanting wildflowers in the spring to the cacophony of migrating waterfowl as winter approaches. Among the notable highlights there are two pairs of American Bald Eagles that return annually to nest along the banks of Coleto Creek. In 2007, members of the Victoria Photography Club assisted Wilfred in erecting several photo blinds at the park, including the Eagles' Nest Blind, which gives hidden nature photographers a bird's eye view of one of the iconic pairs.

Realizing the potential to promote wildlife conservation and photography in low-impact areas across the reservoir, Korth and his staff have consulted with a local Texas Parks & Wildlife Department biologist and a Natural Resources Conservation Service agent to develop and implement plans to improve habitat for wildlife while encouraging a naturally diverse ecosystem. Land stewardship practices include the creation of small ponds to attract animals and to provide additional water sources, prescribed burns to manage invasive plant species and over growth, and strategic brush clearing to provide more habitat edge for wildlife. Weekends from October through December invite bow hunters to the park to help maintain a more balanced and healthy deer population. GBRA's partnership with IPA-Coleto Creek embraces opportunities for greater public use of the land while maintaining a dynamic ecosystem. In addition to promoting wildlife photo opportunities, another goal is to develop a nature education center that teaches area children about land, water, and wildlife in an outdoor classroom setting.

Competing in the ICF Pro-Tour of Nature Photography has allowed Coleto Creek to partner with photographer Keith Szafranski. During the tour, Szafranski spotted a wide range of wildlife against a backdrop of grassy senderos, pastoral oak savannahs, a brushy mix of yaupon, Mesquite, prickly pear and rose hedge, along 61 acres of shoreline. The list of animals includes Bobcats, fox, Coyote, White-tailed Deer, feral hogs, opossum, armadillos, field mice, snakes and alligators. For the bird enthusiast Coleto is a natural haven for numerous species. Osprey, Least grebe, Black-bellied Whistling-duck, herons, pelicans, wood stork, Neotropic Cormorants, Crested Caracaras, woodpeckers, Couch's Kingbird and Vermilion Flycatchers are among the birds that share this reservoir and the land around it.

Coleto Creek offers both the professional and fledgling photographer exceptional opportunities for capturing wildlife moments in this scenic wilderness. Photo workshops are now being offered by the Victoria Photo Club.

Wilfred Korth
Victoria, TX
wkorth@gbra.org

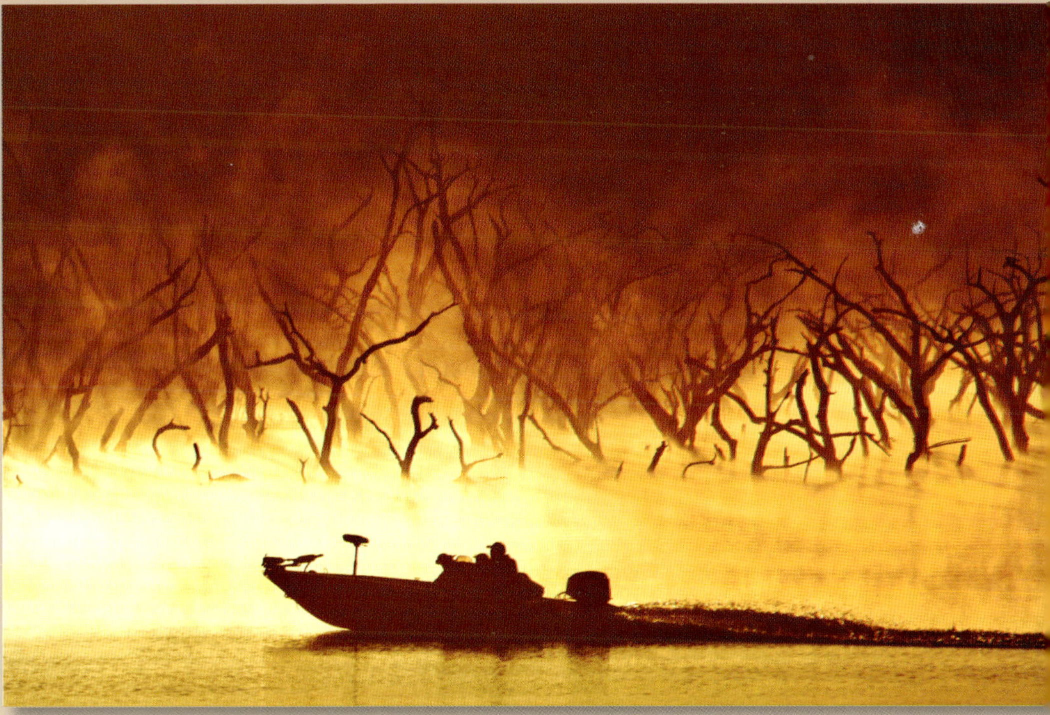

Szafranski

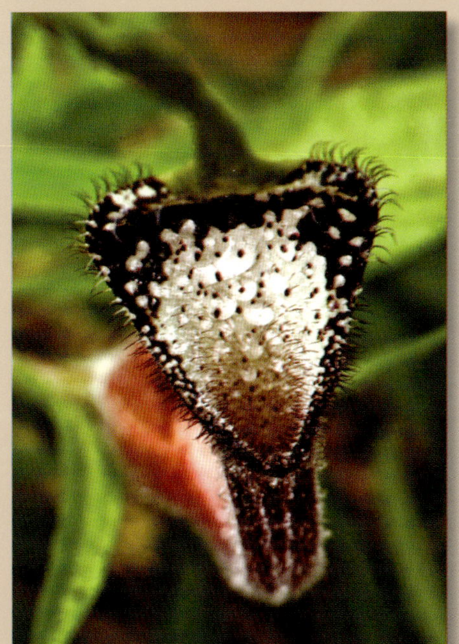

Szafranski | Swan Flower

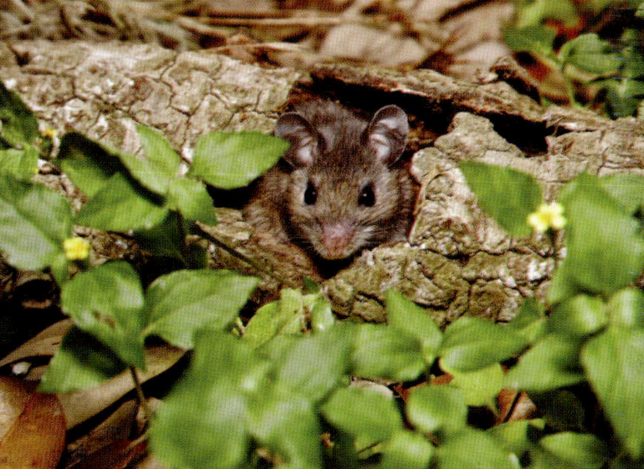

Szafranski | mouse on Straggler Daisy

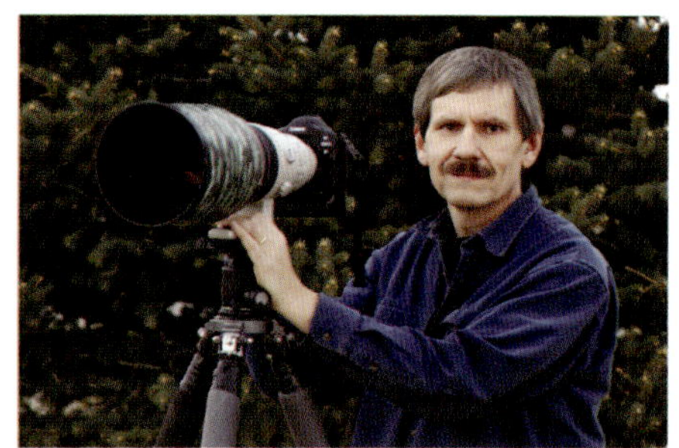

Keith Szafranski

If Keith Szafranski were to sum up his Pro-Tour experience at Coleto Creek in one word "stimulating" would do it. The Montana resident says, "The contest gave me a reason for doing things I hadn't done in a long time and for doing things I'd never done before."

"The type of shooting you do on private land where it's not managed for wildlife is different from the places photographers usually go to, like Yellowstone."

However, adapting to new challenges has never been a problem for the photographer. In 1983, when he made the decision to pursue nature photography as a profession, he moved his family from his native Wisconsin to the wildlife-rich state of Montana.

Keith says that he takes a two-pronged approach to nature photography. "One, I try to capture the essence of my subject. Two, I like to do it in a very personal way. By this I mean I want to be there with my subject and actually see the image through the viewfinder and personally push the shutter button. I never did and hopefully never will care for 'remote' photography where an electronic gizmo actually takes the photograph."

"I was in the blind photographing a little wren singing happily from a woodpile nearby. Suddenly he became quite agitated, flitting back and forth along the woodpile. So I started looking around for what disturbed him. That's when I saw a four-foot rat snake slithering along the edge of the woodpile. Needless to say, I turned my photographic attention to the snake which I probably would not have seen had it not been for the wren's warning and definitely would not have seen if I had been using some electronic gizmo."

To Keith, "being out there instead of being at home watching TV" is a big part of what it takes to be a success in this field.

Livingston, MT
www.mostlywildlifephotos.com
[e] photogsz@msn.com

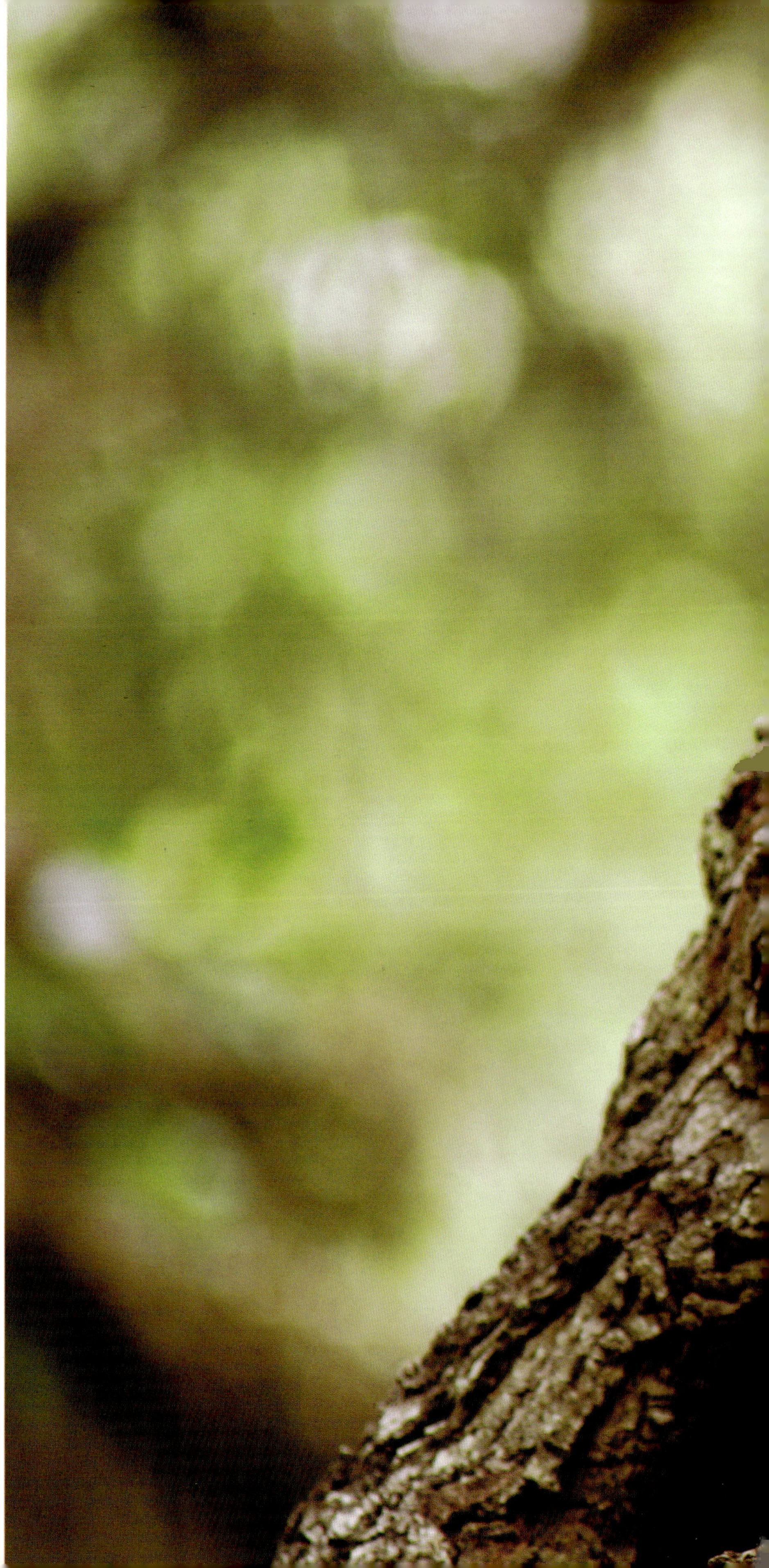

Szafranski | Barred Owl

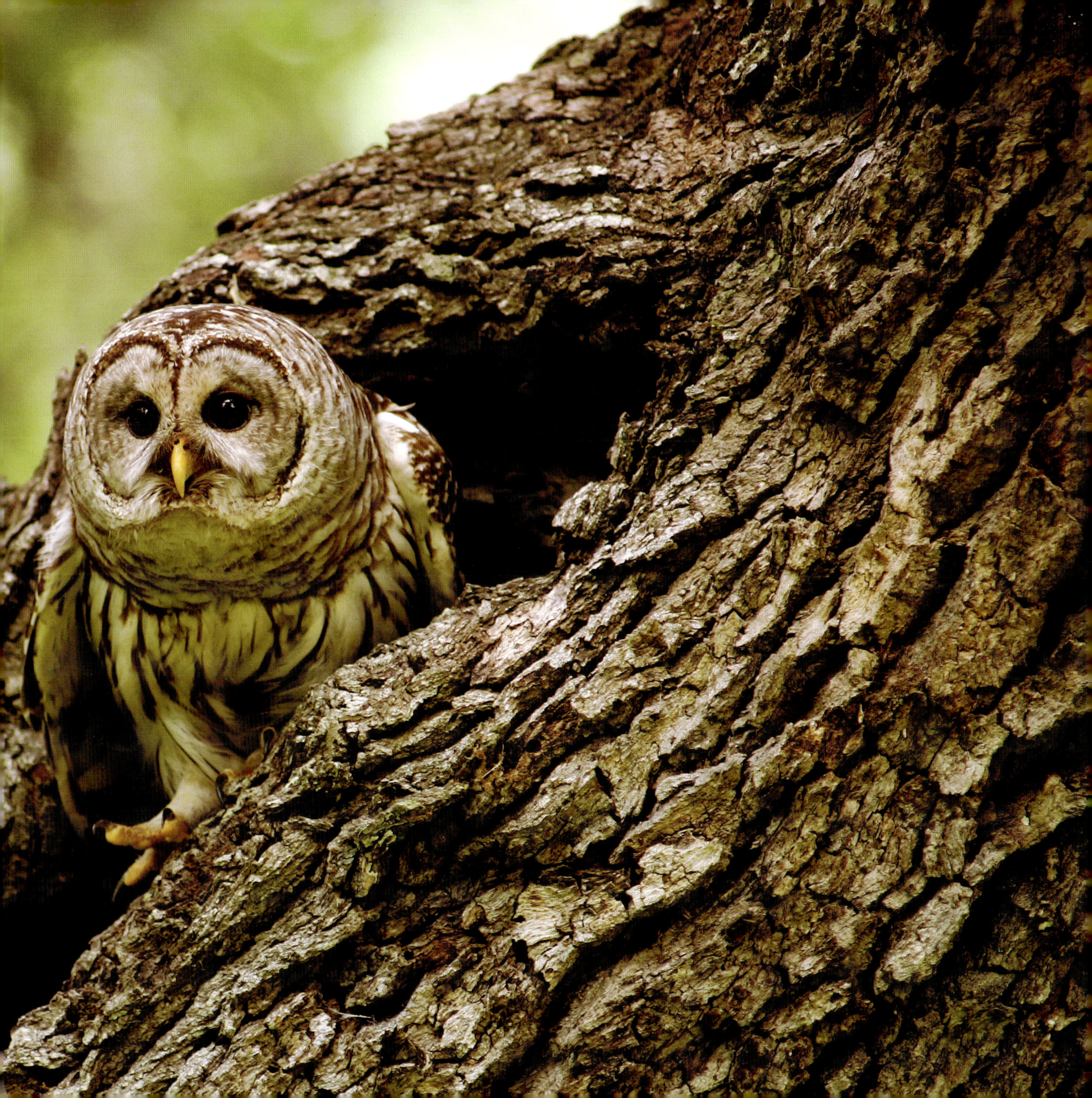

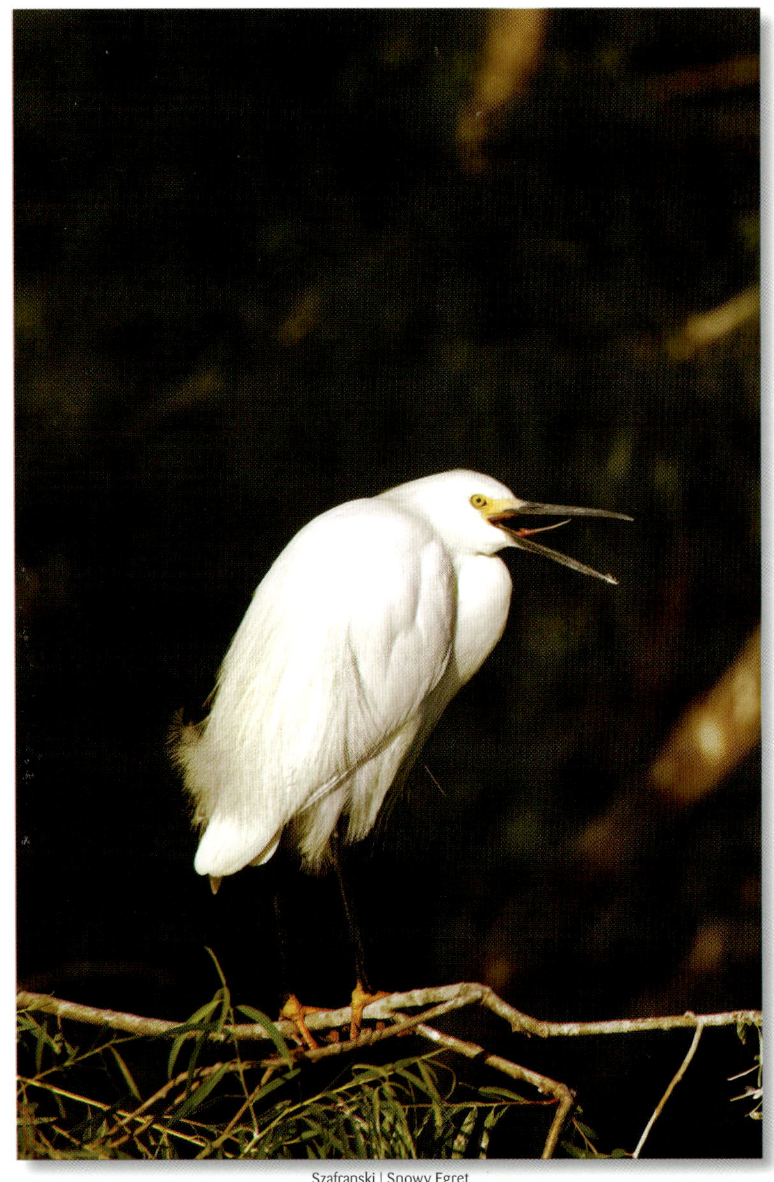

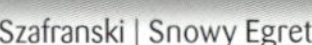

Szafranski | Snowy Egret

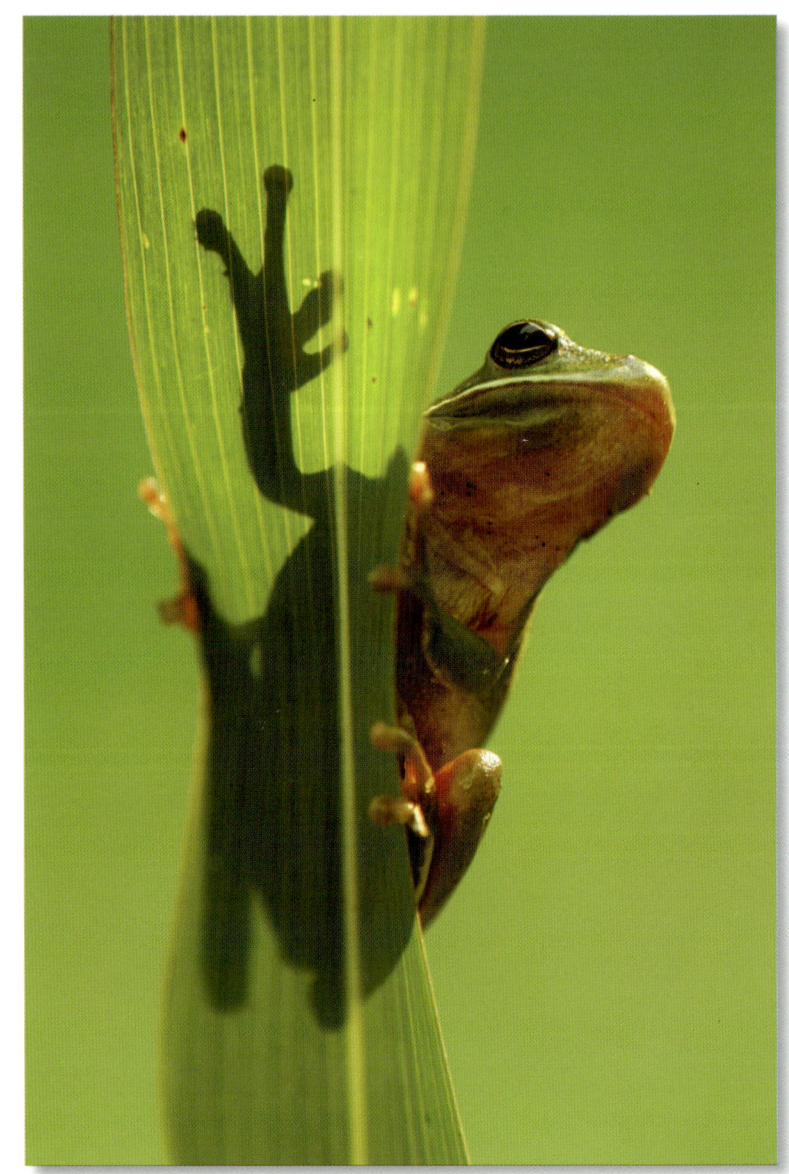

Szafranski | Green Treefrog

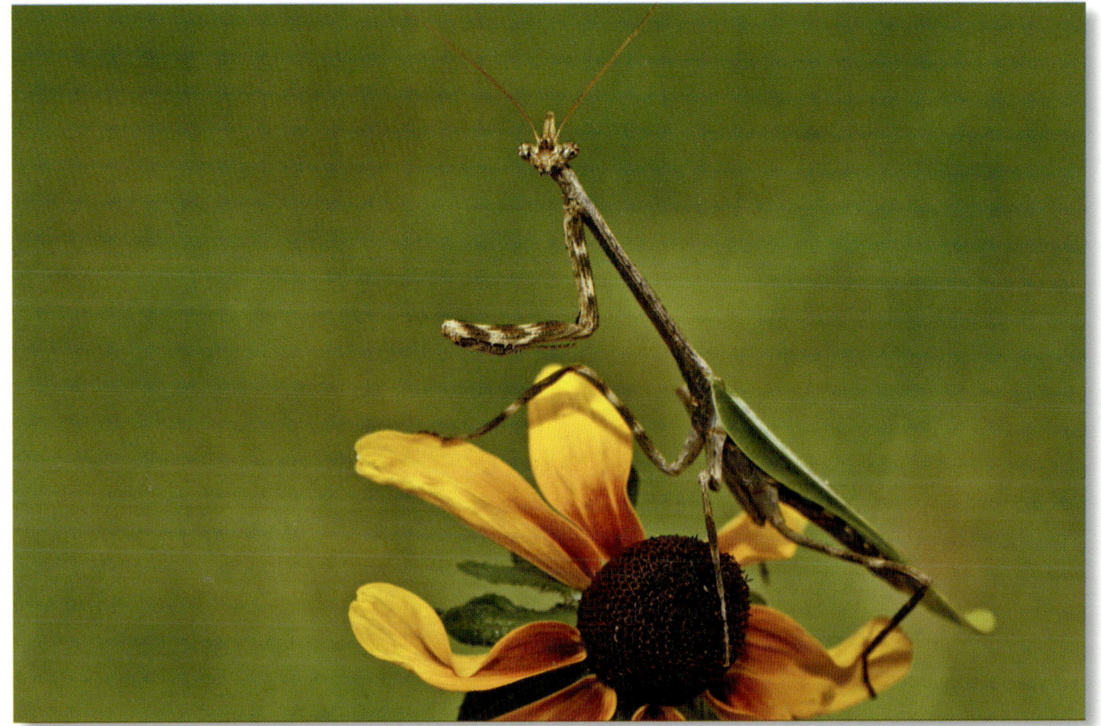

Szafranski | Preying Mantid on Brown-eyed Susan

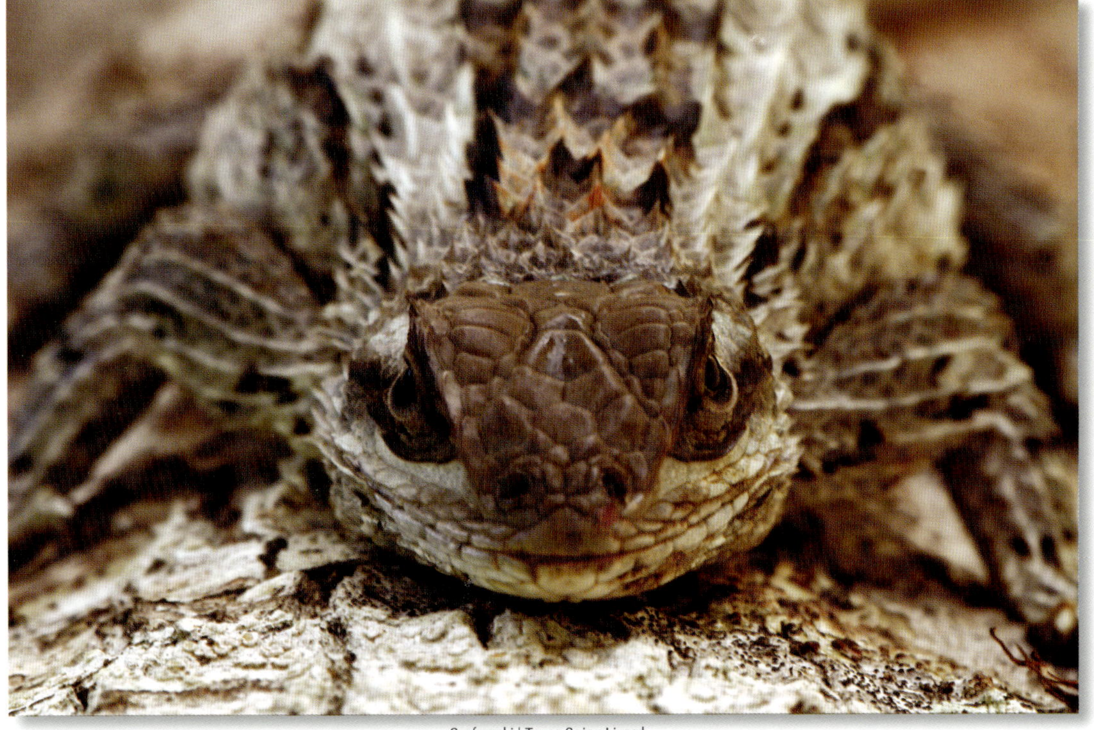

Szafranski | Texas Spiny Lizard

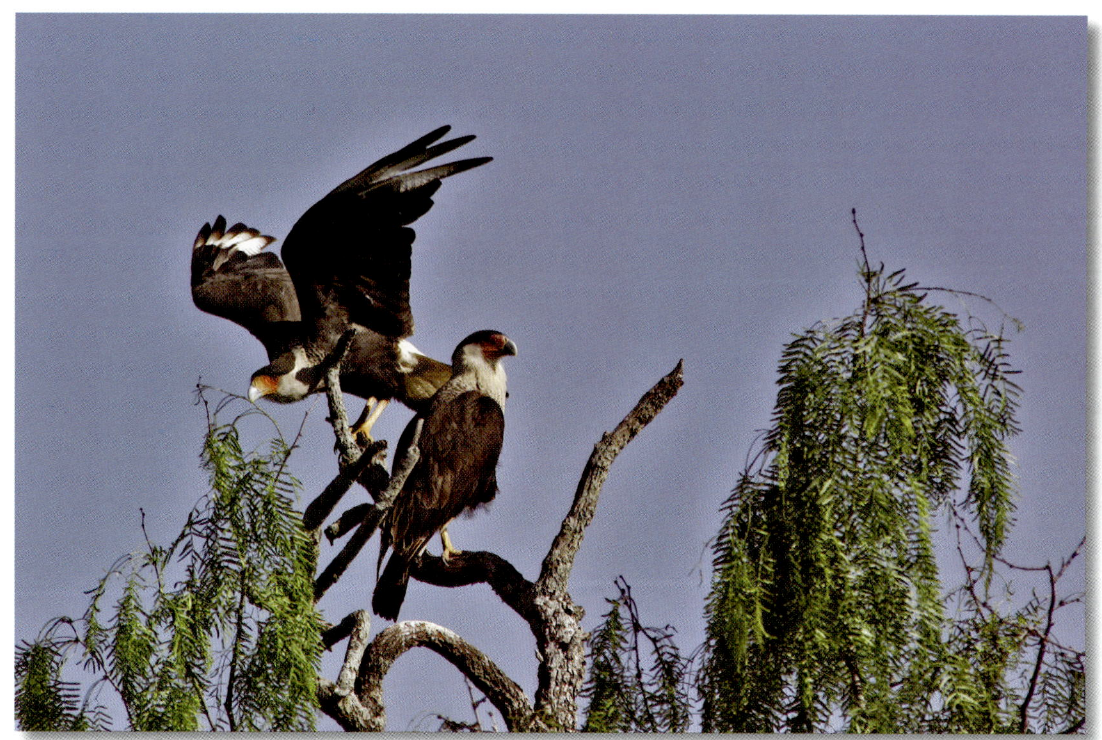

Szafranski | Crested Caracaras in a Mesquite tree

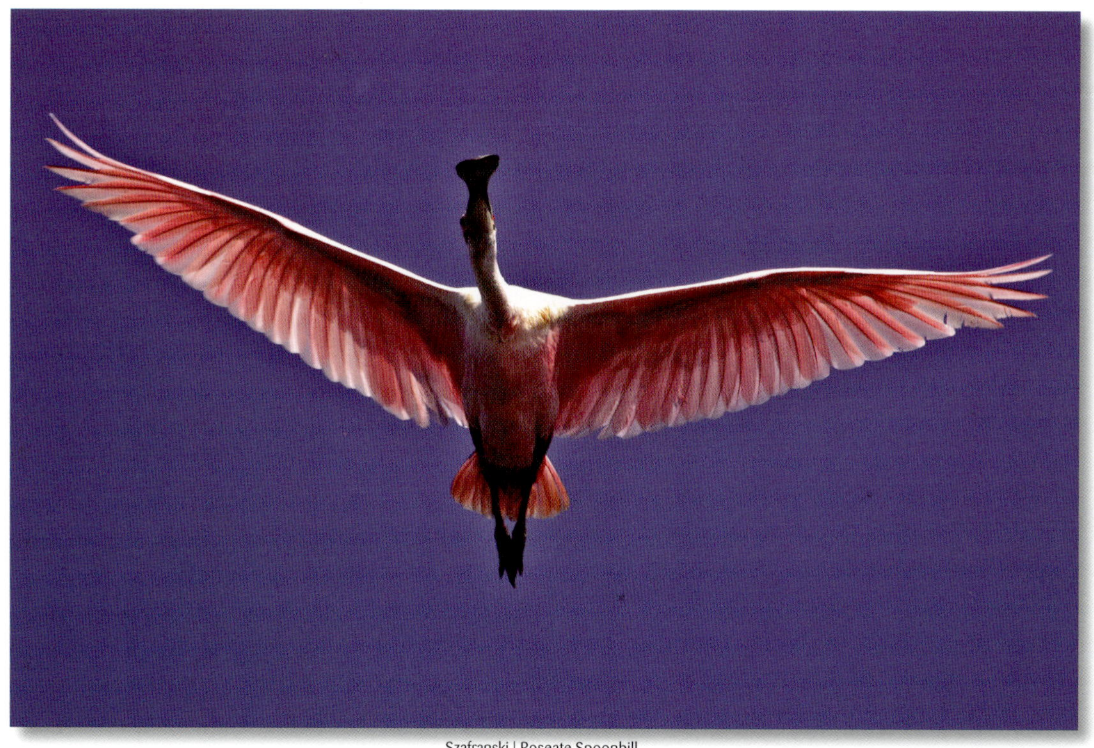

Szafranski | Roseate Spoonbill

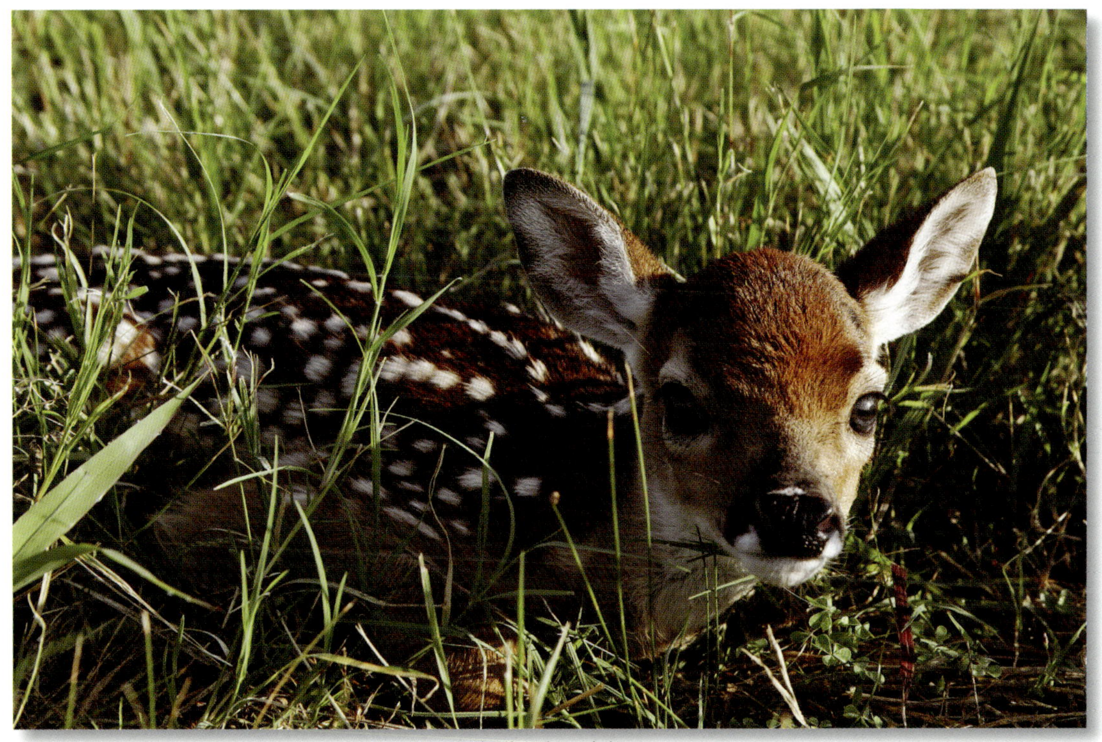

Szafranski | White-tailed Deer

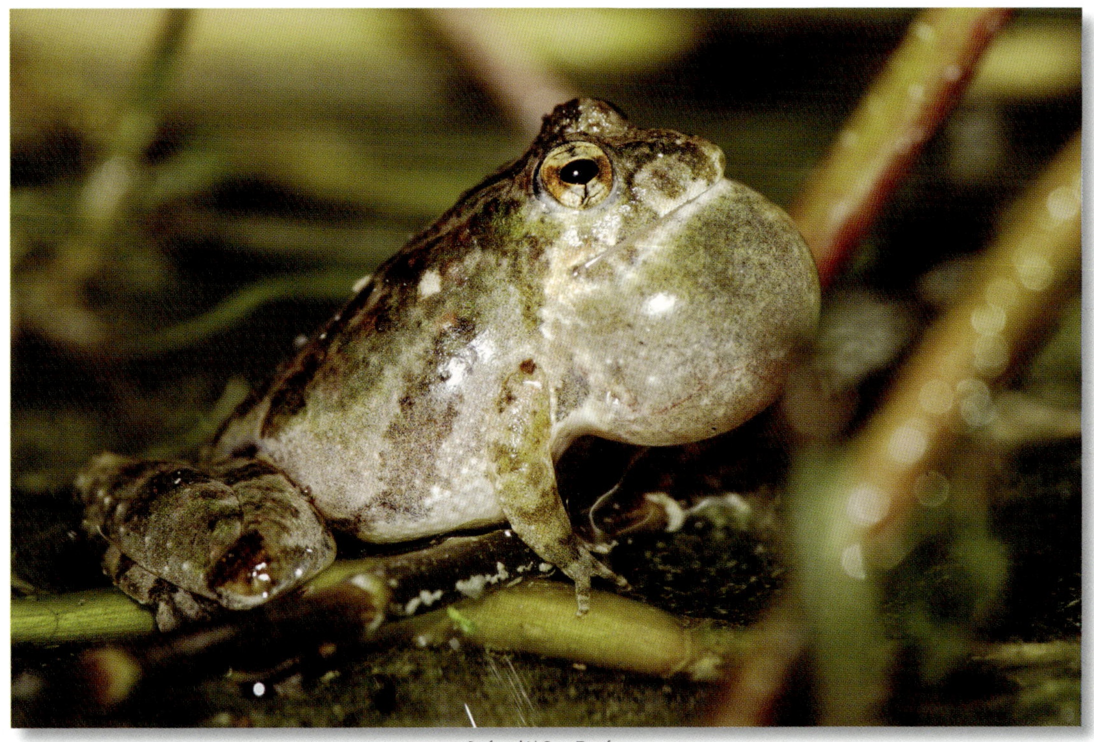

Szafranski | Gray Treefrog

About Flying M Ranch & La Juana Ranch...

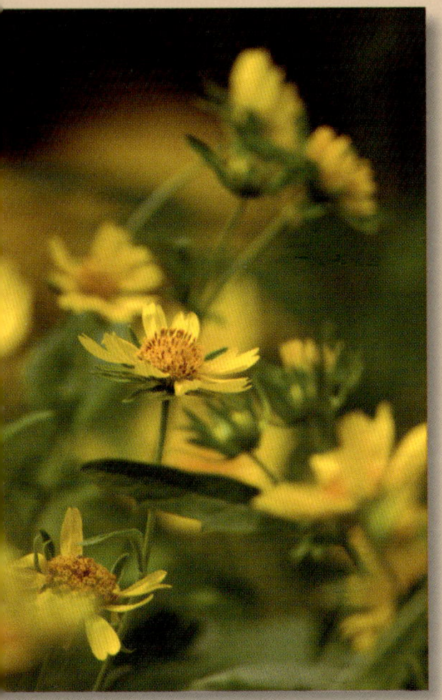

van Kammen | Golden Crownbeard

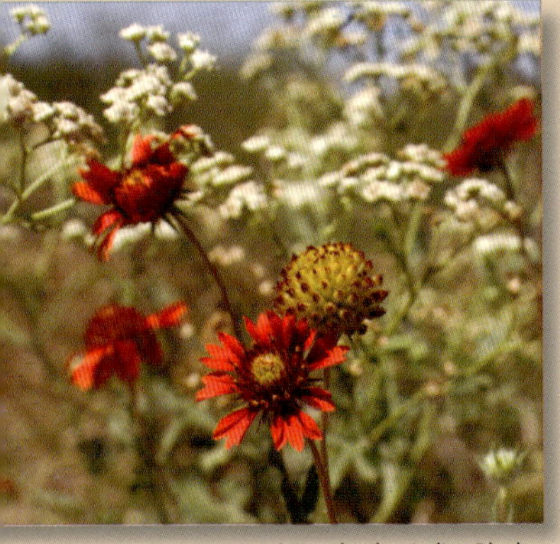

van Kammen | Firewheel or Indian Blanket (seed head behind flowers) and False Ragweed (white flowers)

Flying M Ranch & La Juana Ranch combined to draw photographer Marcel van Kamman from Holland. Traveling the greatest distance, Marcel was one of two photographers from the Netherlands who made the long journey to compete in the 2008 Coastal Bend Pro-Tour of Nature Photography. From this region in Duval County great distances pervade the nearly level panorama with broad vistas that span the South Texas plains in every direction.

Looking beyond the brushy landscape's label, "rattlesnake capital of the world," the adventurous spirit brands this land Big Sky country. Visitors seeking solitude, heavenly sunsets, and star-studded evening skies will find quiet inspiration here.

At the western end of San Diego, Texas, turn north onto County Road 103, and find yourself transported officially off the beaten track. A semi-paved road stretches past brush cloaked in Cenizo, Mesquite, bandaria, cactus, and lime prickly ash.

Passionate about land, music, and family heritage, ranch owner and renowned trombonist, Armin Marmolejo and his wife, Cynthia have a strong connection to this land. Both graduates of Alice High School, they now reside in San Antonio with their children, Andres and Hailey. A professional musician with a PhD from UT Austin, Armin remains steadfast to his roots in San Diego, Texas. He speaks reverently about his Spanish and Irish ancestors who settled here in the 1800s. He finds time to work on ranch ventures when he is not on tour or in the studio. Involving his children in on-going ranch projects promotes their ownership in the ranch, a legacy that hopefully one day they will sustain.

Developing the land for attracting the natural wildlife of this region is the primary focus of Flying M Ranch. Improvements include clearing brush for ranch roads and grazing areas planted with bermuda and millet seed for deer and other wildlife. Every Texas Persimmon on the property is carefully bypassed when shredding brush. Near the entrance Armin and his brother, Noe Marmolejo, who shares ranch ownership, created a fresh water pond in a wooded low area. Deer, Coyotes, badgers, dove, ducks, and egrets number among the various animals spotted quenching their thirst at the watering hole. A seasonal creek runs through the property from the adjacent La Juana Ranch, and roads crisscross through the brush over loamy soils and caliche substrate. Two wood frame houses serve as ranch headquarters near the highest point on their 300 acres. Quaint and comfortable, they offer visitors a cool place to relax either inside or on the screen porch that faces the western frontier. From this vista one can look and listen for armadillos, rabbits, feral hogs, and Javelina patrolling their prickly pathways through the brush. From September to November a variety of hawks, caracaras, vultures, and other birds of prey may be seen 'kettling' in warm columns of air as they make passage to warmer latitudes. Watching raptors of every size gliding in a circular spiral toward the stratosphere is awesome to behold, and on the right autumn day Flying M Ranch & La Juana Ranch would be a perfect place to gather, observe and photograph the avian phenomenon.

Curious about the characteristic plants of the brush and the many species of wildlife that seek shelter here, the Marmolejo family has consulted with a local naturalist.

Mike Howard from the Department of Agriculture in Benavides, Texas avails himself to discuss everything that grows on these rugged plains and which animals use certain plants for various purposes. The Prickly Pear Cactus, for example, has vitamins and minerals that deer can't find in other browsers. Cenizo leaves, also called purple sage, when brewed make a tea that settles an upset stomach. These and other data of Duval County natural history and lore await future adventurous photographers who visit Flying M Ranch & La Juana Ranch.

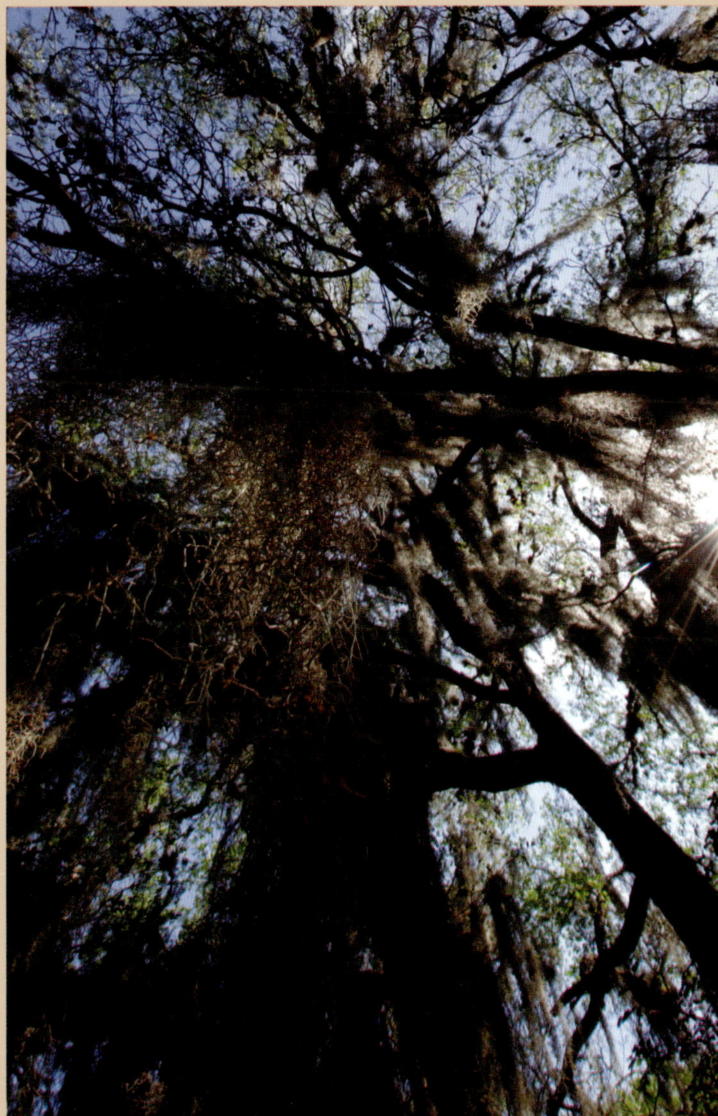

van Kammen | Spanish Moss in Live Oak tree

C. R. Dick Sherron, Armin & Cynthia Marmolejo
Beaumont, TX and San Antonio, TX
[e] cmarmolejo@satx.rr.com

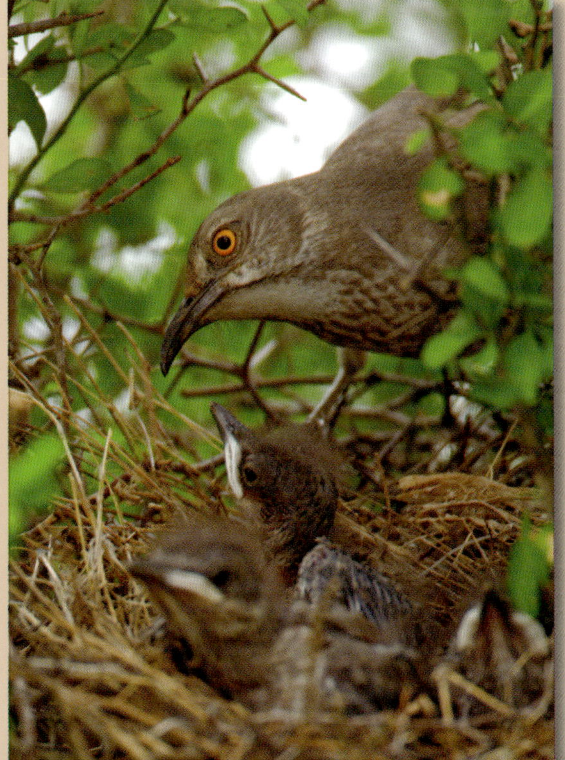

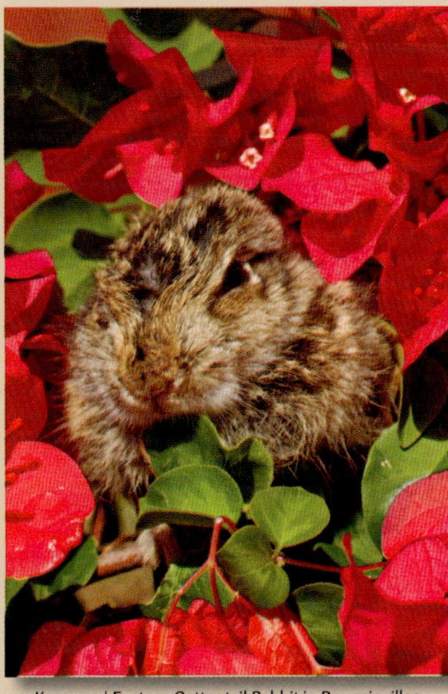

van Kammen | Eastern Cottontail Rabbit in Bougainvillea

van Kammen | Curve-billed Thrasher (adult with nestlings)

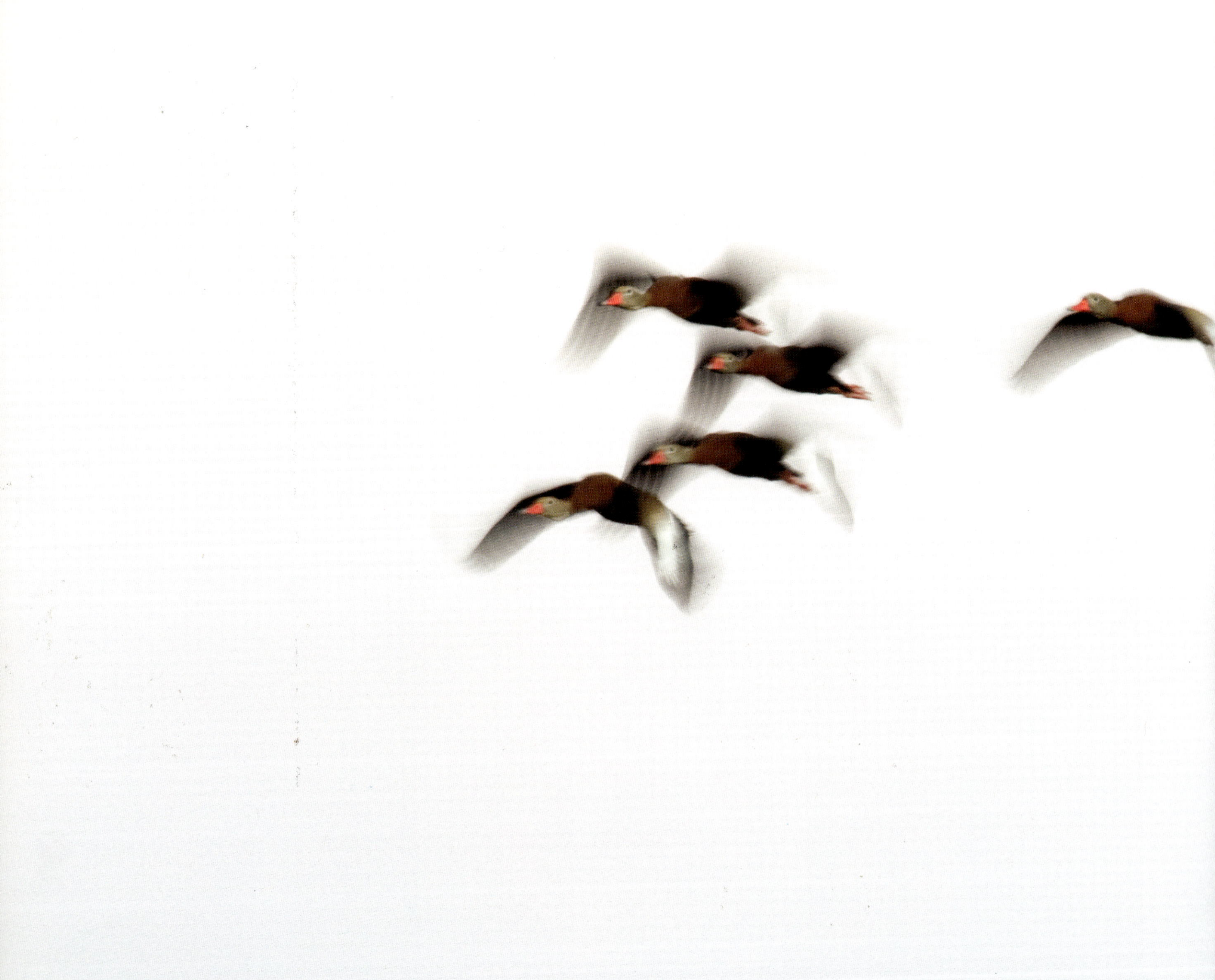

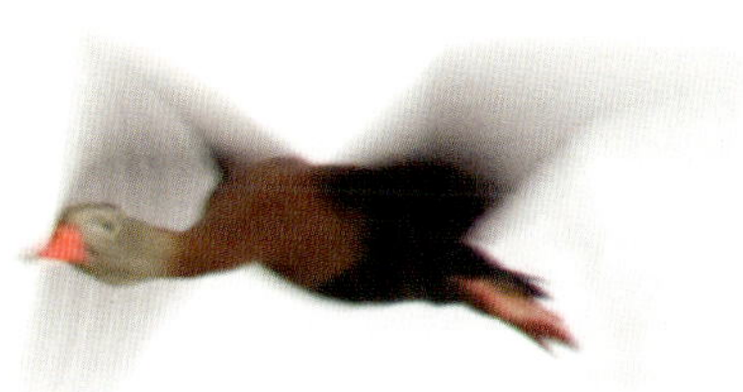

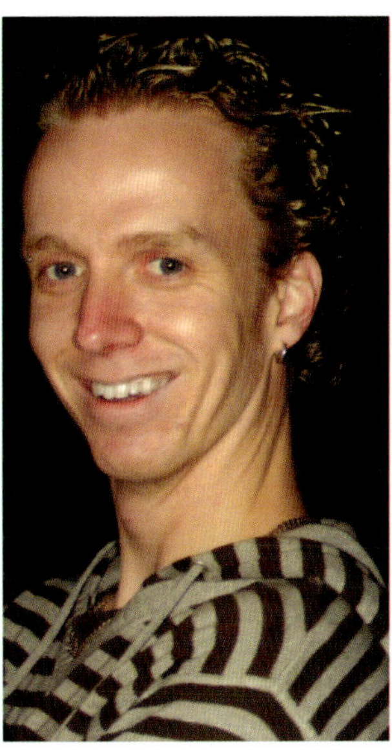

Marcel van Kammen

Marcel van Kammen works for Fotonatura, one of the best known nature photo-stock agencies in the Netherlands. With enthusiasm he says, "I really have a great job as a nature photographer –sitting in the field, watching all those beautiful things out there."

His job was made especially richer by traveling to a place unknown to him. Two animals in this strange land particularly interested him: Coyotes and Bobcats. "I really wanted to get a picture of one of those two species." While he didn't get a photo of either, he was lucky enough to see them both, just not through the eye of his camera.

These weren't the only critters he found appealing. "The Bronzed Cowbird and the Northern Bobwhite are two species that I'll never forget."

"Texans have to be proud of the nature they have. The quantity of birds in this part of America is unique and they need to do the best they can to keep that." He cites the Mountain Lion as another example of the region's unique offerings. "I think it would be a great loss for American wildlife if this mammal were to disappear."

He credits his 30 days at Flying M Ranch and La Juana Ranch with helping to make him a better photographer. "Before I joined the contest, I was mainly interested in birds and mammals. I never took a picture of a flower or an insect. During the contest, I discovered parts of photography that didn't really interest me before, but I really liked doing it during the contest. As the month passed by, I was still getting better at it."

"My landowner taught me a lot about the best places, times and ways to photograph the birds, Javelina and small reptiles. Coming from Holland, I didn't know a lot about the behavior of the birds and mammals. He also inadvertently taught me that the people from America, especially Texas, are much friendlier and open-minded than I had expected."

De Westreen, The Netherlands
m.vankammen@fotonatura.com
www.momentsofnature.nl

van Kammen | Black-bellied Whistling-Ducks

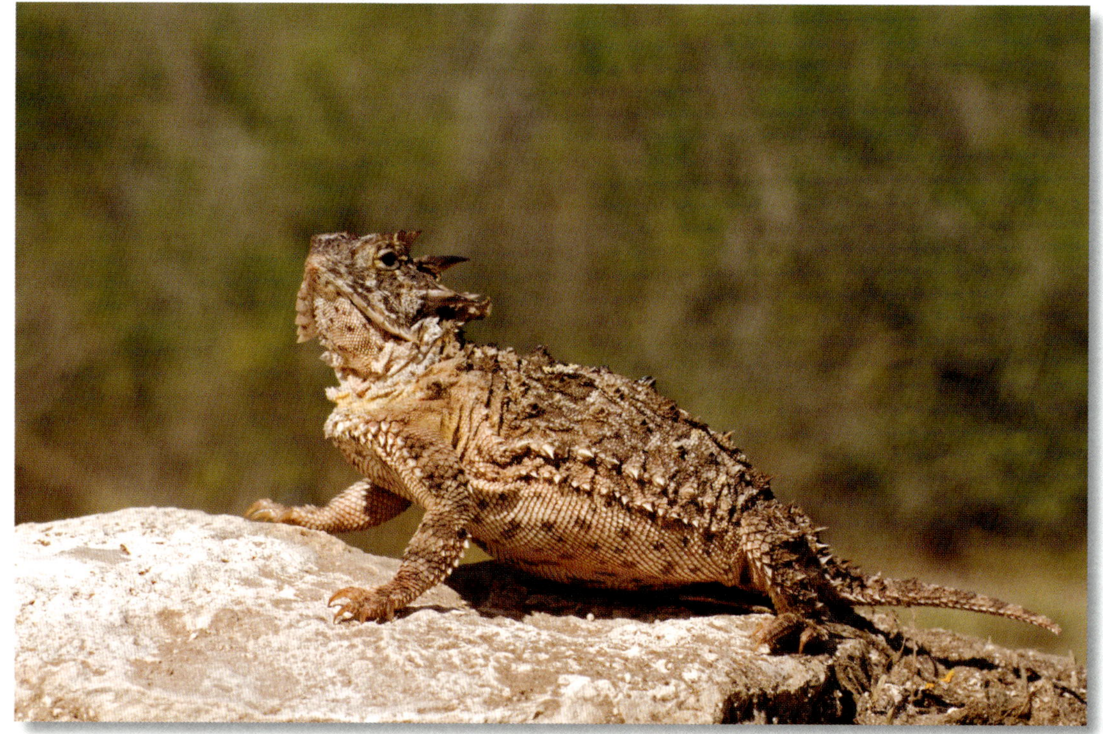

van Kammen | Texas Horned Lizard

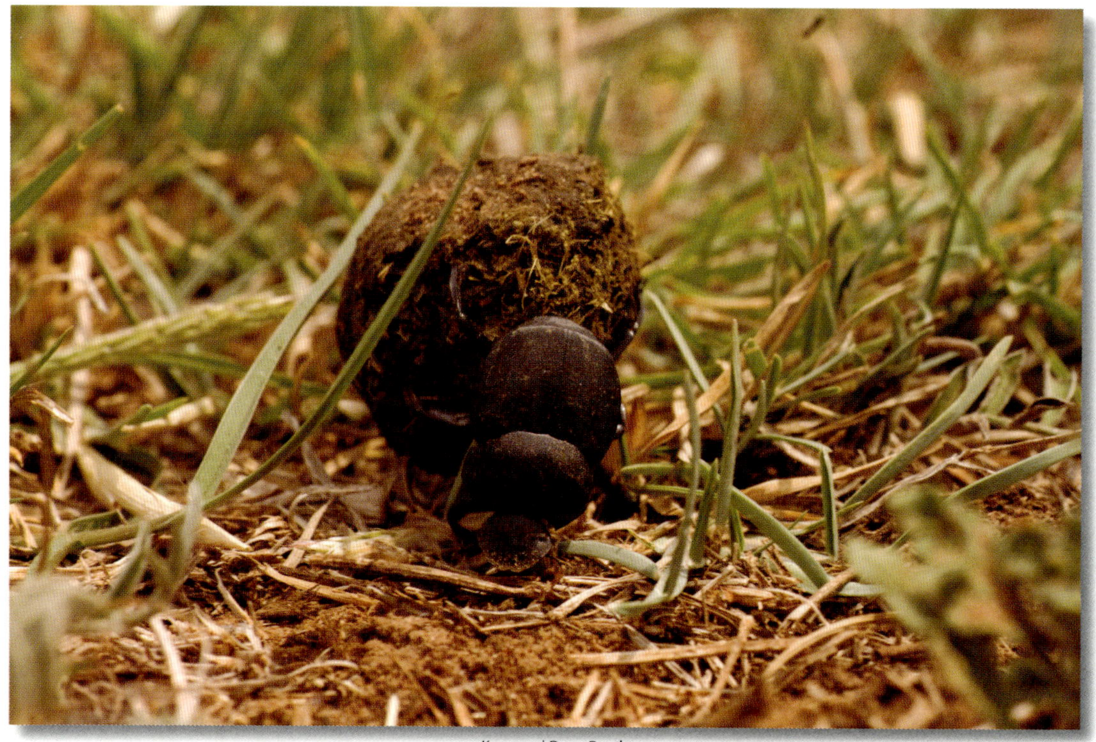

van Kammen | Dung Beetle

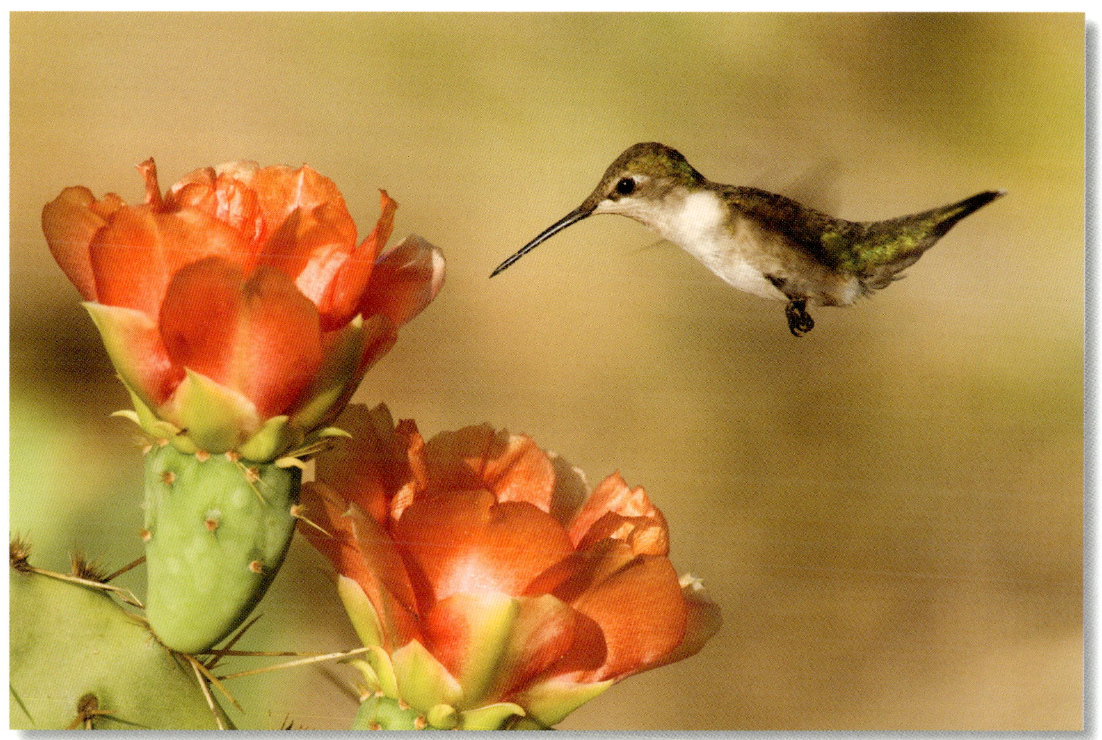

van Kammen | Ruby-throated Hummingbird (female) near Prickly Pear

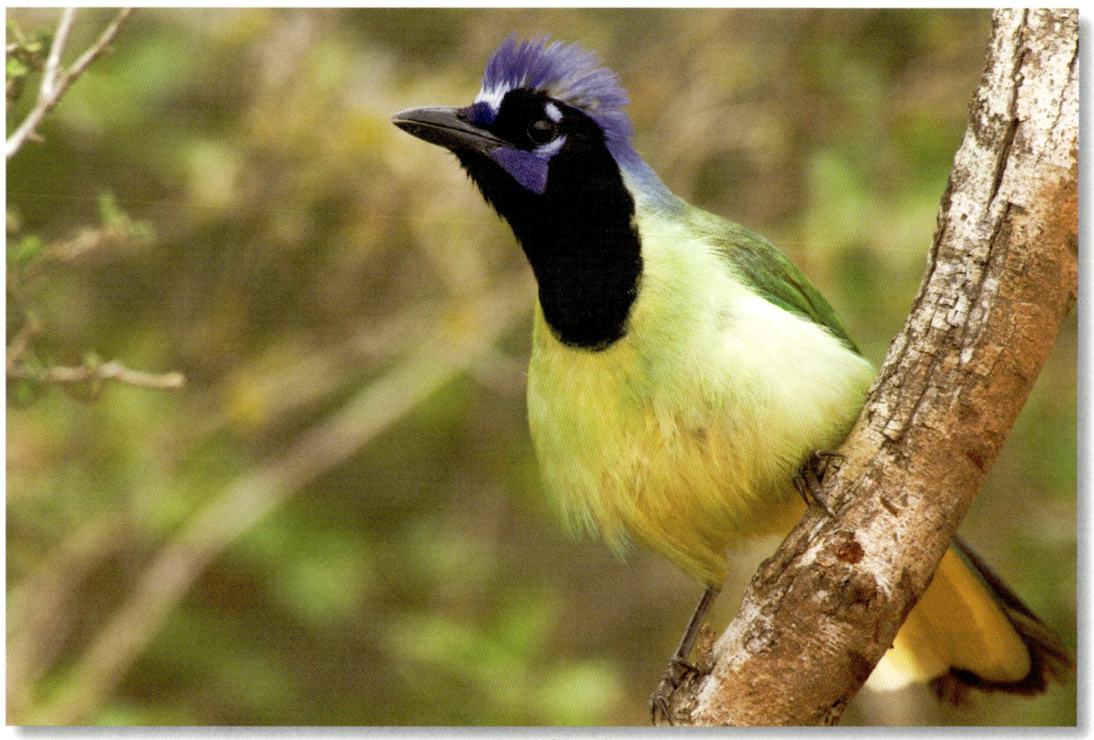

van Kammen | Green Jay

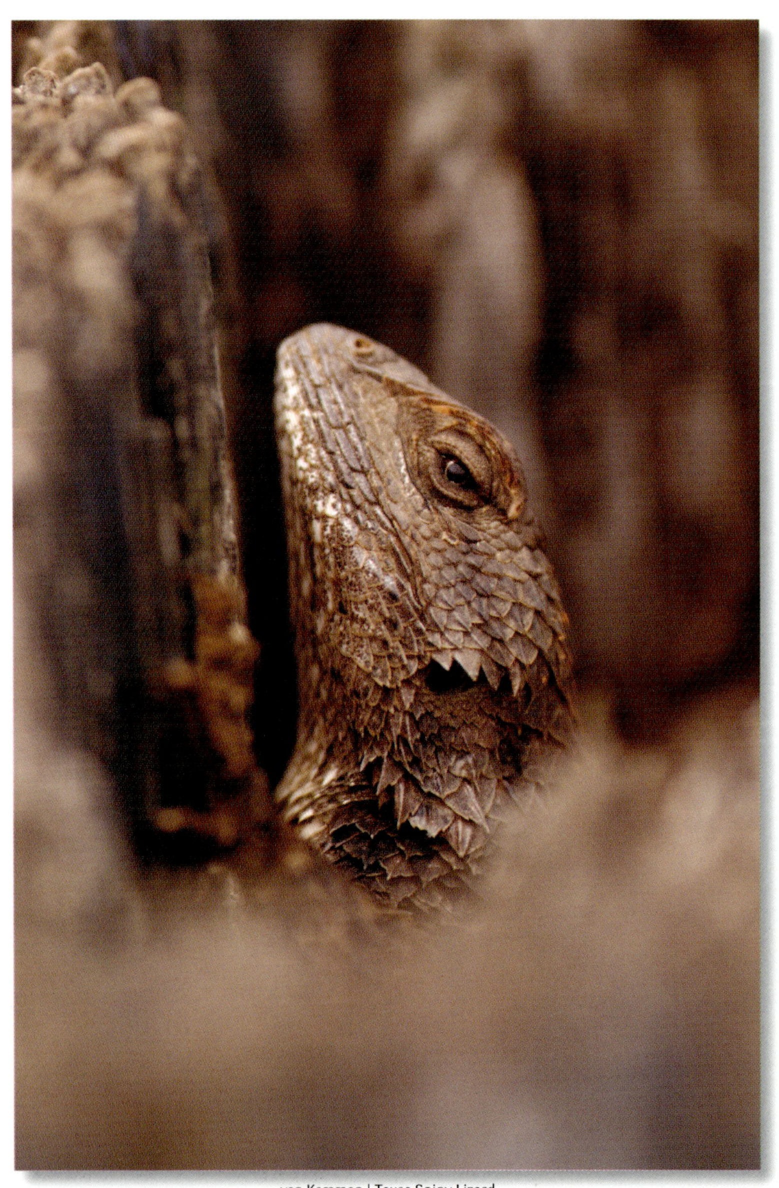

van Kammen | Texas Spiny Lizard

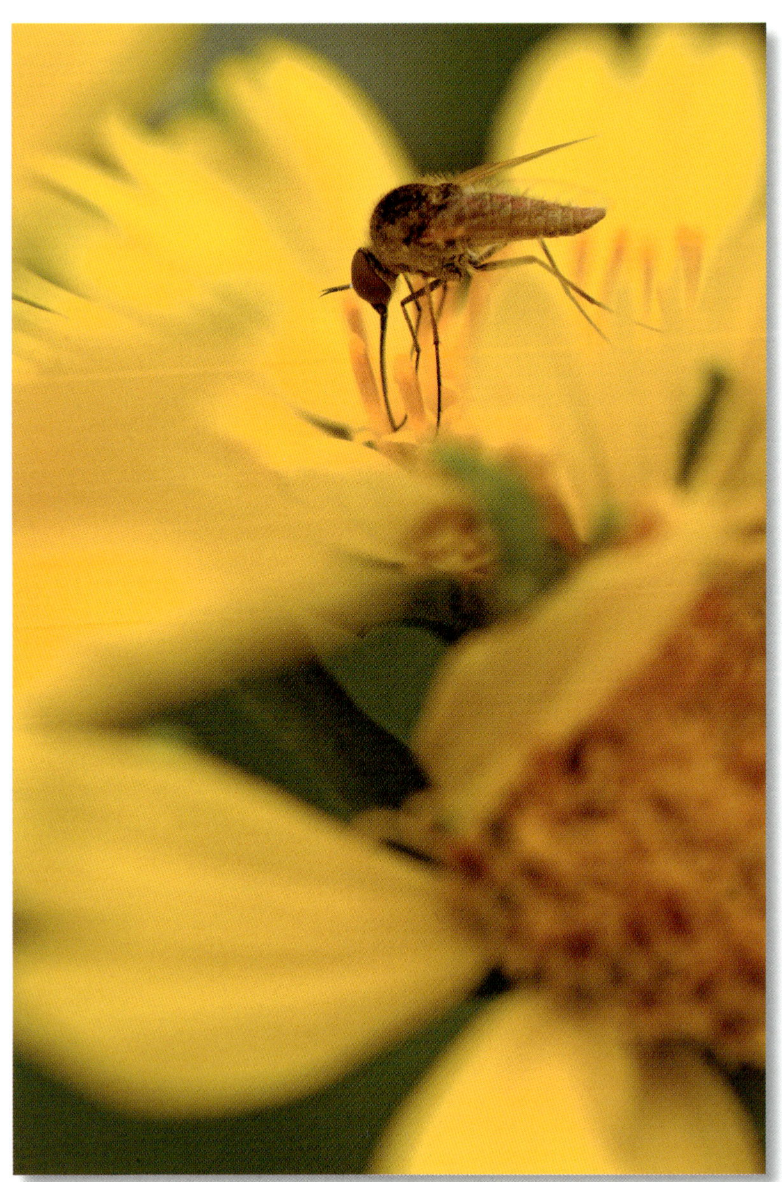

van Kammen | Bee Fly feeding on Huisache Daisy

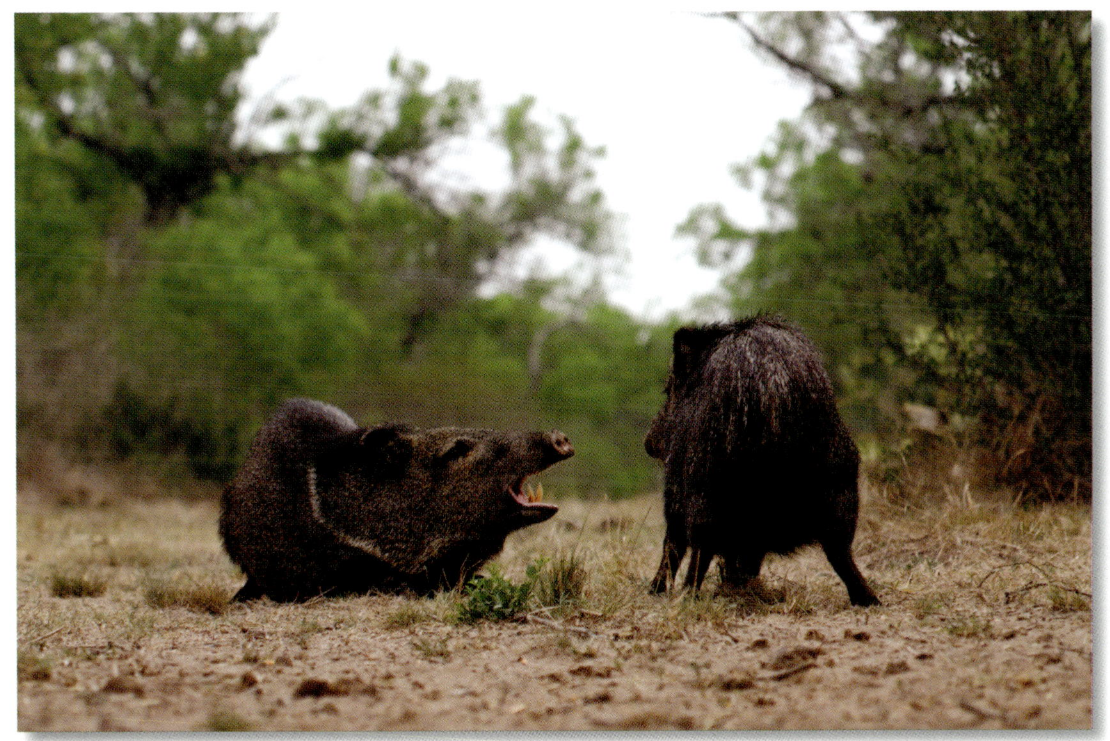

van Kammen | Javelinas

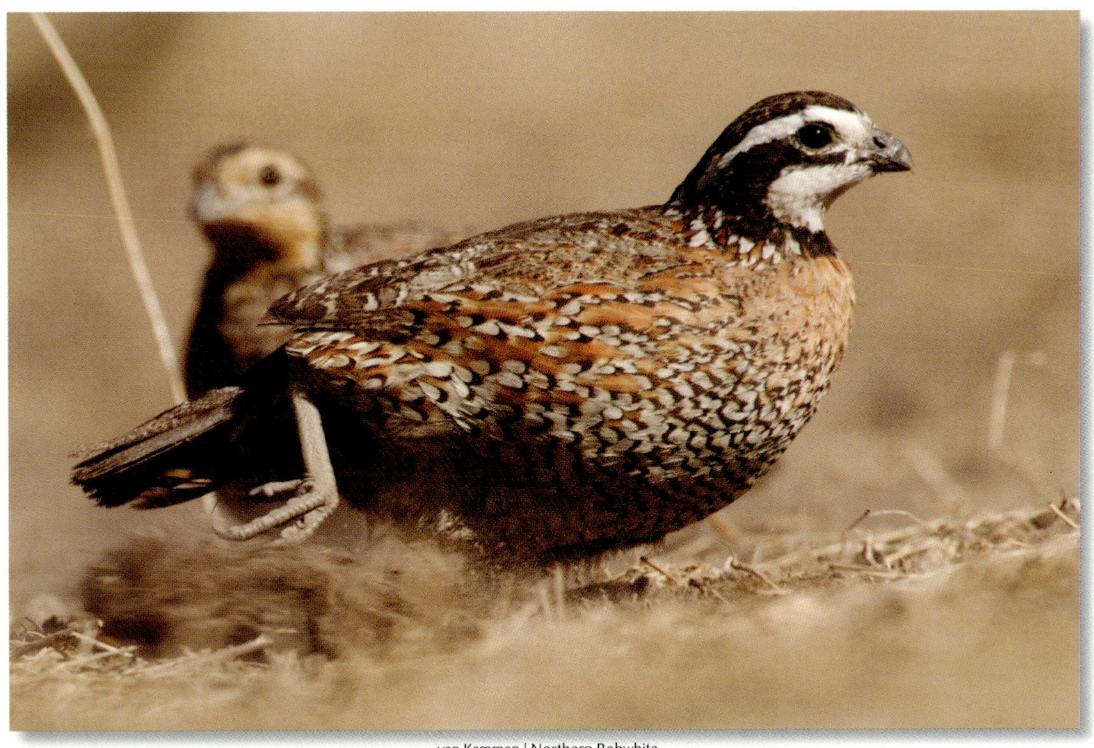

van Kammen | Northern Bobwhite

About Fourth Option Ranch...

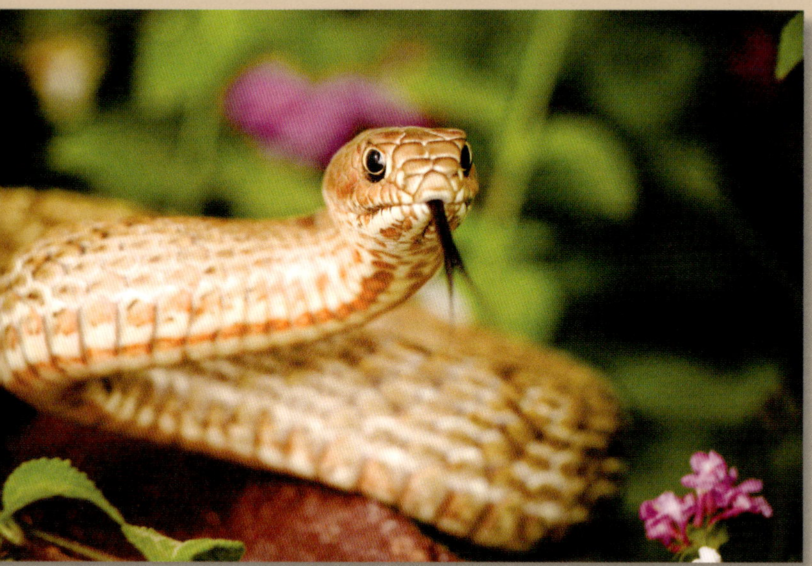
Lightsmith | Western Coachwhip

The possibility of financial reward is not what motivated Darryl and Teresa Haas to open their hearts and their gate to a professional photographer.

For them, the Images for Conservation Fund Pro-Tour of Nature Photography simply was a way to share with others the experience of their Fourth Option Ranch, an experience they enjoy daily at their home.

Life is as good as it gets at their San Patricio County hideaway, the couple is fond of saying.

And even when they're not sharing the land with human guests, they're enjoying the company of the ranch's many cohabitants. The wildlife list is broad and diverse.

"Wildlife," Darryl says, his voice warm and smiling, "That's really all we do here. We're not in any business on the land. We don't run cattle. We're just here to enjoy the place and the wildlife. And we especially like giving others a chance to enjoy it as we do."

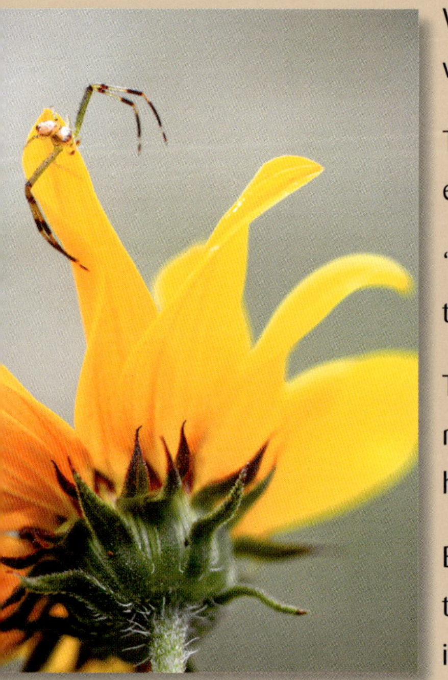
Lightsmith | Crab Spider on sunflower

This certainly applied to photographer Terra Lightsmith, whose insight and friendship the Haases particularly enjoyed. Lightsmith taught them a great deal about their sanctuary.

"She helped us look more closely at what we have here," Darryl said. "She's helped us notice the insects, the little things."

The couple said they began noticing things such as the Praying Mantis. And even months after the photographer returned to her own home, Darryl said they're still enjoying what they learned and are noticing stuff they would have overlooked before.

But, even without the insight of a professional nature photographer, Darryl and Teresa Haas said they knew when they saw the property that it was right for them. They bought the 1,240-acre ranch in 2002, two hours after visiting it for the first time.

"We'd seen only about a third of the ranch, but we knew what we were looking for," Darryl said. "And this was it."

The couple's love for this land becomes apparent when they explain exactly what struck them about the property.

It's a night sky that's black, interrupted only by brilliant stars, planets and the moon. It's the sound of birds in the background, singing, chirping, always there. It's sitting by the water as the sun's last light shines across it. It's listening to the water flowing into the pond.

Most of all, they say, it's the fact that every day on this spiritual place is a good day.

In addition to the peace and wildlife, the original Selee family home, built in 1901, contributes to the property's charm and essence.

"It's a unique old farmhouse," Darryl says, "and it talks to us."

Fourth Option Ranch originally was part of a land grant, which was awarded in 1828 by the Mexican government to 200 Irish-Catholic families. But while the ranch's history is nice to contemplate, Darryl and Teresa Haas say the best part of living here is that it feels like a weekend getaway every day.

"My wife and I never lived in the country," Darryl confesses. "This is our first time. And, it will be our last."

There was not a hint of doubt in Darryl's voice or expression.

Darryl & Teresa Haas
Mathis, TX

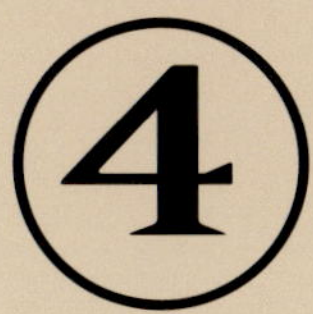

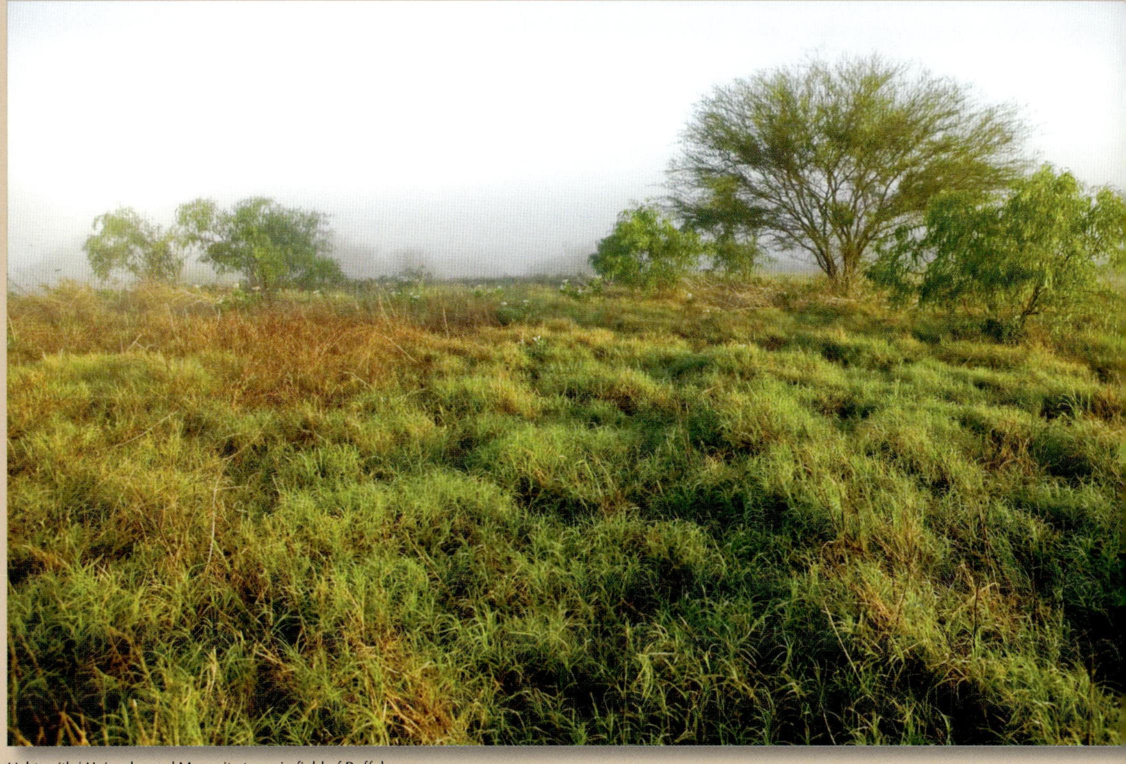

Lightsmith | Huisache and Mesquite trees in field of Buffelgrass

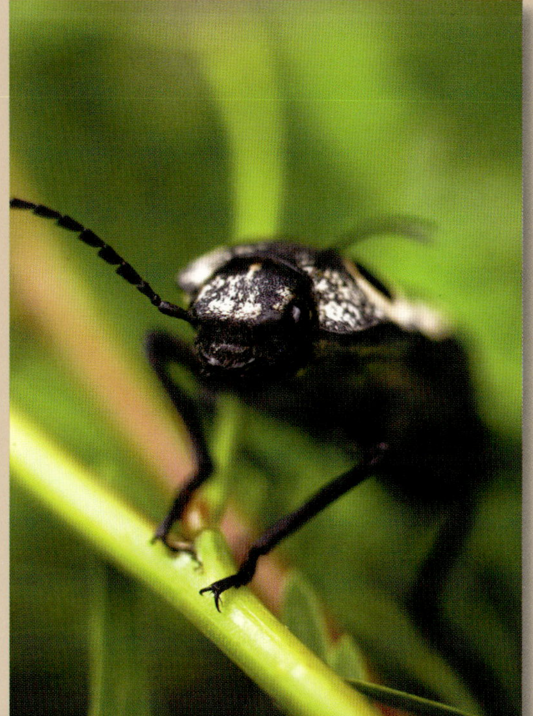

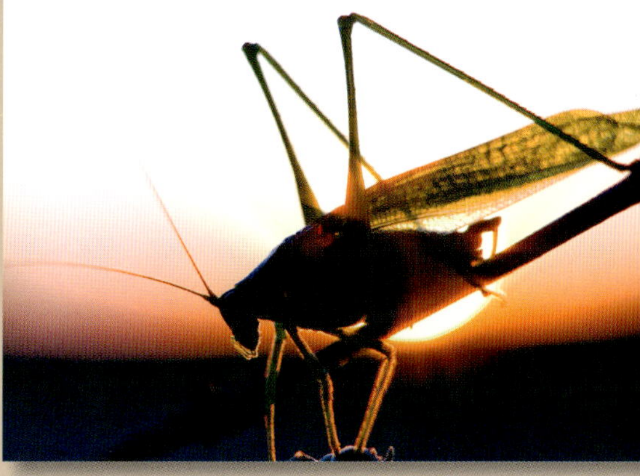

Lightsmith | Katydid

Lightsmith | Eyed Click Beetle

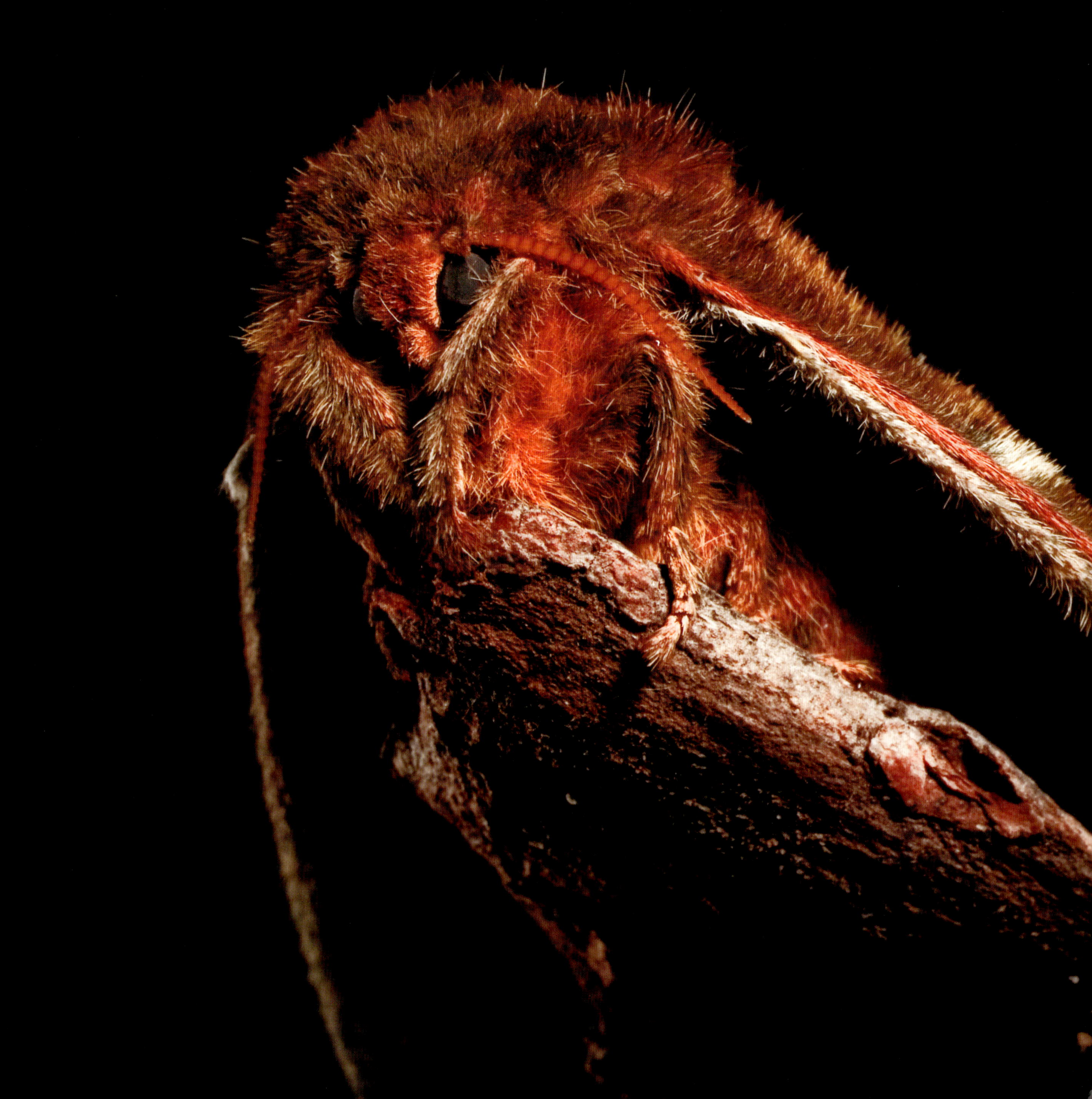

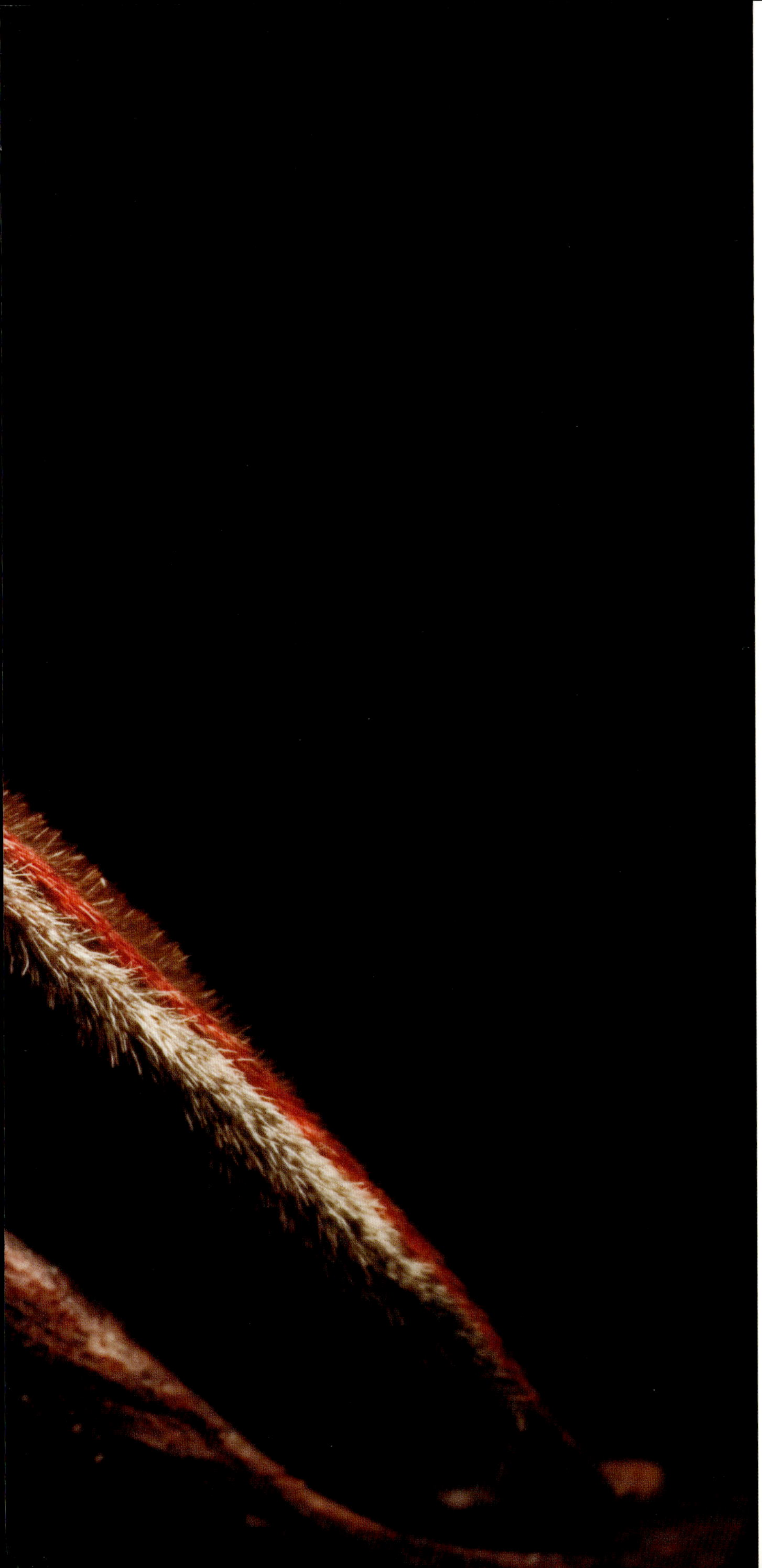

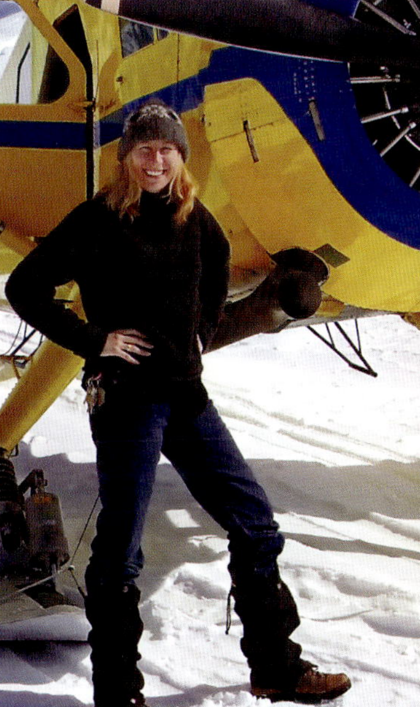

Terra Lightsmith

Terra Lightsmith, the Texas-based photographer, admits she had a passion for nearly every category in the contest just as she's had "a passion for most everything in nature since I can remember."

She says that she came to the Fourth Option Ranch with one set of ideas but soon learned she needed new ones. "My original approach to South Texas wildlife during the contest was to let the creatures become accustomed to me and my lens." However, she says, "This competition threw all such ideas out the window."

"I was able to approach the birds and mammals but as soon as they caught sight of either my tripod or lens, they ran for their lives! The only way to really get close was by using stealth or camouflage and once anything was in view you couldn't move or make a peep. Just my shutter actuations would throw the creatures into a panic, so I often had but one shot to take before I would scare things off."

In this vein, she calls the Pro-Tour "definitely one of the most challenging situations I had ever been in."

Terra has known since she was a six-year-old with her first garage sale camera that photography was her calling. "I spent all of my extra money on film and developing and, combined with my love of nature, thought I may do something meaningful with my experience." The photographer who has "always been preoccupied with the thought of a lost moment and capturing that moment" has found herself driven to do what she does so that she can "capture the essence of an environment."

"There are billions of moments," she philosophizes, "and not one of them the same. Some are more precious than others, all passing by through time and space never to be repeated. I want to save some of these, the fantastic ones, the everyday ones, the quiet ones, the beautiful ones, the traumatic ones. Capturing these moments is part of my life and always will be."

Conroe, TX
denaliphotos@lycos.com
www.denaliphotos.com

Lightsmith | female Lo Moth

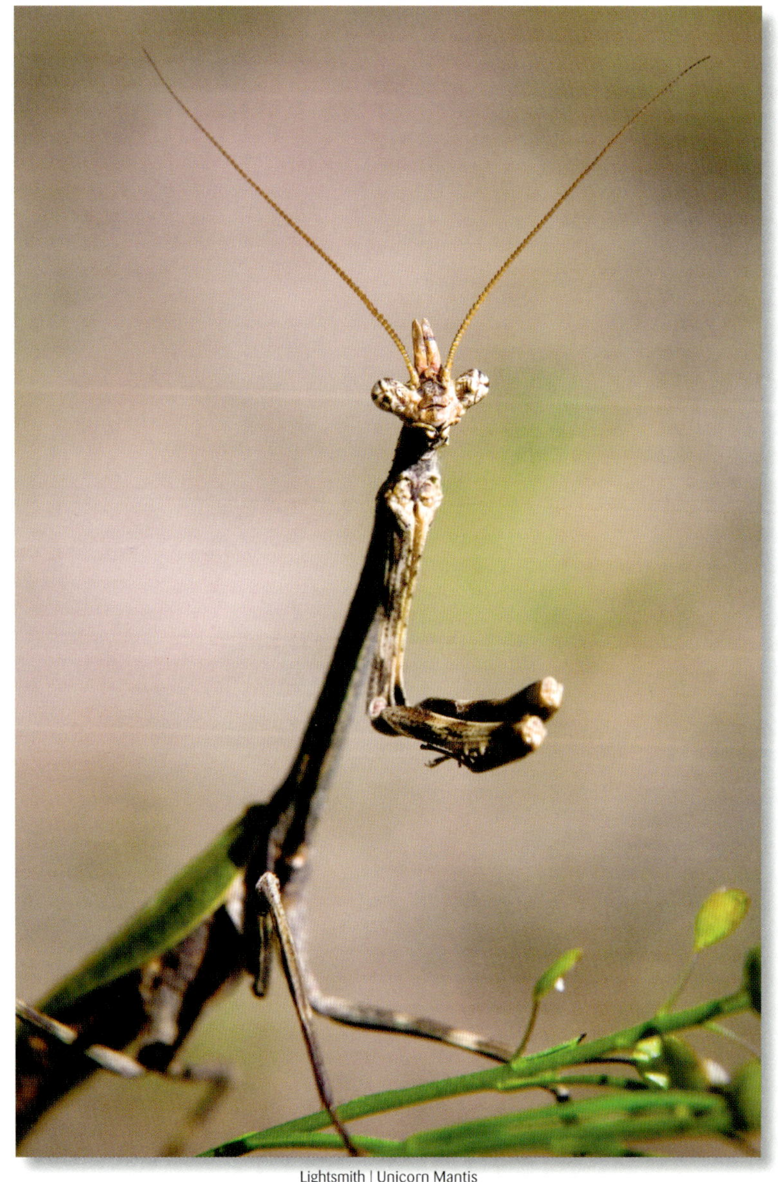
Lightsmith | Unicorn Mantis

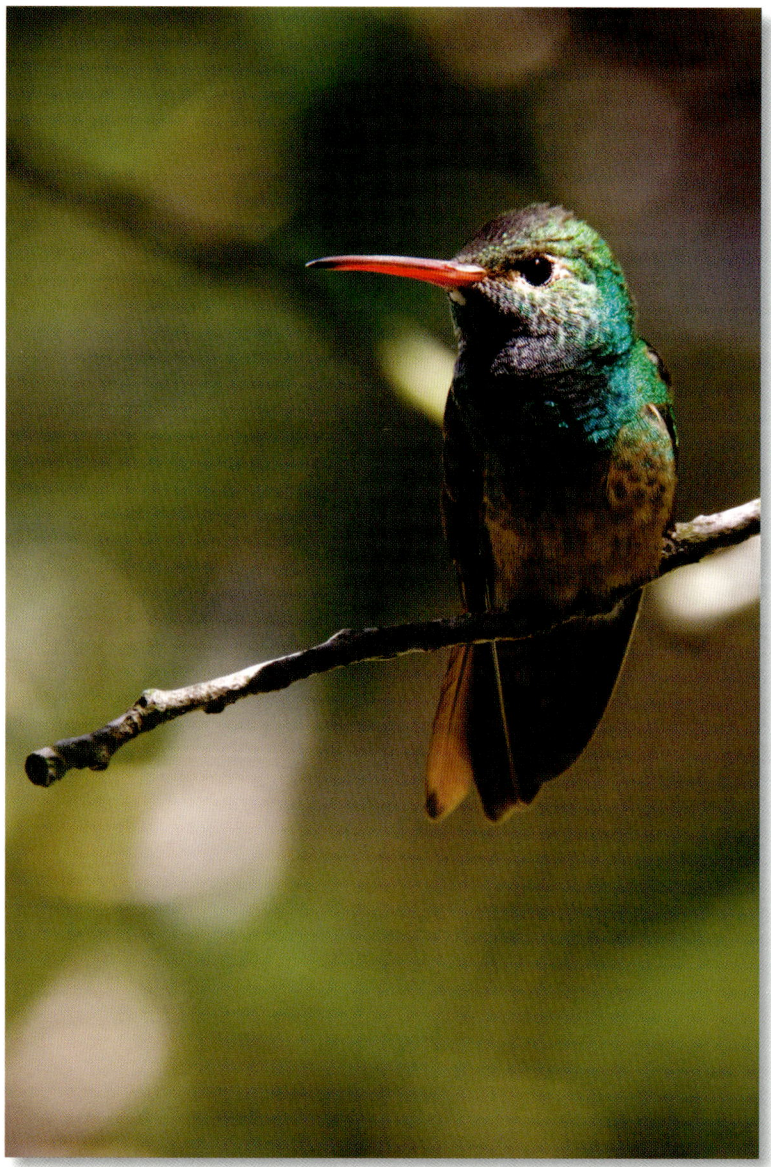
Lightsmith | Broad-billed Hummingbird

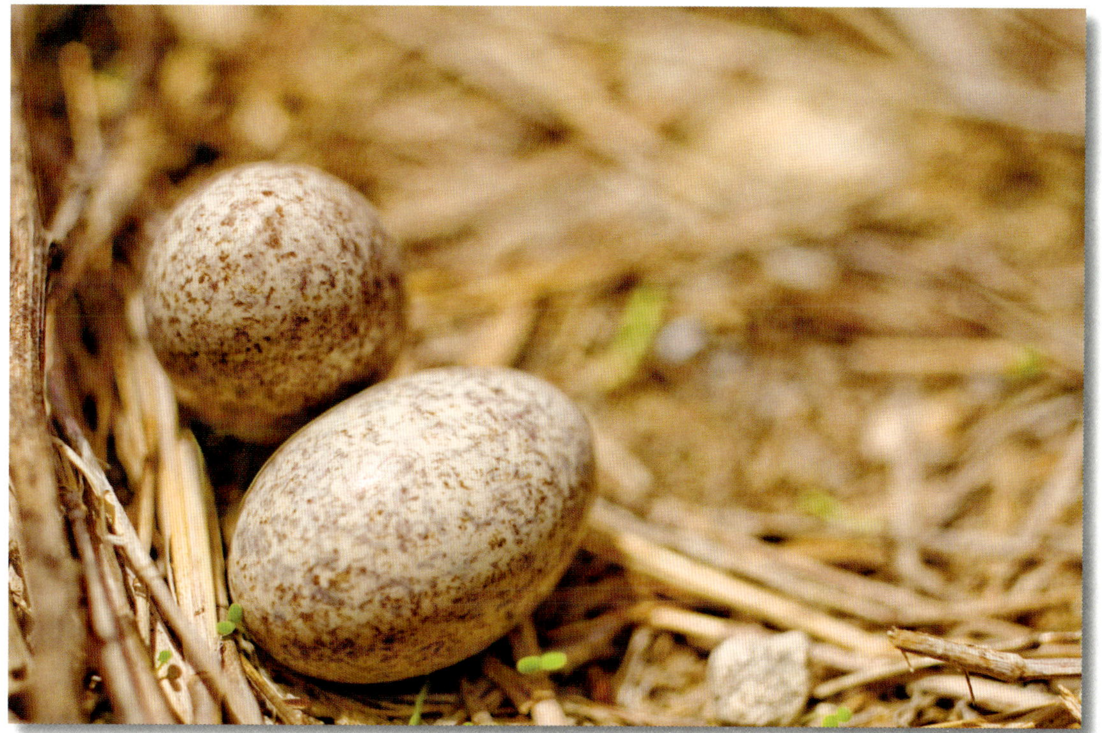

Lightsmith | eggs in a bird nest

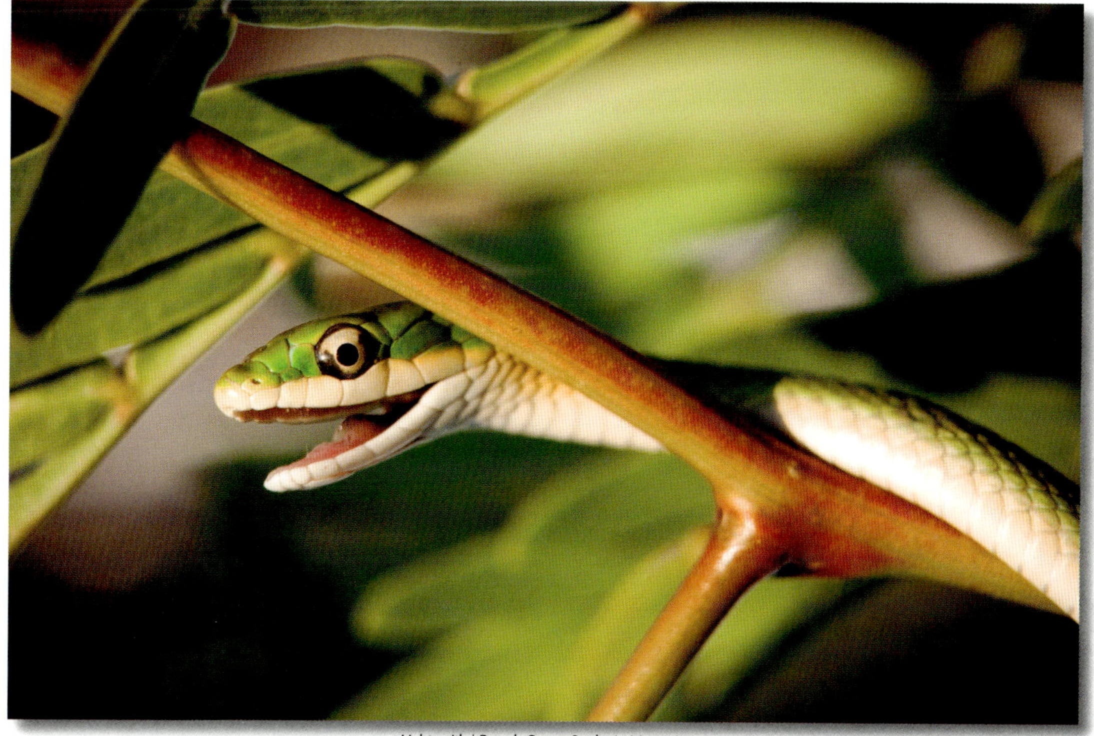

Lightsmith | Rough Green Snake in Mesquite

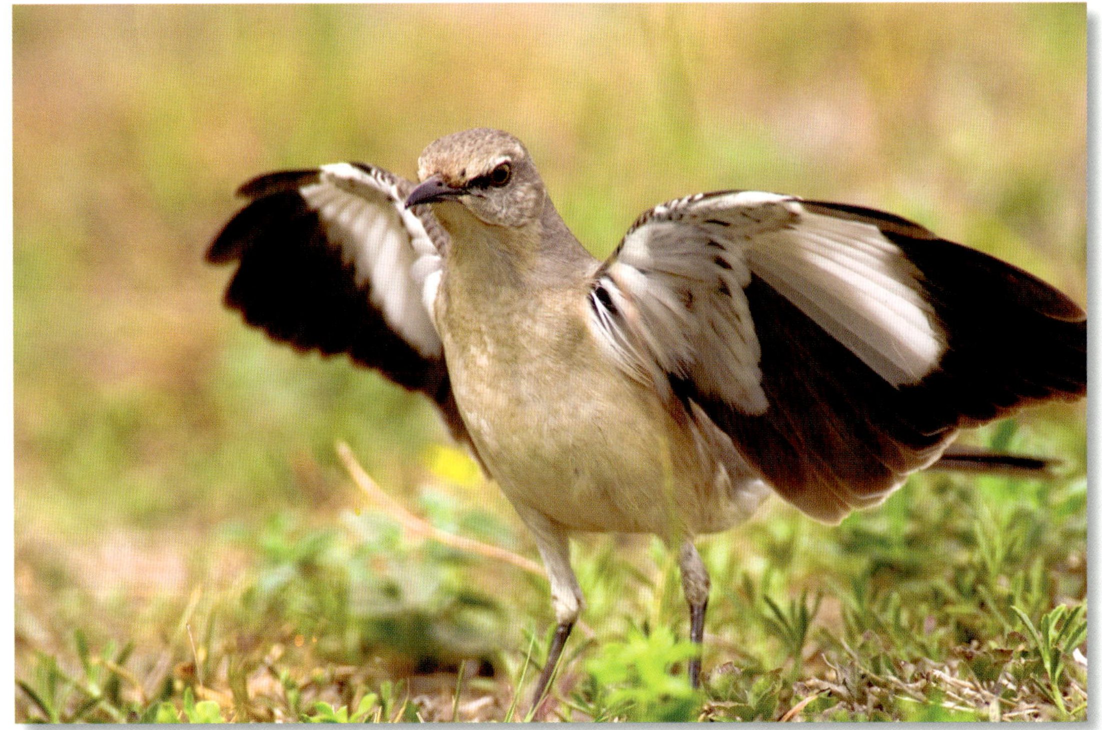

Lightsmith | Northern Mockingbird

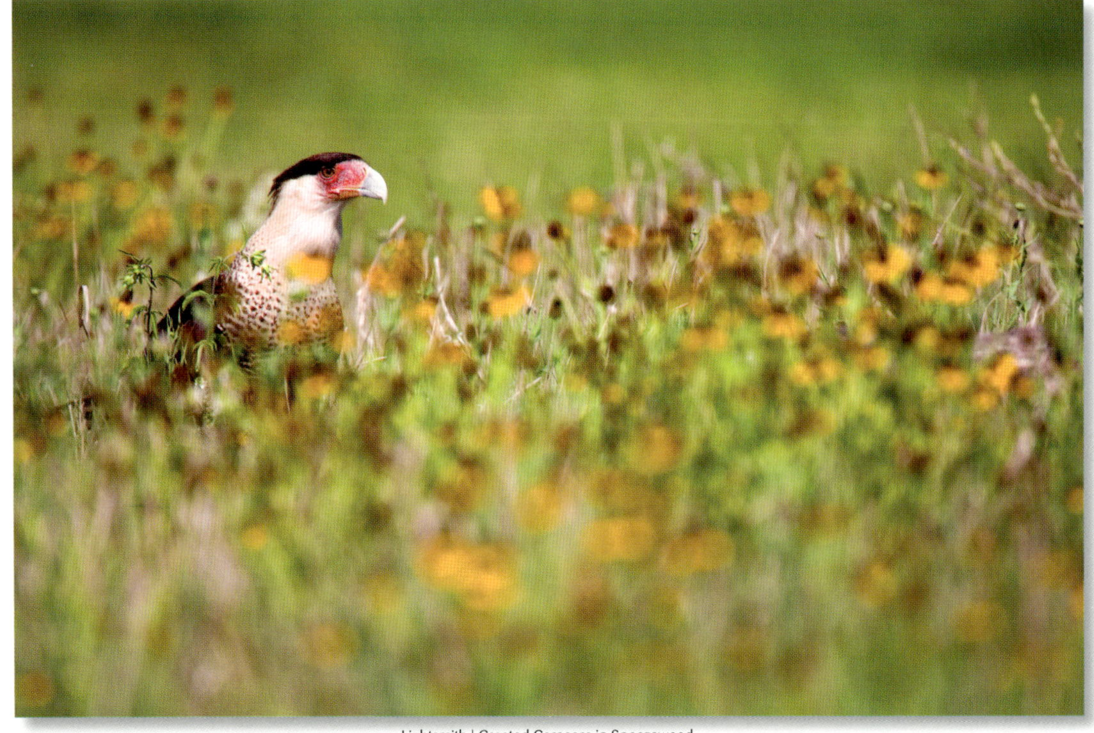

Lightsmith | Crested Caracara in Sneezeweed

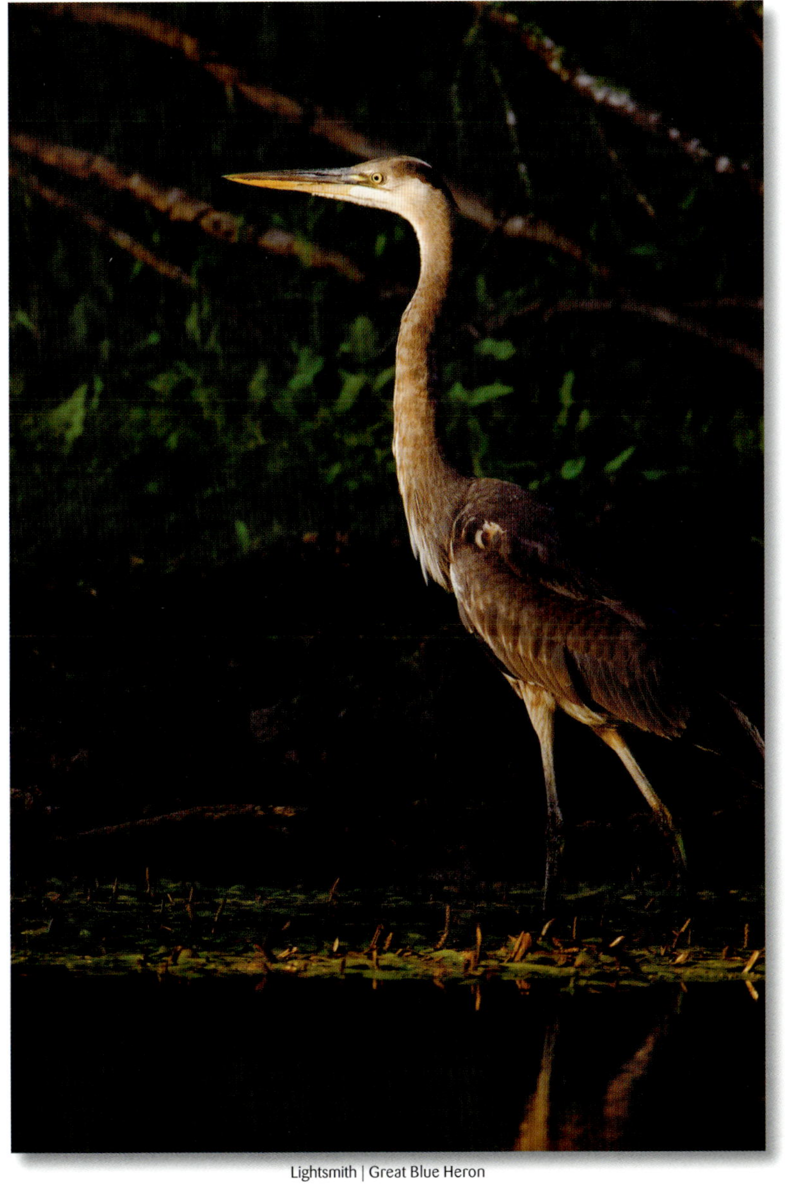
Lightsmith | Great Blue Heron

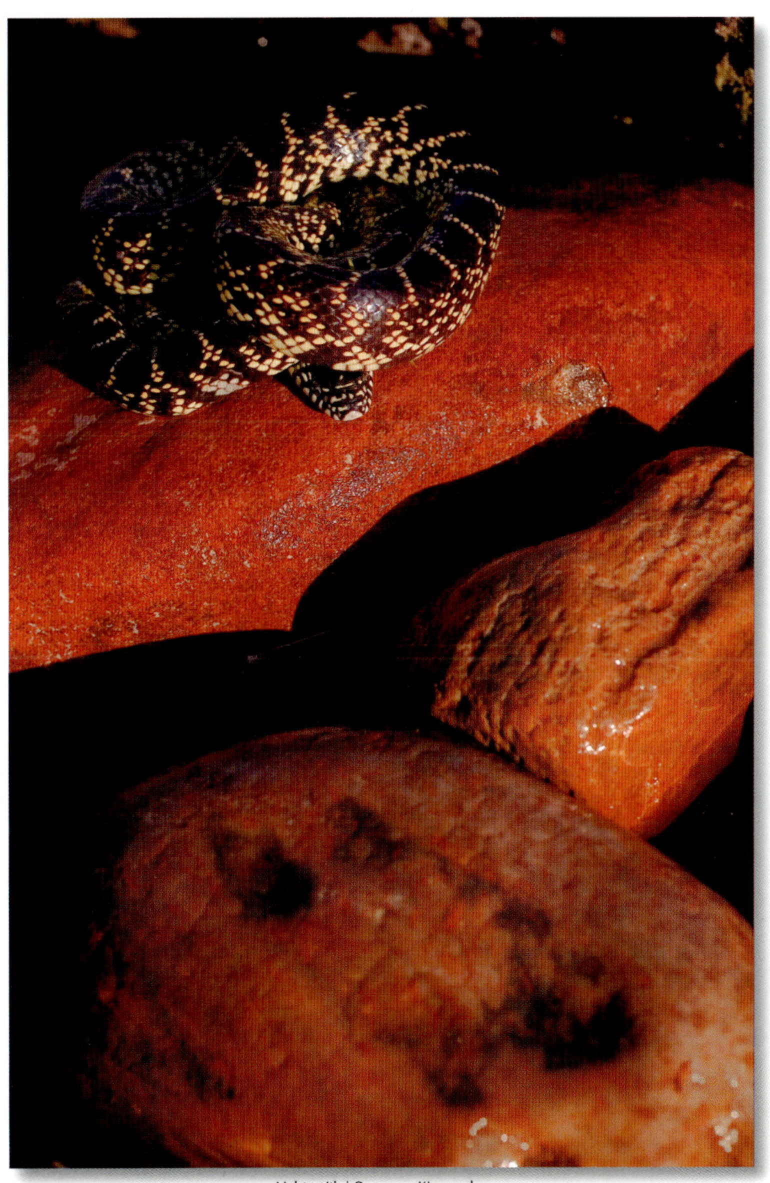
Lightsmith | Common Kingsnake

About Hill Creek Ranch...

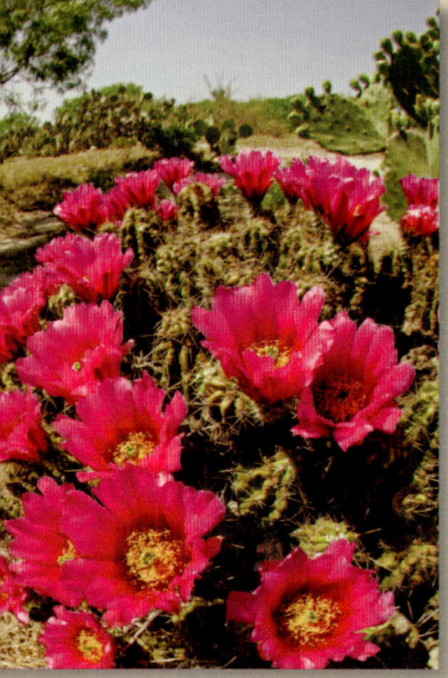

Illg | Hedgehog Cactus

Hill Creek Ranch was founded in 1948 by Clifton Wheeler Sr. The industrious and eager Wheeler embraced hard work, an attitude that allowed him to achieve broad goals in life.

During the 1920s Wheeler managed three stores in town. He was appointed Tilden's postmaster in 1932 and he served as McMullen County judge for many years. Everybody called him Judge. During that time, Wheeler accumulated land in the area. One of his acquisitions involved buying back part of a ranch that was established by his great grandfather in the 1860s. Wheeler's grandson, retired San Antonio physician Peter Swenson, his sister Anne Swenson and their mother Evelyn Swenson own the property today.

The Swenson family primarily uses the ranch for hunting managed game in the fall. But from early spring into summer, Hill Creek Ranch offers comfortable lodging for wildlife photography seminars. Six miles of Hill Creek and nearly two miles of the Nueces River run through portions of this somewhat more than 5,000 acre ranch in eastern McMullen County. The watercourses support riparian habitat and a diverse lineup of native wildlife, including Rio Grande Turkey, White-tailed Deer, Cottontail Rabbits, Coyote, raccoons, alligators and Javelina.

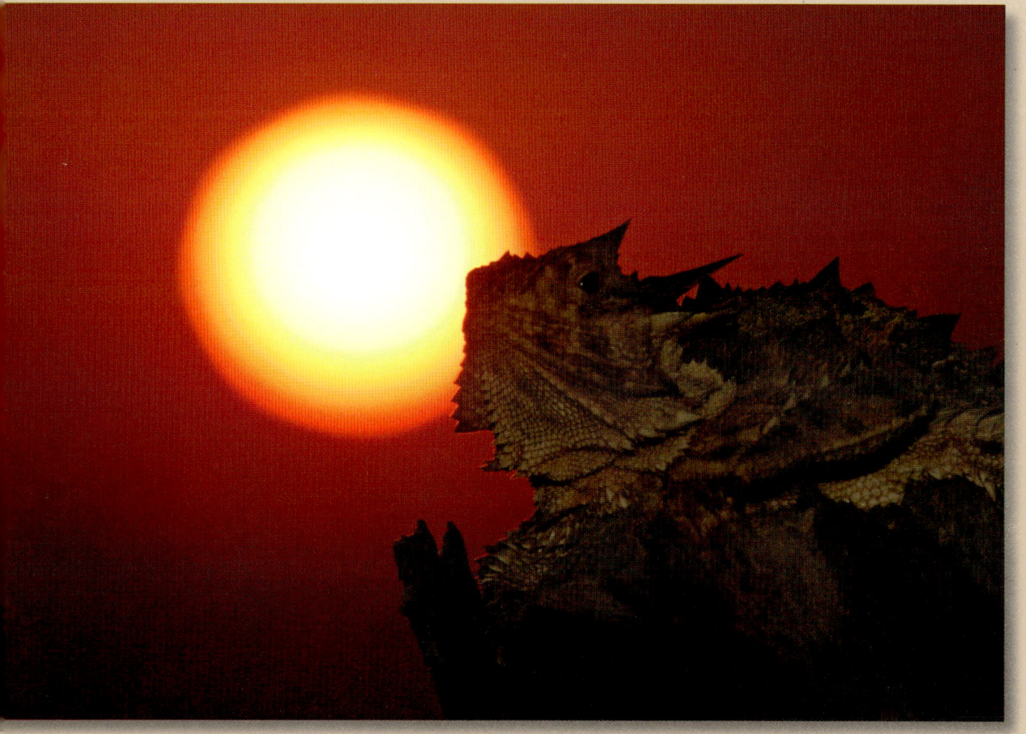

Illg | Texas Horned Lizard

To enhance what the river provides, the family has set water troughs every quarter mile to help maintain healthy cattle and game. There also is a drip water system running continually for birds and wildlife. Eight portable blinds are available for visiting photographers. An on-site wildlife biologist, Case Swaim, manages the deer herd and habitat under the Texas Parks & Wildlife Managed Land Deer Program. Swaim is the son of Wes Swaim, who, has served as ranch foreman for many years.

Peter Swenson fondly recalls boyhood summers spent hunting, fishing and working cattle with his aunts and uncles on the ranch. This connection with the land has evolved into a reverence that Swenson shares with his wife Fran and their daughters Meredith and Karin. Swenson credits much of the family's conservation ethic to his mother Evelyn Swenson an enthusiastic supporter of the Images for Conservation Fund Pro-Tour of Nature Photography.

Miles of Tamaulipan thorn scrub grow from volcanic clay and glass deposits that stretch across the plain to distant horizons. Traveling down ranch roads, Peter identifies the tangled vegetation, noting where deer have browsed. He points to Guajillo bushes whose sweet flowers are pollinated by bees, and to the Guayacan plant, an evergreen shrub with purple springtime blooms. Horned Lizards, the state reptile of Texas, can be spotted sunning near an open cattle tank. Double-crested Cormorants perch on twisted Live Oak limbs, their dark splayed wings reflected in a narrow stretch of the Nueces River below. Life in the chaparral must adapt to the dry climate where nature can be arduous. These often harsh conditions create individuals who are singular and hardy as the Mesquite that thrives here. Some of the characters, landmarks and tales that emerged from this region have provided color to J. Frank Dobie's stories. Remote and ruggedly alluring, this chaparral belies the host of wildlife awaiting the nature traveler.

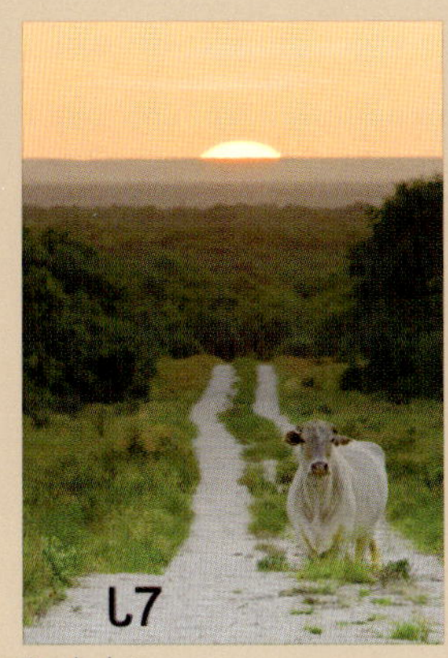

Ranch photo

The lodge and ranch headquarters are north of Tilden, furnishing an ideal setting for group retreats led by professional wildlife photographers. Five bedrooms, four bathrooms, a large kitchen and living area accommodate up to 14 guests. Bird watchers may observe a colorful sampling of avian life attracted to feeders and water just outside the lodge windows. Guests often spot Green Jays, Painted Buntings, roadrunners, orioles, and woodpeckers in this oasis within the South Texas frontier.

Peter Swenson
Tilden, TX
[e] pswsn@sbcglobal.net

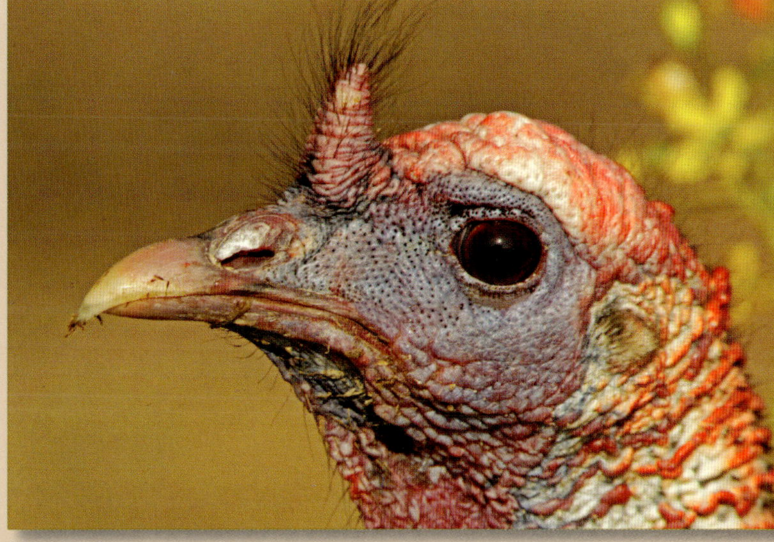
Illg | Wild Turkey

Illg | Eastern Cottontail Rabbit eating Mesquite leaves
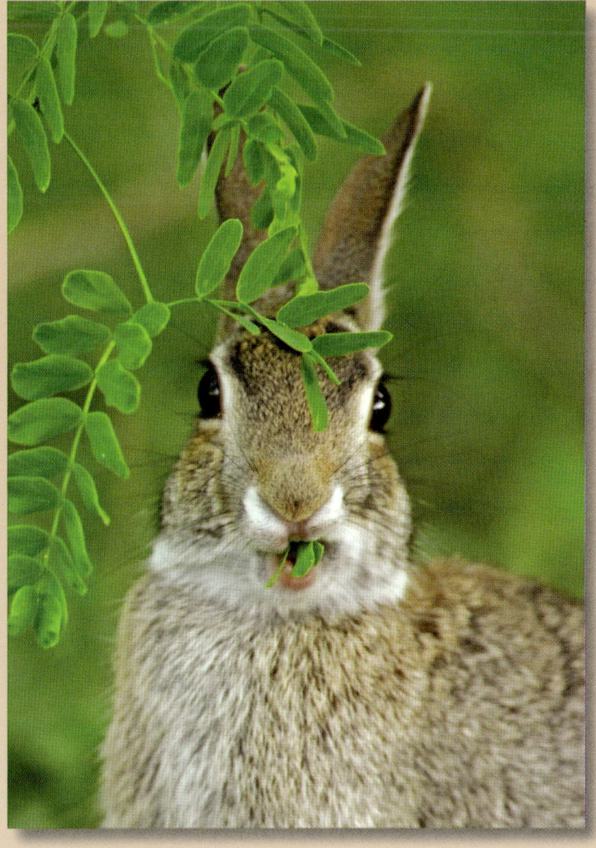

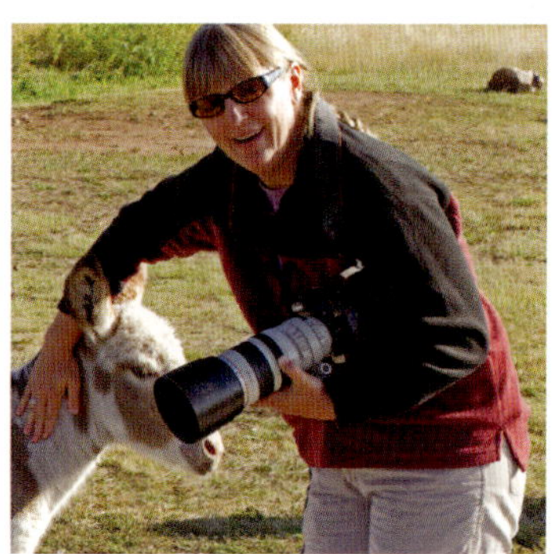

Cathy Illg

Cathy Illg is at ease with a camera in her hands, but the Pro-Tour contest forced her past her comfort zone. “It gets you to do other things you don’t normally do.”

“Macro photography is something I rarely get a chance to do much but with the contest I was able to experiment with it.” And, it’s no surprise that Cathy found such enjoyment in macro; when it comes to bigger critters she says, “I’m a fan of getting in close. I like the action and to see things going on.”

One April morning in particular had a lot going on. “There was a spot where they would put the feral hogs that had been killed and the vultures and caracaras would come to feed. I figured I would go out while it was still dark and wait.” The only problem, Cathy explained, is that it was “really, really cold.” Coming from Colorado to South Texas she says she didn’t expect it to be that nippy.

The drama that unfolded was well worth the four hours of discomfort. “I was amazed at just how involved the fighting was. They were hooking their claws into one another.”

As Cathy sat mesmerized, she noticed how the Crested Caracaras always came out on top. With a touch of surprise in her voice she says “The dominant pair of Crested Caracaras would eat first, then their juveniles, and finally the Turkey Vultures.”

Those four hours were a luxury, albeit a bone-chilling one since, Cathy says, “[During the contest] you have to be so careful with your time. In that way it can be tough. Once you get something usable you have to go on, even if you’re not completely satisfied. You have to go on and hope you have time later to come back to it.”

Moments like the magical morning in the blind, when Cathy’s thumb went numb from so much shooting, are treasured. She admits that her 30 days on the Hill Creek Ranch were “really hard. It’s twenty-four seven for a month. Overall, now that I’ve done it twice, it’s nice to know I can make it through.”

Lakewood, CO
www.advenphoto.com
[e] cathy@advenphoto.com

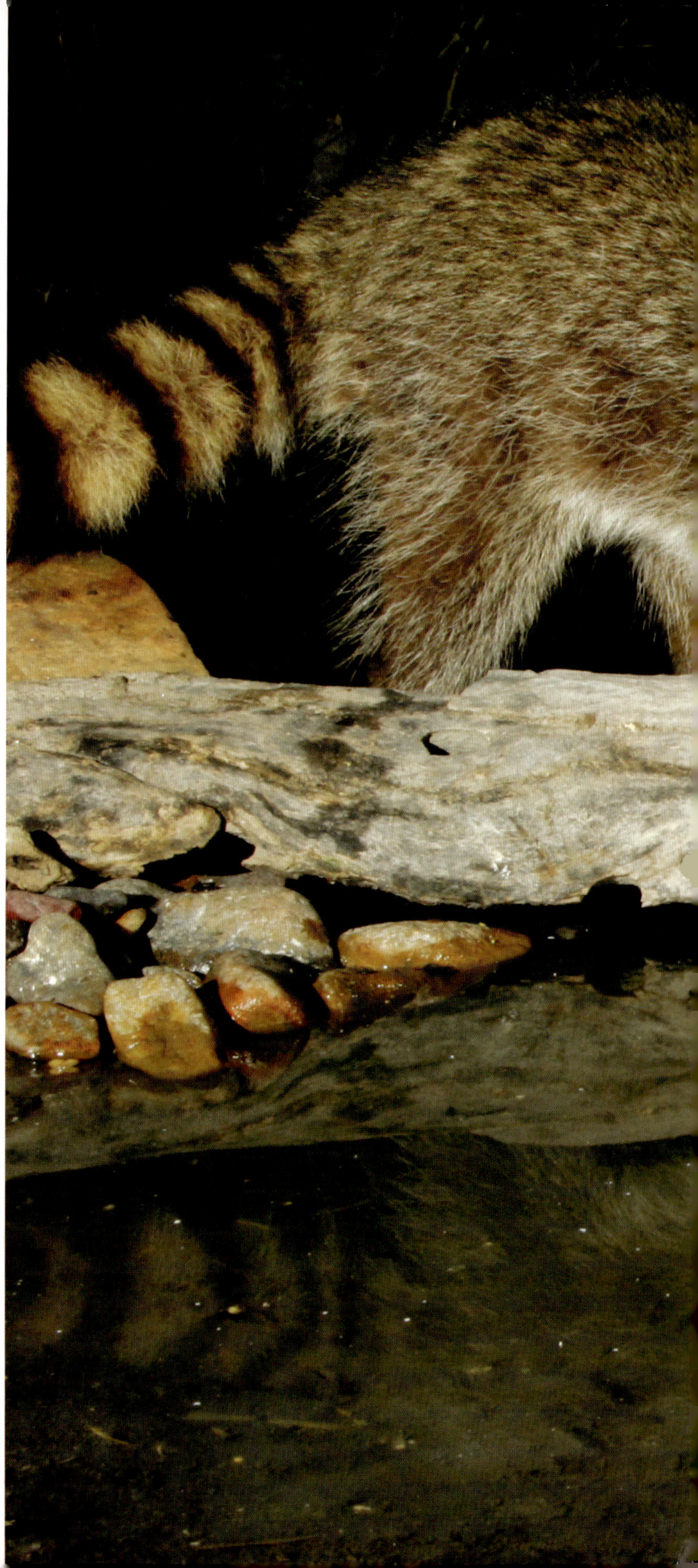

Illg | Common Raccoon

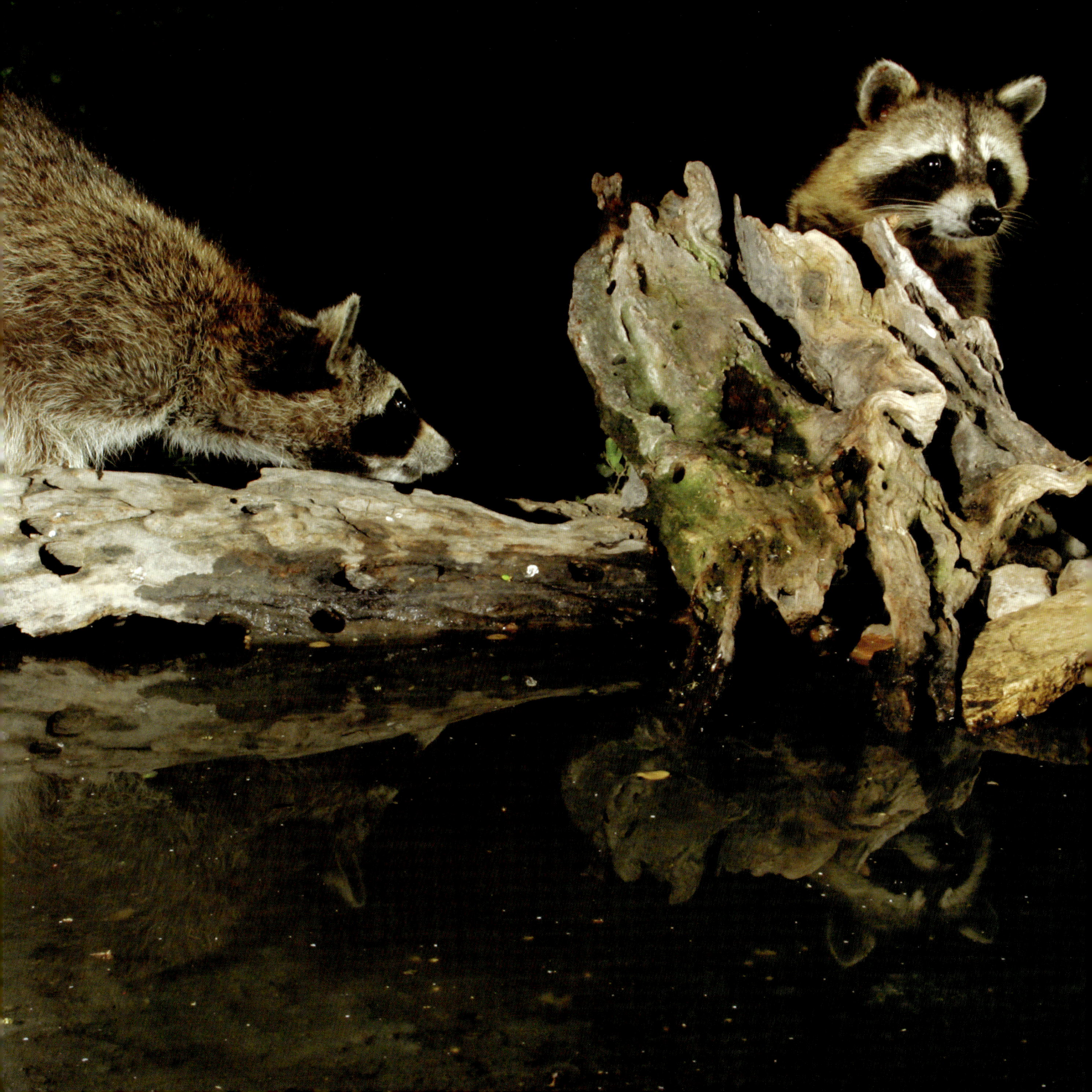

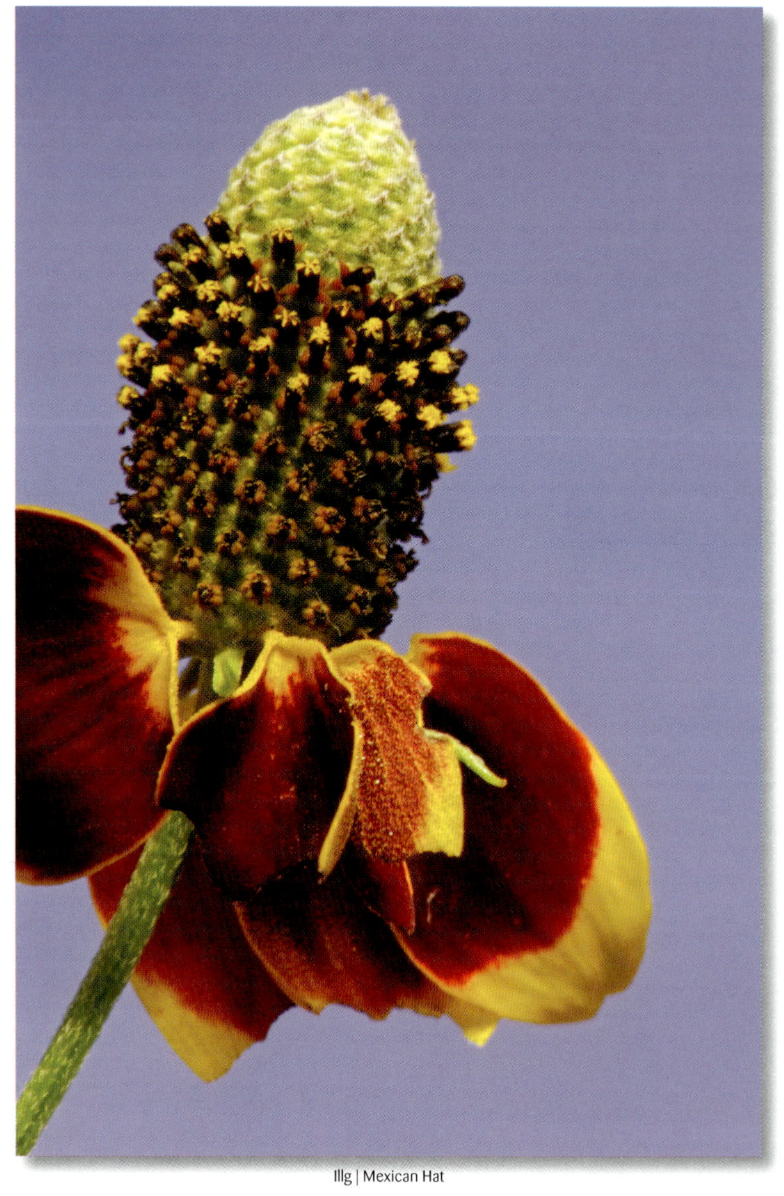

Illg | Mexican Hat

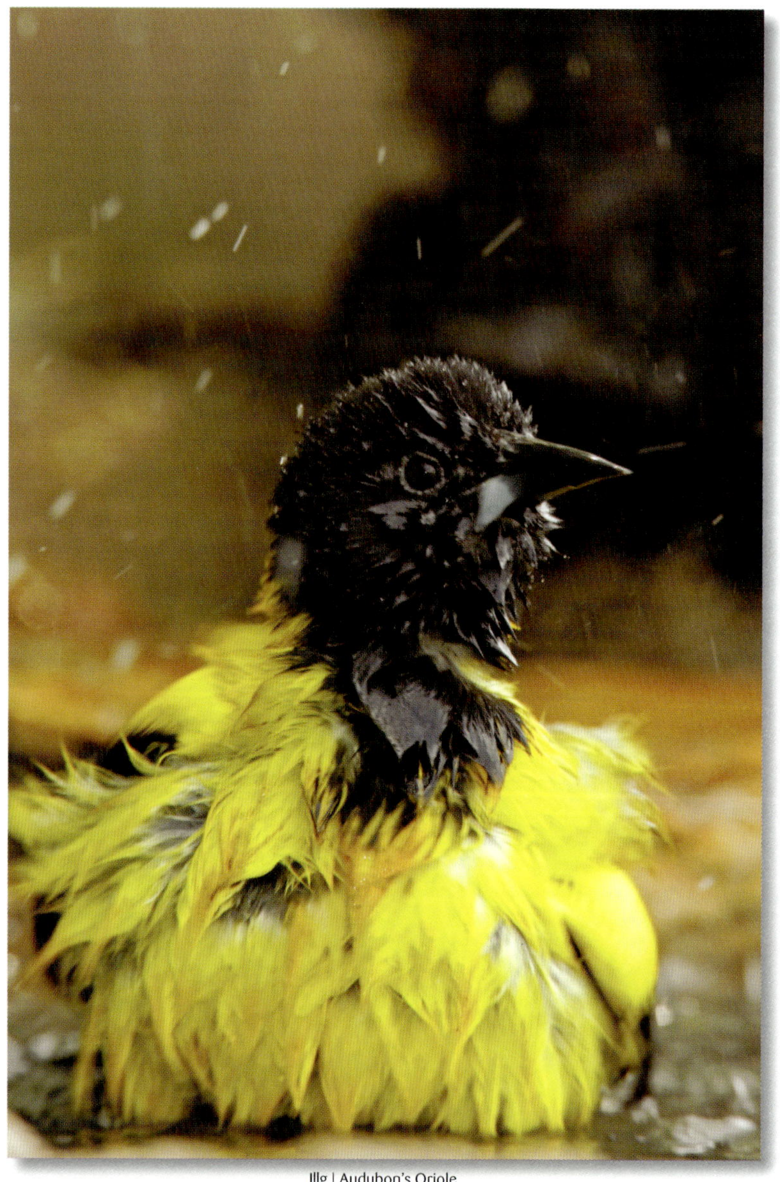

Illg | Audubon's Oriole

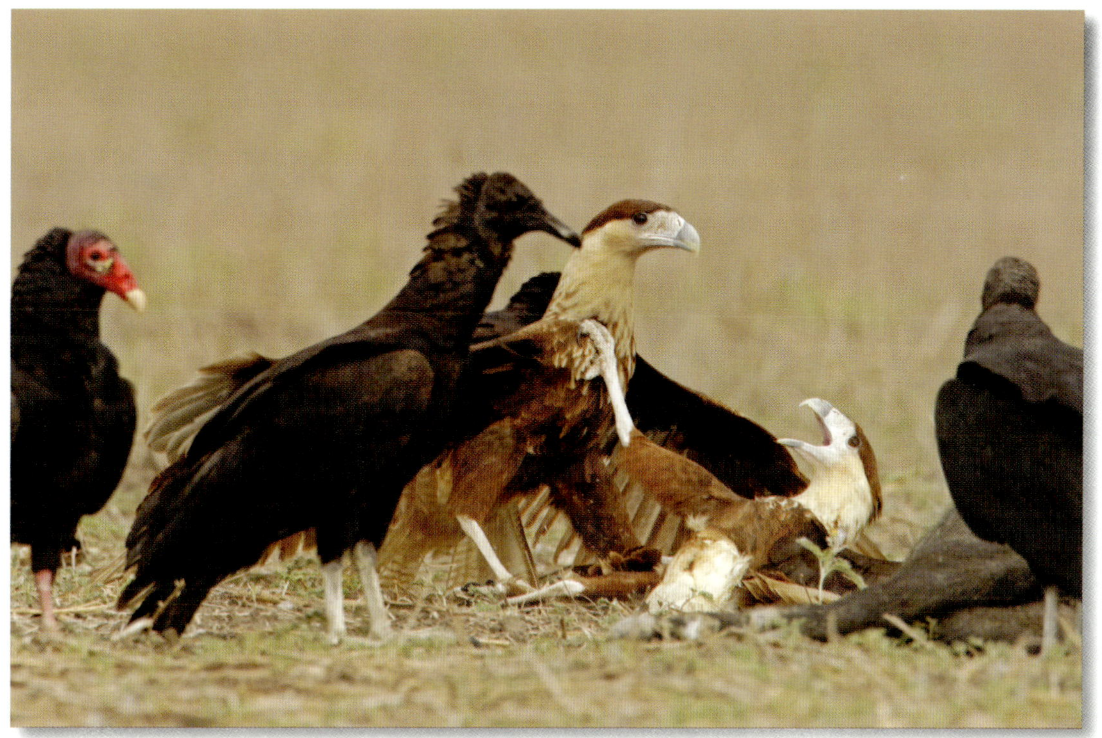

Illg | Crested Caracaras (immatures squabbling), Turkey Vulture (on left with red head) and Black Vultures

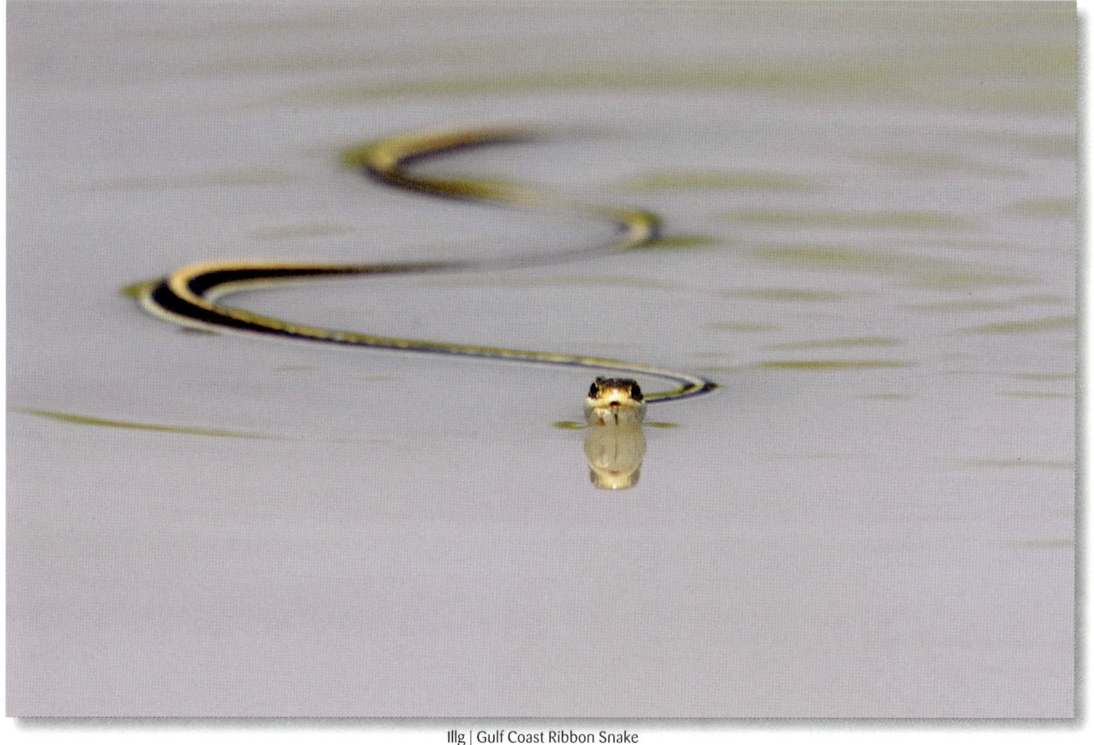

Illg | Gulf Coast Ribbon Snake

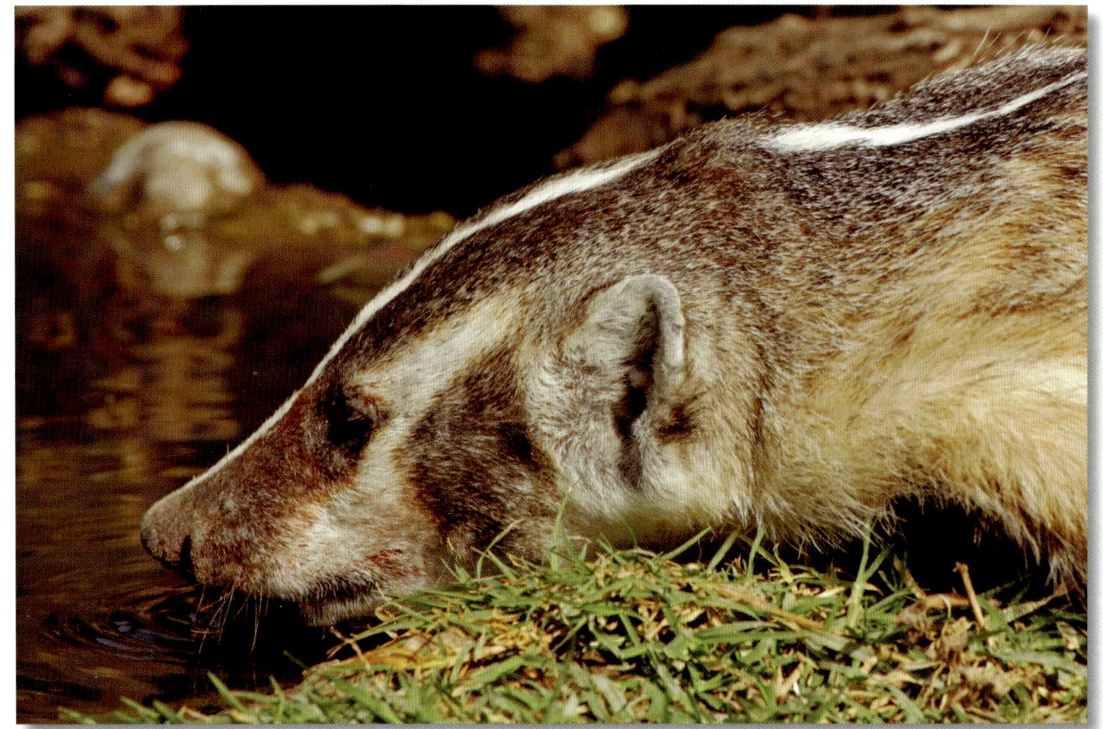

Illg | American Badger

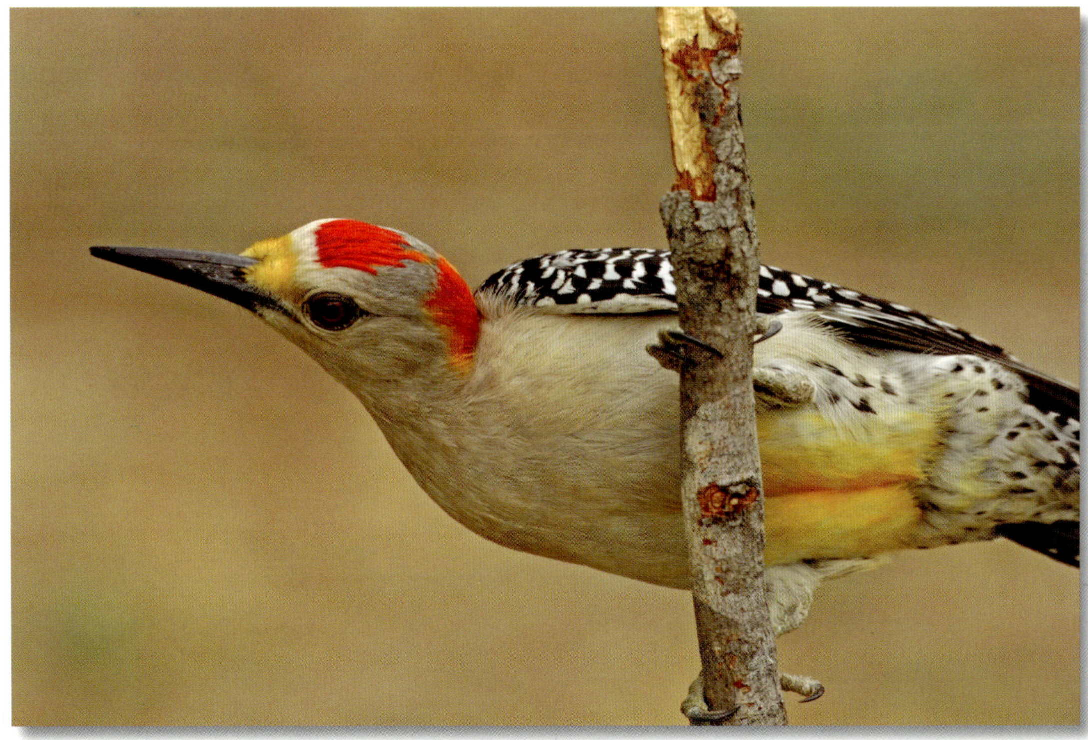

Illg | Golden-fronted Woodpecker

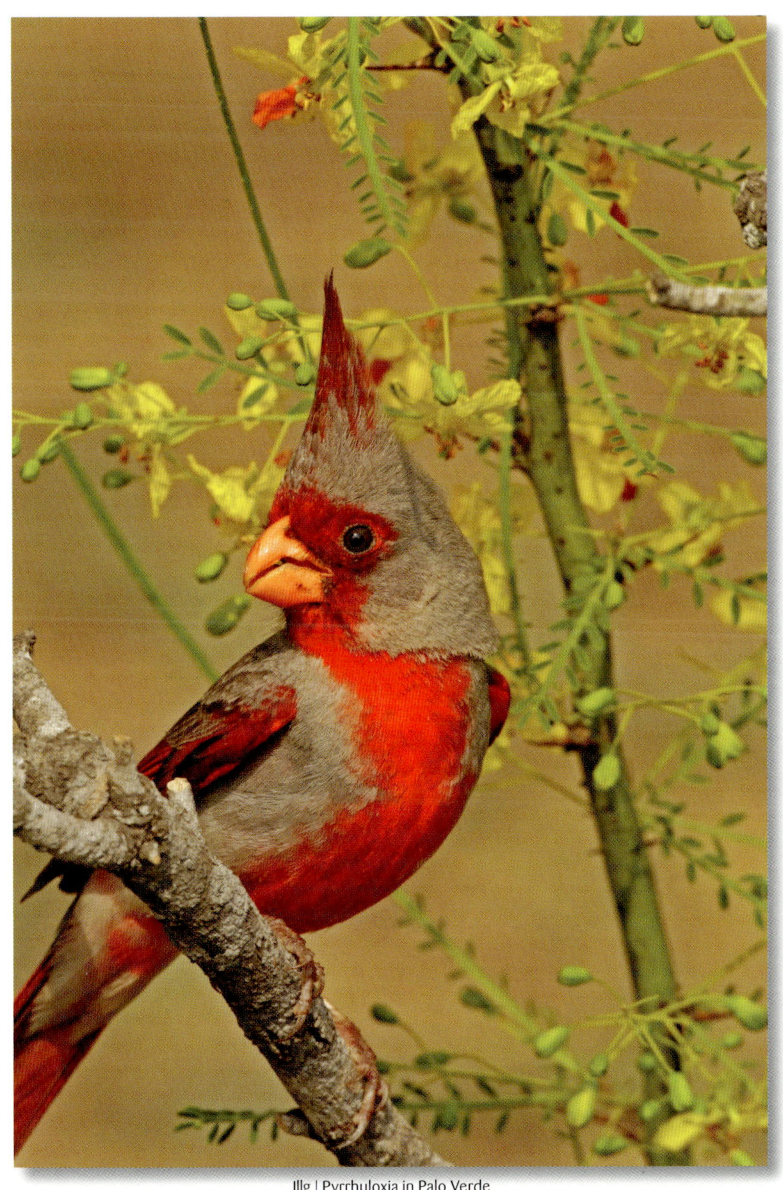

Illg | Pyrrhuloxia in Palo Verde

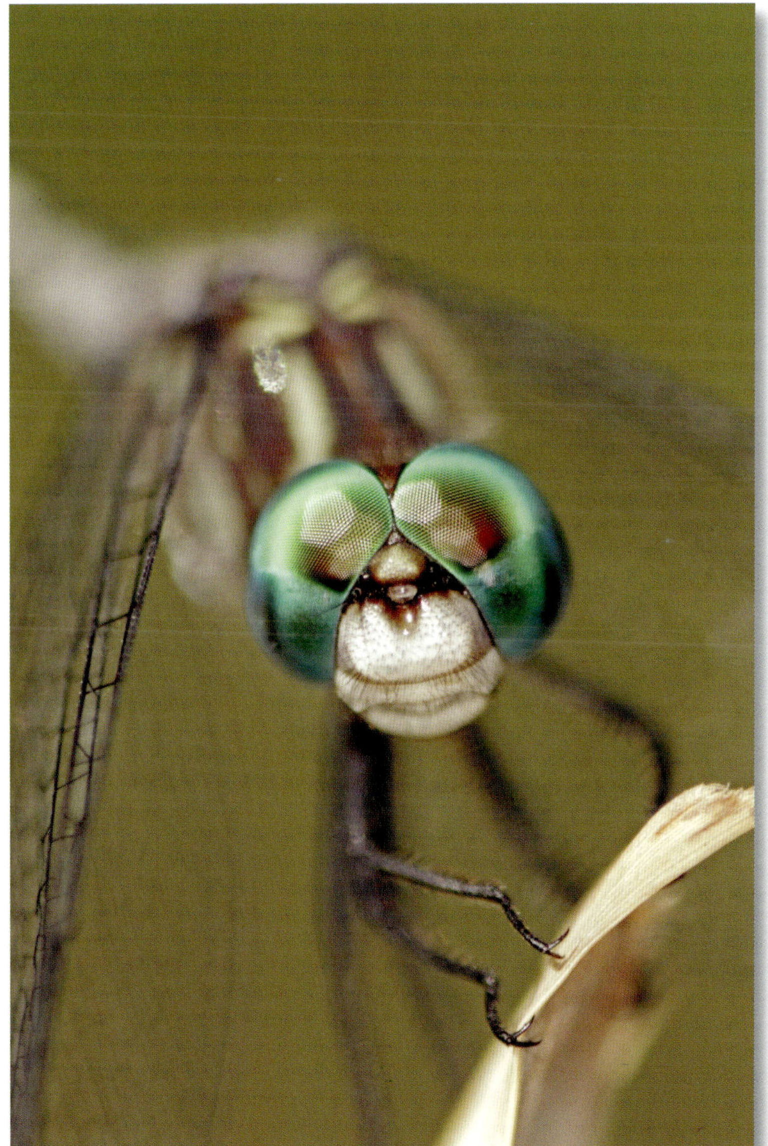

Illg | Thornbush Dancer

About Hoffman Rockin' h Ranches–La Trinidad...

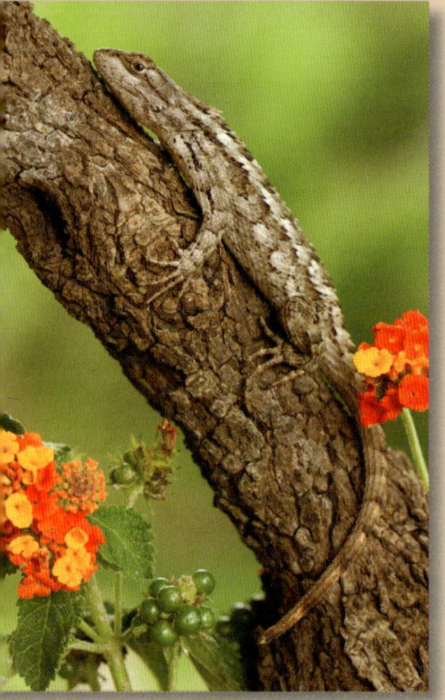
Linstead | Texas Spiny Lizard with Texas Lantana

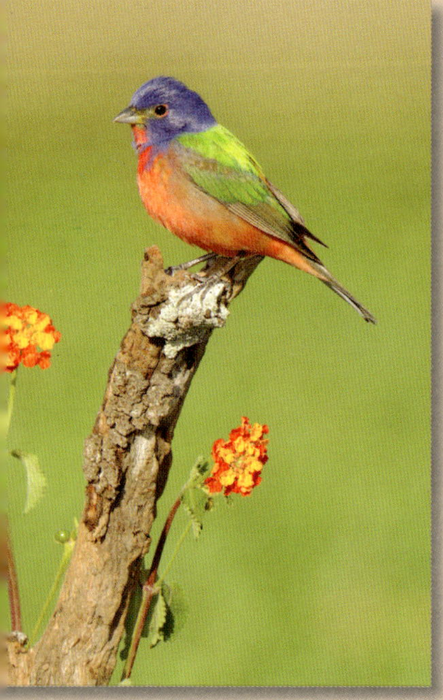
Linstead |Painted Bunting with Texas Lantana

For more than a century the Hoffman family has been ranching the brush country of Jim Wells and Duval Counties. With each generation comes a renewed determination to continue this tradition of innovative and forthright stewardship of the land. The ranch represents a legacy to those who have stood triumphant over this rugged terrain, a testament to those who thrive in it now and a dream to the next generation who wish to celebrate the rewarding and honest lifestyle of ranching and land stewardship.

La Trinidad Division of the Rockin' h is home to hundreds of native species. The brush is a perfect setting for healthy herds of White-tailed Deer, Bobcats, Javelina, Mountain Lions and that suspicious dark gray cat – the Jaguarundi. Though there is no photographic evidence of this rare wildcat on the Rockin' h, several family members believe the opportunity to capture its image will present itself.

Skies above the ranch are alive with countless dove, quail, ducks and geese. Ideal natural roosts attract and sustain impressive flocks of Rio Grande Turkey. A trip to the Rockin' h will almost guarantee visitors a sighting of a Barn Owl or a Great Horned Owl. Many species of hawks also claim territory on the ranch along with a healthy population of roadrunners that call the ranch home. The Rockin' h is a convenient setting to witness wondrous migrations of butterflies and tropical birds. When the earth awakens from her winter sleep nothing can compare with the peaceful and simple beauty of fields painted with South Texas wildflowers. When full, two large tanks and a lake attract wildlife and provide water on the ranch. La Trinidad Creek is one of two long twisting seasonal streams that meander through the property.

The sandy loam soils and mixed brush that cover most of the Rockin' h provides boundless habitat for Texas' many reptiles. From time to time you'll find a Diamondback Rattlesnake; however, their population is closely monitored by the shiny black Texas Indigo, which slithers in abundance on the ranch. The most favored reptile is the Texas Horned Lizard found scurrying across pastures.

When the family decided to focus on raising cattle rather than sheep in the late 19th Century, the Hoffmans chose the horned hereford as their breed. Twice a year, family members mount up for a traditional roundup and work the cow/calf herd to promote good health and to manage range conditions, which should help to provide balanced stewardship of the resources.

During the past five years the Hoffmans have been committed to a more active role in conserving wildlife on the ranch and the habitat that sustains it. Beyond the fences, they have adopted a two-mile stretch of Highway 281 near the ranch, where the family does its part for litter control. They also have joined and supported many conservation organizations, such as Texas Wildlife Association, South Texas Property Rights Association and Images for Conservation Fund. The family also recycles all possible materials at the ranch to help enrich the environment for future generations. The Hoffmans are delighted to welcome the ecotourism industry to their ranch.

They have participated in the local Coastal Bend Wildlife Photo Contest as well as the Images for Conservation Fund Pro-Tour of Nature Photography. They are looking forward to sharing their land for years to come so that others may enjoy it through the images created during these photography contests.

"If you love the land, sharing it with others makes perfect sense!"

Roger H. Hoffman, Sr.
Alice, Texas
[e] bhoffman2@stx.rr.com

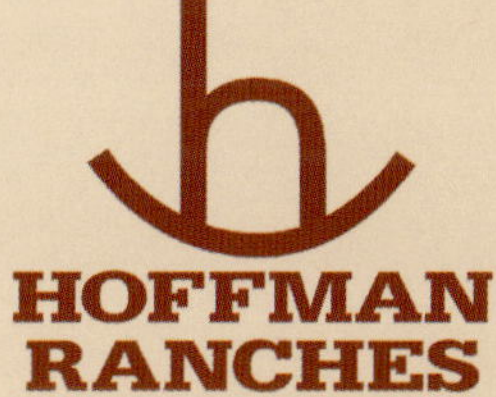

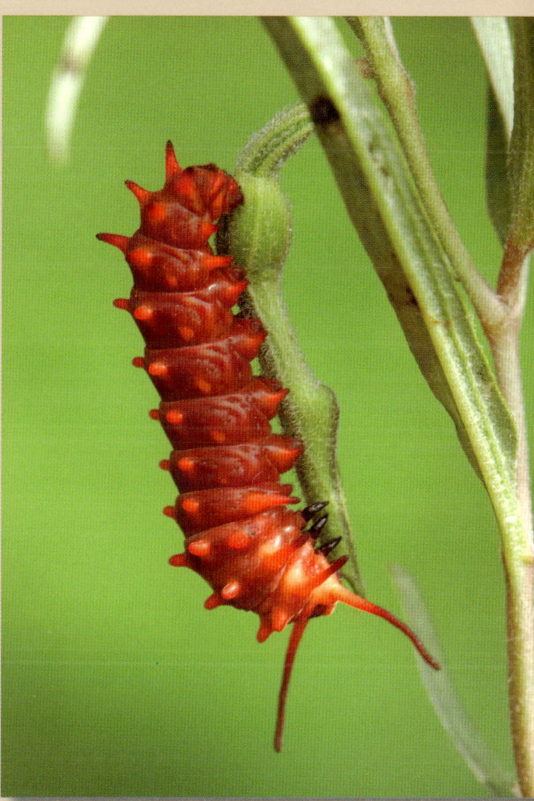
Linstead | Pipevine Swallowtail Caterpillar

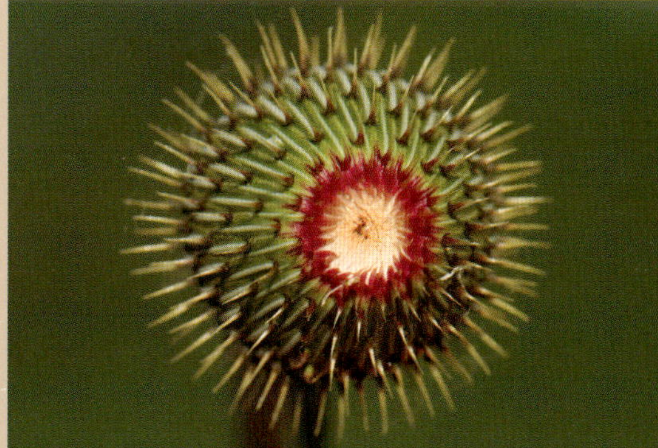
Linstead | Texas Thistle

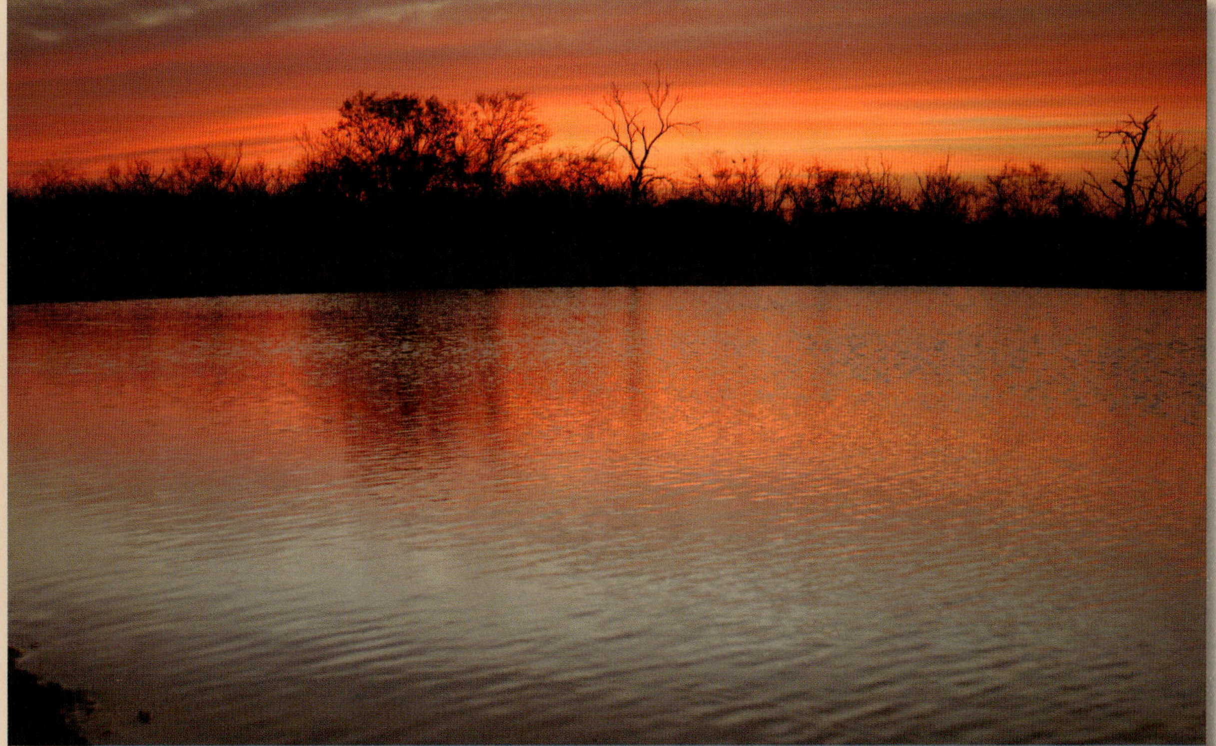
Linstead

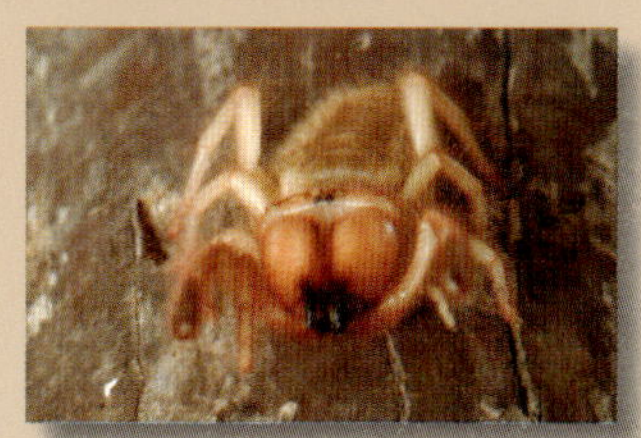
Linstead | Sun Scorpion

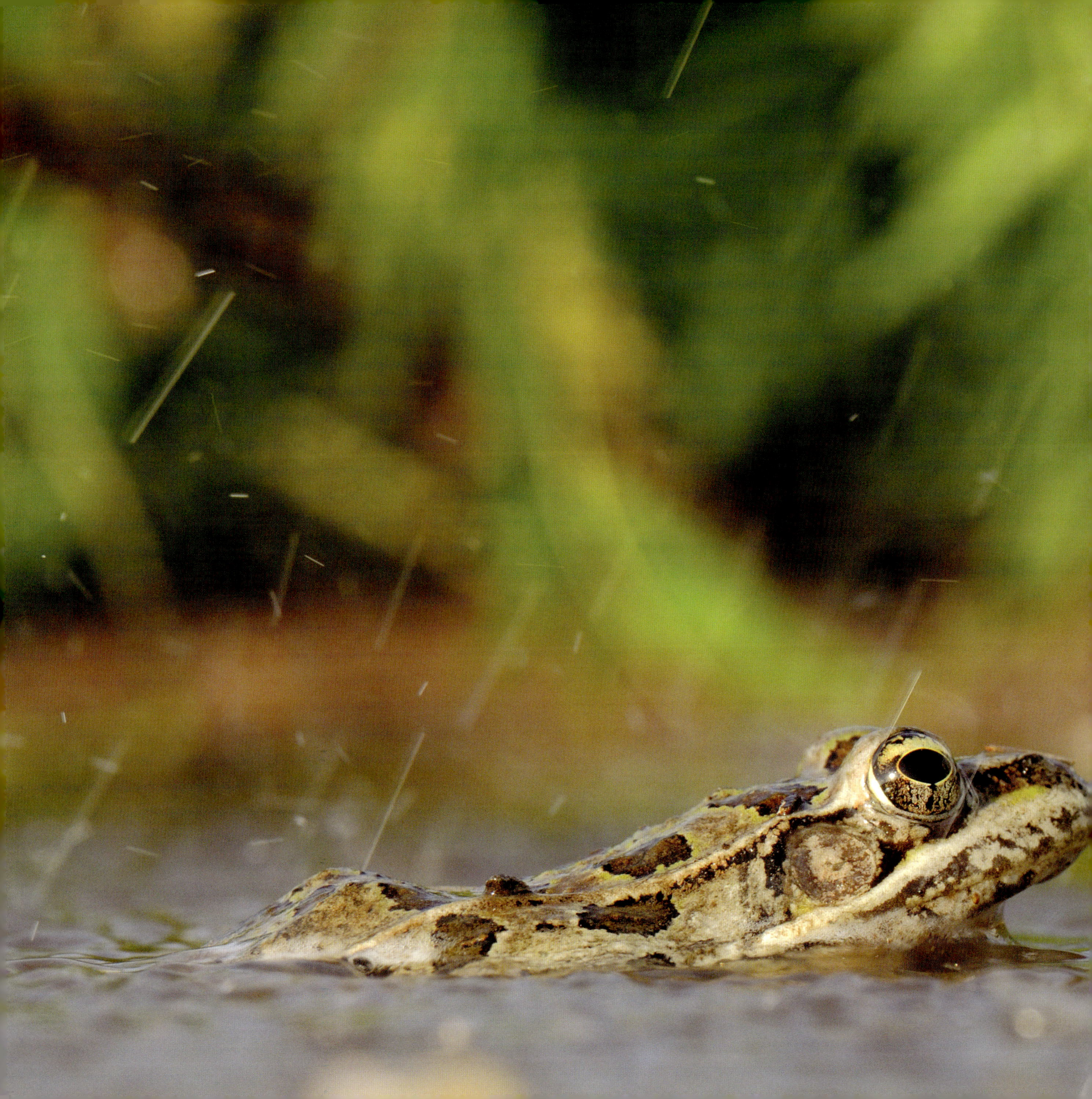

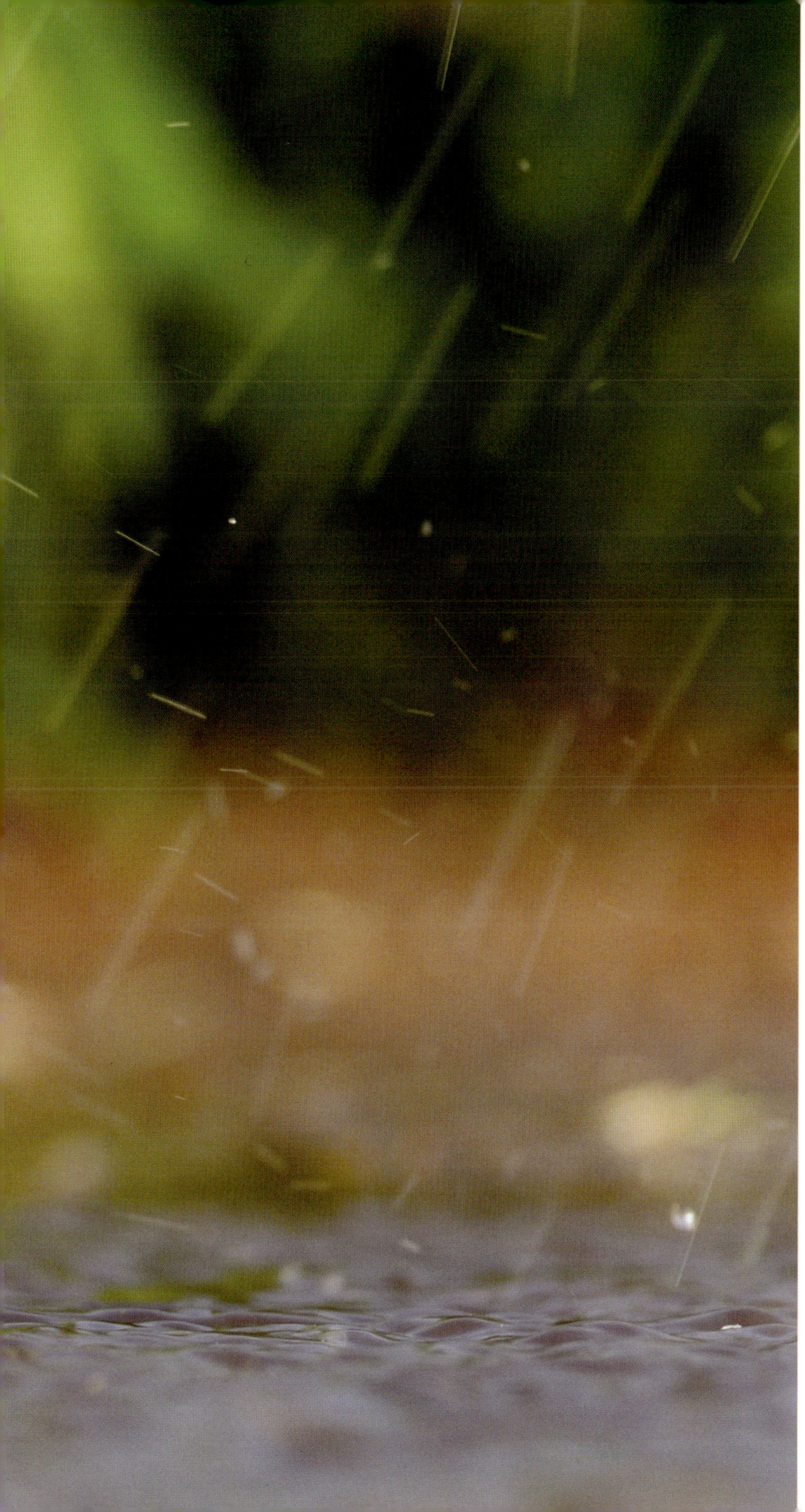

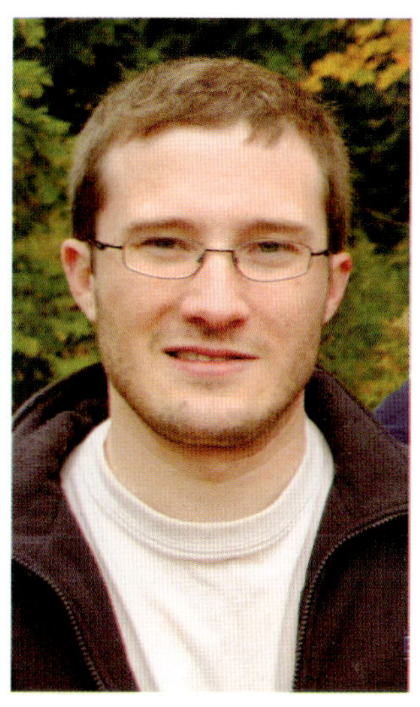

Scott Linstead

When you live in Quebec, Canada, where there's usually snow four months out of the year, you're bound to take water for granted. "One of the things I learned during the contest," explains Scott Linstead. "Is that I'd underestimated how much wildlife water attracted. I know it's obvious to those from South Texas, where water's at a premium, but I didn't realize it until I came."

Among South Texas' critters he coveted during his time on the Rockin' h Ranch was the Painted Bunting of whom says Scott, "The difficulty I had with this species corresponded quite accurately to what I had expected."

The Nine-banded Armadillo was another South Texas native that readily endeared itself to Scott. But, he says, "I was unable to get any decent images of this species and I think the elusive nature of this strange creature somehow heightened my fascination."

Fascination. Obsession. That's Scott. "In order for me to pursue a subject and come home with good results, I have to foster an obsession with it. This obsession will fuel the pre-visualization process and lead me to a specific behavior or pose that I would like to capture."

Scott's photographic obsession began in his late teens when he felt the need to start documenting things as he first began recognizing mortality. But, his real "indulgence into wildlife photography started in 2004" when he says, "I fell in love with the idea of creating an image that had impact on a general audience."

Maple Grove, Quebec, Canada
www.scottyphotography.com
[e] s_linsted@hotmail.com

Linstead | Rio Grande Leopard Frog

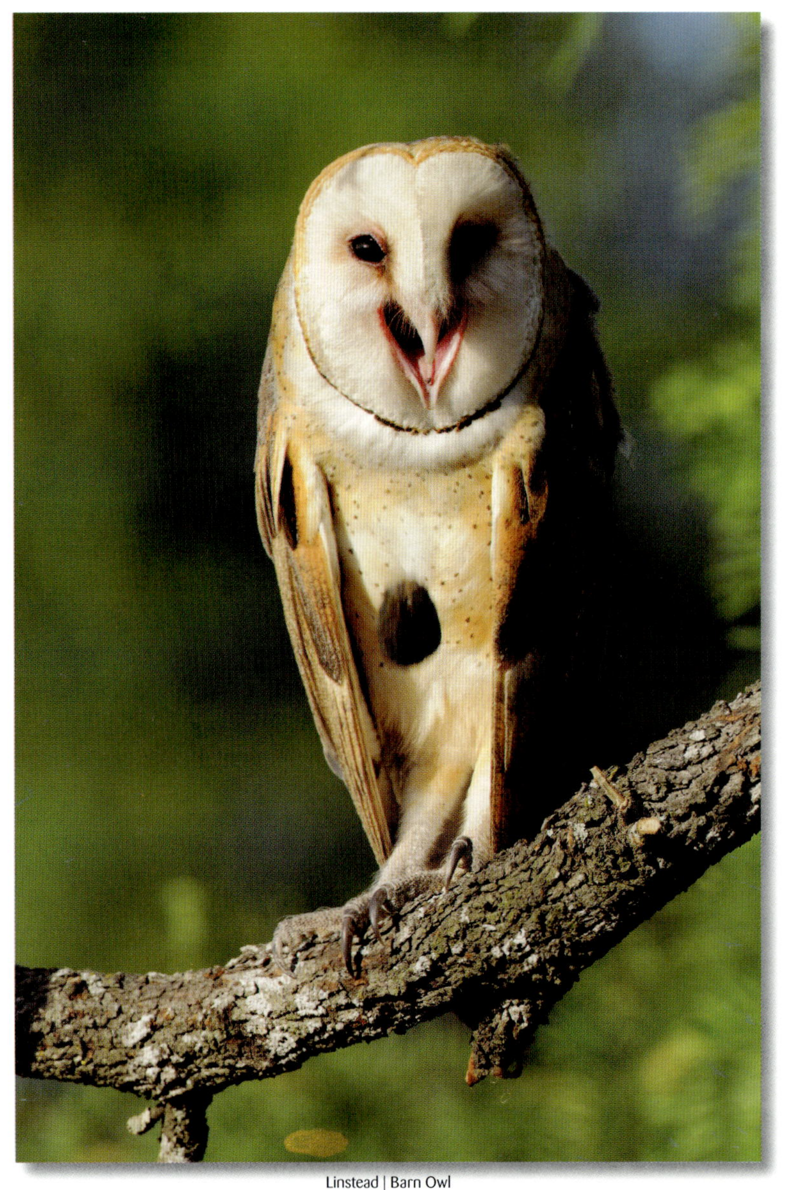

Linstead | Barn Owl

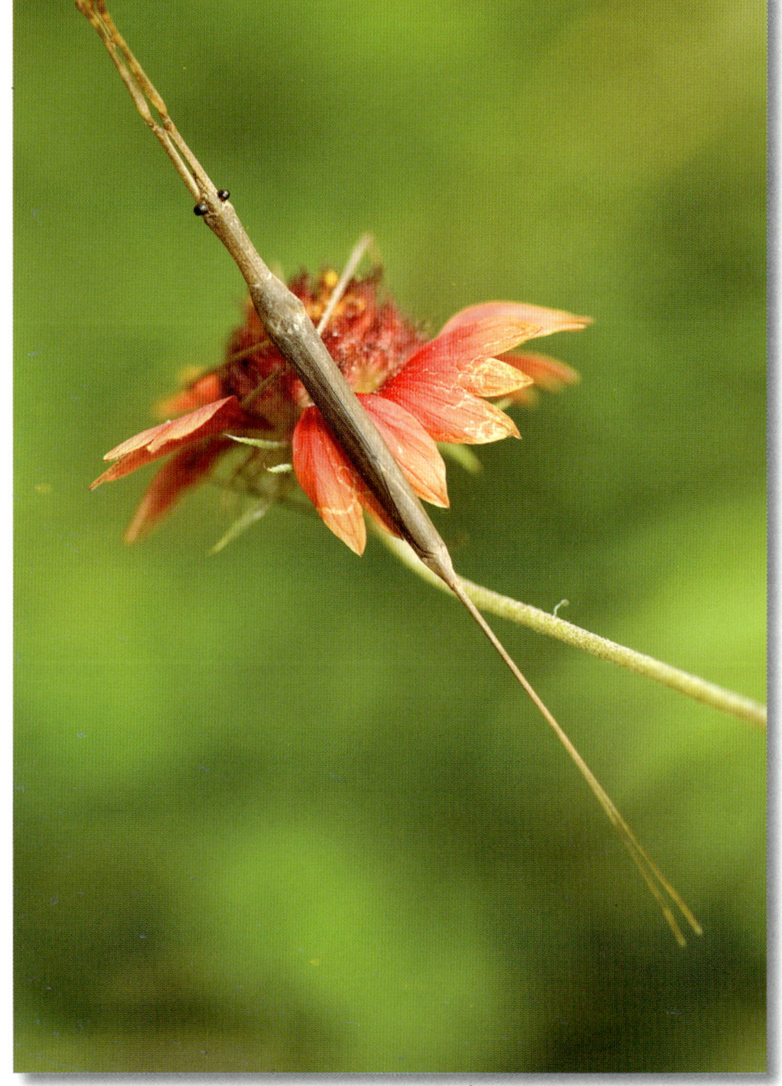

Linstead | Waterscorpion on Firewheel/Indian Blanket

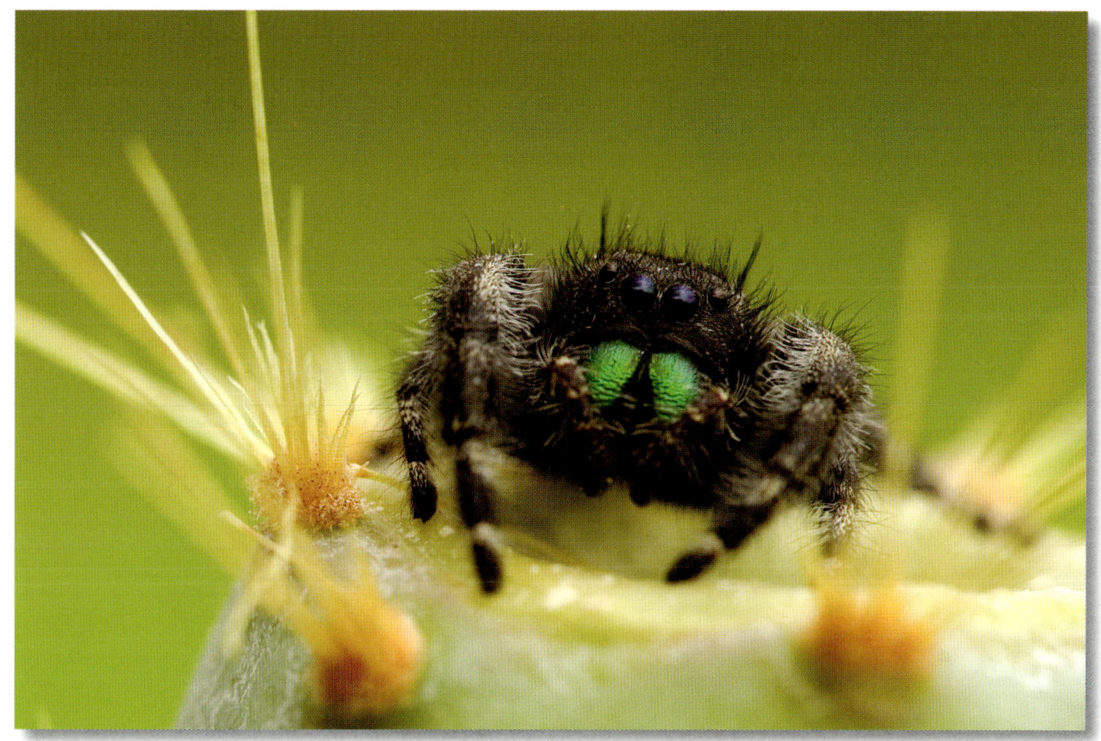

Linstead | Jumping Spider on Lindheimer Prickly Pear

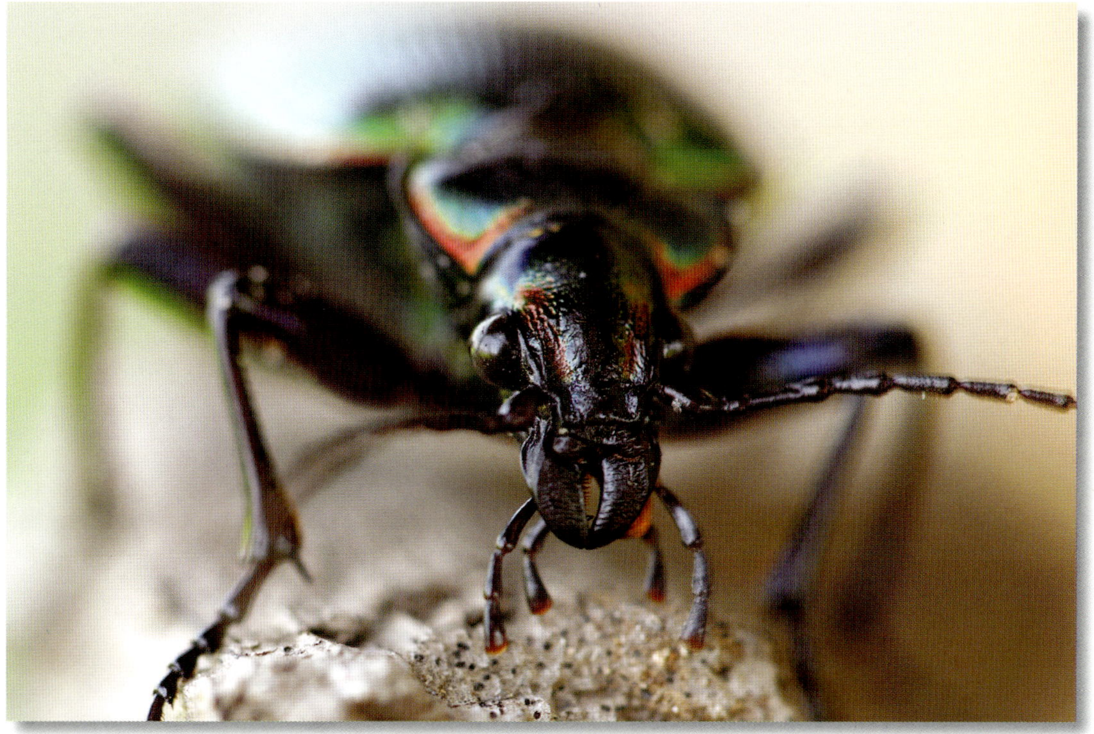

Linstead | Caterpillar Hunter Ground Beetle

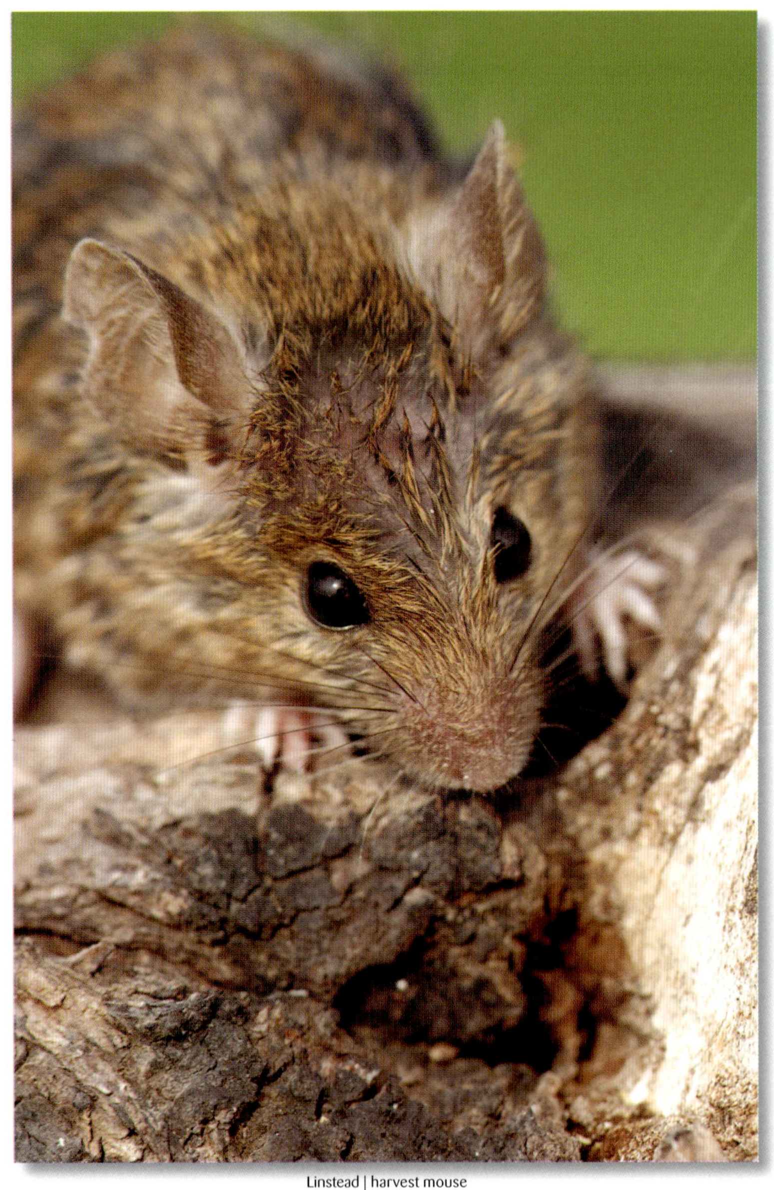
Linstead | harvest mouse

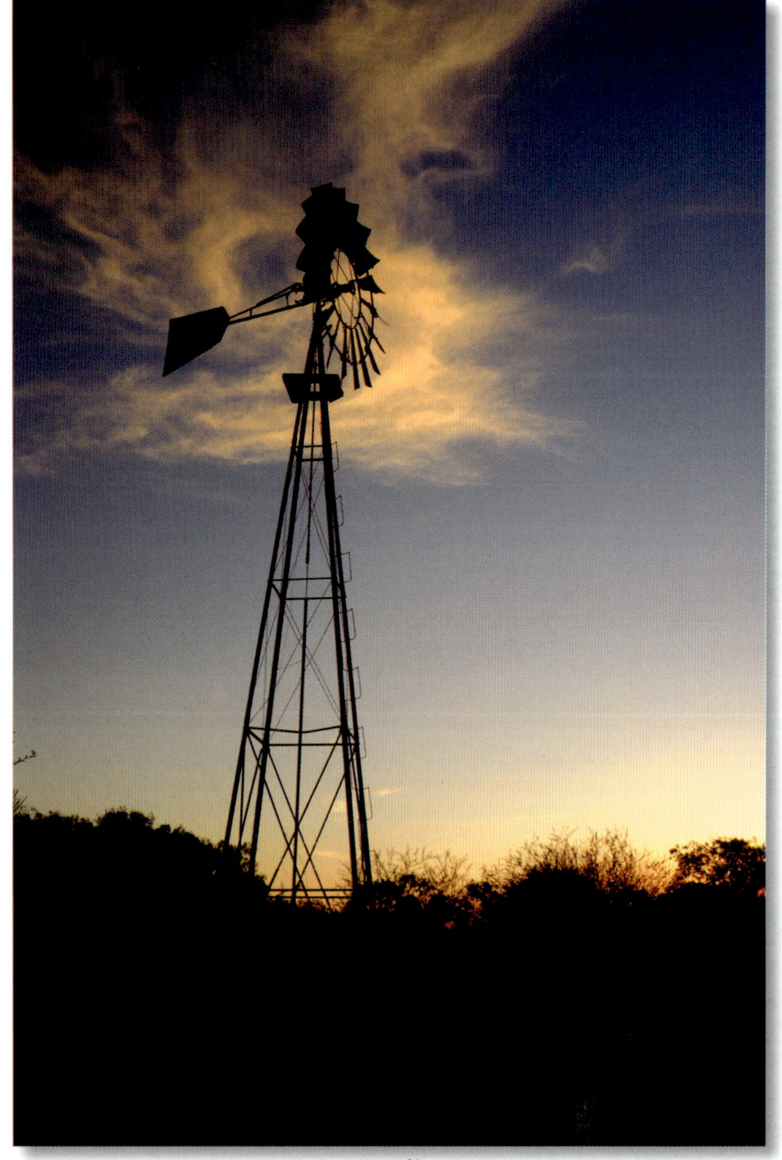
Linstead |

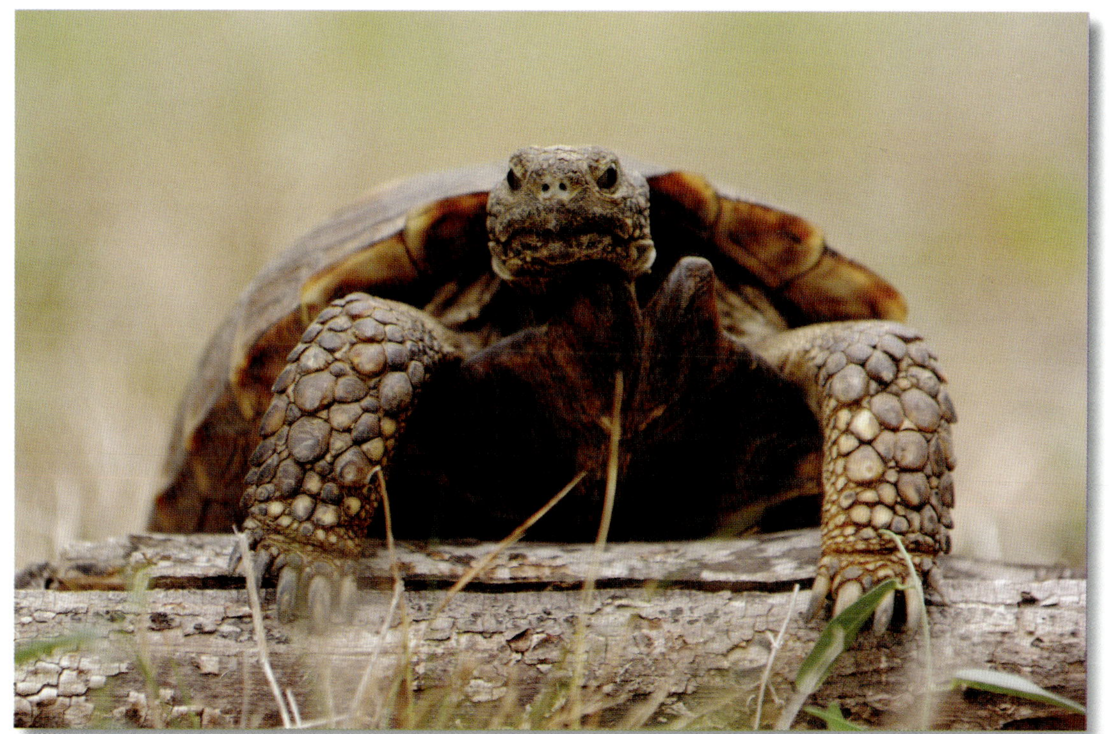

Linstead | Texas Tortoise

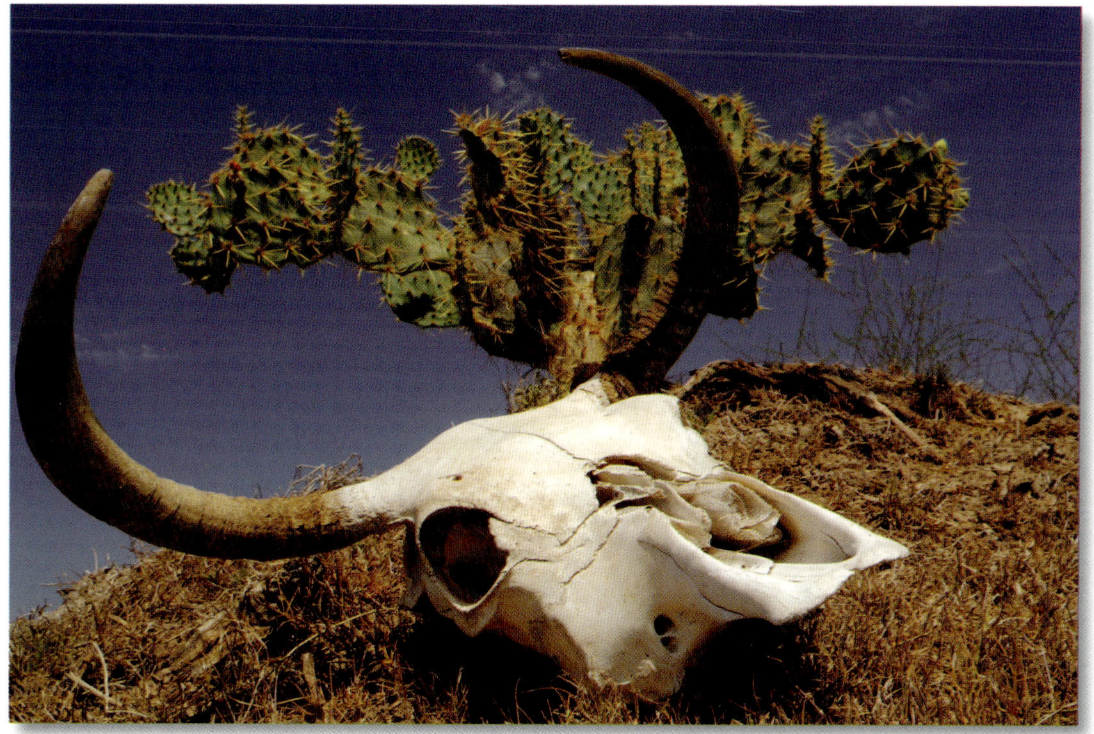

Linstead | Lindheimer Prickly Pear

About Jay Welder Ranch...

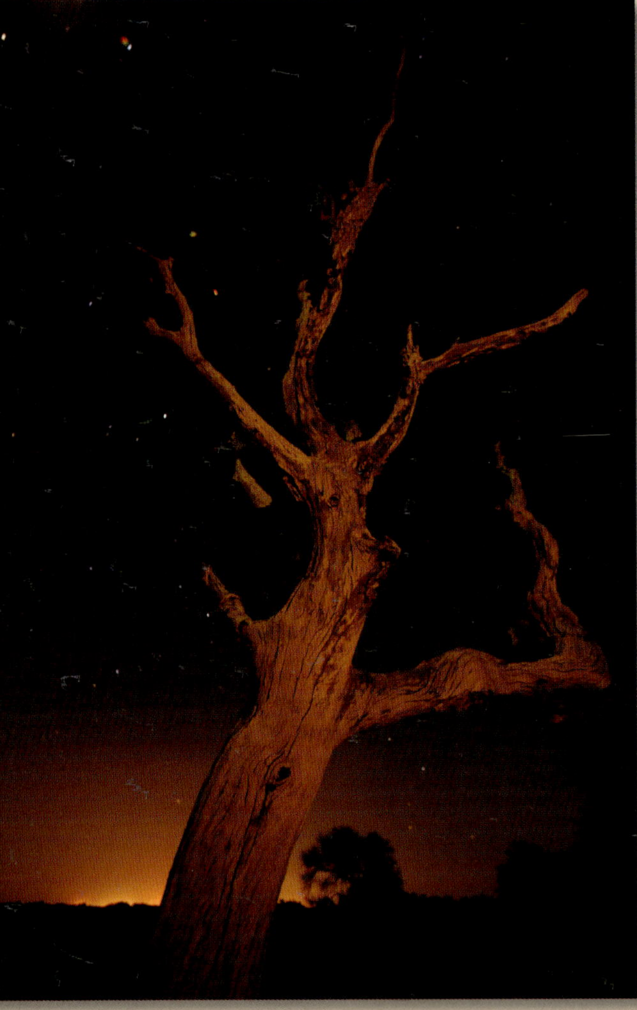

Pryor-Luzier

A coastal gem, the Jay Welder Ranch is located near Seadrift where 8,000 acres of grassland and Live Oaks stretch from Highway 185 toward the Intracoastal waterway.

Near the coast, Shoal Water Pond provides views of Espiritu Santo Bay. Espiritu Santo, which means Holy Spirit, was named by early Spanish explorers. Here Bottlenose dolphins surface for air on shimmering bay waters, ruffled by fresh gulf winds. Clouds billow above the watery horizon in dramatic, ever-changing formations. Roaming thunderstorms or early morning and evening light enhance the colors of the water and sky. Snowy Egrets walk on stilted legs through the salt marsh, which provides nutrients to the many birds and fish that are home in this wetland ecosystem.

Founded in 1910 by John James "Jay" Welder of Victoria, this ranch is one of only two private ranches on the Gulf Intracoastal Waterway between San Antonio Bay and Matagorda Bay. The elder Welder entrusted the ranch to his grandchildren, Kathleen Welder Carey and John Jay Welder V, who entered the property in the Pro-Tour of Nature Photography. This, they said, was a way to open the gates of the family ranch to people with a desire to discover nature and to help promote wildlife conservation along the Texas coast.

After nearly 100 years of primarily farming and ranching, Kathleen and her brother John have embraced the concept of wildlife photography and nature tourism on the ranch.

Their partner/photographer in the Pro-Tour was Maresa Pryor Luzier, who captured a telling array of animals found on the Jay Welder Ranch, including snakes, falcons, shorebirds, blue crabs, armadillos, Jack Rabbits, Sandhill Cranes, Whooping Cranes and Long Billed Curlews. Maresa boasted that during her brief time on the ranch she spotted the greatest number of migratory birds she had seen in any single location. The Jay Welder Ranch is in Calhoun County and is included on the Great Texas Birding Trail. In addition to providing Kathleen and her family with an album brimming with beautiful wildlife images, Maresa devised a comprehensive plan to create wildlife viewing areas in five of the ranch's most scenic locations. This includes several ponds and Whooper's Lookout.

Pryor-Luzier | Green Treefrog on Coral Bean

Biologists and other scientists from Texas Parks and Wildlife and Texas A&M University have documented plant and wildlife species on the ranch including Bobcats, deer, Javelina, snakes, Whooping Cranes, Sandhill Cranes, Common Loons, oyster catchers, marsh wrens, osprey, ducks, gulls, terns, herons and egrets.

The Nature Conservancy helped facilitate the creation of a conservation easement on the property, which legally guarantees the preservation of native ecosystems on the ranch. John manages cattle rotation and controlled salt grass burns and is knowledgeable about all ranch activities.

The tranquil ambiance of this coastal ranch offers exceptional opportunities for bird watching, and photographing wildlife, coastal landscapes and seascapes. For nature tourists, the Jay Welder Ranch offers basic comfortable accommodations in two cabins for as many as 10 individuals.

Kathleen Welder Carey
John Jay Welder, V
Seadrift, TX
[e] tomkatcarey@suddenlink.net

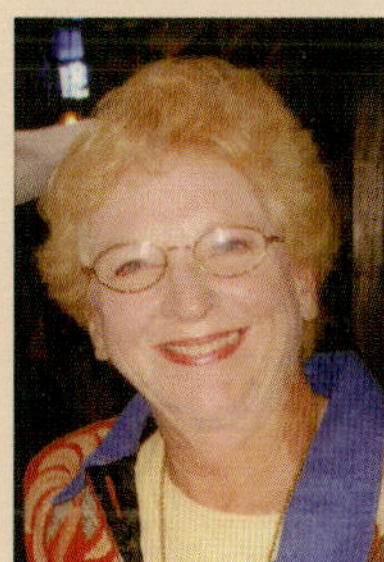

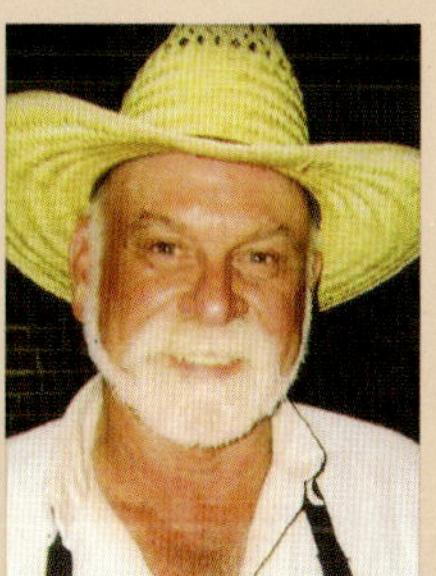

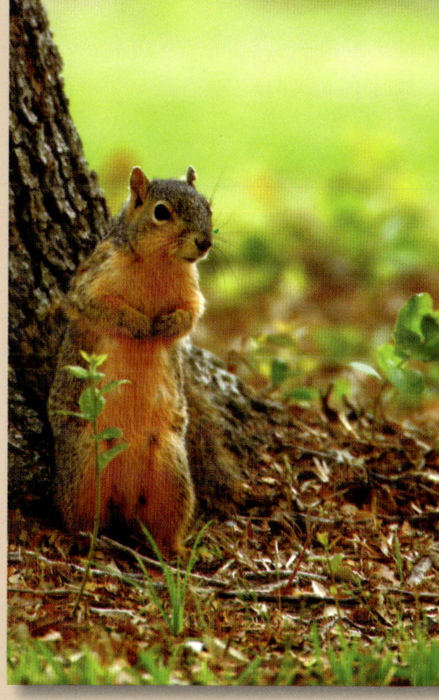

Pryor-Luzier | Eastern Fox Squirrel

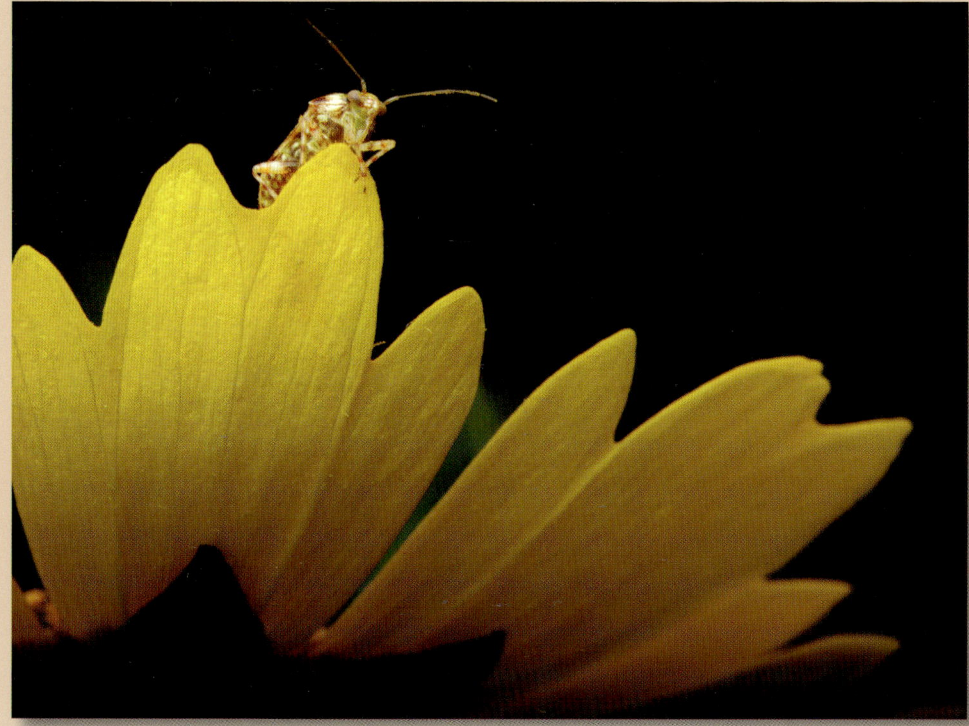

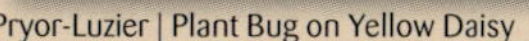

Pryor-Luzier | Plant Bug on Yellow Daisy

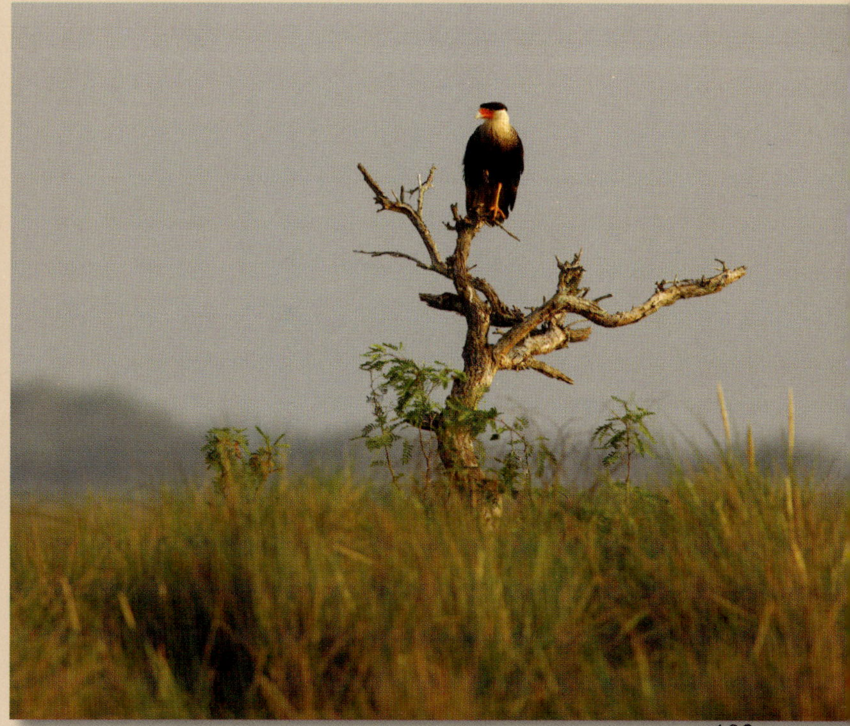

Pryor-Luzier | Crested Caracara

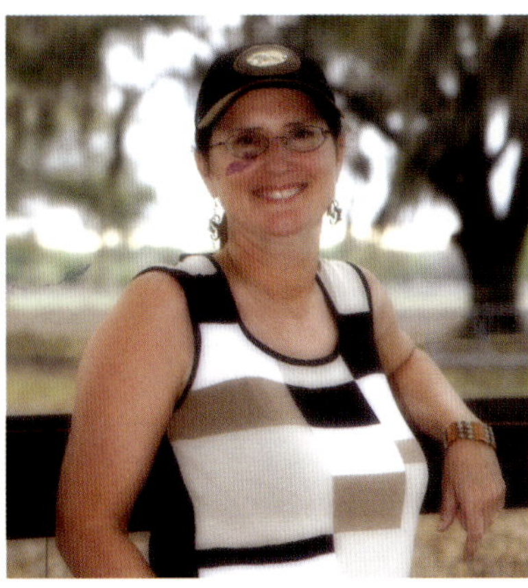

Maresa Pryor-Luzier

"Part of being a good nature photographer," says Maresa Pryor-Luzier, "is realizing that what's going to happen is going to happen."

She had anxiously awaited the Texas Black-tailed Jackrabbit. But, much to her chagrin, the opportunity didn't arise until the very last day of her time on the Jay Welder Ranch. After weeks of not seeing one, she'd resigned herself to going home empty-handed. But, then one entered the picture, quite literally.

"It was the very last day and I was coming back, picking up my blinds and getting ready to go. Then, after all those days of looking I stumbled upon a jackrabbit, I was thinking, 'I'm so excited I'm going to scare him away.'"

Next thing she knew, the jackrabbit flushed out another. While the two interacted Maresa clicked away. "They were so busy with one another they didn't notice me and at times got as close as 10 feet away."

"Doing this sort of contest was very enlightening. I've done much of my photographing in places where wildlife is accustomed to human beings. Here, you're on a thousand acres with wildlife that are used to being hunted or not in communication with people whatsoever. It's a whole other challenge."

"Wildlife was something I just grew up around," she says. A member of the Audubon Society since the age of 16, she really "got" the connection between photography and conservation in Sarasota, Florida while photographing Florida Scrub Jays in order to help save their habitat.

"They were going to develop scrub jay habitat into a park and I worked with others to educate the city leaders about developing without destroying the habitat. I photographed the jays I monitored and these images really helped me speak to the city leaders and explain things." Today, the park does exist, but it's "a nice park that has scrub jays."

Bushnell, FL
www.lwphotogallery.com
[e] mjp@lwphotogallery.com

Pryor-Luzier | white morph Reddish Egret

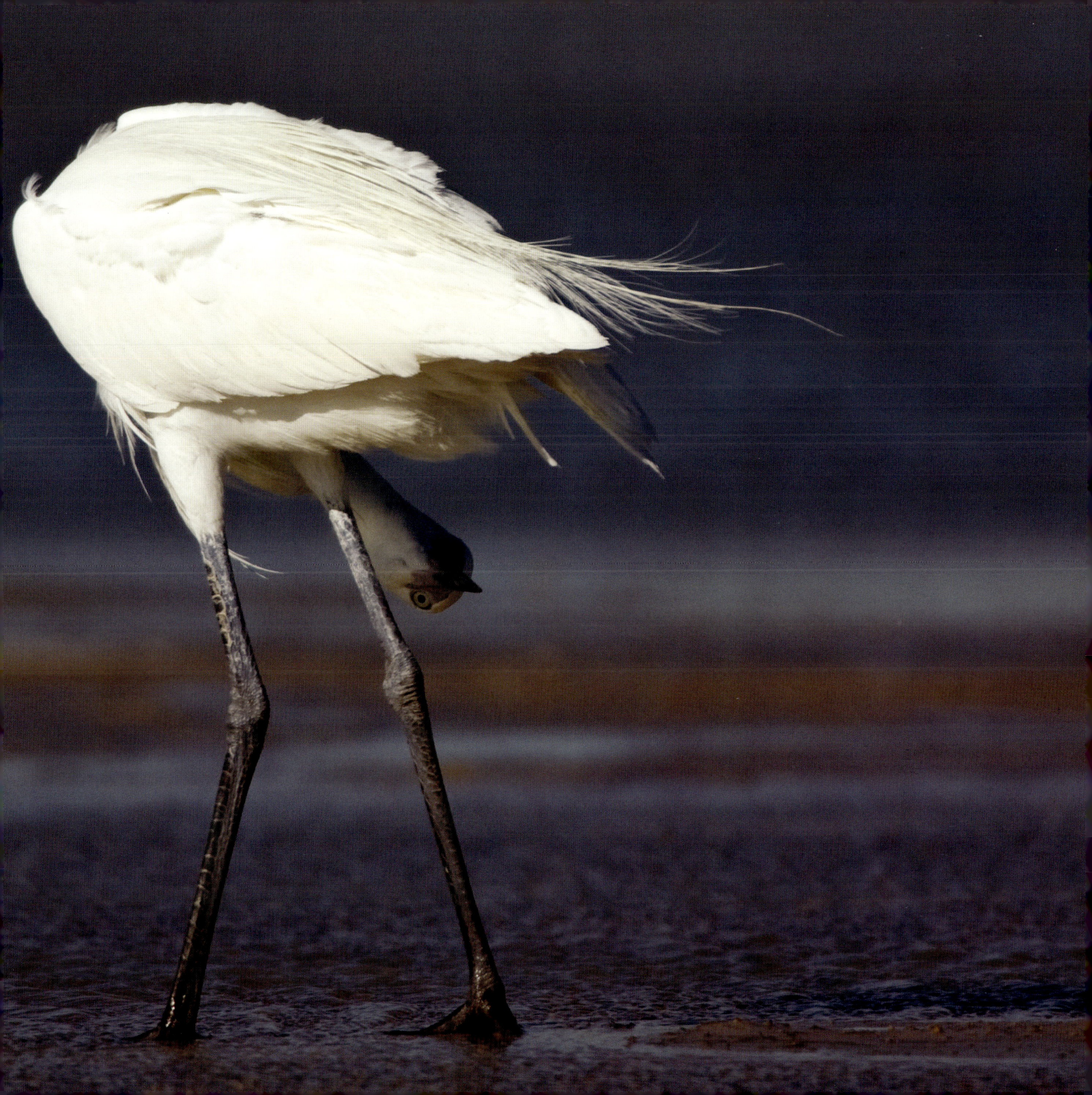

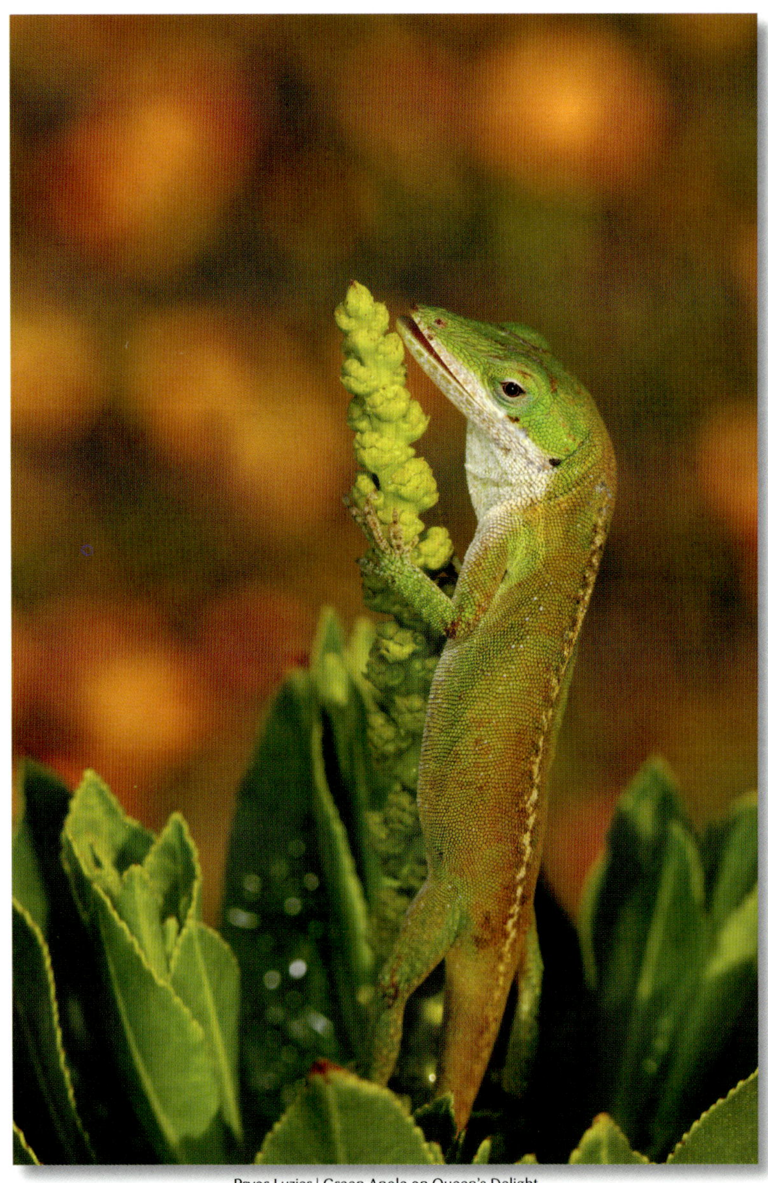

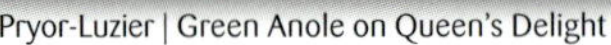
Pryor-Luzier | Green Anole on Queen's Delight

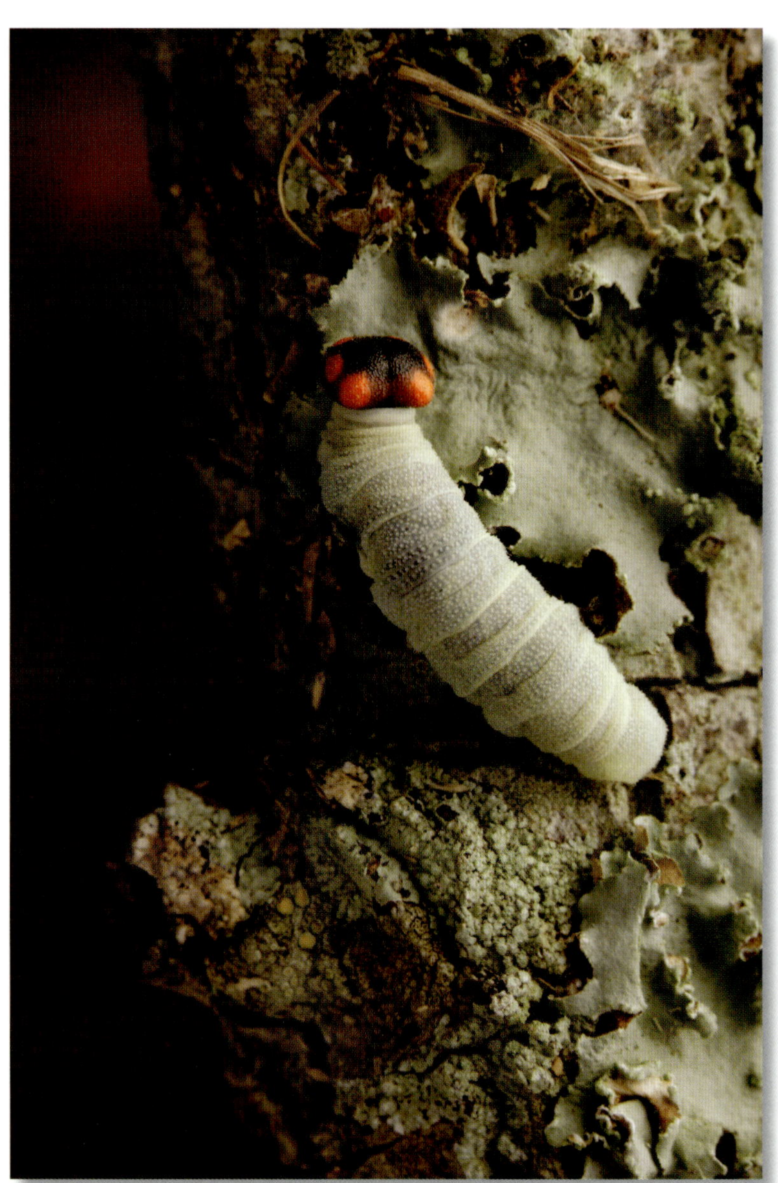
Pryor-Luzier | Skipper Butterfly Caterpillar

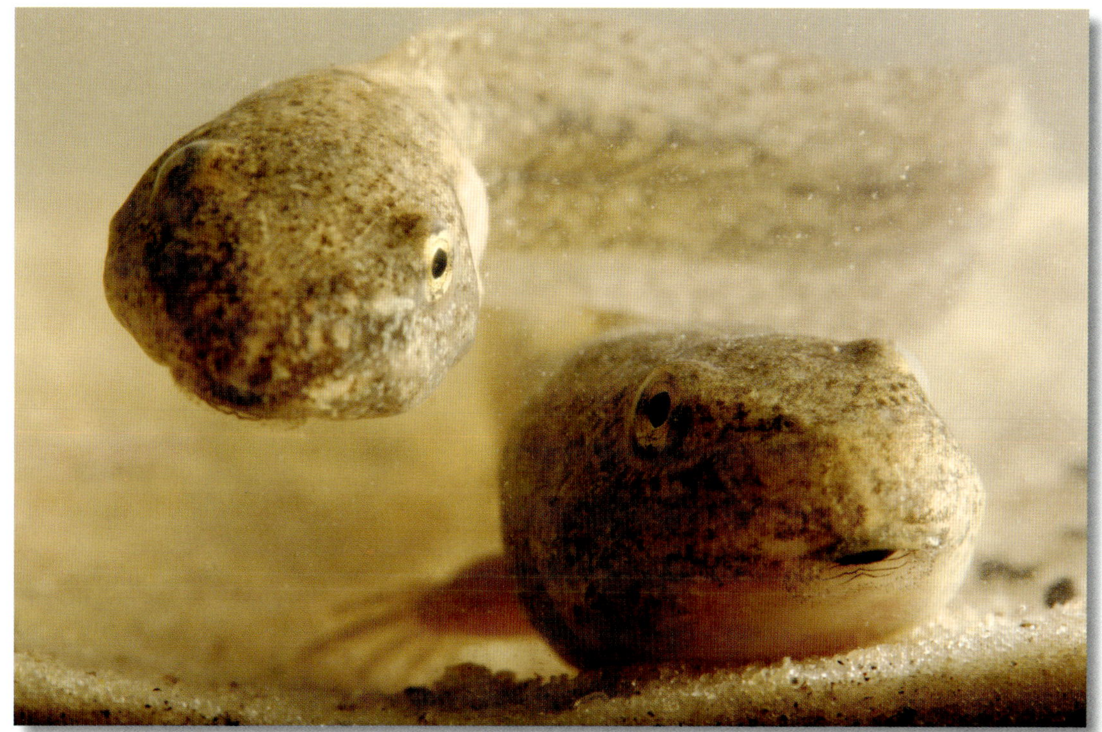

Pryor-Luzier | tadpoles

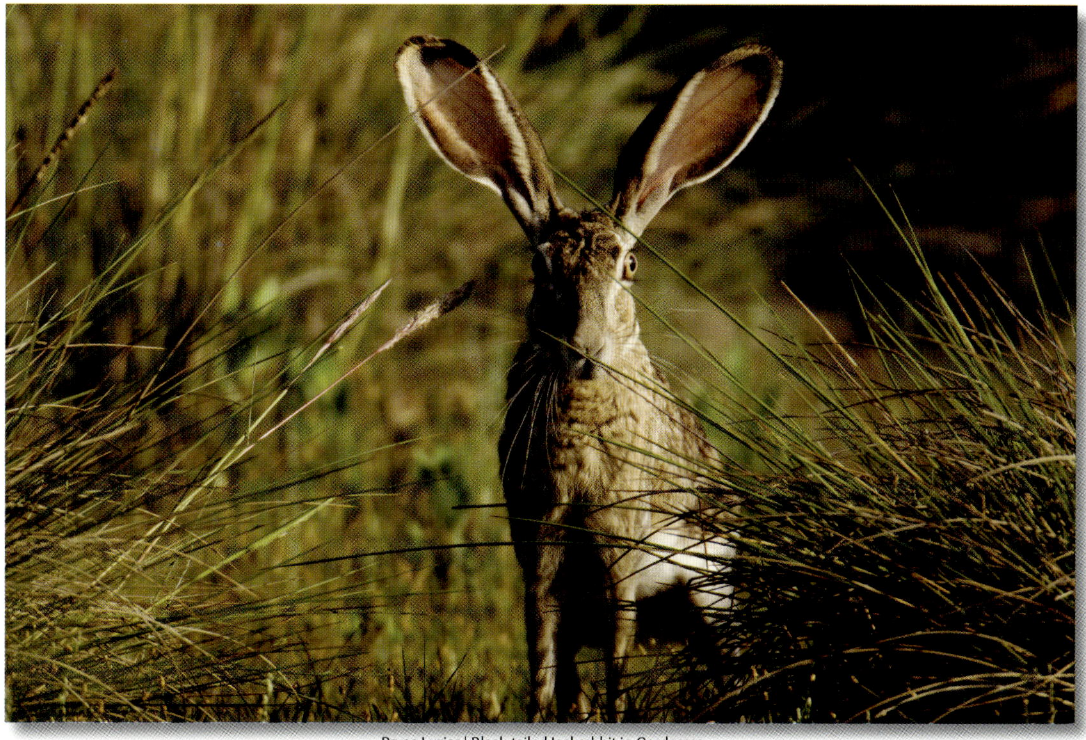

Pryor-Luzier | Black-tailed Jackrabbit in Cordgrass

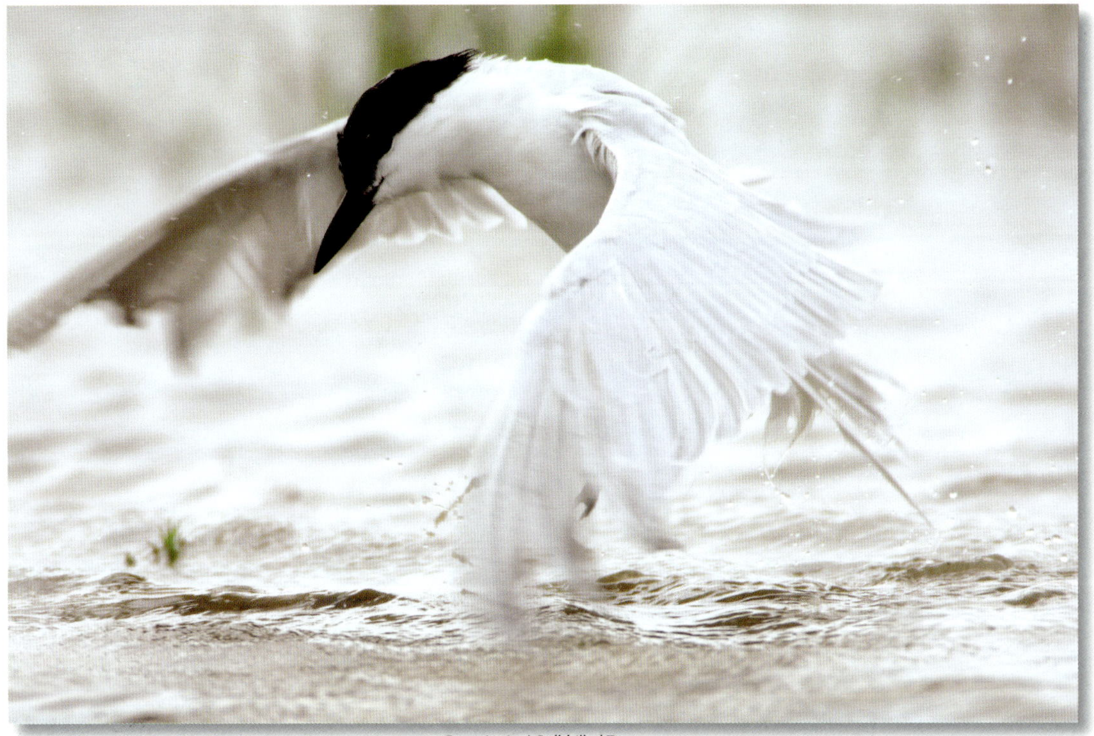

Pryor-Luzier | Gull-billed Tern

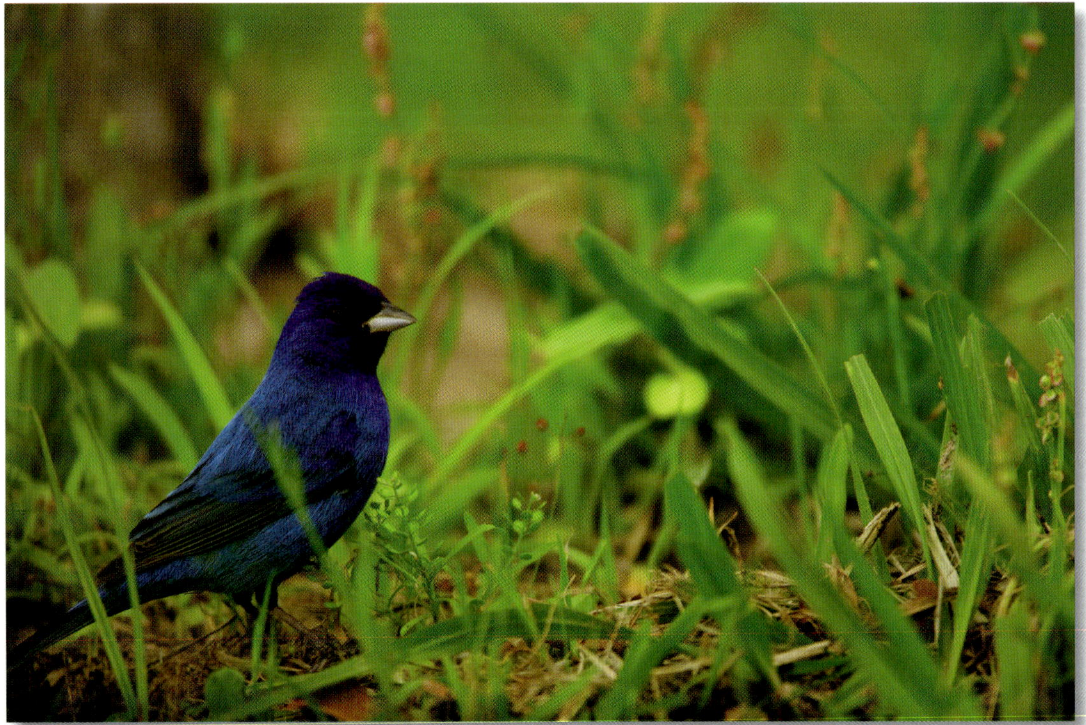

Pryor-Luzier | Indigo Bunting in St. Augustine and Peppergrass

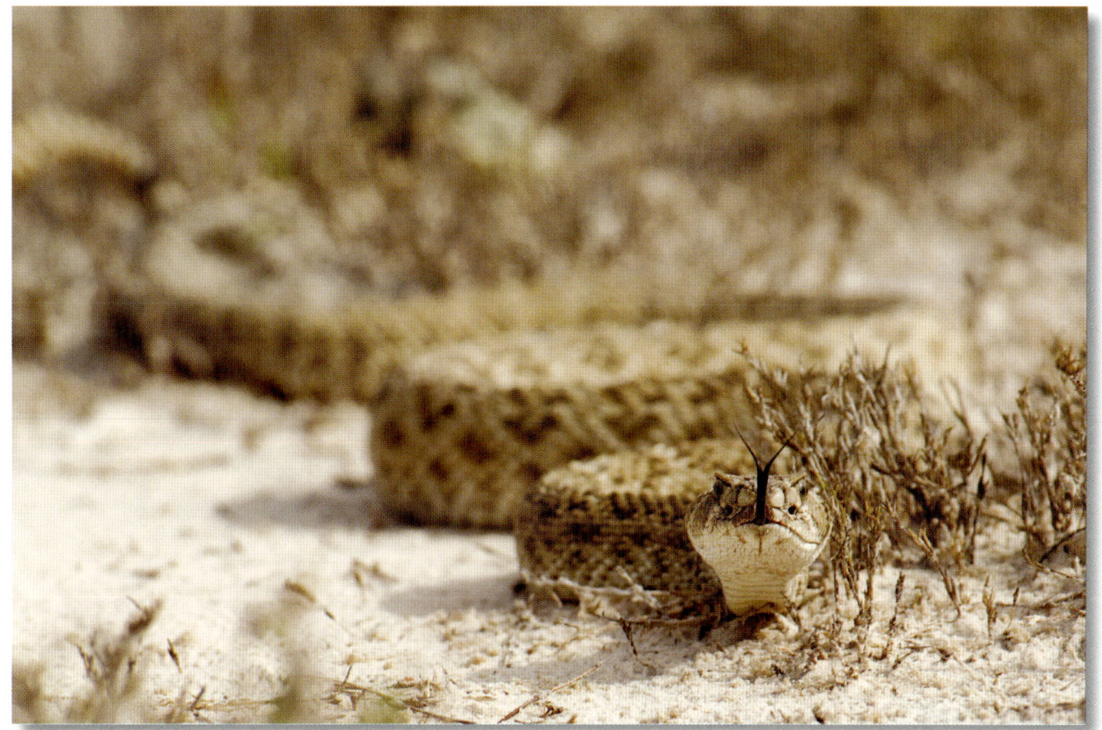

Pryor-Luzier | Western Diamondback Rattlesnake hiding behind shoregrass

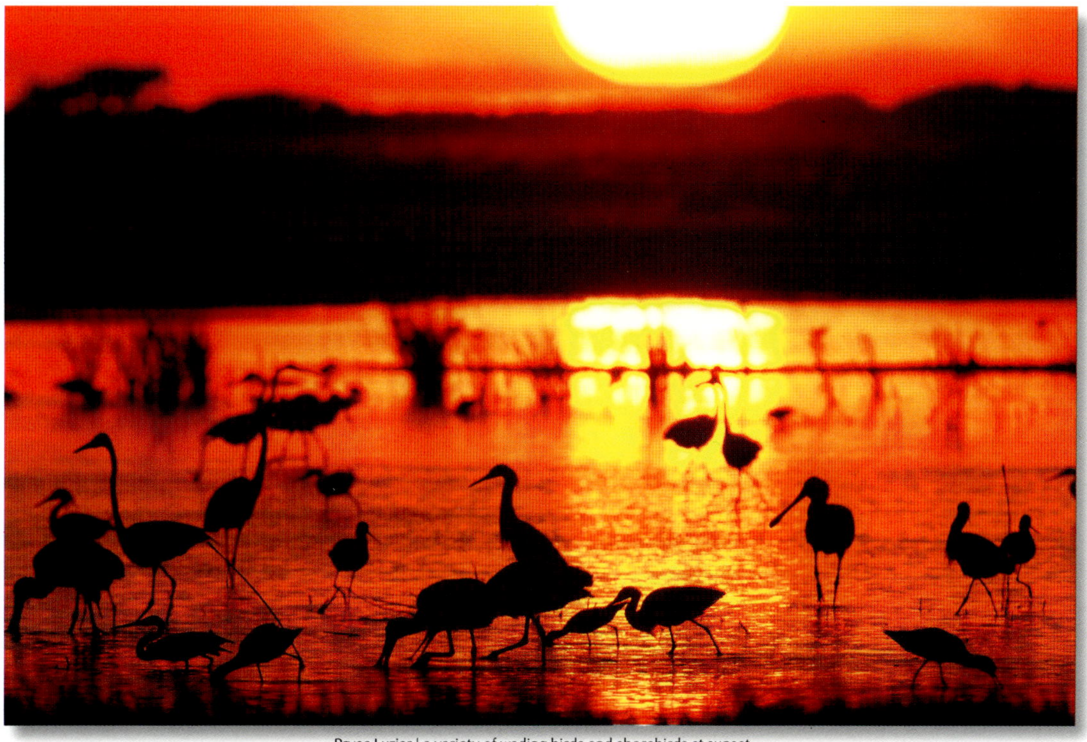

Pryor-Luzier | a variety of wading birds and shorebirds at sunset

About JHA Ranch...

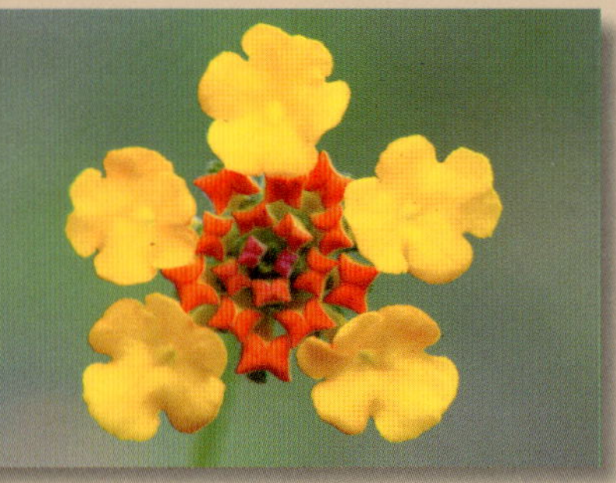

The JHA Ranch is truly a unique and beautiful South Texas ranch that hosts a wide variety of flora and fauna rarely found together in Texas. Comprised of incredibly productive virgin native habitat, the ranch includes a wildlife-rich creek drainage system, native bull Mesquites, large Live Oak trees and a strong diversity of South Texas brush communities. The ranch hosts a variety of soil types ranging from deep sand to heavy clays, resulting in a diverse ecosystem. The JHA Ranch manages this ecosystem to promote and protect the habitat throughout the property to benefit all wildlife and plant species. It is the ranch's truly diverse soil composition, features and habitats that make the ranch an ideal location for observing and photographing many types of plants and animals, including more than a hundred identified bird species. The Anderson family feels very fortunate to have been given the opportunity to be stewards of the ranch and carries forth this responsibility by implementing wildlife, livestock, range and game management practices that enhance the overall habitat for the betterment of all wildlife and plants that depend on it. To that end, the JHA Ranch works closely with a private wildlife biologist who guides these efforts and assists in attaining the family's conservation goals.

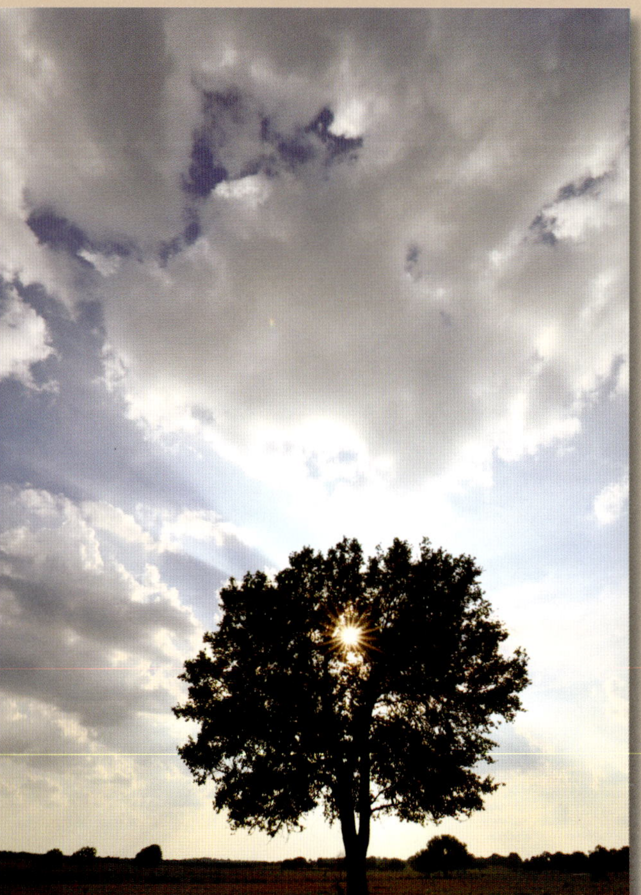

The family-operated ranch is located just south of George West in Live Oak County and was purchased in early 2007 by the Andersons. The JHA Ranch was originally a portion of the vast land holdings of George Washington West, founder and namesake of the nearby town. The terrain is rolling with several higher vantage points yielding beautiful views of the South Texas brush country. The ranch is a mix of improved pasture for cattle and native brush providing excellent habitat for wildlife. There are several prominent draws throughout the ranch, including more than four miles of Spring Creek and its tributaries. The property features abundant White-tailed Deer, Rio Grande Turkey, Green Jays, armadillo, White-winged and Mourning Doves, bobwhite quail, numerous duck species and other game and non-game animals. Sandhill Cranes and a variety of songbirds also winter here. The JHA maintains a year round supplemental feeding program for wildlife and,

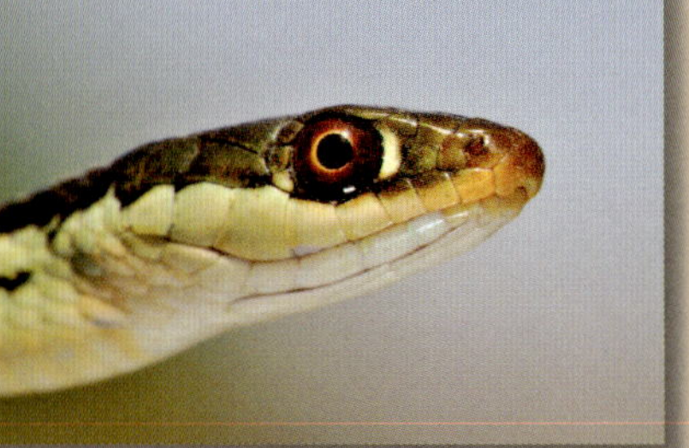

Doest |
(top) Texas Lantana
(middle) Honey Bee
(bottom) Schott's Whipsnake
(right) Live Oak tree

through the Texas Parks and Wildlife Department, participates in the Managed Lands Deer Permit (Level III) program. The ranch has several homes to provide comfortable accommodations for family and friends, an abundance of underground water and miles of buried irrigation pipe to deliver water for wildlife throughout the ranch. Fish are stocked in several beautiful ponds on the ranch.

In addition to preserving and enhancing wildlife found here, the JHA also is a working cattle ranch and operates under the AoK Cattle brand. AoK Cattle Company is a top producer of high quality show cattle that are raised and shown by youth through their local 4-H and Future Farmers of America (FFA) programs. The family also maintains a large herd of registered gray American Brahman cattle. AoK Cattle Company is a member of both the American Brahman Breeders Association and the South Texas Brahman Breeders Association.

Fair Oaks Ranch, TX
Brett Anderson
[e] brett.anderson@att.com

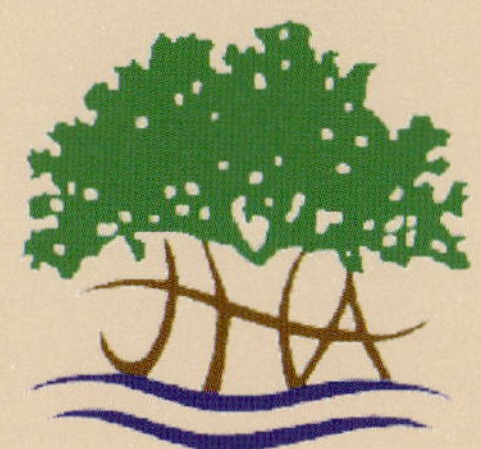

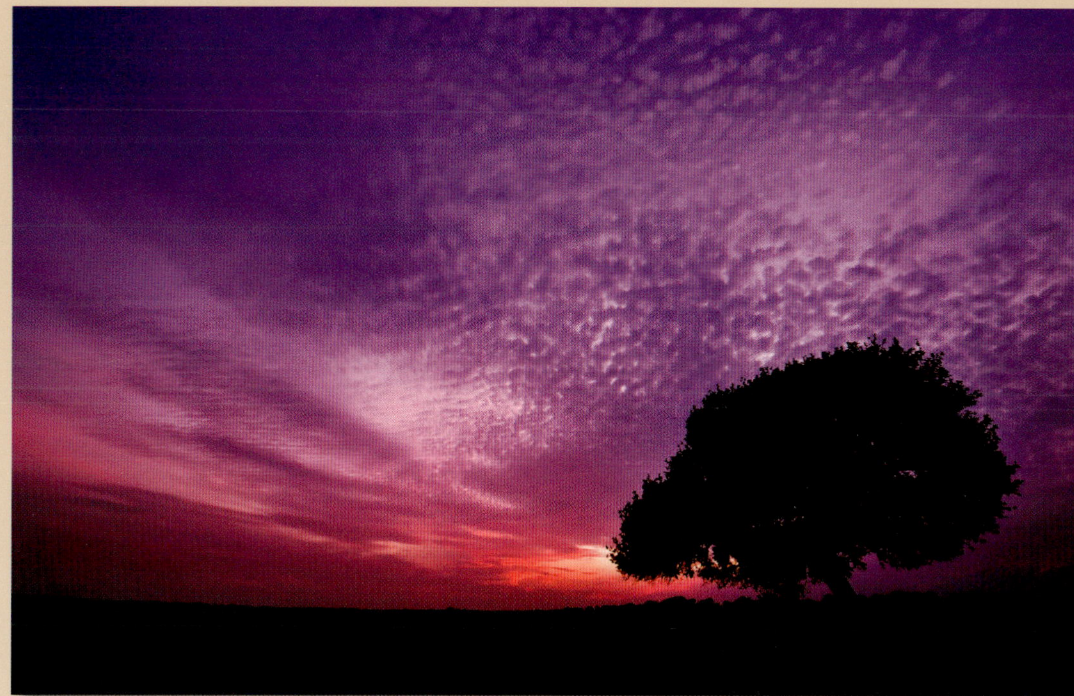

Doest | Live Oak tree

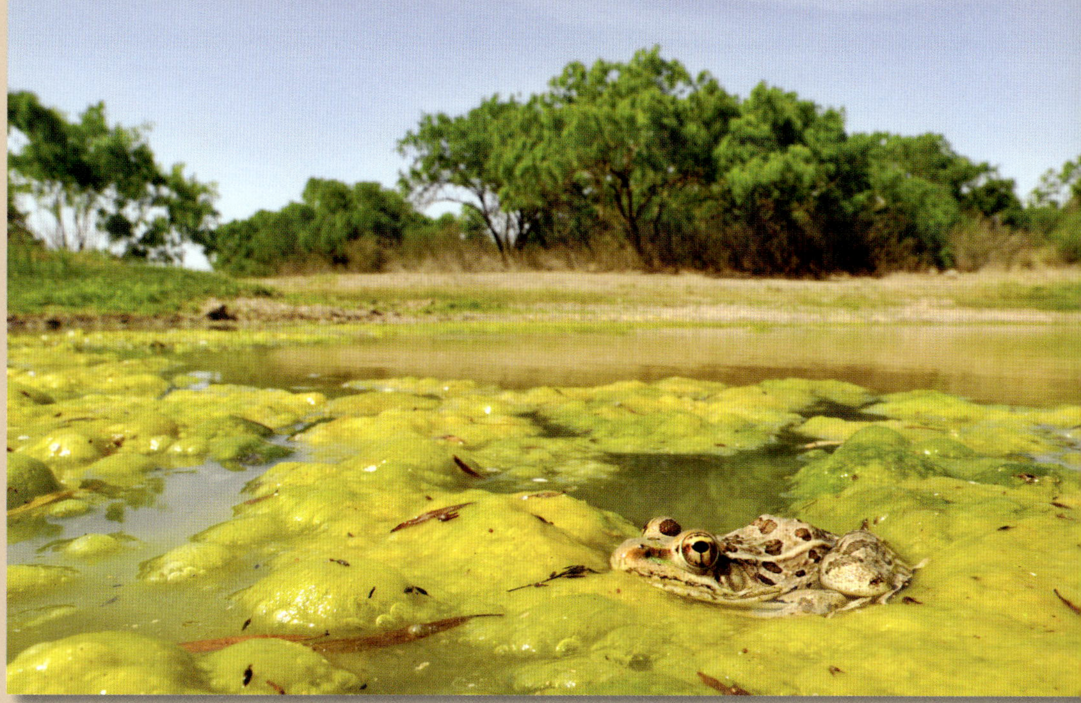

Doest | Rio Grande Leopard Frog

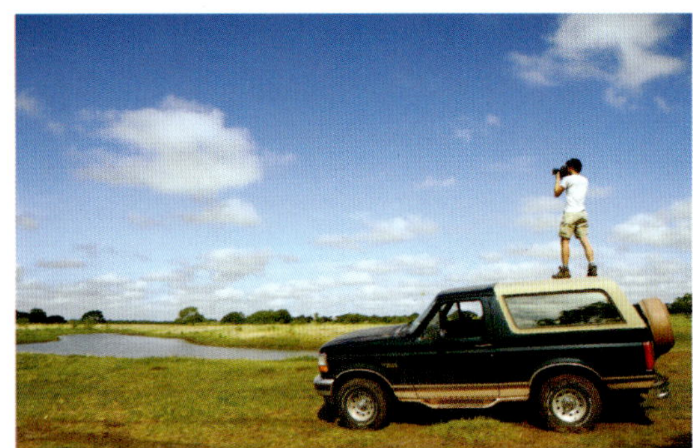

Jasper Doest

The Common Raccoons captivated Jasper Doest. The soft-spoken photographer admits that in spite of the fact that many in the U.S. consider the critters commonplace, "I fell in love with these furry animals and had a great time photographing them."

Part of what made getting to know them especially rich for the Holland resident was "coming from the other side of the pond. Everything, except the photography, was new to me."

Experiences like this are what Jasper craves from his place behind the lens. "For me photography is best when an animal is acting completely natural in his natural environment. I try to do my work with the least disturbance possible."

About a decade ago Jasper got serious about photography, "I was constantly asking myself what I could do better. I'm very competitive. So, I started to ask myself, 'What do I like in photography?' You have to develop your own style." His self-evaluation paid off and he credits winning a national photographic competition with jumpstarting him to the pro-level.

Jasper says as he prepared for South Texas he found himself wondering just how to approach the question of style. "Was I going to adapt my style to the American style of nature photography?" Jasper defines his contest images as a mix of European and American styles.

He was led to the profession by both a love of nature and his studies in biology. While working on a master's thesis on climate change, he discovered that the process "raised a personal awareness that I can tell stories to other people about their environment."

"I think I was able to show the richness in nature of the JHA Ranch to its owners. Red birds will no longer just be red birds. Also, I think that my enthusiasm for Texas wildlife gave my landowner faith that his land might be very interesting for a business in wildlife photography."

Vlaardingen, The Netherlands
www.doest-photography.com
[e] Info@Doest-Photography.com

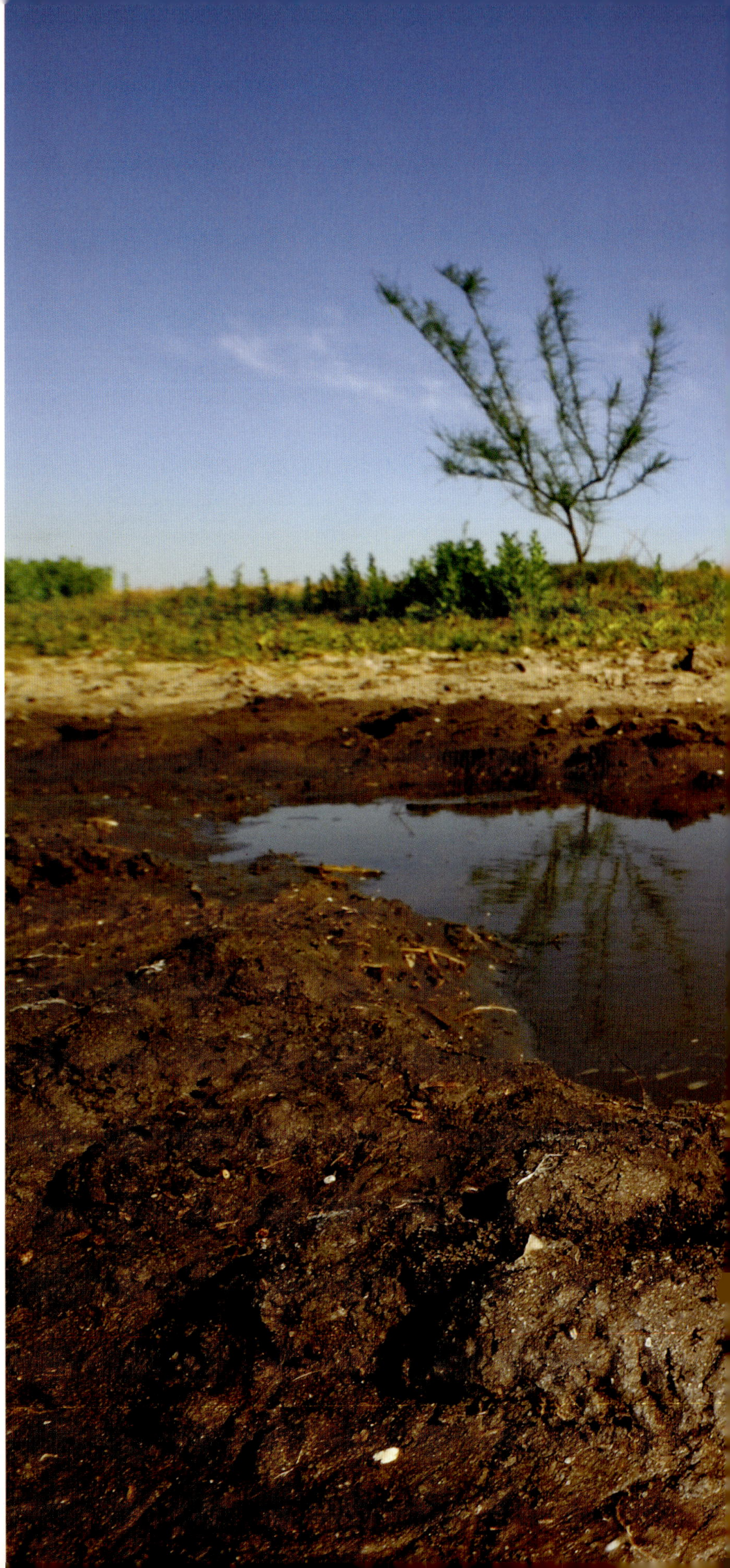

Doest | Red-eared Slider

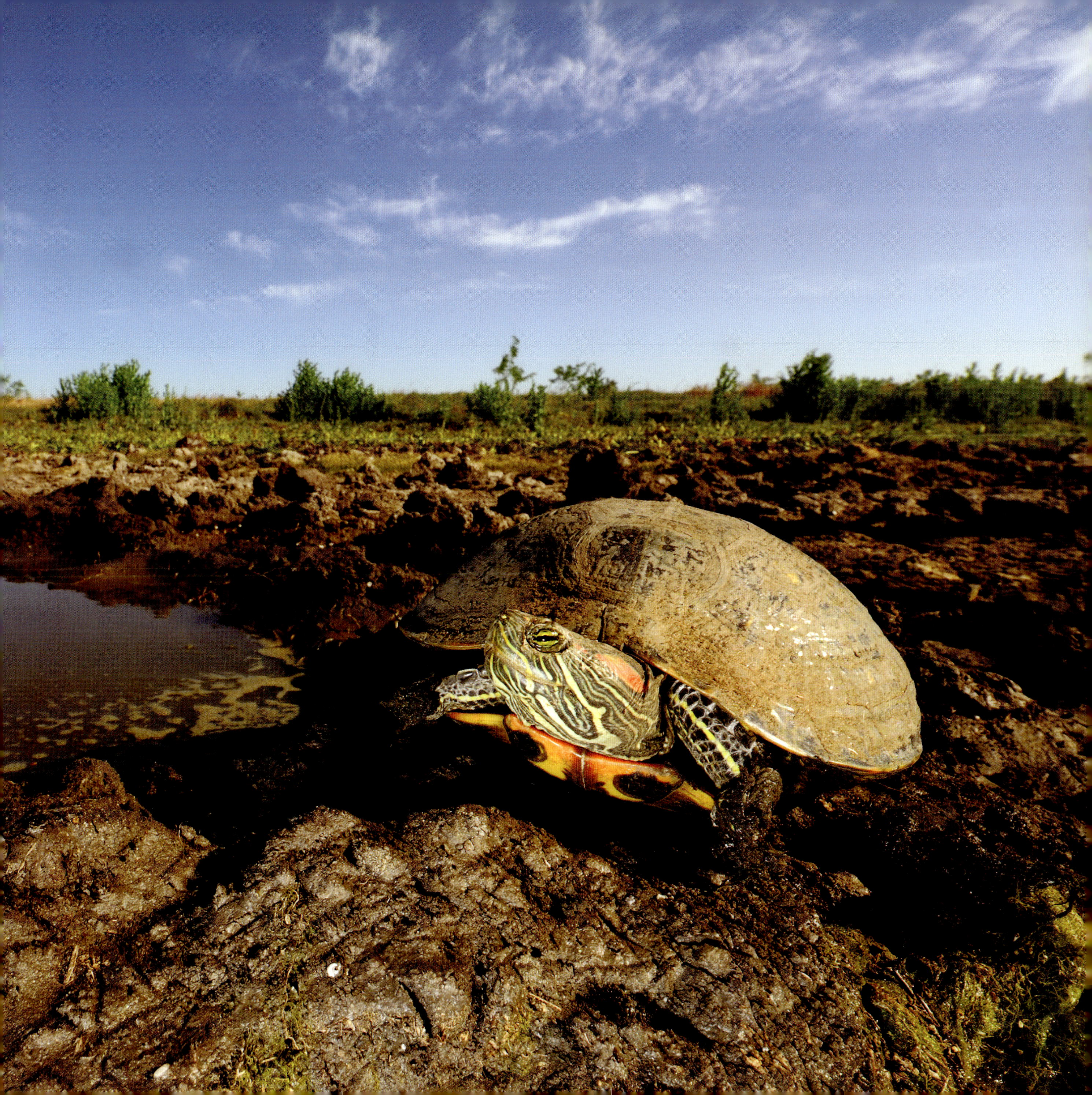

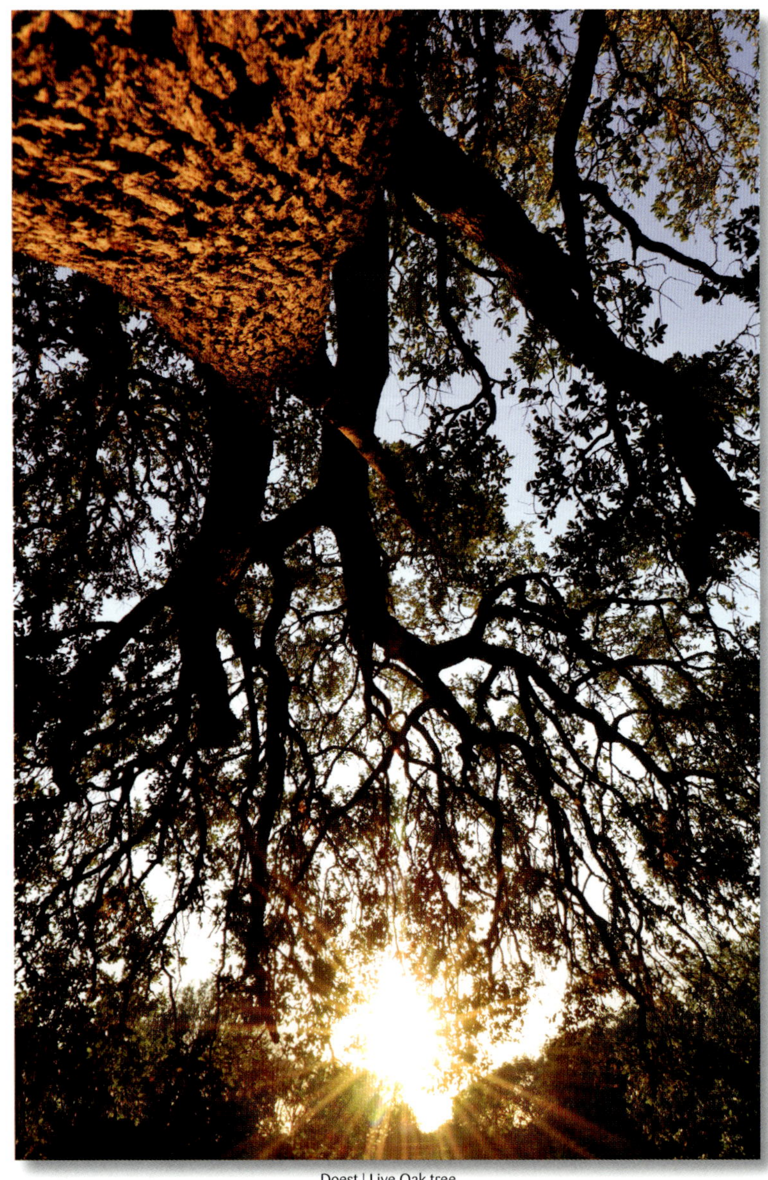

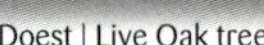

Doest | Live Oak tree

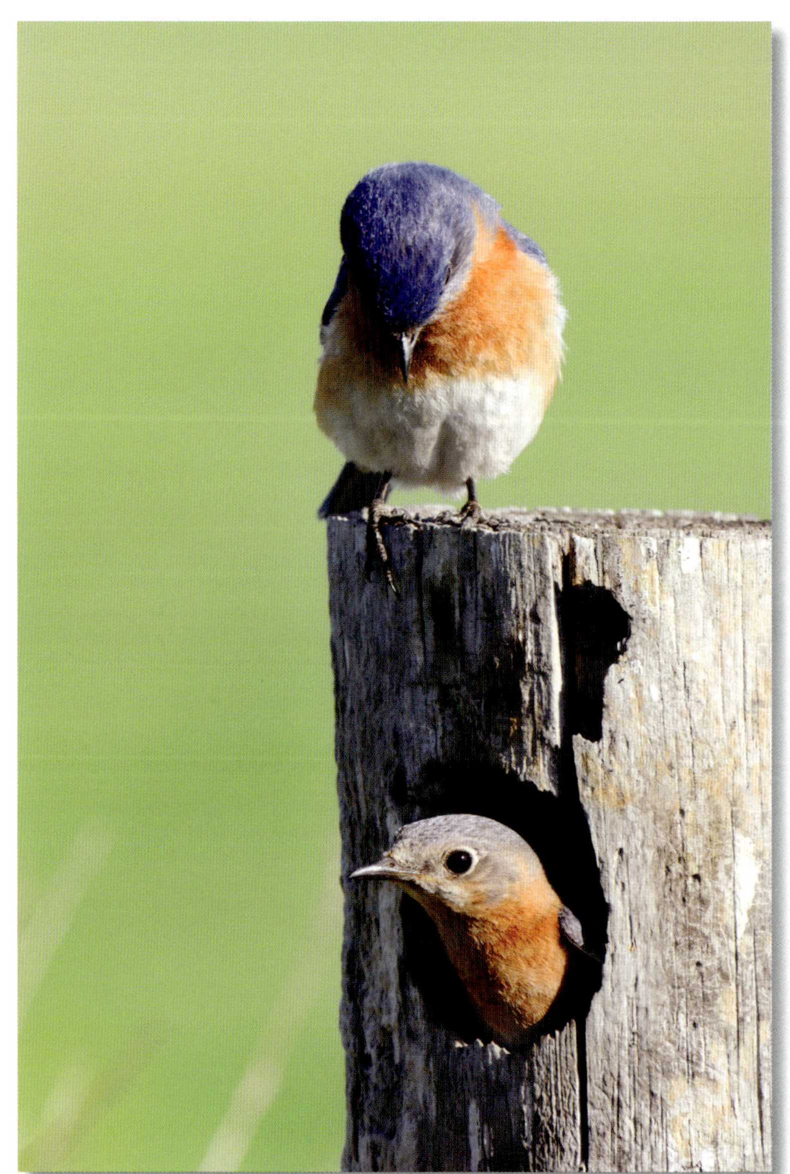

Doest | Eastern Bluebird (male above, female in cavity)

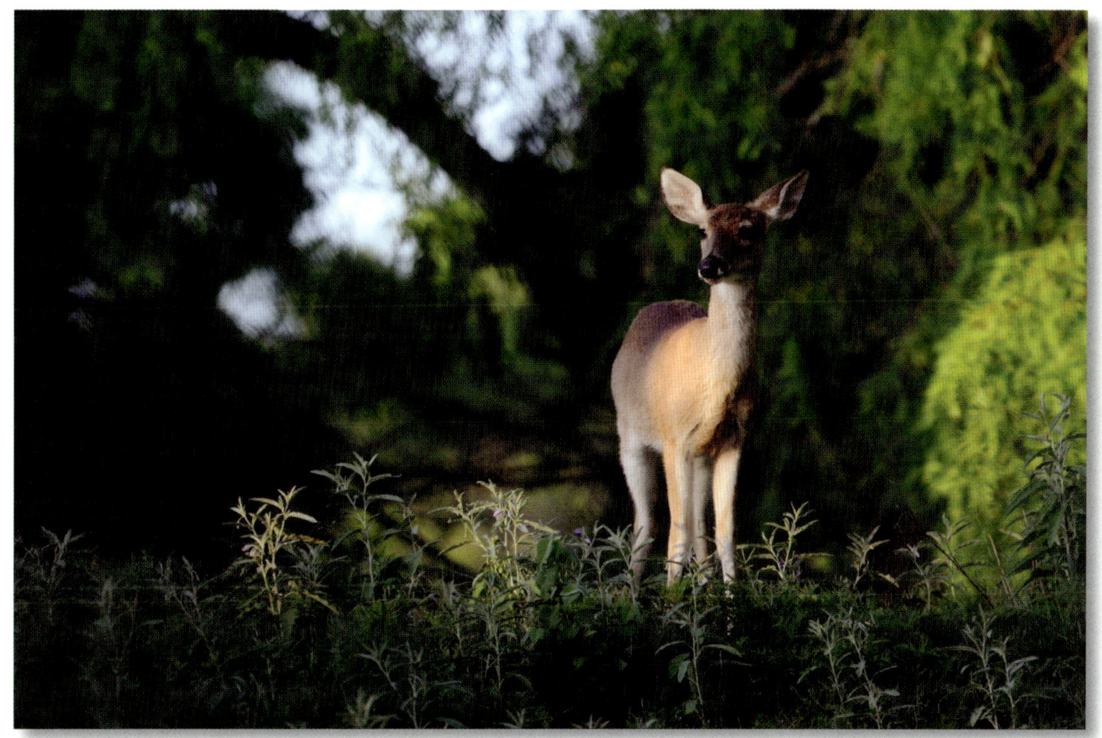

Doest | White-tailed Deer

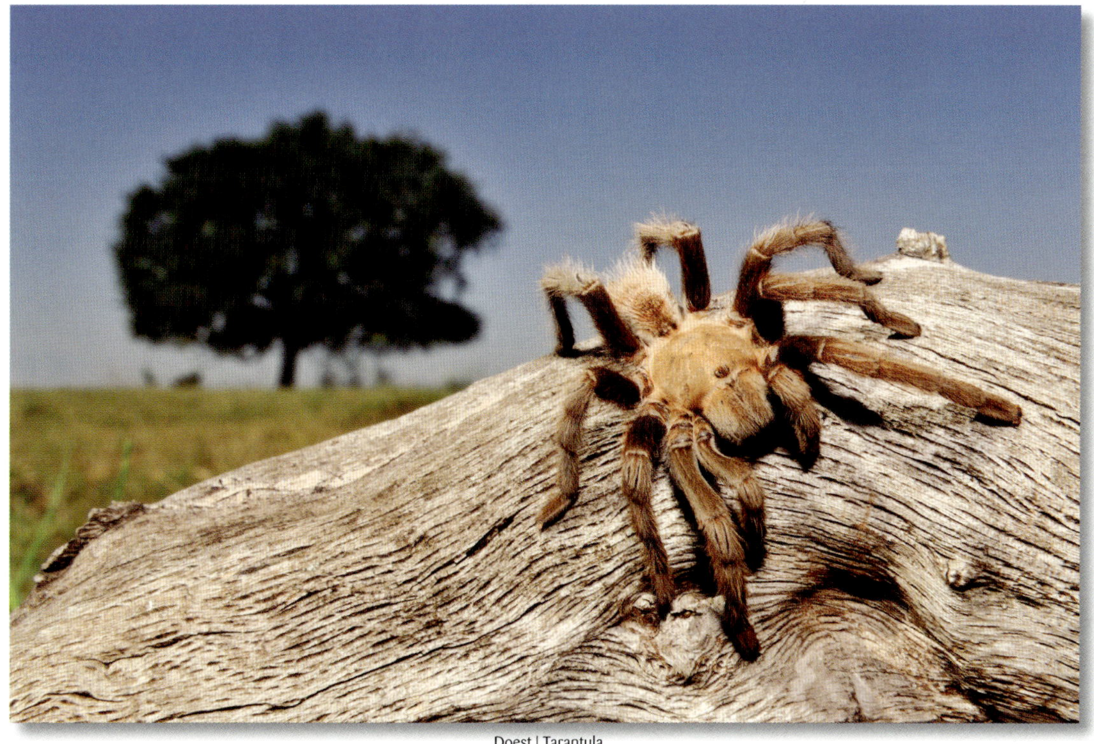

Doest | Tarantula

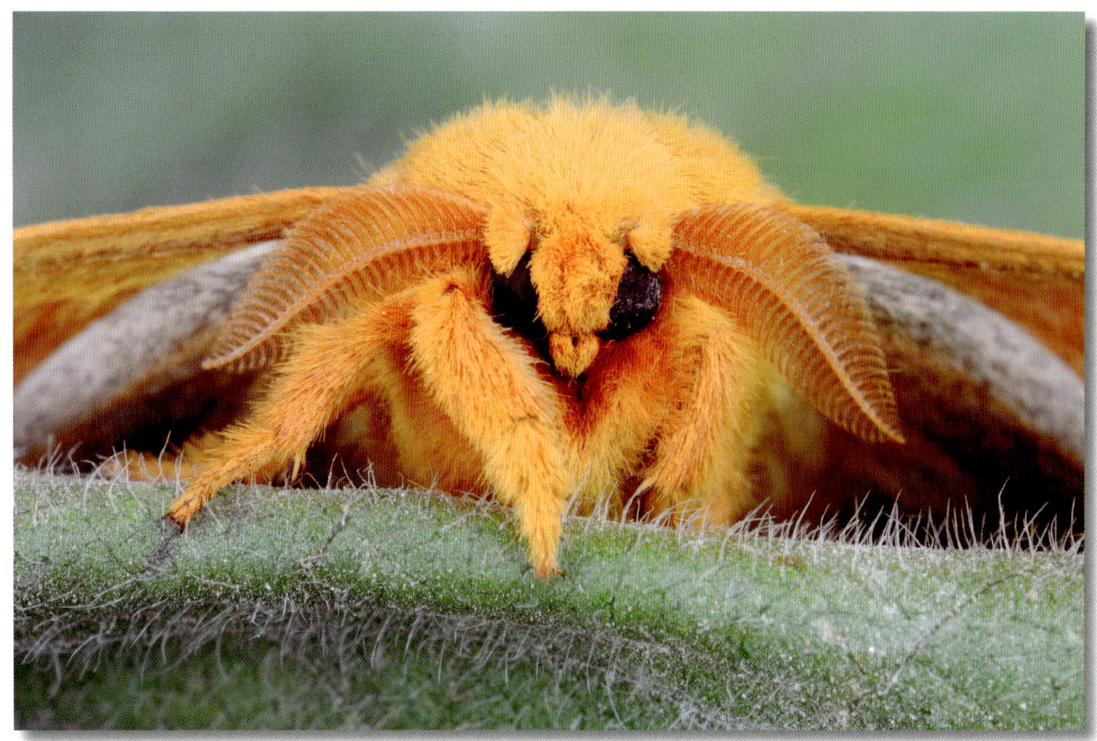

Doest | Native Silkworm Moth

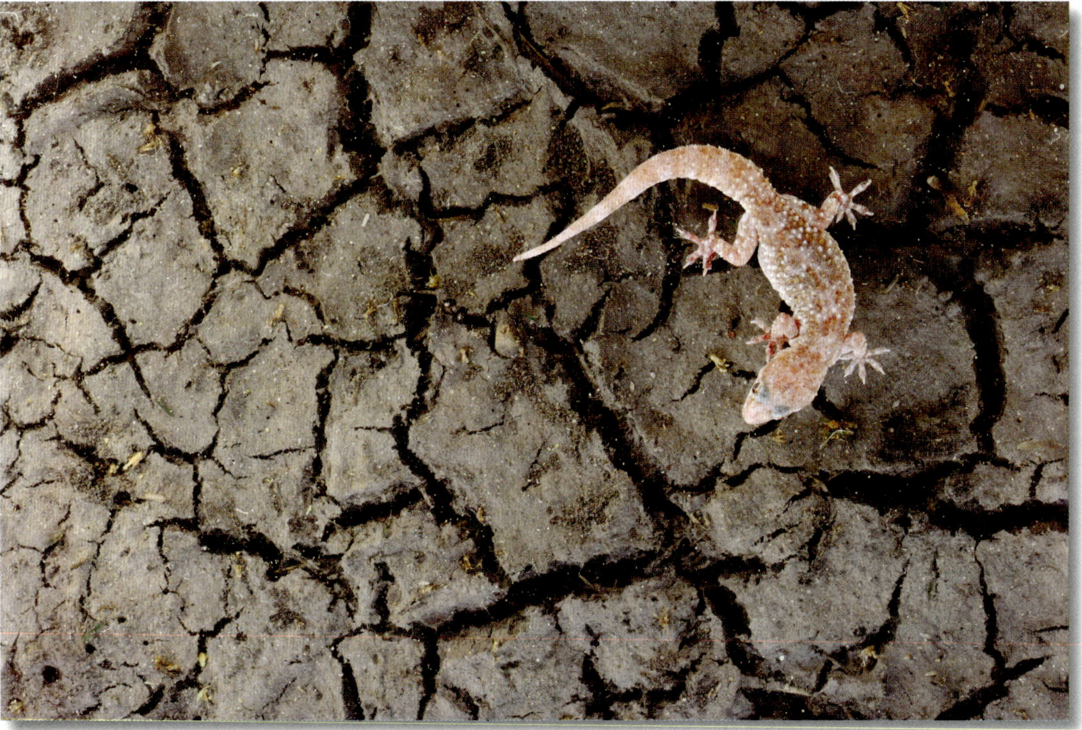

Doest | Mediterranean Gecko

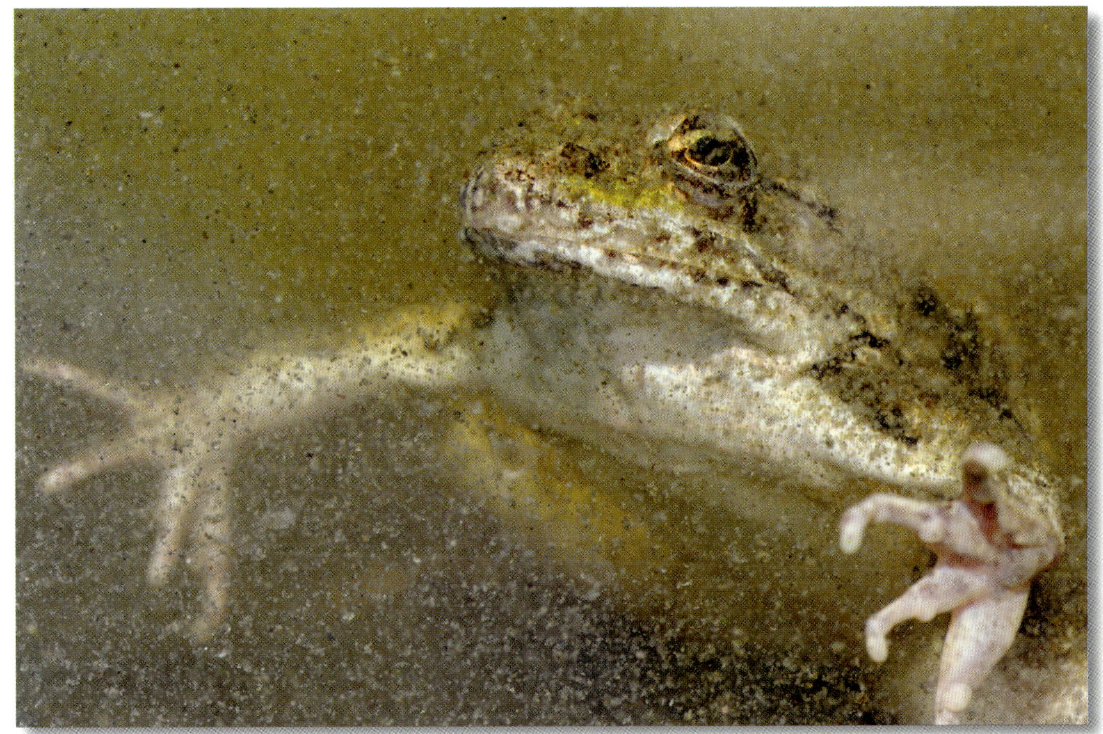

Doest | Rio Grande Leopard Frog

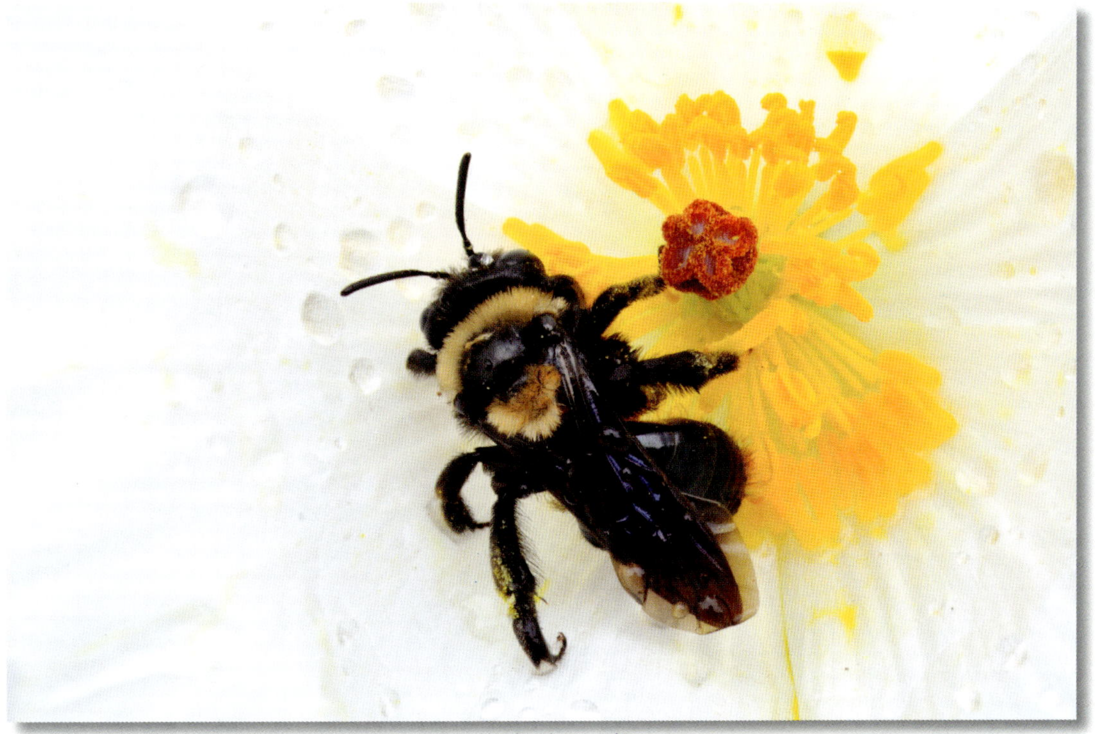

Doest | Rio Grande Leopard Frog

About Knolle Farm & Ranch...

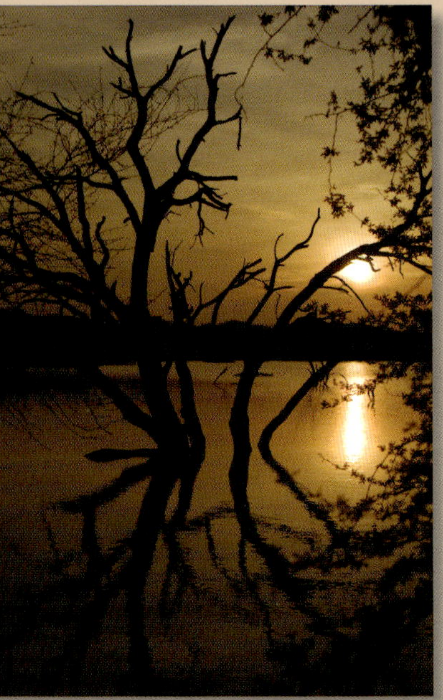
Keeler

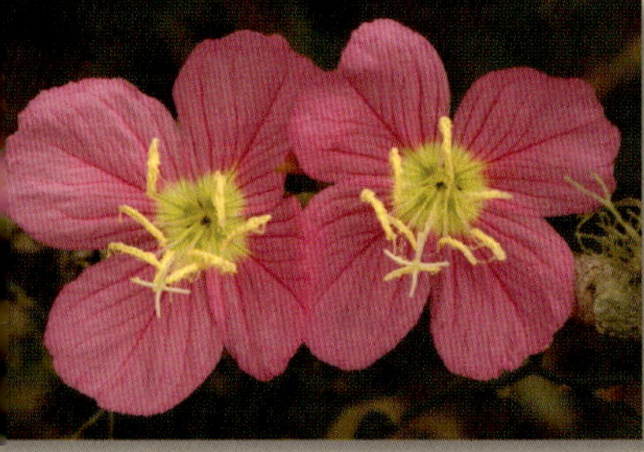
Keeler | Pink Evening Primrose

Knolle Farm & Ranch has a long history of diversified interests, representative of ranches in 21st Century Texas. Four generations have called this land home and each has contributed uniquely to it by nurturing the property for the best purposes possible.

Knolle Farms began as a small agriculture and dairy operation. Mr. Knolle had a special interest in bee keeping. From the 1940s to the 1980s, C.E. "Ed" Knolle and his brother Henry Knolle expanded the family property along with its dairy herd, pushing the limits of superior breeding and modern milking and processing. Knolle Jersey Farms became known as having the world's largest Jersey herd. The name Knolle became an important fixture in South Texas home life, supplying the highest quality Jersey dairy products, while the farm itself became a beautiful retreat where thousands of school children and Boy Scouts camped, toured and learned about agriculture and nature.

During the 1980s, part of the Knolle clan went into the beef cattle business. Changing times, mounting governmental regulations and increased production costs urged the family into new business ventures. Knolle Farm & Ranch was reborn in the 1980s, with a goal of producing high quality beef cattle and ultimately of putting a good piece of beef on a plate.

The death of Charles Knolle Jr. in 1997 was a blow to the family that eventually opened new doors. The business expanded again, with an emphasis on hospitality added to cattle ranching. Knolle Farm & Ranch Bed, Barn & Breakfast is the result of the family's legacy to always strive for superiority. "Our doors are open to guests longing for a gentle pastoral experience that is a part of the history of this farm and ranch. What a blessing it is to introduce

Keeler | Green Anole

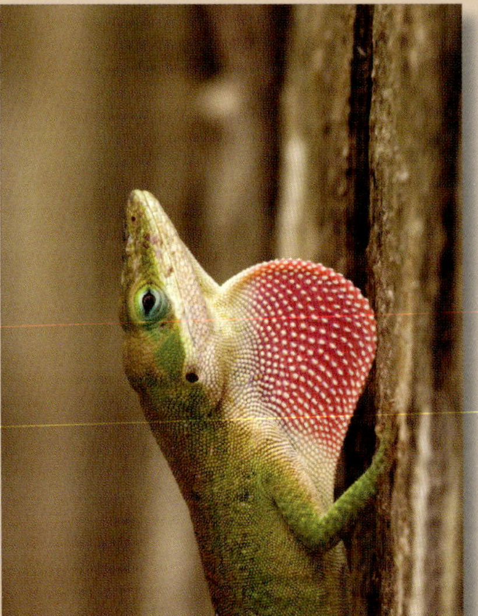

Keeler | White-tailed Deer

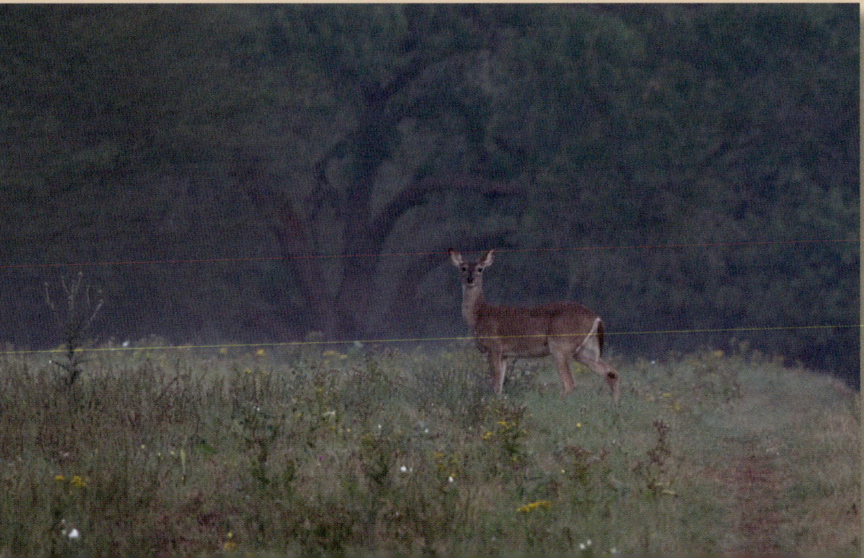

visitors to the livestock, wildlife and the gorgeous and varied countryside we call home," says Beth Knolle Naiser. The operation offers guided hunts, birding, hiking, kayaking, photography, meticulously orchestrated weddings and events and promises guests an opportunity to soak in God's presence in His creation.

Also on the menu are sumptuous meals. Guests are pampered daily with a bountiful breakfast delivered to their quarters. Or they may stretch their culinary experience to include lovely dinners or cooking classes. Guests with a desire may choose hand-gathered eggs and freshly picked vegetables, from the farms own chicken house and organic garden, prime beef or fresh seafood served with 400 count linens. Or perhaps a relaxing massage surrounded by glorious countryside is more to your liking.

As a final note on current events at the farm, there are new babies to provide promise of a next generation and a wonderful new husband. Stephen Naiser brings many talents to Knolle Farm & Ranch, as he explores expanded improved pastures, planting thousands of acres of pasture grass all over Texas and surrounding states. What a great partnership this makes, as Stephen pours his energies into every facet of this operation.

"Yes, over the years Knolle Farm has diversified," says the family. "Along with the blessings we enjoy come the responsibilities of caring for the land and finding new ways to share it. We welcome guests here and are continually looking for ways to help further nature tourism. Please join us at our home and in our effort to protect this natural gift."

Stephen & Beth Knolle Naiser
Sandia, TX
[e] knollefarm@the-I.net

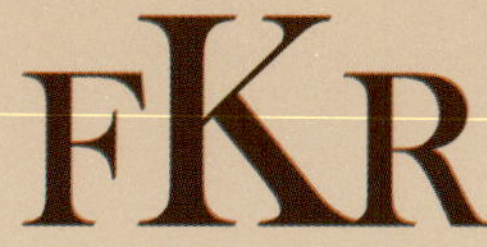

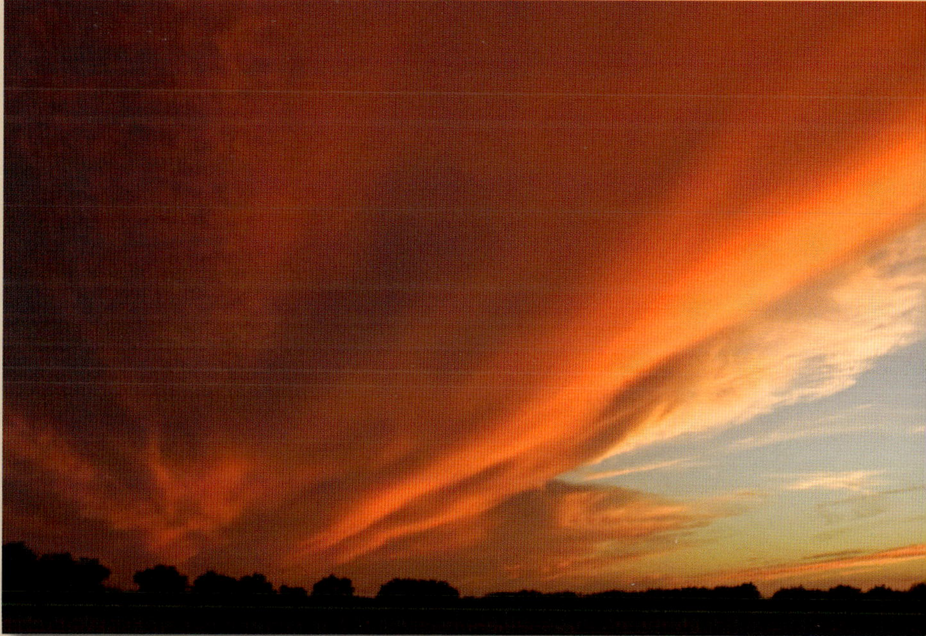

Keeler

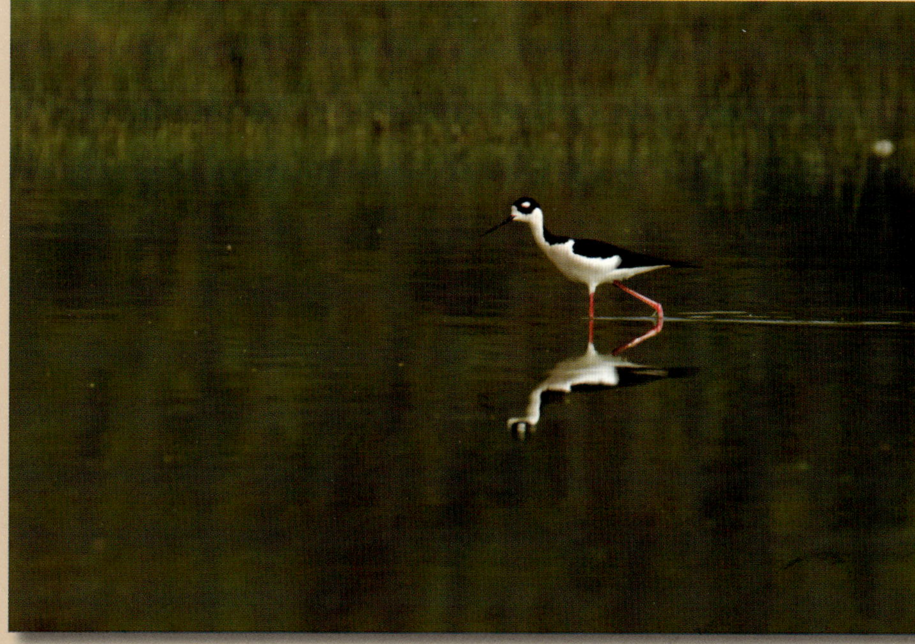

Keeler | Black-necked Stilt

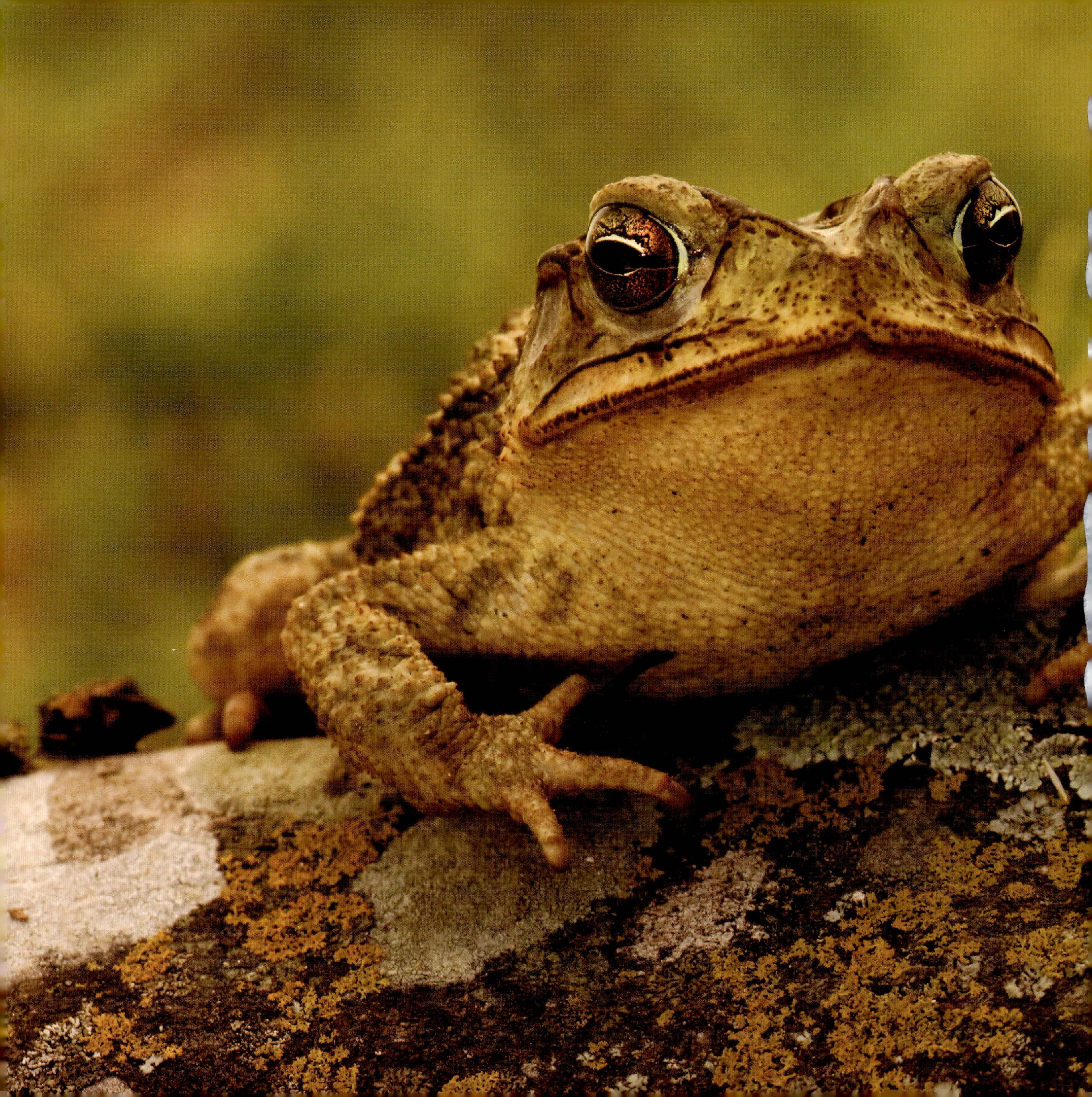

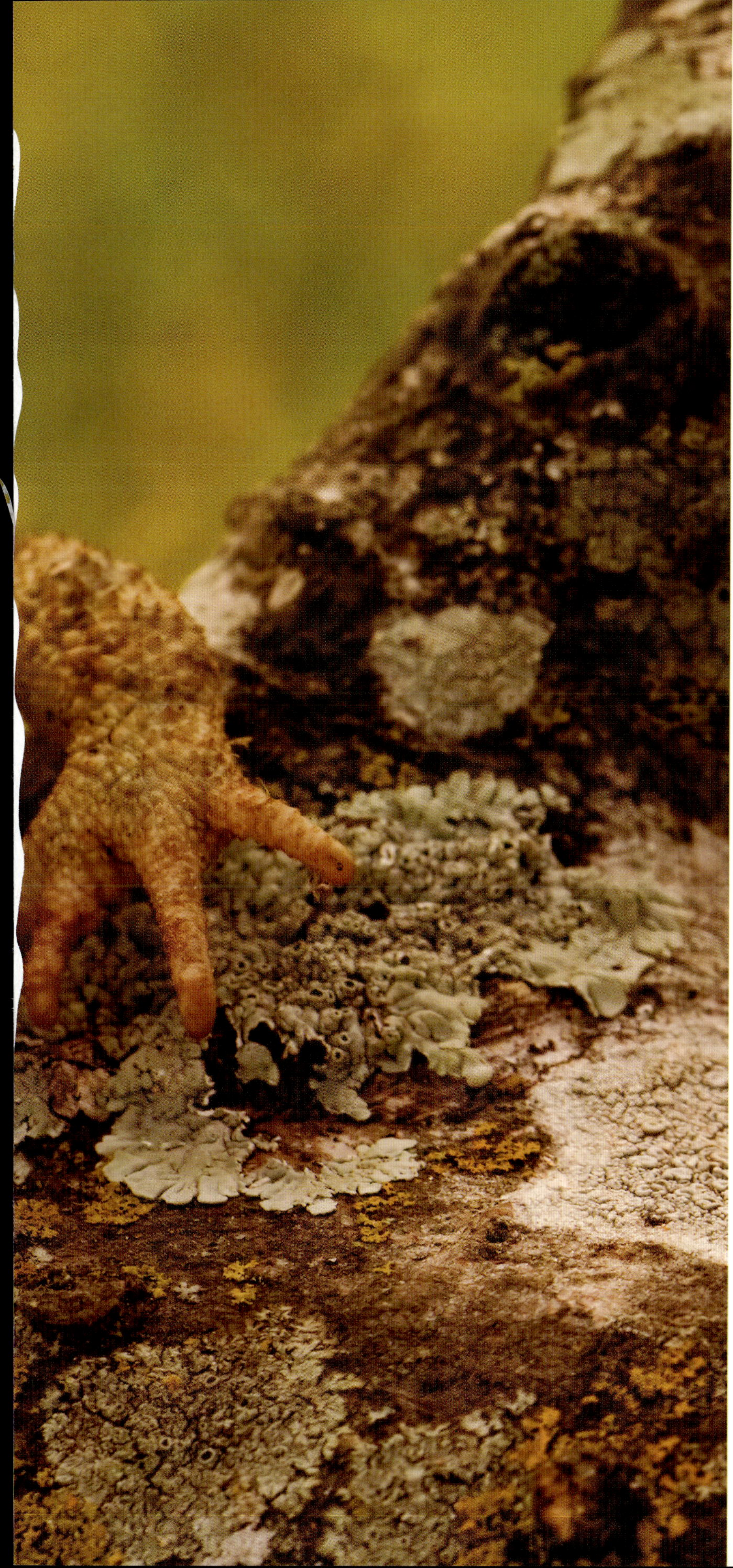

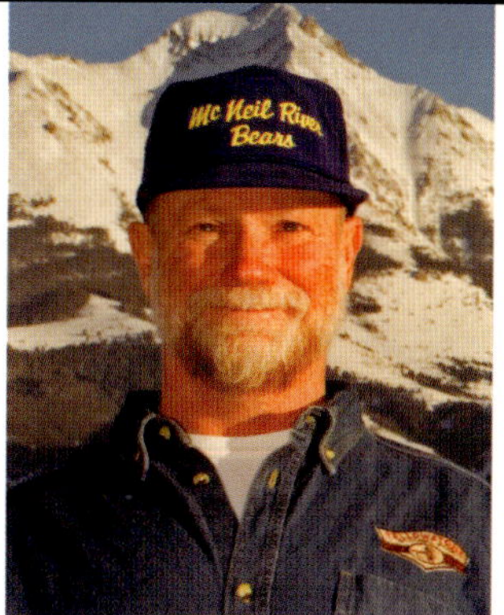

Leo Keeler

Leo Keeler's favorite moments are those in which nature's uniqueness unfolds while he's there to see it. It's those snatches of time when the nuances of nature expose themselves that make it especially magical to him.

One of his favorite Pro-Tour shots happened under the auspices of such magic. The image features a Bold Jumping Spider feeding on a Honeybee. As usual, there's more to the photograph than meets the eye, beginning with the synchronic fact that the spider, the bee, and Leo all happened to be in the same frame of time together.

"I have an eye to capture unique moments," Leo admits, "And, it was a unique moment, one where happenstance and circumstances came together."

It's moments like these, he says, that sometimes "cause me to stop thinking photography and get into the moment versus simply focusing on the process of capturing the image." He says that, even after over 40 years in photography, he still has moments like that. "And, I hope I never stop having them."

A Founding Fellow of the International League of Conservation Photographers, Leo explains how important it is to him to help others see nature differently. "One of the things I've enjoyed with photography is taking people out and getting them to see rather than look."

As part of helping others see better, Leo's approach to the contest was to "document the variety of species on the land and do that in a way that was appealing." He believes he helped the folks at Knolle Farm, "understand how to improve a visitors or photographer's experience while on their property."

The photographer grew up in Southeast Arizona and says he's had a love of the natural world as long as he can recall.

One part of that world that's always fascinated Leo is predation. He says the interest stems, in part, from a desire to "take a closer look at the way things have evolved. I guess I just like to explore how things have changed, including how man's influence plays a part. Man can be benign or destructive."

Emigrant, MT
[e] info@akwildlife.com
www.akwildlife.com

Keeler | Gulf Coast Toad

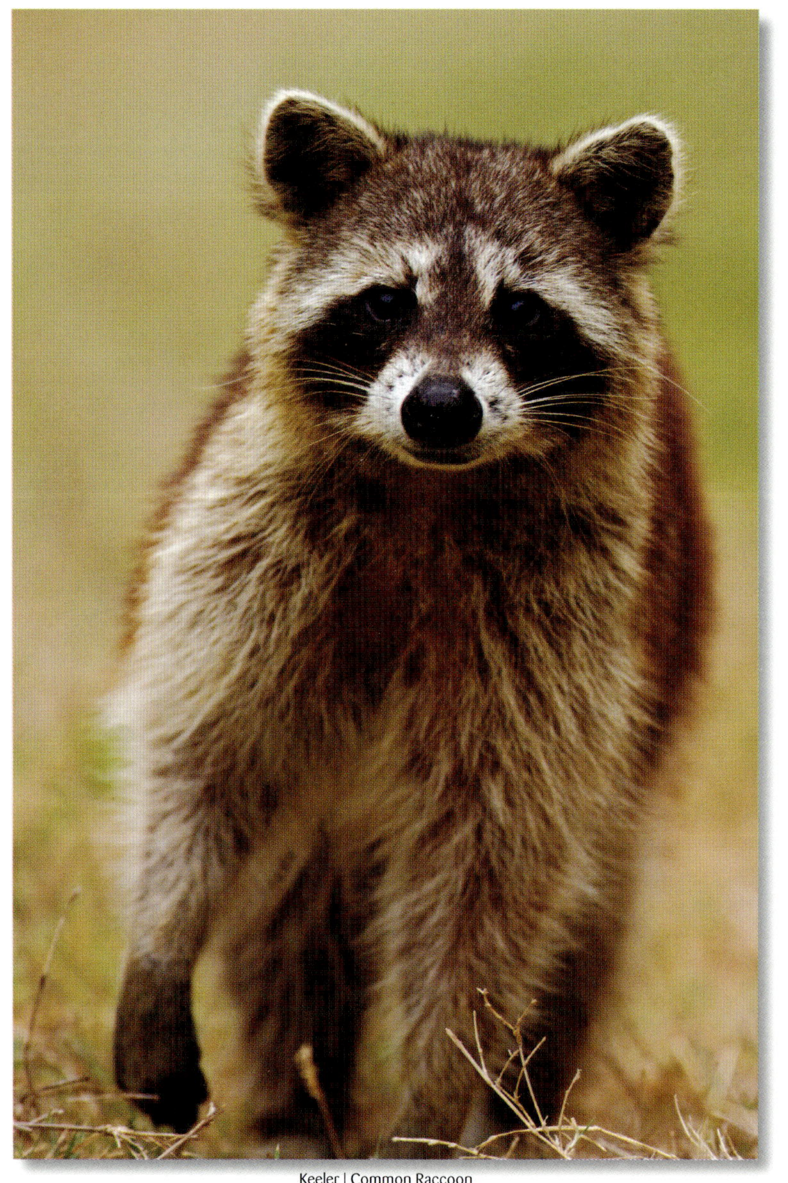

Keeler | Common Raccoon

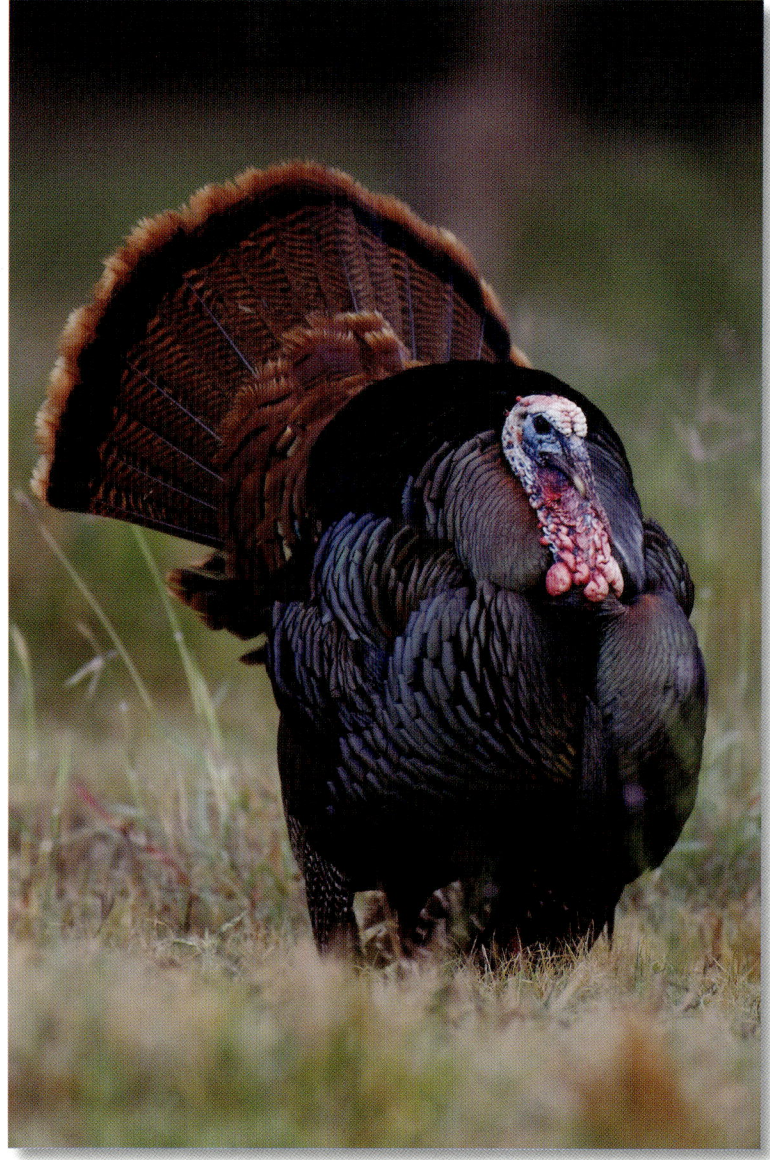

Keeler | Wild Turkey

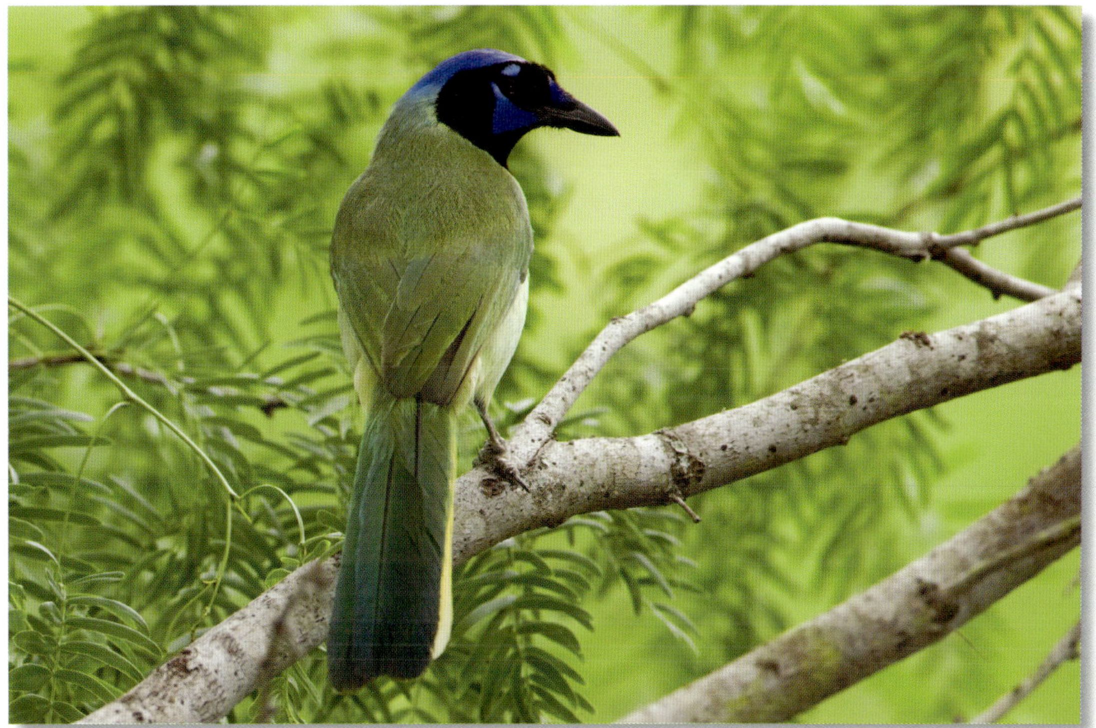

Keeler | Green Jay in Mesquite

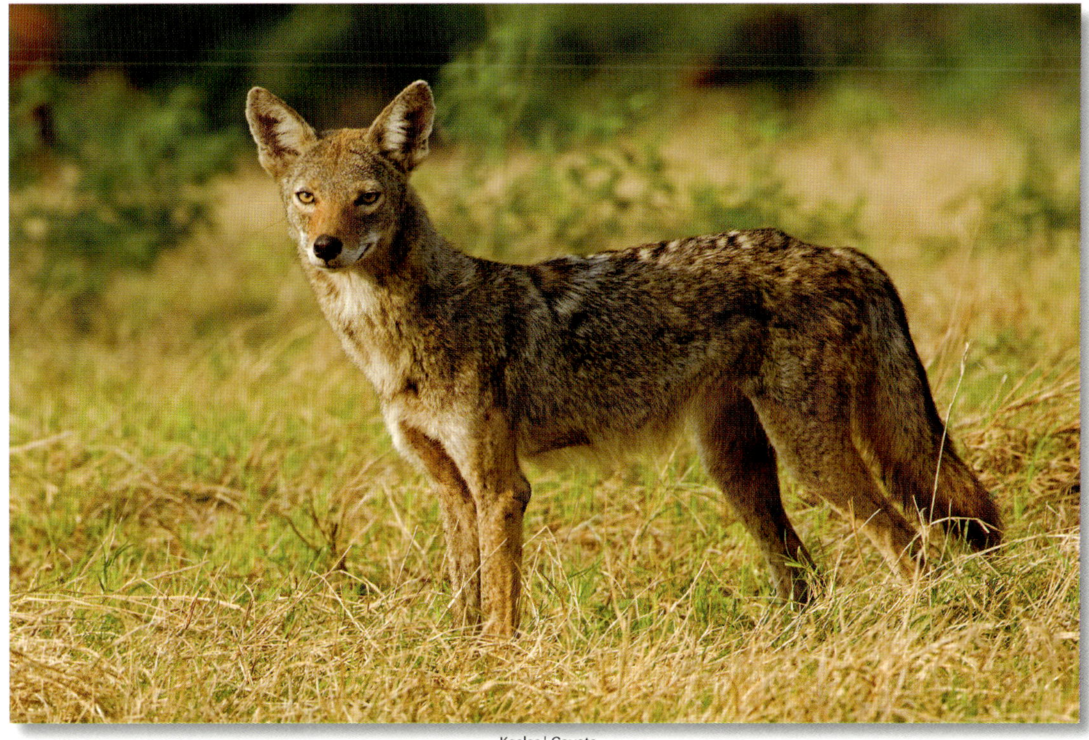

Keeler | Coyote

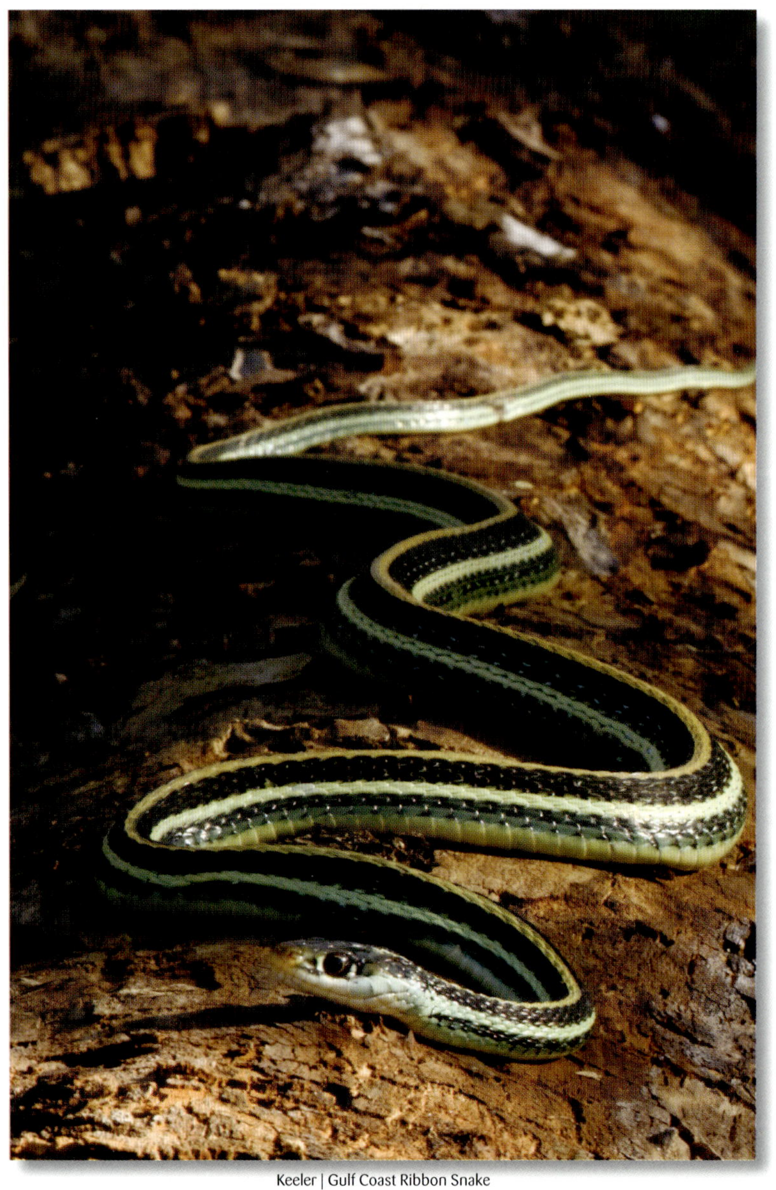

Keeler | Gulf Coast Ribbon Snake

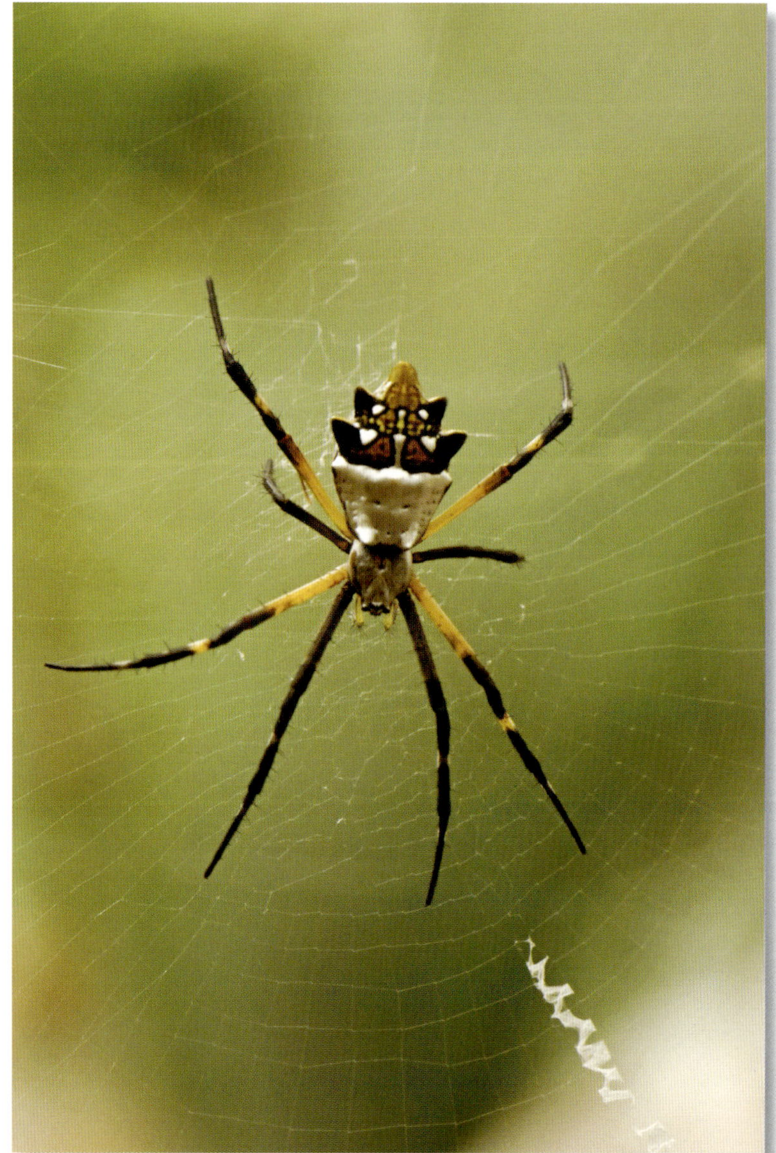

Keeler | Silver Garden Spider

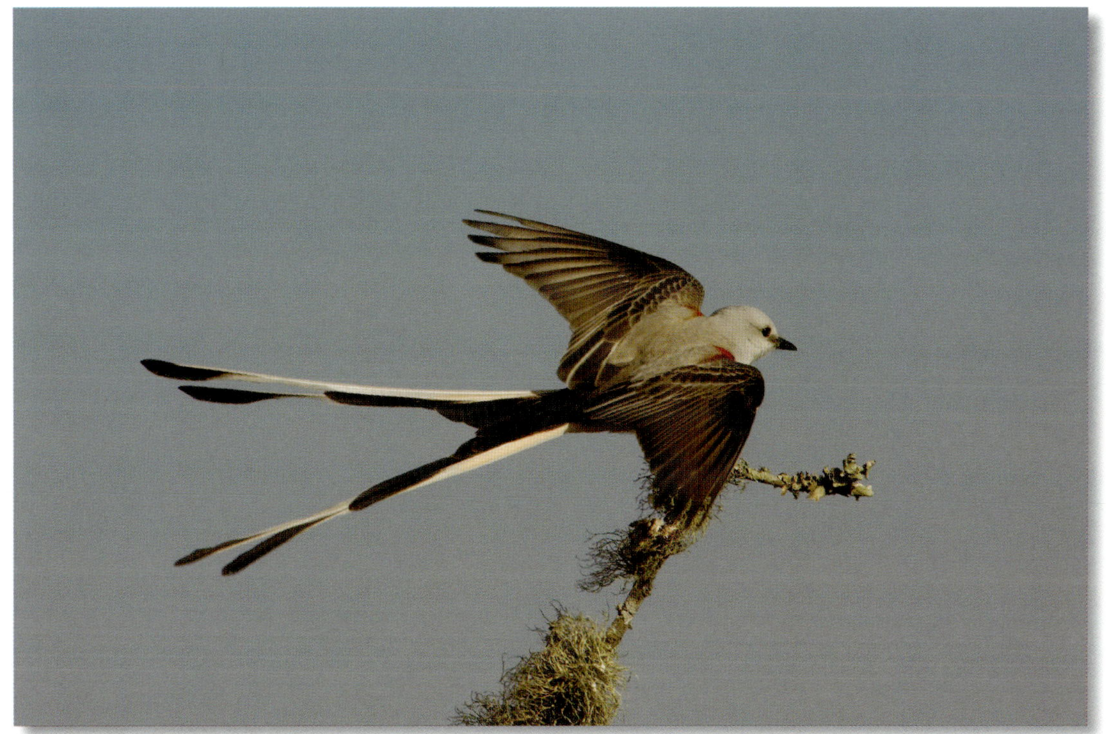

Keeler | Scissor-tailed Flycatcher

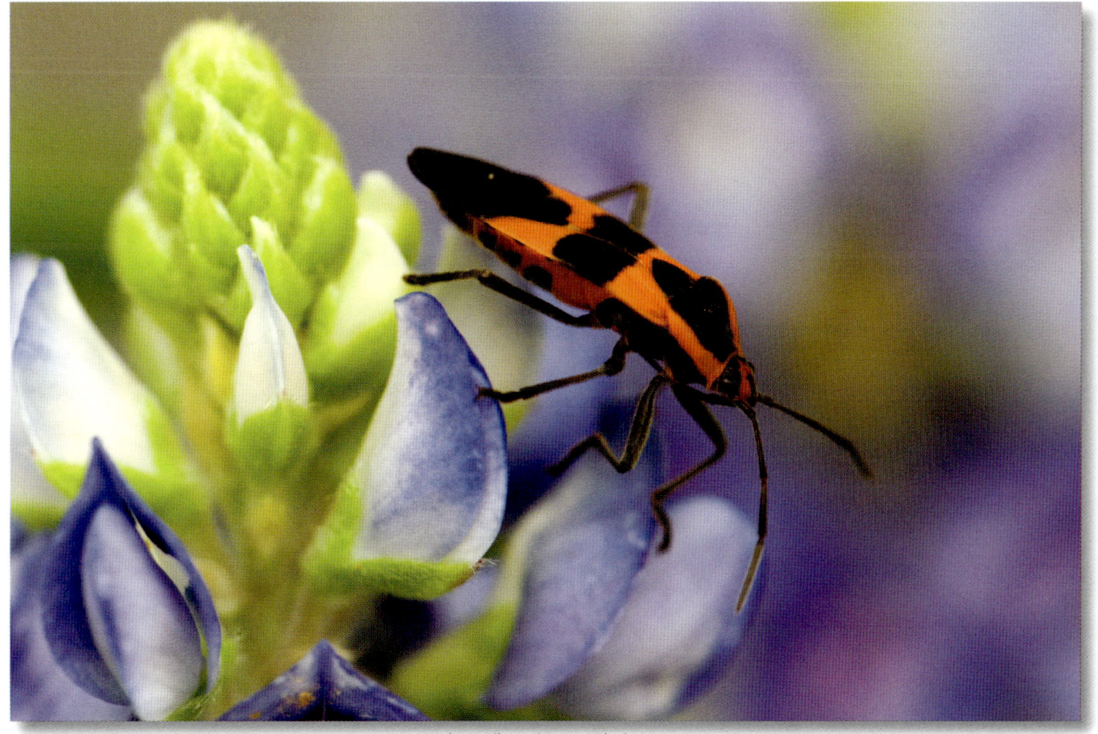

Keeler | Milkweed Bug on Bluebonnet

About La Campana Ranch...

Hamrick

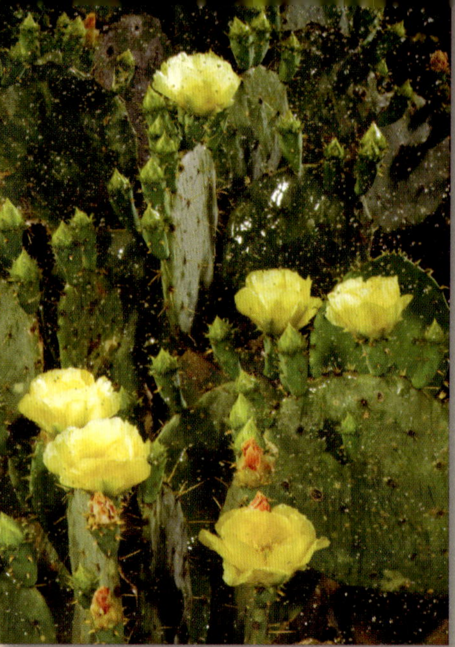
Hamrick | Lindheimer Prickly Pear

Rolling hills dotted by South Texas Mesquite are the first things you see upon approaching La Campana Ranch. The ranch stretches across McMullen, Duval and Live Oak counties and represents classic South Texas brush land. The ranch's northwest corner features a local landmark known as La Chusa Hill. To the north is Devil's Water Hole, which actually is a seep included in the writings of author J. Frank Dobie.

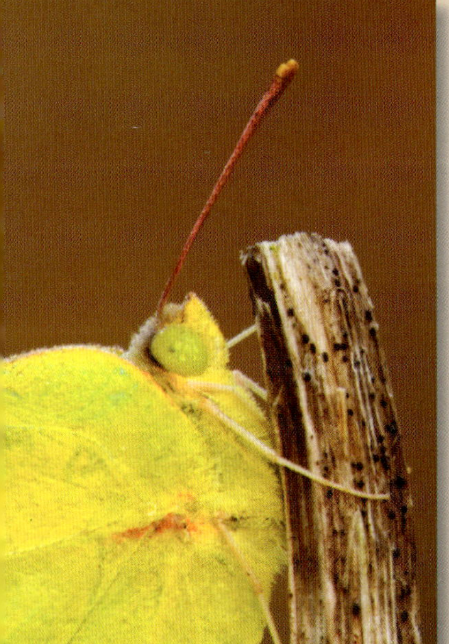
Hamrick | Sulphur Butterfly

Four generations of the Martin family have worked on La Campana Ranch. The second, third and fourth are proud to still call it their home. On January 9, 1875, title to the property that would become La Campana Ranch was transferred by land scrip from the State of Texas as payment for "opening and cleaning out a channel in the Sabine River." It then was sold a week later for 12 cents an acre to William Rogers of Corpus Christi. In the early 1900s, land speculators from Houston, playing off the fertile farming operations in the Taft coastal plains, purchased large tracts of land in the area. They intended to subdivide the land into smaller farm tracts. Prospective buyers were told that the land was ripe for raising large cotton and citrus crops.

As a young boy in the early 1900s, Jeff Martin, the patriarch of the family's ranching heritage, worked for Mr. Jim Dobie on the Dobie Ranch in La Salle and McMullen counties. He was too young for much of the ranch work, so he became a frequent companion of Mr. Dobie on trips to San Antonio. While in San Antonio, Martin would run errands for Mr. Dobie and could frequently be found assisting at Mr. Dobie's regular poker games with the local bankers. As Martin got older and the cattle business collapsed, farmers realized their newly acquired land was not the rich agricultural land they had been promised. Martin reconnected with the bankers of his youth and began the process of purchasing the ranch. As a result, the Martin family has been stewards of the land for more than 70 years. During those years, they have continued acquiring contiguous tracts to create the La Campana of today.

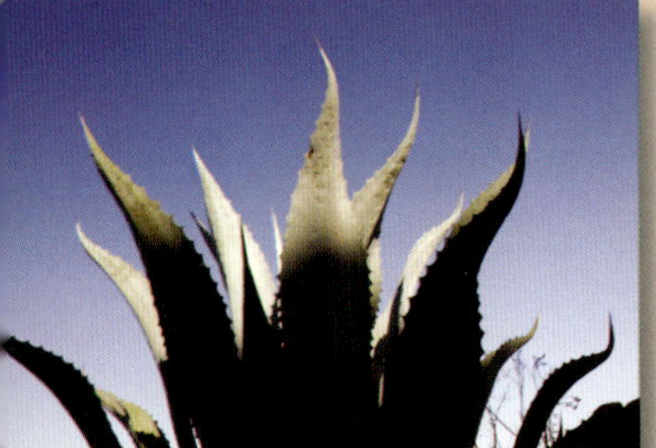
Hamrick | Agave

The ranch house and headquarters, like the ranch itself, has undergone many changes. It has seen 12 renovations and additions over the years. Most recently the family added a stucco chapel, which houses the original family Bible. The chapel is a site of peace and respite for the Martin family and ranch employees. La Campana means bell in Spanish. The origin of this name is steeped in Texas lore, which states that when the land belonged to William Rogers a bell was found on the property. Rogers initially named his ranch the Rogers Ranch, but upon discovery of the bell he renamed it La Campana. The bell supposedly was moved to a large cathedral in Corpus Christi and was lost in the hurricane of 1919. The Martin's chapel features a bell in the tower, a modern symbol of the land's rich history.

In those early years, Rogers operated the ranch primarily as a sheep and goat farm. However, this use soon gave way to the raising of cattle. Today the Martin family owns a small herd of purebred Santa Gertrudis cattle and still maintains a commercial Santa Gertrudis cattle operation. But you can't have South Texas brush without a little hunting. So the family also maintains a hunting operation on a part of the ranch.

"The land is our life and our future is the ranch," Tom Martin said. "If a person loves the land he is committed to its conservation, it's a way of life. You will always do what is necessary to enhance your life's blood. Having control over a relatively large piece of land is like being in charge of a small third-world country. There are lots of struggles, but also many opportunities. It's a cornucopia of possibilities."

Through the support of Alan Turner, the Martins chose to participate in the 2008 Pro-Tour. Alan convinced them that in addition to being another potential opportunity to generate income, the photo contest is a way to showcase nature on the ranch. Through the Pro-Tour, the Martins have come to feel more in touch with and knowledgeable about some of the more overlooked inhabitants of their ranch. Tom's wish is that the land would remain the same for many generations, only wetter.

Tom Martin Family & Alan Turner
George West, TX
[e] campana@granderiver.net

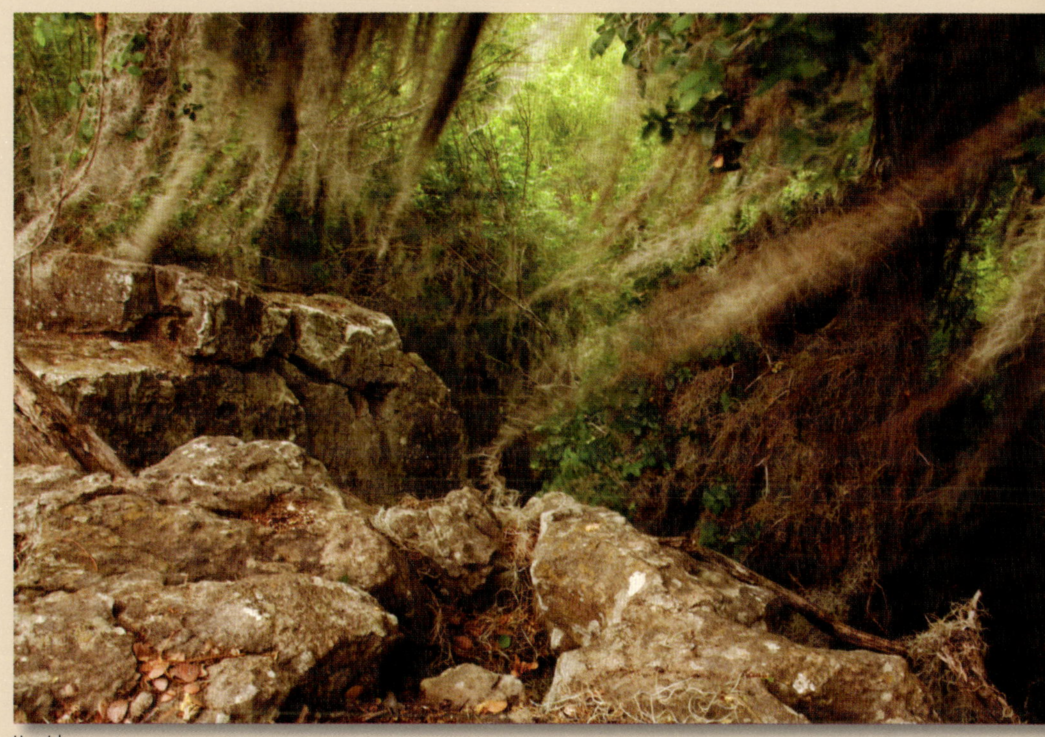
Hamrick

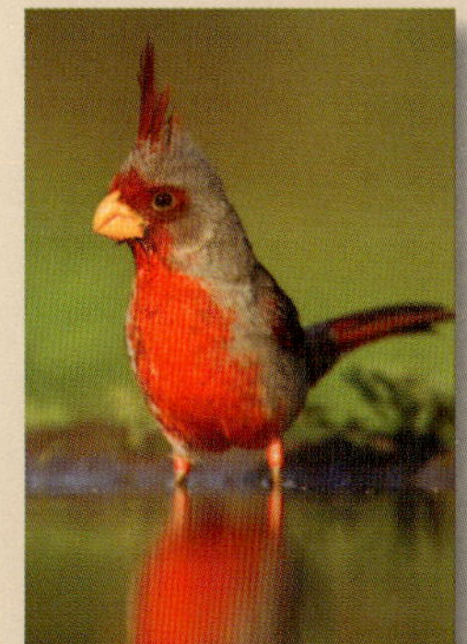
Hamrick | Pyrrhuloxia

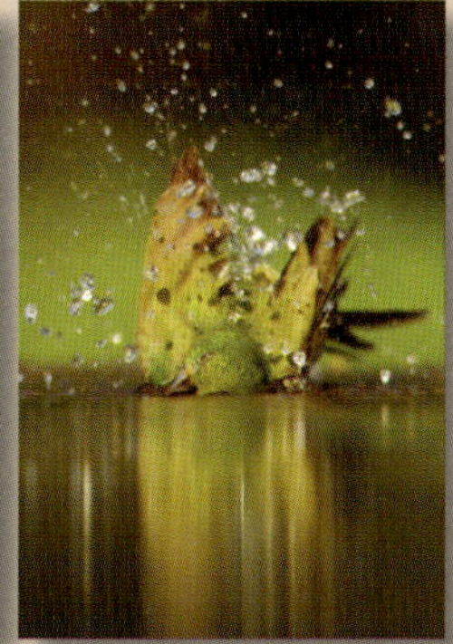
Hamrick | Painted Bunting (female)

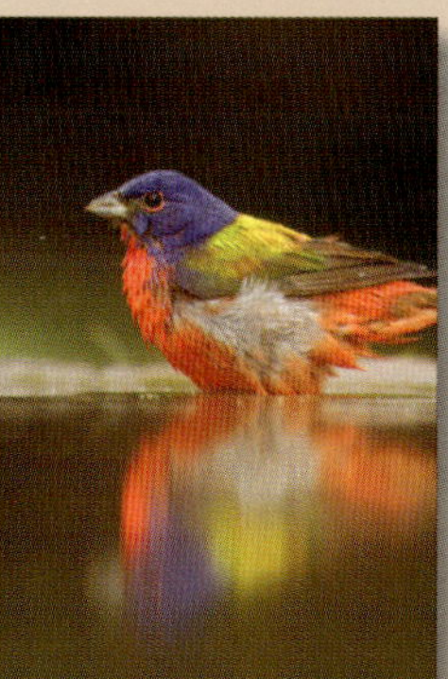
Hamrick | Painted Bunting

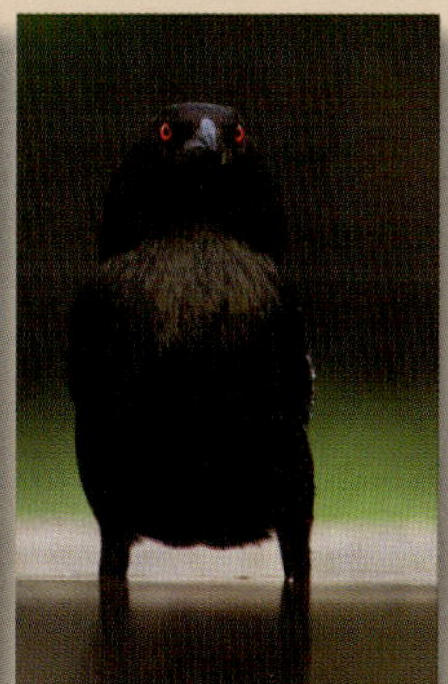
Hamrick | Bronzed Cowbird

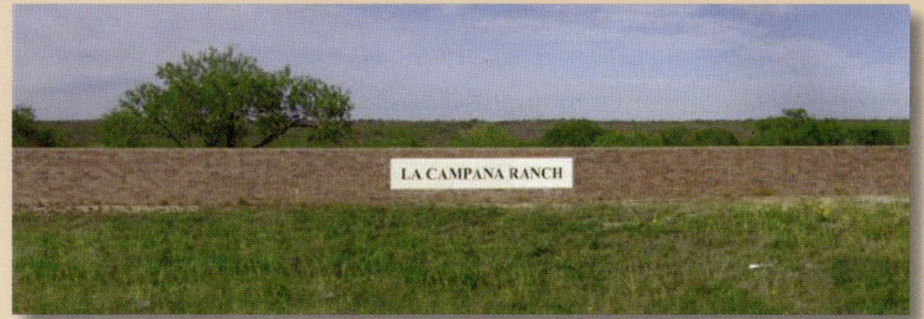

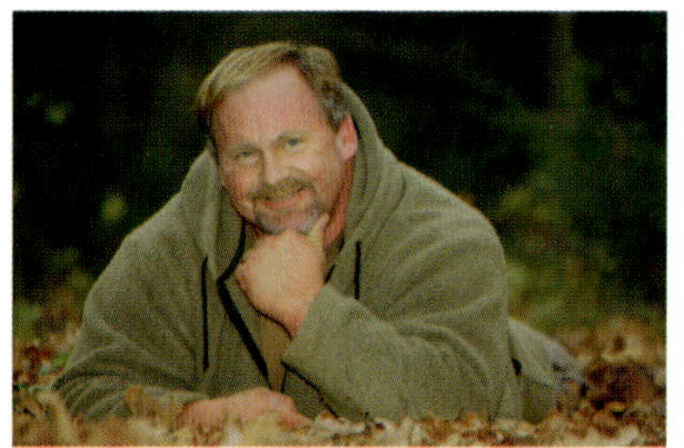

Derrick Hamrick

Intense is a word that's synonymous with Derrick Hamrick. "I'll do what I need to do to get the shot, no matter how much work or how much it costs. If I want it, I'll get it," Derrick says, but adds, "Well, usually. Nature doesn't always cooperate."

It turns out that during his month on the La Campana Ranch, nature's cooperation wasn't the issue. Instead, Derrick faced a comedy of errors that wasn't a bit funny. For starters, he spent the first two days so sick that he couldn't do a thing. About the time he got well enough to work, his brand new trolling motor in his floating blind stopped working. The coup de grâce was the fact that, after two weeks of shooting, Derrick discovered he'd been shooting in the wrong format. He admitted that after 25 years as a film photographer, he was making the switch to digital at a rather inopportune time.

"I'm old-school," he says, "Instead of taking a sloppy shot and just thinking 'I'll fix it later with Photoshop' I believe in doing what it takes to get the shot right up front." For instance, of his award-winning photo of an owl on a fence post, Derrick says, "There was a lot of work involved in getting that shot right from the start. I found a deer blind that some Barn Owls were nesting in. I kept watching them and I'd watch and wait for the mother to leave so I could start building a structure. I'd observe her flight path so I could see what direction she'd be coming from. Building my set-up was slow-going because I worked on it a little bit at a time so as not to disturb them."

While taking shots of the owls at night, Derrick was faced with yet another challenge: "All but two of my flashes had gone out and one of those wasn't working right either. I was down to the nitty-gritty on my flashes." In the end, Derrick's dogged determination, what he calls "my intensity," paid off. He got the shot of the owl and it's one he's proud of.

While his passion for photography didn't start until he had his first "little Keystone as a teenager," his passion for nature has been with him as long as he can remember. "I've always been this way about nature."

"I just believe that you have to do something you want to do. And that's what I'm out here doing."

Raleigh, NC
[e] imagesofthewild@aol.com

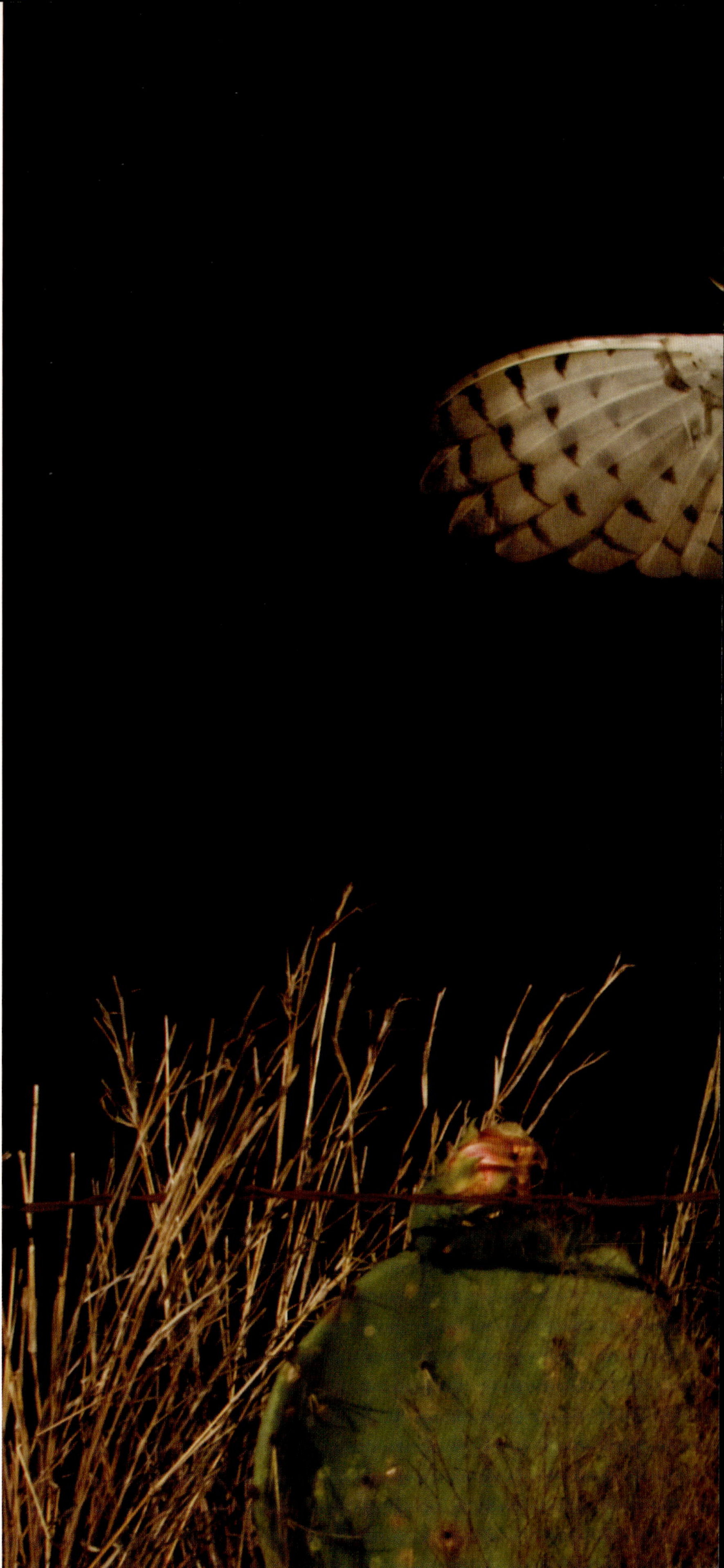

Hamrick | Barn Owl
(flying over Lindheimer Prickly Pear and Little Bluestem)

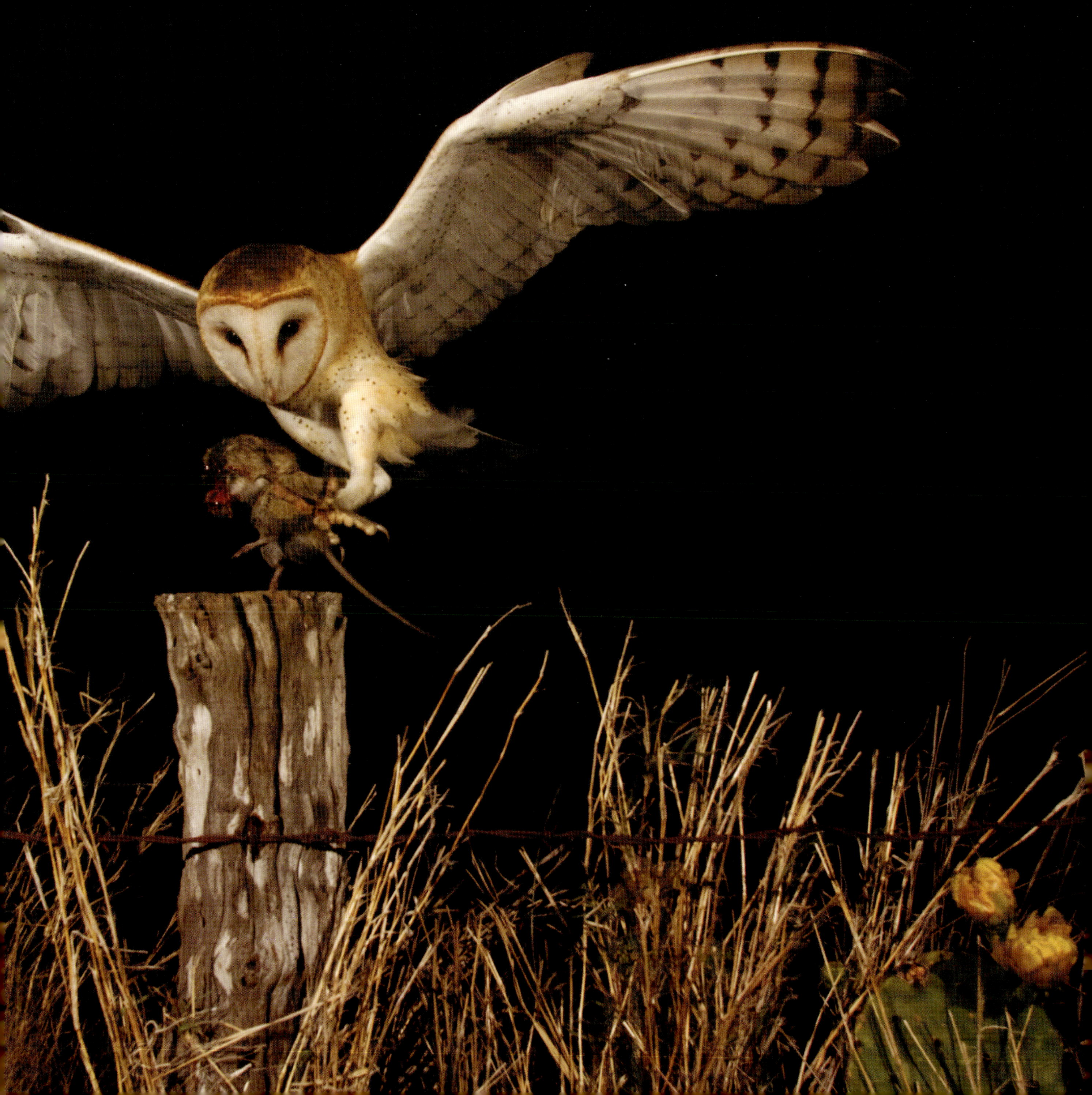

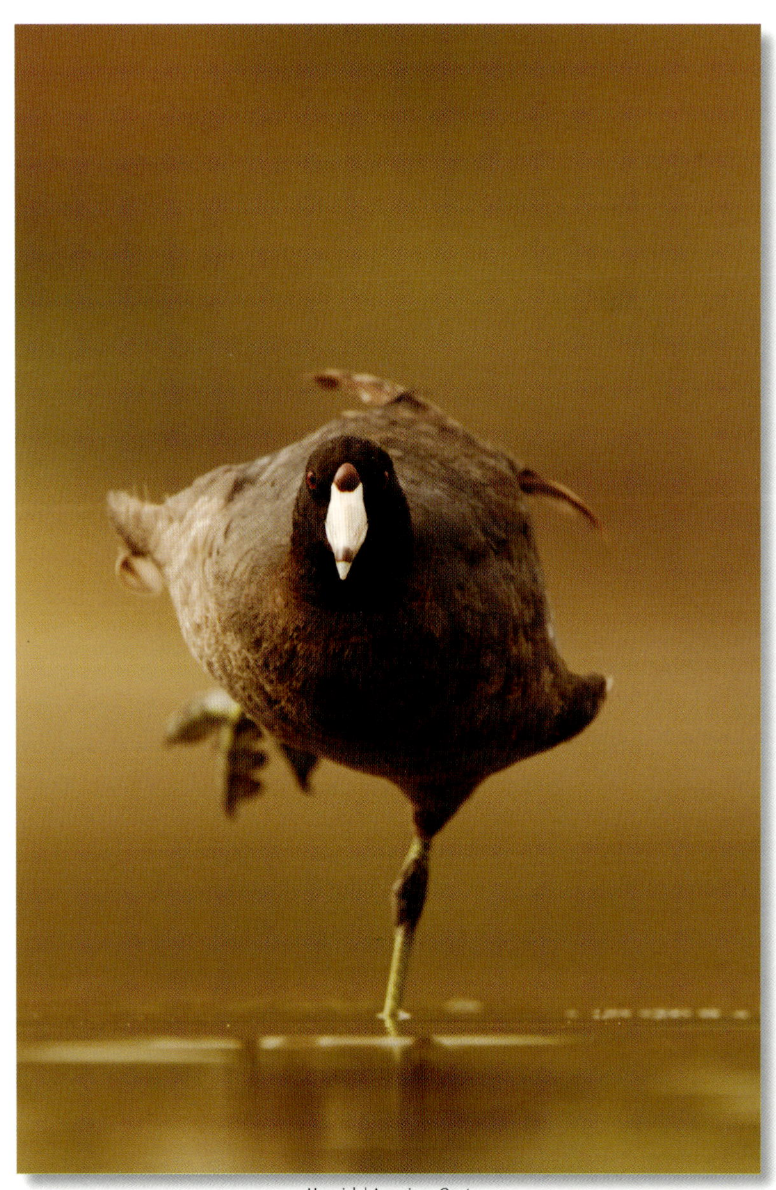

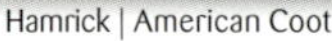
Hamrick | American Coot

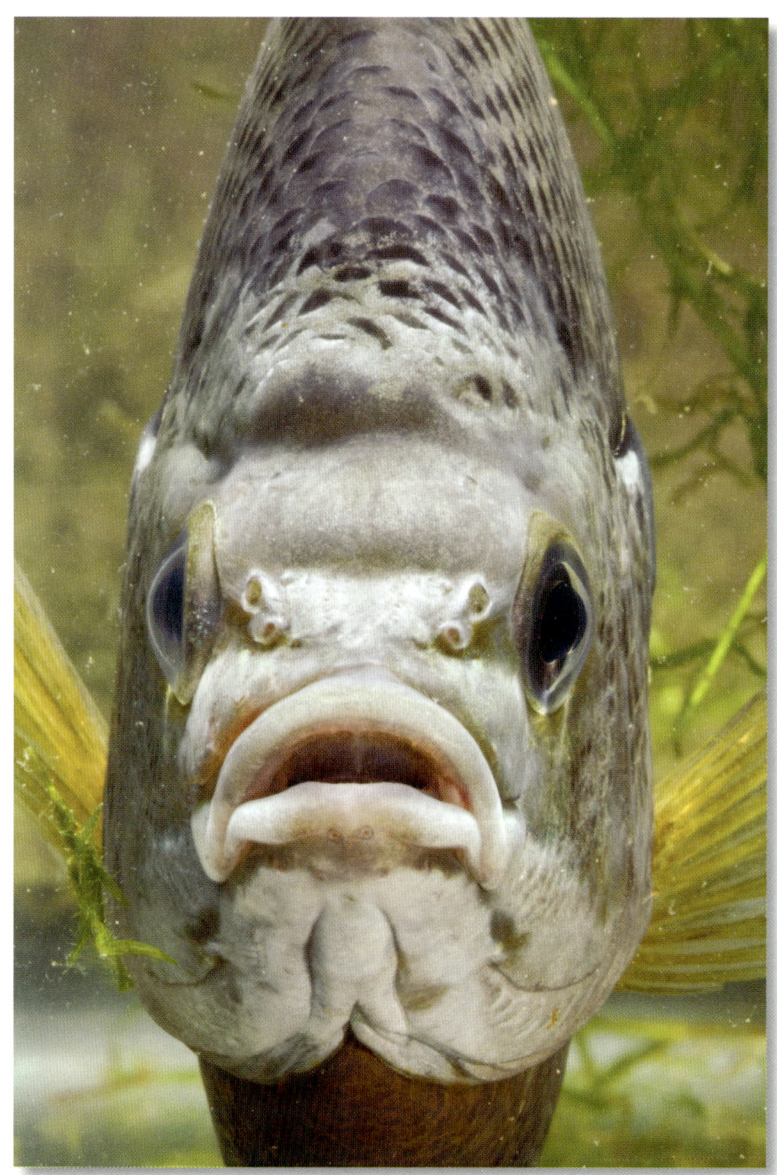
Hamrick | male Bluegill in breeding colors

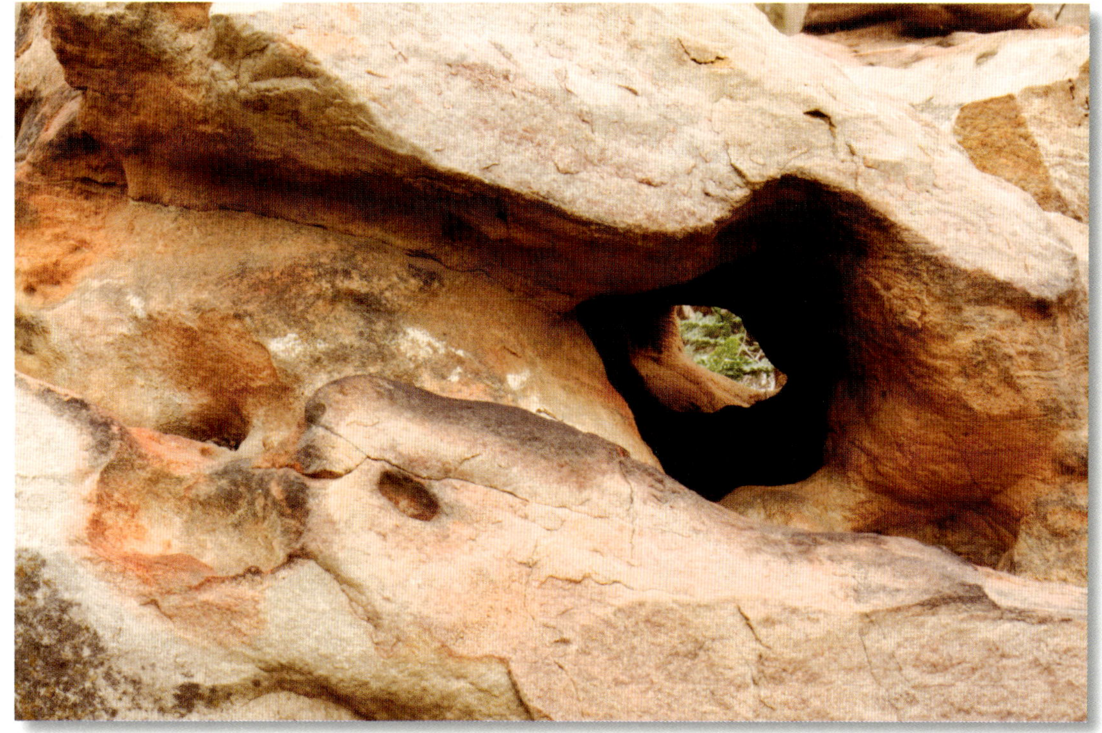

Hamrick

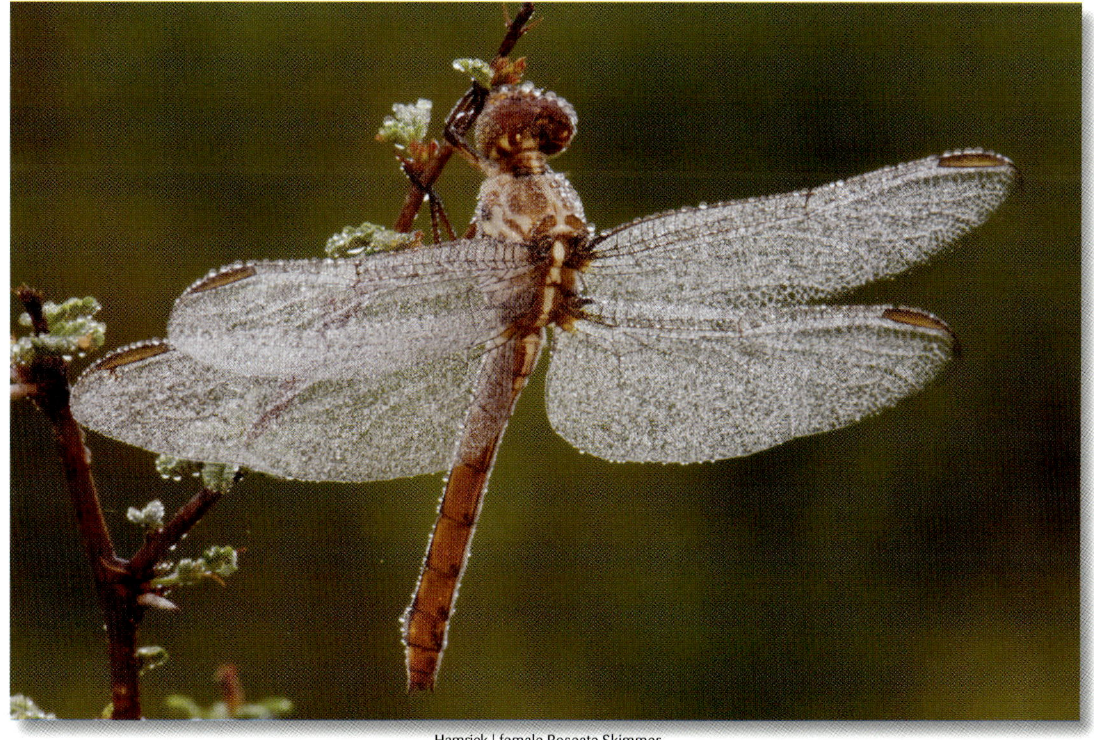

Hamrick | female Roseate Skimmer

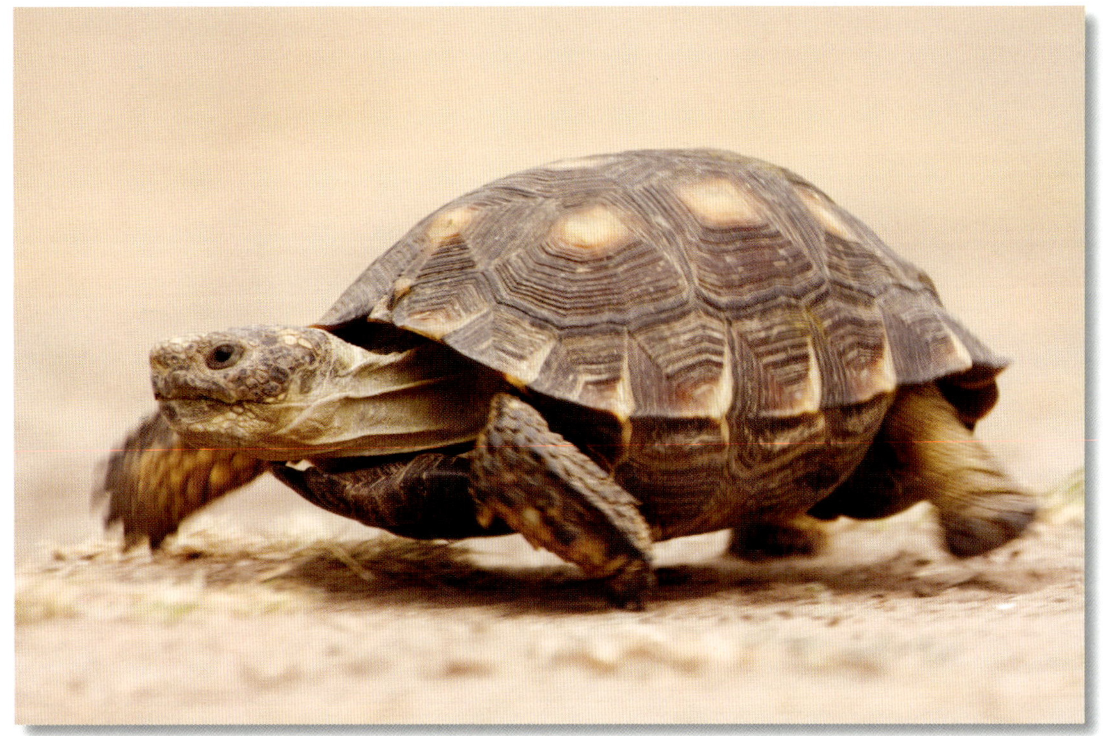

Hamrick | Texas Tortoise

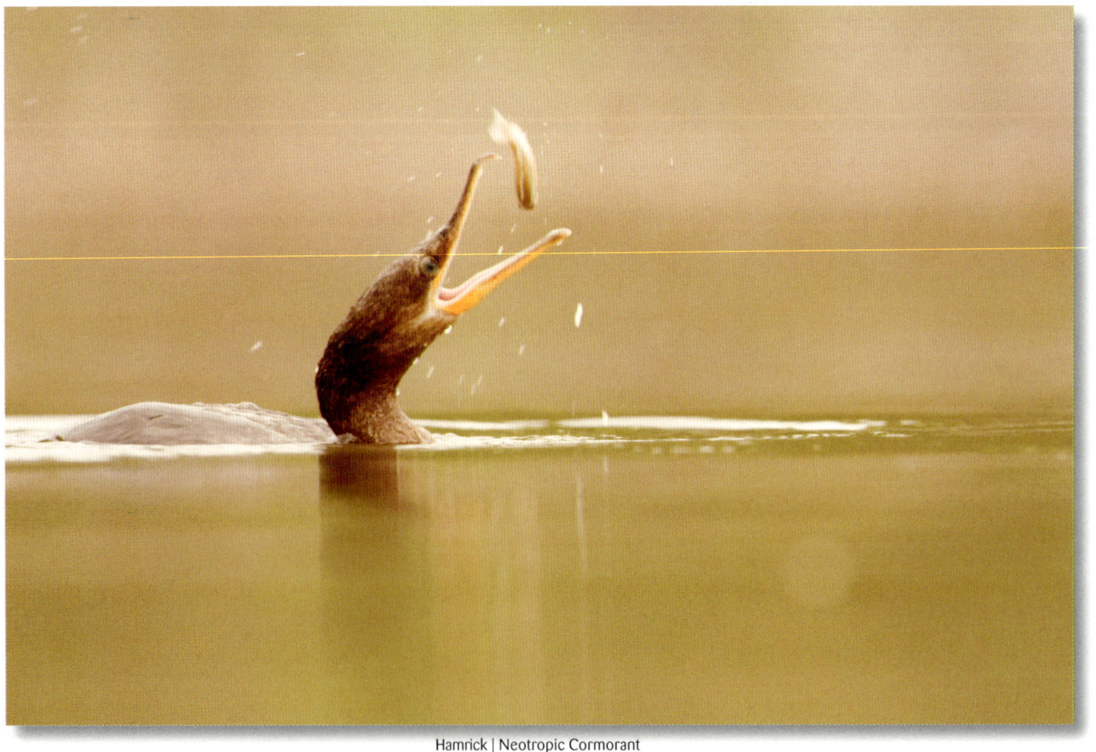

Hamrick | Neotropic Cormorant

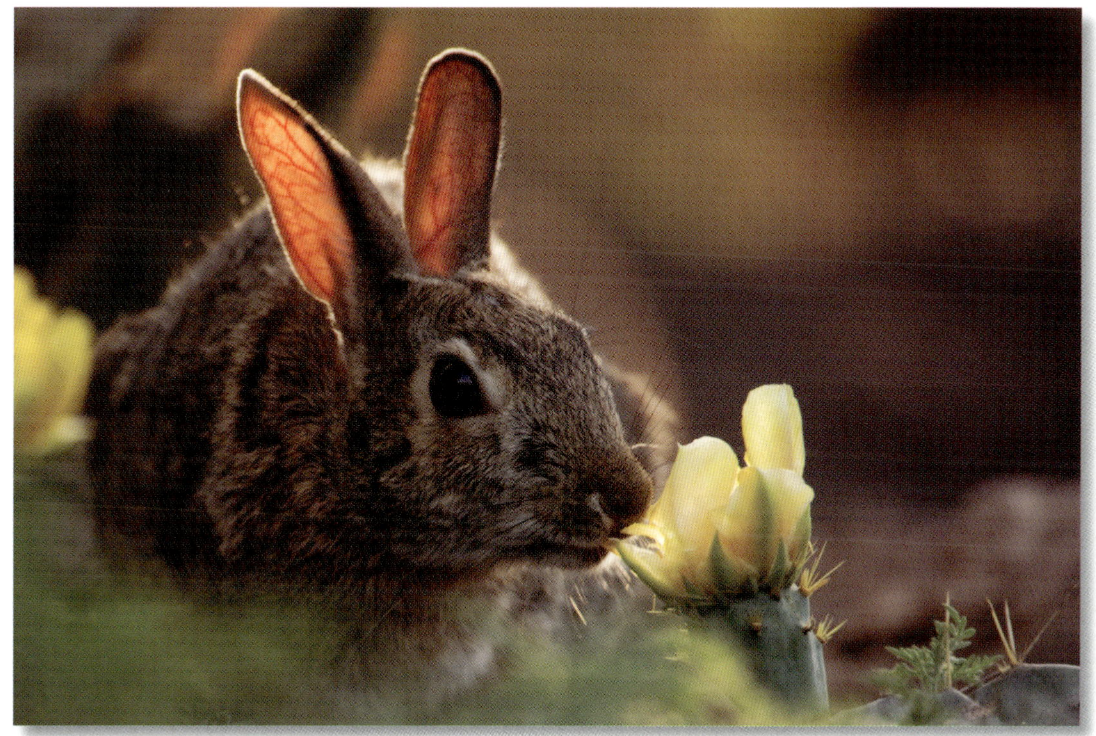

Hamrick | Eastern Cottontail Rabbit sniffing Lindheimer Prickly Pear

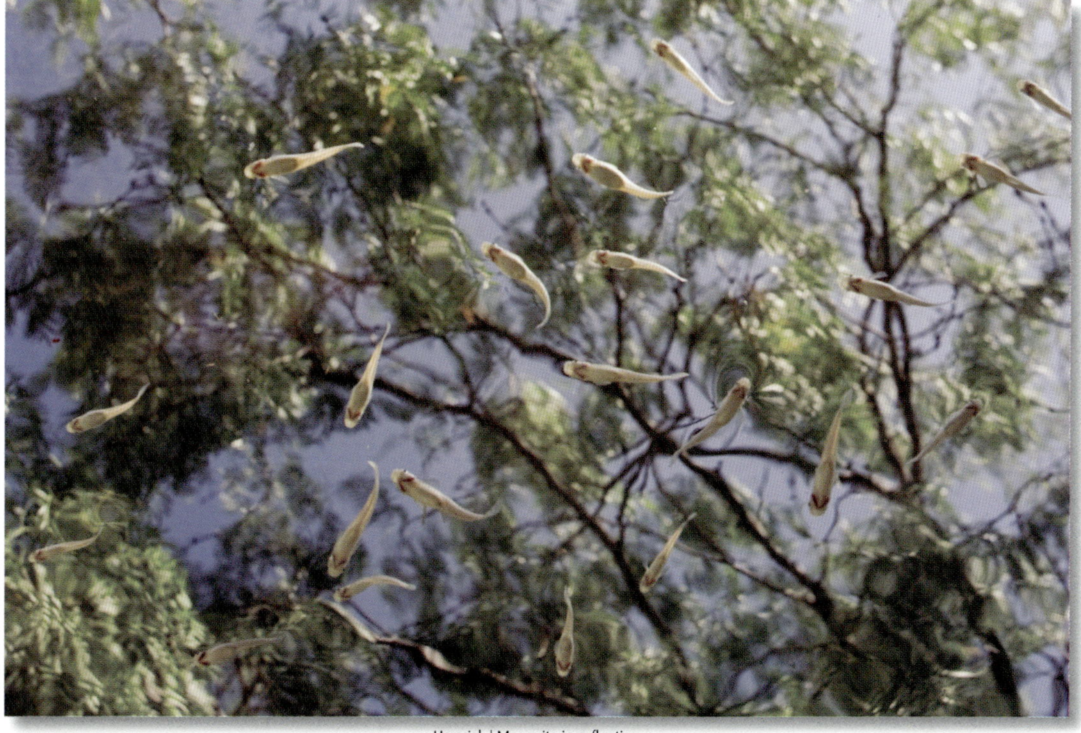

Hamrick | Mesquite in reflection

About La Ramireña Ranch...

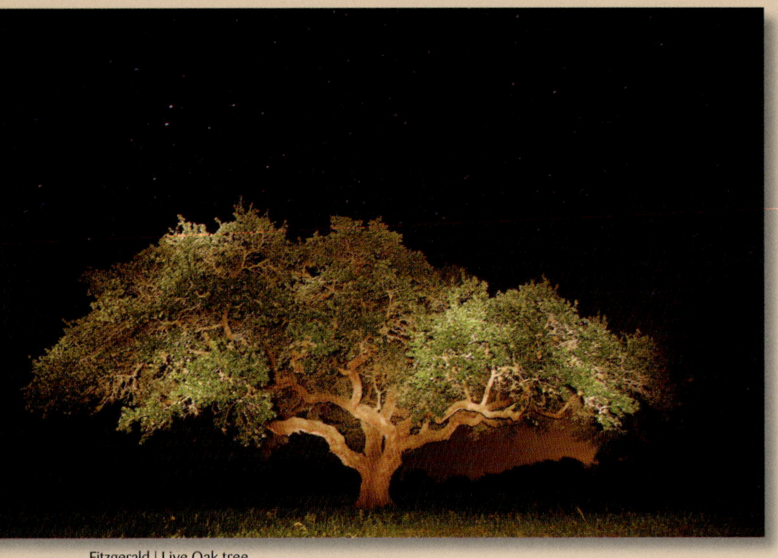

Fitzgerald | Live Oak tree

Ruggedly beautiful, La Ramireña Ranch is located in southern Live Oak County west of Lake Corpus Christi. Ramireña Creek, which meanders for two miles through the property, is a familiar landmark in many of author J. Frank Dobie's tales of Texas lore. The meaning of Ramireña is debatable, but it may be a corruption or combination of the Spanish words for "queen" and "brush." Queen of the brush seems a fitting name for the land that invites nature lovers to discover the natural wonders of this remote South Texas wilderness.

A push-button entrance at gate No. 3 off Farm-to-Market Road 534 welcomes visitors up the caliche drive to the ranch home of Patricia and Richard Phillips. Here family and friends relax in a porch swing and rocking chairs overlooking the lake and sweeping vistas in every direction.

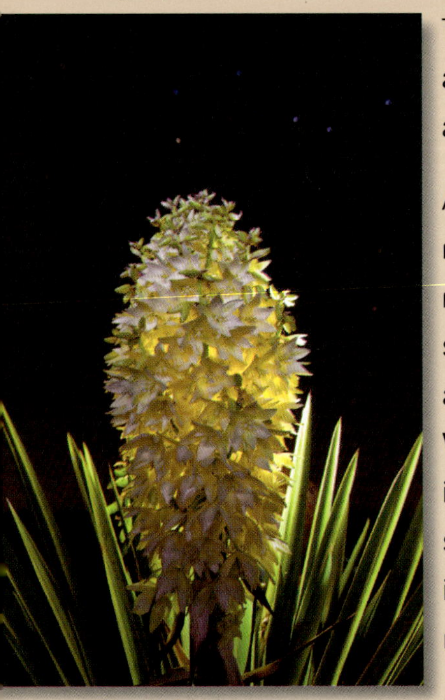

Fitzgerald | Spanish Dagger

The Phillips family acquired the ranch in 2000. Today the limited cattle operation is subordinate to resident wildlife and its natural habitat. The Phillips plant millet, redtop cane and other grains for birds and other animals. And they allow very limited harvesting of deer, turkey, quail and dove while protecting all other wildlife.

About 10 miles of all-weather roads provide access to the 1,026-acre property. A prominent caliche ridge trends north and south along the eastern portion and is shrouded in Mesquite, Cenizo, various species of acacia, mountain laurel, Prickly Pear Cactus, lantana, Spanish and Buckley yucca, huisache, Guajillo and many other shrubs and cacti native to the South Texas plains. This ridge of low brush gives way to sharp relief and rolling hills as vegetation evolves into open Live Oak savannahs, ranging 125 feet in elevation from the lowest to highest point. Willow trees, cedar elms, and large Mesquite groves grow along the creek, providing habitat for a variety of wildlife in this transitional riparian forest. Wild Turkey, White-tailed Deer, Bobcats, raccoons, snakes of all descriptions, sizes and dispositions, Horned Lizards, turtles, alligators, Javelina, Coyotes and cottontails frequently are spotted in this rugged terrain. Visitors and family occasionally spot a Mountain Lion, adding a rare treat to the list of wild residents whose territory includes La Ramireña Ranch.

More than 60 species of birds have been recorded on the ranch. The most common resident birds include roadrunners, Crested Caracara, hawks, Wild Turkey, Cactus Wrens, Painted and Indigo Buntings, bobwhite quail, cardinals, Green Jays, five varieties of dove, herons, egrets, kingfishers, mottled ducks, and Black-Bellied Whistling Ducks. Migratory birds include a variety of humming birds, hawks, ducks, Sandhill Cranes, geese, wood storks,

Scissor-tailed and Vermilion Flycatchers, making La Ramireña an ideal place for year round bird-watching.

The ranch has several water features available for its abundant wildlife. In addition to Ramireña Creek and its seasonal gully washers, the ranch has four tanks supplemented by wells and windmills. The jewel in the lacy Mesquite crown is an artesian well that has poured a gallon of water per minute into a nearby pond since it was drilled in 1984.

The Phillips family has enjoyed being involved in the semi-annual Coastal Bend Wildlife Photo Contest. During the ICF Pro-Tour of Nature Photography, they were honored to have award-winning nature photographer Sean Fitzgerald setting up blinds and working diligently to capture the magic of wildlife moments on the ranch. It is the Phillips' sincere wish that through the extraordinary images selected from these photo competitions, naturalists will be inspired to discover La Ramireña Ranch for themselves. The ranch offers visitors a comfortable bunk house that sleeps four, photo blinds and vehicles for ranch transportation. Outdoor grilling on the poolside patio provides a rewarding end to a day of hiking, birding or fishing in the catch and release bass pond. After the sun sinks into the distant horizon, the night sky becomes alive with stars allowing primal senses to stir like the brilliant Milky Way, reminding observers what is most important in this vanishing landscape.

Richard Phillips
Dinero, TX
[e] rpsanpat@intcomm.net

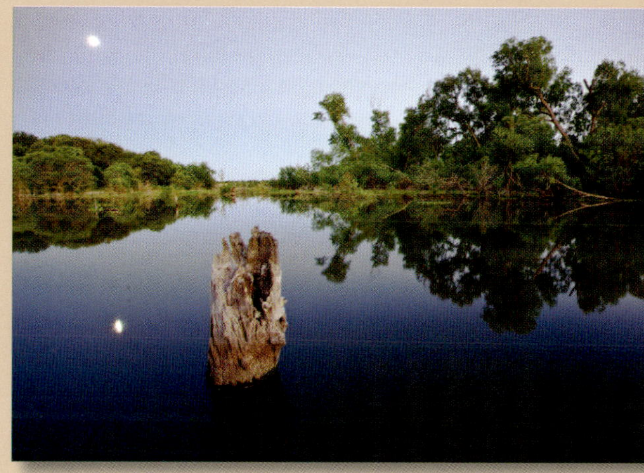

Fitzgerald

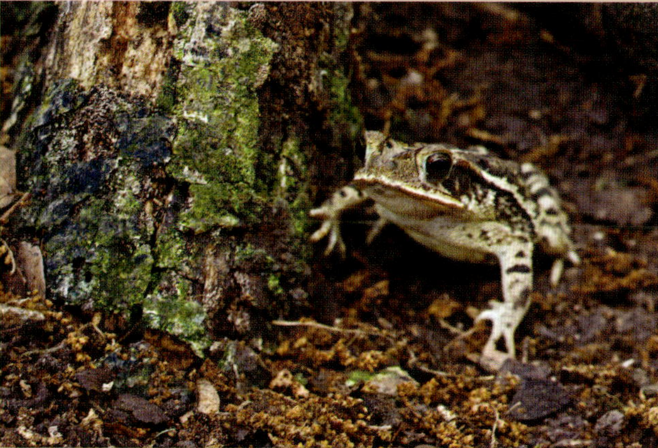

Fitzgerald | Gulf Coast Toad

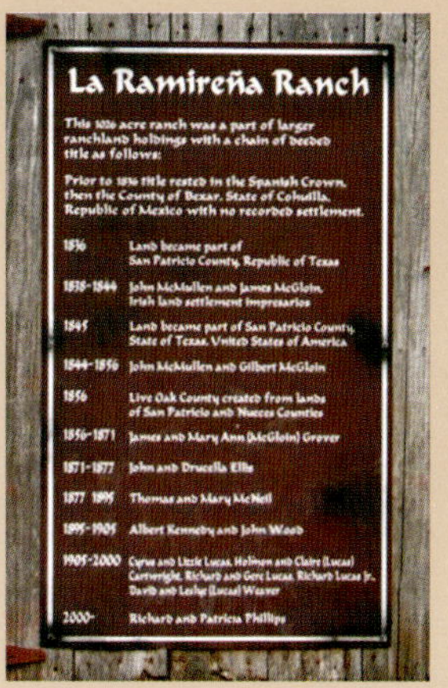

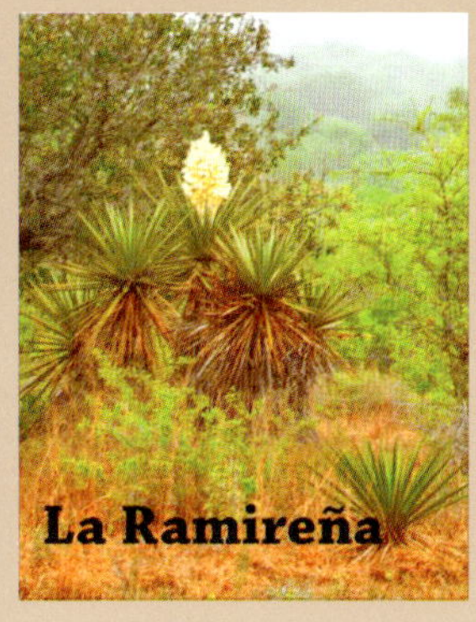

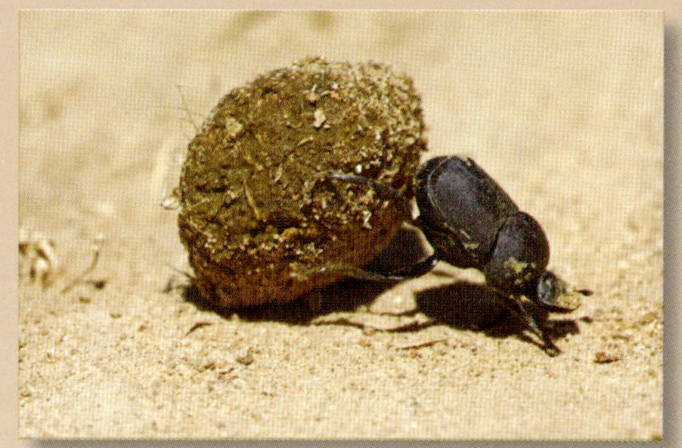

Fitzgerald | Dung Beetle

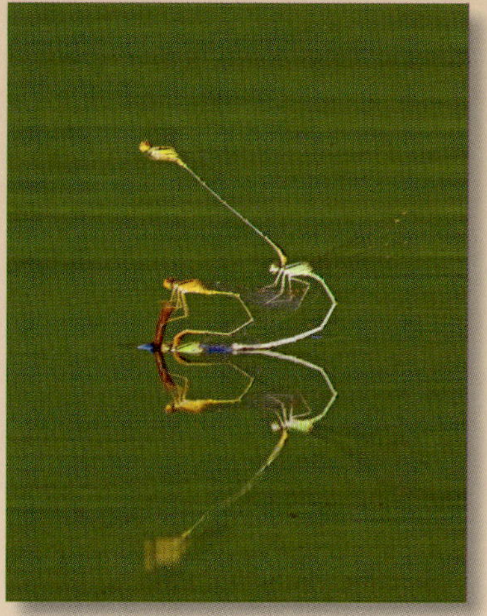

Fitzgerald | Orange Bluet

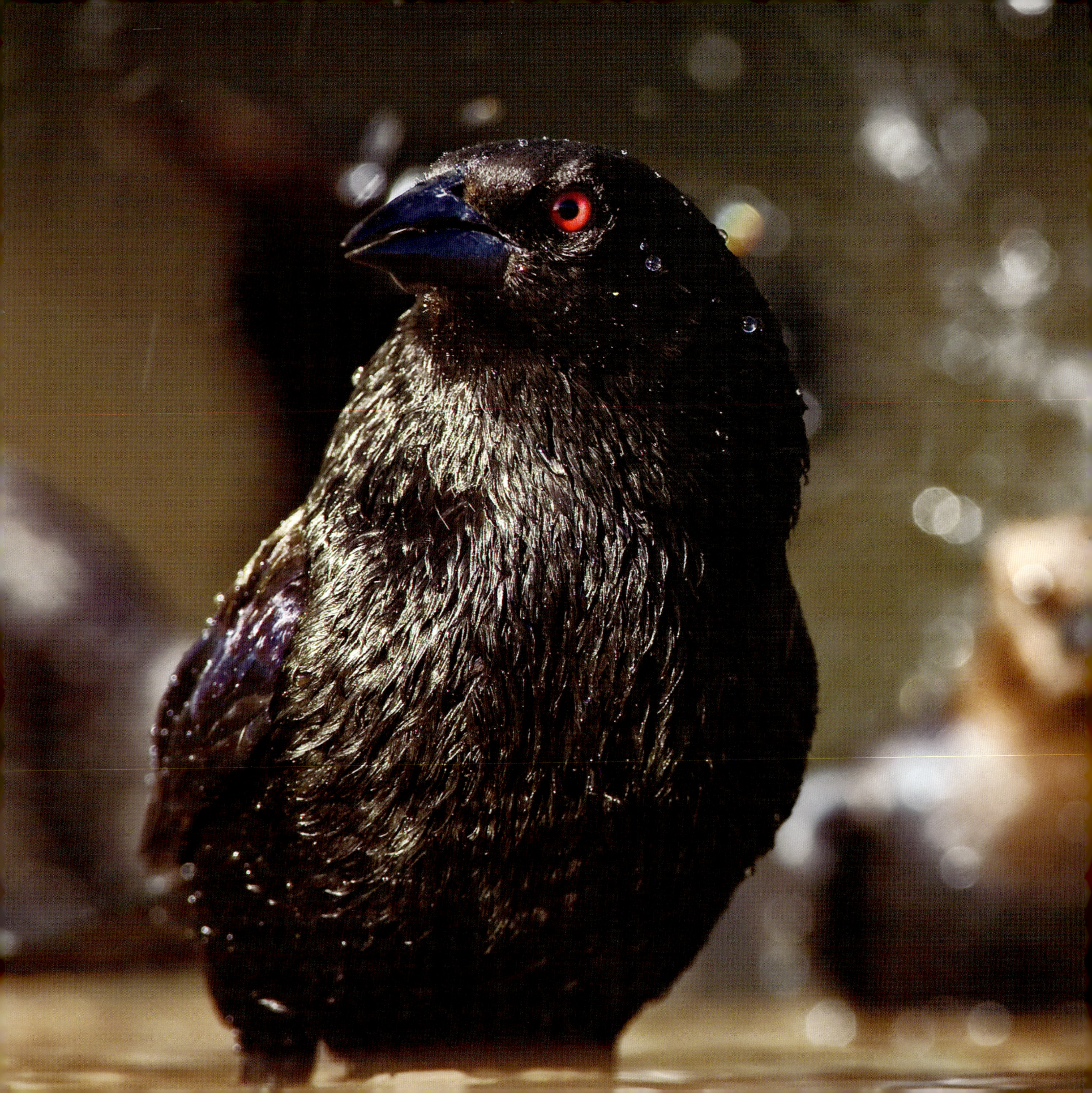

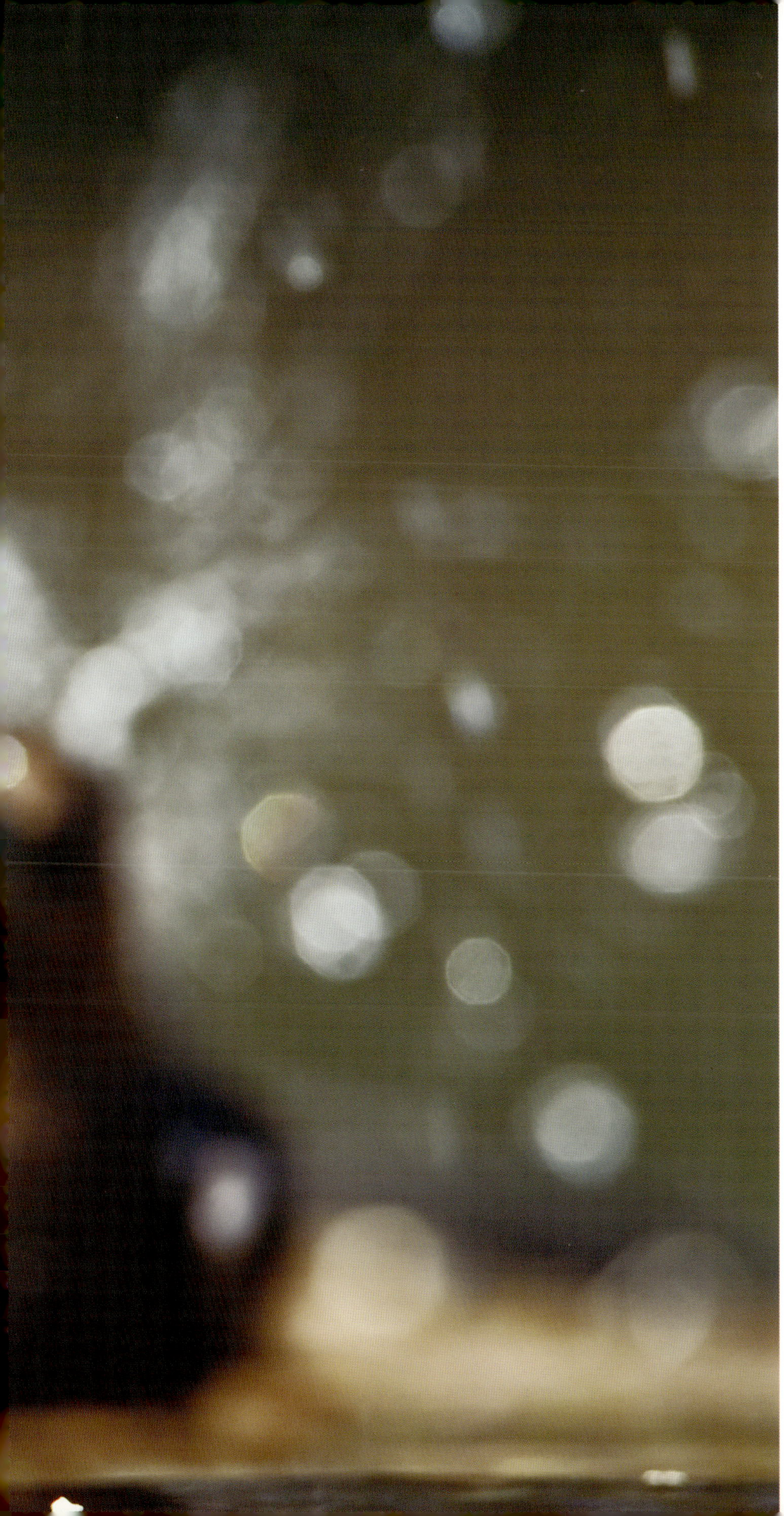

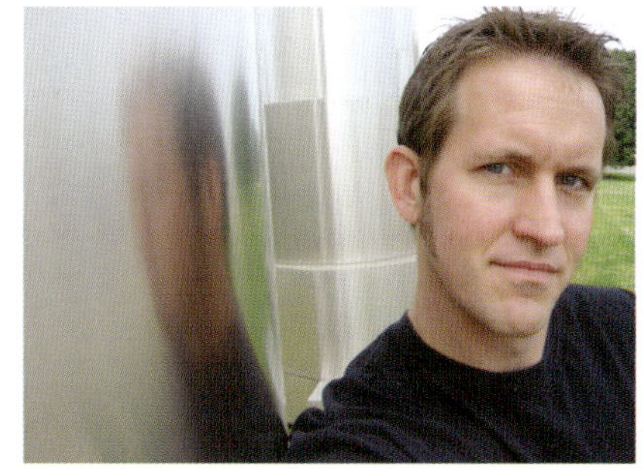

Sean Fitzgerald

To Sean it's simple: his photography is his art. A surprise, perhaps, even to himself since, he confesses, "I didn't have any exposure growing up. I had only blue collar experiences."

For many photographers the approach is more technical, but for Sean it truly is all about the creating. "I come at it emotionally."

He says that five years ago he would have said his favorite influences were impressionists, but, as he's changed, that too has changed. These days, "I prefer the work of the realists, the type who push the bounds, who are pushing around the edges."

For him, his work in nature photography encompasses "more the abstract, the emotional. What feeling do I get when I see this animal? I look for images that show something more. Images that tap into what, in my mind, I see in the essence of that animal or that living thing."

One of his Pro-Tour images does a particularly good job of demonstrating this Zen-like approach. It's a dramatic night-time shot of a yucca plant in bloom. "If you've ever seen the white blossoms of the yucca up close you've noticed how full they are, how much they give. The yucca uses all its energy up. That kind of flowering display, well, I wanted to show the giving of that energy."

"The result," he says, "is an image rendered so that it speaks with some relevance to what the yucca is all about." Shooting at night, Sean used a flash at the back and a flashlight in the front so that it "had a kind of inner glow."

As he continues to grow professionally and artistically, Sean says that he finds himself reaching further past "literal documentation." I find myself gravitating more toward learning how to better document while still expressing something more."

Dallas, TX
www.seanfitzgerald.com
[e] sean@seanfitzgerald.com

Fitzgerald | Bronzed Cowbird (foreground) and male Brown-headed Cowbird (background)

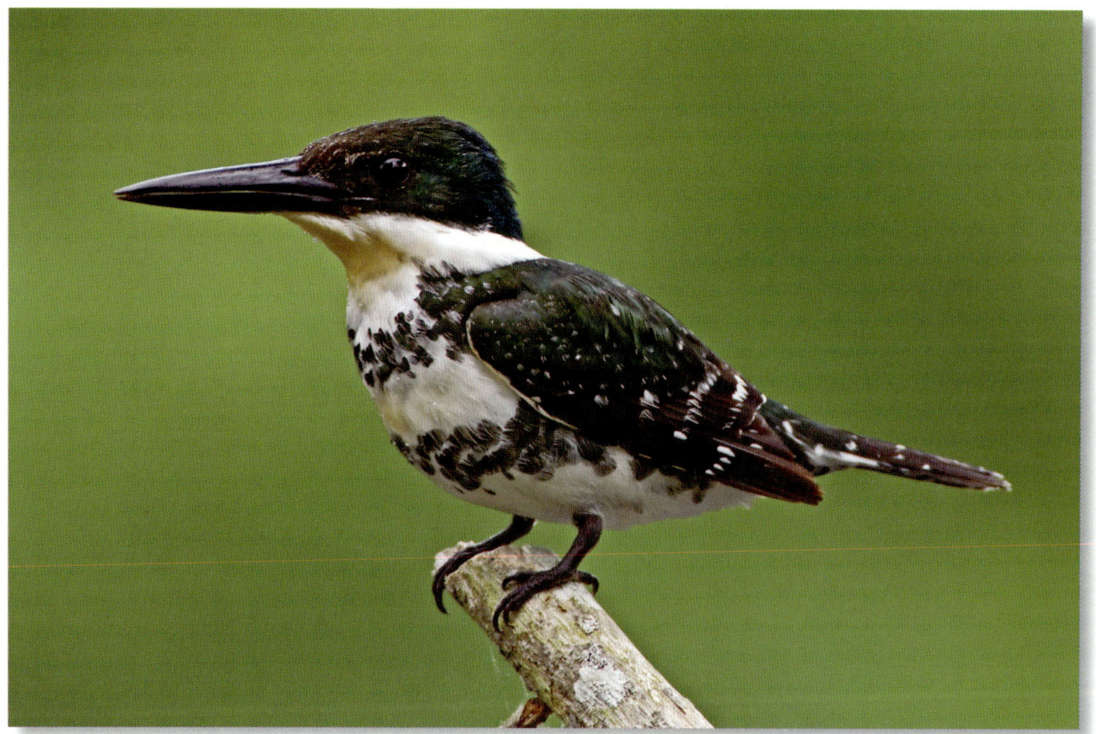

Fitzgerald | Green Kingfisher

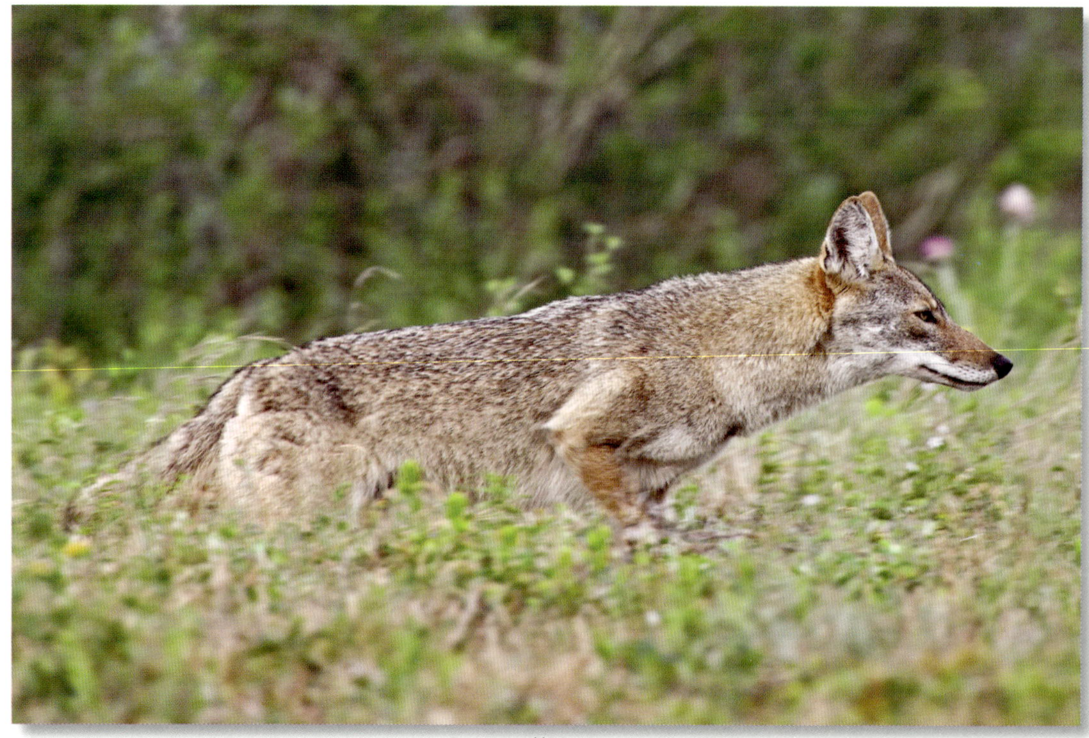

Fitzgerald | Coyote

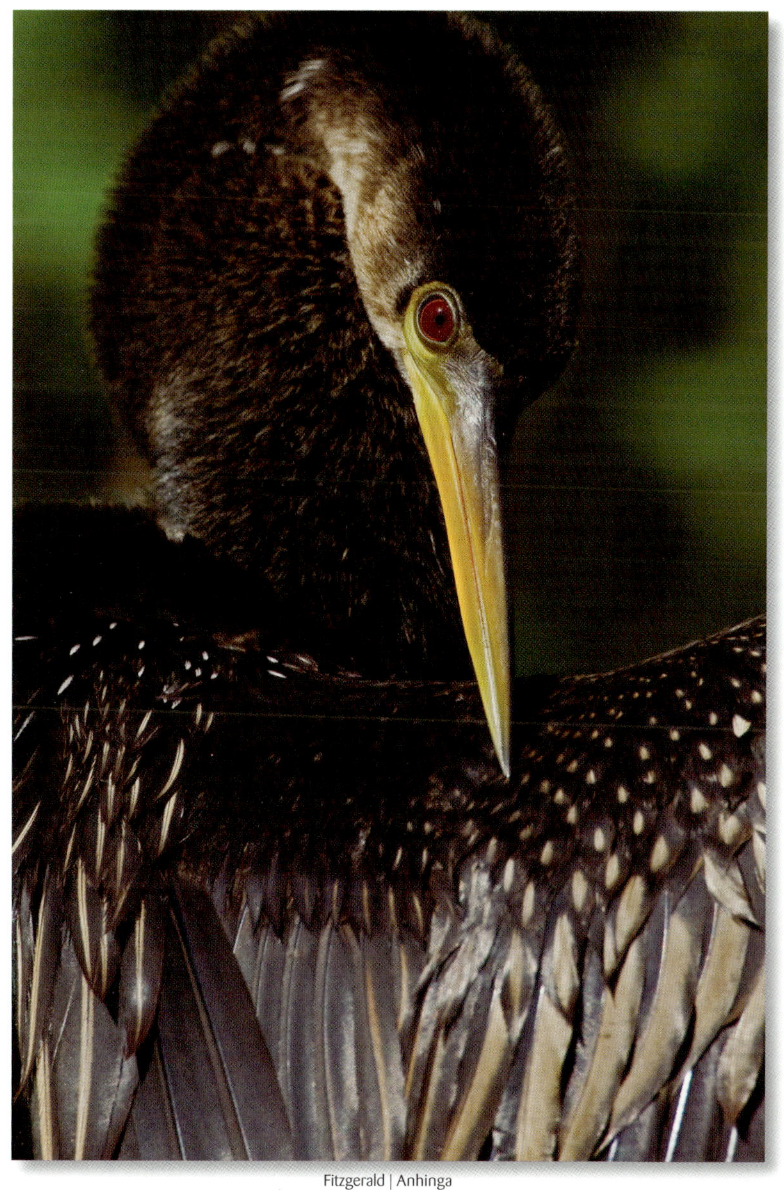
Fitzgerald | Anhinga

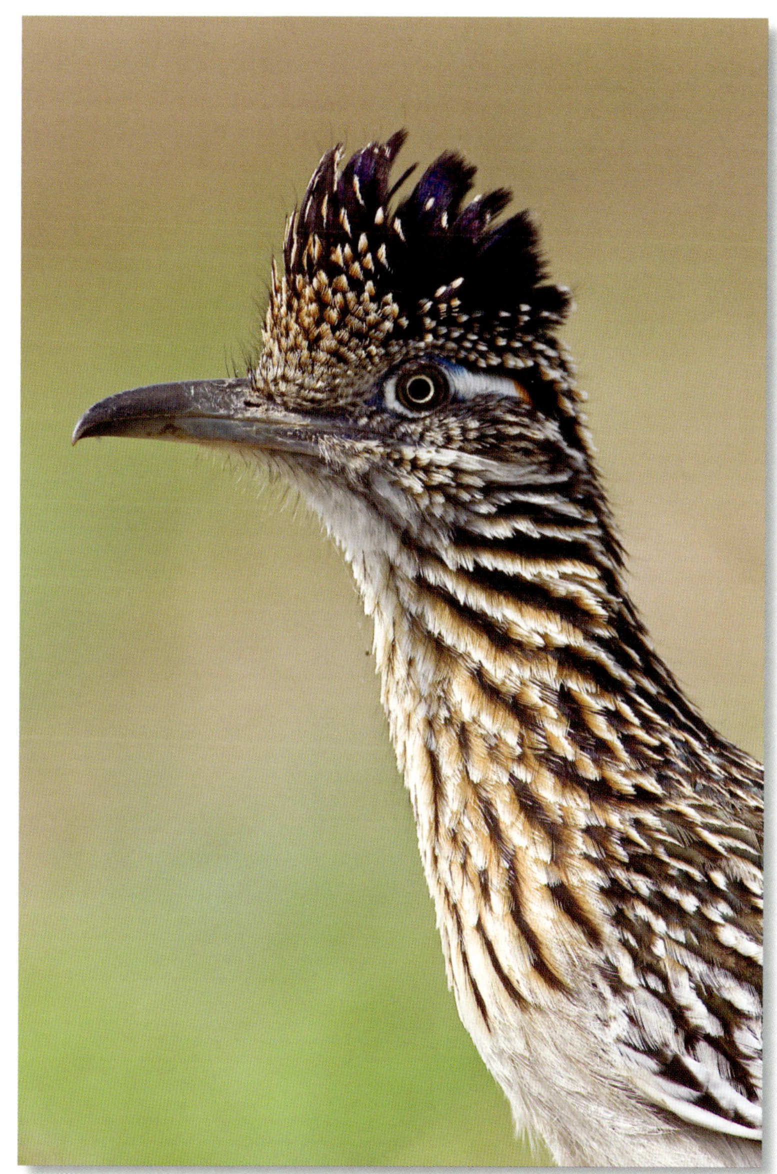
Fitzgerald | Greater Roadrunner

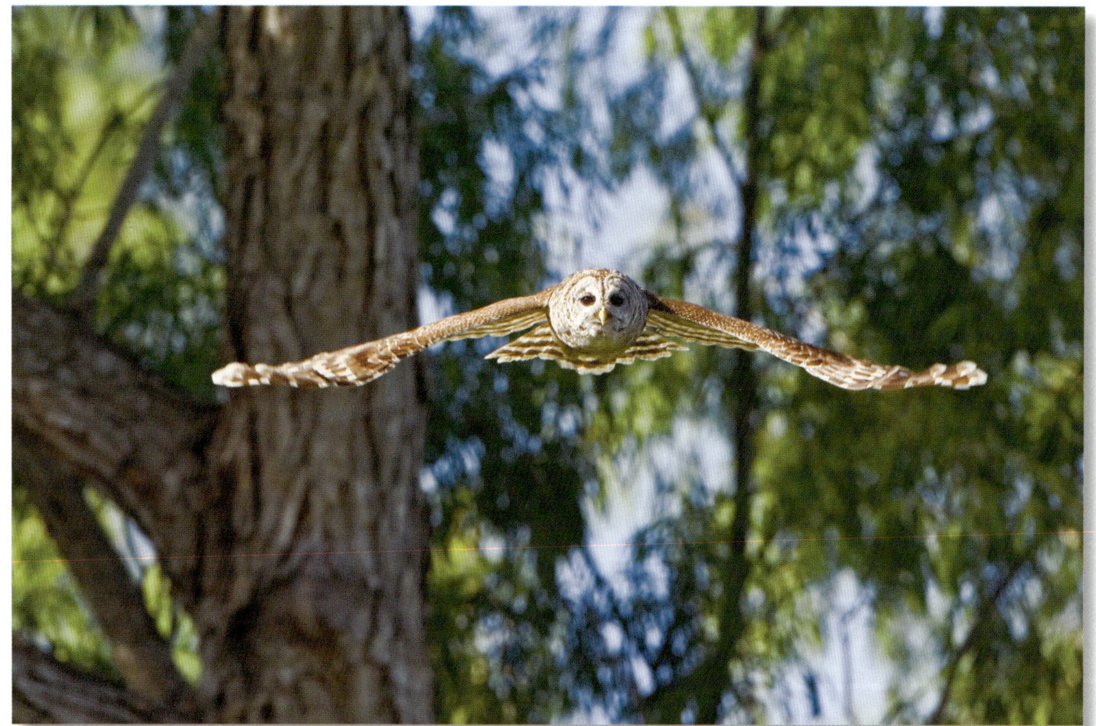

Fitzgerald | Barred Owl

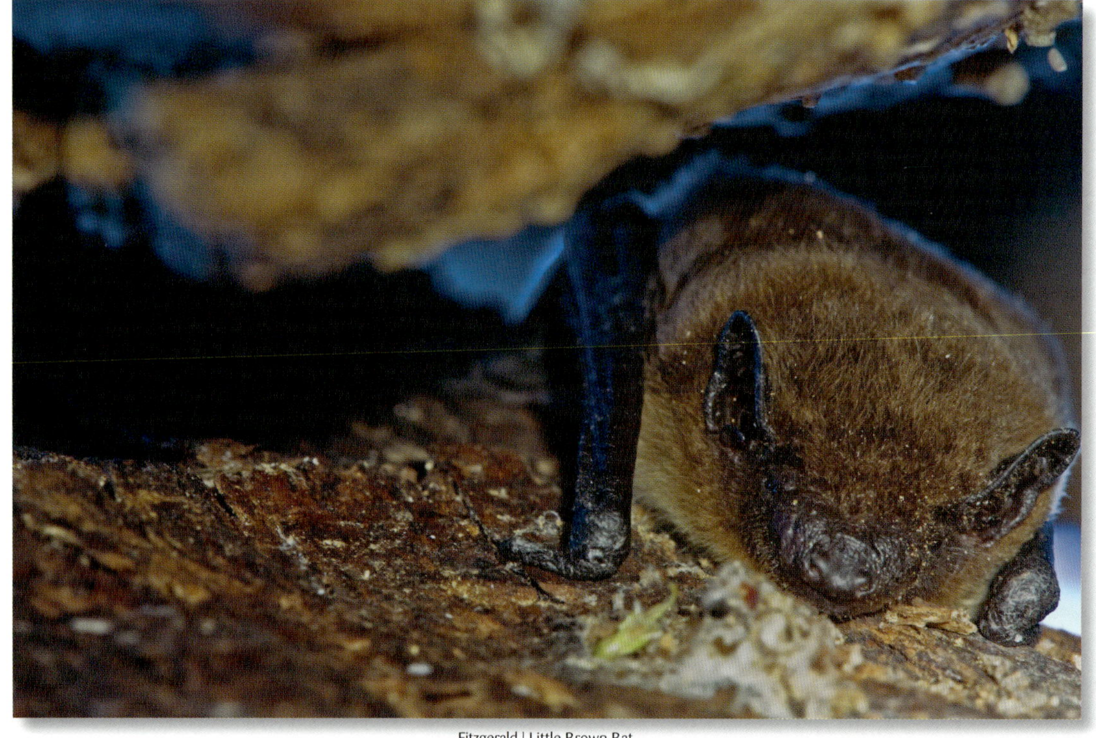

Fitzgerald | Little Brown Bat

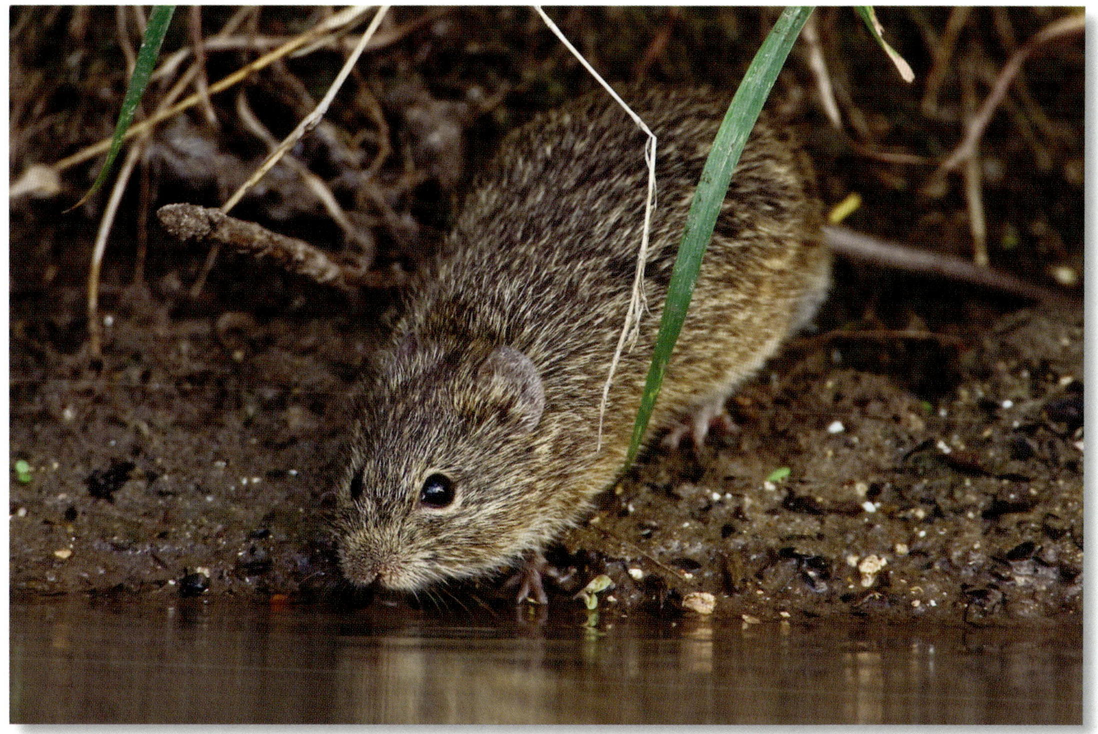

Fitzgerald | Cotton Rat

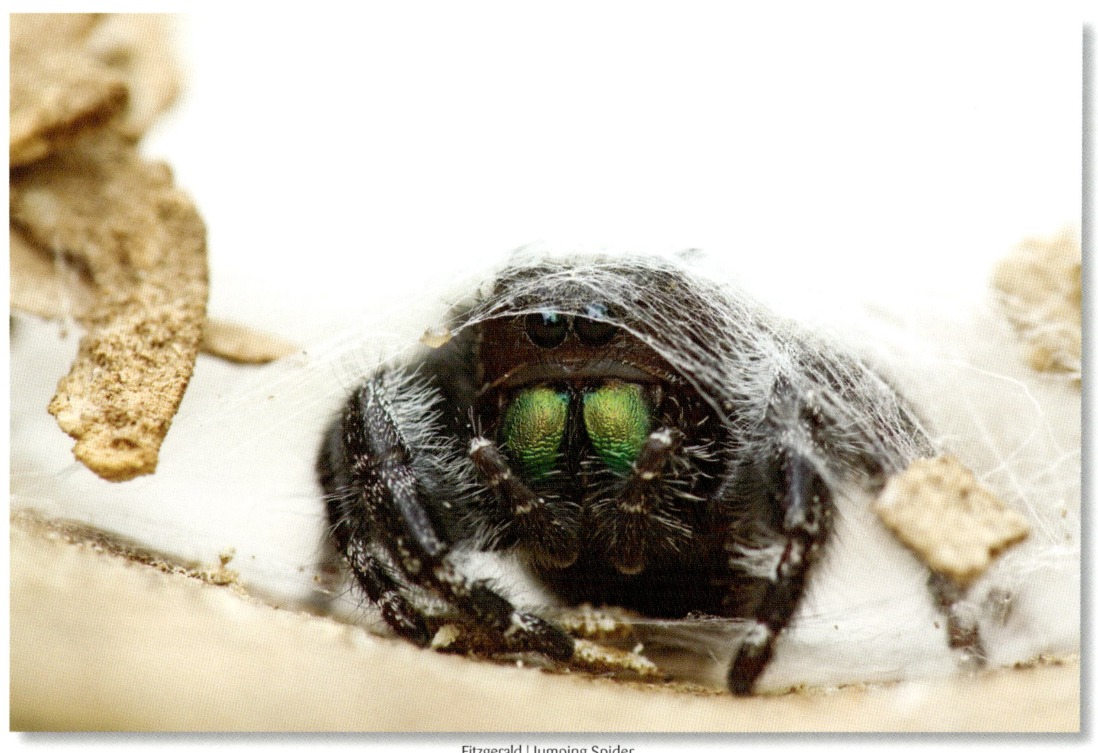

Fitzgerald | Jumping Spider

About Pedrotti-Sorgente Ranch...

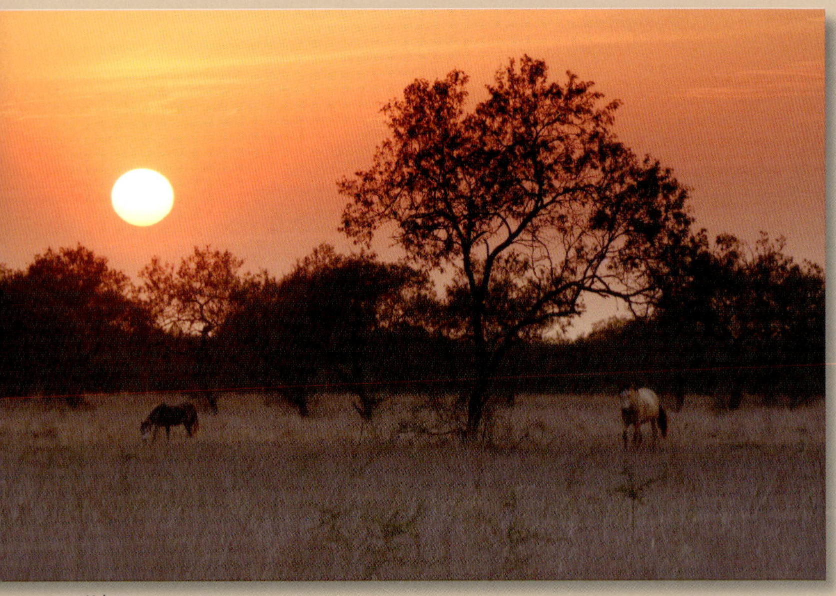

Hahn

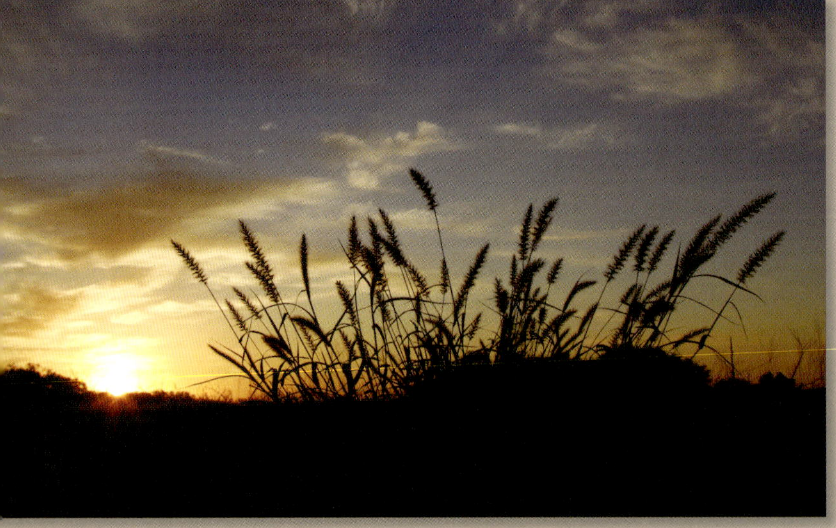

Hahn | Buffelgrass

Upon discovery of a naturally flowing artesian water well, stock tanks filled and water wells flourished on a piece of South Texas property that ultimately fulfilled a dream for Dan Pedrotti. In honor of his Italian heritage, Pedrotti named his ranch Pedrotti-Sorgente. In Italian, sorgente suggests naturally flowing water. The ranch's P-S brand also stands for Pete and Sue, the childhood names of Pedrotti and his wife from their early life in Del Rio.

Habitat on the Pedrotti-Sorgente Ranch east of Concepcion in Duval County is typical of South Texas brush country. Guests are greeted by a gentle rolling countryside with little elevation to disturb the picturesque sunsets. A dry creek bed on the ranch leads to a lake affectionately named La Playa, Spanish for The Beach; farther downstream is El Toro Lake. While providing water is always a challenge in South Texas, the lakes are a reliable source for the abundant wildlife and for the Pedrotti family. The land is dotted with Mesquite trees adding lime green to the color palette dominated by cactus and sage.

The Pedrotti's 4,500-acre ranch is carved from the original 11,000-acre Gus Glasscock property. Glasscock was a circus performer, who gave up performing during the early stages of the oil and gas business in Texas. Glasscock created the first offshore mobile drilling rig for use in the Gulf of Mexico. His company became Marine Drilling Company, headed by the illustrious Jimmy Storm. Gus also became a legend among South Texas ranchers. He accumulated his land in three separate parcels. Texas lore has it that 2,000 acres of the 11,000 was won in a poker game. Dan selected his 4,500 acres because of the amenities it offered. Featuring a five bedroom home, barns and a foreman's house, it seemed to be the perfect fit for his family with four children. Before closing on the land purchase in January 1996 the real estate broker invited Dan, his wife and their children to stay in the home over the Christmas holidays and to enjoy the hunting and fishing as though they already owned the property. While the family had a wonderful time sharing Christmas, Dan shot a Boone & Crocket Club record book white-tail buck, which sealed the deal. Soon afterwards, Dan and Sue began updating the 1937 homestead to meet modern standards. All of the main buildings, including the garage, guest house, water tower and power room feature matching brick and red tiled roofs. To modernize and minimize the straight lines reminiscent of 1930s architecture, the Pedrottis added verandas and a porte-cochere, giving the structures an entirely different appearance. To complete the modernization, the Pedrotti's converted the garage into a playroom for the children. For nearly 50 years, the ranch has enjoyed the loyal service of the same foreman, whose love of the land is apparent in the care he provides.

While the Pedrotti's consider their ranch as a retreat and a source of great pleasure, they also do a little farming. About 700 acres of the property is dedicated to agriculture. They grow grain, peas and watermelon. Between 15 and 20 horses graze on the land alongside five goats and three steers. All the animals are for recreational pleasure and seem to thoroughly enjoy life with the Pedrottis.

One of the Pedrottis philosophical goals is to prevent further fragmentation of large pieces of land across Texas. The more the land is broken into smaller portions the further the natural habitat is disturbed or destroyed. Awareness of climate change and its potential effects on wildlife is something all landowners must be attuned to and the Pedrottis' diligently support any conservation effort that educates landowners about such issues. When asked years ago about how he envisioned this land in 50 years, Pedrotti described a scene in which he and his grandson are sitting in a deer blind, while both anticipate the pleasure of a young boy bagging his first deer. Dan wanted to see his grandson as an adult sitting in that same deer blind with his own grandson sharing the same experience.

Through the Pedrotti family's commitment to conservation, it's likely this will happen.

Daniel A Pedrotti
Corpus Christi, TX

PEDROTTI-SORGENTE
P-S
RANCH

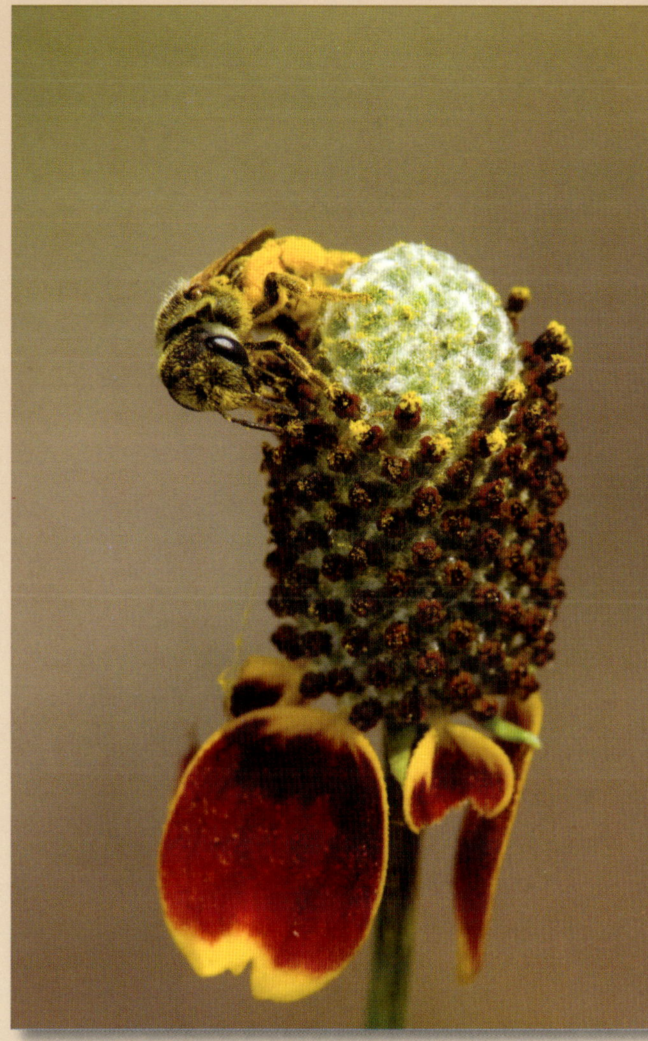

Hahn | bee on Mexican Hat

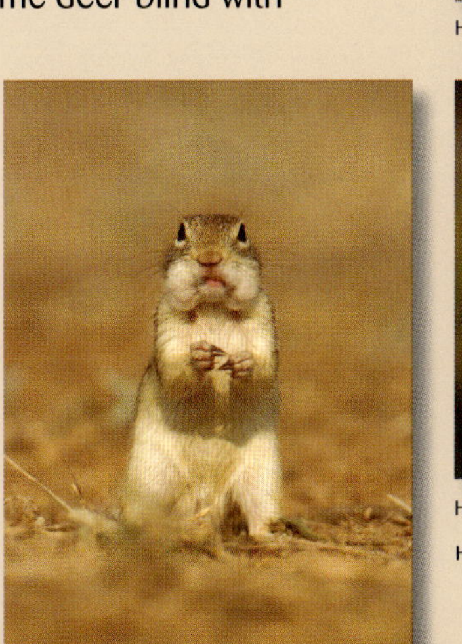

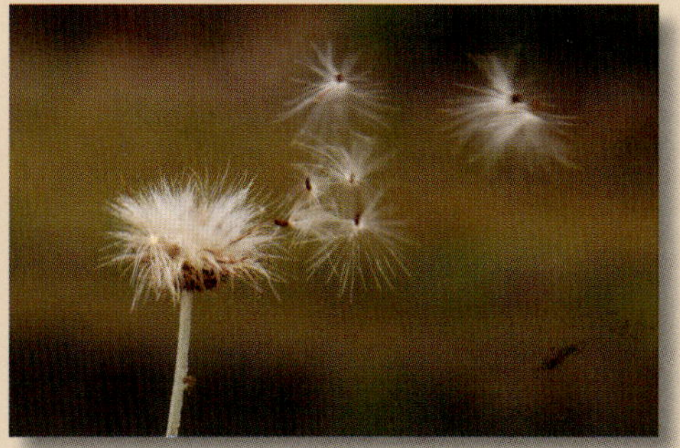

Hahn | thistle seeds dispersing

Hahn | ground squirrel

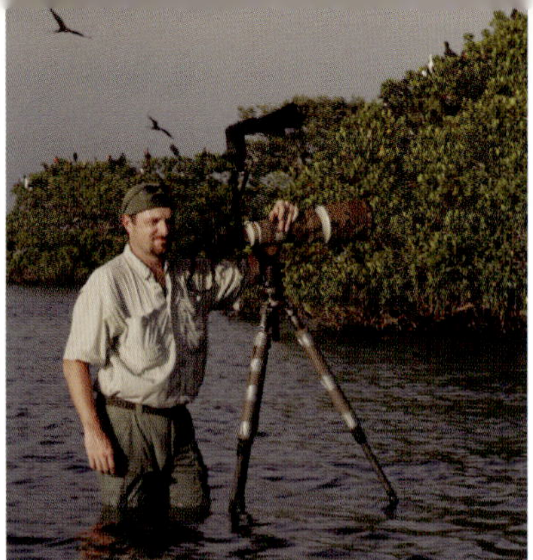

Jason Hahn

Jason Hahn confesses that he walks around with a "laundry list of shots" in his head.

"I always have a composition in mind, that compositional side of things is the hardest part." Jason is also an instructor and says he finds this to be true with his students as well. "When I teach my photo workshops, it's easier to teach the technical side of things." But, when it comes to the creative process, "there's just no mathematical formula for art."

Jason focuses on the formulaic side of things long before he utilizes it. "My approach is to make the technical side intuitive so I can focus purely on form, motion, composition – what all that other stuff is really building up to."

And, for Jason, that "other stuff," when done well, will leave the viewer with the sense that there's more than what meets the eye.

"Everything technical is just to get me there, to that place."

While at the Pedrotti-Sorgente Ranch, Jason did what he often does: he put hunters' tricks to work. "I figure people have been hunting for ten-thousand or so years and hunters have learned a lot of tricks. No sense in reinventing the wheel. After all, I've got to get as close, if not closer, than a hunter."

But, when it comes to utilizing tricks to get his shots, Jason draws a strong ethical line. "If I'm not comfortable explaining how I got a photo, there's a good chance there's an ethical issue there," he cautions. "Animals, especially the ones in South Texas where conditions are so harsh, are concerned with one thing: their routines of survival. So, something like the birdcalls I used to get my owl shots should only be used with minimal impact and after trying other means. Like, I would never use them on a nesting bird. I wouldn't want to pull the bird from her nest and expose the chicks to danger."

His voice gets a determined edge as he adds, "As a photographer you've got to think of the welfare of the animal first and of getting the shot second."

Land O'Lakes, FL
www.HahnNaturePhotography.com
[e] jason@hahnnaturephotography.com

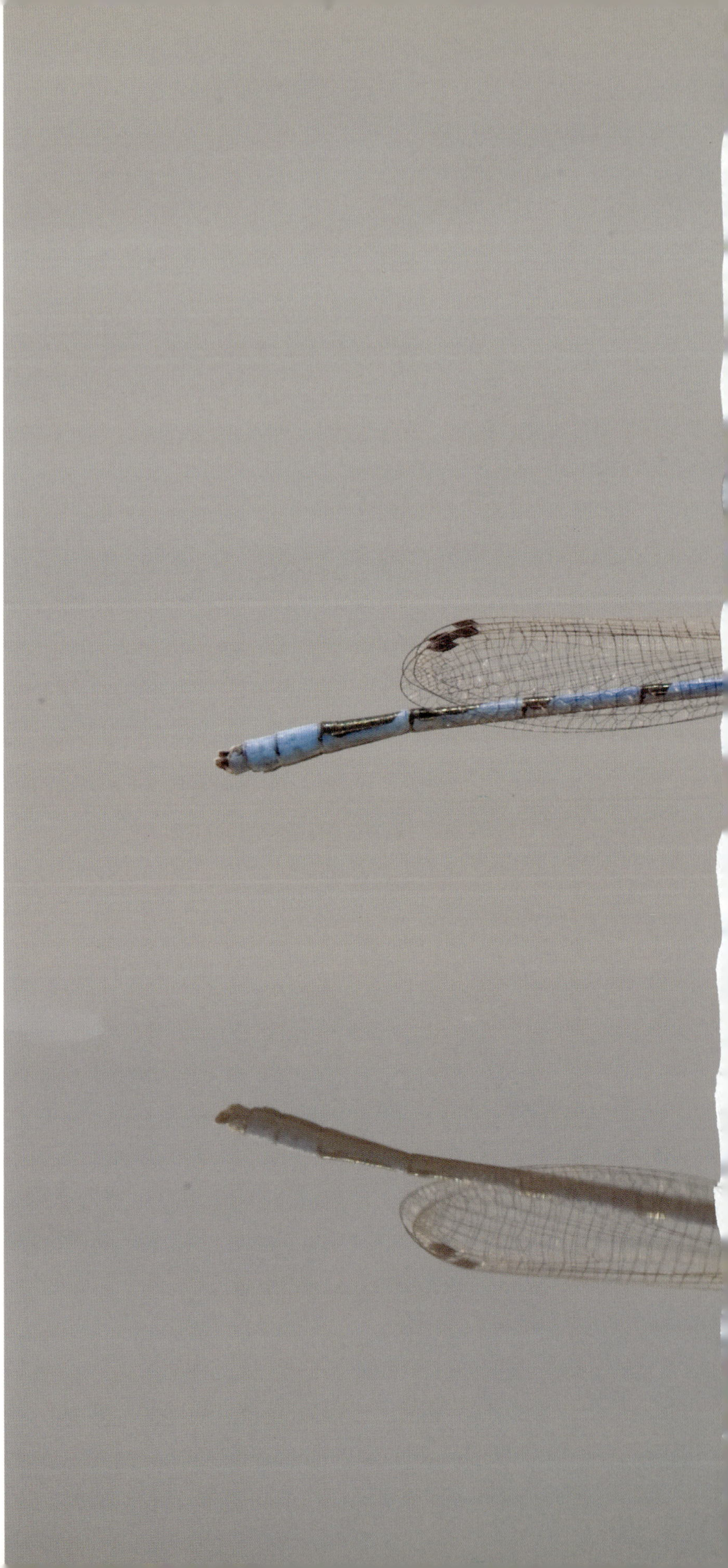

Hahn | male Familiar Bluets

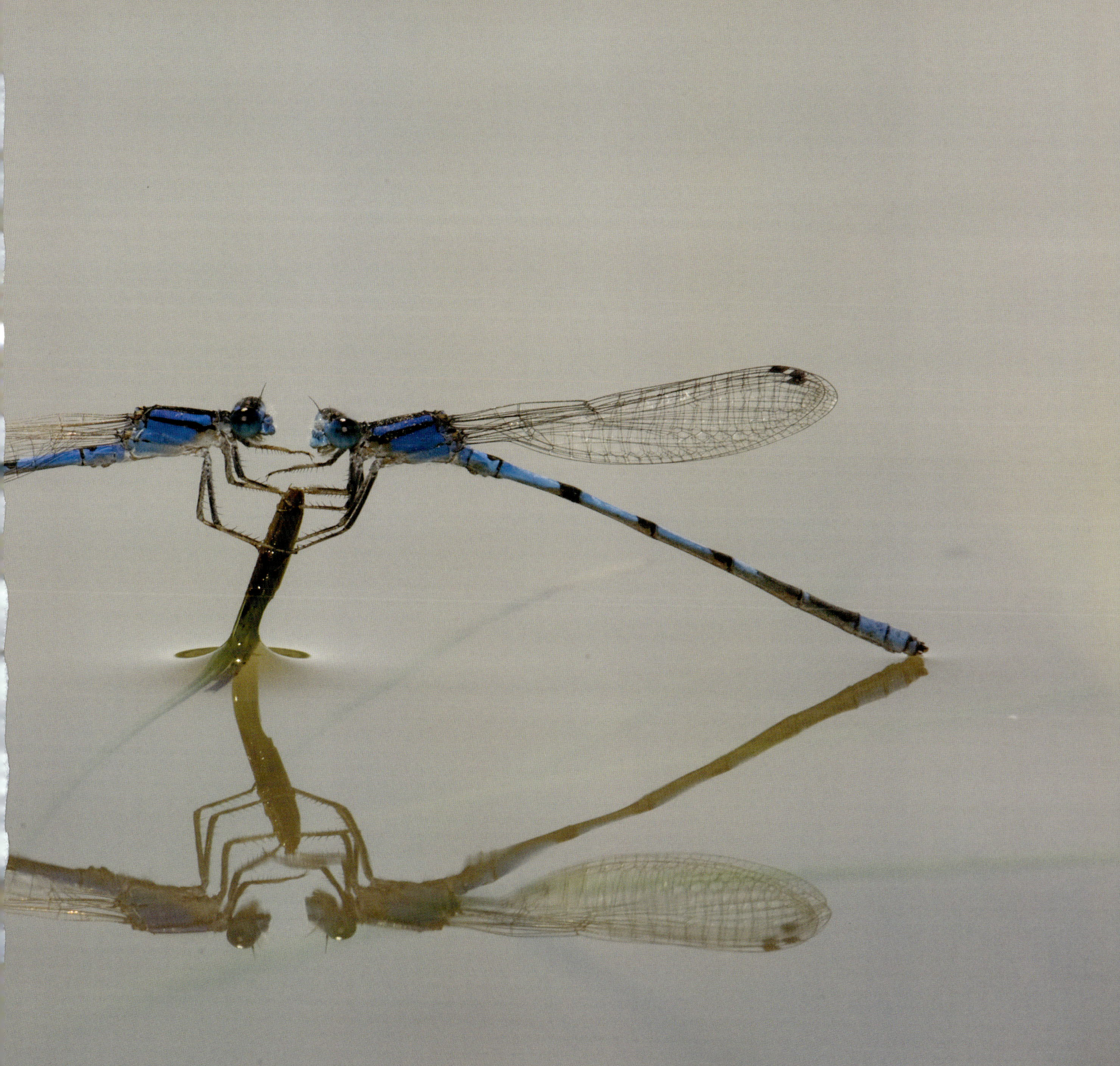

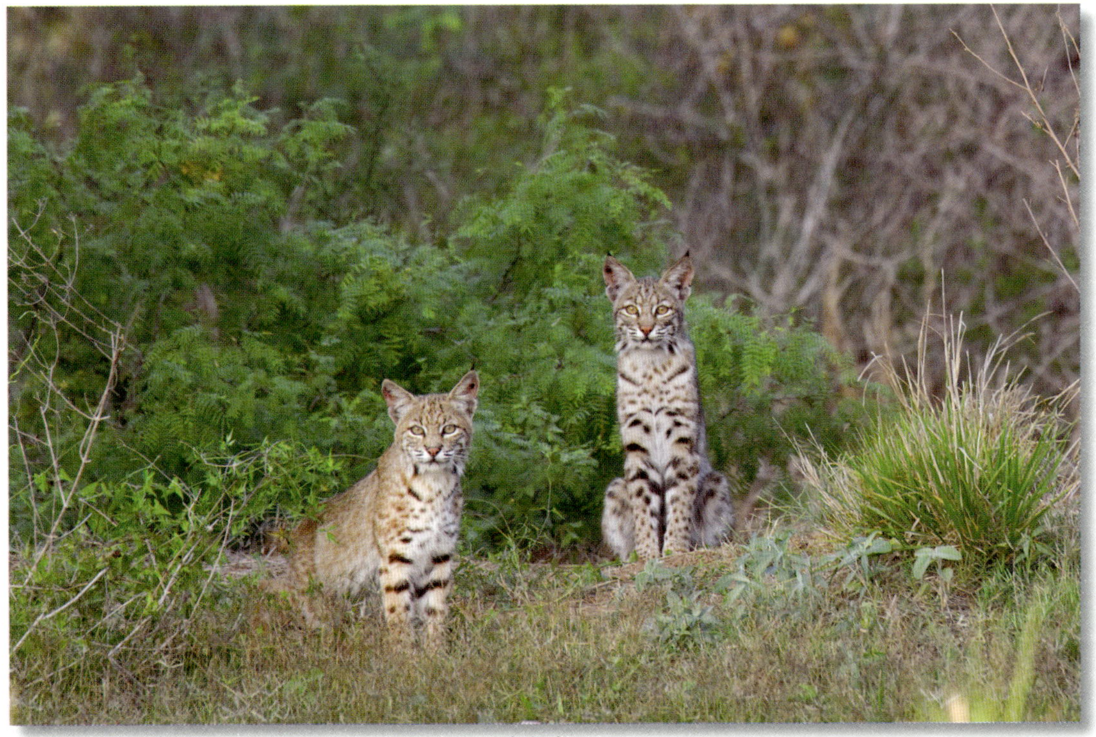

Hahn | Bobcats

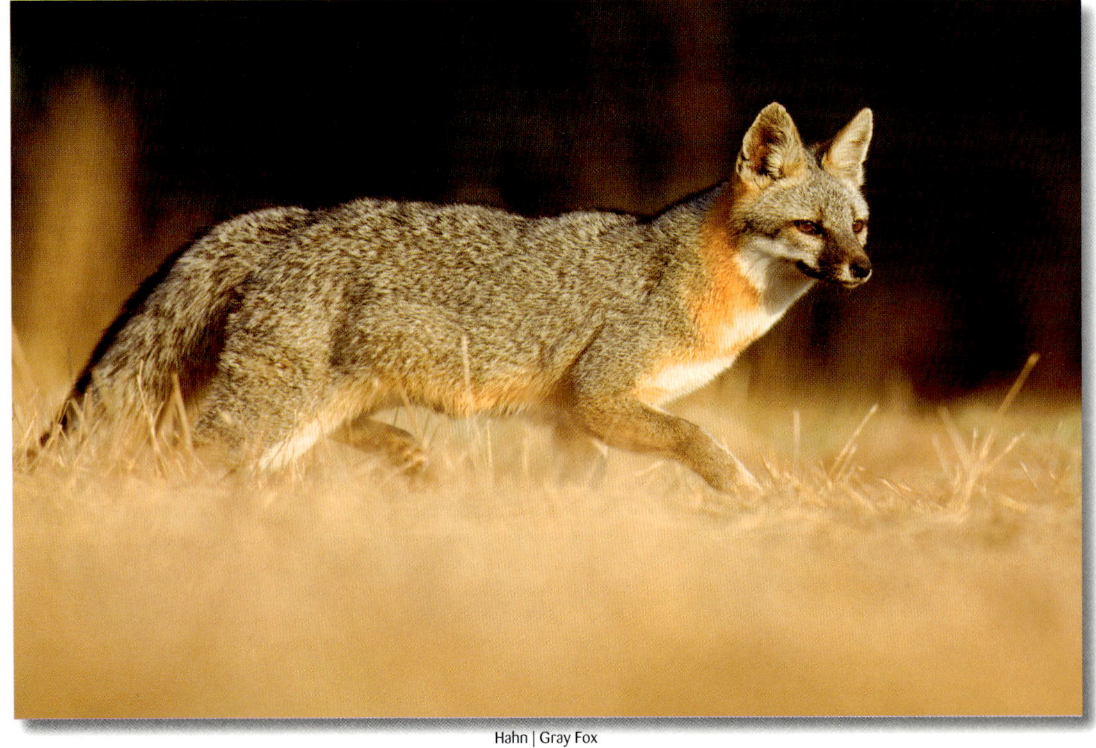

Hahn | Gray Fox

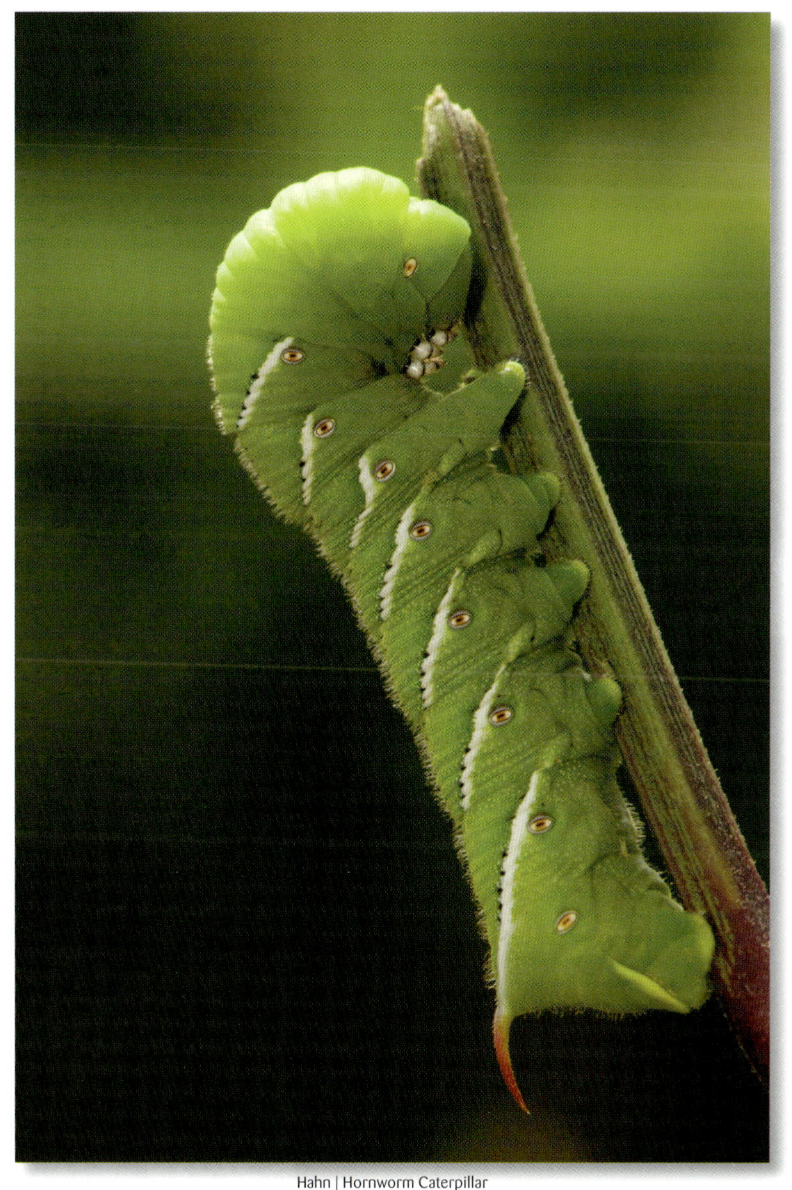

Hahn | Hornworm Caterpillar

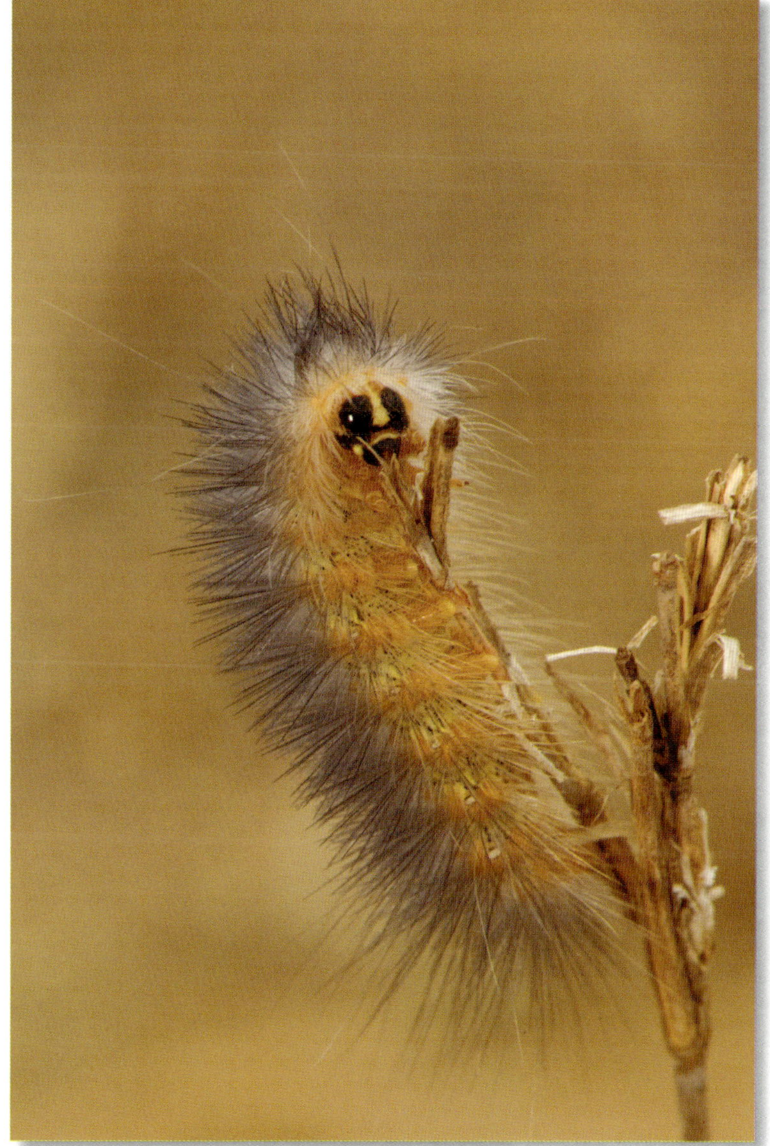

Hahn | Saltmarsh Caterpillar

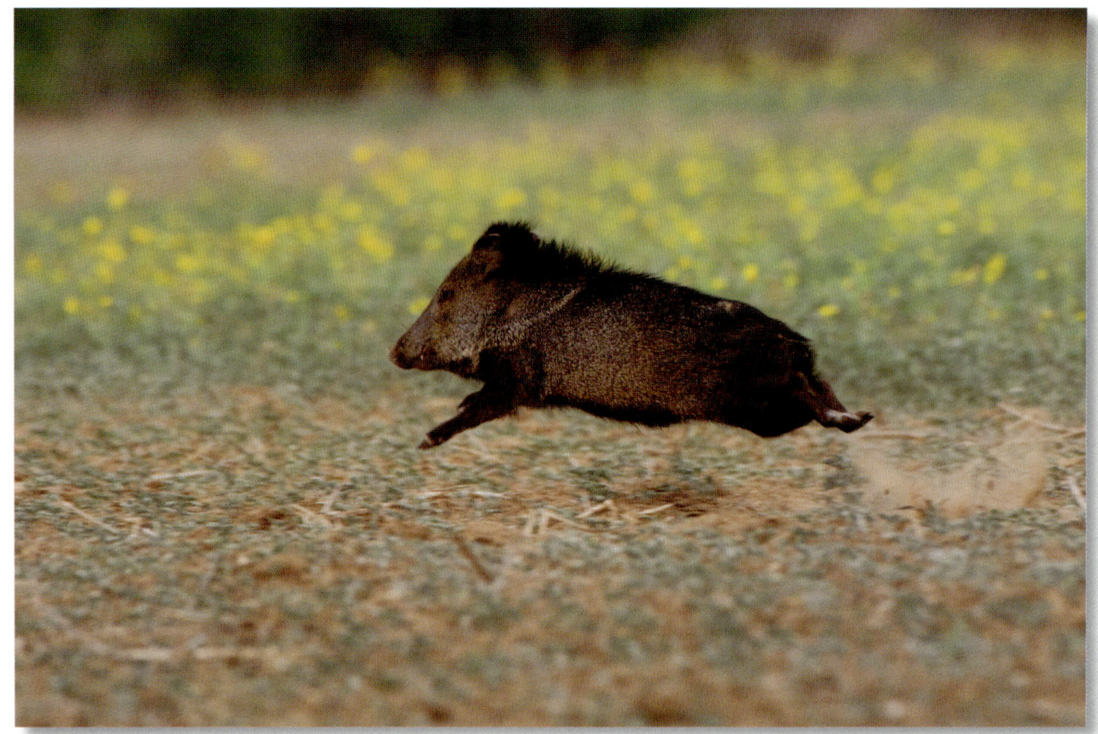

Hahn | Javelina

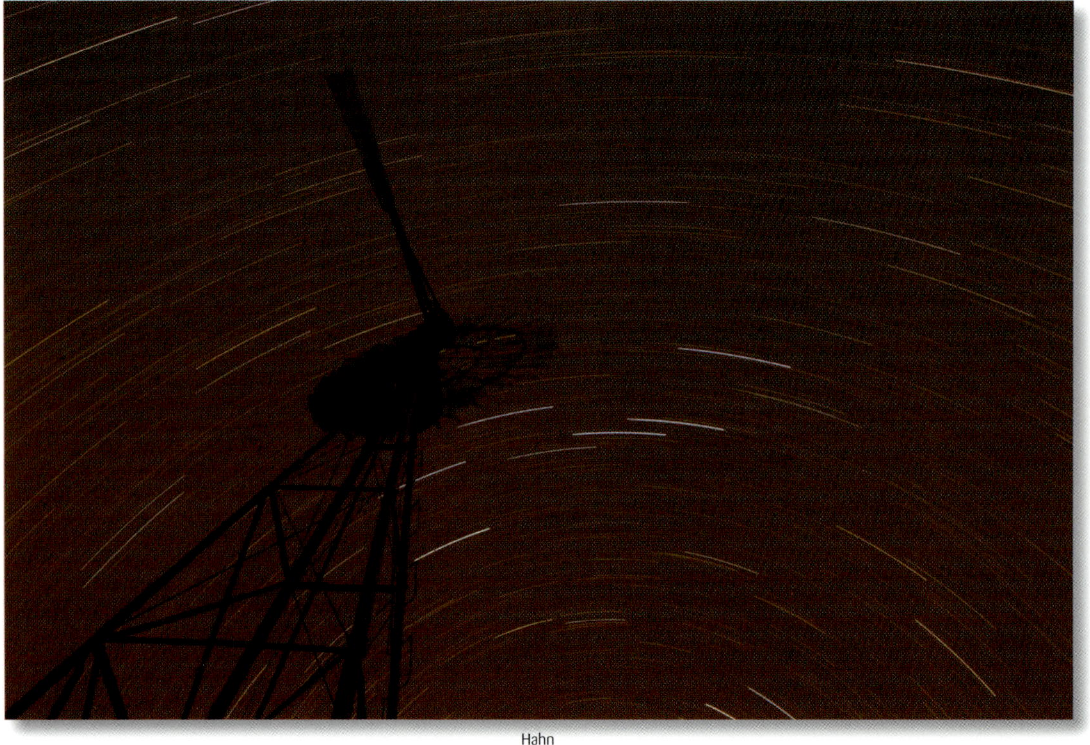

Hahn

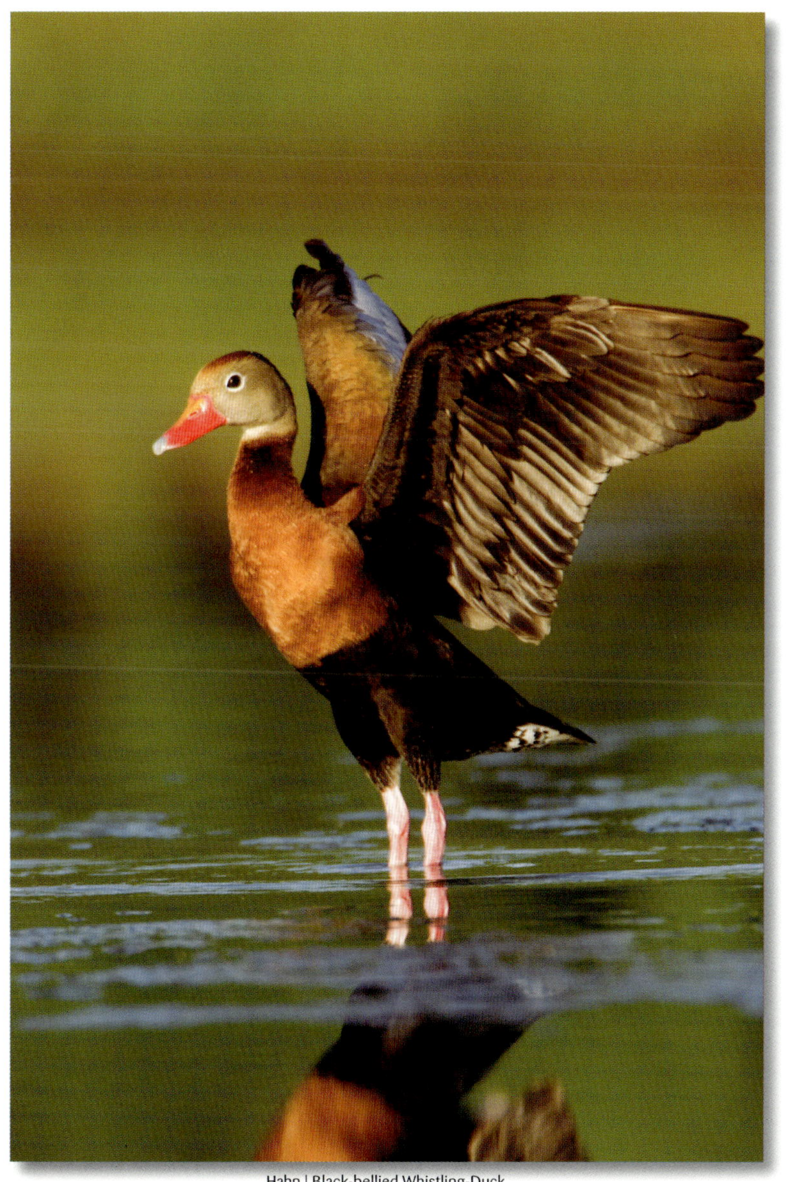

Hahn | Black-bellied Whistling-Duck

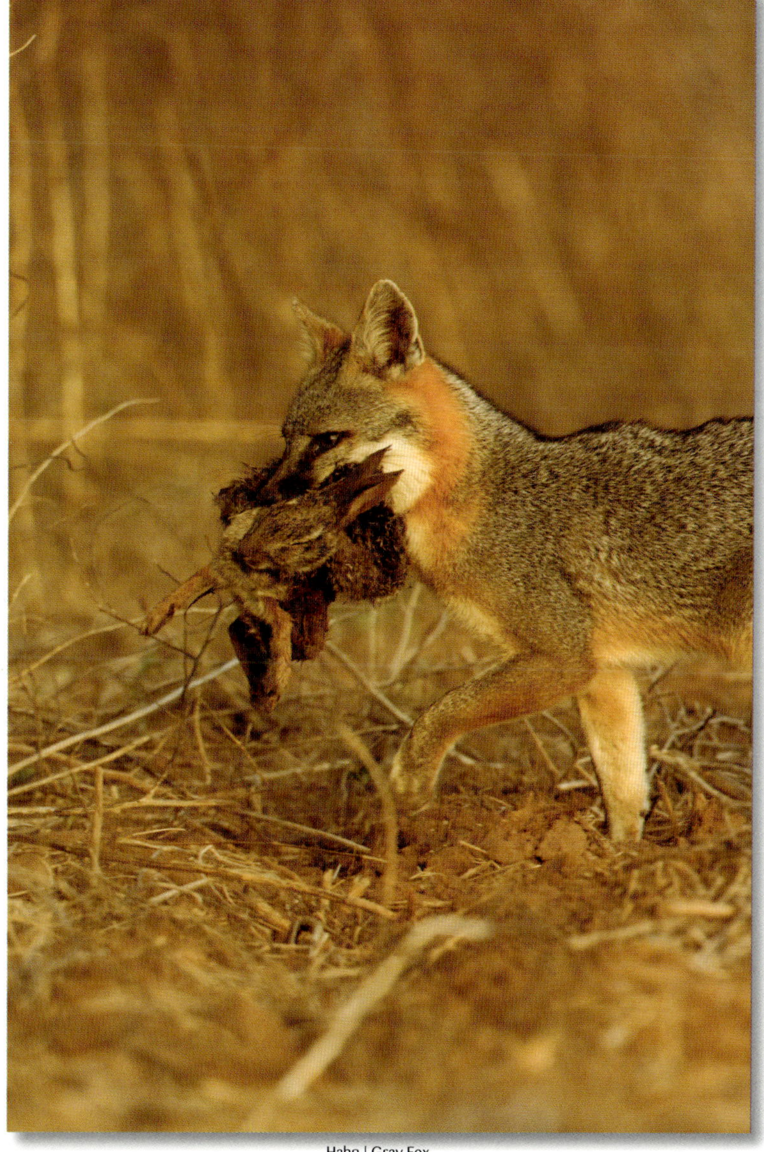

Hahn | Gray Fox

About Pierce Ranch...

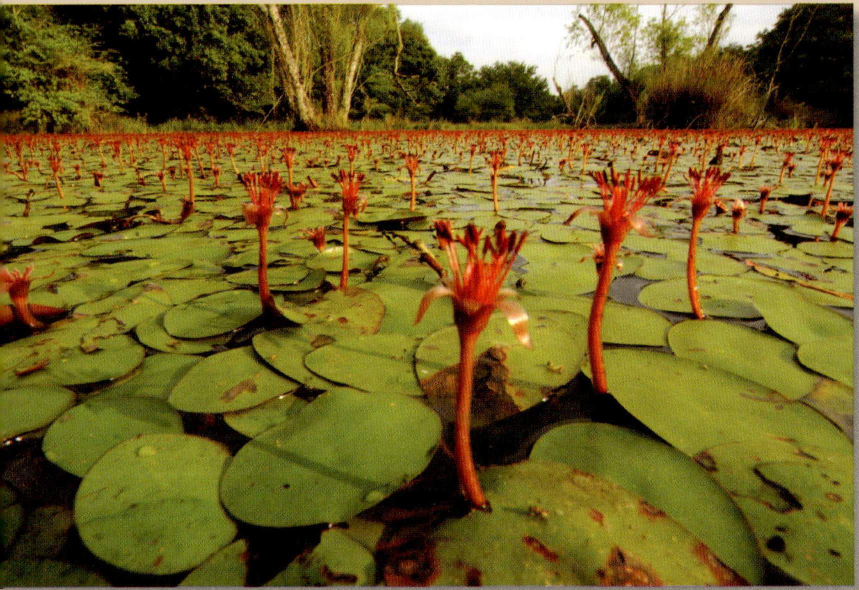

Ulrich | Water Lilies

Laurance Armour prefers surveying the Pierce Ranch by air, enjoying a bird's-eye view from a two-seat airplane. From this vantage he can follow the Colorado River as it winds through coastal woodlands like a silvery-red ribbon among towering hardwoods that provide a vast green canopy of ancient oaks, pecan, elm, and cottonwood.

Flying south, timberlands retreat and the landscape evolves into a giant patchwork of wetlands and native prairie grasslands.

In addition to migrating waterfowl such as geese and ducks, cranes and their allies and many neo-tropical varieties, Pierce Ranch supports a wide array of terrestrial wildlife throughout its diverse ecosystems. Herds of deer roam and elusive feral pigs root for tender shoots in the alluvial soils. Eagles, hawks, owls and other birds of prey also inhabit the ranch. Ten miles of the Colorado River flow along its eastern boundary. Other water sources on the ranch include Jones Creek, Blue Creek, Pecan Slough, and 50 miles of canal systems for rice and row crop irrigation.

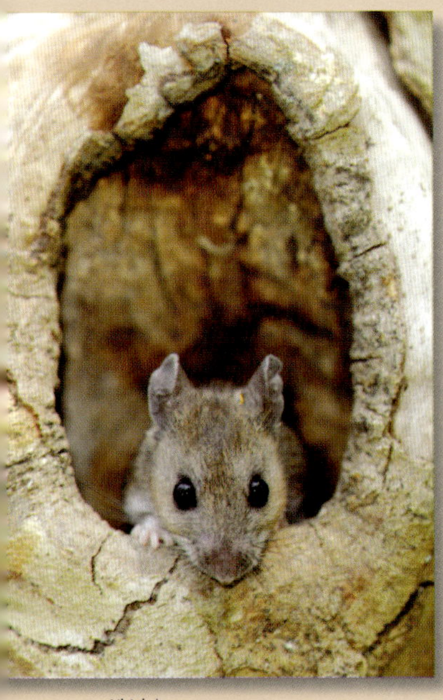

Ulrich | mouse

Pierce Ranch, the northernmost link in the chain of Coastal Bend ranches celebrated in this book, is located near Wharton and was founded by Armour's great-great grandfather, Abel Head 'Shanghai' Pierce in the late 1800s. Branded as one of the most colorful cattlemen in early Texas history, Shanghai amassed land that at one time consisted of half a million acres, spanning Wharton, Matagorda, Calhoun and Galveston counties. The name Shanghai Pierce became synonymous with cattle from Texas to Missouri as he spearheaded large cattle drives northward across the country.

Today, family members lend a hand in daily management of a variety of agricultural enterprises at the ranch. Steven Armour handles oil and gas interests. Laurance oversees the daily operations of agriculture, which includes rice, row crop and native grass seed production. About 15,000 acres is dedicated to crops, while 17,000 acres is set aside for the ranch's cattle operations. Laurance's sons, Russ Hawes and Andrew Pierce Armour, have embraced the family business, pursuing degrees in range and wildlife management and agriculture business. Brooks Armour Diesel lives on the ranch with her husband Hank and three children. With the fifth generation on the ground, the Armours hope to honor the family legacy by sustaining all facets of their historic working ranch. In every ranch endeavor, Pierce descendants practice a partnership with wildlife habitat.

A strong example of that partnership is the family's affiliation with the Texas Rice Industry Coalition for the Environment, or R.I.C.E. Co-founded by Laurance Armour in 1994, the non-profit organization helps landowners establish wetland habitats and native grass prairies. These man-made wetlands supply more than 300,000 acres of vital Texas wetlands. Rice and native grass seed crops grown in the summer become the feeding and roosting grounds of millions of ducks and geese during winter. Grounded in the axiom that we all depend on a clean and healthy environment, the mission of R.I.C.E. is to continually seek ways to improve our understanding of the interaction between the rice industry and the environment.

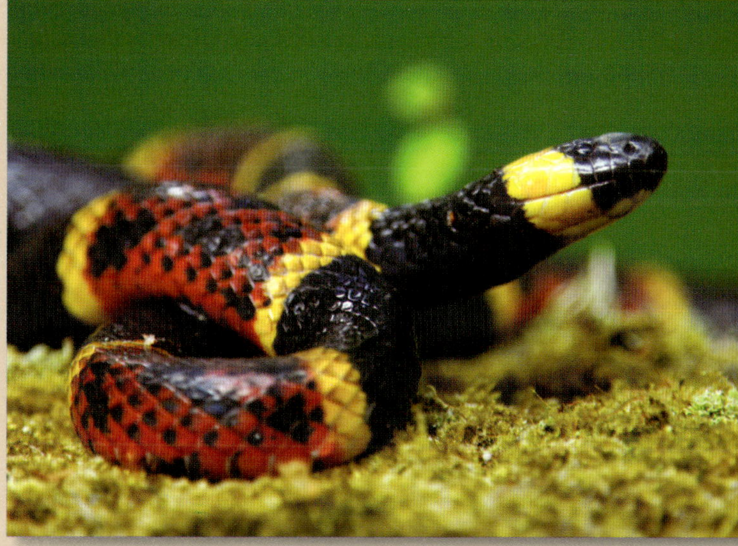

Ulrich | Texas Coral Snake

Intrigued by the concept of the ICF Pro-Tour of Nature Photography, Laurance entered Pierce Ranch in the contest and was teamed with photographer Tom Ulrich. Although viewing the ranch from a helicopter was not the joy ride for Tom that Laurance had expected, Tom used his talents on the ground, bringing into focus his trademark fusion of wildlife, nature and rustic ranch elements in vivid images. Aided by local naturalist Bill Stransky, Tom embraced the potential for a winning shot each day with contagious alacrity, winning the admiration of the Armour family.

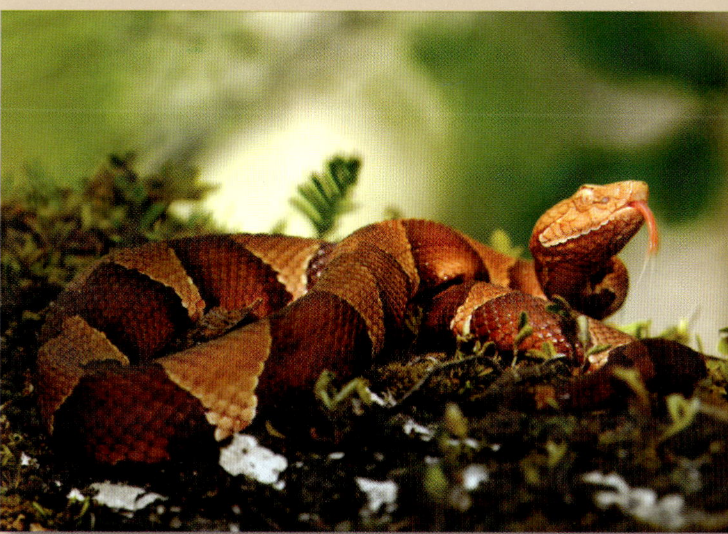

Ulrich | Southern Copperhead

For those interested in visiting Pierce Ranch, the Karankawa Plains Outfitting Company, also run by the Armour family, offers full-service hunting and nature tourism opportunities. Bird watching, wildlife viewing, canoeing, hiking, and horseback riding are available during spring and summer. Here riders bring their own horses where they can enjoy miles of woodland trails. From November 1 to February 15, the ranch is reserved for waterfowl and wild game hunts. Lodging is available year round in two secluded cabins or in lodges nearer ranch headquarters for up to 35 guests. The original ranch house is honored with a medallion from the Texas Register of Historic Places and is the current home of Laurance's sister Brooks and her family.

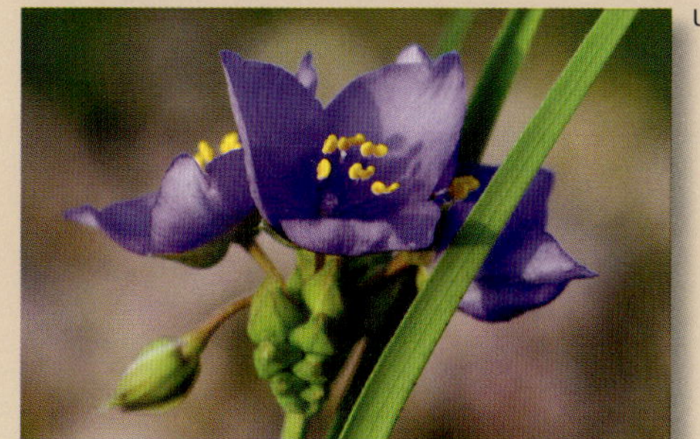

Ulrich | Spiderwort

Laurance Armour III
Pierce, TX
www.karankawa.com
[e] la3a@flash.net

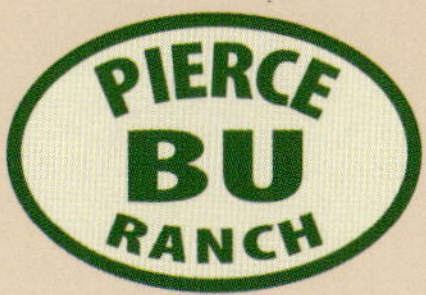

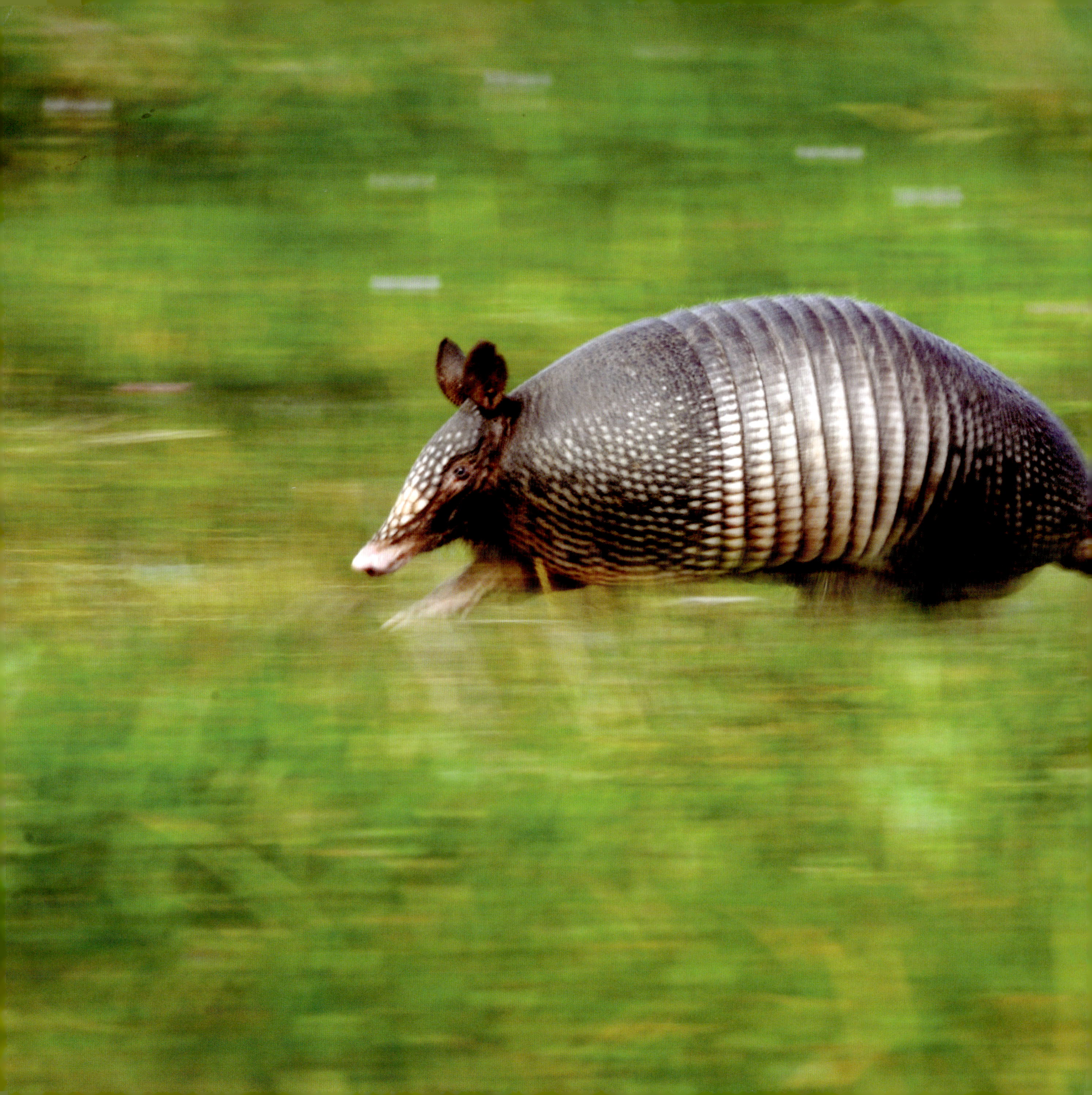

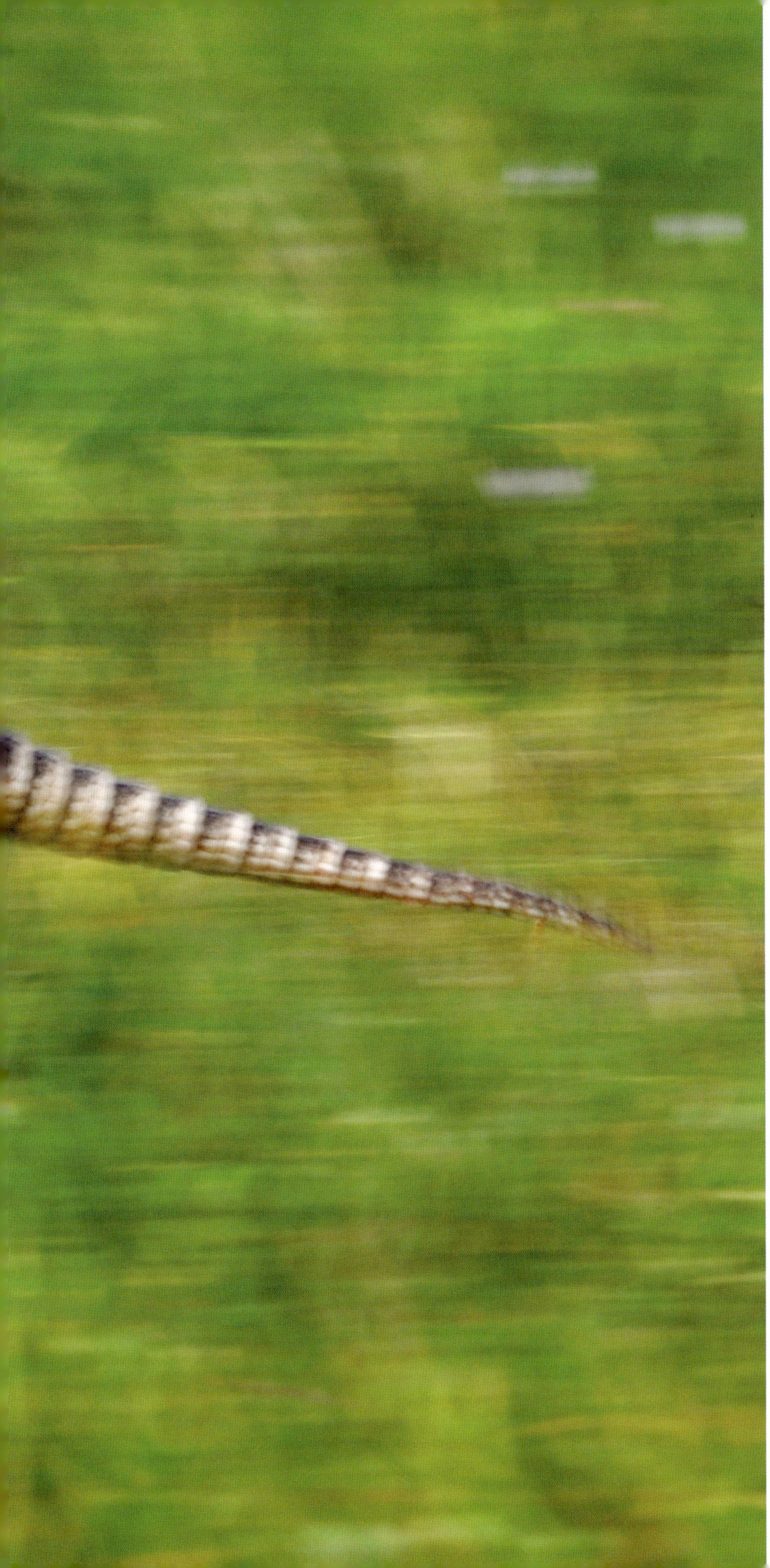

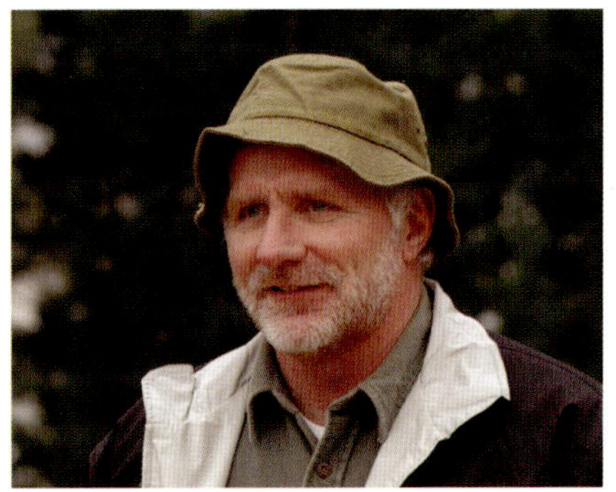

Tom Ulrich

After 35 years in the trenches of professional photography, Tom Ulrich still found himself digging outside his comfort zone at Pierce Ranch during the ICF competition.

"I've done the contest twice," he says, "and both times noticed how different it is compared to traditional photography. The competition is really good. You have to be out there in the dark, and before light."

The contest forced Tom to expand in other ways, too. He found himself pointing his camera toward the smaller flora and fauna such as insects and flowers. "During a contest like this you can be a great bird photographer but if you don't do well in the other categories you won't do well."

However, it's apparent that Tom's perspective is different than it was three and half decades ago. "When I first started, I wasn't environmentally and conservation minded because it wasn't that big of an issue back then. But, now it is. So much land has gone under pavement and concrete."

"I transitioned to digital about six years ago," he says. "You can take more risks with digital, but I still like to do my composing in the camera rather than on the computer." He confesses that he still likes to meter and use manual focus.

"Photography," he explains, "allowed me to get closer to birds in a way I couldn't have otherwise." Even though he has come to view images as valuable conservation tools, he says, "I really started as a way to enjoy the birds more myself."

"I would be walking down the street and see a bird and then it would be gone. I wouldn't have the time to really enjoy it. With photography I could get another look. I can go back and enjoy the feather patterns, the beak, the feet."

"I also found," he adds, "that I could share it with the public."

West Glacier, MT
www.tomulrichphotos.com
[e] tjulrich@cyberport.net

Ulrich | Nine-banded Armadillo

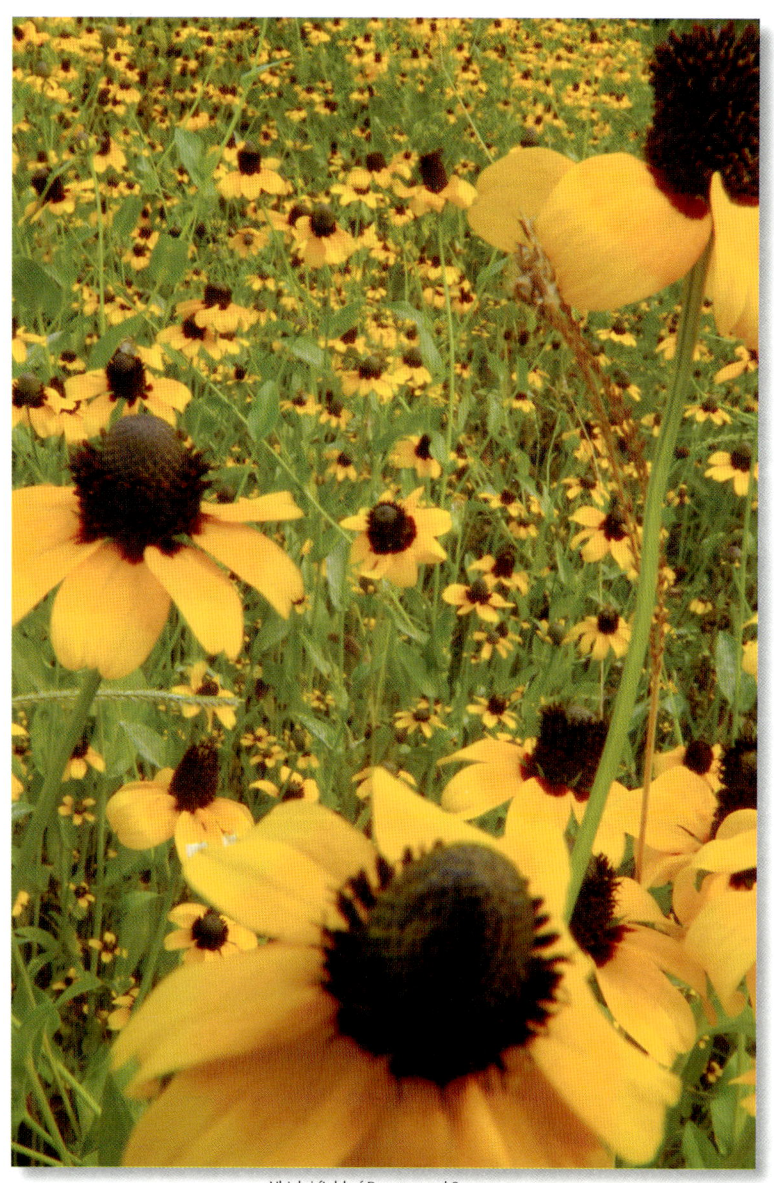

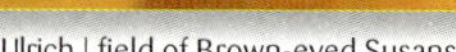

Ulrich | field of Brown-eyed Susans

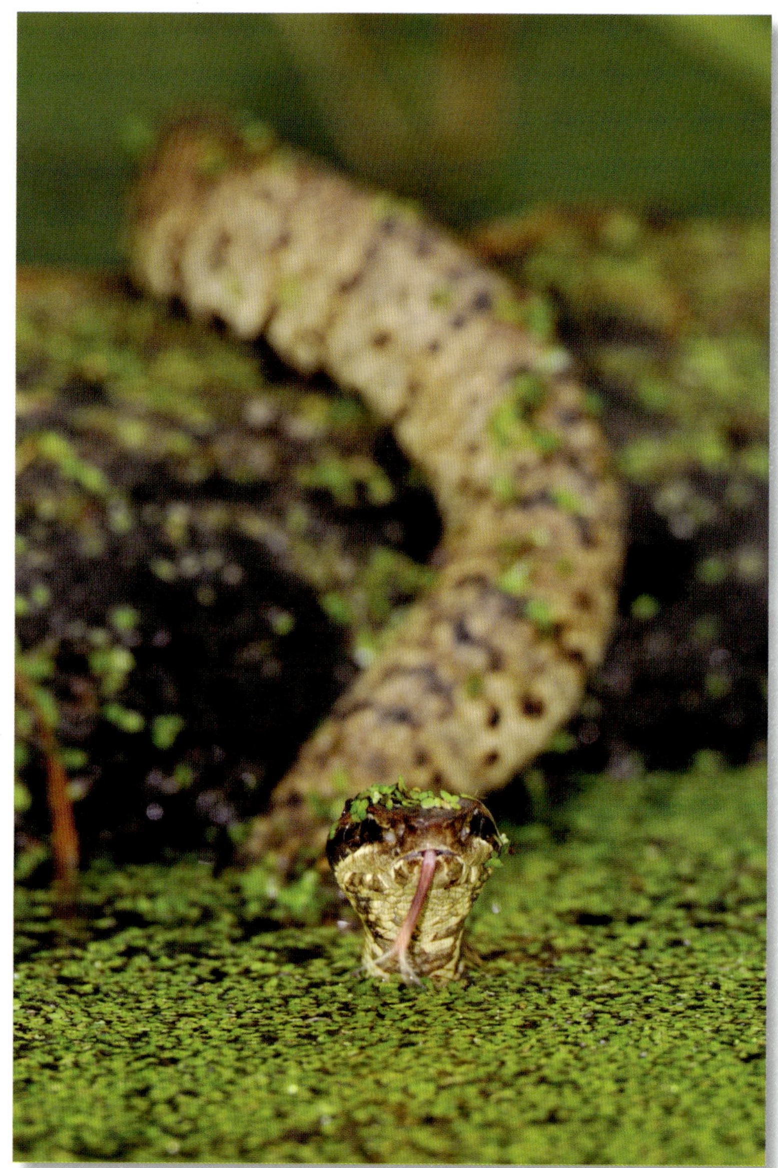

Ulrich | Western Cottonmouth

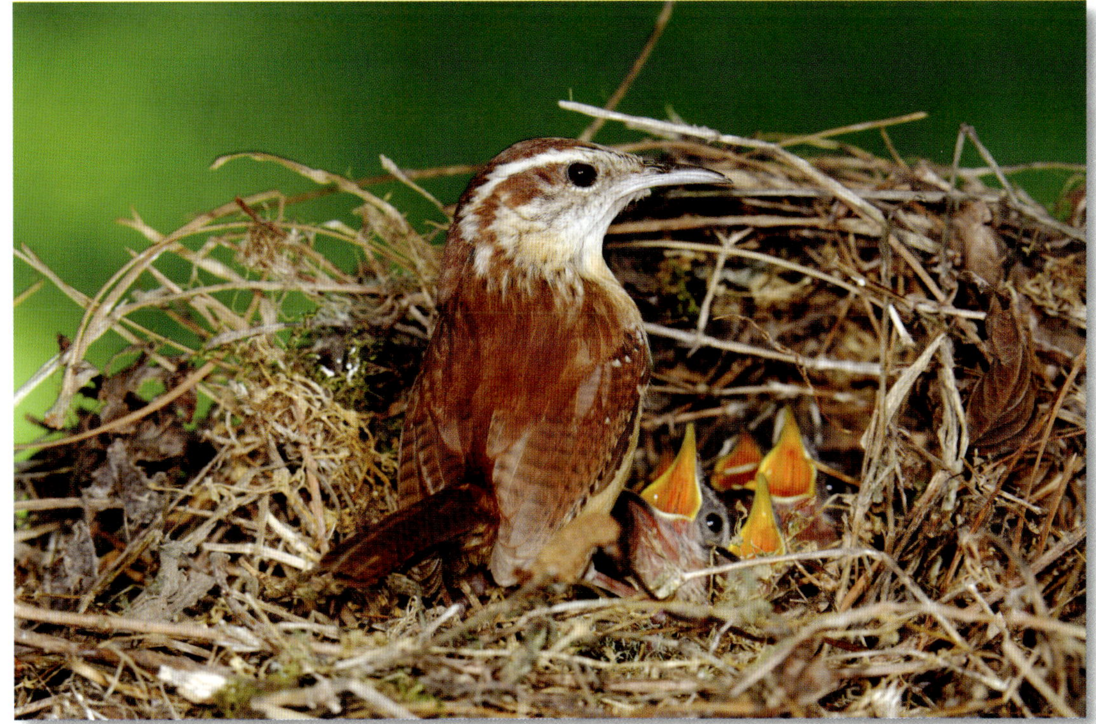

Ulrich | Carolina Wren (adult feeding nestlings)

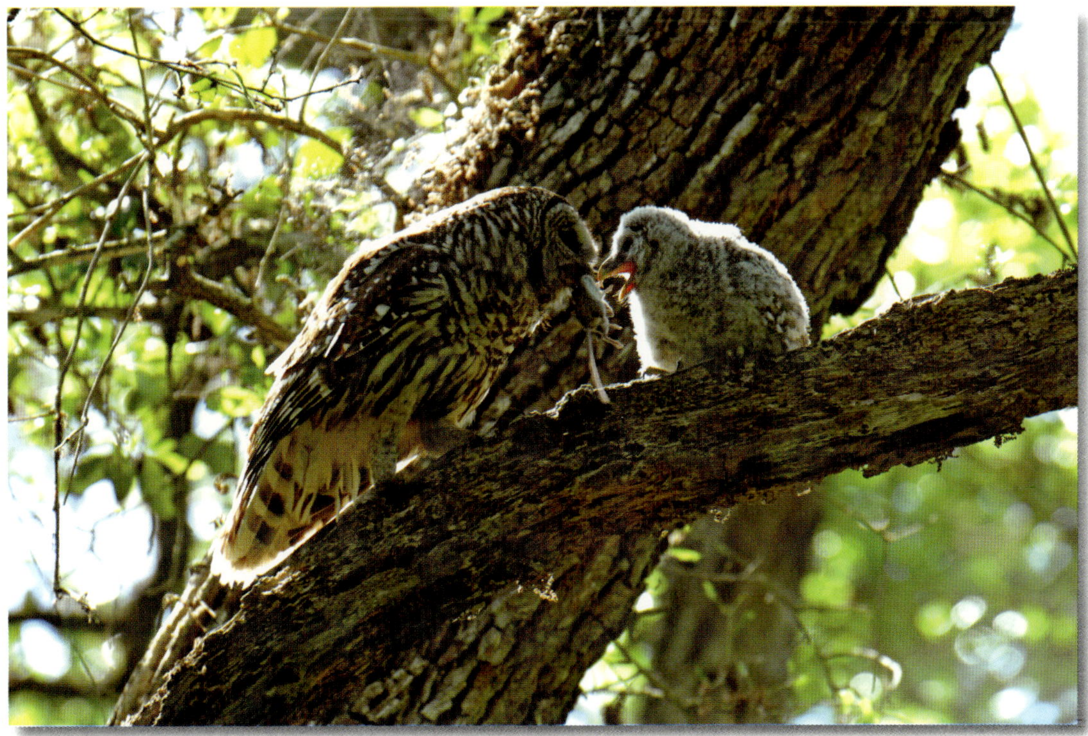

Ulrich | Barred Owl (adult feeding nestling on right)

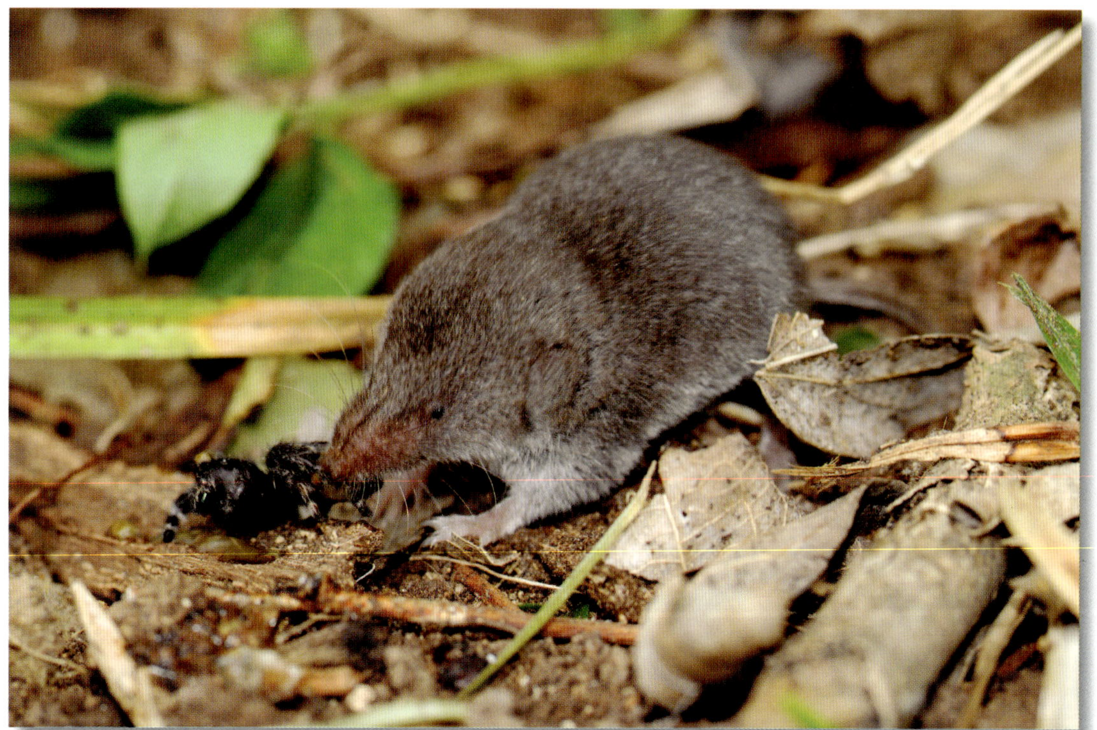

Ulrich | Least Shrew and Jumping Spider

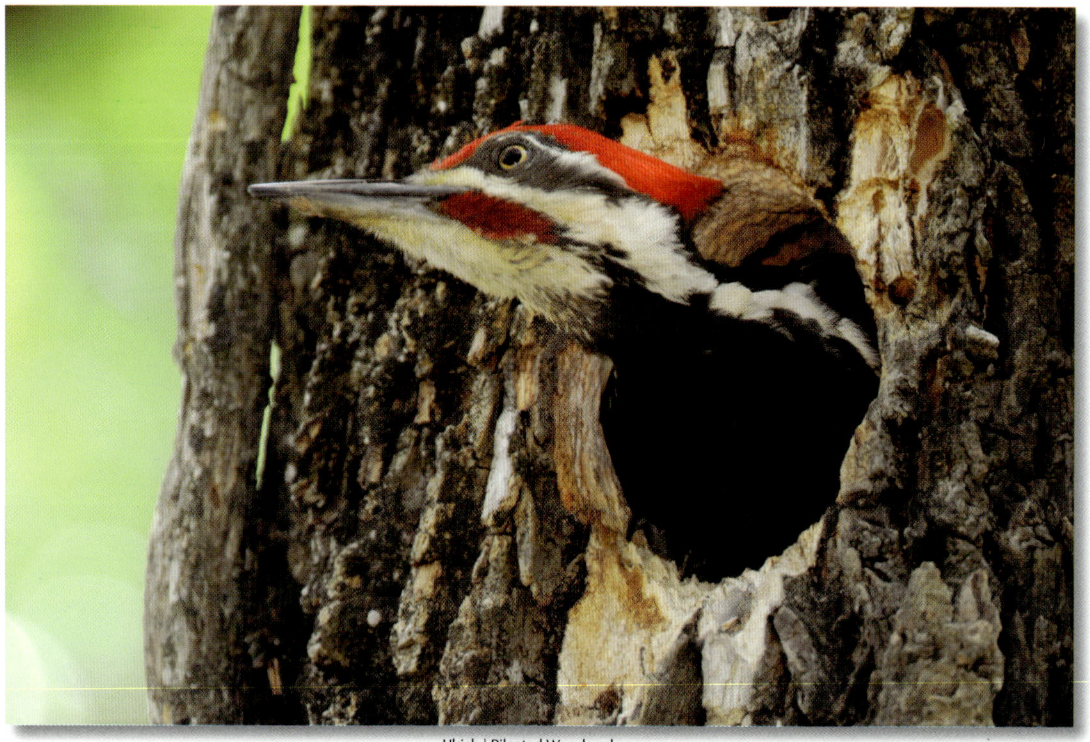

Ulrich | Pileated Woodpecker

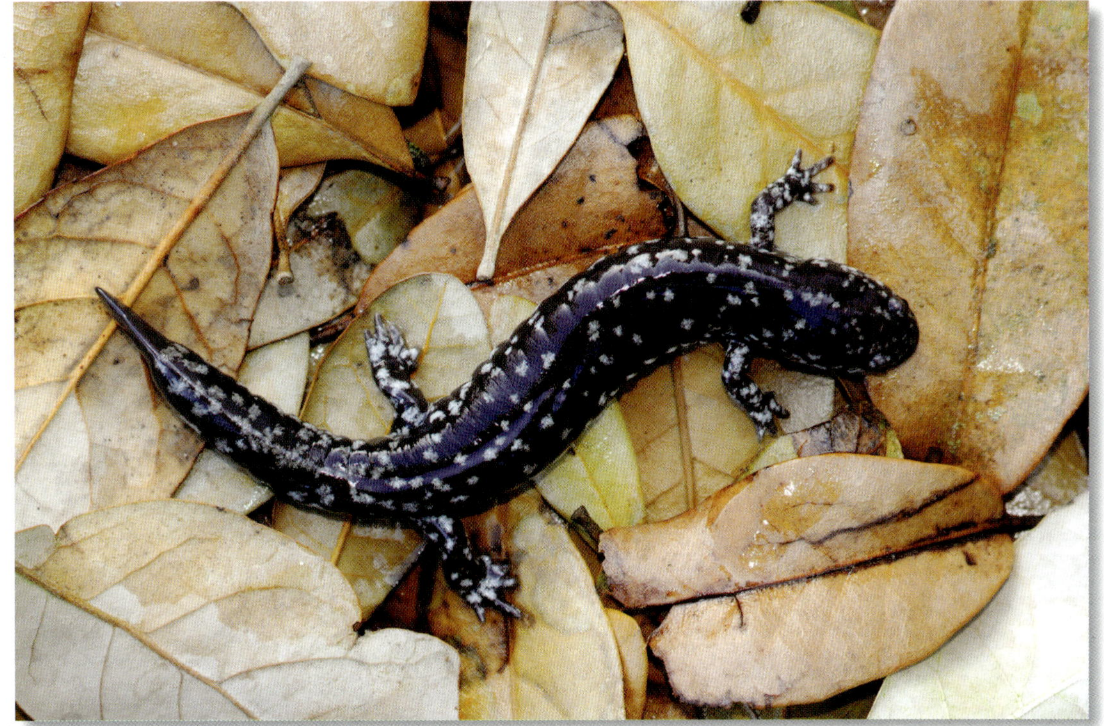

Ulrich | Western Slimy Salamander on fallen Live Oak leaves

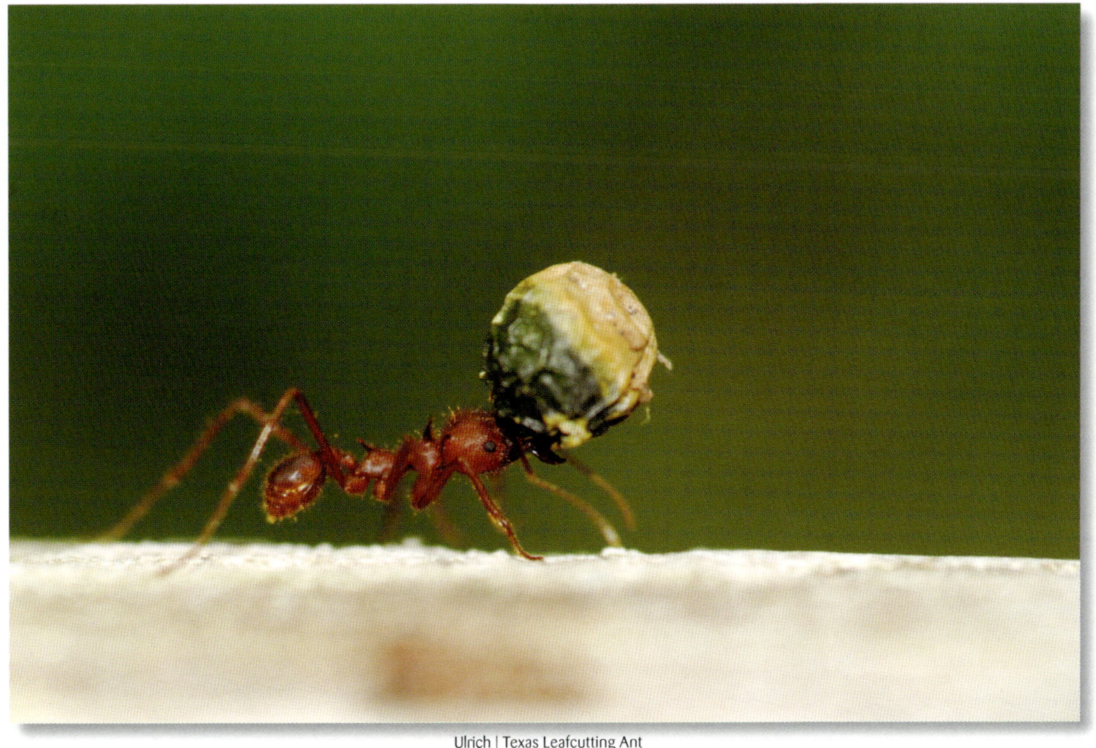

Ulrich | Texas Leafcutting Ant

About Rancho Lucero...

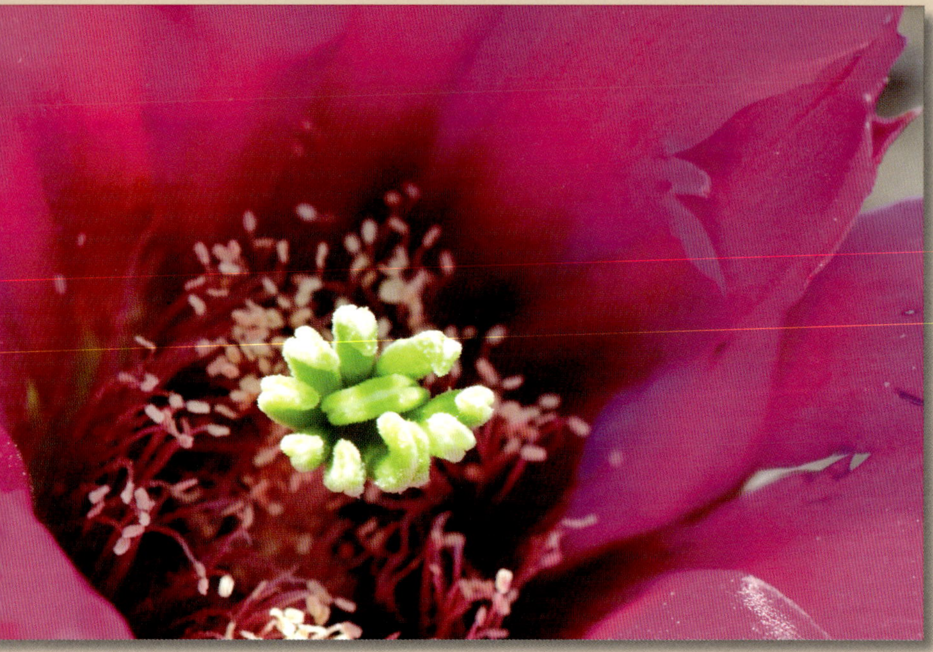
Anderson | Hedgehog Cactus flowers

Located 15 miles southwest of Freer down a long gravelly road you'll find beautiful Rancho Lucero. Translated in English it means the Bright Star Ranch. And on peaceful nights with a crisp clear evening sky when the stars shine brightly over the region you'll agree this is the perfect name. When Tim and Amy Ehrman bought the property, which is a little more than 3,100 acres carved from the 10,000-acre Peters Ranch, they dreamed of creating a wildlife sanctuary. They wanted their three beautiful children to enjoy the unique landscape and pass on the South Texas legacy for generations to come.

Their dream became reality. The ranch no longer is over grazed by cattle and truly has become a wildlife haven. On the Lucero you'll find silent Bobcats, howling Coyotes and rooting Javelinas. The ranch has a healthy population of Texas Indigo snakes that control the Texas Diamondback Rattlesnakes among other indigenous species. The ranch has a one-acre pond surrounded by enormous Palo Blanco trees that shelter wildlife from the blazing sun of this semi-arid desert land. Since its acquisition, the family has transformed Rancho Lucero from an over-extended pasture with three water sources to a well developed wildlife habitat with 16 watering holes scattered throughout the ranch. These water sources not only attract wildlife that call the Lucero home, they attract migrating visitors such as the Bullocks Oriole, Blue Grosbeak and Painted Bunting, for which this region is well known. Among the traveling birds you'll also spot Green Jays, Pyrrholoxia, cardinals and flycatchers, to name a few.

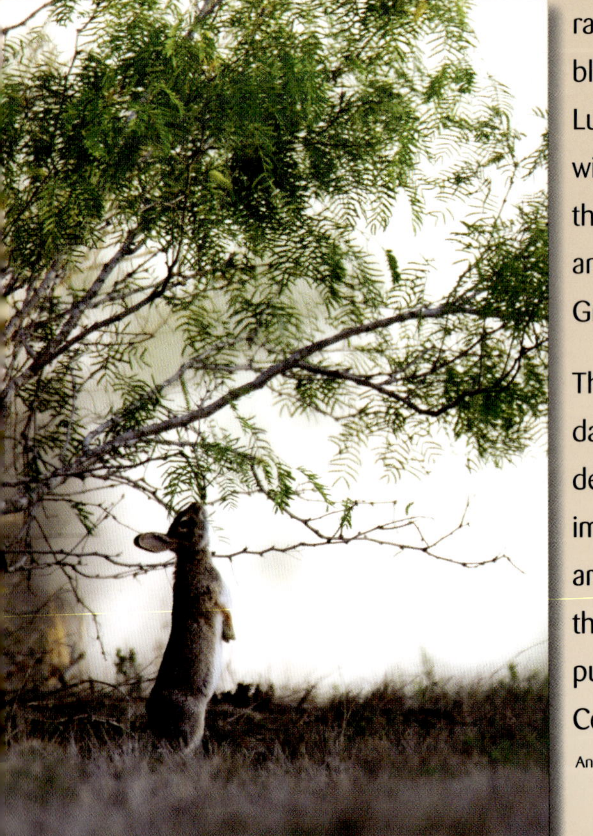

The rolling hills of this region provide breathtaking views that extend for hundreds of miles. On a clear day, you can glimpse the hilltops of northern Mexico. This interesting landscape appears bleak and desolate during drought, but erupts with lushness from the slightest touch of rain. Some of the more impressive native plants of Texas reside on Rancho Lucero. In early spring, visitors feel like their noses are playing tricks on them when they smell the strikingly sweet aroma of Texas Mountain Laurel that thrive in abundance on the ranch. This is a slow growing evergreen tree that blooms with dazzling purple blossoms that look like grape clusters. Another well known native that speckles the ranch is Cenizo, with its gray green foliage and purple flowers that grace the ranch throughout summer. The

Anderson | Eastern Cottontail Rabbit eating Mesquite leaves

Lucero also hosts several varieties of cacti, such as the Horse Crippler, Strawberry Cactus and the very rare Fishhook Cactus.

The Ranch is high fenced with a healthy herd of the famous South Texas White-tailed Deer, which enjoy choice cuisine on the Lucero. The Texas Kidney Wood and Guayacan are common brush plants on the ranch and are two of the prime browsing choices for white-tail. The Ehrmans have created supplemental feeding opportunities for their deer, with food plots and free choice feeders.

The headquarters at Rancho Lucero will accommodate several guests. The ranch also boasts a state-of-the-art game handling facility. The Ehrmans enjoy the ranch with their family and strive to be honorable stewards of the land.

Tim Ehrman
Corpus Christi, TX
tjehrman@aol.com

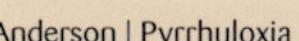

Anderson | Pyrrhuloxia

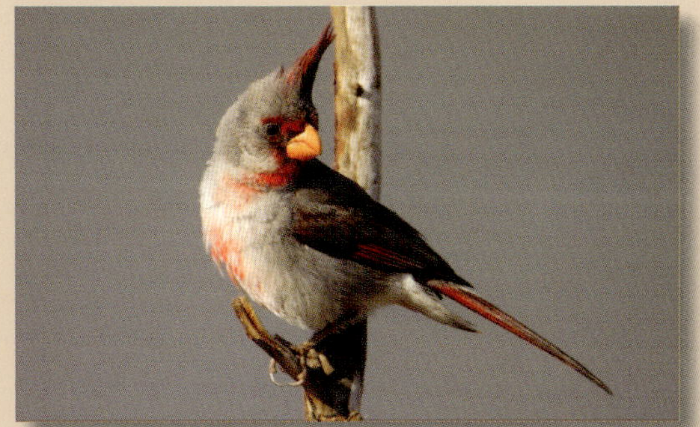

Anderson | Northern Cardinal

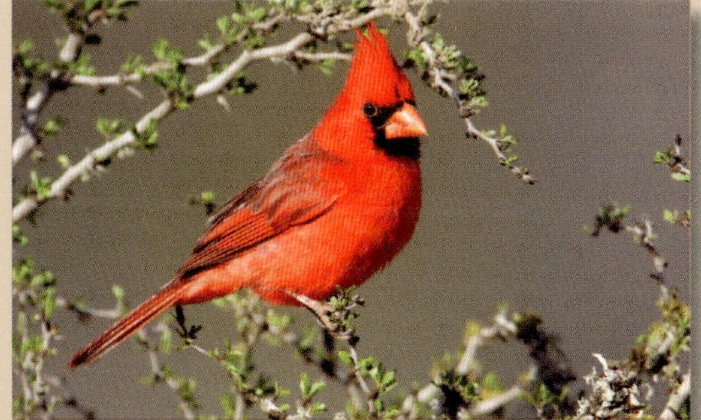

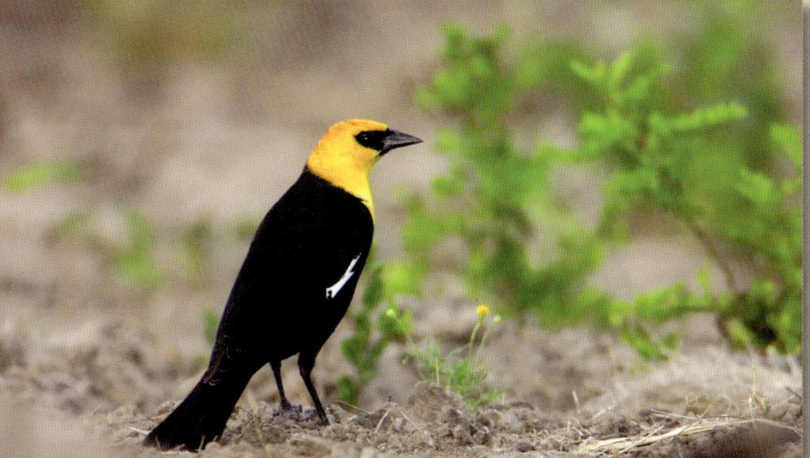

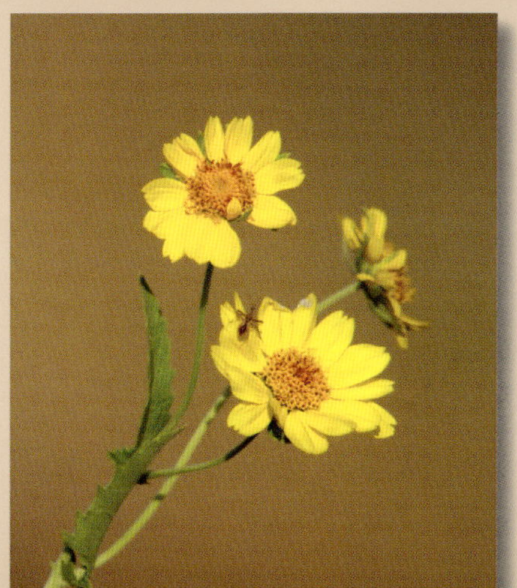

Anderson | White-tailed Deer (above)
Anderson | Yellow-headed Blackbird (left)
Anderson | Cowpen Daisy (right)

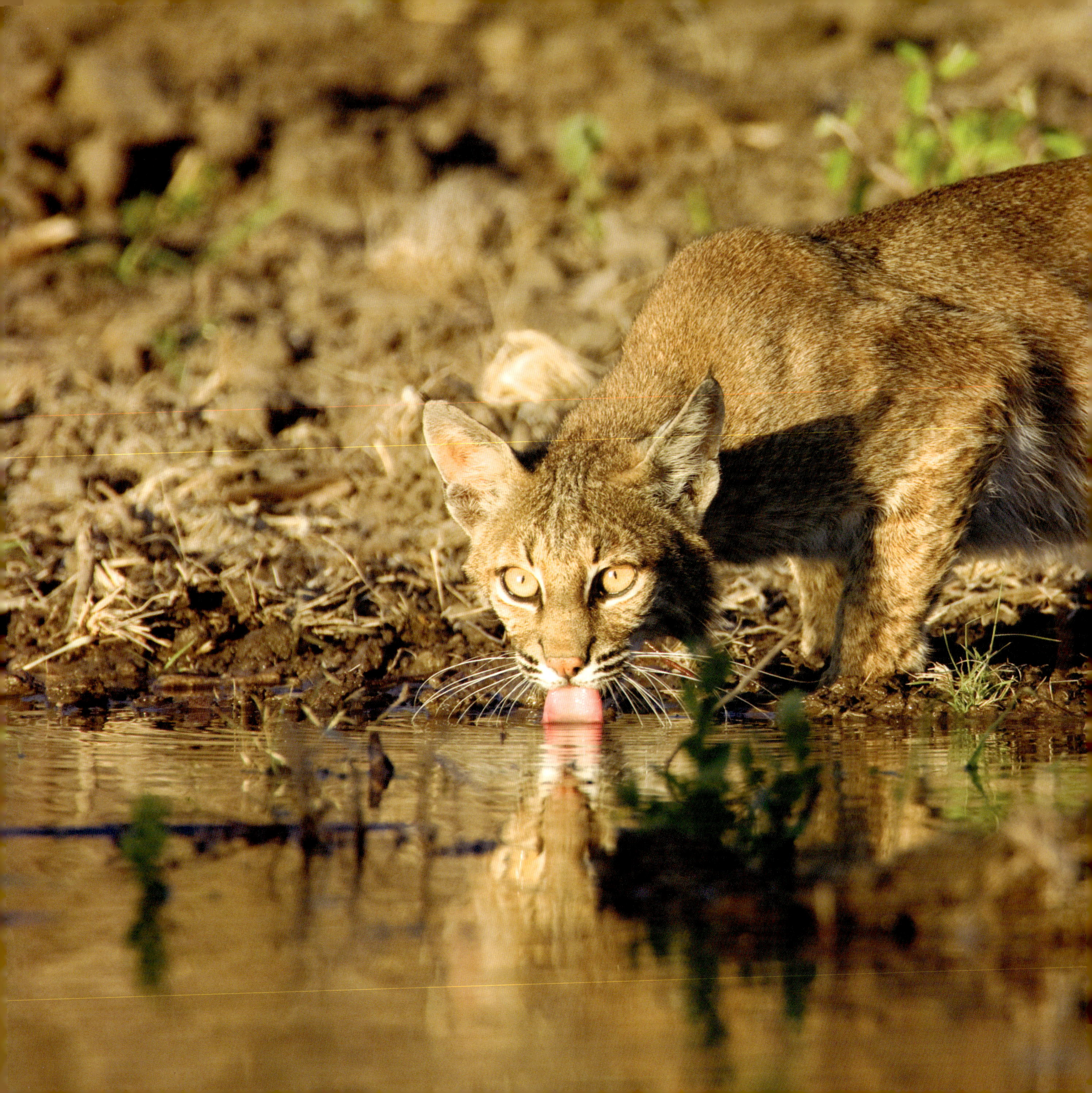

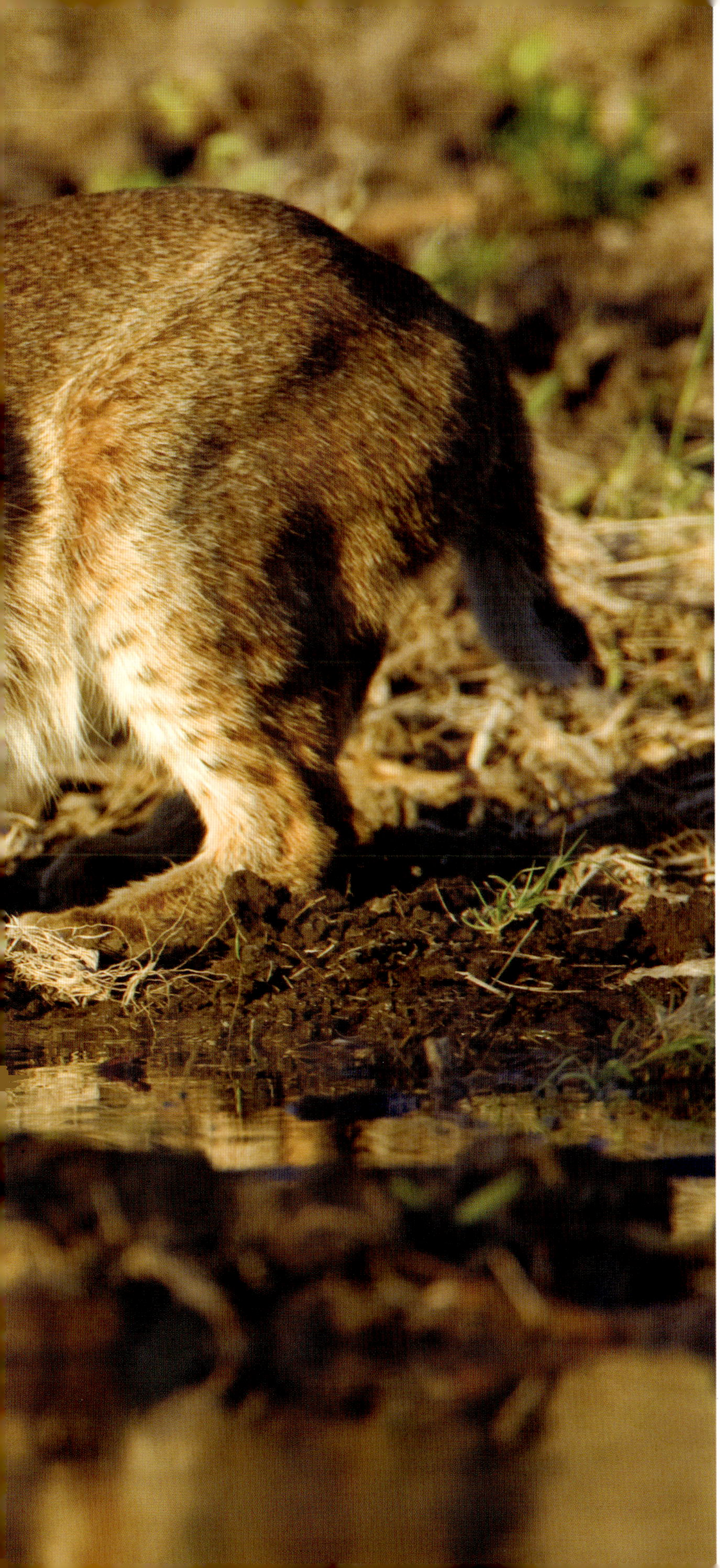

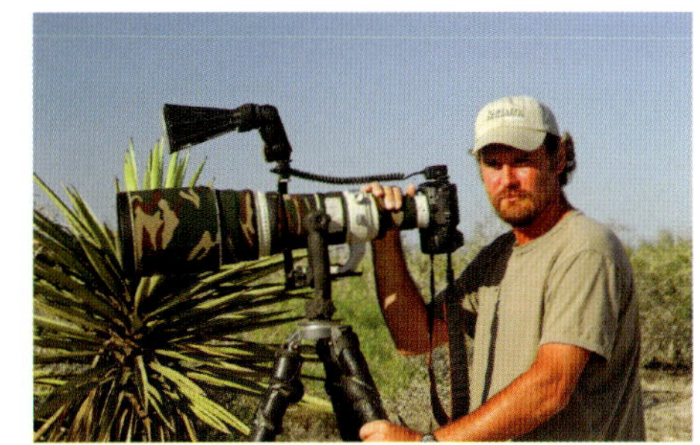

Joshua Anderson

It was the idea of "conserving wildlife and wildlife habitat through sustainable development" which caught Joshua Anderson's attention when he heard of the ICF Pro-Tour. With so much of Texas' land in the hands of private stewards, says Joshua, "it's imperative that [landowners] find ways to make land preservation profitable." He wanted to help do his part.

And, Joshua credits Jim Erhardt, publisher of Nature Photographers Online Magazine (NPN), with helping him by sponsoring him in the contest. He explains that the community-based website, much like ICF, focuses on using "photography for habitat conservation and environmental photojournalism."

He remained leery of a showdown with one of the region's most famous residents: the Western Diamondback Rattler. "I was very eager to photograph one, but I also didn't want to walk up and surprise one." A great relationship with the folks at Rancho Lucero helped to quickly educate him on how to safely travel around in the "the bush" the native reptile calls home.

"I also learned that I have a lot more patience than I realized. I spent the better part of 13 days in a single blind waiting for a specific animal to photograph." His perseverance paid off, and he "ended up getting over 40 marketable images in seven minutes of consistent shooting."

That animal was a Bobcat and it made its appearance at the best time, "Late evening, superior lighting."

The photographer sees his work more as art, rather than documentation. Lighting and its nuances are his loves. "If I am photographing animals or landscapes, the light is the most important element. Beautiful, moody light can make a mundane scene look like something out of a fairy tale, while harsh midday light can ruin the most pristine landscape ever seen."

"Without a doubt I feel my photography improved while I was in South Texas. There was not a single morning or evening that went by in those 30 days that I did not spend photographing. With so much shooting you definitely begin to see the world from a different perspective."

Chillicothe, OH
www.joshuaandersonphotography.com
[e] janderson@mail.gsn.k12.oh.us

Anderson | Bobcat

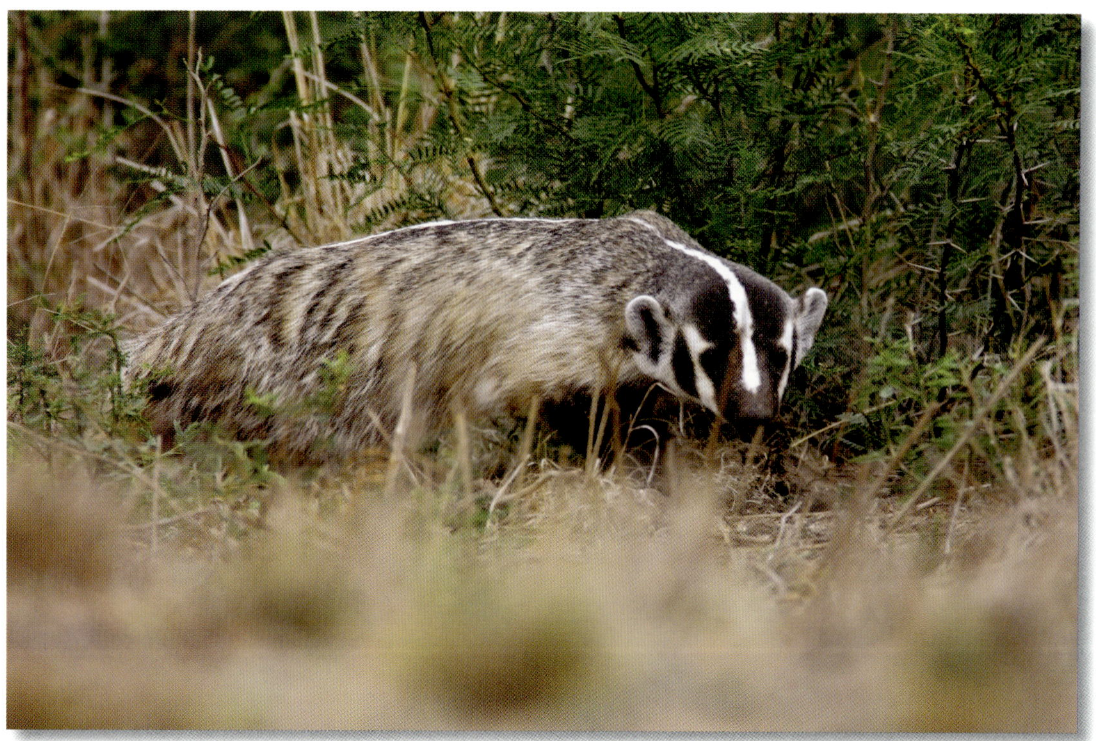

Anderson | American Badger

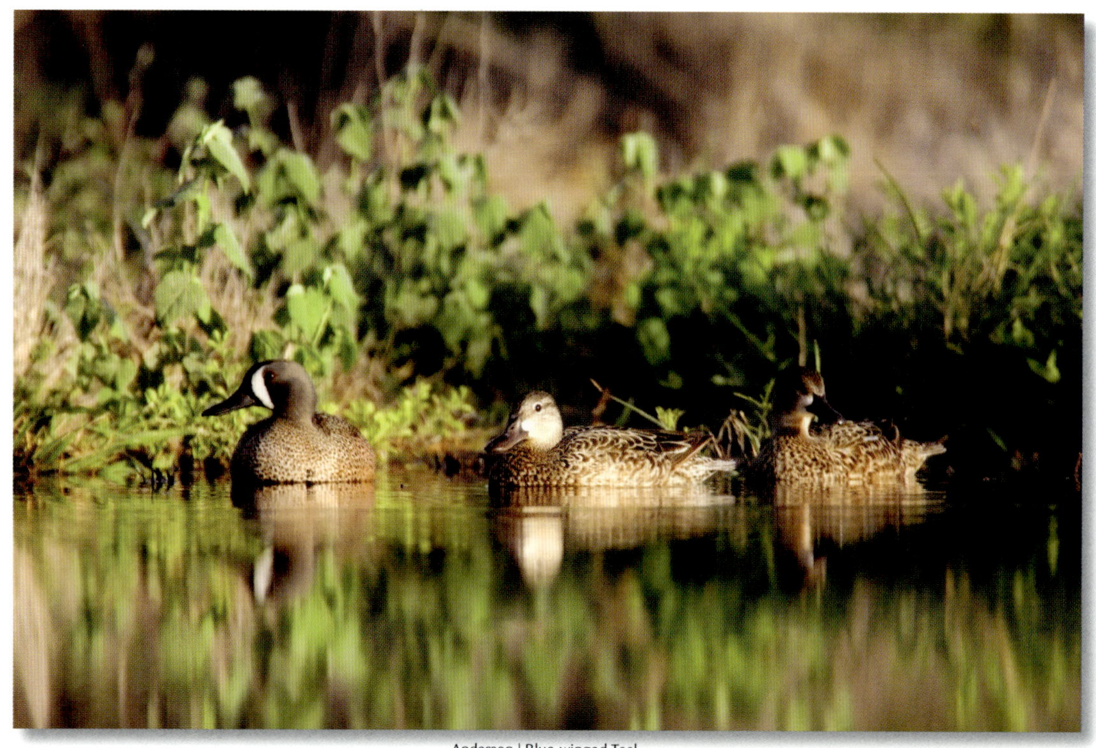

Anderson | Blue-winged Teal

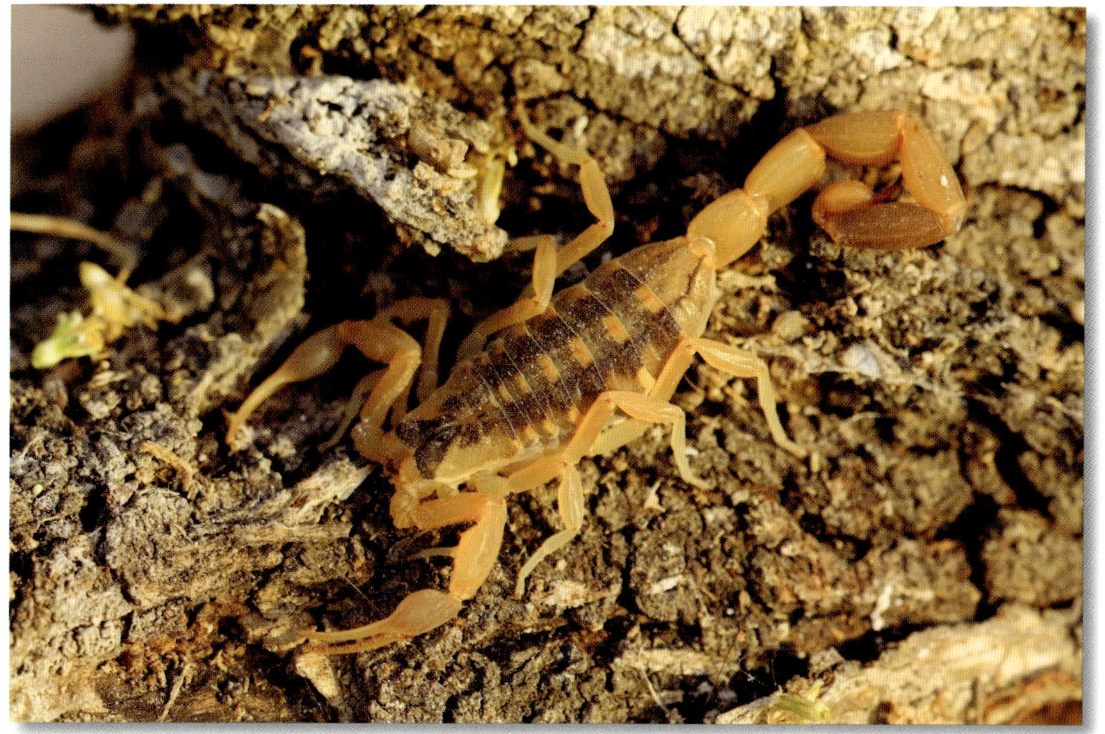
Anderson | Striped Bark Scorpion

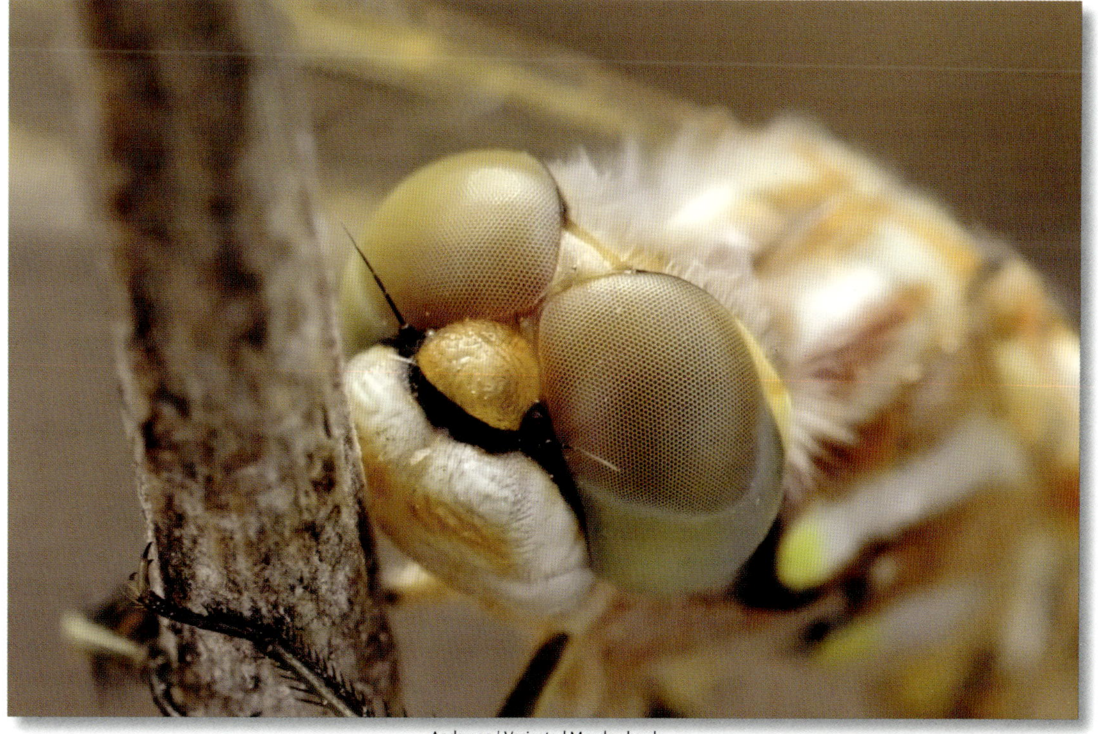
Anderson | Varigated Meadowhawk

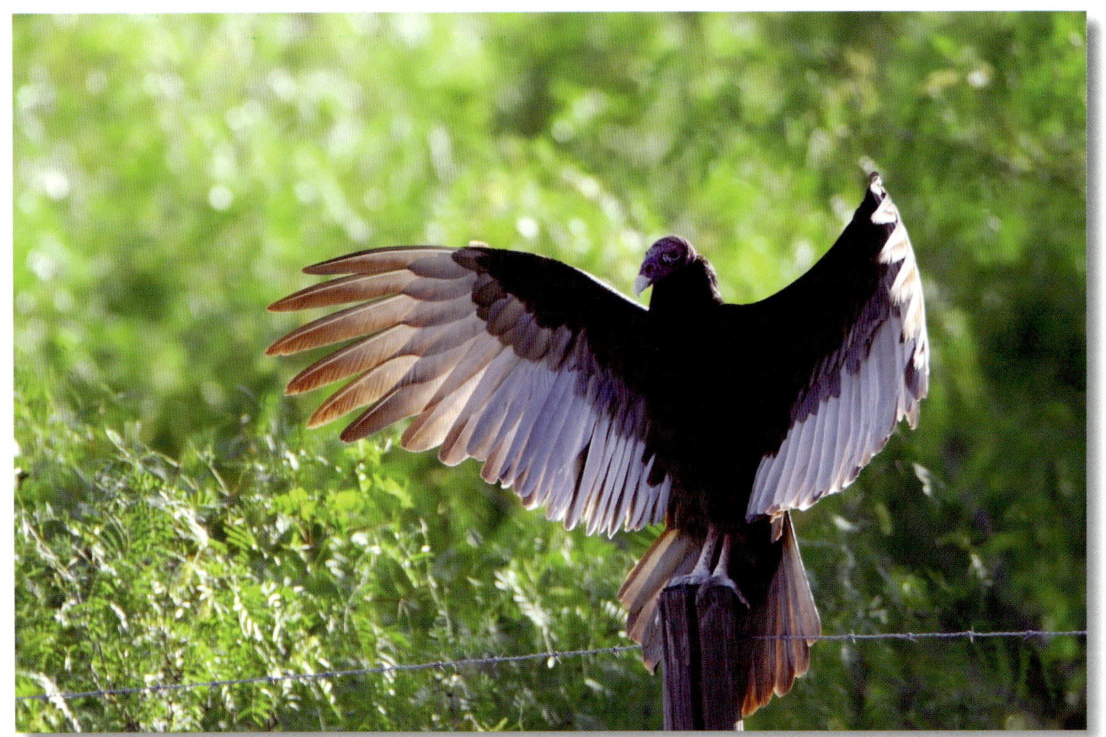

Anderson | Turkey Vulture

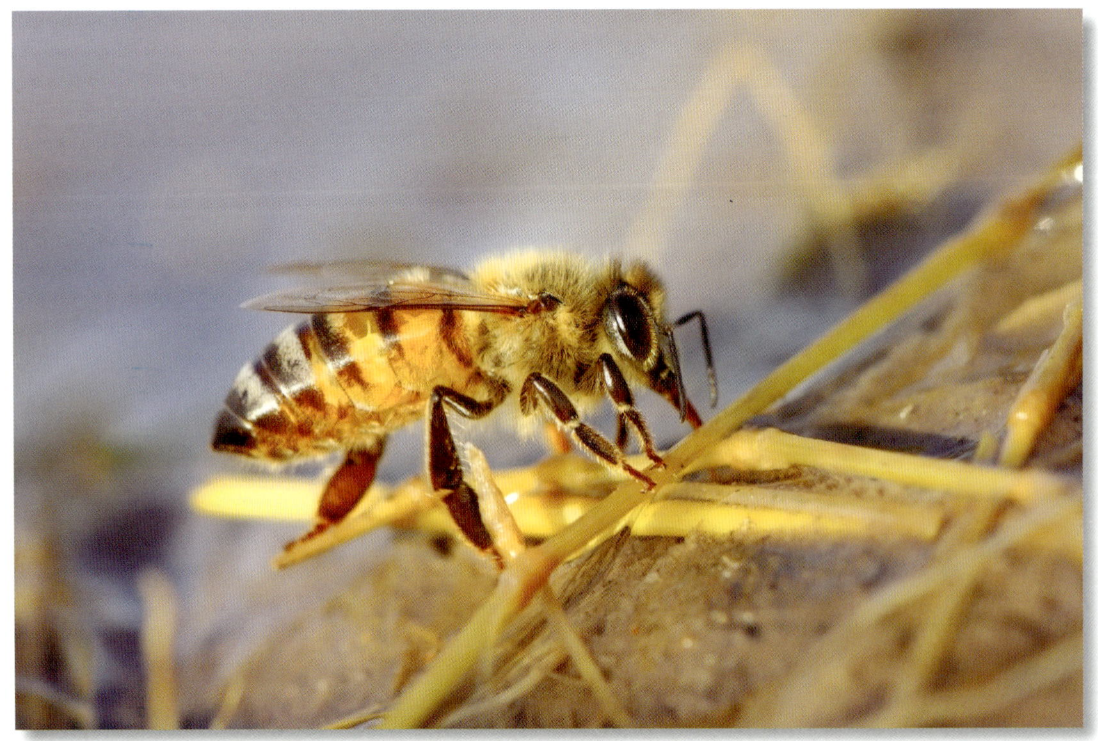

Anderson | Honey Bee

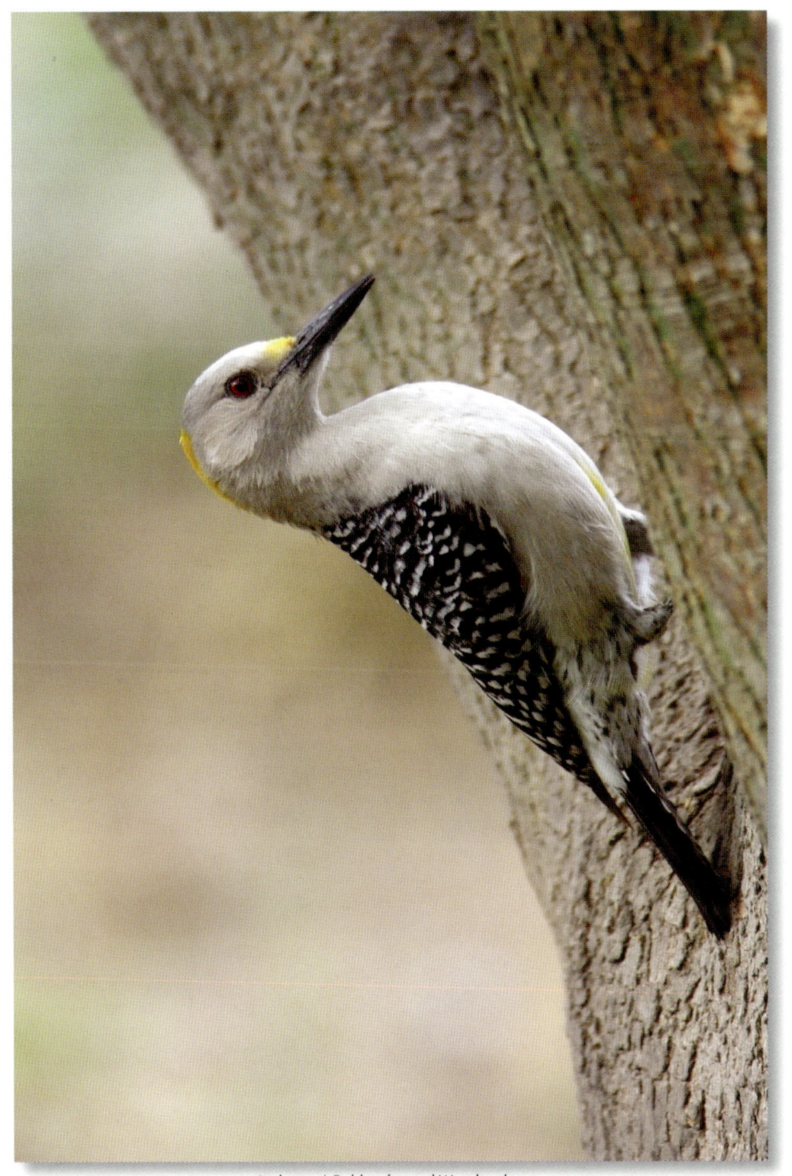

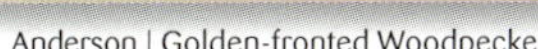

Anderson | Golden-fronted Woodpecker

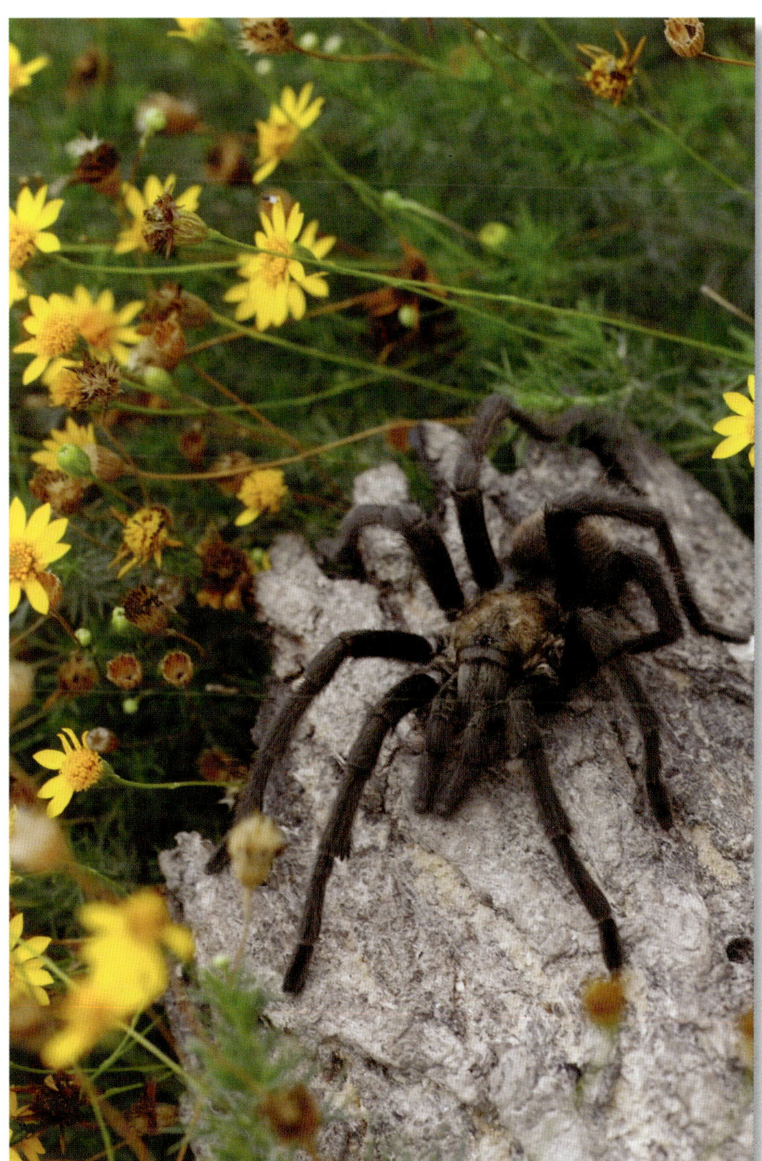

Anderson | Tarantula by Dogweed (flowers)

About Sick Dog Ranch (Dale Land & Cattle)...

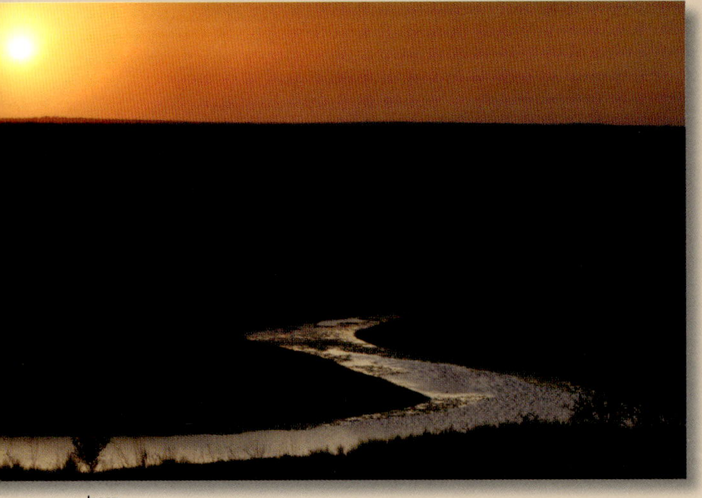

Isern

Grandpa Dale was fond of telling his twin grandsons that not everyone has to enjoy deer hunting as he did, but that he hoped every man, including the two boys, would find something they love as much as their grandfather loved deer hunting.

This was among the many life lessons involving the outdoors that Grandpa Dale left with his grandsons. Memories of their grandfather's lessons and wise sayings continue to resonate in the minds of the Dale brothers as they enjoy the beautiful family ranch in northern Jim Wells County. Mitchell Dale said there isn't a day that passes at the ranch that he doesn't reminisce about the values his grandfather taught him. Their dream of owning a ranch became a reality in the early 1990s. The Dale Brothers are successful businessmen, both working as the third generation of family members at McRee Ford in Dickinson. Mitchell's daughter Molly, son Carter and son-in-law Dain also are involved in the business. Like the ranch, the dealership is a family affair.

Isern | Lindheimer Prickly Pear

The scenic rolling hills of the Sick Dog Ranch (Dale Land & Cattle) are part of the rich history of the original Wild Horse Desert, where the first horses of North America roamed freely. The breathtaking views of this 7,500-acre ranch boast the original headquarters of the historic Freeborn Ranch. A few of the original structures from the 1800s remain on the ranch. In the nearby home pasture is a beautiful stucco and stone ranch house. This impressive home represents the epitome of family living, told in pictures and artwork hung on the walls of a hearty kitchen. Talavera tiles pay homage to the region's Spanish heritage through the home. The home's design was a family project but the interior decor came from the brilliant eye of Michael Dale.

The Dale family cherishes their land, which hosts many native plant and wildlife species such as White-tailed Deer, Javelina, Bobcats, Mountain Lions, armadillos and reptiles that include Diamondback Rattlesnake, Texas tortoise and a Texas favorite, the Horned Lizard.

During the past 12 years the Dale family has become exceptional stewards of the land, striking a healthy balance between their cattle operation and the wildlife management. Family members are blessed to have lifelong friend, Emmit Heffron and his wife Cynthia manage the day-to-day ranch operations. The cattle rotationally graze for optimum use of the native grasses and forbs. The family has developed fenced food plots planted annually for deer, turkey and quail. Managers at the Sick Dog Ranch (Dale Land & Cattle) enhance the habitat through prescribed burns, aerating, chopping and fallow discing to create ideal wildlife conditions. They survey the ranch annually by helicopter to determine the viability of the ranch's native populations. And cattle are rounded up by helicopter twice a year.

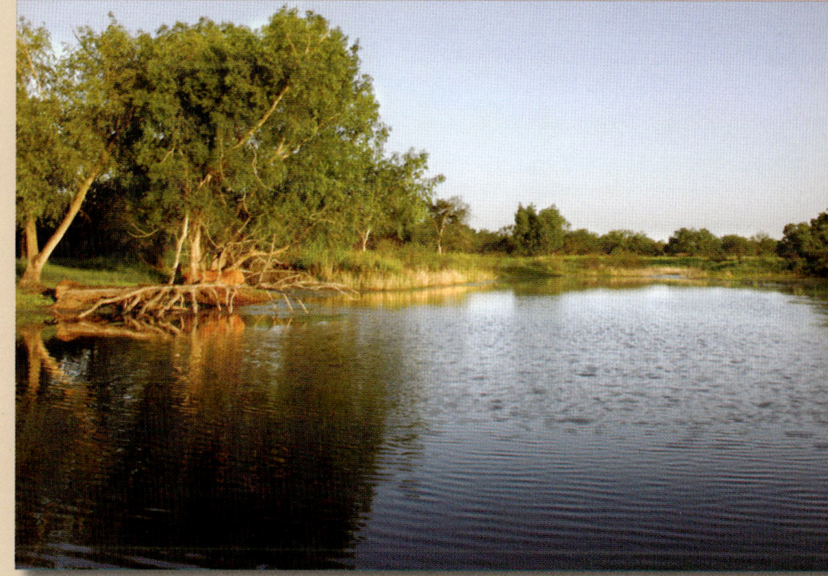

Isern

In addition to the commercial calf-cow herd, the ranch is home to about 50 registered Texas Longhorns. So along with being exceptional land stewards, the Dales also have nurtured and benefited thousands of children through a program called the Longhorn Project. This is an agriculture program that provides life lessons to students from elementary through high school in the Clear Creek School District by encouraging them to raise Texas Longhorn cattle. The Dales, who breed Longhorns, offer their livestock for free to a youngster in exchange for the student's commitment to raise, groom and show them at major livestock shows. The prize money and premiums students win from the competition and sale of these animals go directly towards collage scholarships for these students. The Dales love their Longhorn herd, which actually originated from their grandson. Carson, who started showing cattle in the peewee division, is responsible for the purchase of the Dale's first Longhorn named Freckles. The Longhorns are not a part of the family beef operation. For now, the herd of 20 to 30 Longhorns are bred and raised exclusively for pleasure and distributed to students in the name of education.

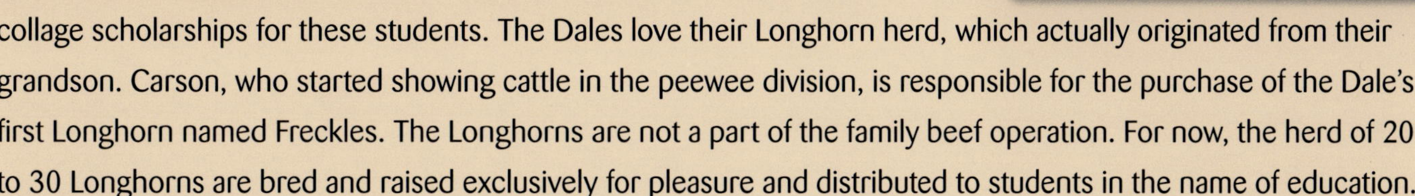

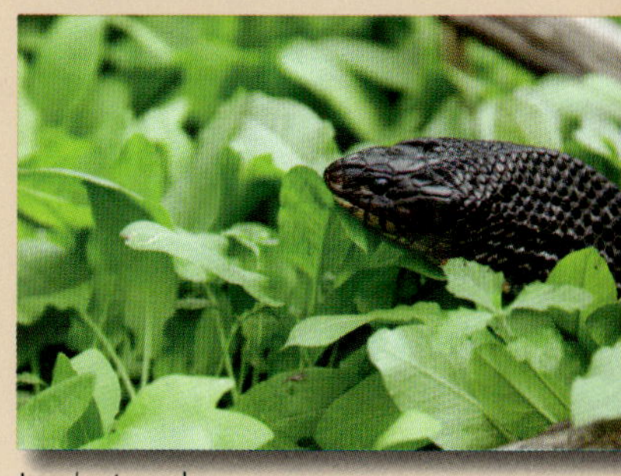

Isern | water snake

The Sick Dog has a certain ring to it that makes folks who hear it for the first time tilt their head like a curious puppy. The name was born as the Dale family enjoyed a cold winter day with close family friends at a ski resort. Three of the family members were riding up a ski lift when one challenged the other to take a look at the only way down, a double black mogul. Someone responded that only a sick dog would go down such a treacherous slope. The name stuck. The Sick Dog Ranch (Dale Land & Cattle) receives five-star reviews from biologist and photographer guests alike. It's a quiet retreat where anyone can enjoy the serene vistas, seven tanks and the trickling rhythms of seasonal creeks. The Dales strongly believe in conservation and are involved in many organizations that support these efforts, such as the Texas Wildlife Association, Images for Conservation Fund and South Texas Property Rights Association. They plan to continue opening their ranch to the Coastal Bend Wildlife Photo Contest so that others may enjoy its wonders.

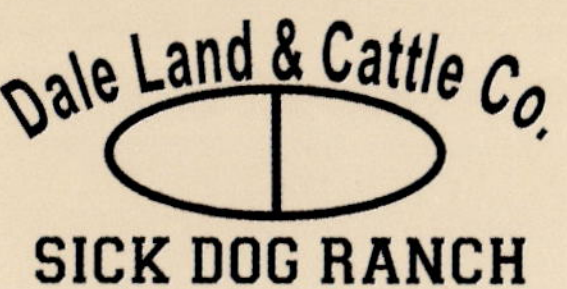

Mitchell M. Dale
Dickinson, TX
[e] mdale@mcreeford.com

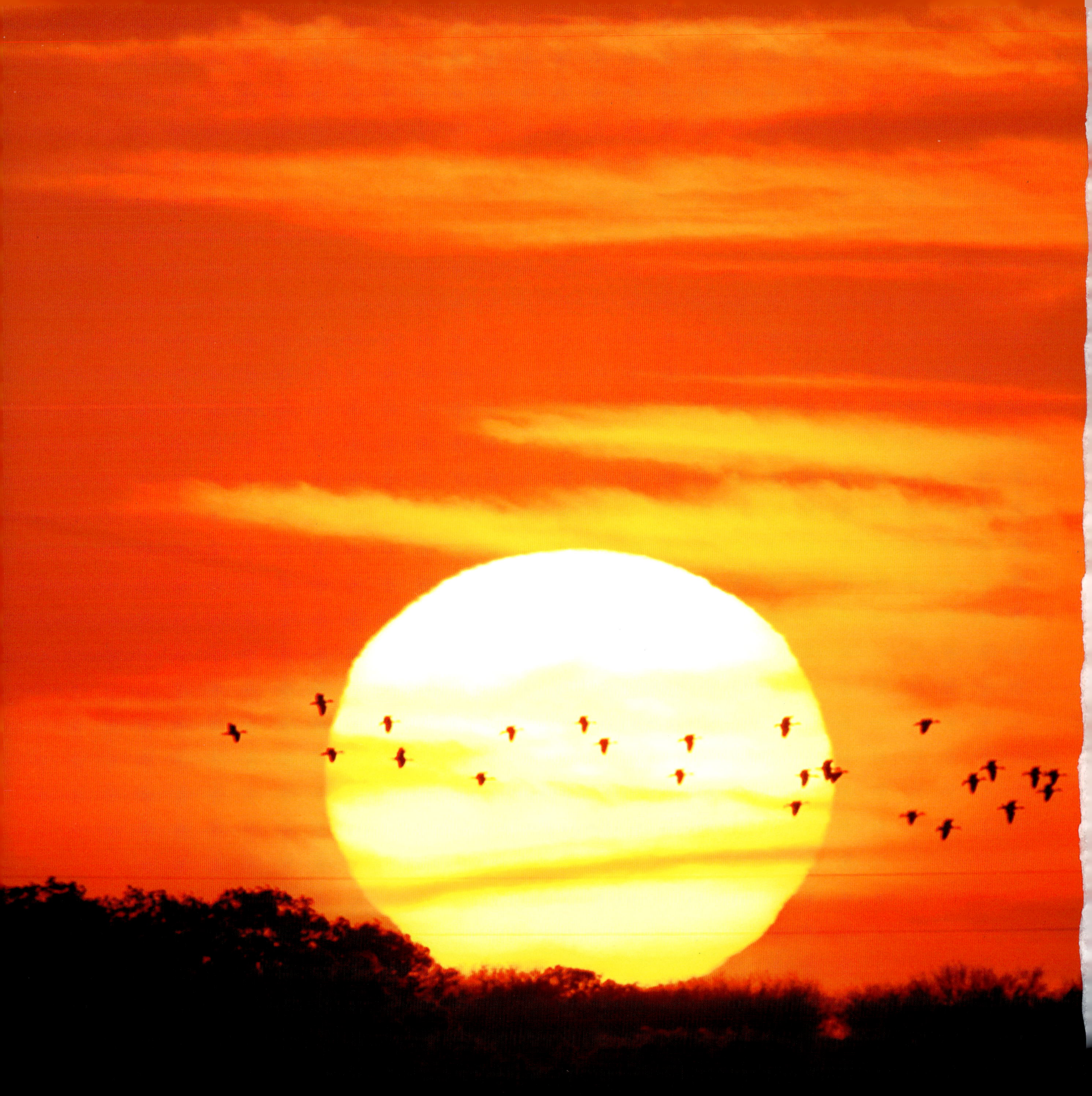

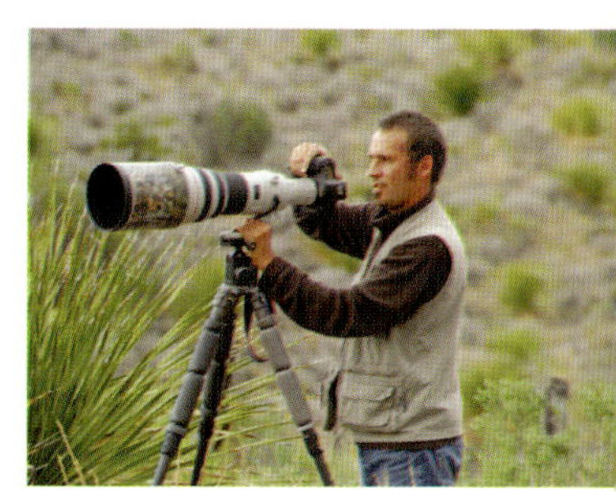

Santiago Gibert Isern

During his days on the Sick Dog Ranch (Dale Land & Cattle), Santiago Gibert Isern says, "I learned cattle ranchers are interested in business and appreciate nature." He also discovered it's possible to integrate cattle management and conservation.

That was good news to the photographer and conservation biologist. He uses the power of his images to help people "appreciate the excellence found in nature so they'll value it and respect it."

Six years ago the native of Spain moved from Barcelona to northern Mexico to do conservation biology there. "At present I'm collaborating with CEMEX on a project in El Carmen. We're studying the conservation and reintroduction of species such as the Bighorn Sheep, the Black Bear, and the Golden Eagle."

"This area is in Coahuila on the border with Texas, across from Big Bend National Park and Black Gap Management Area; it forms one of the biggest international protected areas in the world."

Santiago has joined forces with the International League of Conservation Photographers. Together with some of his Mexican colleagues, he formed Tierra Silvestre, A.C., an association that helps carry out various projects focused on northeastern Mexico.

When he arrived in Mexico, he says, "I started to take images as a hobby." He soon discovered he was as passionate about photography as he was about conservation. This passion led him to the ICF Pro-Tour, which he feels is "the way to seriously promote conservation."

During the contest, Santiago says, "I learned that sometimes the most important thing is not to win but to focus on my true purpose, which is the conservation of wildlife and wild areas." He remains hopeful that we aren't too late to "preserve the marvelous biodiversity of the planet on which we live. Today, in general, people are more conscious about conserving the planet and its components so that we're able to live better."

Linares, Nuevo Leon, Mexico
[e] santigibert@hotmail.com

Isern | whistling ducks flying by sunset

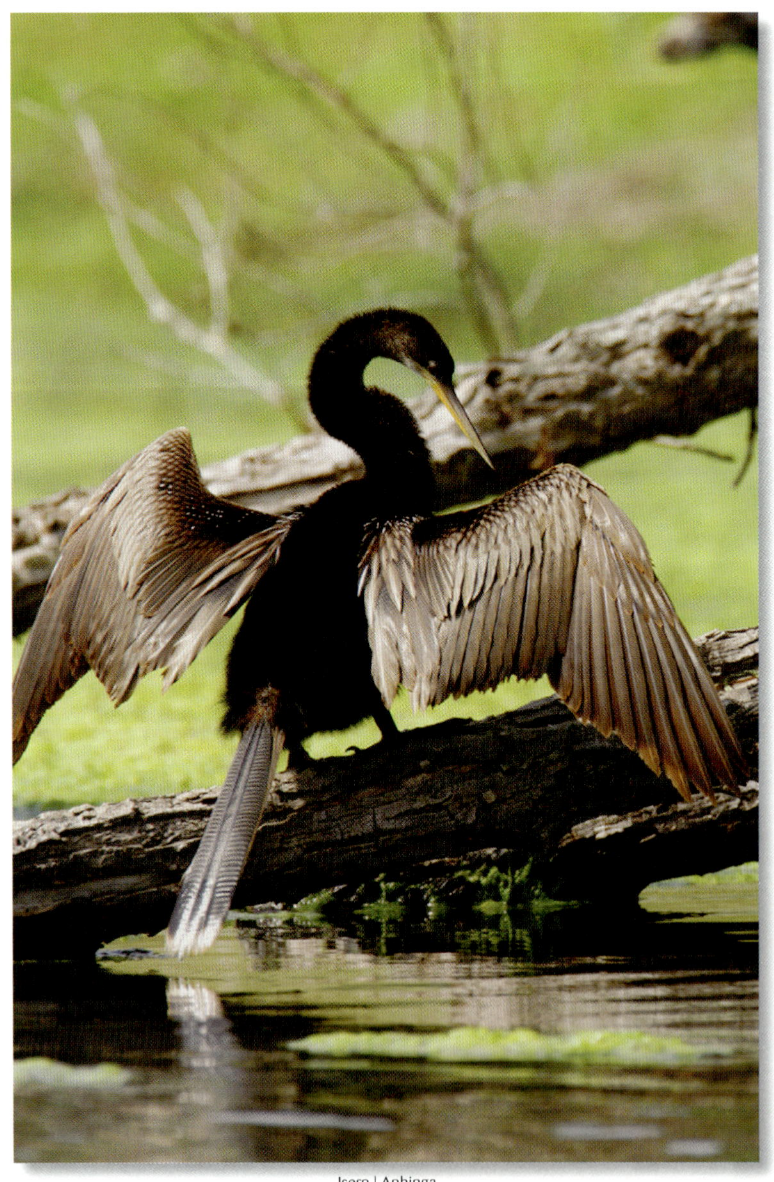

Isern | Anhinga

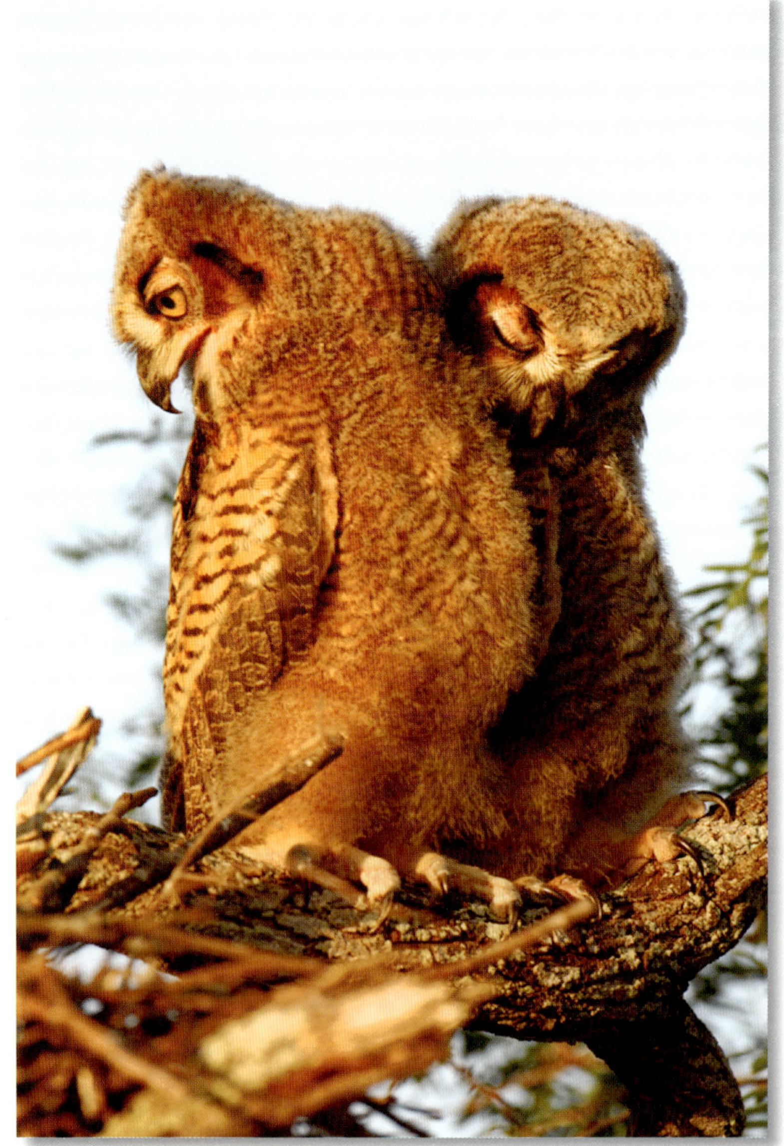

Isern | Great Horned Owl nestlings

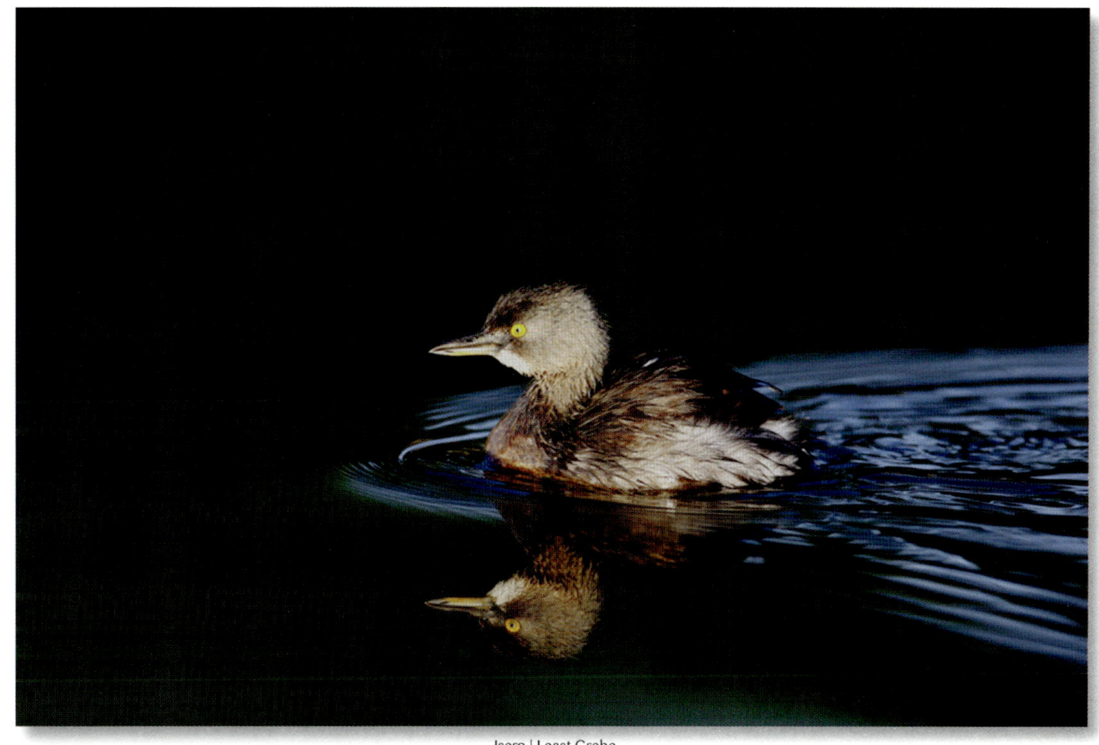

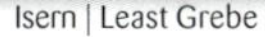
Isern | Least Grebe

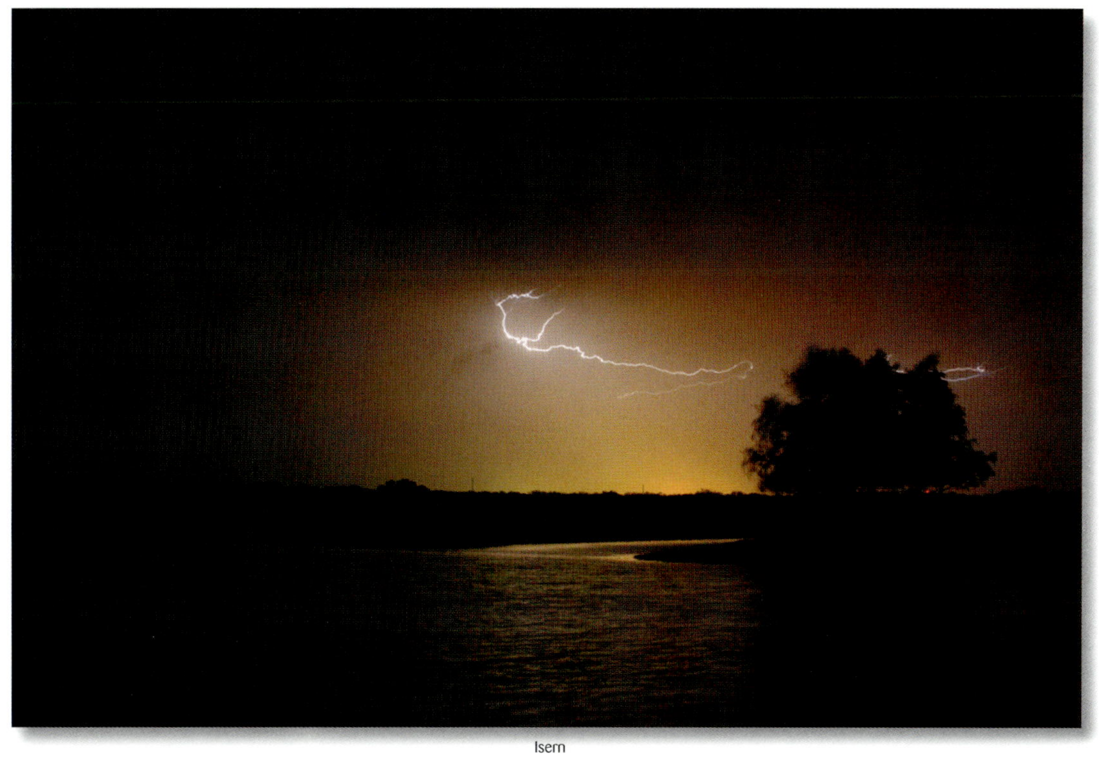

Isern

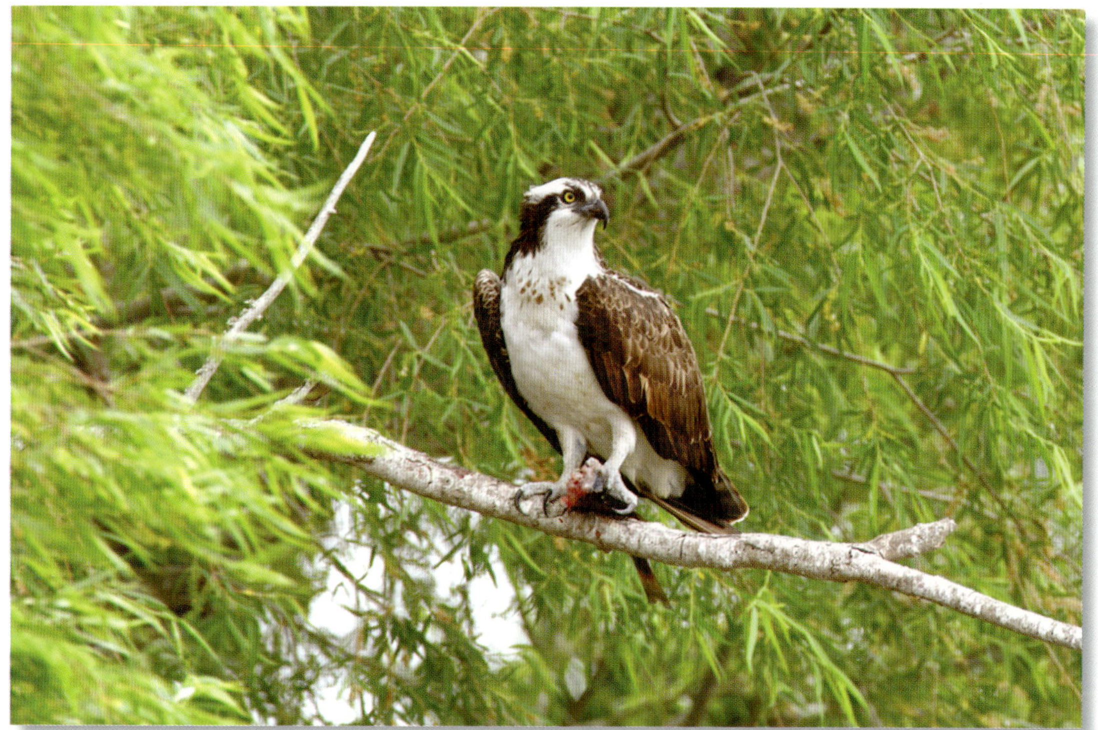
Isern | Osprey in Willow

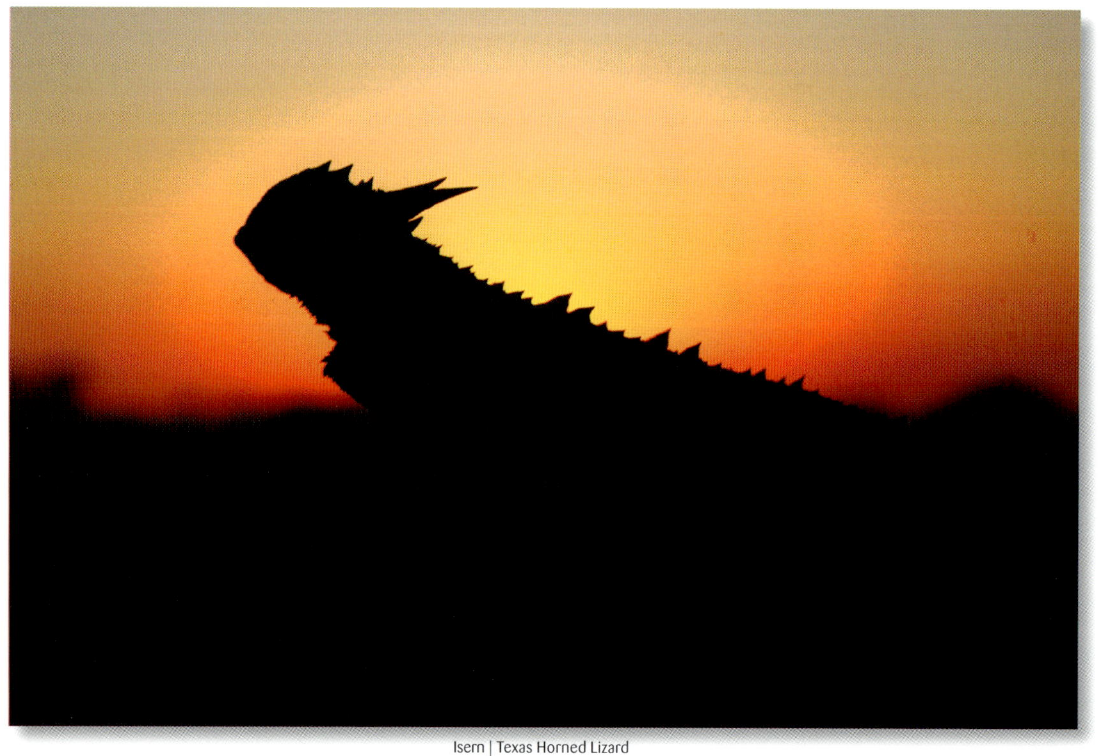
Isern | Texas Horned Lizard

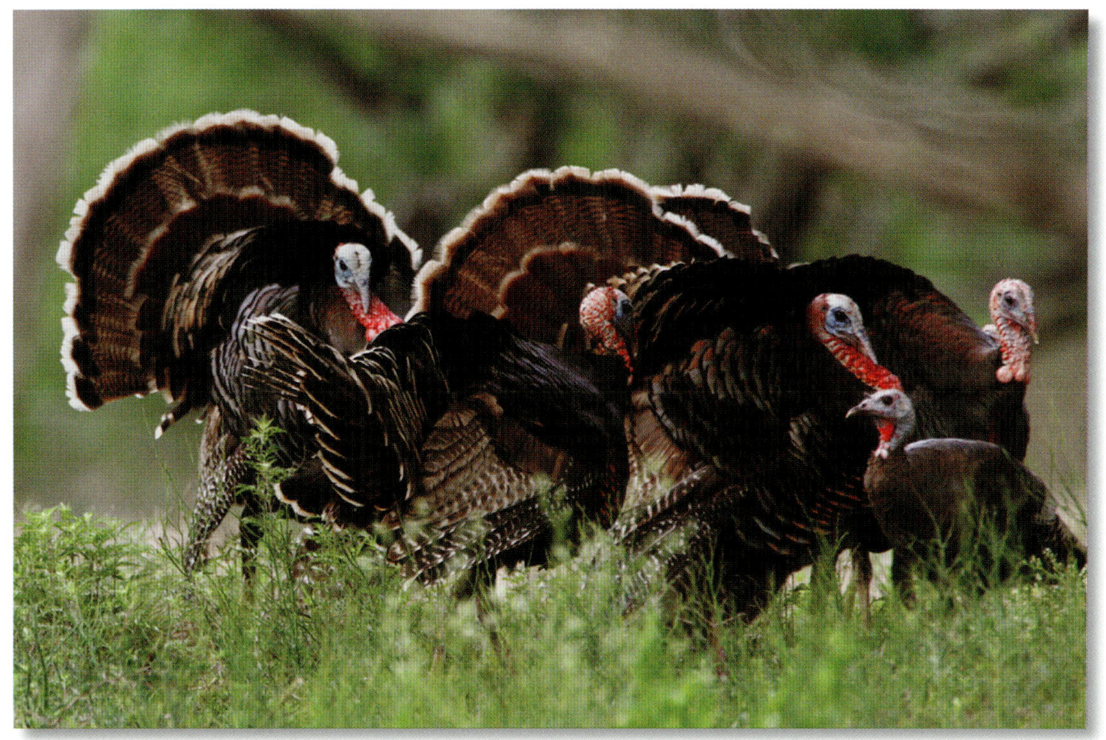

Isern | Wild Turkey

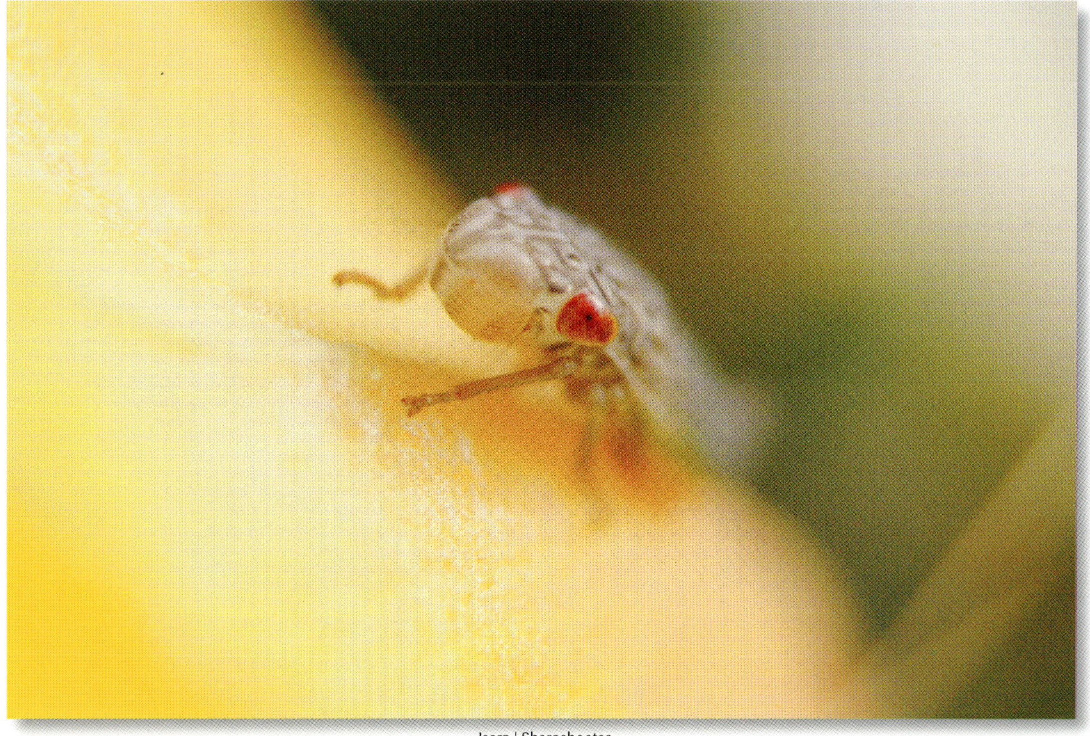

Isern | Sharpshooter

About Twin Oaks Ranch...

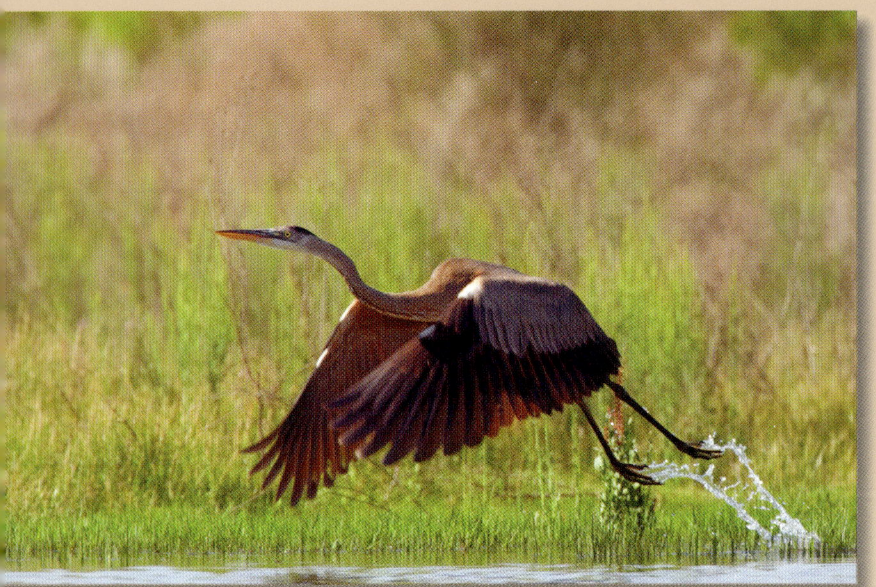

Perry | Great Blue Heron

Twin Oaks Ranch stretches across the heartland of the Texas Coastal Plains. The Nueces River runs along its eastern border as it flows gradually into Lake Corpus Christi. This Live Oak County ranch landscape covers rolling hills, sandy windswept savannahs, cultivated pastures, alluvial plains, and wet weather marshes. In 1914 Claire Cartwright received the ranch as a wedding gift from her husband Holman Cartwright. They named their property Twin Oaks after the majestic 500 year-old oak tree with two trunks by which they built their home and began a tradition of hospitality and innovative land management that continues today. J. Frank Dobie from the neighboring Dobie Ranch would often stop by to visit and talk about world affairs and reminisce about when he and Holman cowboyed together.

Lon Cartwright arrived at Twin Oaks in 1938 at the age of 16 to work the ranch with his Aunt Claire and Uncle Holman Cartwright. In 1955 Lon brought Mary Leigh Zerbee to Twin Oaks as his bride. They worked together for over 40 years to create a ranch that would welcome family and friends for many generations.

Perry | immature White Ibis

From the 1950s, Lon and Holman Cartwright worked as partners in Cartwright Cattle Company implementing advances in ranch programs, a process that Loncito, Lon's son, watched from an early age. Lon, Holman, and Loncito were early advocates of using prescribed burning as a tool for range and brush management. Their innovative methods augment the Cartwrights' deep commitment to conservation, sustainable farming and agriculture practices. The ranch's diversity includes cow, calf and stocker enterprises as well as hunting and direct marketed grass-fed lamb. In addition to prescribed burning and rotational livestock grazing, ranch wildlife management focuses on habitat preservation by creating strip edge areas of different densities in the brush, identifying and encouraging native wildlife forage, and using hunting as a tool.

A new addition to Twin Oaks Ranch is a state-of-the-art multi-use facility, Triple B Lodge. In addition to Triple B Services LLP, the Cartwrights have enjoyed working jointly with the Farm Bureau, National Conservation Resource Services, the Texas A&M Experimental Stations, Texas Parks and Wildlife, and the Caesar Kleberg Institute on projects at the ranch. Texas and Southwestern Cattle Raisers and Texas Wildlife Association have also helped the Cartwrights to be admirable stewards of their land and its resources. Opening their gates for these organizations as well as Audubon Society, Boy Scouts, Girl Scouts, churches, and other groups in the South Texas community has been a tradition of fun and friendly hospitality for the family.

Participating in the Coastal Bend Wildlife Photo Contest, this year Twin Oaks also hosted the judges' party for the Pro-Tour contest. Lon's daughter Claire Vaughan beams, "We all love the photo contests because the photographers, like us, love to share the beauty of the wild on our ranch…and we hope to keep doing it forever." The Cartwrights and Vaughans look forward to opening Twin Oaks Ranch for photo-hunt adventures guided by experienced photographers.

Visitors to the ranch are likely to see an amazing array of wildlife. Birders with the Audubon Society have spotted from 60-160 species of birds on the ranch. Traveling up from Cartwright Cove one might see cottontails dart across the road, armadillos dig along a sandy creekbank, or even the elusive horned toad sunbathing along a deer path. Always beware of rattlesnakes! As the landscape climbs, watch Crested Caracara's glide on thermals to lofty heights. Observe the hawk/raptor migration on Blania Hill where 360 degree views sweep the rolling hills of South Texas.

There at the summit Lon Cartwright feels as though he were standing on top of the world. "My wife Leigh and I loved to watch the sunsets from here."

"This land is my life. It's hard work, but I don't know what I would do anywhere else. This is home."

Lon Cartwright
Dinero, TX
www.inflightoutfitters.com
[e] david@inflightoutfitters.com

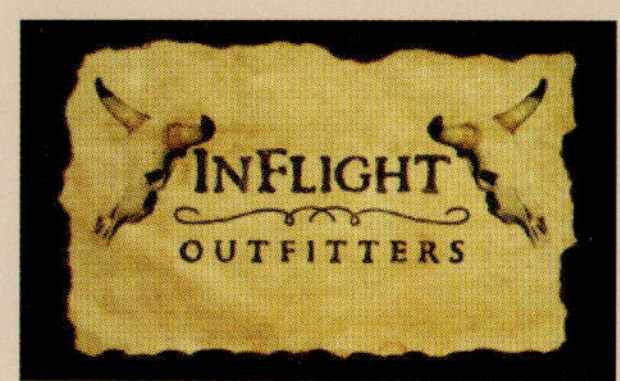

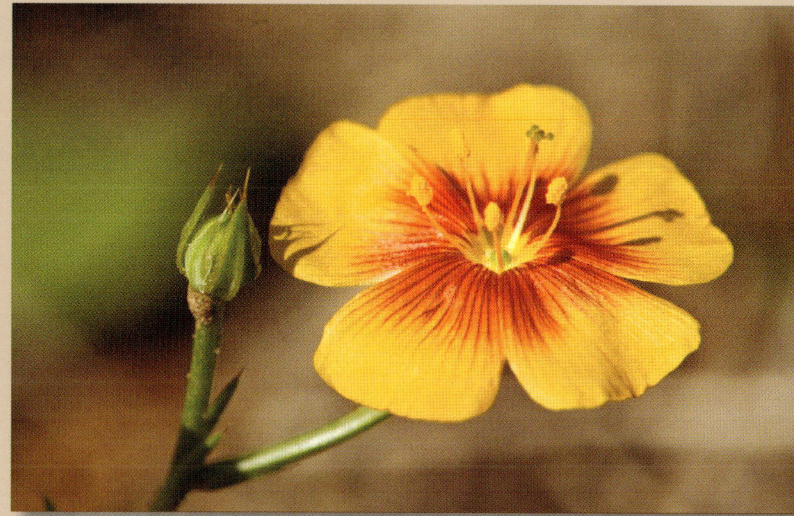

Perry | Wild Flax

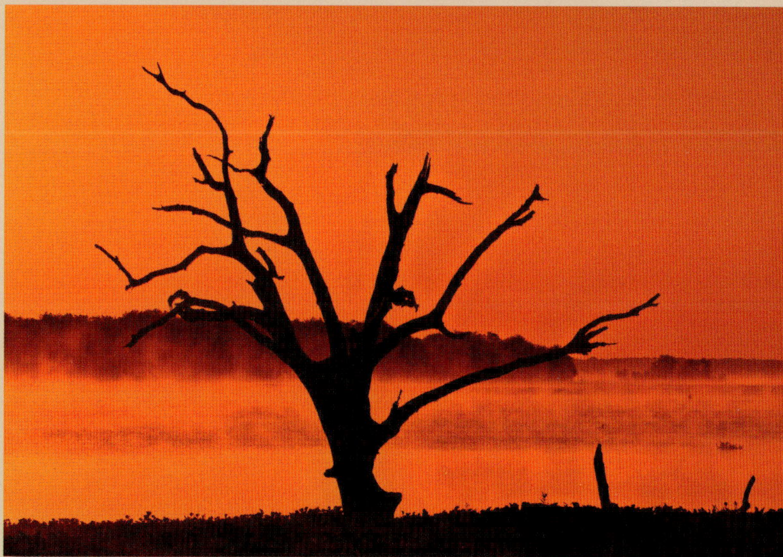

Perry

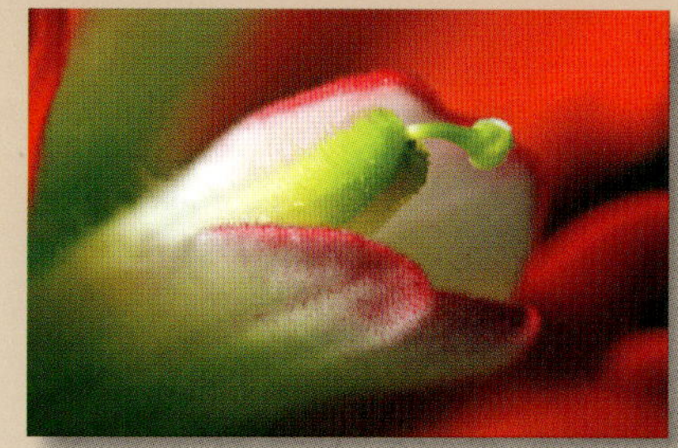

Perry | Indian Paintbrush flower close-up

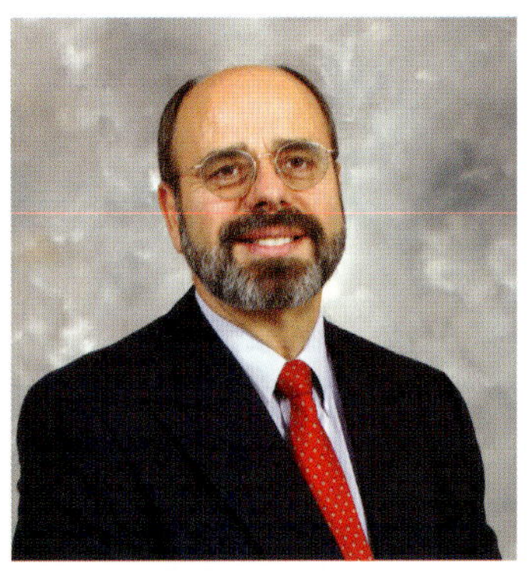

Al Perry

“My photography is so much better when the animals aren’t stressed,” shares veteran photographer Al Perry. “Just like we say candids of people are better, I think candids of animals are too.”

But, don’t let the word “candid” make you think that great shots like his just happen. “There’s a lot of preplanning to visualize. You’ve got to have some idea of what you want to accomplish and that takes a lot of work. Once you find the right set of conditions you’ve got to be ready to execute it.”

Al laughs and confesses, “Of course, things don’t always go according to plan and the truth is I rarely get what I set out to get.” And, he cautions, speaking from nearly 40 years of experience, “You’ve got to not imagine too much or you’ll miss out on the moment.”

When he headed to South Texas, the Indiana photographer says he was particularly interested in capturing two Texas natives with his lens: a Bobcat and a Texas Horned Lizard. To most folks, seeing a Bobcat would be much more exciting than seeing a “horny toad,” but to Al, the fact that each were firsts “made seeing them both exciting to me. I’d never photographed a horny toad before and there’s something so exciting about that first-time opportunity.”

Part of what drove him, he says, was that “I felt a responsibility to the land I was on. I didn’t want the owners of Twin Oaks Ranch to be underrepresented in the contest.” Taking part in this sort of competition allowed him to get to know the ranch people and how tough it is for them to make a living today. “I wanted them to benefit from good imagery.”

Such imagery was tricky at times, especially when he wanted to faithfully represent the animal in its environment. “You’ve got to be creative to come up with something different.” Such a desire goes back to Al’s propensity for the purity of candid-like moments.

Evansville, IN
www.alperry.com
[e] alperry@alperry.com

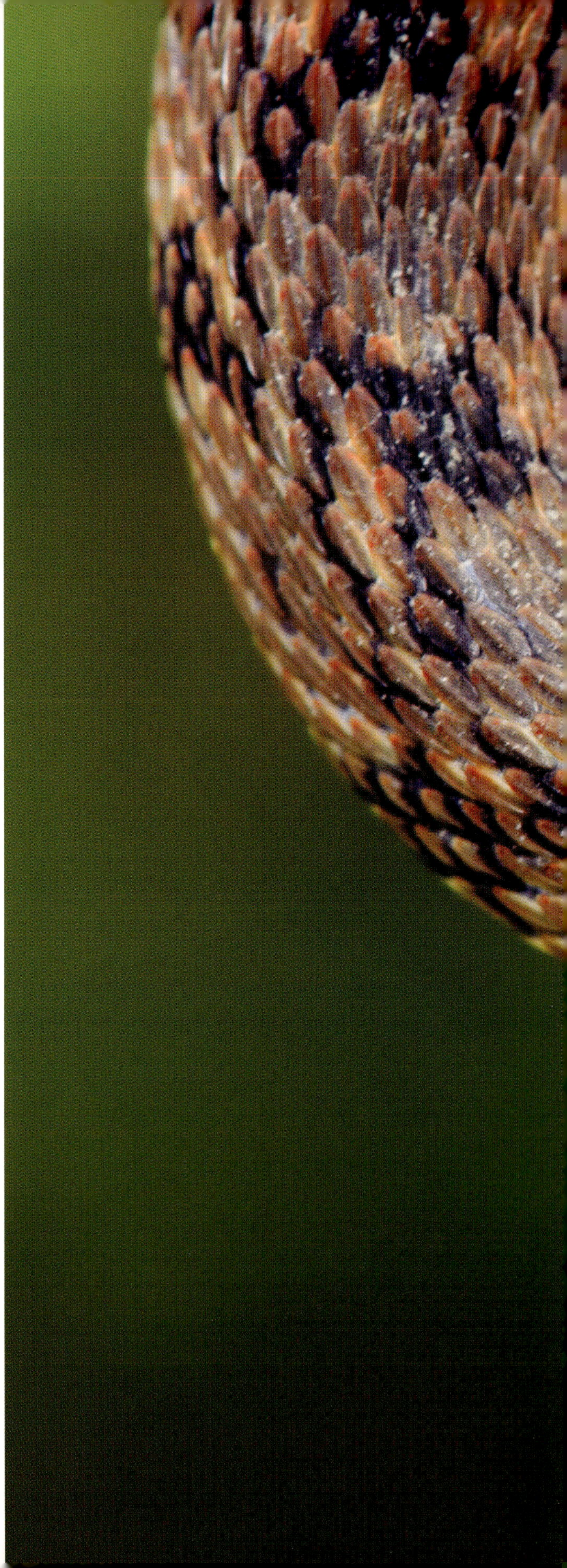

Perry | Diamondback Water Snake

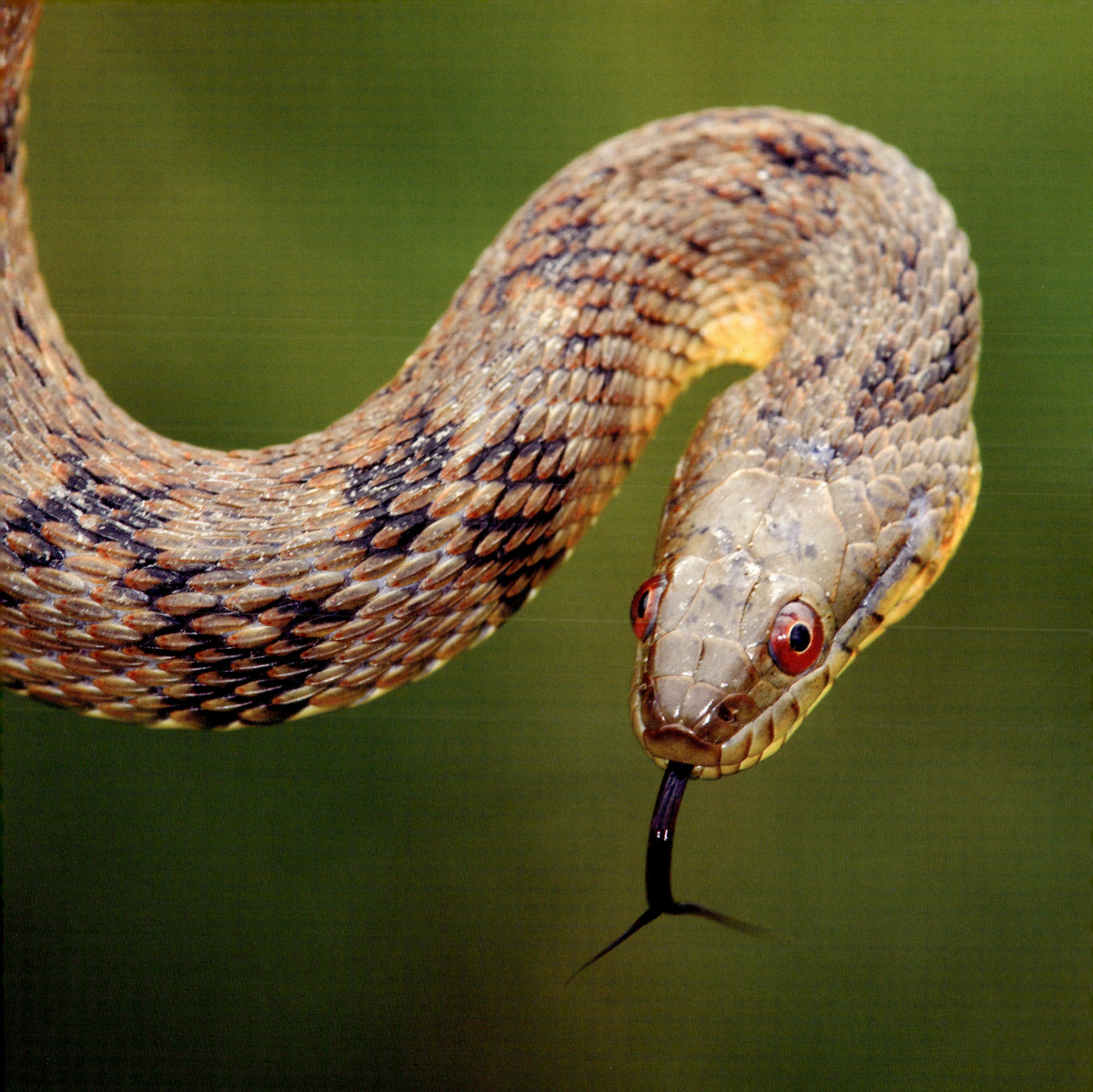

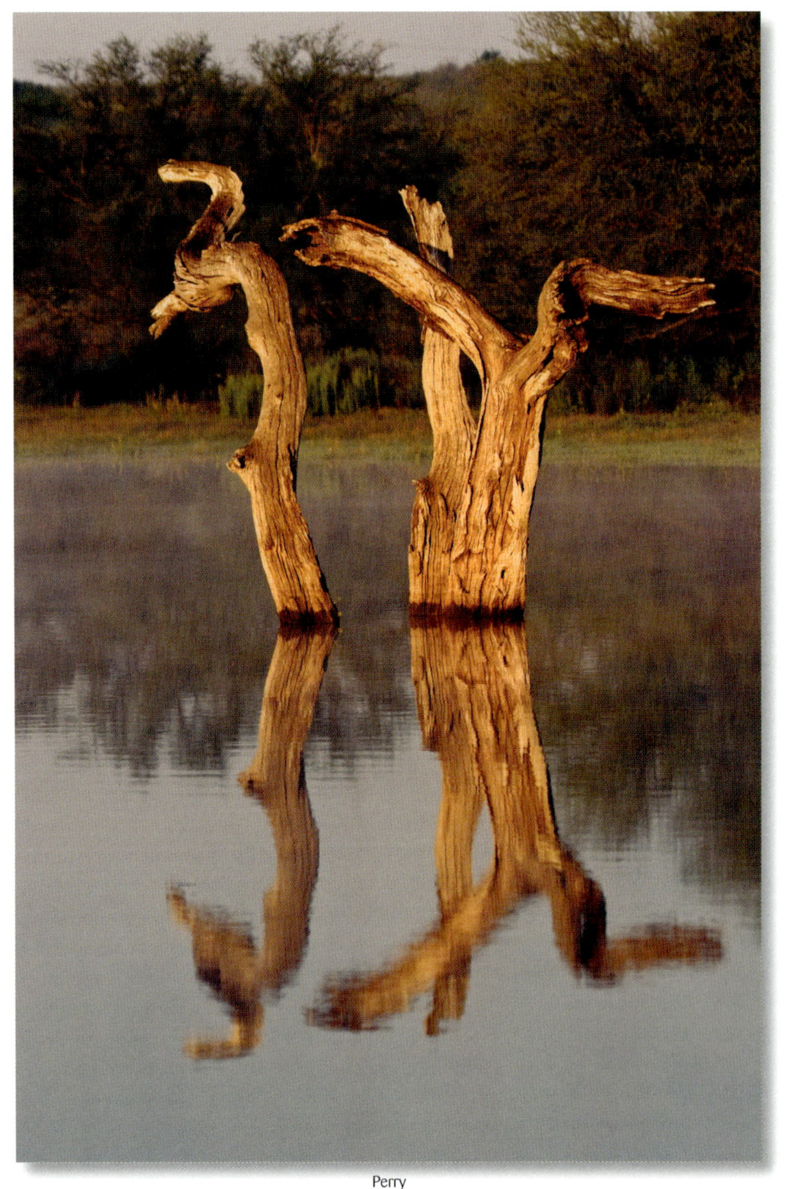
Perry

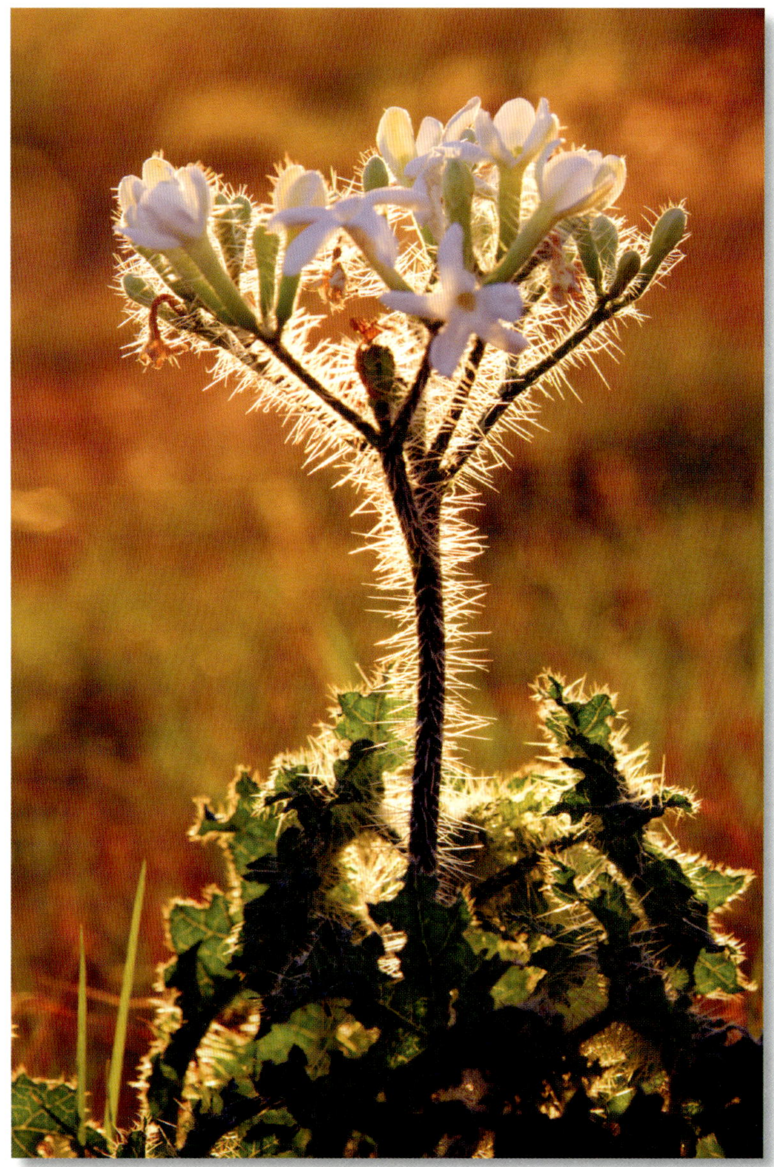
Perry | Bull Nettle (also called Mala Mujer)

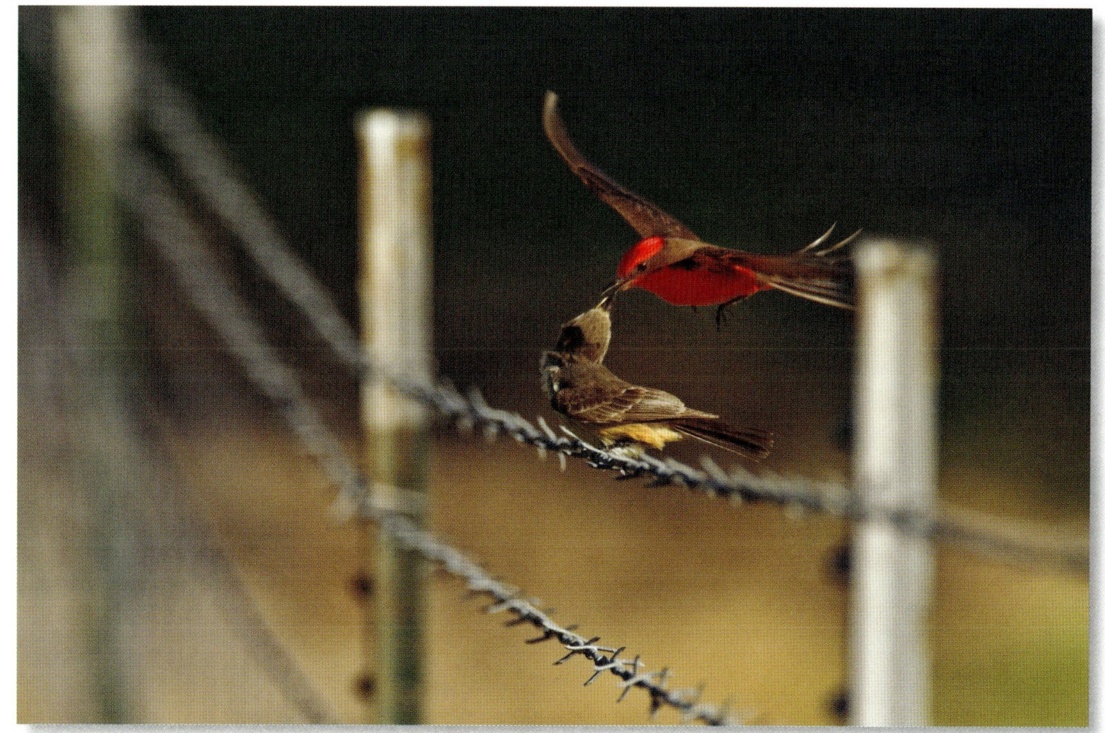

Perry | Vermilion Flycatchers (male aloft, female perched)

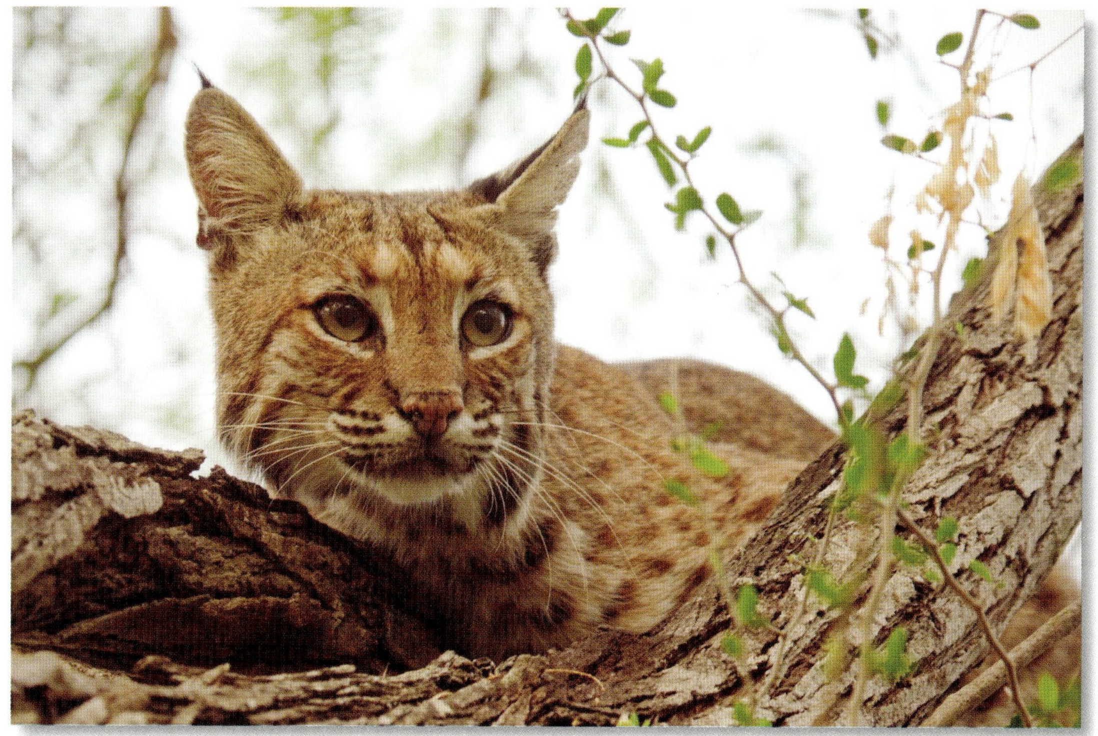

Perry | Bobcat

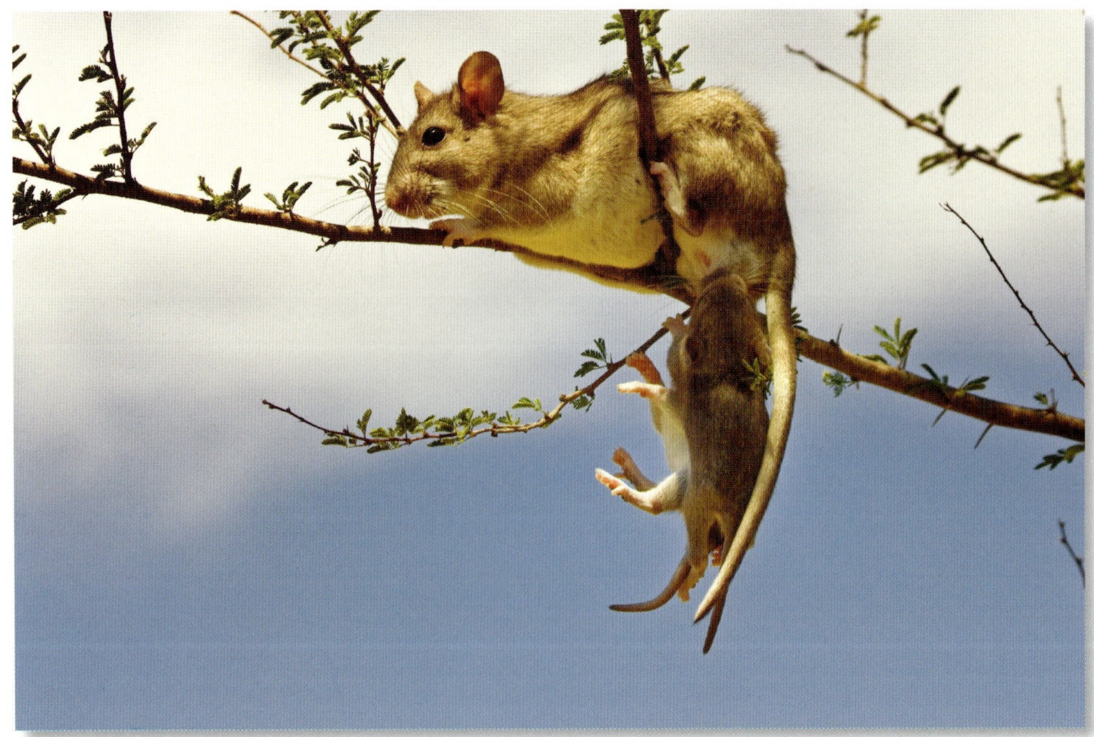

Perry | wood rat

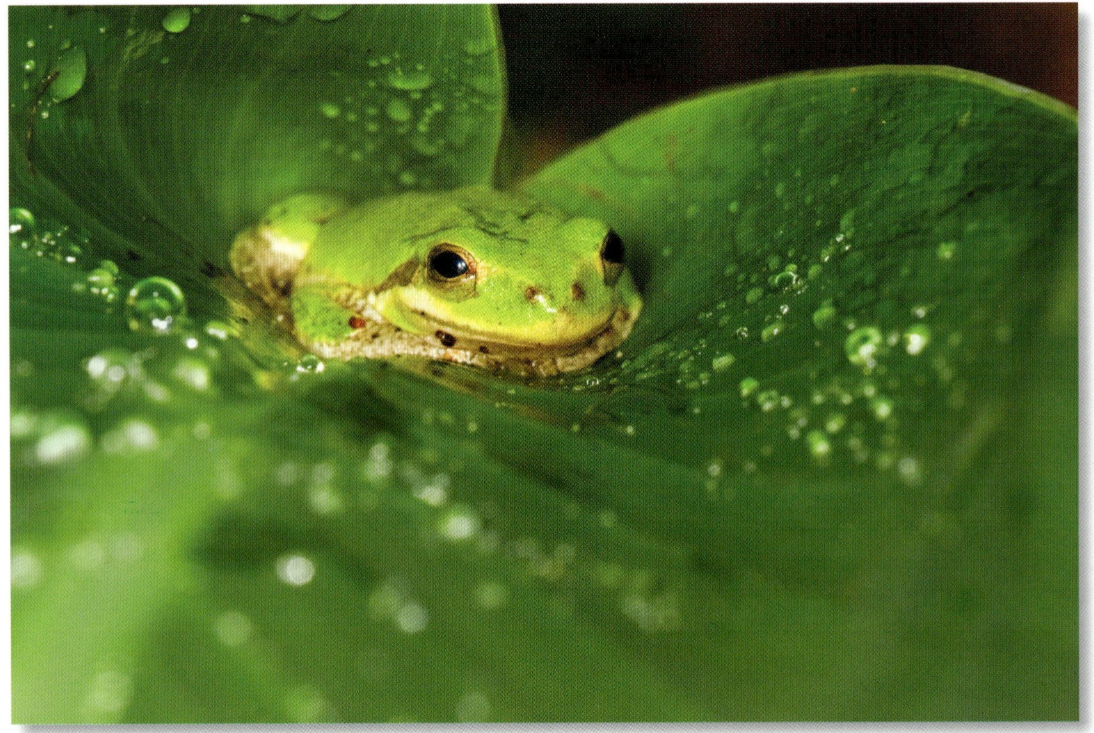

Perry | Green Treefrog

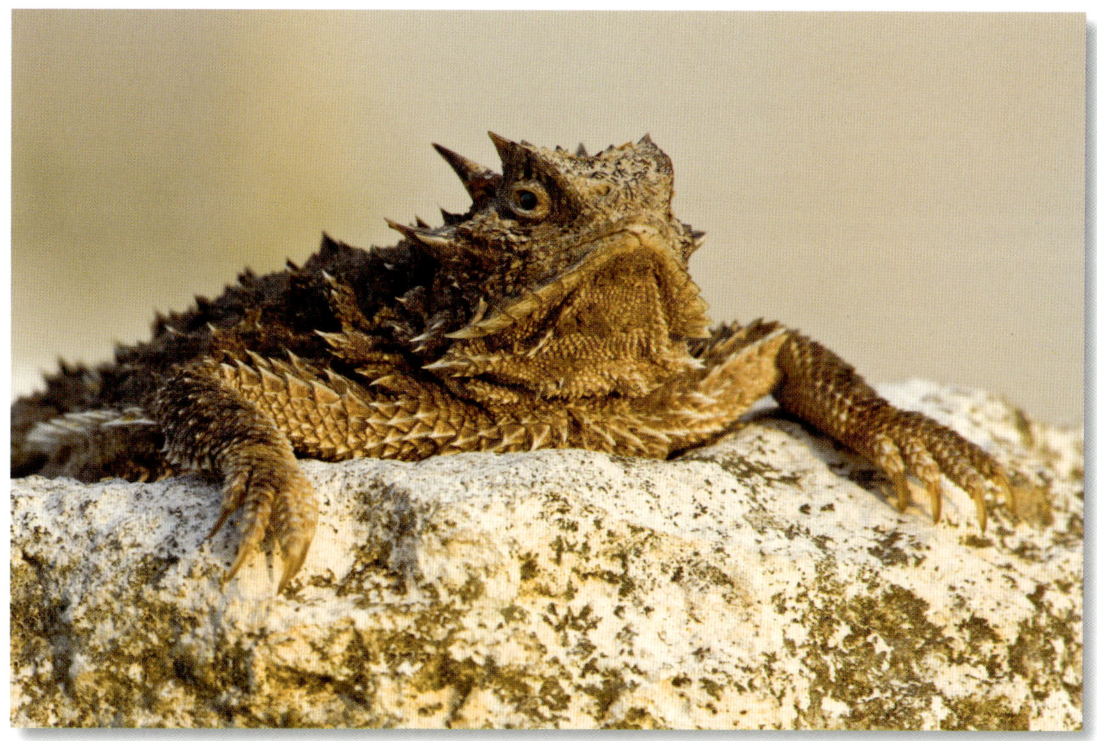

Perry | Texas Horned Lizard

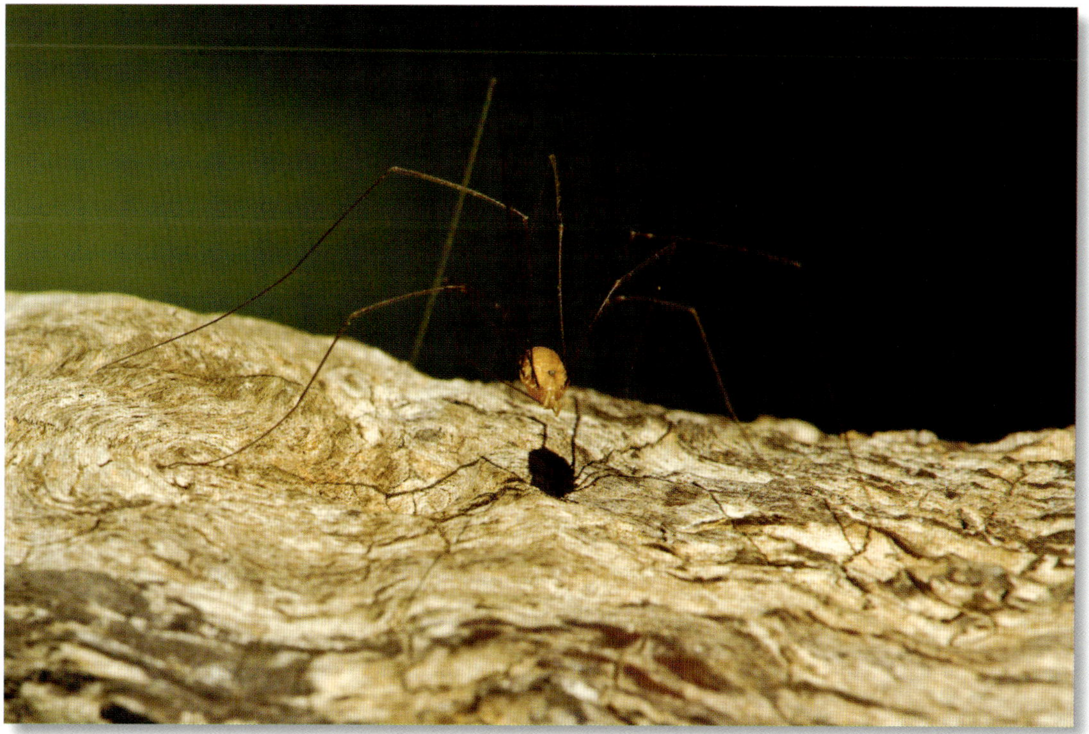

Perry | Harvestman

Images for Conservation Book Two Dedication Party Sponsor

South Texas Money Management, Ltd.

"Helping Individuals, Individually."®

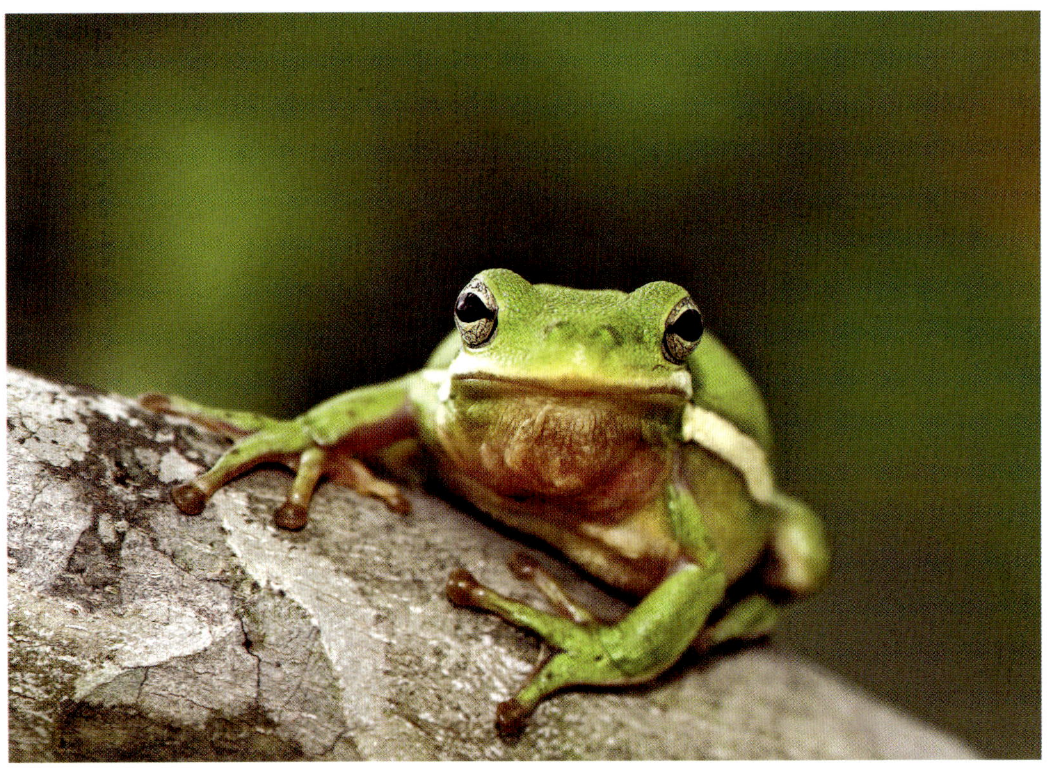

Szafranski | Green Treefrog | Coleto Creek Project

South Texas Money Management is proud to support the dedication party for *Book Two: Coastal Bend Edition.* The stunning collection of photographs represents the unique beauty of the land and the wildlife that we have in Texas.

The state of Texas encompasses diverse land and wildlife. The photographers and landowners have truly captured its treasures in this book.

We also applaud David Langford to whom this book is dedicated. He works tirelessly on behalf of Texas wildlife and conservationism, as well as shares his beautiful talent in photography. He is an exceptional leader and most deserving of this honor.

Enjoy!

Jeanie Wyatt, CFA
CEO & Chief Investment Officer
South Texas Money Management

Richard M. "Cardo" Kleberg IV
Senior Investment Advisor
South Texas Money Management

ICF Book Dedication Party Sponsors

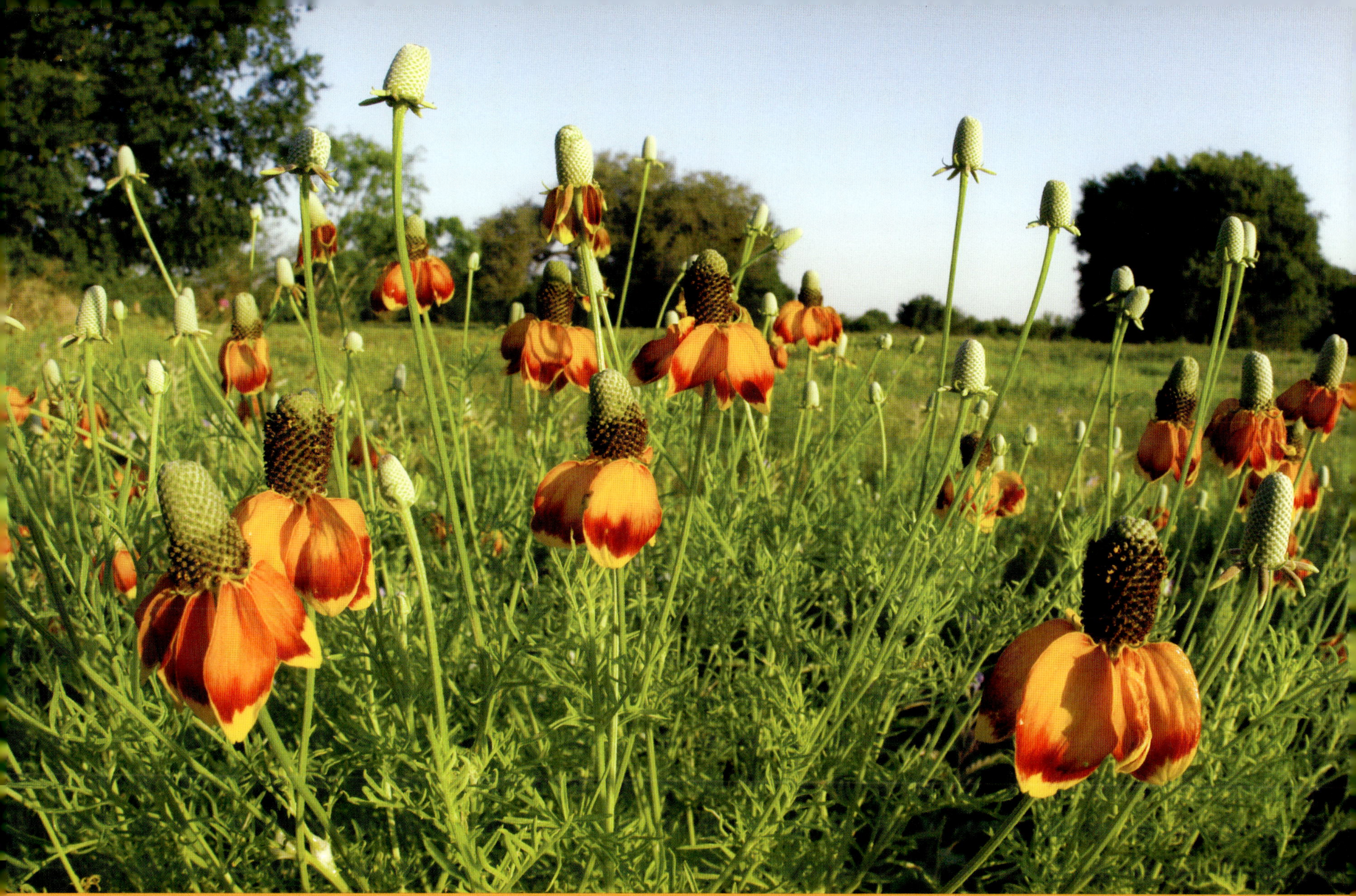

PROUD SPONSOR OF THE 2008 PRO-TOUR OF NATURE PHOTOGRAPHY

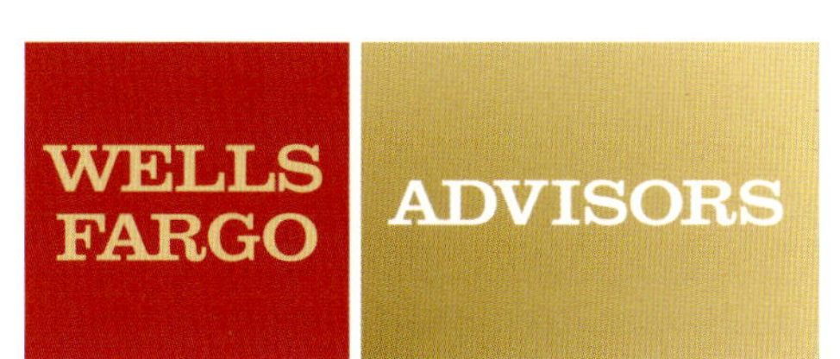

Bruce & Gail Hoffman

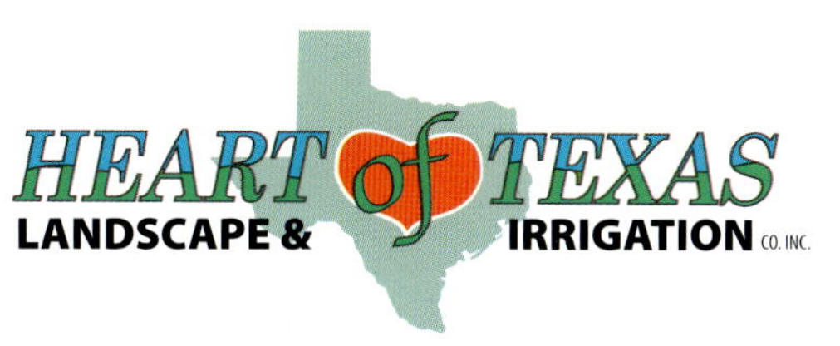

Belton, Texas

Perry | Mexican Hat | Twin Oaks Ranch

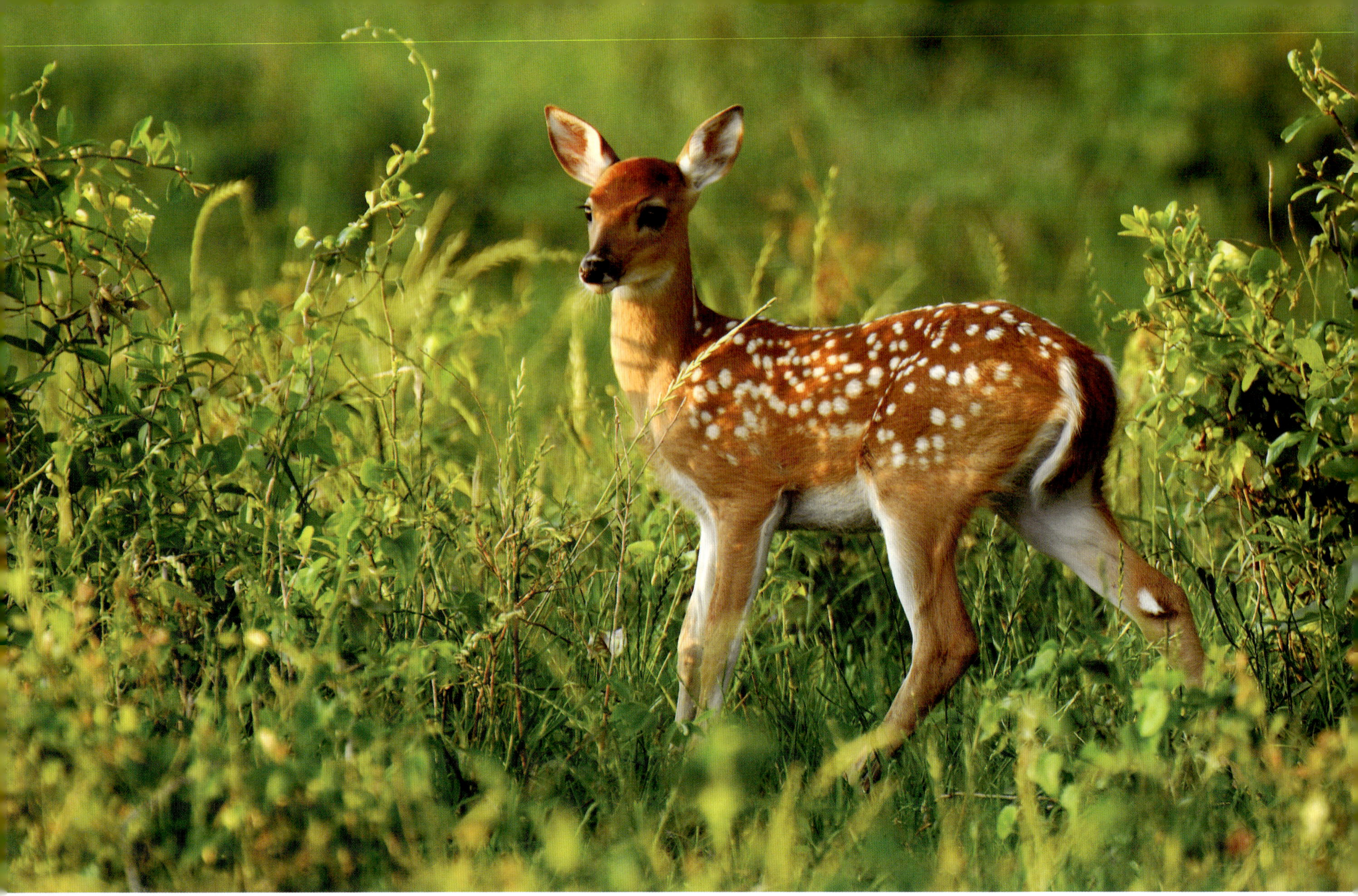

Ulrich | White-tailed Deer fawn | Pierce Ranch

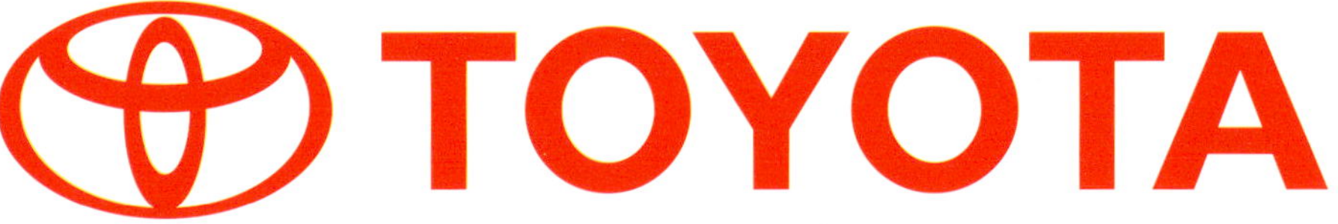

Gulf States Toyota, a distributor of Toyota cars, trucks and sport utility vehicles in Arkansas, Louisiana, Mississippi, Oklahoma and Texas, is proud to be a sponsor of Images for Conservation Fund Pro-Tour of Nature Photography.

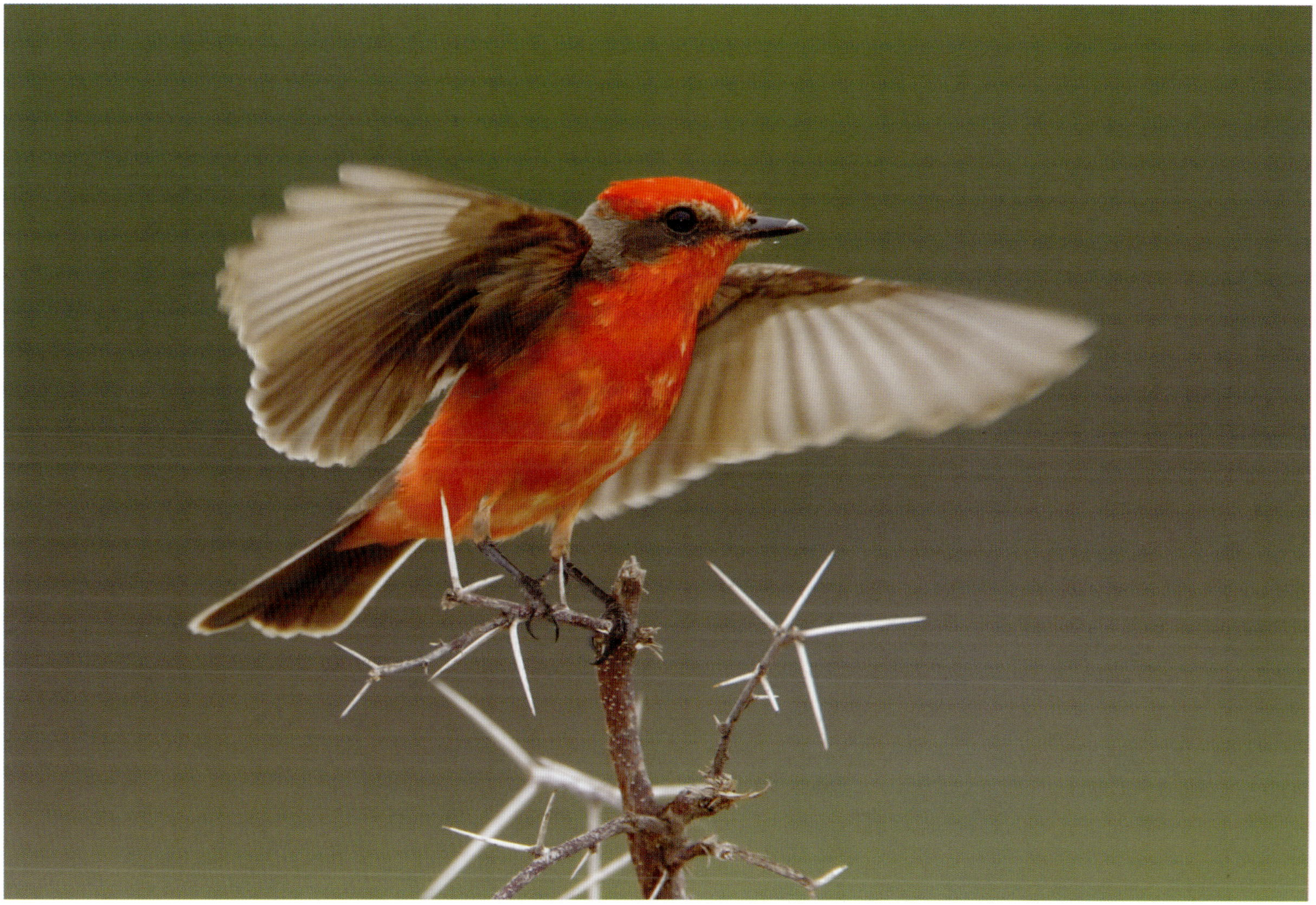

Hahn | Vermillion Flycatcher | Pierce Ranch

John and Audrey Martin

in honor of their parents and Georgia Mason

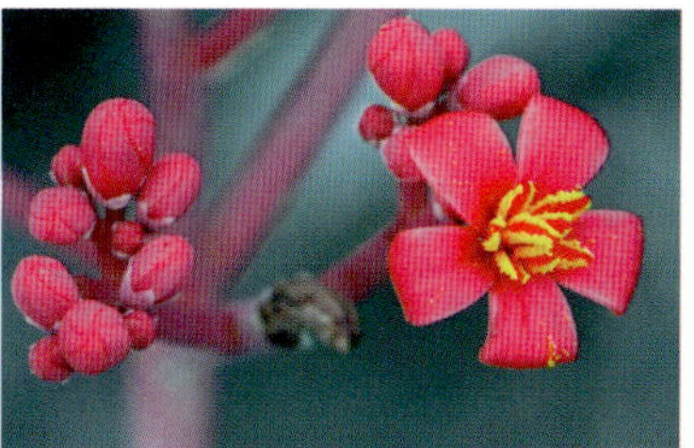

Illg | Berlandier's Nettlespurge | Hill Creek Ranch

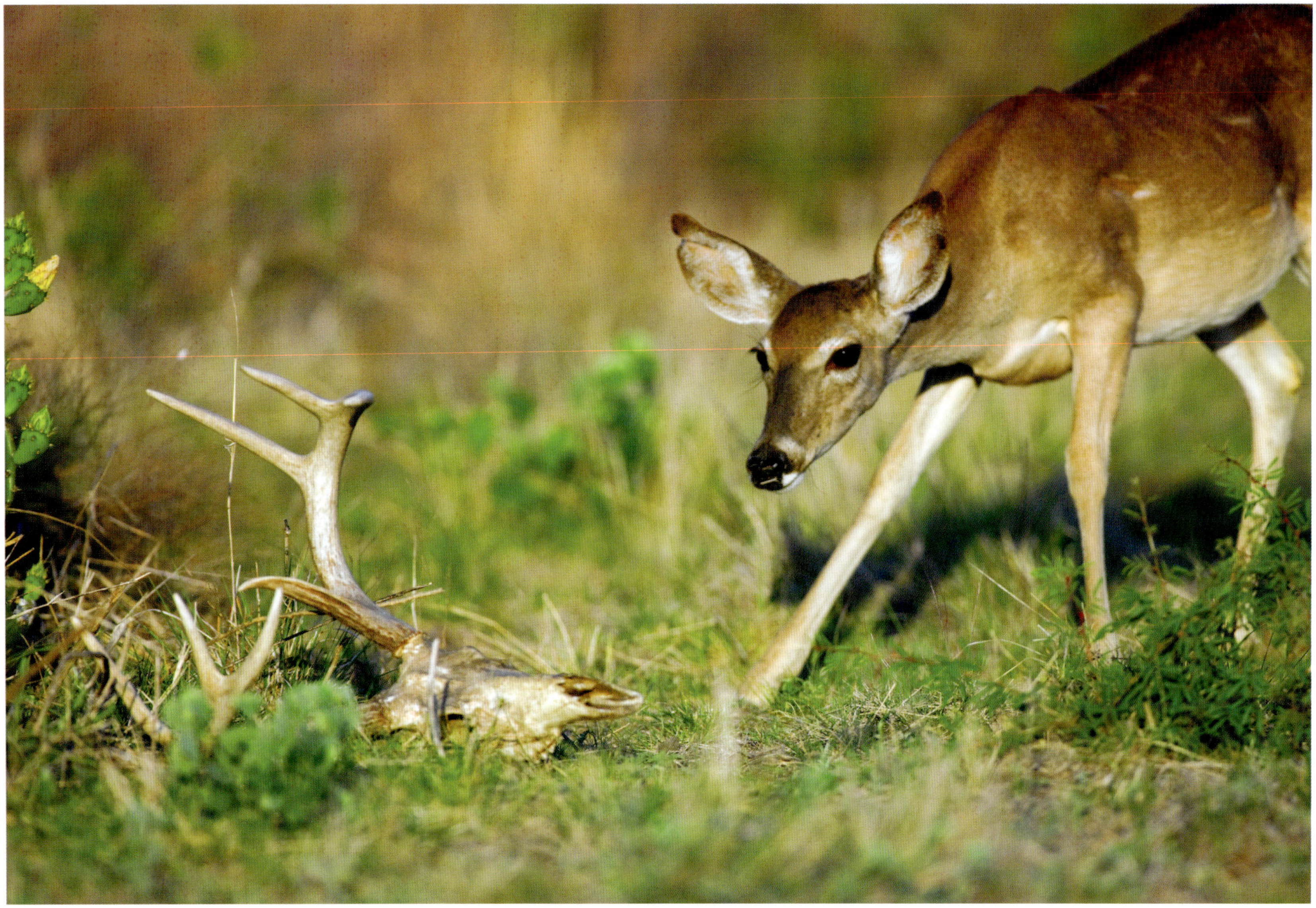

Steele | White-tailed Deer | Butler Ranch

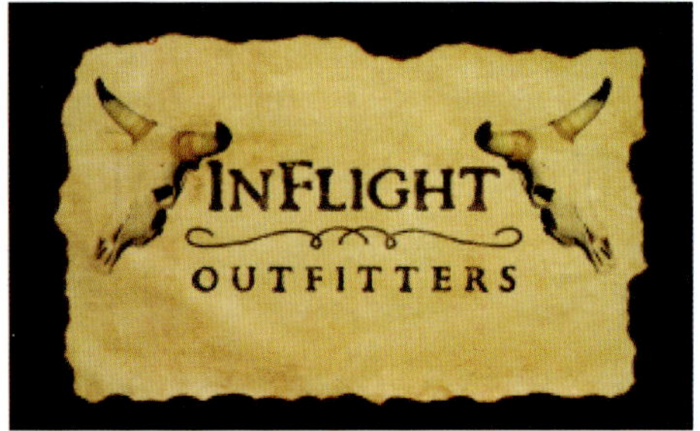

Twin Oaks Ranch

ICF Meet the Judges
Party Sponsors
and Judging Host Site

Claire Vaughan Volunteer Leadership Award

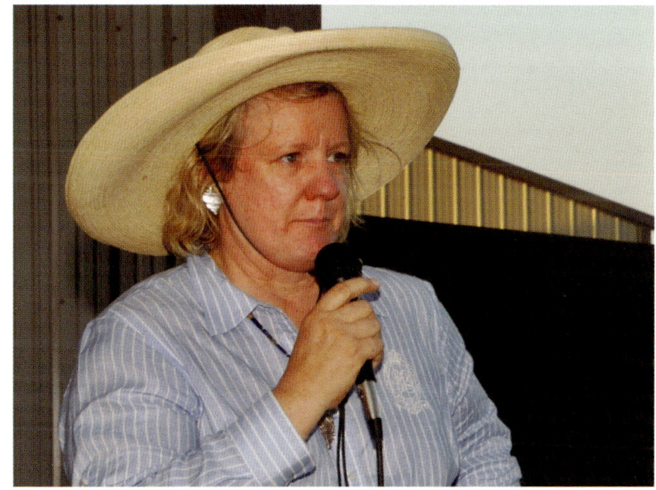

Non-profit organizations all know their volunteers are their life-blood. Without the help of those committed to the organizations' success, there would be a perpetual uphill battle.

The Images for Conservation Fund has had a proponent since the inception of the first Pro-Tour of Nature Photography. Claire Vaughan was there every step of the way. She recruited more volunteers, she hosted events, she attended a multitude of meetings, her family's ranch participated in the contest and her list of volunteer time to ICF goes on and on.

It only seemed fitting to name our award for an outstanding volunteer –"Claire Vaughan Volunteer Leadership Award." Thank you, Claire, for showing everyone how it's done.

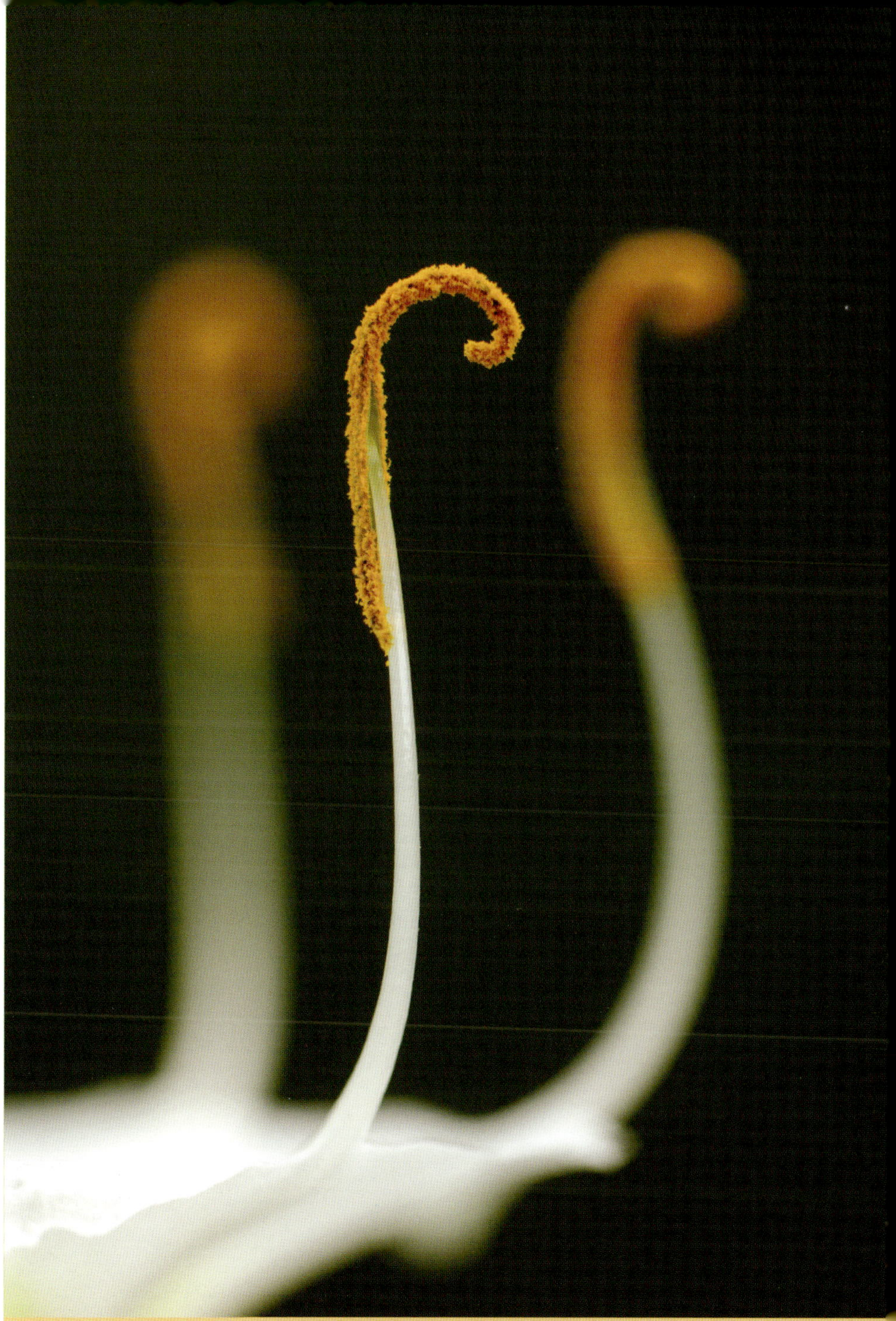

Nussbaumer | spiderlily | Fennessey Ranch

Art & Jenny Cahoon

are proud to be a sponsor of
the Images for Conservation Fund
Pro-Tour of Nature Photography

The Images for Conservation Fund
Pro-Tour of Nature Photography
thanks

Roger Zessin

for his continuing support.

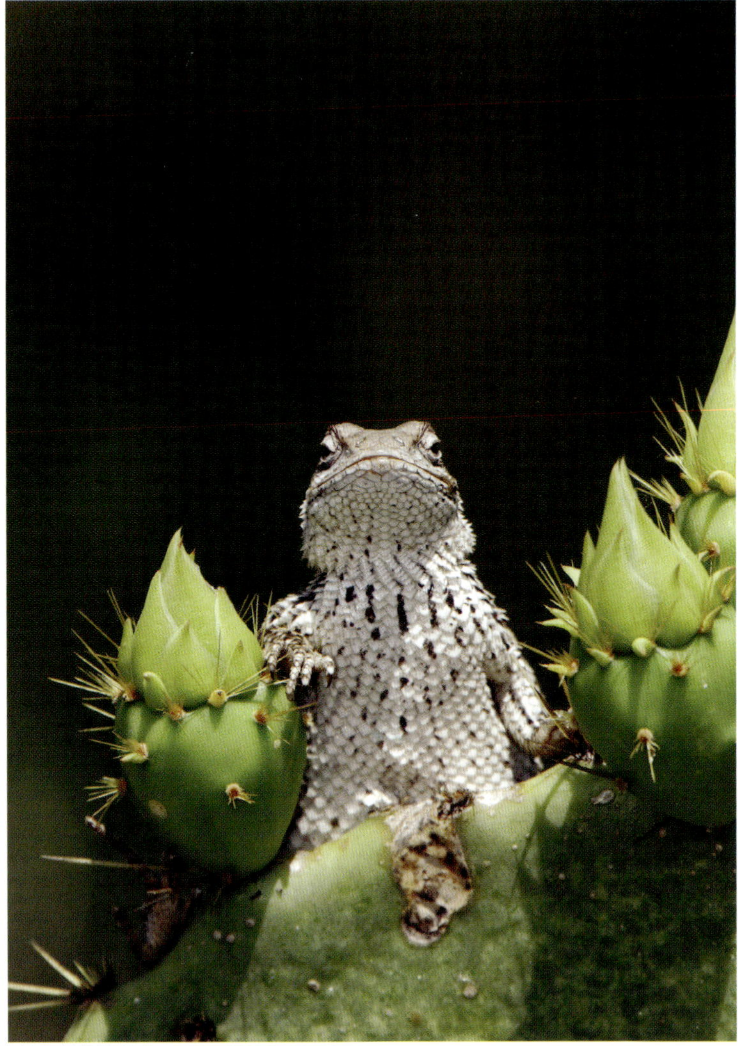

Szafranski | Texas Spiny Lizard | Coleto Creek Project

George & Claire Vaughan

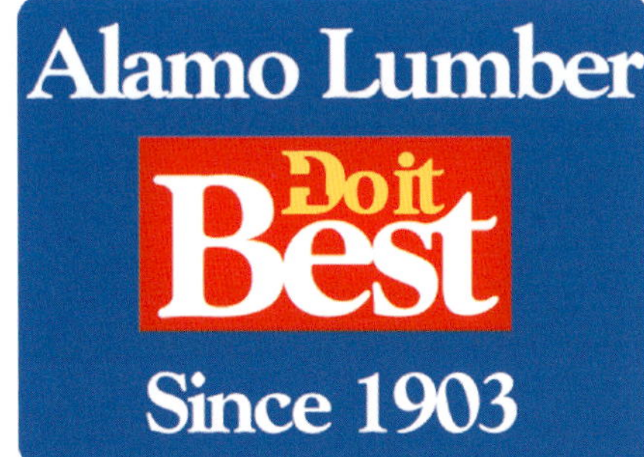

Alice, Bay City, Beeville, Carrizo Springs, Cuero, Eagle Pass,
El Campo, Falfurrias, Freer, Hebbronville, Kenedy,
Mathis, Nixon, Raymondville

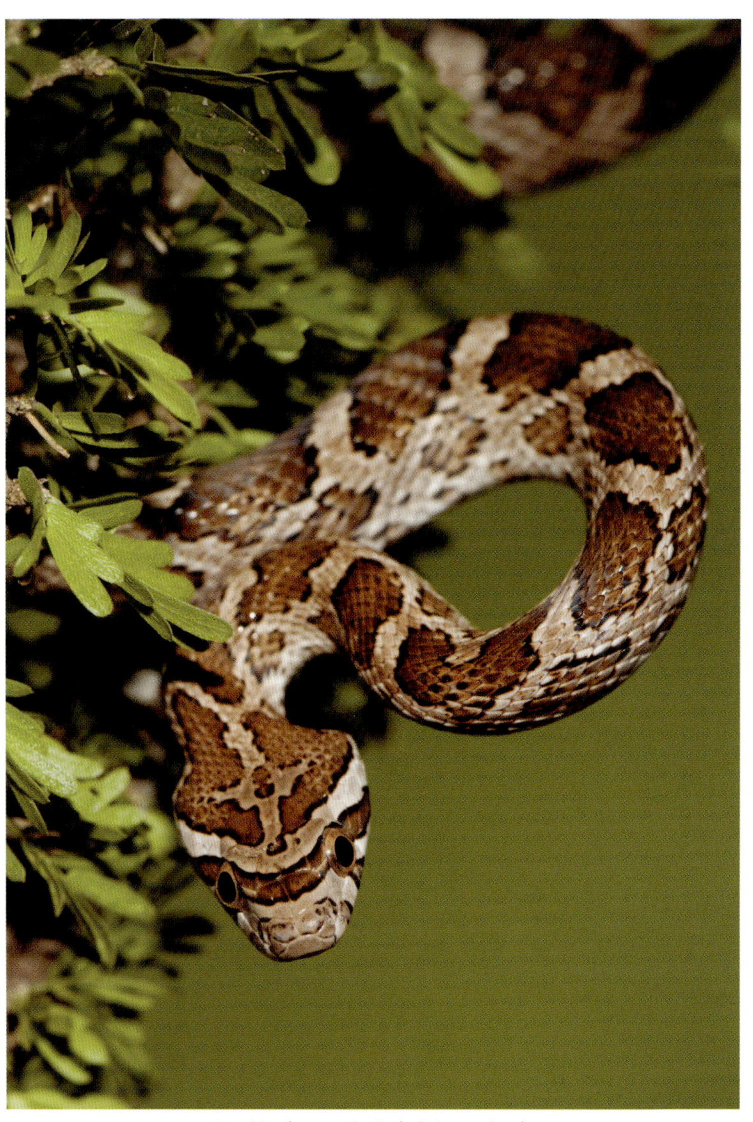

Franz | Southwestern Rat Snake | Mustang Ranch

Business & Foundation Sponsors

AEP Texas
South Texas Money Management
IBC Bank
Heart of Texas Landscape
Wells Fargo Advisors
Burke Enterprises/Inflight Outfitters
Toyota
Alamo Lumber Company
The Loring Cook Foundation
Corpus Christi Convention & Visitor's Bureau
Valero Energy
Muñoz Investment Banking Group
Texas State Aquarium
Harvey Weil Foundation
CopyZone
Exelon Nuclear
Ellis Koeneke Ramirez, LLP
Kingsville Convention & Visitor's Bureau
Nature Photographer's Network
First Victoria Bank
Alimento Catering
University of Houston-Victoria
King Ranch Institute for Ranch Management
L & F Distributors
Caesar Kleberg Wildlife Facility
Digett Marketing
Jim Lago, Lago in the Morning 1360 KKTX
O'Connor & Hewitt Foundation

Individual Sponsors

John & Audrey Martin
Todd & Alexis Hunter
Diane Smith
John Welder
Kathleen Welder Carey
David Sikes
Carol Rausch
Art & Jenny Cahoon
Roger Zessin
George & Claire Vaughan
Bruce & Gail Hoffman
Elaine Fox

Book Patrons

South Texas Money Management
Bill Martin, Mark Southwell, Justin Capadona – Morgan Stanley
Corpus Christi Regional Economic Development Corporation
Caroline Schreiber
Corpus Christi Medical Center
Ellis Koeneke Ramirez LLP
Bruce Hoffman – Wells Fargo Advisors
Dale & Lorri Franz
Mitchell Dale – Sick Dog Ranch
Sue Butler Carter – Butler Ranches
Fennessey Ranch
Rolf & Karen Nussbaumer
Kingsville Convention & Visitors Bureau
USDA Natural Resources Conservation Services
Texas Parks & Wildlife Foundation
Texas Park & Wildlife Department Employees
John & Audrey Martin
Terry Blankenship – Welder Wildlife Foundation
Kevin Pena – Advisors Asset Management
Muñoz Investment Banking
Carol Rausch & Miguel Nevarez
Barry Dunn PhD – King Ranch Institute for Ranch Management
Carol Bailey, Attorney at Law
Vaughan & Sons
Marshall Company Inc
Richard Bothe – IBC Bank – Victoria
Hugo & Laura Berlanga – Mustang Ranch
Tim & Amy Erhman – Rancho Lucero
Danny Startz – Enterprise Rent-A-Car
Richard Folmar – Wells Fargo Advisors
T. J. Martin, Jr.
Valerie Barrett
Museum of the Coastal Bend
Peter C. & Fran G. Swenson – Hill Creek Ranch
Michael Portman – Wells Fargo Advisors
Brent Hoffman – Rockin' h Ranch Services
Mark Hiler – Capital Farm Credit
Katharine Armstrong Love
Lawrance Armour III – JHA Ranch
Texas Wildlife Association
Julio Reyes – AEP Texas
IBC Bank
King Ranch Saddle Shop
Fred Santos
Guadalupe Blanco River Authority

Thanks to the following people for their help in making sure our book was accurate – Janice Odom, Audrey Martin

2008 Pro-Tour Partners

We are grateful and indebted to our partners – those people and organizations who contributed time and effort to the mission of ICF and to making this project a success. They signed on early and did what they said they would do. It would not have happened without them.

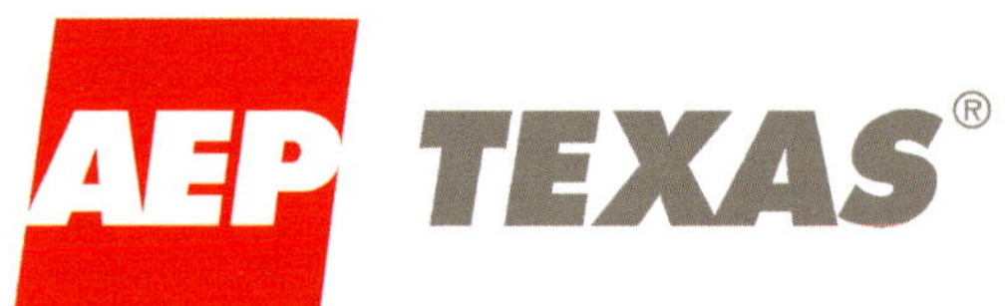

A unit of American Electric Power

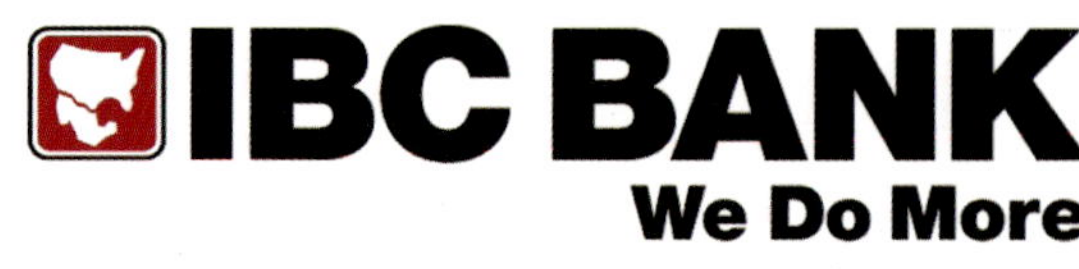

www.ibc.com

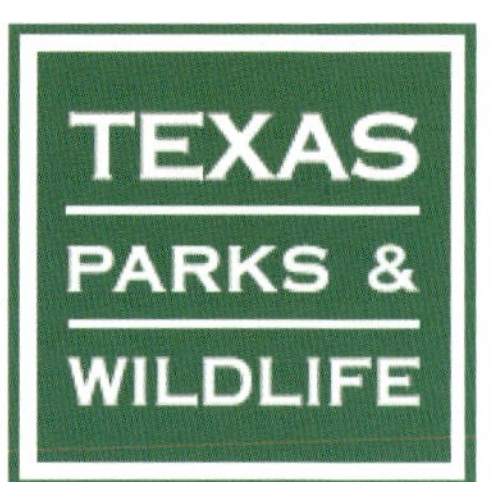

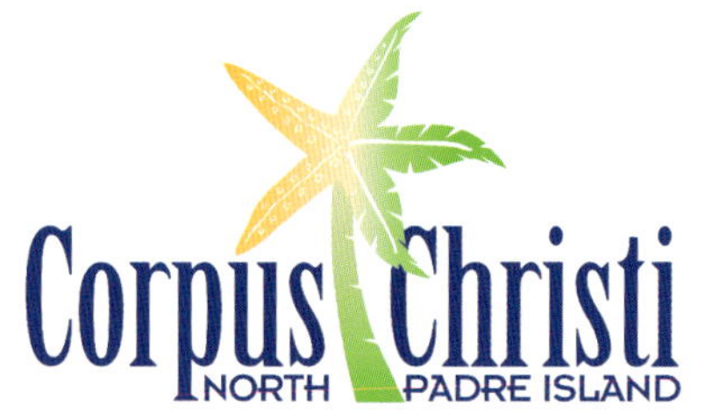

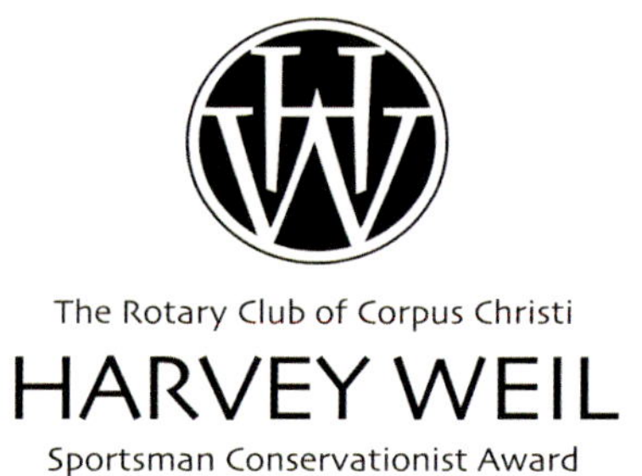

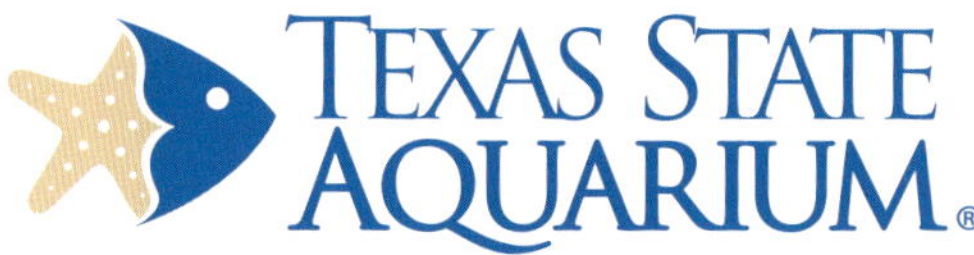

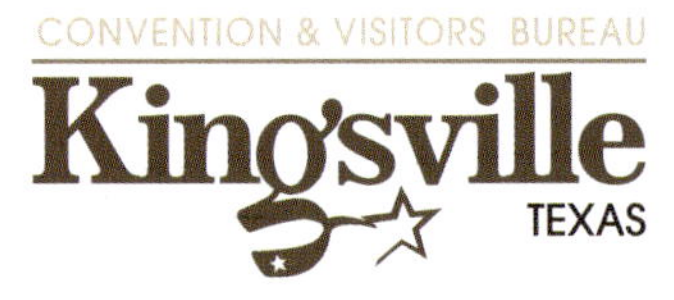

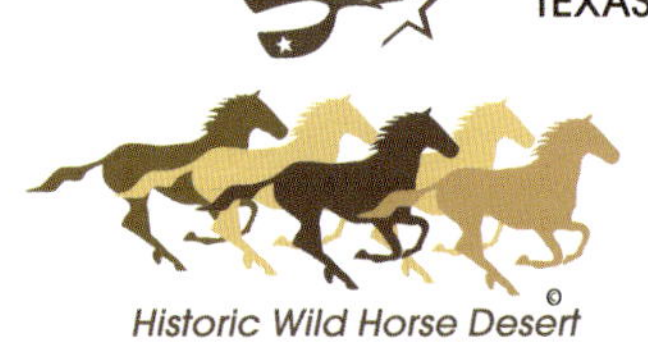

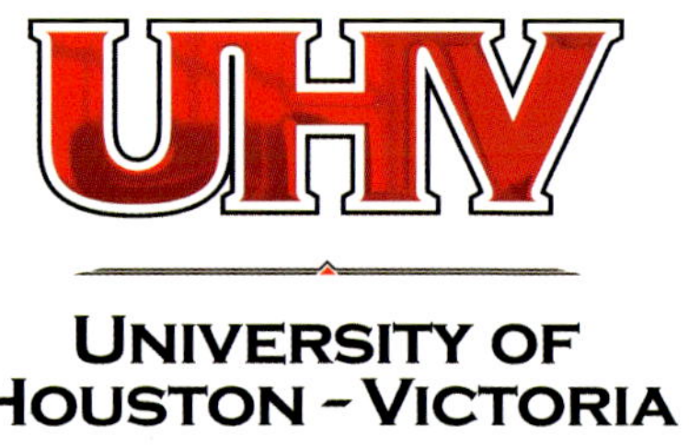

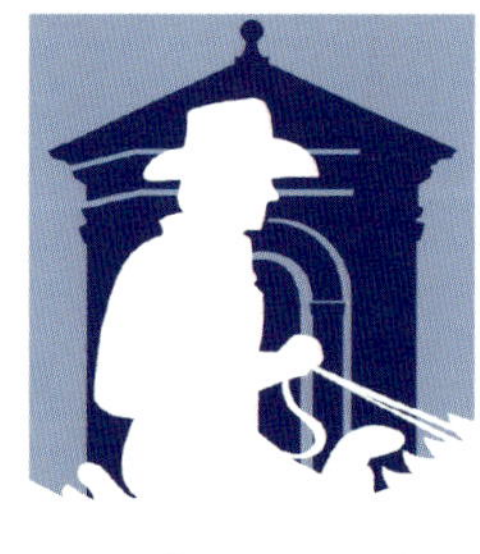

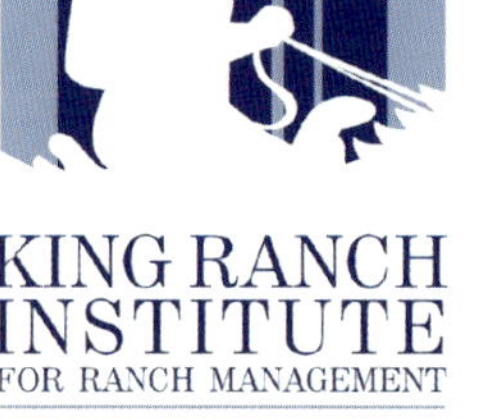

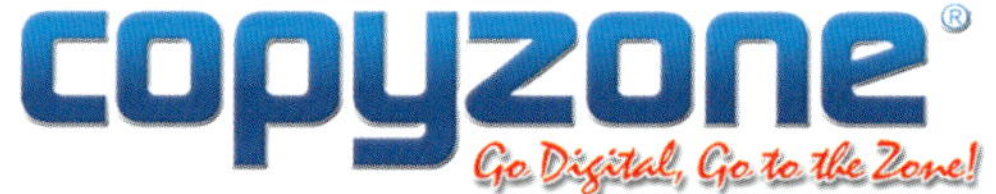

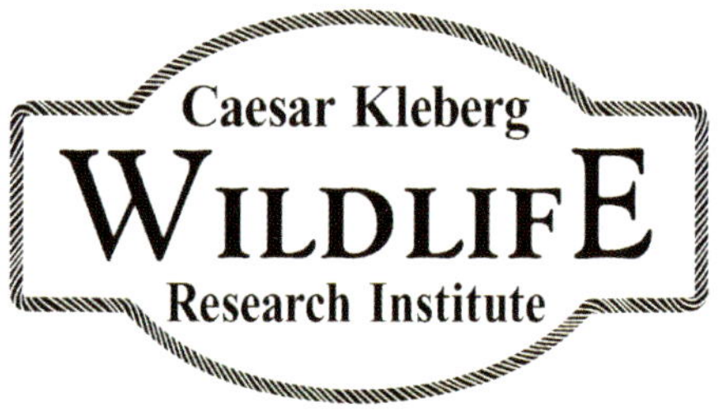

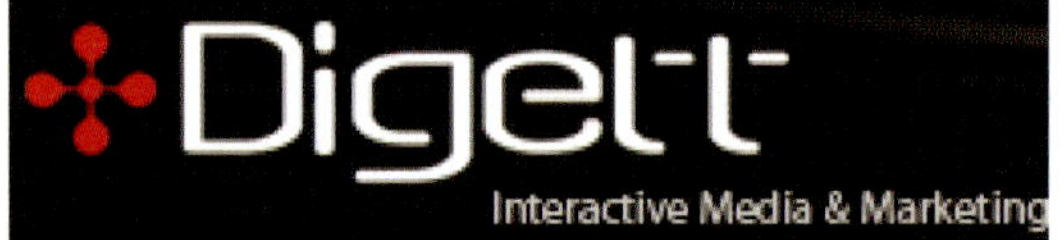

Nature Photographers *Online Magazine*

L & F Distributors - Budweiser | Jim Lago, Lago in the Morning, 1360 KKTX

Carter Smith, TPWD

Alimento Catering (John Welder) | Kathleen Welder Carey | Elaine Fox | Todd & Alexis Hunter

O'Connor & Hewitt Foundation | Ellis Koeneke Ramirez, LLP | Carol Rausch | David Sikes | Diane Smith

Victoria Convention & Visitors Bureau | Texas Co-Op Power Magazine | Texas Wildlife Association

PERC Reports | Miles Phillips | Smith, Fankhauser, Voight & Watson, PLLC

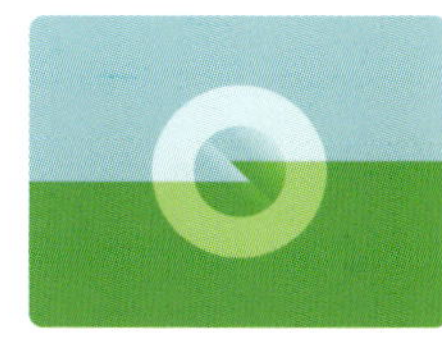

ICF National Board of Directors

John F. Martin, Chair, Edinburg, TX
Connie K. Bransilver, National Vice-Chair, Naples, FL
Carol Rausch, Secretary, McAllen, TX
Miguel A. Nevárez, PhD, Treasurer, Edinburg, TX
Katharine Armstrong, Austin, TX
Arthur L. Cahoon, Jacksonville, FL
Thomas D. Koeneke, McAllen, TX
Edward H. Muñoz, Leesburg, VA
Susan Muñoz, Leesburg, VA
Gabby Salazar, Youth Director, Pleasant Garden, NC
Roberto Zambrano, Monterrey, Mexico
Roger A. Zessin, Corpus Christi, TX

ICF Coastal Bend Advisory Board

Gail & Bruce Hoffman, Co-Chair, Fundraising
Claire & George Vaughan, Co-Chair, Events
John F. Martin, Chair & Founder, Images for Conservation
Alexis Hunter, Launch Co-Chair
Kathy Lorenz, Launch Co-Chair
Gayle Neessen, Launch Co-Chair
Kathleen Welder Carey, Awards Chair
Gail Hoffman, Book Dedication Chair

Keith Arnold
Jane Buchek
Keith Burke
Lynn Drawe
Barry Dunn, PhD
Jane Dunn
Alicia Hoover
Michelle Horine
Todd Hunter
Bebe Canales Inkley
Larry Jones
Cardo Kleberg
Glenn Mayo
Mo Morehead
Judy Newton, PhD
Miles Phillips
Shelley Plante
Pat Rangel
Tom Schmid
Caroline Schreiber
David Sikes
Diane Smith
Adair Sutherland
Fran Swenson
Pete Swenson, MD
Heather Welder
Roger Zessin

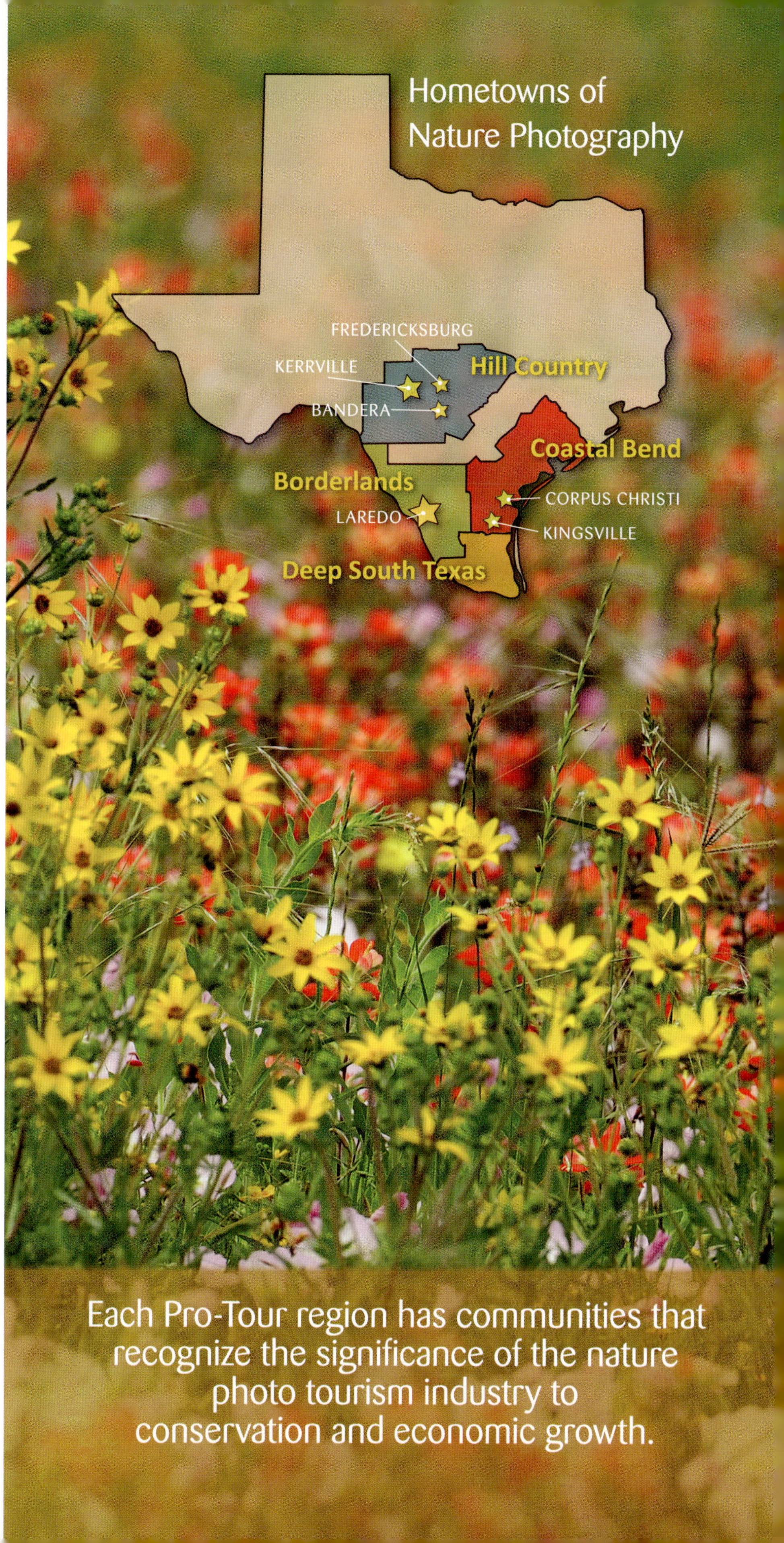

Ulrich | Pierce Ranch

Each Pro-Tour region has communities that recognize the significance of the nature photo tourism industry to conservation and economic growth.

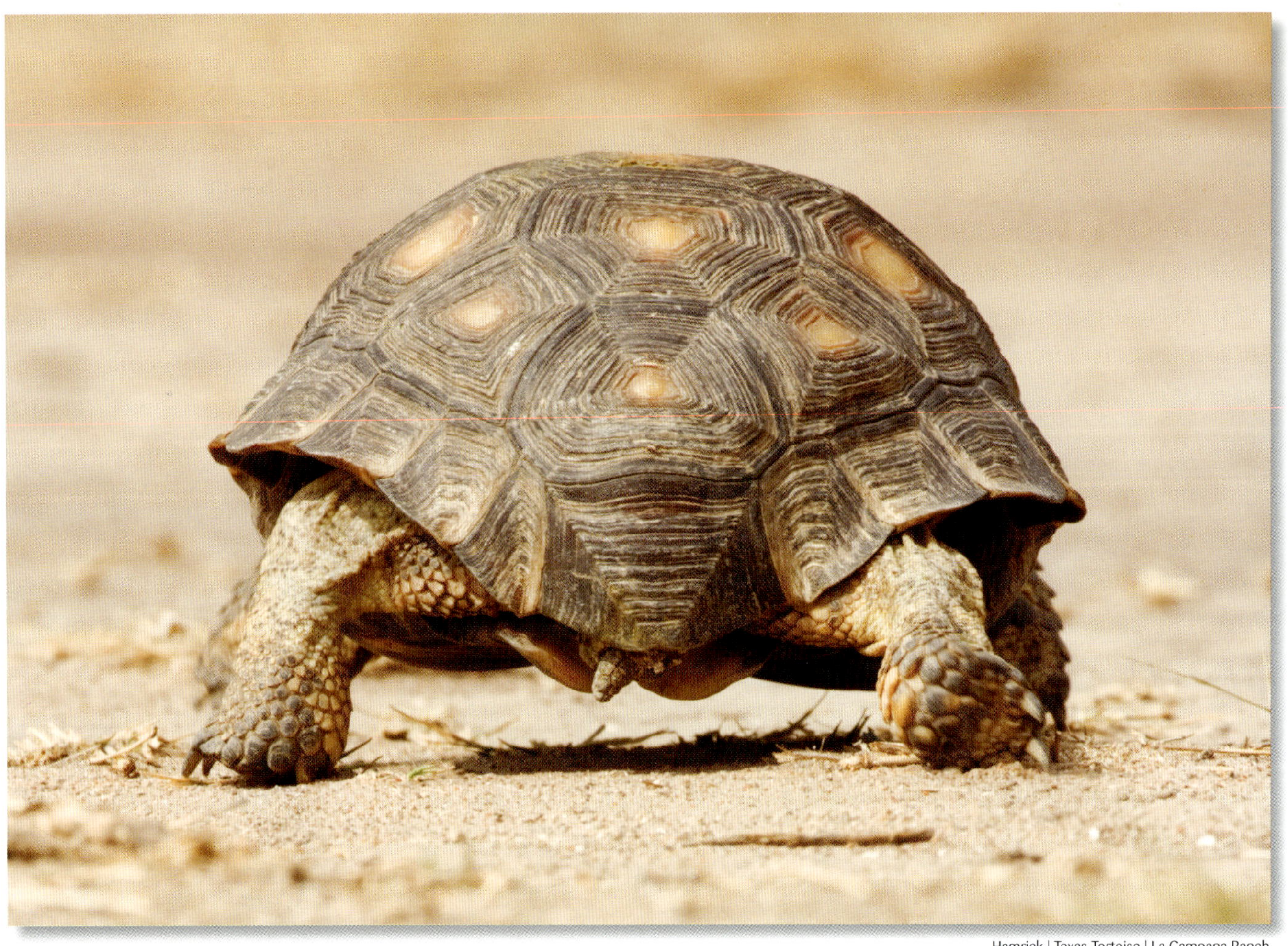

Hamrick | Texas Tortoise | La Campana Ranch

Distinguished Judges...

Mark Godfrey

Director of Photography
The Nature Conservancy

The Nature Conservancy's Director of Photography Mark Godfrey worked for several newspapers before covering the Vietnam War for the *Associated Press* and *LIFE Magazine*. He was a member of the photographer's cooperative *MAGNUM Photos* and later Director of Photography for *U. S. News & World Report*. He has photographed a number of books for The National Geographic Society.

Kevin Schafer

Professional Nature Photographer

Kevin Schafer is a professional natural history photographer, whose work has appeared in all of the most respected science and nature magazines in the U.S., including *National Geographic, Smithsonian, Audubon* and *Natural History*. He has written and photographed more than 10 books, including *Penguin Planet*, which received the 2000 National Outdoor Book Award. His most recent book is *Living Light*, published in 2006.

Bob Tope

Photo Editor
Nature's Best Magazine

Bob Tope has been a professional photographer, artist, and writer for more than 30 years, focusing his talents on natural history and conservation. Over the years his award-winning work has been published in more than 30 books and hundreds of articles, and is held in the permanent collections of the Smithsonian, the National Park Service, and the National Geographic Society.